NEW YORK
ACCESS®

Orientation	4
Lower Manhattan	16
Chinatown/Lower East Side/Little Italy	40
SoHo/TriBeCa	54
Greenwich Village	78
East Village	98
Union Square/Gramercy/Murray Hill	112
Chelsea	132
Theater District/Garment Center	142
Midtown	170
East Side	216
Upper East Side	246
Central Park	256
West Side	266
Upper West Side	286
Heights/Harlem	292
Boroughs	306
Index	320

D1367514

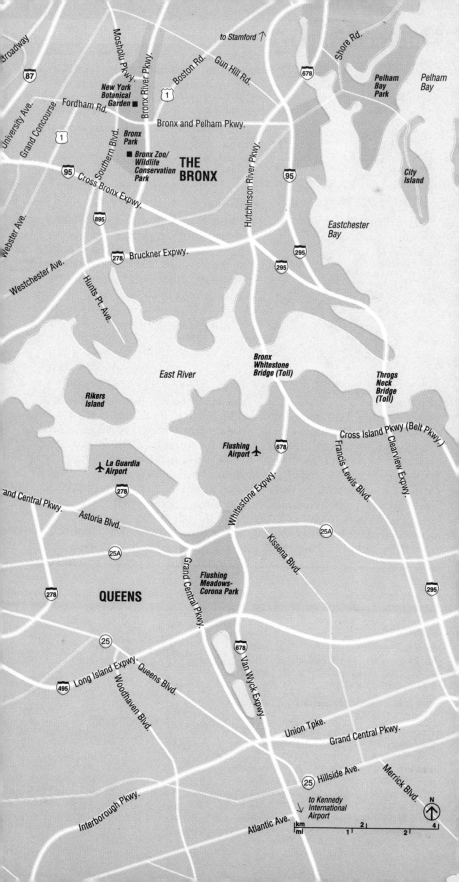

Orientation

Michael Storrings

Sophisticated and brutal. Exhilarating and oppressive. Earthy and aloof. A thorough description of New York City might exhaust the largest vocabulary. New York is indeed a city of dynamic contrasts, from the sleek granite high-rises of **Wall Street** and **Midtown** to the decaying old tenements of the **Bowery** and the **Bronx**, from the bohemian spirit of **Greenwich Village** to the old-money atmosphere of the **East Side**, and from the avant-garde art galleries of **SoHo** to the graffiti-covered subway stations of **Harlem**.

Weighted down by wall-to-wall buildings and seven million people, New York in its density may seem relentless and chaotic to first-time visitors. But it's essentially a city of small neighborhoods best explored one at a time. Don't exhaust yourself by trying to race from one end of the city to the other in the hopes of seeing "everything." Instead, make a list of must-sees in each neighborhood and enjoy all they have to offer before moving on to the next.

One of New York's chief attractions is the overwhelming number of places to visit. Every night on the town doesn't have to include dinner at a four-star restaurant and a Broadway show to be memorable, and you don't have to spend your days splurging in the expensive shops on **Fifth Avenue**. Some of New York's greatest pleasures are simple, and often inexpensive: sitting on the front steps of the **Metropolitan Museum of Art** and watching a mime while eating a hot dog; whiling away an hour in a cafe, sipping a cappuccino as the world goes by the window; walking through **Central Park** on a clear day and gazing up at the brilliant blue sky above the tall buildings; and, when you've said and done as much as you can, waving good-bye to the **Statue of Liberty** from the window of a departing plane, humming "New York, New York."

Area code 212 unless otherwise noted.

Getting to New York City

Airports

For convenient money-saving ways to get to the following airports, call **AIR RIDE** at 800/AIR.RIDE for information on buses, trains, and car, minivan, and limousine services.

John F. Kennedy International Airport (JFK)

The area's largest airport, almost always referred to as simply JFK, is located about 15 miles east of **Manhattan** in the borough of **Queens** and, depending on traffic, travel time can take anywhere from 35 to 90 minutes; average time is one hour. Most transatlantic flights, as well as many domestic flights, arrive and depart from JFK. Terminals are connected by free shuttle buses; if time is short, taxis are available.

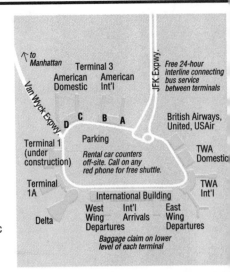

↖ to Manhattan

Van Wyck Expwy.

JFK Expwy.

Terminal 3 — American Domestic — American Int'l

Free 24-hour interline connecting bus service between terminals

D C B A

British Airways, United, USAir

Terminal 1 (under construction)

Parking

Rental car counters off-site. Call on any red phone for free shuttle.

TWA Domestic

Terminal 1A

Delta

International Building

West Wing Departures — Int'l Arrivals — East Wing Departures

TWA Int'l

Baggage claim on lower level of each terminal

How To Read This Guide

NEW YORK CITY ACCESS® is arranged so you can see at a glance where you are and what is around you. The numbers next to the entries in the following chapters correspond to the numbers on the maps. The text is color-coded according to the kind of place described:

Restaurants/Clubs: Red   Hotels: Blue

Shops/ Outdoors: Green   Sights/Culture: Black

 ♧ **Wheelchair accessible**

Wheelchair Accessibility

An establishment (except a restaurant) is considered wheelchair accessible when a person in a wheelchair can easily enter a building (i.e., no steps, a ramp, a wide-enough door) without assistance. Restaurants are deemed wheelchair accessible *only* if the above applies *and* if the rest rooms are on the same floor as the dining area and their entrances and stalls are wide enough to accommodate a wheelchair.

Rating the Restaurants and Hotels

The restaurant star ratings take into account the quality, service, atmosphere, and uniqueness of the restaurant. An expensive restaurant doesn't necessarily ensure an enjoyable evening; however, a small, relatively unknown spot could have good food, professional service, and a lovely atmosphere. Therefore, on a purely subjective basis, stars are used to judge the overall dining value (see the star ratings at right). Keep in mind that chefs and owners often change, which sometimes drastically affects the quality of a restaurant. The ratings in this guidebook are based on information available at press time.

The price ratings, as categorized at right, apply to restaurants and hotels. These figures describe general price-range relationships among other restaurants and hotels in the area. The restaurant price ratings are based on the average cost of an entrée for one person, excluding tax and tip. Hotel price ratings reflect the base price of a standard room for two people for one night during the peak season.

Restaurants

★	Good	
★★	Very Good	
★★★	Excellent	
★★★★	Extraordinary Experience	
$	The Price Is Right	(less than $15)
$$	Reasonable	($15-$20)
$$$	Expensive	($20-$30)
$$$$	Big Bucks	($30 and up)

Hotels

$	The Price Is Right	(less than $100)
$$	Reasonable	($100-$150)
$$$	Expensive	($150-$250)
$$$$	Big Bucks	($250 and up)

Map Key

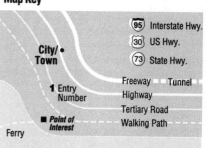

Airport Services

Airport Emergency	718/244.4225/6
Business Service Center	Contact individual airline
Complaints	800-498-7497
Currency Exchange	718/656-8444
Customs	718/553.1648
Dental Service	718/656.4747
Ground Transportation	800/247.7433
Immigration	718/553.1688
Information	718/244.4444
Interpreters/Translators	Contact individual airline
Lost & Found	718/244.4225
Lost or Damaged Baggage	Contact individual airline
Medical Clinic	718/656.5344
Paging	Contact individual airline
Parking Availability	718/656.5699
Police	718/244.4225/6
Traveler's Aid	718/656.4870

Airlines

Air France (AF)	247.0100, 800/237.2747
Air India (AI)	751.6200, 800/442.4455
Alitalia (AZ)	903.3300, 800/223.5730
American Airlines (AA)	800/235.9292
America West (HP)	800/247.5692
British Airways (BA)	800/247.9297
Delta (DL)	239.0700, 800/221.1212
El Al (LY)	768.9200, 800/223.6700
Finnair (AY)	499.9026, 800/950.5000
Icelandair (FI)	967.8888, 800/223.5500
Japan Airlines (JL)	838.4400, 800/525.3663
KLM Royal Dutch Airlines (KL)	800/374.7747
Lufthansa (LH)	800/645.3880
Northwest (NW)	
Domestic	800/225.2525
International	800/447.4747
Swissair (SR)	800/221.4750

TWA (TW)
　　Domestic 290.2121, 800/221.2000
　　International 290.2141, 800/892.4141

United Airlines (UA) 800/241.6522

USAir (US) 800/428.4322

Getting to and from John F. Kennedy International Airport

By Bus Bus service includes **Carey Transportation, Inc.** buses (718/632.0500, 800/284.0909), which depart JFK every 30 minutes (sometimes more frequently; call for information) from 6AM to midnight ($13). All buses drop off and pick up at **Grand Central Terminal** (Park Ave at E 41st St), a number of principal **Midtown** hotels, and **Port Authority Bus Terminal.** Buses also depart to and from **Queens** (**Long Island Railroad Jamaica Station**) every 30 minutes (5:30AM to 11PM) and to and from **Brooklyn** (scheduled stops include **Pierpont Plaza** and at **Williamsburg Savings Bank**) every two hours (8:30AM to 8:30PM). The last departure from **Grand Central** to JFK is 1AM. Travel time is about an hour but allow extra time for the hotel-hopping route. **Gray Line Air Shuttle Buses** (315.3006) run to and from the airport to nearly 50 hotels on the **East** and **West Side** between **23rd** and **63rd Streets** in Manhattan every 15 minutes from 7AM to 11PM, and hourly from Manhattan to the airports ($16). Travel time is about an hour, though its hotel stops are time-consuming.

By Car The most direct way into and out of Manhattan is by car. From the airport, take the **Van Wyck Expressway** to the **Grand Central Parkway (GCP),** which connects with the **Long Island Expressway (LIE).** Those going to downtown Manhattan (or to Brooklyn) should exit the LIE onto the **Brooklyn-Queens Expressway (BQE).** The BQE, in turn, feeds into the **Williamsburg, Manhattan,** and **Brooklyn Bridges.** For Midtown destinations, continue on the LIE, which connects with the **Queens-Midtown Tunnel.**

Rental Cars Most car rental agencies offer free shuttles from the arrivals terminal to their airport locations. The following companies can be reached by using the red phones in any terminal, or for advance reservations call:

Avis ....718/244.5400 or 800/331.1212

Budget ....718/656.6010 or 800/527.0700

Dollar ....718/656.2400 or 800/800.4000

Hertz ....718/656.7600 or 800/654.3131

National ....718/632.8300 or 800/227.7368

By Helicopter National Helicopter (800/645.3494) offers helicopter charters for four to six passengers to and from the airport at its **East 34th Street Heliport** for $299; additional departure and arrival sites in Manhattan include the **West 30th Street Heliport** and Wall Street area. Call for information.

By Limousine Car services and limousines provide transportation to, though not as frequently from, the airport. They're a good bet when you must leave for the airport during rush hour, when taxis usually can't be found. Rates are set in advance and are typically the same—at times even cheaper—than a cab ride ($25 to $35 for a standard car, or $50 to $80 for a limousine). Many companies accept credit cards and offer standard as well as luxury cars and limousines. Here are some car service and limousine companies:

All City Transportation 718/402.4747

Carey 718/632.0500

Carmel 662.2222

City Ride 861.1000

Davel 645.4242

Fugazy 661.0100

G&G Limo 800/LIMO-NEED

London Towncars 988.9700

Minute Man 718/899.5600

Olympic Limousine .....800/872.0044 or 995-1200

Tel Aviv 505.0555

Timely Wheels 645.9888

By Taxi Taxis from the airport can be found outside all major domestic and international arrival buildings. An airport employee is usually on hand if you have any questions or need assistance. A cab ride for up to four people to midtown Manhattan is approximately $30 to $35, plus tunnel or bridge tolls and a tip (generally 15 percent). Not all taxis will want to make the trip from Midtown (and should never ask you to compensate for their return trip into town), so allow yourself time to find one so inclined. See limousines (above) to reserve private car service for the same price, or less.

Subway/Bus This is the cheapest way to get into town; you'll need to catch a free shuttle bus marked **Howard Beach Station,** where you'll connect with the **A** train ($1.50) subway, making stops along **Eighth Avenue** at **West 59th, West 42nd,** and **West 34th Streets.** To coordinate your trip from Midtown, call 800/247.7433 for departure times for the bus from **Howard Beach Station** to the airport.

La Guardia Airport (LGA)

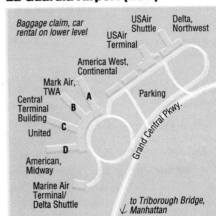

Located closer to Manhattan in northwest Queens, **La Guardia** is eight miles northeast of the city, or about a 30-minute drive. Most airlines serving other American cities use the two-level main terminal. **Delta Airlines** shares a terminal with **Northwest**, and **USAir** has a shuttle terminal. Terminals are connected by free shuttle buses.

Airport Services

Airport Emergencies 718/533.3900

Currency Exchange Information 718/533.3400

Customs/Immigration 718/476.4378,
. . . . .718/476.5211

Ground Transportation 800/247.7433,
. . . . .718/533.3705

Information .718/533.3400

Lost or Damaged Baggage . . Contact individual airline

Medical Office 718/476.5575

Paging . . . . .Contact individual airline

Parking 718/533.3400

Police 718/533.3900

Traveler's Aid 718/476.5575

Airlines

Air Canada (AC) 800/776.3000

American Airlines (AA) 800/235.9292

Continental (CO) 800/525.0280

Delta (DL) 239.0700, 800/221.1212

Midway (JI) .800/446.4392

Northwest (NW) 800/225.2525

TWA (TW) 290.2121, 800/221.2000

United (UA) .800/241.6522

USAir (US) 800/428.4322

Getting to and from La Guardia Airport

By Boat Delta Water Shuttle (800/543.3779) is a high-speed boat that departs the **Marine Air Terminal** several times each weekday morning and early evening ($20 one way; $30 roundtrip). Travel time is approximately 25 minutes to 34th Street and 40 minutes to Wall Street, and is available as well for those not flying with Delta.

By Bus Carey Transportation, Inc. (718/632.0500) runs buses between **La Guardia** and Manhattan every 20 minutes from 6:45AM to midnight ($9.50), to Queens every 30 minutes from 6:30AM to 11PM, and to Brooklyn every 60 minutes from 9:15AM to 9:15PM ($7.50). **Gray Line Air Shuttle Buses** (315.3006) run from the airport to nearly 50 hotels in Manhattan every 20 minutes from 7AM to 11PM, and also hourly from Manhattan to the airports ($13). Travel time is about an hour.

By Car If you're traveling to the city by car, you could take Grand Central Parkway to the **Triborough Bridge,** then travel south on the **FDR Drive.** Or, if you want to save time and the toll, get off at the **Van Dam Street** exit just before the Triborough Bridge, turn south on Van Dam/21st Street, and take the **Queensboro Bridge (59th Street Bridge)** into Manhattan. To go downtown (**SoHo** or Wall Street), take the Brooklyn-

Queens Expressway to the **Williamsburg Bridge,** which exits at **Delancey Street.**

Rental Cars The following companies have desks on the lower level by baggage claim; reservations are required:

Avis . . . . .718/507.3600 or 800/331.1212

Budget . . . . .718/639.6400 or 800/527.0700

Dollar . . . . .718/779.5600 or 800/800.4000

Hertz . . . . .718/478.5300 or 800/654.3131

National . . . . .800/227.7368 or 800/227.7368

By Limousine Car and limousine services are also available, a standard car costing approximately $15-$20. See **JFK Airport** above for more information.

By Taxi Taxis depart from in front of **La Guardia**'s major terminals around the clock. The cost to Midtown is generally $15 to $25, plus bridge and tunnel tolls and tip (15 percent).

By Subway/Bus Buses include **Triborough Coach** (718/335.1000), which runs a 5AM-to-1AM bus service from **La Guardia**'s main terminal to the **Jackson Heights 74th Street** subway station (the **E, F, R, G** and **7** all stop here) in Queens for connections into and out of Manhattan ($1.50). The trip takes about 30 minutes.

Newark International Airport (EWR)

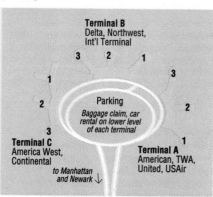

Local traffic snafus are making **Newark** a popular choice, especially if your final destination is the West Side or downtown Manhattan. Located on Newark Bay, 16 miles southwest of Manhattan in New Jersey (30 minutes to an hour traveling time), it has one international and two domestic terminals, with shuttle bus connections and easy public transportation options to and from Midtown.

Airport Services

Airport Emergencies 201/961.6633

Currency Exchange 201/961.4720

Customs 201/645.3409

Ground Transportation 800/247.7433

Immigration .201/645.3239

Information .201/961.6000

Lost & Found . . . . .Contact individual airline

Paging . . . . .Contact individual airline

Parking 201/961.4751

Police 201/961.6230

Airlines

Air Canada (AC) 800/776.3000

Alitalia (AZ) .800/223.5730

American West (HP) 800/235.9292

British Airway (BA) 800/247.9297

Carnival (KW) 800/824.7386

Continental (CO) 800/525.0280

Delta (DL) 800/221.1212

Kiwi (KP) 800/538.5494

Mexicana (MX) 800/531.7921

TWA (TW)
    Domestic 800/221.2000
    International 800/892.4141

Virgin Atlantic (VS) 800/862.8621

Getting to and from Newark International Airport

By Bus Bus service includes **New Jersey Transit** (201/762.5100; in New Jersey, 800/772.2222), which offers 24-hour bus service every 15 to 30 minutes to the **Port Authority Bus Terminal**. It also offers rail service to Newark's **Penn Station** every 10 to 15 minutes from 6AM to 1AM, and every 30 to 60 minutes between 1AM to 6AM ($7). **Olympia Trails** (964.6233) runs buses from **Newark** to **1 World Trade Center** every 30 minutes (Monday to Saturday 6:45AM to 8:45PM; Sunday, holidays 7:15AM to 8:15PM) and **41st Street** at **Park Avenue,** and 34th Street at Eighth Avenue every 20 to 30 minutes daily from 6:15AM to midnight ($7.00). The ride lasts from 30 to 45 minutes. **Gray Line Air Shuttle Buses** (315.3006) run from the airport to nearly 50 hotels in Manhattan every 20 minutes from 7AM to 11PM; also hourly from Manhattan to the airports ($18). Travel time is about an hour, mostly due to in-town hotel stops.

By Car The route to Manhattan by car is fairly straightforward. Take the **New Jersey Turnpike** and follow the signs to either the **Holland Tunnel** (downtown) or the **Lincoln Tunnel** (Midtown).

Rental Cars The following are located in the baggage-claim area and are open daily from 7AM to midnight (the return lots are open for 24 hours):

Avis 201/961.4300, 800/331.1212

Budget 201/961.2990, 800/527.0700

Dollar 201/824.2002, 800/800.4000

Hertz 201/621.2000, 800/654.3131

National 201/622.1270, 800/227.7368

By Limousine These services may be obtained at booths within individual terminals. To reserve in advance, see car and limousine companies that service **JFK Airport.**

By Taxi To Manhattan it will cost $25-$35; taxi stands are located in front of the arrivals building.

By Train There is currently no rail service for transportation to or from **Newark Airport** to Manhattan, though current negotiations are underway to create a monorail line, an extension of the one now under construction that will connect all terminals.

Getting Around New York City—and Beyond

Perhaps the most crucial element of your stay is mastering the city's transportation services and routes. The five major ways of getting around are subway, bus, taxi, car service, and foot. Of these, walking is the most highly recommended, and sometimes the quickest. Manhattan is laid out in a rather easy-to-grasp grid of north/south avenues and east/west numbered streets. **Fifth Avenue** is the dividing line between east and west.

Bicycle Bicycle-riding in Midtown is a hazardous art that should be left to the pot-hole–hardened bicycle messengers known for their derring-do.

Bus Criss-crossing the city, New York City's network of buses may be slower than subways, but you have the satisfaction of seeing where you're going and enjoying a more pleasant mode of travel. A sign on the front of each bus gives its route number and final destination, and stops are clearly marked on the street, sometimes with maps showing the route served (although not every bus serves every stop). In addition to the longer-distance routes that run on the north-south avenues, there are many crosstown bus routes. (Request a transfer from the driver when you get on, so that if you're going, say, north and then west across town, you don't have to pay a second fare on the crosstown route, or vice versa.) During rush hours, buses marked "Limited" function like express subway lines and stop only at major intersections. Exact change, a $1.50 bus/subway token, or **Metrocard** is required.

The **Port Authority Bus Terminal,** located between **West 40th** and West 42nd Streets and Eighth and **Ninth Avenues** (with principal entrance on Eighth Ave), is the departure and arrival point for all long-distance buses, commuter buses, and bus links to the airports.

Car Think twice about driving a car to get around Manhattan. Traffic is nightmarish, parking on the street is impossible, and parking garages are outrageously expensive. If you must arrive by car, it's best to stash it away in a parking garage and then use alternative means of transportation. Hotels sometimes offer discounted parking rates to their guests (even the most expensive hotels charge extra). Parking tickets are given without mercy, so don't park at a meter that isn't working, and be sure you understand the convoluted restrictions posted on parking signs so your car isn't towed—something that happens all too frequently.

Car Service These so-called gypsy cabs (generally owner-operated and not as strictly controlled as licensed cabs) have sprung up in town simply because yellow cabs are sometimes scarce or will sometimes not go where you wish to go—particularly to the outer boroughs or to Harlem and Washington Heights. Or you may find yourself visiting until a late hour and wish to have a car at your door rather than trying to hail one on the avenue. Car services and gypsy cabs are identified by their "livery" license plates. Car services are listed on page 6 or in the Yellow Pages and gypsy cabs can be hailed on the street—if you have to. Confirm the fare in advance on the phone when reserving a car for a "drop off" or an hourly booking.

Ferry Ferries can be a good bet for crossing water. The **Staten Island Ferry** is still one of the cheapest thrills (50¢) in New York City, running every 20 to 30 minutes 24 hours daily from the foot of **Whitehall Street** (next to **Battery Park**); you can stay on round-trip at the same fare. Other popular ferry services include the following:

Delta Water Shuttle 800/543.3779

Express Navigation (Sandy Hook, New Jersey)
. . . . .800/262.8743

Hoboken-Battery Park City Ferry 201/420.6307

Port Imperial (Weehawken, New Jersey)
. . . . .800/533.3779

Staten Island Ferry 806.6940

Parking Almost all hotels have either private parking or a special arrangement with a nearby lot, so check before arriving. Parking lots are not hard to come by, though they are expensive. Ask about daily rates or try to strike a deal if you'll be leaving your car there, unused, for more than 24 hours. If you opt to park on the street, make sure you understand the restrictions posted and the risk you run with frequent burglaries. "Alternate side of the street parking" means you'll have to get there by 8AM the next day to move it.

Subway Subways may be loud, dirty, and crowded, but they are the most efficient way to conquer longer distances within Manhattan. Actually, most of the graffiti-riddled cars have been replaced with sleeker modern ones that are air-conditioned in the summer and heated in winter.

The New York City system is complicated and not always immediately decipherable. Entrance requires the purchase of a $1.50 token, which allows you to travel its length and breadth (and to make unlimited connections). Tokens are available at token booths at most stations as well as at some **McDonald's** restaurants and at newsstands. It's wise to purchase tokens in 10-packs if you're planning to ride often. The city recently introduced **Metrocard**, for prepaid subway access; it is available in $5 increments up to $80, and at press time was planned to be accepted in 169 of 469 stations. The subway system is open 24 hours, although principal service is between 6AM to midnight. After hours, wait for your train in designated areas on the station platform.

Taxi They seem to rule the streets of New York City. In fact, there are nearly 12,000 licensed cabs—a meaningless number if you can't find one when you need one. Licensed cabs are bright yellow and signal their availability with a light on the roof. Cabs may be hailed anywhere on the street, except for crosswalks and intersections, and by law they are supposed to take you wherever you wish to go. But be forewarned—New York cab drivers are an independent bunch. The taxi rates are posted on the side of the cab ($1.50 for the first 1/5 mile, 25¢ for each additional 1/5 mile, and 20¢ for each minute in standstill or slow traffic). A 50¢ nighttime surcharge is applied 8PM to 6AM. A cab ride in New York can be colorful, amusing, and efficient, or hellish and frustrating, depending on the traffic and the driver. Most cabbies are recently arrived immigrants and, though they must pass a language proficiency test, communication can occasionally be a problem; make sure the driver understands where you want to go.

Tours There's something here for everyone. Additional information on a large variety of tours geared toward everything from architecture to history, culture, and the homes of the stars, is available at the **New York Convention and Visitors Bureau** (see page 11). Here is a sampling of what's offered:

Adventure on a Shoestring (265.2663) celebrates everything that is wonderful and positive about the city. Walking tours include chats with members of the community toured. **Doorway to Design** (221.1111, daytime; 718/339.1542, evenings) customizes a behind-the-scenes tour of the interior design, fashion, and art worlds as well as walking tours with an architectural historian. **Gray Line of New York** (297.2600) offers two- to eight-and-a-half-hour Manhattan tours in English and a number of foreign languages. **Harlem Gospel & Jazz Tours** (757.0425) provides visits to historic sites, gospel church services, soul-food restaurants, and jazz clubs. **Municipal Art Society** (935.3960) gives walking tours (one hour to all day) with an architectural orientation. **92nd Street YM/YWHA** (415.5628 or 415.5599) focuses on ethnic, cultural, architectural, social, and historical facets of New York and also offers bus tours to Manhattan environs. **Urban Park Rangers** (427.4040) features walking tours of parks in all five boroughs, with an emphasis on botany, geology, and wildlife. For hikers, there's **Heritage Trails New York** (767.0637), which offers four different tours in a 40-page guide: Colored dots (blue, green, orange, and red) link some 50 historic sites in lower Manhattan. Call for more information. **Museum of the City of New York** (534.1672 ext 206) provides walks of varying lengths geared to the museum's current exhibitions. Historian Joyce Gold of **Historic Walks** (242.5762) conducts walking tours of lower Manhattan, **Greenwich Village, Chelsea,** and **Harlem. Spirit Cruises** (727.2789) will wisk you to sail **New York Harbor** and catch a glimpse of the breathtaking New York skyline. Manhattanites Mimi Dalva and Barbara Raynor (988.4571) conducts tours of the city—lots of history and a bit of tradition.

Train Grand Central Train Terminal (E 42nd St, between Vanderbilt and Lexington Aves) in the heart of Manhattan is the hub of the **Metro-North Commuter Railroad.** The **New Haven, Harlem,** and **Hudson Lines** service New York State and Connecticut. For train schedule and fare information, call 532.4900.

Pennsylvania Station (between W 31st and W 33rd Sts, and Seventh and Eighth Aves) services all long-distance trains, including **Amtrak** (800/872.7245) and **Metroliner** (800/523.8720), plus the **Long Island Railroad** (718/558.7400) and **New Jersey Transit** (201/762.5100) commuter trains.

Walking To get a true sense of New York City, you're best off hitting the pavement, where one minute you'll find yourself dwarfed by Midtown skyscrapers and the next winding your way through narrow Greenwich Village streets. Most museums are conveniently close to one another, and parks and gardens offer good resting places for tired legs and aching feet. You can easily stroll from the Upper West Side to Midtown in about an hour; the most scenic route is along **Central Park West** to **Central Park South,** then on to Fifth Avenue. Warning: Beware bicycle messengers who have a habit of not yielding the right-of-way to pedestrians!

FYI

Accommodations New York City's hotels come in all sizes and locations. See above for price categories, though never overlook the often-advertised bargain rates. When booking ask if there are any special deals—Broadway tickets and breakfast, or special summer or week-end rates—not always publicized. With year-round conventions, trade fairs, and ever-growing numbers of tourists, never underestimate the importance of booking in advance: Even during slow months, hotels can be booked solid.

Climate The best months to visit New York are May, June, September, and October. July and particularly August can be oppressively hot, with high humidity and temperatures hovering in the 90s. December through February are the coldest months, with blustery winds and temperatures in the 20s and below.

Months	Average Temperature (°F)
December-February	34
March-May	55
June-August	83
September-November	68

Drinking The legal drinking age is 21, and many bars, restaurants, and clubs require ID. Bar hours vary (all are closed before noon on Sunday), but the legal limit for closing is 4AM. On Sunday, restaurants may not serve alcohol until noon, and liquor stores are closed, but beer, which is sold in grocery stores, may be purchased after noon.

Hours It's a good idea to call ahead to find out if a particular restaurant or shop will be open the day and time you plan to visit. Although this book provides business hours for shops, museums, galleries, and other places, keep in mind that this information may change with the seasons, the economy, or even the whim of the owner.

Money Most Citibank, Chemical, and American Express branches will exchange foreign currency at current market rates. Most banks won't charge a fee if the amount changed is more than $200. Traveler's checks may be purchased at most banks, whose standard hours are Monday to Friday, 9AM-3PM. Call *Chequepoint* (800/544.9898; open daily) for

their different locations around town. *Thomas Cook's* various locations often include Saturday and Sunday hours as well; call 265.6049.

Personal Safety Cities attract every type of person, and that includes the worst. It is perhaps less a commentary about New York than about the times to say that you have to be alert on the street (and in buildings, the subways, etc.) and to try not to advertise helplessness, naiveté, or confusion, lest you risk attracting unsolicited assistance. Common sense dos and don'ts: Don't display your good jewelry on the subway. Don't make eye contact with people who impart a sense of danger or derangement, even though they may seem exotic to you. (View the scene from a safe distance, if you must.) Carry your purse in front of you with the clasp side against your body. Don't carry your wallet in a back pants pocket or in a way that causes it to bulge. Don't let strangers carry packages for you and never leave your bag or bags unattended if even for a moment. If you see trouble coming, avoid it.

Publications There are three daily papers: *The New York Times,* the *New York Post,* and the *Daily News;* and a number of weekly publications, including *New York* magazine, *The New Yorker, Variety, Backstage,* and *The Village Voice,* have excellent listings and information.

Restaurants Those restaurants garnering three- or four-star ratings usually warrant a reservation; when booking, check on their dress code. In the area of the Theater District and the blocks that surround it, restaurants often offer a pre-theater price (and recommend reservations to assure a seat); others offer prixe-fixe meals during certain hours.

Shopping The trendiest shopping area in New York City is Fifth Avenue with its exclusive department stores and boutiques. Not far behind is **Madison Avenue,** well known for its high fashion and art galleries. Each neighborhood may determine the hours certain stores follow, as will the season. The period between Thanksgiving and Christmas commonly see extended hours; neighborhoods with a lot of foot-traffic such as **Columbus Avenue** or areas of Greenwich Village may have longer hours. Stores may shut tight on Sunday on Madison Avenue, but it's a popular shopping day for SoHo's boutiques. If you're making a special trip during off hours, call first to verify the store's hours.

Smoking It is illegal to smoke on all public transportation, in the lobbies of office buildings, in enclosed public places, in taxis, in designated areas of theaters, and in most shops. In early 1995, a much-contested city law was passed that limits smoking to restaurants seating less than 35, or in the bar areas of certain larger restaurants if they are sufficiently separated from the main dining area.

Street Plan Manhattan is laid out in an easy-to-follow grid of north/south avenues and east/west numbered streets. Bear in mind that Fifth Avenue is the dividing line between east and west. Below **Houston Street,** the numbered streets end, and parts of downtown (Greenwich Village in particular) can get a little tricky.

Taxes There is an 8.25-percent sales tax on almost everything except supermarket food. The hotel tax is five percent plus a charge of $2 per room/per night.

Telephone As of this writing, it costs 25 cents to make a local call from a pay phone. Manhattan is in the 212 area code; calls to Brooklyn, the Bronx, Queens, and Staten Island require dialing 1, and then the 718 prefix. Response to advertisements with exchanges such as 394, 540, 550, etc. will cost you extra; the same goes for 900- and 700-prefixes.

Tickets Theater tickets can be obtained at the box office, through ticket agencies (see Yellow Pages), or at **TKTS** (West 47th St, between Seventh Ave and Broadway, 768.1818). Tickets are not available for all shows; you may have a better chance close to curtain time, when producers release unused house seats. The same applies for music and dance tickets. However, for same-day performances for music, dance, sports, and entertainment, stop at the **Music & Dance Tickets Booth** in **Bryant Park** (W 42nd St at Sixth Ave, 382.2323). Other ticket outlets include **Telecharge** (239.6200) and **Ticketmaster** (307.4100)

Time Zone New York City is on Eastern Standard Time.

Tipping A 15- to 20-percent gratuity is standard. In restaurants, most people simply double the sales tax (8.25 percent). Taxi drivers are tipped a minimum 15 percent of the meter reading. Hotel bellhops and station porters expect a dollar for each bag they carry. A tip is a reward for service; if you don't get it, don't pay for it.

Visitors' Information Center For information, brochures, maps, lists of special events, theater discount coupons, and knowledgeable help, stop by the **New York Convention and Visitors Bureau** at 2 Columbus Circle, on Central Park South at Central Park West, or call 397.8200. Hours are Monday through Friday from 9AM to 5PM, and Saturday and Sunday 10AM to 3PM (397.8222). Also at 226 West 42nd Street, between Seventh and Eighth Avenues, in the old Harris Theater. Open daily 10AM to 7PM.

Phone Books

Emergencies
Ambulance/Fire/Police 911
TDD 800/342.4357, 800/662.1220
AAA Road Service (members only) . .800/222.4357
Animal Medical Center 838.8100
Dental 679.3966
Hospitals
  Bellevue Hospital Center 561.4141
  Mt. Sinai Medical Center 241.6500
  New York Hospital–Cornell Medical Center
  . . . . .746.5454
  NYU Medical Center 263.5000
  St. Luke's–Roosevelt Medical Center . .523.4000
  St. Vincent's Hospital & Medical Center 604.7000

Pharmacy (24-hour) 604.8376
Police (Non-Emergency) 374.5000
Poison Control 764.7667, 340.4494

Visitors' Information
American Youth Hostels 932.2300
Amtrak 582.6875
Better Business Bureau 533.6200
Convention and Visitors' Bureau 397.8200
George Washington Bridge Bus Station . .568.5323
Greyhound Bus 971.6318, 800/231.2222
Handicapped Visitors' Information 397.8222
NYC Taxi & Limousine Commission 302.8294
NYC Transit Authority
  subway and bus information 718/330.1234
  lost and found and other services
  . . . . .718/330.3000, 718/625.6200
Time 976.1616
US Customs 466.5550
US Passport Office 399.5290
Weather 976.1212
Western Union 800/325.6000

Manhattan Address Locator

To locate avenue addresses, take the address, cancel the last figure, divide by two, then add or subtract the key number below. The answer is the nearest numbered cross street, approximately. For example, to find the cross street to 1650 Broadway, take half of 165 (roughly 83) and subtract 30 as indicated below. The answer is 53rd Street.

To find addresses on numbered cross streets, remember that numbers above Eighth Street increase east or west from Fifth Avenue, which runs north-south. Below Eighth Street, Broadway is the dividing line.

Avenues A, B, C, D . . . . .Add 3

First Avenue . . . . .Add 3

Second Avenue . . . . .Add 3

Third Avenue . . . . .Add 10

Fourth Avenue . . . . .Add 8

Fifth Avenue

   Up to 200 . . . . .Add 13

   Up to 400 . . . . .Add 16

   Up to 600 . . . . .Add 18

   Up to 775 . . . . .Add 20

   775-1286 . . . . .Cancel last figure and subtract 18

   286-1500 . . . . .Add 45

   Above 2000 . . . . .Add 24

Avenue of the Americas (Sixth Avenue) . .Subtract 12

Seventh Avenue

   Below 110th Street, ...Add 12

   Above 110th Street, ...Add 20

Eighth Avenue . . . . .Add 10

Ninth Avenue . . . . .Add 13

10th Avenue . . . . .Add 14

Amsterdam Avenue .Add 60

Audubon Avenue . . . . .Add 165

Broadway (23rd-192nd Streets) . . . . . . .Subtract 30

Columbus Avenue . . . . .Add 60

Convent Avenue . . . . .Add 127

Central Park West . . . . .Divide house number by 10
and add 60

Edgecombe Avenue .Add 134

Ft. Washington Avenue . . . . .Add 158

Lenox Avenue . . . . .Add 110

Lexington Avenue . . . . .Add 22

Madison Avenue . . . . .Add 26

Manhattan Avenue . . . . .Add 100

Park Avenue . . . . .Add 35

Pleasant Avenue . . . . .Add 101

Riverside Drive

(up to 165th Street) . . . .Divide house number by 10
and add 72

St. Nicholas Avenue . . . . .Add 110

Wadsworth Avenue .Add 173

West End Avenue . . . . .Add 60

York Avenue . . . . .Add 4

iloveinns.com/bed_and_breakf
www.wymanhouse.com

New York, Home Style

Due to ever-escalating hotel rates, many travelers have turned to bed-and-breakfast inns. A time-honored tradition in Europe, these alternative services are becoming increasingly popular here, placing visitors in the homes of accommodating New York hosts. Aside from the obvious attraction of saving money, most guests enjoy meeting new people in the relaxed atmosphere of a home, which can make a world of difference to travelers who find the city daunting.

Here are some of the bed-and-breakfast services with listings in the New York area. You must call or write well in advance of your arrival and send a deposit. Most agencies also offer "unhosted" (and therefore slightly more expensive) stays, where furnished apartments are rented by the day, week, or month.

Abode Bed & Breakfast, Ltd. *4 nt. minimum*
PO Box 20022, New York, NY 10021. 472.2000, 800/835.8880 (good only outside of tri-state area)

City Lights Bed & Breakfast. *.com*
PO Box 20355, Cherokee Station, New York, NY 10021. 737.7049; fax 535.2755

New World Bed & Breakfast, *.com*
150 Fifth Ave, Suite 711, New York, NY 10011. *emailed*
675.5600, 800/443.3800; fax 675.6366

Urban Ventures, Inc. *.com*
38 W 32nd St, Suite 1412, New York, NY 10001. 594.5650; fax 947.9320
no site

New York Speak

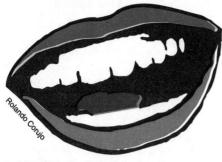

Rolando Corujo

Standing on line Known everywhere else in the world as "standing in line."

Fashion victim Someone whose clothes and makeup are too trendy to wear anywhere but at a photo shoot.

East Village type The flip side of "fashion victim"; someone whose clothes and makeup are too urban funky to wear anywhere but on **Avenue D.**

In George Orwell's *1984,* society is undermined by a language called "newspeak," sophisticated words and phrases that actually mean nothing at all.

New Yorkers have taken the opposite tack by cultivating a series of unique and simple phrases that, once understood, speak volumes. Here, then, is a guide to some of the more trenchant vocabulary:

Sample sales Sales of leftover or sample merchandise held by manufacturers in the Garment District. Although some garmentos like to keep the best sales a secret (more for them), they are often advertised to the public in the back of *New York Magazine* and on flyers handed out on the street or pasted on lampposts and mailboxes.

Greetings and Such

Yo Could mean "Pardon me," "Watch it, you," or "Pleased to see you, my good man."

Cuisine

Grab a slice To purchase and consume pizza.

The Original Ray's Refers to a famed establishment on Sixth Avenue at 11th Street, whose name has since been used by dozens of imitators. See "grab a slice."

A schmear Refers to a small portion of cream cheese to be smeared upon a bagel.

A regular A cup of coffee with milk, no sugar.

A black A cup of coffee with sugar, no milk.

Wait on them Contrary to popular practice, something that waiters tell customers to do, as in "You're gonna have to wait on them fries."

Geography

The Island (Long Island). Not used to refer to Staten Island. Never, but never, used to refer to Manhattan.

Uptown When used in Greenwich Village or points south, refers to the entire area that stretches above 14th Street.

Upstate Refers to anywhere north of New York City, within New York State.

Over there New Jersey.

Consumerism

Bloomie's Bloomingdale's department store, as in "I saw her in Bloomie's." Not to be confused with underwear.

Lotto fever An affliction that compels people to wait "on line" for hours for a one-in-26-million chance at wealth, although it's more likely they'll be crushed by a meteor while watching *Jeopardy* that night. Its seriousness increases as the jackpot grows—in 1994 it reached an unprecedented $70 million.

Two-fer A theater coupon that entitles the bearer to two tickets for the price of one (plus a surcharge) to the show for which the two-fer is issued. Available at the **Convention and Visitors Bureau** at Columbus Circle.

Our Fair Streets

Don't block the box Anti-gridlock warning to drivers meaning "Do not drive into the intersection until there is room to cross it."

Gridlock The traffic jam that results when someone "blocks the box."

Don't even THINK of parking here Courteous street sign provided by the city. Usually ignored.

Alternate parking Rules in which the side of the street one may park on is determined by the hour and day of the week.

Bridge-and-tunnel people Commuters from New Jersey and Long Island. See "Over there."

BBQs Those who commute into Manhattan from the boroughs of Brooklyn, the Bronx, and Queens.

No radio Posted on car windows as an appeal to thieves who might be tempted to break in without checking to see that the radio has been removed.

Main Events

January

National Boat Show, Jacob Javits Center; **Winter Antiques Show,** Seventh Regiment Armory.

February

Chinese New Year, Chinatown; **New York International Motorcycle Show,** Jacob Javits Center; **Westminster Kennel Club/ Westminster Dog Show,** Madison Square Garden; **Black History Month,** events all throughout the city.

March

Ringling Bros. and Barnum & Bailey Circus, Madison Square Garden; **St. Patrick's Day Parade,** Fifth Avenue; **New York Flower Show,** Hudson Passenger Piers at West 53rd Street; **Greek Independence Day Parade,** Fifth Avenue.

April

Easter Parade, Fifth Avenue; **Greater New York International Auto Show,** Jacob Javits Center; **Cherry Blossom Festival,** Brooklyn Botanic Garden; **Annual Flower Show,** Macy's; **New York City Ballet** (spring season) begins, State Theater, Lincoln Center; New York **Mets** (Shea Stadium) and New York **Yankees** (Yankee Stadium) open baseball season.

May

Washington Square Outdoor Art Show, University Place; **Rose Week/Orchid Show,** New York Botanical Garden, Bronx; **All City Beaches** open for the summer; **Memorial Day Parade,** Fifth Avenue; **Ninth Avenue International Festival,** between West 37th and West 57th Streets, is a weekend of food and fun.

June

Metropolitan Opera/New York Philharmonic concerts, city parks; **Belmont Stakes,** Belmont Park, Long Island;

July

Macy's Annual 4th of July Fireworks, East River; **American Crafts Festival,** Lincoln Center; **Shakespeare in the Park,** Delecorte Theater, Central Park.

August

US Open Tennis Championships, Flushing Meadows, Queens.

September

New York Philharmonic season opens, Avery Fisher Hall, Lincoln Center; **San Gennaro Festival,** Little Italy; **Washington Square Outdoor Art Show,** University Place; **New York Film Festival,** Alice Tully Hall, Lincoln Center; **New York Jets/Giants** season begins, Giants Stadium, Meadowlands, NJ; **New York is Book Country Fair,** Fifth Avenue, between 48th and 57th Streets; **Metropolitan Opera** opens, Metropolitan Opera House, Lincoln Center.

October

Ice skating begins at Rockefeller Center; **Halloween Parade,** Greenwich Village; **Columbus Day Parade,** Fifth Avenue; **New York Rangers** season begins, Madison Square Garden.

November

New York City Ballet (fall season) begins, State Theater, Lincoln Center; **New York City Marathon** begins at Verrazano-Narrows Bridge and ends in Central Park; **Macy's Thanksgiving Day Parade,** Broadway; **Virginia Slims Women's Tennis Championships,** Madison Square Garden; **Veteran's Day Parade,** Fifth Avenue; **The Christmas Spectacular** featuring the Rockettes, Radio City Music Hall.

December

Lighting of the Christmas Tree, Rockefeller Center; **Nabisco Masters Tennis Championships,** Madison Square Garden. **New Year's Eve** celebrations at Times Square and throughout the city.

Bests

Cindy Adams
Syndicated Columnist for the *New York Post*/
WNBC-TV "Today in New York" Correspondent

For celebrity-watching: Lunch at **Le Cirque.**

For jewelry-watching: The **Diamond Center,** West 47th Street between Fifth and Sixth Avenues.

For people-watching: Bench in front of the **Plaza Hotel** around noon.

For kid-watching: **FAO Schwarz.**

For view-watching: **Rainbow Room.**

For lox/bagel/pastrami/salami-watching: **Stage Deli.**

For window-shopping: **Madison Avenue** going uptown from East 57th Street.

For shopping: **Trump Tower.**

For culture: **Lincoln Center.**

For color: **Greenwich Village.**

For architecture: **Seagram's Building** (supermodern glass and chrome), **Chrysler Building** (Art Deco), **Guggenheim Museum** (Frank Lloyd Wright), **World Trade Center** (tallest).

For VIP high-rises, where people from Phil Donahue to me dwell: Walk **Fifth Avenue.**

For caviar: **Petrossian's.**

For seafood: **The SeaGrill.**

For steaks: **Gallagher's.**

For Chinese: **Fu's.**

For Japanese: **Inagiku** at the Waldorf.

For Russian: **Russian Tea Room.**

For atmosphere: **The Water Club.**

For what's no place else in the whole world but in New York: **Statue of Liberty, Radio City Music Hall, United Nations, Rockefeller Center** skating rink, the **Theater District, Empire State Building.**

And read the *New York Post.*

Brendan Gill
Writer, *The New Yorker*

Downstairs at the **21 Club.**

A midsummer night's sail from the **South Street Seaport Museum.**

Openings at the **Clocktower Gallery,** high above Broadway.

Sunday brunch at **Mortimer's.**

The latest theater piece at **La Mama E.T.C.,** with Ellen Stewart presiding.

A ramble in the **Ramble,** in Central Park.

The **Big Apple Circus.**

The sound of brasses on Sunday morning at the **Cathedral of St. John the Divine.**

Crossing the windswept boardwalk of the **Brooklyn Bridge.**

The successful flagging down of a taxi at twilight on **Park Avenue.**

Books & Company, a shop eager to serve customers even on Sunday.

Architectural exhibitions at the **Urban Center** in the historic **Villard Houses** on Madison Avenue.

Ninth Street, west of **Fifth Avenue.**

Lunch in the **Rose Room** of the **Algonquin.**

The **New York Society Library.**

The annual festival of the **Film Society of Lincoln Center.**

The **Café des Artistes.**

A big winter opening at the **Whitney Museum of American Art.**

Brandy at **Jim McMullen's.**

The delectable smell of **Bendel's.**

The pillared Palladian folly on **West 57th Street** that leads one into the **Parker Meridien** hotel.

Bradley's bar, on University Place.

Upstairs at the **21 Club.**

Edward Kosner
Editor-in-Chief, *Esquire* magazine

Lunch in the **Grill Room** of the **Four Seasons Restaurant.**

Chili and a bacon-cheeseburger in the back room of **P.J. Clarke's.**

The **Carousel** in **Central Park.**

The **Cloisters.**

Café des Artistes.

The gallery with the fountain at **The Frick Collection.**

Fifth Avenue from 12th Street to **Washington Square.**

The promenade at **Battery Park City.**

Le Cirque at lunch.

The view of **Midtown Manhattan** from the riverside in **Long Island City.**

The **Metropolitan Opera** in top form.

The **Oak Bar** at the **Plaza** at dusk on a winter evening.

Madison Square Garden when the Knicks are hot.

Each of the 11,787 licensed yellow cabs in New York City (a number frozen since 1937) pays a medallion fee of $140,000. Unlike London cabbies, who undergo a rigorous two-year program (while managing to retain their politeness), New York City drivers sign up for an obligatory 40-hour training course. When possible, give the cross street when telling the driver your destination—don't be surprised if he asks *you* how to get there.

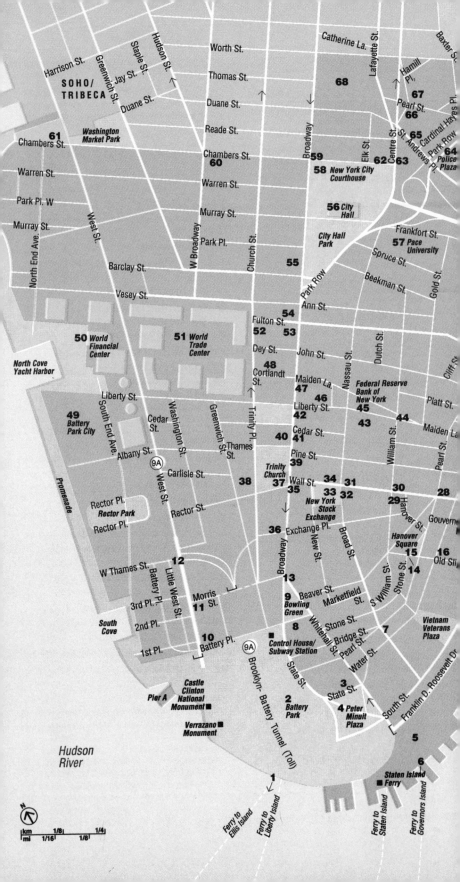

SOHO/
TRIBECA

Harrison St.

Greenwich St.

Jay St.

Staple St.

Hudson St.

Worth St.

Thomas St.

Duane St.

Reade St.

Catherine La.

Lafayette St.

Baxter St.

Hamill Pl.

Pearl St.

67

66

68

Chambers St.

61

Washington
Market Park

Duane St.

Elk St.

Centre St.

St. Andrews Pl.

Cardinal Hayes Pl.

Park Row

65

64 Police
Plaza

Warren St.

Park Pl. W

Murray St.

North End Ave.

West St.

Duane St.

Chambers St.

60

Warren St.

Murray St.

W Broadway

Park Pl.

Church St.

Broadway

59

58 New York City
Courthouse

62 **63**

56 City
Hall

Barclay St.

Vesey St.

55

City Hall
Park

Park Row

Frankfort St.

57 Pace
University

Spruce St.

Beekman St.

Gold St.

North Cove
Yacht Harbor

50 World
Financial
Center

51 World
Trade
Center

Fulton St.

52

54

53

Dey St.

John St.

Nassau St.

Dutch St.

Ann St.

Platt St.

Cliff St.

48
Cortlandt
St.

Maiden La.

47

46

Federal Reserve
Bank of
New York

Liberty St.

Battery Park City

49

South End Ave.

Liberty St.

Cedar
St.

Greenwich St.

Trinity Pl.

Liberty St.

42

45

43

William St.

44

Maiden La

Pearl St.

Albany St.

Washington St.

Thames
St.

Cedar St.

40

41

Pine St.

Promenade

9A

Carlisle St.

West St.

Rector St.

38

Trinity
Church

37

Wall St.

35

34

33

32

31

New York
Stock
Exchange

30

Hanover St.

29

28

Gouverne

Rector Pl.

Rector Park

Rector Pl.

Rector St.

36

Exchange Pl.

Broadway

New St.

Broad St.

Hanover
Square

15

14

Stone St.

S. William St.

16
Old Sli

W Thames St.

Battery Pl.

Little West St.

12

Morris
St.

11

13

9
Bowling
Green

Beaver St.

Marketfield
St.

Whitehall St.

Stone St.

Bridge St.

Pearl St.

Water St.

7

Vietnam
Veterans
Plaza

3rd Pl.

2nd Pl.

South
Cove

1st Pl.

10
Battery Pl.

9A

8

Control House/
Subway Station

State St.

2
Battery
Park

3
State St.

4 Peter
Minuit
Plaza

South St.

Water St.

Franklin D. Roosevelt Dr

5

Pier A

Castle
Clinton
National
Monument

Verrazano
Monument

Hudson
River

Brooklyn- Battery Tunnel (Toll)

1

6

Staten Island
Ferry

N

km

mi

1/8

1/16

1/4

1/8

Ferry to
Ellis Island

Ferry to
Liberty Island

Ferry to
Staten Island

Ferry to
Governors Island

Mott St.

E Broadway

Catherine St.

Henry St.

Oliver St.

St. James Pl.

Madison St.

Monroe St.

Market St.

Cherry St.

Water St.

South St.

**CHINATOWN/
LOWER EAST SIDE/
LITTLE ITALY**

Finest

Robert F. Wagner Sr. Pl.

Franklin D. Roosevelt Dr.

Dover St.

21 Brooklyn
Bridge

22

23

Peck Slip

Pearl St.

Water St.

Front St.

South St.

Beekman St.

20 Fulton
Fish Market

Fulton St.

19 South Street
Seaport

18

Pier 18

John St.

24

Pier 17

tcher St.

Pier 16

Pier 15

5
Wall Street
Plaza

17

Pier 14

6

Pier 13

7

Pier 11

Pier 9

**Wall Street
Heliport**

■ Pier 6

*East
River*

Lower Manhattan

It all began on Lower Manhattan Island, bounded by **Chambers Street** and the **East** and **Hudson Rivers.** Here, at the confluence of these majestic waterways, the earliest explorers—Giovanni da Verrazano, Esteban Gómez, and Henry Hudson first touched land. And it was also here, in 1625, that the Dutch set up **Fort Amsterdam** to protect the southern perimeter of their settlement, called **Nieuw Amsterdam.** The skyscrapers and canyons of today's **Financial District** stand where the tiny Dutch settlement, and later the prime residential enclave of post-Revolutionary New York, once flourished.

The narrow alleys of the Financial District are a reminder of the scale of colonial America. But, except for a few fragments of old foundations, not a single building erected during the 40 years of Dutch rule remains. When the British Army withdrew in 1783 after seven years of occupation, the village of New York—which covered 10 blocks north from what is now **Battery Park**—lay almost totally in ruins. But once New York City pulled itself together and began to push north, the city grew swiftly. Two blocks of low-rise commercial buildings from this early surge of development have survived: the **Fraunces Tavern** block and **Schermerhorn Row.**

When **City Hall**—the one still in use today—was being built in 1811 on the northernmost fringe of town, the north side of the building was covered with common brownstone instead of marble, because no one ever expected the building to be seen from that side. But by 1820, New York City had expanded another 10 to 15 blocks, and by 1850 the limits had pushed two miles north to 14th Street and city planners with foresight began to assign numbers to the streets. A fire in 1835 leveled most of Lower Manhattan, but even that didn't halt the expansion of what had become the leading commercial center and port in the new country after the War of 1812. **Pearl Street** took its name from its location as the original shoreline of the East River. Landfill added **Water Street**, then **Front Street**, and finally **South Street**, where by the 1820s a thick forest of masts congested the port. The **South Street Seaport Museum** evokes that maritime era. By 1812, lawyers, insurance companies, merchants, and financiers were crowding out families in what quickly became the Financial District, whose symbolic and geographic center was the intersection of **Broad** and **Wall Streets** (named for the wooden wall that served as the northern fortification of Nieuw Amsterdam). The construction of the **Merchants' Exchange** in 1836 speeded up the area's transition to a commercial district.

Today, you can visit the current stock exchanges, but in the limestone-and-glass caverns of Wall Street, only a few of the old public buildings remain: **Federal Hall**, the former **US Custom House** on **Bowling Green**, the famous **Trinity Church** (an 1846 incarnation, several times removed from the original), and the less well known but earlier **St. Paul's Chapel**. A 20th-century masterpiece worth going out of your way to look at is the **Woolworth Building**, also located in this area.

The **Whitehall Building** is architecturally reminiscent of Dutch governor Peter Stuyvesant's mansion (renamed by his English replacement), which was on nearby **Whitehall Street. Bowling Green**, a cattle market in Dutch days, and then a green for bowling and recreation at the center of a desirable residential area, is now an egg-shaped park at the foot of **Broadway**; its 1771 fence is still intact. And the **Civic Center**—the cluster of old and new government buildings, some handsome, some horrendous—just north of the Financial District, has become the western boundary of **Chinatown**.

Created by landfill, the present **Battery Park** offers cooling breezes, welcome greenery, and a panoramic view of **New York Harbor**. It's the jumping-off spot for the ferries to **Liberty Island, Ellis Island**, and **Staten Island**, the best sightseeing buy for close-ups of the **Statue of Liberty** and the New York City skyline. The observation deck at the **World Trade Center** can't be beat for an aerial perspective of Manhattan Island and its surroundings. Nearby, two massive developments, residential and commercial **Battery Park City** and the **World Financial Center**, symbolize Lower Manhattan's emergence as the new epicenter of downtown activity.

1 Ellis Island National Monument On 1 January 1892, when a boat carrying 148 steerage passengers from the SS *Nevada* pulled into the new pier on **Ellis Island,** Annie Moore, a 15-year-old Irish girl, became the first immigrant to set foot on the island. More than 16 million souls followed in her footsteps before the island was closed in 1932. In 1907, its peak year, 1,285,349 people were admitted. The original station burned to the ground in 1897, and the **Ellis Island National Monument** was erected by **Boring & Tilton** in 1898. The present complex of buildings was already decaying during the World War II years when German aliens were imprisoned there. When it finally closed in 1954, vandals moved in and did their best to destroy what was left. In 1990,

after eight years of restoration (at a cost of $156 million, with much of the funding spearheaded by Lee Iacocca), the main building opened as a museum. The fate of the other 32 buildings is undetermined, although plans to turn the hospital (where immigrants were often detained) into an international conference center have been discussed. ♦ Ferry: fee includes visits to both Ellis Island and the Statue of Liberty. Daily 9:30AM-3:30PM. Take Statue of Liberty Ferry from Castle Clinton in Battery Park. 269.5755

On Ellis Island:

Ellis Island Museum of Immigration Visitors can now follow the footsteps of their ancestors upon arrival in America: from the **Baggage Room,** where they dropped off what

were often all of their worldly belongings, to the **Registry Room,** where they underwent 60-second medical and 30-question legal examinations, and on to the **Staircase of Separation,** which led to the ferryboats that transported the immigrants who were granted admittance (98 percent of those who arrived here) to either Manhattan, New Jersey, or points farther west. Also on view are exhibitions tracing the immigration experience: *Islands of Tears* is a poignant film that documents the voyage to America; *Treasures from Home* contains personal property brought here by immigrants; the *American Immigrant Wall of Honor* is inscribed with the names of more than 420,000 American immigrants who were commemorated by their descendants through a donation to the Statue of Liberty–Ellis Island Foundation (call 883.1986 for more information). A new extension of this wall was added to accommodate an additional 75,000 names. In the **Oral History Studio** visitors are given the opportunity to listen to immigrants reminisce about their experiences here.
♦ Free. Daily 9:30AM-3PM. 363.3200 &

1 Statue of Liberty National Monument
Officially named *Liberty Enlightening the World,* the figure alone (supported by a steel skeleton engineered by Gustave Eiffel) is 151 feet high, not counting the pedestal, which adds another 89 feet. It is a full 30 feet taller than the Colossus of Rhodes, one of the Seven Wonders of the Ancient World. French sculptor Frederic Auguste Bartholdi's original idea was to design a statue of a peasant woman holding the Lamp of Progress to Asia and place it at the entrance to the Suez Canal, an idea that was rejected by the sultan of Egypt. When Bartholdi came to the New World from France looking for a site for the statue, he traveled up and down the Eastern Seaboard and as far west as Salt Lake City, but he never for a moment seriously considered any place but Bedloe's Island, which he saw as his ship sailed into New York Harbor. It was finally placed on its pedestal, designed by **Richard Morris Hunt,** in 1886.

Bartholdi cleverly situated it so that when a ship rounds the Narrows between Brooklyn and Staten Island, she appears on portside, striding forward in a gesture of welcome. As the vessel passes directly in front of her, she seems suddenly erect and saluting. It is truly one of the most impressive optical illusions in the world.

The island, which was renamed **Liberty Island** in 1956, was used as a quarantine station in the early 18th century. After 1811, it was the site of **Fort Wood,** which is the star-shaped structure that forms the pedestal's base. In the years between, it was a popular place to hang pirates.

Since the statue's restoration (completed in 1986), climbing the spiral staircase to its crown is easier than it had been for a hundred years, but there are still 22 stories (300-plus steps) to climb, and in very closed quarters. The windows at the crown are small but the view is worth it, although the panorama on the ground is impressive, too, as is the outlook from the open promenade around the top of the pedestal, just under Miss Liberty's feet. The line forms on the left to walk up to the crown; the line on the right is for the 10-story ascent by elevator to the top of the pedestal. Both lines can be quite long in the summer; you may be turned away if you arrive after 2PM, so plan to visit in the morning. ♦ Ferry: fee. Ferry: daily every 30 minutes in the summer; every 45 minutes in the winter. Ferry service from Castle Clinton in Battery Park. 269.5755

Within the Statue of Liberty:

The Statue of Liberty Museum Beginning with the arrival of the Dutch, the museum chronicles the full spectrum of immigration to the New World. It also contains exhibitions on the statue itself, including the original torch, which was re-created and replaced during the 1986 restoration. ♦ Free. Daily. 363.3200 &

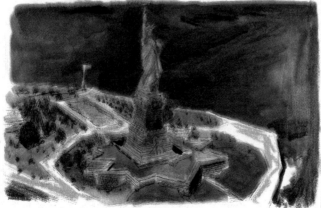

Liberty Island

Michael Storrings

2 Battery Park The Dutch began rearranging the terrain the moment Peter Minuit bought Manhattan for trinkets valued at $24 from the Native Americans in 1626. When they dug their canals and leveled the hills, they dumped the dirt and rocks into the bay. Over the next 300 years or so, more than 21 acres were added to the tip of the island, creating the green buffer between the harbor and the dark canyons of the Financial District. The park takes its name from a line of British cannons that once overlooked the harbor in the late 1600s. The 100,000-rose **Hope Garden**, a living memorial to those who have died of AIDS, was planted in 1992. A **World War II Memorial** and **Korean War Memorial** stand in the park. Despite its bellicose moniker, the park has always been a place for those described by Herman Melville as "men fixed in ocean reveries" (Melville was born nearby at 17 State Street in 1819). ◆ Bounded by Whitehall St and Hudson River, and Battery Pl

Within Battery Park:

Staten Island Ferry This trip provides an excellent visual orientation to New York City. The ferry leaves from the southern tip of Manhattan, weaves through harbor traffic— from tug to sailboat, yacht to cruise ship— and travels past the **Statue of Liberty** and **Ellis Island** to the northeast edge of Staten Island, then back again. En route, passengers have a glorious view of the city's celebrated skyline. The price is still one of the best bargains around, even if you bring your car. ◆ Fee. Daily 24 hours. Off South and Whitehall Sts. 718/390.5253 ♿

Verrazano Monument During the Hudson-Fulton Festival, an extravaganza marking the 300th anniversary of Henry Hudson's trip up the river, New York's Italian-Americans placed this heroic group by Ettore Ximenes at the edge of the harbor in 1909. It commemorates their countryman, who got here first in 1524. The female figure representing *Discovery* is trampling a book labeled *History*. ◆ At the southwest corner of Battery Park

During the peak years of immigration on Ellis Island, the record of languages spoken by a single official interpreter was 15. One interpreter was Fiorello La Guardia, who would later become the famous—and possibly the most beloved—mayor of New York City, responsible for cleaning up the corruption of Tammany Hall. He worked at Ellis Island for an annual salary of $1,200 from 1907 to 1910. He was the first mayor to serve an until-then unprecedented three terms, from 1935 to 1945.

Castle Clinton National Monument Originally known as **West Battery,** this structure served as a defense post housing 28 cannons within eight-foot-thick walls. It faced **Castle William** on Governors Island, and the pair were fortified to block the harbor from enemy attack. In 1811, **John McComb Jr.** designed the original building, which fell into disuse when no enemy appeared. The structure was redesigned as an entertainment venue called **Castle Garden;** the main hall was used for the American premiere performance of singer Jenny Lind, presented by showman P.T. Barnum. For several years, it was the **Emigrant Landing Depot,** processing more than seven million immigrants before giving up that role to **Ellis Island** in 1892. In one of its final incarnations, from 1896 to 1941 the building housed the **New York Aquarium** (now at Coney Island in Brooklyn). Finally, as need for repairs became apparent and its historical importance was realized, the building was designated a National Historic Landmark in 1950. It has since been restored as a fort and is under the care of the National Park Service. Park rangers conduct free walking tours on weekdays. It also serves as an information center and a ticket office for the *Statue of Liberty Ferry*. ◆ Daily. Battery Pl (between State and St and the Hudson River). 344.7220 ♿

Battery Park Control House One of two surviving ornate entrances to the original **IRT** subway (the other is at West 72nd Street and Broadway), this structure was built in 1905 and was designed by **Heins & LaFarge.** The term "control house" was coined by engineers who designed them to control crowds coming and going in two directions at once. ◆ State St and Battery Pl

3 Church of Our Lady of the Rosary This pair of Georgian town houses, originally designed in 1800 by **John McComb Jr.,** was restored in 1965 as a shrine church dedicated to Elizabeth Ann Seton. Canonized in 1975 as the first American-born saint, Seton lived here with her family in the early 1800s. The exterior of each building, faithfully returned to its original condition with columns presumably cut from ship masts, provides a small reminder of the character of this fashionable residential neighborhood at the beginning of the 19th century. ◆ 7-8 State St (at Water St). 269.6865

3 New York Unearthed In 1990, a permanent archaeological display (administered by the **South Street Museum**) opened in an annex behind 17 State Street. Visitors enter at street level, where they view 10 dioramas, created by graphic designer Milton Glaser, that hold such items as medicine vials, crucibles, cannon balls, and

Restaurants/Clubs: Red   Hotels: Blue
Shops/ 🍴 Outdoors: Green   **Sights/Culture:** Black

bottles, all excavated on or near this site. On the **Lower Gallery,** a glass-enclosed space reveals conservationists hard at work, while at the **Stratigraphy Wall,** visitors can view a three-dimensional cross-section of an archaeological site. Museum-goers may also board the **Unearthing New York Systems Elevator,** which takes them on a simulated dig, four centuries back into New York history. ♦ Free. M-Sa noon-6PM. 17 State St (at Water St). 748.8628 ♿

4 Peter Minuit Plaza This small park honors the man who bought Manhattan from the Native Americans for a small price in 1626. Sent by the Dutch West India Company to oversee its holdings in the New World, Minuit eventually made Nieuw Amsterdam its center. He later died at sea. The flagpole is a memorial to the first Jewish settlers, who arrived in

1654. They had been expelled from Portugal to a Dutch colony at Recife in Brazil, but were driven from there in a Portuguese conquest. On the way back to Holland, their ship was attacked by pirates, and the survivors were taken to the nearest Dutch colony, Nieuw Amsterdam, where they were allowed to stay. ♦ South and State Sts

5 Battery Maritime Building The sheet-metal-and-steel facade of this Beaux Arts ferry terminal has been painted green to simulate copper. Before the Brooklyn Bridge was built, there were 17 ferry lines between Lower Manhattan and Brooklyn. Until 1938, one of them operated out of this terminal, which was designed by **Walker & Gillette** in 1906. Today, it houses the small fleet of white ferries that serves Governors Island. ♦ 11 South St (at Whitehall St)

On a Clear Day You Can See. . .

When the streets get a little too littered, the air a bit too smoggy, and the crowds just too intense, remember that everything looks better from a distance—and New York City's no exception. Unlike the aging actress whose left profile is better than her right, the Big Apple shines every which way, especially from the following vantage points:

Circle Line
Pier 83, W 42nd St at the Hudson River. 563.3200

Columbia Heights
Pineapple St (at Orange St), Brooklyn Heights

Empire State Building Observatories
Fifth Ave and W 34th St. 736.3100

Fort Tryon Park and The Cloisters
Washington Heights

Liberty State Park
South of the Holland Tunnel, New Jersey

Promenade
East River, Brooklyn Heights

The Rainbow Room Restaurant
30 Rockefeller Plaza (between W 49th and W 50th Sts). 632.5000

River Café
1 Water St (on East River, under the Brooklyn Bridge), Brooklyn Heights. 718/522.5200

Riverside Church
490 Riverside Dr (at W 122nd St). 222.5900

Roosevelt Island Tramway Station
Second Ave and E 59th St. 832.4543

Staten Island Ferry
Leaves from South St and State St, Battery Park. 806.6940

Statue of Liberty
Liberty Island. 363.3200

The Terrace
400 W 119th St (at Morningside Dr). 666.9490

Top of the Sixes Restaurant
666 Fifth Ave (between 52nd and 53rd Sts), 39th floor. 757.6662

Triborough Bridge
Above Wards Island (entrance at E 125th St and Harlem River Dr)

The View Restaurant
1535 Broadway (at W 45th St). 704.8900

Windows on the World Restaurant
1 World Trade Center (Church St, between Liberty and Vesey Sts), 107th floor. 938.1111 (slated to reopen by press time)

World Trade Center Observation Deck
2 World Trade Center (Church St, between Liberty and Vesey Sts), 107th floor. 435.7397

6 Governors Island When the Dutch arrived here in 1624, they established their first toehold on what they called **Nut Island.** But even before the Dutch governor surrendered Nieuw Amsterdam to them in 1665, the British established their own governor here. In addition to the British **Governor's Mansion,** another historic landmark on the island is the 1840 **Admiral's House,** home of the commanding general of the army garrison stationed here from 1790 until 1966. The island is now the headquarters of the US Coast Guard, which is responsible for all the waterways in the country east of the Continental Divide.

The island is an idyllic place with sweeping lawns and fine old houses on traffic-free roads, a few hundred yards from the tip of Manhattan. But, alas, as a government reservation, it is closed to the public except for one day a year, usually in May or June, when they polish up the brass and welcome visitors for the annual open house. For further information, call 668.3402. &

7 Fraunces Tavern This Georgian brick building (illustrated above), erected in 1719, became the tavern of Samuel Fraunces in 1763, and was made famous when George Washington said farewell to his officers here on the second floor on 4 December 1783. Washington returned six years later to the old **City Hall,** five blocks away, to take the oath of office as the first president of the new nation. The building was refurbished in 1927 in the spirit and style of the period rather than as an accurate restoration. ♦ 54 Pearl St (at Broad St)

Within Fraunces Tavern:
Fraunces Tavern Restaurant ★$$$
Samuel Fraunces, George Washington's steward, opened a tavern in this 1719 Georgian brick building in 1763. Today, Wall Streeters congregate here for such dependable American fare as steaks, chops, and seafood, amid Colonial-era decor. ♦ American ♦ M-F breakfast, lunch, and dinner. Reservations recommended. 269.0144

Fraunces Tavern Museum Above the restaurant, permanent and changing exhibitions of decorative arts, period rooms, paintings, and prints and manuscripts from 18th- and 19th-century America are on display. ♦ Admission. M-F; Sa noon-4PM. 425.1778

8 United States Custom House This 1907 building (illustrated at right) by **Cass Gilbert** has been called one of the finest examples of the Beaux Arts style in New York City, and it is instantly apparent why. The granite facade is surprisingly delicate, despite an ornate frieze and Ionic columns with Corinthian capitals along the face. Four seated female figures, representing Africa, Asia, Europe, and America, are Daniel Chester French and Adolph Weinman's contribution to the magnificent structure. Reginald Marsh painted the murals in the wonderful oval rotunda. ♦ Broadway and Bowling Green. No phone

Within the United States Custom House:
National Museum of the American Indian The comprehensive collection of artifacts linked to the indigenous peoples of the Americas is part of Washington, DC's Smithsonian Institution. The artifacts were assembled over a 54-year-period by George Gustav Heye, a New York banker. Opened in 1994, this facility, which features changing displays of its one million objects, also stages educational workshops, film and video festivals, and performances of Native American dance and theater. Among the permanent exhibits on display are Navajo weavings and blankets; stone carvings from the Northwest; basketry and pottery from the Southwest; gold from Colombia, Peru, and Mexico; and jade objects from the Olmec and Maya cultures. Although the concentration is on North, Central, and South American peoples, there are ethnological materials from as far away as Siberia. ♦ Free. Daily. 825.6700 &

9 Bowling Green In 1734, a group of citizens leased the space facing the **Custom House** as a bowling green for an annual rent of one peppercorn. In the process it became the city's first park. In 1729, the park was embellished with an equestrian statue of England's King George III, which was demolished by a crowd that assembled here to listen to a reading of the *Declaration of Independence* on 9 July 1776 (the park's fence dates to 1771). The statue was melted down to make bullets that, according to some contemporary accounts, were responsible for the killing of 400 British soldiers during the war that followed. ♦ Broadway and Battery Pl

At Bowling Green:

The Charging Bull In response to the stock-market crash of 1987, Arturo DiModica sculpted this 3.5-ton bronze bull to attest to the "vitality, energy, and life of the American people in adversity." It has been put up for sale; since the city is not allowed to buy works of art, they are half-heartedly looking for a patron.

Michael Storrings

United States Custom House

10 Whitehall Building A 1930s real-estate guide said that the tenants of this 1903 building, which at the time included the Internal Revenue Service, Quaker Oats, and the Bon Ami Cleanser Co., had "an intimate relationship with the landlord," and no one ever moved out. There has been some turnover since the guide was written, but tenants are still (understandably) reluctant to give up offices boasting what may be the best views of New York Harbor. Originally designed by **Henry J. Hardenbergh,** the rear section was designed by **Clinton & Russell** in 1910. ♦ 17 Battery Pl (between Washington and West Sts)

11 Downtown Athletic Club The arched ground-floor arcade and the window treatment of this Moorish-influenced Art Deco masterpiece, designed by **Starrett & Van Vleck** in 1926, are perfection itself, and the interior by Barnett-Phillips is even better. The rooms are reminiscent of a 1920s ocean liner. In addition to an enclosed roof garden, the building originally contained a miniature golf course. Off-limits to women until 1978, the club now boasts a coed, cross-cultural membership. ♦ 19 West St (between Battery Pl and Morris St). 425.7000 ♿

12 Brooklyn-Battery Tunnel In the early 1930s, builder Robert Moses announced that he was going to construct a bridge between Lower Manhattan and Brooklyn to connect his Long Island parkway system with his West Side Highway, which reached a dead end at **Battery Park.** Preservationists were appalled. City officials, noting that the city would lose $29 million a year in real-estate taxes, also opposed it. The battle raged until 1939, when President Roosevelt stepped in and denied

federal funds for the project. The bridge became a tunnel, and **Battery Park** was saved. When the tunnel—engineered by Ole Singstad in 1949—finally opened, it carried more than 15 million cars in its first year. ♦ From West St (between Morris and Rector Sts), Manhattan to Hamilton Ave, Brooklyn

13 26 Broadway This graceful giant, which was first built in 1885 and altered in 1922 by **Carrère & Hastings,** actually curves along to follow the street line. The most important business address in the world for half a century, this was where John D. Rockefeller said that he had revolutionized the way of doing business "to save ourselves from wasteful conditions and eliminate individualism." There is no denying he accomplished his goal, and at the same time built one of the world's greatest fortunes behind these walls, the headquarters of Standard Oil. When the Supreme Court dissolved the trust in 1911, the building became home to Socony Mobil, one of the new companies that rose from Standard Oil's ashes. ♦ At Bowling Green

14 India House **Richard J. Carman** built this beautiful brownstone (one of the largest in the city) as headquarters for the Hanover Bank in 1854. At other times it was used as the New York Cotton Exchange and the main office of W.R. Grace and Co. It is now a private club. ♦ 1 Hanover Sq (between Pearl and Stone Sts)

The first slaves brought from Africa arrived in New York in 1625. The practice grew, and the first slave market was established at the foot of Wall Street in 1711; it was not until 1827 that slavery was abolished in New York.

15 Hanover Square Named for the English royal family of the Georges, this was once a small London-style park at the center of a residential neighborhood. Homeowners included Captain William Kidd, who was considered a solid citizen in New York but something quite different by the British, who hanged him for piracy in 1701. Captain Kidd has gone down in popular history as the most bloodthirsty of pirates, and even today people poke around beaches along the coast in hopes of finding the fabulous treasure he supposedly buried. The square was also the home of New York's first newspaper, the *New-York Daily Gazette,* established in 1725. George E. Bissell's statue of *Abraham de Peyster,* a one-time mayor of the city, was moved here from Bowling Green. ♦ Old Slip (between Pearl and Stone Sts)

16 United States Assay Office Built in 1930 and designed by **James A. Wetmore,** this is a division of the United States Mint for refining gold and silver bullion and melting down old coins. It is also a storehouse that contains about 55 million troy ounces of gold, worth more than $2 billion at the official government price. ♦ Old Slip (between Front and Water Sts)

17 HRC (New York Health & Racquet Club) Tennis Nonmembers are allowed to reserve tennis courts here 24 hours in advance, but be prepared to pay high rates for the privilege—especially during the peak hours after 5PM weekdays. ♦ Daily 6AM-midnight. Nominal charge for nonmembers. Piers 13 and 14 (off Wall and South Sts). 422.9300

Sloppy Louie's

18 Sloppy Louie's ★$$$ Before the renaissance of **South Street Seaport** forced Louie to clean up his act and raise his prices, this was a no-nonsense restaurant that catered to the people who worked in the area's markets. The bouillabaisse and shrimp scampi, among other dishes, are still good enough for the most demanding fishmonger, but now the ambience is more genteel. ♦ Seafood ♦ Daily lunch and early dinner. Reservations recommended for six or more. 92 South St (between John and Fulton Sts). 509.9694

On 16 December 1835, fire engulfed Lower Manhattan, scorching everything south of Wall Street and east of Broadway. More than 650 buildings were burned. The conflagration took nearly 20 hours to bring under control; final loss of property was some $20 million.

19 South Street Seaport Back when sailing ships ruled the seas, New York's most active ports were along this stretch of the East River. With the coming of steamships, the deeper piers on the Hudson River attracted most of the seafaring traffic, and the East River piers fell into decline. In 1967, a group of preservation-minded citizens banded together to buy the rundown waterfront buildings and a collection of historic ships. Twelve years later, commercial interests moved in and provided funds to restore the old buildings and add some new ones. The result, thanks to the ingenuity of architects **Ben** and **Jane Thompson,** is a lively historic site—complete with cobblestone streets—that has revitalized a derelict neighborhood, transforming it into one of New York's most fascinating enclaves. Especially active after 5PM, the place is a magnet for young Wall Streeters who drift by for an after-work drink. ♦ Daily. East River to Water St (between Fletcher and Dover Sts). 669.9400 &

Within South Street Seaport:

Titanic Memorial Lighthouse This structure originally overlooked the harbor from the Seamen's Church Institute on Water Street at Cuyler's Alley. A memorial to the 1,500 who died when the **White Star Line**'s *Titanic* struck an iceberg in 1912, it was moved here in 1976 to mark the entrance to the seaport. ♦ Fulton St and Water St &

Brookstone The ultimate hardware store, this place displays one of each tool or gadget in stock like an objet d'art next to a card describing its virtues. Each is the best in its class. Pick up a clipboard when you enter and write down your order as you go. At the end, the goods are delivered via a dumbwaiter from the loft above. ♦ Daily. 18 Fulton St (between Front and Water Sts). 344.8108. Also at 620 Fifth Ave (between W 47th and W 48th Sts). 262.3237

South Street Seaport Museum America's nautical heritage and the city's evolution are exhibited in three galleries, a children's center, a crafts center, and a library. The museum is housed in a former warehouse built in 1868. ♦ Museum: admission. Library: free. Museum: daily. Library: M-F. 213 Water St (at Fulton St). Museum 748.8600; Library 748.8648

Abercrombie & Fitch Sports clothing has kept this chain in business since 1892. ♦ Daily. 199 Water St (at Fulton St). 809.9000.& Also at: 725 Fifth Ave (between E 56th and E 57th Sts, Fifth floor). 832.1001

Cafe Fledermaus $ Perfect for people watching, this unpretentious spot for coffee, pastries, salads, and sandwiches has tables on the Fulton Street promenade. ♦ Cafe ♦ Daily. 1 Seaport Plaza (at Water St). 269.5890 &

Strand Bookstore The downtown branch of New York's landmark bookstore stocks a large selection of discounted books, plus remainders and review copies. ♦ Daily. 159 John St (at Front St). 809.0875. Also at: 828 Broadway (at E 12th St). 473.1452.

South Street Seaport Museums Shops New York's best source for fiction and nonfiction about ships of all kinds and the waters they sail, recently relocated here. You'll also find rare prints, ship models, and otherwise hard-to-find books on New York City and its history. ♦ Daily. 12 Fulton St (between South and Front Sts). 748.8663 &

Fulton Market The 1882 building on this spot used to house a fresh produce and meat market, filled with merchandise brought from Long Island farms on the now-defunct *Fulton Ferry*, which connected Fulton Street in Manhattan with Fulton Street in Brooklyn. The reconstructed building (illustrated below) now houses shops, restaurants, and stalls selling fresh food. Outlets in the market include **Zaro's Bread Basket**, the **Fulton Market Retail Fish Market, Rocky Mountain Chocolate Factory**, and **Ferrara** (for Italian pastries). ♦ Daily. 11 Fulton St (between South and Front Sts). 732.8257

The Ships Ships visiting **Piers 15, 16,** and **17** make this an ever changing experience, but the seaport's permanent collection includes two tall ships open to the public: *Peking*, a steel-hulled, four-masted bark built in 1911 (and the second-largest sailing ship ever built), and *Wavertree*, a full three-masted iron-hulled ship built in 1885. Also here is *Ambrose*, the steel, floating lighthouse that was anchored at the entrance to the harbor from 1908 until 1963, when she was replaced by a permanent tower. Tickets, available on **Pier 16** and at the **Visitors' Center** at Fulton and Water Streets, allow admission to **Museum Galleries** (see above) and daily changing events. Other ships in the **South Street Seaport**

fleet include the working tugboat *W.O. Decker* and the schooner *Lettie G. Howard. Pioneer,* a former cargo schooner, makes 90-minute daytime and twilight sails in the harbor late March to mid-November. Hours vary according to season. Reservations can be made within 14 days of a sail; unreserved tickets are sold each day starting at 10AM at **Pier 16** (669.9400). Special exhibitions are scattered throughout the **Seaport;** there are also special holiday events. Two separate walking tours guide you to them. ♦ Admission. Daily. East River (off South and Fulton Sts). 748.8600, 748.8659

Schermerhorn Row A row of Federal-style warehouses and countinghouses (shown above) built by **Peter Schermerhorn** in 1812 have been restored. At various times in their history, the buildings were used as stores, taverns, rooming houses, and hotels. Greek Revival cast-iron storefronts were added later when the *Fulton Ferry* brought more stylish customers into the area. The upper floors are the least altered from the original, but the mansard roof at the western end was added in 1868 when **2 Fulton Street** was the **Fulton Ferry Hotel.** The ground floor currently houses a variety of interesting shops, including **The Nature Company, The Body Shop,** and **The Sharper Image.** ♦ Fulton St (between South and Front Sts)

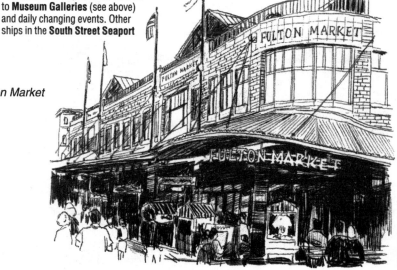

Fulton Market

Michael Storrings

Spectacular Spans

Brooklyn Bridge
Completed 1883; total length 3,455'6"; center span 1,595'6"; maximum clearance above water 133'.

George Washington Bridge
Completed 1931; total length 4,760'; center span 3,500.'; maximum clearance above water 212'.

Manhattan Bridge
Completed 1909; total length 2,920'; center span 1,470'; maximum clearance above water 135'.

Queensboro Bridge
Completed 1909; total length 3,724'; major span 1,182.'; maximum clearance above water 135'.

Verrazano-Narrows Bridge
Completed 1964; total length 6,690'; center span 4,260'; maximum clearance above water 228'.

Williamsburg Bridge
Completed 1903; total length 2,793'6"; center span 1,600'; maximum clearance above water 135'.

All bridge art by Michael Storrings

Seaport Liberty Cruises A number of 60-minute cruises of the harbor depart here March through December. In the warmer months there are longer cruises with music and live entertainment on Saturday nights. ◆ Fee. Daily 12, 1:30, 3, and 4:30PM; Sa-Tu also at 6PM. Tickets available at Pier 16 kiosk. Pier 16. 630.8888

Pier 17 Modeled after the recreation piers of the last century, this development was built directly over the water. In good weather, it's packed with people enjoying the pleasures of the waterfront. Such shops and food stalls as **Cindy's Cinnamon Rolls, Minter's Ice Cream Kitchen, Bain's Deli,** and the Chinese fast-food **Wok N'Roll** fill the inside. During the summer, the pier becomes a venue for concerts and other special activities. There are many busy restaurants here as well, offering spectacular scenery at spectacular prices, although the food is generally no better than average. ◆ Daily. East River (between Fulton and Beekman Sts). 732.8257 ᕪ

20 Fulton Fish Market Established in 1821, this venerable institution has been at this location since 1907. It was given the name **Tin Building** by old salts who still remembered the wooden structure it replaced. The market was located here to conveniently receive the daily haul from local fishing boats, but today the catch (from cleaner waters) arrives via refrigerated truck. Daytime visitors find the market a quiet place, but it is positively frantic between midnight and 8AM. Early risers can watch the activity wind down by taking guided tours at 6AM on the first and third Thursdays of each month from May through October; reservations are required. ◆ Daily. South St (between Fulton and Beekman Sts). Tour information 669.9416

21 Brooklyn Bridge This milestone in civil engineering, built from 1869 to 1883 and designed by **John A. Roebling** and his son **Washington Roebling,** is an aesthetic, as well as a structural, masterpiece. The bridge (illustrated at left) gets its dynamic tension from the massive strength of its great stone pylons and Gothic arches contrasted with the intricate web of its woven suspension cables. In 1855, John Roebling's proposal for a bridge across the East River was met with derision, but far-sighted residents of Brooklyn (then a separate city) pushed the idea after the Civil War. The Roebling family's fate was inextricably tied up with that of the bridge. John died as the result of an accident on a Brooklyn wharf before work on the bridge began, but his son, Washington, carried on, even when he got the bends during construction and became partially paralyzed for the rest of his life; his mother then took over the operation (plaques at both ends of the bridge commemorate the Roebling trio's dedication). The Brooklyn Bridge was the first

to use steel cables. For 20 years it was the world's longest suspension bridge; for many more its span was the longest. The subject of many poems, paintings, paeans of praise, and bad jokes, the bridge still gives a special lift to the bicyclists, walkers, and marathoners who cross it. If you care to stroll across the bridge, the entrance is on Park Row: The left side is for pedestrians, the right for bikers. ◆ From Park Row, Manhattan to Cadman Pl, Brooklyn

BRIDGE CAFE

22 Bridge Cafe ★★$$ The walk to this aptly named cafe situated under the Brooklyn Bridge can take you down some streets that look a bit rough and deserted. But don't be put off—the food, including dishes like pecan and cornbread trout, and duck with red wine and green peppercorn sauce, is probably the best in the **Seaport** area. ◆ Continental. ◆ M-F lunch and dinner; Su brunch and dinner. Reservations recommended. 279 Water St (at Dover St). 227.3344 ᕪ

23 Seaport Inn $$ For the traveler who wants easy access to historic downtown Manhattan, or the businessperson who would rather walk to those early morning Wall Street appointments, this handsomely restored 19th-century building houses 65 tastefully decorated rooms offering a warm and comfortable refuge. Some rooms have terraces with views of the Brooklyn Bridge. There is no restaurant. ◆ 33 Peck Slip (at Front St). 766.6600, 800/HOTEL.NY ᕪ

24 127 John Street A huge electric display clock designed by Corchia–de Harak Associates, in addition to the nearby colorful steel patio furniture, adds a touch of whimsy to the Water Street streetscape. ◆ View from Water St (between John and Fulton Sts)

25 Wall Street Plaza This 1973 white-aluminum-and-glass structure by **I.M. Pei & Associates** richly deserved the award presented by the American Institute of Architects for its classical purity, rather rare in the new buildings in this area. The 1974 sculpture in its plaza, by Yu Yu Yang, consists of a stainless-steel slab with an opening that faces a polished disk. It is a memorial to the **Cunard** liner *Queen Elizabeth,* whose history is outlined on a nearby plaque. ◆ 88 Pine St (between Front and Water Sts)

Restaurants/Clubs: Red **Hotels:** Blue

Shops/ ⁇ Outdoors: Green **Sights/Culture:** Black

26 Seaport Suites Hotel $$$ Located in the heart of the historical district that harks back to New York's early days, this suites-only hotel is just a two-minute walk from Wall Street. Suites come in four sizes, from an oversize double room to a miniature apartment that can sleep four people. All 408 suites have fully equipped kitchens, and many have a separate living room for business meetings. The **Rainbow Lounge** has a limited menu. ♦ 129 Front St (at Wall St). 742.0003, 800/777.8483; fax 742.0124 ఉ

27 St. Maggie's Cafe ★$$ With its carved plaster, brown-and-cream walls, and antique chandeliers, the opulent decor of this eatery would be oppressive were it not for the huge windows that let in sunlight and views of the East River. Young Wall Streeters come here for such light fare as the Mulberry Street grilled chicken salad, and for seafood dishes, including Maryland crab cakes with tequila-chili mayonnaise or angel-hair pasta with sea scallops, shrimp, and crab in Sherry-lobster sauce. ♦ American ♦ M-F lunch and dinner. Reservations recommended. 120 Wall St (at South St). 943.9050

28 74 Wall Street The nautical decoration around the arched entrance of this solid-looking 1926 building by **Benjamin Wistar Morris** is a reminder that it was built for the Seamen's Bank for Savings, the second-oldest savings bank in the city. It was chartered in 1829 as a financial haven for sailors, who usually arrived in the port with their pockets full of back pay accumulated while they were out at sea. The official address of the property was 76 Wall Street, but before it was changed, superstitious seamen refused to leave their money there because the numbers added up to 13. ♦ At Pearl St

29 55 Wall Street One of the first buildings in the area after the Great Fire of 1835 leveled 700 structures between Wall and South Streets, Coenties Slip, and Broad Street, this building was designed by **Isaiah Rogers** in 1836. It was built as a three-story trading hall for the **Merchants' Exchange,** and later became the **Custom House.** In 1907, its height was doubled when it was remodeled and expanded by **McKim, Mead & White,** and it became the headquarters of First National City Bank, which still maintains an impressive-looking branch here under its new name, Citibank. ♦ Between Hanover and William Sts

"Going down Wall Street you pass what looks like an alley called New Street. The street is hardly new. The name was bestowed in 1647 because the street was the first in this part of town laid out by the new English government."

Joyce Gold,
From Windmills to the World Trade Center

30 Bank of New York The bank has occupied several buildings on this site since its founding by Alexander Hamilton in 1784. Commodore Vanderbilt used one of them as his banking headquarters. The present Georgian building, built in 1927 and designed by **Benjamin Wistar Morris,** is easily one of the most attractive in the area, with tall, arched windows and a broken pediment framing a handsome galleon lantern. ♦ 48 Wall St (at William St). 495.1784 ఉ

31 40 Wall Street The tower was built in 1929, the same time as the **Chrysler Building** uptown, and was secretly designed by **H. Craig Severance** and **Yasuo Matsui** to be two feet higher, which would have made it the tallest in the world. (But the **Chrysler**'s builders outfoxed the bankers with a secret plan of their own: They pushed a 123-foot stainless-steel spire through a hole in their roof.) This was the headquarters of the Bank of the Manhattan Company, which eventually merged with Chase National Bank. The Manhattan Company was founded in 1799 by Aaron Burr, who was blocked by political rivals when he tried to charter a bank. Instead he received legislative permission to establish a water company. In the charter's fine print, he was granted the power to loan money to property owners who wanted to connect their buildings to his wooden water mains. Before he had dug up too many streets, Burr abandoned the water business and became what he had always wanted to be: a banker. ♦ Between William and Nassau Sts

31 30 Wall Street When this structure was built as the United States Assay Office in 1921 by architects **York & Sawyer,** the facade of its predecessor, the Bank of the United States, designed in 1826 by **Martin E. Thompson,** was dismantled and eventually reconstructed in the **American Wing** of the **Metropolitan Museum of Art.** Additions were made in 1955 by the firm of **Halsey, McCormack & Helmer.** ♦ Between William and Nassau Sts

31 Federal Hall National Memorial This Americanization of the Parthenon is one of New York City's finest examples of Greek Revival architecture and a fitting National Historic Landmark. At the front of the building, which was designed in 1842 by **Town & Davis,** John Quincy Adams Ward's statue of *George Washington* marks the spot where the Revolutionary War general became the country's first president. An early 18th-century building at this site (demolished in 1803) served as the United States governmental seat in the days when New York City was the nation's capital; it was here that the House of Representatives and the Senate first met. Today, Doric columns climbing 32 feet high span the building's face. Enter for a self-guided tour of the interior of the building, which was designed by John Frazee and Samuel Thompson, as well as exhibitions organized by both the Historic Hudson Valley and the **Museum of the American Constitutional Government.** ♦ M-F. 15 Pine St or 26 Wall St (at Nassau St). 825.6888 ♿

32 Morgan Guaranty Trust Company If ever a single man epitomized the American capitalist, J.P. Morgan (1837-1913) was that man. His son, John Pierpont Morgan Jr., took control of the empire in 1913, the year this building was built by **Trowbridge & Livingston.** Like his father, John Jr. was apparently not without enemies. On 16 September 1920, at the height of the lunch hour, a carriage parked on Wall Street suddenly exploded, killing 33 people, and injuring 400. The marble walls of the building still have scars from the bomb, noticeable on the Wall Street side of the building. No reason was ever determined, and the owner of the carriage was never found. The bank survived unscathed, as did Morgan who was out of town at the time. ♦ 23 Wall St (at Broad St)

33 New York Stock Exchange The Exchange's giant portico, colonnade, and sculptures express austerity and security—key design goals in 1903, when this building (pictured at right) was designed by **George B. Post,** and when the upper section was designed in 1923 by **Trowbridge & Livingston.** The solemn facade masks the leading-edge technology that drives the exchange today. That technology, integrated with the judgment and skills of the trading floor's professionals, provides investors with the broadest, most open, and most liquid equities market in the world. Before entering the gallery that overlooks the trading floor, visitors go through an exhibition area that includes video presentations and frequent lectures on the history and workings of the institution. A multilingual, pre-recorded explanation of what's happening three floors below is provided from a glass-enclosed observation gallery overlooking the frenzied action on the trading floor. More than two thousand companies deal on the exchange; it is the world's largest, with stock valued at more than $3 trillion. The tickets for tours are dispensed at 20 Broad Street; there are a limited number for each session. ♦ Free. Visitors Gallery M-F 9:15AM-2:45PM. Tours M-F 9:15AM-2:45PM. 20 Broad St (at Wall St), Third floor. 656.5168 ♿

34 Bankers Trust Building The pyramid on top of this 31-story tower, built in 1912 by **Trowbridge & Livingston,** became the corporate symbol of Bankers Trust and remained its logo even after the bank moved its main headquarters up to 280 Park Avenue in 1963. ♦ 16 Wall St (at Nassau St)

Within the Bankers Trust Building:

La Tour D'Or ★$$$ This staid restaurant on the 31st floor was once J.P. Morgan's pied-à-terre. Its views extend in every direction, but the best is from the comfortable bar that overlooks the harbor and the **Statue of Liberty.** The menu, featuring such classic dishes as *duck à l'orange,* seems not to have changed in decades, which is exactly as the regulars like it. ♦ French ♦ M-F lunch; dinner if arranged in advance. Reservations recommended. 233.2780 ♿

35 Irving Trust Company Building/The Bank of New York **Ralph Walker**'s only skyscraper was built in 1932 on what was called the most expensive piece of real estate in the world in the 1930s. He said his design was one of superimposed rhythms, a steel frame draped outside with rippling curtains of stone. The gold, red, and orange Art Deco mosaics created by Hildreth Meière in the banking room off Wall Street make a visit rewarding even if you are not a depositor. ♦ 1 Wall St (at Broadway)

36 Waldenbooks The Lower Manhattan branch of the national chain is spacious, and many of its departments are separated by alcoves. Especially strong in business, the bookstore also offers wide selections in cooking, history, and sports, with many remainder and sale books. ♦ M-F. 57 Broadway (at Exchange Pl). 269.1139

Michael Storrings

New York Stock Exchange

New York City on Screen

New York was a thriving film production city long before the sunny skies of Hollywood began to lure producers and filmmakers west in the early 1900s. D.W. Griffith loved to shoot here, and Mack Sennett's *Keystone Cops* ran rampant through **Coney Island.**

The city goes out of its way to court the film industry: there's a special mayor's office to act as an industry liaison, to provide police protection for stars and production crews, and even to help arrange scenes ranging from helicopter chases to historical location settings. The number of feature films shot here has quadrupled since 1977, and movie, TV, and commercial production ranks among the city's top five growth industries.

It's no wonder then that many visitors to movieland's Gotham get a feeling of déja vu. Here are a few of the movies and locations you may remember:

After Hours (1985) takes place in **SoHo** with an adventurous Rosanna Arquette leading Griffin Dunne on the most hellish date of his life.

America, America (1963), Elia Kazan's portrayal of his own family's immigration to the US, incorporates **Ellis Island** locales.

Angie (1994), in which Geena Davis portrays an Italian-American in search of her inner self.

Annie Hall (1977) depicts Woody Allen on Woody Allen—growing up under the Cyclone roller coaster at Coney Island.

Arthur (1981), in which Dudley Moore questions his date's (Liza Minnelli) profession just a bit too loudly in the **Oak Bar** at the **Plaza Hotel.**

Big (1988) stars Tom Hanks and Robert Loggia performing a charming impromptu musical number at **FAO Schwarz.**

Bonfire of the Vanities (1990), based on Tom Wolfe's novel, captures Sherman McCoy's world of **Upper East Side** privilege and debauchery. Courtroom scenes were filmed on location in the **Bronx.**

Breakfast at Tiffany's (1961) Audrey Hepburn and George Peppard find love on **Fifth Avenue.**

Bright Lights, Big City (1988) finds Michael J. Fox in the fast lane in the film adaptation of Jay McInerney's best-selling novel.

A Bronx Tale (1993) marks actor Robert De Niro's directorial debut.

Citizen Kane (1941) rallies political support at **Madison Square Garden** in Orson Welles's classic film.

Crocodile Dundee (1987) Paul Hogan checks in at the **Plaza** while visiting from Down Under.

Crimes and Misdemeanors (1989) is Woody Allen's view of life, death, and infidelity against the backdrop of the New York City skyline.

Daniel (1983) is Sidney Lumet's adaptation of E.L. Doctorow's novel where nearly 4,000 extras attend a protest staged at **Union Square.** Stars are Timothy Hutton and Lindsay Crouse.

Desperately Seeking Susan (1984) portrays Rosanna Arquette as a suburban housewife and her unexpected adventures with Madonna in **Battery Park.**

Die Hard with a Vengeance (1995) Bruce Willis and Samuel L. Jackson track down a mad bomber (Jeremy Irons) on the streets of New York.

Do the Right Thing (1989) is director Spike Lee's tale of racial strife starring Danny Aiello, Ossie Davis, Ruby Dee, and Giancarlo Esposito. Filmed on location in the Bedford Stuyvesant section of **Brooklyn.**

Dog Day Afternoon (1975) stars Al Pacino and two cohorts who turn a simple Manhattan bank robbery into chaos.

Fort Apache, The Bronx (1981) Paul Newman fights the bad guys in this crime-ridden part of the **Bronx.**

The French Connection (1971) casts Gene Hackman as the unforgettable cop Popeye Doyle as he tracks drug smugglers in a spectacular car chase along Brooklyn's **Stillwell Avenue.**

Funny Girl (1968) Barbra Streisand shares the spotlight with the **Statue of Liberty.**

Ghostbusters (1984) Bill Murray, Dan Aykroyd, and Harold Ramis move into (and blow the roof off of) the **No. 8 Hook and Ladder Firehouse** in TriBeCa and finally come to terms with these supernatural beings at **55 Central Park West.**

The Godfather (1972) is the first of a trilogy staring Marlon Brando, James Caan, Diane Keaton, Robert Duvall, and Richard Castellano in Mario Puzo's look at the mob.

The Godfather, Part II (1974) returns to **Little Italy** where Robert De Niro plays young mob boss Don Corleone.

GoodFellas (1990) Robert DeNiro, Ray Liotta, and Joe Pesci rise in the mob ranks in this Martin Scorsese film.

Green Card (1990) stars Gerard Depardieu and Andie MacDowell in Peter Weir's tale of love after marriage.

Hannah and Her Sisters (1986) Carrie Fisher, Diane Wiest, and Sam Waterson star in Woody Allen's Manhattan-based family drama. Mia Farrow, Barbara Hershey, and Michael Caine add to the angst.

Home Alone II (1993), directed by Chris Columbus, continues Macauley Culkin's escapades—this time in New York City. Co-stars are Joe Pesci, Daniel Stern and Brenda Fricker.

Kramer vs. Kramer (1979) shows **P.S. 6** on Madison Avenue at East 81st Street, as Dustin Hoffman drops his son off at school, while his soon-to-be-ex-wife Meryl Streep watches from across the street.

The Lost Weekend (1945) Ray Milland suffers the DTs at **Bellevue Hospital** after a three-day bender.

Madigan (1968) takes place in **Spanish Harlem** and stars Richard Widmark as a tough cop.

Manhattan Murder Mystery (1993) features Woody Allen as a New York book editor, with Dianne Keaton, as his wife, delving into the mysterious disappearance of their neighbor.

Mean Streets (1973) A slice of life in Little Italy starring Robert De Niro.

Midnight Cowboy (1969) Dustin Hoffman and John Voight stop traffic at **West 58th Street** and **Sixth Avenue.**

Miracle on 34th Street (1947) is the classic tale that proves there really is a Santa Claus. A young Natalie Wood co-stars with Maureen O'Hara.

Moonstruck (1987) Cher finds love at the **Metropolitan Opera.**

The Naked City (1948) stars Barry Fitzgerald, Howard Duff, and Don Taylor in the oft-imitated police thriller, which has a famous final scene on the **Williamsburg Bridge.**

Next Stop, Greenwich Village (1976) captures the lure of artsy bohemia for a Brooklyn boy.

On the Town (1949) is the quintessential New York picture with Frank Sinatra, Gene Kelly, and Ann Miller dancing from **Wall Street** to **Rockefeller Center.**

Panic in Needle Park (1971) strikes heroin addicts at **Broadway** and **Amsterdam Avenue.** Al Pacino stars.

The Pawnbroker (1965) is Sidney Lumet's film of a Jewish concentration camp survivor (Rod Steiger) running a pawnshop in **Harlem.**

Prince of Tides (1991) A New York psychiatrist (Barbra Streisand) helps high school football coach (Nick Nolte) to uncover his darkest secrets.

Prisoner of Second Avenue (1975) tells the story of two victims of the city with Jack Lemmon and Anne Bancroft starring.

Prizzi's Honor (1985) showcases the **Brooklyn Heights Promenade** and stars Kathleen Turner, Anjelica Huston, and Jack Nicholson.

Rosemary's Baby (1968) highlights the **Dakota Apartments** (West 72nd Street and Central Park West) in Roman Polanski's film starring Mia Farrow and John Cassavetes.

Saboteur (1942) Alfred Hitchcock's chilling tale includes a dangling climax from the **Statue of Liberty**'s crown.

Saturday Night Fever (1977) shows John Travolta's life as he tries to escape his dead-end career as a disco king. His identity crisis reaches a climax atop the **Verrazano-Narrows Bridge** when a friend falls to his death.

Scent of a Woman (1992) pits Chris O'Donnell and Gabrielle Anwar with Al Pacino in his Oscar winning role as a blind man.

Serpico (1974) Al Pacino fights corruption in the NYPD, with location shots at **New York University.**

Slaves of New York (1989) stars Bernadette Peters as an aspiring hat designer lost in the artificiality of the SoHo art world.

Sophie's Choice (1982) stars a very Victorian-looking Meryl Streep and Kevin Kline who reside in **Flatbush** (101 Rugby Road).

Splash (1983) captures Daryl Hannah, as a mermaid, trying to tell Tom Hanks her name while shopping at **Bloomingdale**'s. The resulting fish-squeal shatters every TV set in the store. She later chooses the name "Madison" while walking down that avenue with him.

Superman (1978) finds Clark Kent, the mild-mannered reporter for the Daily Planet, saving the world—and Lois Lane. The former **Daily News Building** is featured.

The Sweet Smell of Success (1957) Tony Curtis and Burt Lancaster dine at **21.**

The Taking of Pelham Bay 1-2-3 (1974) finds subway riders at the mercy of extortionists on the **Pelham Bay Line.**

Taxi Driver (1976) Robert De Niro discovers his talents for cleaning up New York's crime-ridden streets in this Martin Scorsese film.

A Tree Grows in Brooklyn (1945), based on Betty Smith's novel, stars Dorothy McGuire and Joan Blondell in the depiction of a troubled family.

An Unmarried Woman (1978) portrays the trauma of a suddenly single female on the **Upper East Side.**

The Wedding Banquet (1993) stars Mitchell Lichstenstein and May Chin in a marriage of convenience, shot at various locations in the city.

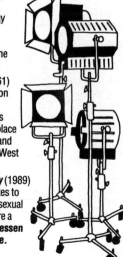

West Side Story (1961) pits two street gangs on the **Upper West Side.** Director Robert Wise's opening scene takes place between Amsterdam and West End Avenues at West 68th Street.

When Harry Met Sally (1989) Meg Ryan demonstrates to Billy Crystal the art of sexual deception as they share a meal at **Katz's Delicatessen** on the **Lower East Side.** A memorable scene.

37 Trinity Church This historic architectural and religious monument has a strong square tower punctuated by an exclamation point spire, and the good fortune to stand at the head of Wall Street. The shaded grassy cemetery, a welcome open space in this neighborhood, offers a noontime haven for office workers. The cemetery came first, and such notables as Alexander Hamilton, William Bradford, and Robert Fulton are buried here (marked by placards that are especially helpful where gravestone inscriptions have worn away). This is the third church with this name on this site. The original was built in 1698, paid for by taxation of all citizens, regardless of religion, because the Church of England was the official religion of the colony. It burned in 1776. The second was demolished in 1839. A small museum behind the main altar documents the church's history.

The present structure was designed in 1846 by **Richard Upjohn; Richard Morris Hunt**'s brass doors were added later. The **Chapel of All Saints,** designed by **Thomas Hash,** was built in 1913; and the **Bishop Manning Memorial Wing** by **Adams & Woodbridge** was erected in 1965. In 1993, work was completed on a time-consuming effort to restore the building to its original appearance. Workers steamed away a layer of paraffin that was mistakenly applied to the building in the 1920s to keep it from crumbling; beneath the paraffin were layers of coal dust and pollutants that had made this building blacker than many other historic buildings. The result of the cleaning process—rosy sandstone as **Upjohn** had intended—was quite a surprise to the thousands of Wall Streeters who, every day for years, had been walking past what they believed to be a very dark building. Classical concerts are often given here on Sundays during the winter months. ♦ Services: daily. Museum: M-F 9-11:45AM, 1-3:45PM; Sa 10AM-3:45PM; Su 1-3:45PM. Broadway and Wall St. 602.0800 ♿

On 7 August 1974, circus performer Philipe Petit took a 45-minute walk on a 131-foot steel cable running between the North and South Towers of the World Trade Center. When asked why, he explained, "When I see three oranges, I have to juggle, and if I see two towers, I have to walk." In July 1975, Owen Quinn, a skydiver and dock builder, dove from the 110th floor of the North Tower. At about the 60th floor, after he had gained enough momentum, he opened his parachute. The entire trip took two minutes. On 27 May 1977, mountain climber George Willig scaled the South Tower in a three-and-a-half-hour climb. "I thought I'd like to try it," he said.

Restaurants/Clubs: Red **Hotels:** Blue
Shops/♥ Outdoors: Green **Sights/Culture:** Black

38 American Stock Exchange The building was known until 1953 as the "Curb Exchange" because before 1921 brokers stood at the corner of Wall and Broad Streets and communicated with one another through hand gestures. The present building was designed in 1930 by **Starrett & Van Vleck.** ♦ 86 Trinity Pl (between Rector and Thames Sts). 306.1000

38 Syms Located in the heart of the Financial District, this famous discount house is primarily for men and women with conservative tastes. Sizes range from lean and trim to portly, at discounts of 30 to 50 percent. Unlike in some discount stores, here you'll find the original labels on the stock. Selections include double-breasted and single-breasted suits in conservative pinstripes, herringbones, and Harris tweeds, as well as double-pleated slacks, jeans, and all the accessories to go with them. But the greatest strength is the shirt department, which takes up nearly the entire second floor. On the third and fourth floors are the women's departments. ♦ Daily. 42 Trinity Pl (at Rector St). 797.1199. Also at: 400 Park Ave (at E 54th St). No phone at press time

39 Bank of Tokyo Trust Alterations that took place in 1975 by **Kajima International** modernized **Bruce Price**'s 1895 building. The eight Greek ladies by J. Massey Rhind still guard the building from their perch on the third floor. Look farther up and you'll find more of them on an even higher level. ♦ 100 Broadway (at Pine St). 766.7916 ♿

40 Trinity and US Realty Buildings The **Trinity Building** by **Francis H. Kimball** replaced **Richard Upjohn**'s five-story 1840 building of the same name, which was the first office building in the city. After the present Gothic structure was built in 1906, its developer, US Realty Company, acquired a similar 50-foot plot next door and constructed an identical 21-story building for their own use, with a shared service core along Thames Street. Fantastic creatures sporting lions' heads and eagles' wings watch as you approach the entrance to the **Trinity Building.** ♦ 111 and 115 Broadway (at Cedar St)

41 Equitable Building The massive structure is noteworthy not for any particular stylistic qualities but for its size, which changed the history of building in New York. This 40-story block contains 1.2 million square feet of office space on a site of slightly less than one acre. The public outcry when it was completed in 1915 by **Ernest R. Graham** caused the creation of the 1916 zoning laws, the first ever in the country, to ensure a minimum of light and air on city streets in the future. ♦ 120 Broadway (between Pine and Cedar Sts)

42 Marine Midland Bank One of Lower Manhattan's more successful modern-style steel-and-glass high-rises, this one was designed by **Skidmore, Owings & Merrill** in 1967. The sleek black building has an appropriateness of scale, largely due to a spandrel design that helps it fit into its older, more ornate surroundings. A vermilion cube by sculptor Isamu Noguchi enlivens the plaza. ♦ 140 Broadway (at Liberty St). 658.1641 ♿

43 Chase Manhattan Bank Built in 1960 as a catalyst to revitalize the aging Wall Street area, the bank's aluminum-and-glass face rises an impressive 813 feet, and it is still a fittingly imposing base for the Rockefeller banking empire. The designers, **Skidmore, Owings & Merrill,** gave the tower a trend-setting feature, its large plaza, which is home to *A Group of Four Trees* by Jean Dubuffet and a sunken sculpture garden by Isamu Noguchi. ♦ 1 Chase Manhattan Pl (between William and Nassau Sts). 552.2222 ♿

44 Louise Nevelson Plaza This small triangular park with large steel sculptures created by the late Louise Nevelson is a popular lunch spot. ♦ Bounded by Maiden La and Liberty and William Sts

45 Federal Reserve Bank of New York This is the banker's bank, where the nations of the world maintain the balance of trade by the storage and exchange of gold, which is housed on five underground floors that occupy an entire city block. The unimaginable riches inside this Fort Knox are reflected in the building's exterior, modeled after a 15th-century Florentine palazzo, with Samuel Yellin's finely detailed ironwork adding to the serene beauty of the limestone-and-sandstone facade (designed by **York & Sawyer** in 1924). Free one-hour tours of the building and gold vaults are available weekdays on a limited basis. Reservations are required at least one week in advance. ♦ 33 Liberty St (between William and Nassau Sts). 720.6130 ♿

46 Chamber of Commerce of the State of New York Designed by **James B. Baker** in 1901, this ornate Beaux Arts edifice is ponderous from its heavy stone base to its massive top, with Ionic columns adding to its almost predatory look. ♦ 65 Liberty St (at Liberty Pl)

47 McDonald's $ Believe it or not, this is the home of the golden arches, despite the tuxedo-clad doorman, glass-and-wood dining room, and classical pianist serenading diners. With the exception of espresso and cappuccino served from silver trays and the pastries from **Dumas** (an Upper East Side bakery), the food is standard Ronald McDonald fare. Serious investors will appreciate the Dow Jones ticker tape, informing them of market fluctuations as they munch their Big Macs. ♦ Fast food ♦ Daily breakfast, lunch, and dinner. 160 Broadway (near Maiden La). 385.2063 ♿

48 Century 21 A larger version of the Brooklyn discount department store, this place has three bustling floors of top-quality housewares and appliances, in addition to clothing, toys, and electronics. ♦ M-Sa. 22 Cortlandt St (between Broadway and Church St). 227.9092. Also at: 472 86th St (between Fourth and Fifth Aves), Brooklyn. 718/748.3266

49 Battery Park City When this eclectic complex of 14,000 rental apartments and condominiums is finally complete, it will support a population larger than that of Bozeman, Montana (the residential population will be approximately 25,000). The total development cost of this 92-acre landfill site (see map on page 34) adjacent to the Financial District is estimated at $4 billion, including the privately financed $1.5-billion **World Financial Center.** The master plan devised in 1979 by **Cooper, Eckstut Associates** divides the blocks into parcels, with individual developers for each one, thus avoiding a superblock appearance. About 30 percent of the site is open parkland with parks linked by the 1.2-mile landscaped waterfront. **The Esplanade** was designed by landscape architects **Stanton Eckstut** between Liberty and West Thames Streets; **Eckstut, Susan Child Associates,** and artist Mary Miss at the South Cove; and **Carr, Lynch, Hack & Sandell** between North Cove Yacht Harbor and Chambers Street); it extends the entire length of the site, providing a perfect place to relax and watch the river traffic. Access for the disabled has been incorporated into the overall design.

The first completed section was **Gateway Plaza** (1982), a trio of 34-story towers and three six-story buildings that provide 1,712 residential units. The structures, designed by **Jack Brown** and **Irving Gershorn,** were begun before the current master plan was established.

New York's first subway (one car, seating 22 passengers) was fueled by a blast of air from a huge steam-driven fan, which would suck the car back when it reached the end of the line. It traveled 10 miles an hour and ran under Broadway from Warren to Murray Streets, a distance of 312 feet. It was conceived and constructed in 1870 by Alfred Ely Beach, a publisher and the inventor of the typewriter.

Wall Street's first financier was probably Frederick Phillipse, whose house was at the northern end of Nieuw Amsterdam. Indian wampum, made from Long Island clam shells, was the legal tender of the colony, and in 1665, Phillipse bought several barrels of it, creating an artificial shortage. Anyone who needed any wampum to settle debts and continue in business had to buy it from Phillipse, at his rates.

BATTERY PARK CITY

The architects who worked on **Rector Place** (1988), the second phase of residential construction, included **Charles Moore; James Stewart Polshek; Gruzen; Ulrich Franzen; Conklin Rossant; Mitchell Giurgola;** and **Davis, Brody & Associates.** Developed under the master plan, this nine-acre plot contains 2,200 apartments grouped around one-acre **Rector Park,** designed by landscape architects Innocente & Webel.

The third phase, **Battery Place** (scheduled for completion near the year 2000), consists of 2,800 residential units on nine parcels located between **Rector Place** and Pier A. The architects involved in the initial three buildings are **The Ehrenkrantz Group & Eckstut, Gruzen Samton Steinglass,** and **James Stewart Polshek & Partners.** The southern end of this area will include the **Machado & Silvetti**–designed **The Living Memorial for the Holocaust/Museum of Jewish Heritage;** a hotel; a residential building; and the three-acre **South Gardens** park designed by landscape architect Hanna Olin. ♦ Bounded by West St and the Hudson River, and Pier A and Chambers St. 416-5300 ♿

50 World Financial Center More than eight million square feet of office, retail, and recreational space have been created on landfill produced by the construction of the **World Trade Center** across West Street. Designed by **Cesar Pelli & Associates** and completed in 1981, the complex includes four 33- to 50-story office towers, two nine-story buildings designated as gatehouses, a four-acre plaza, and a vaulted and glass-enclosed **Winter Garden,** whose most dramatic feature is 15 Washington robusta palm trees. The only ones of this size in the city, they are each a uniform 45 feet high. Tenants include **Bally of Switzerland, Caswell-Massey, Godiva Chocolatier, Manufacturers Hanover Trust, Rizzoli International Bookstore,** and **Plus One Fitness Clinic.** The **Courtyard,** a two-level outdoor piazza, houses four international restaurants and cafes. The **World Financial Center Plaza** is a stellar example of public space design: 3.5 beautifully landscaped acres of parkland on the Hudson River with twin reflecting pools. The center presents an ongoing series of music, dance, and theater events as well as visual arts installations, and is world headquarters for such companies as American Express, Merrill Lynch, and Dow Jones. ♦ Daily. West St (between Liberty and Vesey Sts). 945.0505 ♿

Within the World Financial Center:

Hudson River Club ★★★$$$$ The menu specializes in food from the Hudson River Valley: fillet of salmon in woven potatoes, T-bone of Millbrook venison trout, and roast free-range chicken with red-beet risotto. The regional wine list is exceptional. The clublike setting, with its plush banquette seating and

34

armchairs, has a breathtaking view of **North Cove Harbor Marina** and the **Statue of Liberty.** ♦ American ♦ M-F lunch and dinner; Sa dinner; Su brunch. Reservations required; jacket required. 4 World Financial Center, Upper Level (enter at 225 Liberty St). 786.1500 ♿

Le Pactole ★★$$$ This 10,000-square-foot restaurant with giant windows overlooking the Hudson features the estimable talents of French chef Andre Laurent. In the dignified, rose-colored dining room, expect such classic French dishes as terrine of duck with pistachio nuts and tournedos of beef with black truffle sauce, as well as newer creations that include grilled tuna steak with a ginger and cucumber *coulis* (a thick pureed sauce). Next door is the gourmet shop, **Le Pac to Go** (945.9387), which delivers to offices and homes in the area. ♦ French ♦ M-F lunch and dinner; Su brunch. Reservations recommended. 4 World Financial Center, Second Level (enter at 225 Liberty St). 945.9444 ♿

Pipeline ★$$ Designed by Sam Lopata to look like an oil refinery, this vast space seats 120 indoors and 150 more outside. The interior features brightly colored pipes, catwalks, ladders, and a great video/jukebox system. Chef Gonzalo Figueroa creates such dishes as corn chowder, and penne with tuna and white-bean salad; for dessert the chocolate truffle cake and bread pudding are musts. Also featured are "Battery Park Picnic Baskets," which are special lunch and dinner take-out boxes. ♦ American ♦ M-F lunch and dinner; Sa-Su brunch and dinner. Reservations recommended. 2 World Financial Center, Ground floor. 945.2755 ♿

Au Mandarin ★$$ The authentic Mandarin menu served here—particularly the tangy, spicy chicken; diced chicken marinated with minced garlic, ginger, and peppercorns; and Peking duck—is popular at lunchtime. ♦ Mandarin ♦ Daily lunch and dinner. 2 World Financial Center, Courtyard. 385.0313 ♿

Donald Sacks ★$$ Good potpies, salads, and grilled sandwiches are served at this outpost of SoHo's famed take-out shop. Relax in the elegant mahogany-and-marble room while enjoying the river view. ♦ American ♦ Daily lunch and dinner. 2 World Financial Center, Courtyard. 619.4600 ♿

Tahari This designer's full line of sophisticated clothing for women, including scarves, jewelry, and handbags, is stocked here. The shop is decorated with antiques (not for sale) from Ellie Tahari's private collection. ♦ Daily. 2 World Financial Center, Upper Level. 945.2450 ♿

The World Trade Center has more than a half-million square feet of glass.

Downtown Sound The music store stocks lots of CDs—which you can listen to on the headphones that hang from the wall—and fast, computer-aided service, plus audio equipment and accessories. ♦ M-F. 4 World Financial Center, Lobby. 587.0093 ♿

51 **World Trade Center (WTC)** Seven buildings, including the **Vista Hotel** and the two landmark towers, make up this massive complex set on a semicircle around a five-acre plaza. Designed by **Minoru Yamasaki & Associates** and **Emery Roth & Sons, WTC** was begun in 1962 and finished in 1977. At 110 stories, the monolithic twin towers are the tallest in the city (shown on page 36). All the structures are connected underground by the concourse—a vast pedestrian mall filled with shops, banks, public spaces, and restaurants, including branches of **Au Bon Pain** and **Ben and Jerry's.** Beneath it all are parking garages, where on 26 February 1993, a terrorist bomb went off in **One World Trade Center,** killing six people, injuring many more, and causing millions of dollars of damage. At press time, the dining spots listed below in **One World Trade Center** were undergoing renovation; the doors at all three restaurants were scheduled to reopen in early 1996. Call 435.4170 for updated information. ♦ Church St (between Liberty and Vesey Sts). 435.4170

Within the World Trade Center:

The Observation Deck Floor-to-ceiling windows at the top of the more southerly of the twin towers are marked with unobtrusive diagrams explaining what you are seeing. With this kind of competition, no one pays much attention to the walls behind you on all four sides of the building, displaying the history of world trade. The view from the deck has been called the best in the world, but if you want an even better one, take the escalator up to the open rooftop observatory (open only in good weather), the tallest outdoor platform in the world. Another thrill: Take the quarter-mile, 58-second elevator ride from the mezzanine level of **2 WTC** to the 107th floor. ♦ Admission. Daily 9:30AM-9:30PM. Tickets are sold on the mezzanine level of 2 World Trade Center. 2 World Trade Center. 435.7377 ♿

The Restaurant at Windows on the World For years it's been one of the most spectacular restaurants in New York, although, frankly, it was about due for a face-lift. When the restaurant closed after the bombing, Joseph Baum and Michael Whiteman Company (the original designers) got busy. And now it's even more stunning than before, and still featuring those breathtaking panoramic views. There's no reason to believe that this hiatus will cause the kitchen's standards to do anything but rise, and the wine list, heretofore boasting over 600 selections, should be just as extensive. ◆ Continental ◆ Reservations required; jacket and tie required. 1 World Trade Center. No phone at press time

The Hors d'Oeuvrerie at Windows on the World When the renovation is complete, no doubt this place will be a great spot to sip a cocktail and marvel at the views to the south and west. The revamped bar area will feature a light menu and a dance floor. ◆ Continental ◆ Cover. Jacket required. 1 World Trade Center. No phone at press time

Cellar in the Sky Previously, this small 40-seat dining room within **Windows on the World** was located in a windowless wine cellar, but when it reopens, it will have moved to an area with floor-to-ceiling windows that have "The View." ◆ Continental ◆ Reservations required; jacket and tie required. 1 World Trade Center. No phone at press time

TKTS Half-price day-of-performance tickets are available here for evening performances of Broadway and Off-Broadway shows. Wednesday, Saturday, and Sunday matinee tickets are sold from 11AM to closing the day before the performance. ◆ M-F 11AM-5:30PM; Sa 11AM-3:30PM. 2 World Trade Center, Mezzanine. 768.1818. Also at: Broadway and 47th St ♿

 Austin J. Tobin Plaza This five-acre space between the towers is graced with a fountain that surrounds a 25-foot bronze construction by Fritz Koenig. The granite pyramid at the entrance is by Masyuki Nagare, and the stainless-steel abstract sculpture is by James Rosati. Also note the Alexander Calder stabile just outside on Church Street. Other sculpture is often temporarily displayed on the windy plaza, which is frequently used as a setting for concerts and other events. Other works of art commissioned for the **World Trade Center** include Louise Nevelson's *Sky-Gate New York* on the mezzanine of **1 World Trade Center,** and a three-ton tapestry by Joan Miró, which hangs in the mezzanine of 2 **World Trade Center.**

World Trade Center

Michael Storrings

Vista International Hotel $$$$ Now reopened after a $65-million renovation and bomb repair, this sleek yet welcoming 820-room Hilton affords views of the Hudson River from the highest floors. Designed in 1981 by **Skidmore, Owings & Merrill,** it is packed during the week with businesspeople who want proximity to Wall Street and the **World Trade Center;** on weekends, visitors come to experience the sights and charms of old New York. Free weekend shuttle buses uptown make it a pleasure to venture out of the neighborhood, too. A fitness center provides a free indoor swimming pool, jogging track, sauna, and exercise rooms (fee for racquetball and massage), along with spectacular views of the harbor. The business center offers secretarial services, personal computers, and cellular phones. The **Executive Floors** boast a special lounge with complimentary cocktails, breakfast, and other perks. The adjacent concourse of the **World Trade Center** is a bazaar of stores and restaurants. And there's a comfortable spot in the lobby for express breakfast or lunch. ◆ 3 World Trade Center. 938.9100, 800/469.8478; fax 444.3444 ㅊ

Within the Vista International Hotel:

Greenhouse Cafe ★$$ This gardenlike, sun-drenched cafe has a skylight roof that gives an unusual view of the **Twin Towers** soaring above. Executive chef Walter Plendner has put together an eclectic menu, featuring such dishes as glazed duck breast and andouille sausage over greens with pumpkin dressing. There are also daily curries and a buffet featuring roasted meats, as well as a daily-changing antipasto that is likely to include mozzarella and sun-dried tomatoes, various smoked fish, and a variety of salads. ◆ American ◆ Daily breakfast, lunch, and dinner. 3 World Trade Center, Plaza Level. 938.9100

Tall Ships Bar & Grill ★$$ As befits the name, the decor is strictly nautical, with canvas sails draped overhead, polished mast-worthy woods, and stripes on the walls. The food is simple, including blackened or broiled swordfish steak with grilled vegetables, barbecued chicken medallions with spring onions and corn sticks, and freshly baked pies for dessert. ◆ American ◆ M-F lunch and dinner; Sa-Su dinner. 3 World Trade Center, Lobby level. 938.9100

52 **The Millenium Hilton** $$$$ Fifty-five stories high, this sleek lodging has overlooked downtown New York since being built in the shadow of the **World Trade Center** in 1992. It offers 561 nicely appointed guest rooms and suites, an indoor pool and health center, an executive business center, and other amenities. The hotel's restaurants include the casual **Grill.** ◆ 55 Church St (between Dey and Fulton Sts). 693.2001, 800/752.0014; fax 571.2316

Within the Millenium Hilton Hotel:

Taliesin ★$$$ This formal, pretty room with wood paneling and etched glass is the setting for ambitious cooking, some of which succeeds. Try the clam and corn chowder lightly scented with thyme, tuna carpaccio with vegetable relish and black-olive croutons, and grilled swordfish with shrimp, clams, and mussels in a shellfish broth. ◆ American ◆ Daily breakfast, lunch, and dinner. 312.2000 ㅊ

53 **195 Broadway** There are more columns on the facade of this building than on any other building in the world, with even more inside (the lobby is like an ancient Athenian temple). It was designed in 1917 by **William Welles Bosworth** as headquarters for the American Telephone & Telegraph Company. The ornamental panels over the Broadway entrance, as well as the bronze seals on the lobby floor and the other interior decorative elements are by Paul Manship, whose best-known work in New York is the *Prometheus* fountain in **Rockefeller Plaza.** ◆ Between Dey and Fulton Sts

54 **St. Paul's Chapel** Built in 1766 by **Thomas McBean,** this is Manhattan's only remaining pre-Revolutionary War church—it even survived 1776's Great Fire—making it the oldest public building in continuous use. The chapel is not only a rare Georgian architectural gem; it is also historically important. Said to be the most impressive church in the colony when built, its grandeur loses nothing in the shadow of that neighboring temple of commerce, the **World Trade Center.** It's humbling to remember that in 1750 this site was a wheat field; the cemetery once extended to the Hudson River; and George Washington came here to pray after his inauguration as the country's first president on 30 August 1789. **McBean**'s plan for the edifice was much influenced by St. Martin-in-the-Fields in London, designed by his teacher, **James Gibb.** The interior, lit by Waterford crystal chandeliers, is one of the city's best. Come here for the concerts of classical and church music Monday and Thursday at 12:10PM (donation requested), or for services Sunday at 8AM. ◆ Broadway (between Fulton and Vesey Sts). 602.0800 ㅊ

55 **Woolworth Building** One of the city's most dramatic skyscrapers and one of the world's most ornate commercial buildings, it was designed by **Cass Gilbert** in 1913 as the headquarters of Frank W. Woolworth's chain of five-and-dime stores. The building, known in its day as a "cathedral of commerce," is a Gothic celebration inside and out, with picturesque details enhancing the forceful massing and graceful vertical thrust, which culminates in a perfectly composed crown. Inside, the lobby features a soaring glass

mosaic ceiling and marble walls awash with more Gothic detail. An added surprise are the caricature bas-reliefs, including one of **Gilbert** himself with a model of the building and another of Frank Woolworth counting nickels and dimes. The Woolworths were so pleased with **Gilbert's** work that they paid for it in cash ($1.5 million); they still maintain an office here. It's well worth a visit. ♦ 233 Broadway (between Barclay St and Park Pl)

56 City Hall Surprisingly, New York City is still doing business (with a little help from the nearby **Municipal Building**) in the same building that was its headquarters in 1811 when the building was completed. This elegant scaled-down palace by **Mangin and McComb,** a winning entry in a design competition, successfully combines the Federal style with French Renaissance details. The central hall has a sweeping twin-spiral marble staircase under a splendid dome, making it the perfect setting for public functions and grand entrances. Kings, poets, and astronauts have been received here. Upstairs, the grand **City Council Chamber** (also used by the Board of Estimate) and the **Governor's Room—** now a portrait gallery with paintings by Sully, Trumbull, Inman, and others—are worth a visit. There are always exhibitions with historical or artistic themes. Interiors were restored and refurbished between 1902 and 1920, and the exterior was restored and repaired by **Shreve, Lamb & Harmon** in 1959. What is known today as **City Hall Park** has always been the city's village green or town common; equally grand in scale, the park sets off the mass of **City Hall.** ♦ M-F. City Hall Park (between Park Row and Broadway)

57 Pace University Originally founded as an accounting school, this university now offers courses in the arts and sciences as well as business, education, and nursing. The welded copper sculpture on the facade, by Henri Nachemia, represents *The Brotherhood of Man.* The building itself was designed by **Eggers & Higgins** in 1970. ♦ 1 Pace Plaza (at Nassau St, between Spruce and Frankfort Sts). 346.1200 &

58 New York City Courthouse The building was known as the **Tweed Courthouse** because Tammany Hall chieftain William Marcy Tweed escalated its cost to 52 times the appropriated amount, most of which went into his own bank account. Because of the scandal, the building became a symbol of graft and has always been something of a municipal stepchild. Recent attempts to restore it have been halfhearted, but it has been saved from destruction. The original building, designed by **John Kellum** and constructed in 1872, had a grand staircase in front; the staircase was removed in 1955 to make room for the widening of Chambers Street, leaving a blank space that ruins the

facade. ♦ 52 Chambers St (between Centre St and Broadway)

59 Ellen's Cafe and Bake Shop ★$ Ellen Hart Sturm, a former Miss Subways beauty queen, runs this bustling upscale cafe and bakery across from **City Hall;** the walls are lined with photos of former Miss Subways (Ellen sponsors yearly reunions). Try the "Mayor's Special" (toasted Thomas's English Muffin halves layered with tuna salad and tomato slices and topped with melted cheese). Be sure to save room for Ellen's pecan pie. If you like the food here, try **Ellen's Stardust,** at 1377 Sixth Avenue (307.7575). ♦ American ♦ M-Sa breakfast, lunch, and early dinner. 270 Broadway (at Chambers St). 962.1257 &

60 Ecco $$$ This restaurant has none of the downtown funkiness of its nearby Tribeca neighbors. Carved mahogany, beveled mirrors, and a two-story-high tin ceiling provide a clubby, 19th-century atmosphere. The waiters bustle through the crowd: equal parts Wall Streeters and art dealers. Stick with pasta and dessert. ♦ Italian ♦ M-F lunch and dinner. Sa dinner. Reservations required. 124 Chambers St (between Church St and W Broadway). 227.7074

61 Stuyvesant High School Built in 1991 by **Alexander Cooper & Partners,** this is the new location of one of the most prestigious and progressive public high schools in the country. Since the difficult-to-earn Westinghouse scholarships were first awarded, this school's students have routinely finished the competition among the top 10 from all over the US. Graduates include Nobel laureates Joshua Lederberg and Raoul Hoffman. The building is not open to the public. ♦ 345 Chambers St (at West St). 312.4800.

62 Surrogate's Court Monumental sculptures, including a pair by Philip Martiny at the entrance—one representing *Britannia* (an English soldier and a maiden), the other *America* (a Native American and a Pilgrim)— along with an array of cherubs, eagles, festoons, ship prows, and shields, let you know something important is going on here. The French Empire facade, reminiscent of the Paris Opera, is only the beginning. The interior has an Egyptian-tile mosaic ceiling with the 12 signs of the zodiac by William de Leftwich Dodge, as well as marble walls and floors and allegorical reliefs. The huge double stairway is yet another touch borrowed from the Opera. Intended to be the last resting place of important city records, the building, which was designed in 1911 by **John R. Thomas** and **Horgan & Slattery,** also serves as the Surrogate's Court. Over the years this became its primary function, as the need grew for more space to probate wills and administer guardianships and trusts. ♦ 31 Chambers St (at Centre St). 374.8233

63 Municipal Building McKim, Mead & White created this Neo-Classical skyscraper (illustrated below) in 1914 to house city government offices. The building straddles Chambers Street and coexists quite happily with neighboring, smaller **City Hall** without upstaging it. The almost Baroque confection is topped with a fanciful cluster of colonnaded towers capped by Adolph Weinman's gilded statue. ♦ 1 Centre St (at Chambers St)

64 Police Plaza At three full acres, this is the largest public plaza in New York. On the south side is a prison window from the 1763 **Rhinelander Sugar Warehouse,** which was on this site until 1895. (The original building was used by the British to house American prisoners of war during the Revolution.) The five interlocking oxidized-steel disks, a 1974 creation by Bernard Rosenthal, represent the five boroughs of the city. Just beyond, an eight-foot waterfall marks the entrance to a multilevel parking garage under the plaza, which was designed in 1973 by **M. Paul Friedberg.** ♦ Chambers St (pedestrian mall between Municipal Building and Police Headquarters)

65 St. Andrew's Church The Roman Catholic church was established here in 1842 to minister to the needs of Irish immigrants. Its mission has changed along with the neighborhood. The present church was designed in 1939 by **Maginnis & Walsh** and **Robert J. Reiley.** ♦ 20 Cardinal Hayes Pl (between St. Andrews Pl and Pearl St). 962.3972

66 United States Courthouse Here's another Lower Manhattan structure trying to be a temple. Designed in 1936 by **Cass Gilbert** and **Cass Gilbert Jr.,** this civic building presents a traditional, stately image with rows of Corinthian columns as a base for a tower crowned with a gold pyramid. ♦ 40 Centre St (at Foley Sq)

67 New York County Courthouse A National Historic Landmark, this hexagon-shaped building was designed by **Guy Lowell** in 1926. The Roman style of the building—particularly the Corinthian portico—works much better here than at the neighboring **United States Courthouse.** ♦ 60 Centre St (at Pearl St).

68 Jacob K. Javits Federal Building The smaller building on the left houses the **US Customs Court,** and the taller one with the strange windows is filled with government offices. Both buildings were designed by **Alfred Easton Poor** and **Kahn & Jacobs** in 1967. ♦ 26 Federal Plaza (between Duane and Worth Sts)

Municipal Building

Michael Storrings

Chinatown/Lower East Side/

Little Italy

In New York's early days, the swampy territory just northeast of **City Hall** was considered worthless. But as waves of immigrants began arriving in the middle of the 18th century, the former marshes became valuable to the real-estate developers who packed the newcomers into crowded tenements. The distinct ethnic flavors of Chinatown, the Lower East Side, and Little Italy were established as each immigrant group settled the area roughly bounded by the **East River** and **Lafayette, Chambers,** and **Houston Streets.**

Nearly every part of New York has metamorphosed several times during the last two centuries. But in this area, it's mainly the populace, rather than the architecture, that has changed. During the 1860s, thousands of Germans arrived, forcing the long-settled Irish farther uptown. Between 1881 and 1910, 1.5 million Jews fled Romania, Hungary, and Russia, creating the largest Jewish settlement in the world on Manhattan's Lower East Side. Italians, Greeks, Poles, and Turks were among the other settlers. The neighborhood continues to be a first stop for newly arrived immigrants; today's predominantly Hispanic population fills streets that still carry the legacy of the Jews they have replaced.

The southwestern portion of this area is a magnet for Chinese immigrants, who began arriving from San Francisco during the 1870s. Since immigration laws were changed in the mid-1960s, the neighborhood has welcomed more of them than ever. Once covering three square blocks and now 40 square blocks and growing, the area's more than 150,000 Chinese residents make Chinatown the largest Chinese community outside of Asia. The need for more living space has caused new arrivals to cross **Canal Street** into the enclave traditionally reserved for immigrants from Naples and Sicily. The result is that the neighborhood called Little Italy is now filled with hundreds of sweatshops and other businesses identified by Chinese ideograms. (Distressed about this

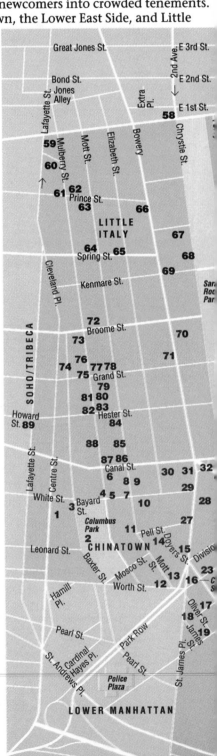

situation, Italian community leaders have requested that signs along **Mulberry Street** be posted only in Roman letters, so that the neighborhood retains what little character is left despite ambitious Chinese landlords.)

Chinatown is a neighborhood that thrives on street life, but except for pagoda telephone booths, don't expect quaintness. What you will find is a warren of shops selling exotic vegetables and bargain-basement Chinese clothing and housewares, along with Formica- and vinyl-filled restaurants, many of which

prepare wondrous dishes. The largest crowds appear on Chinese New Year, in late January or early February.

The Lower East Side is roughly the area below East Houston Street, from the **Bowery** to the East River. During the 1880s and 1890s, immigrants from Eastern Europe flooded into the cramped redbrick tenements. At the turn of the century, this was the world's largest Jewish settlement, a slum that later became a center of culture and community (documented by, among others, critic Irving Howe in his 1976 study "World of Our Fathers") that spawned many writers, businessmen, and intellectuals. Most of the upwardly mobile Jewish immigrants left as quickly as possible; now the Lower East Side is home to Chinese, Latin Americans, and African-Americans. However, although many synagogues remain empty, the old crowd comes back for a steak at **Sammy's Famous Roumanian Jewish Steakhouse** or to shop: **Orchard Street** is still discount heaven for everything from fabrics to designer dresses. In observation of the Sabbath, most nonreligious sites on the Lower East Side are closed Friday afternoon and all day Saturday.

Mulberry Street is the main drag of Little Italy (bounded by Canal, Lafayette, and East Houston Streets and the Bowery), a bustling residential area filled with neighborhood stores and old Italian social clubs. Former residents and visitors come for the food—to buy salamis, cheeses, and pasta, to dine in one of the plentiful restaurants, or to linger over an espresso and pastry in a *caffè*. The area was settled mainly between 1880 and 1924 by immigrant families, many of whom have moved on. But they always come back—especially for the Feast of San Gennaro, a week-long religious celebration held each September that is famous for its eating, drinking, and merrymaking.

1 Criminal Courts Building Called the "Tombs" after its Egyptian Revival ancestor across the street, this giant ziggurat is the third Manhattan jail, the last built before prisoners were housed at Riker's Island. Designed by **Harvey Wiley Corbett** in 1939, it is an elegant Art Moderne structure (you'll recognize **Corbett**'s hand in **Rockefeller Center**). In its day, the Tombs' 835-cell jail was considered a standard for penal reform: Each cell housed only one prisoner. ♦ 100 Centre St (between Leonard and White Sts). 374.5880

By 1643, 18 languages were spoken in New York City. More than 75 are spoken today.

"Gotham," a term for New York, was coined by Washington Irving in his satire *A History of New York* written in 1807. In it he also introduced the word "Knickerbockers" for New Yorkers. Also the author of *Rip Van Winkle* and *The Legend of Sleepy Hollow*, Irving's works garnered some of the first serious international recognition for American literature.

Restaurants/Clubs: Red   **Hotels:** Blue

Shops/ 🌳 Outdoors: Green   **Sights/Culture:** Black

2 Columbus Park The only real open space in Chinatown provides a setting for ballplaying and outdoor entertainment, and is a staging area for the dragon dancers during Chinese New Year. It replaces Mulberry Bend, once a red-light district and part of the 19th-century slum neighborhood known as Five Points. ♦ Bounded by Mosco and Bayard Sts, and Mulberry and Baxter Sts

3 Thailand Restaurant ★$$ Some of the best and cheapest Thai food Chinatown has to offer is served here. All of the dishes are reliable, but a specialty is *koong kratiam* (garlicky shrimp and peppers). Vegetarian dishes are also available. ♦ Thai ♦ Daily lunch and dinner. 106 Bayard St (at Baxter St). 349.3132 &

4 Saigon House Restaurant ★★$ A little interior decoration couldn't hurt this place, but the food is authentic Vietnamese. Appetizers and soups are best: crisp spring rolls, shrimp with sugar cane, cold shrimp and pork roll, and seafood and chicken soups with lemongrass. ♦ Vietnamese ♦ Daily lunch and dinner. 89-91 Bayard St (at Mulberry St). 732.8988

5 Museum of Chinese in the Americas Begin your visit to Chinatown by exploring this small museum founded in 1980, or join one of their walking tours, organized for groups of 20 or more. The museum now houses the nation's largest research collection of oral histories, photographs, and artifacts relating to the Chinese-American experience. ♦ Nominal admission. M-F, Su noon-5PM; closed Nov-Apr. 70 Mulberry St (at Bayard St). 619.4785

6 Kam Man Food Products, Inc. Even if you're not planning to buy, drop in to see the astonishing selection of fresh vegetables, dried fish of all kinds, herbs, teas, noodles, and kitchenware. The barbecued duck and chicken available for takeout are delicious. ♦ Daily. 200 Canal St (at Mulberry St). 571.0330 ♦

7 Bo Ky Restaurant ★$ The specialty of this popular restaurant, owned by Chiu Chow people from Vietnam, are the big bowls of steaming hot rice noodles topped with shrimp, fish, shrimp balls, or sliced roast duck. ♦ Vietnamese ♦ Daily breakfast, lunch, and dinner. No credit cards accepted. 80 Bayard St (at Mott St). 406.2292

8 Mandarin Court ★★$ Sisters Kitty and Carol Chan from Hong Kong offer such well-prepared dishes as shrimp baked with spicy salt, clams with black-bean sauce, and pork chops Hong Kong–style. The dim sum is also especially good and served without the bustle of larger dim sum palaces in the neighborhood. ♦ Hong Kong ♦ Daily breakfast, lunch, and dinner. 61 Mott St (between Bayard and Canal Sts). 608.3838

9 Tai Hong Lau ★$ This is a great place for inexpensive Cantonese cooking. Try the Winter Melon Treasure, a curved piece of white melon atop a mixture of mushrooms, roast duck, chicken, pork, and shrimp, surrounded by broccoli florets. ♦ Cantonese ♦ Daily breakfast, lunch, and dinner. 70 Mott St (between Bayard and Canal Sts). 219.1431

9 Eastern States Buddhist Temple of America, Inc. The sparkling gold mountain of Buddhas in the window beckons you into this temple with more than a hundred statues of Buddhas and other religious articles in the back. Neighborhood worshipers come here to pay their respects and light incense. ♦ Daily. 64 Mott St (between Bayard and Canal Sts). 966.4753 ♦

10 New Lin Heong ★$ The greasy-spoon restaurant—heavy on the oyster sauce and sweet-and-sour—is popular because of the low prices and heaping plates of delicious *chow fun* (wide noodles). Also try the big batter-dipped fried fantail shrimp. ♦ Cantonese ♦ Daily breakfast, dinner, and late-night meals. No credit cards accepted. 69 Bayard St (at Mott St). 962.8195

11 Lung Fong Bakery Most of the beautiful sweets offered here, like black-bean doughnuts, are acquired tastes, and this

is the best bakery in Chinatown to start garnering them. For the less adventurous, the huge, melt-in-your-mouth almond and walnut cookies are a sure bet. ♦ Daily. 41 Mott St (at Pell St). 233.7447 ♦

12 Hunan Garden ★★$ This friendly restaurant has a large and interesting menu featuring spicy Hunan specialties and Cantonese favorites, among them Peking Duck, spicy lobster in Hunan sauce, and sautéed chicken and shrimp in a bird's nest. ♦ Hunan/Cantonese ♦ Daily lunch and dinner. 1 Mott St (at Worth St). 732.7270 ♦

13 20 Mott Street ★★$ This is as close to the Hong Kong dining experience as you'll find in New York. Specialties include baked conch stuffed in its own shell and salt-baked shrimp. The dim sum is among the best in the neighborhood. ♦ Cantonese ♦ Daily breakfast, lunch, and dinner. 20 Mott St (between Park Row and Pell St. 964.0380

13 Peking Duck House ★★$ As the name suggests, this is the place to come for Peking Duck. The thoroughly crisped delicacy is carved tableside and is served with the traditional accompaniments: thin pancakes in which to roll the duck, slivered cucumbers, and a scallion brush to swab the duck with *hoisin* (a sweet brown sauce). Also great as an appetizer, one order serves six hearty diners. Preparation takes a while, so get some steamed pork dumplings to munch on while you wait. ♦ Beijing/Szechuan ♦ Daily lunch and dinner. 22 Mott St (between Park Row and Pell St). 227.1810

14 Doyers Street The narrow little street with a wishbone-shaped curve was once known as "Bloody Angle." Opium dealers who thrived in the area during the last century lured their competitors here, where they could be ambushed beyond the blind turn. ♦ Between Bowery and Pell St

14 Nam Wah Tea Parlor ★$ After 75 years, this is the oldest and most colorful—if a bit seedy—Hong Kong dim sum parlor in the area. The funky atmosphere is the lure here rather than the food, which is not as good as at other restaurants in Chinatown. ♦ Dim sum ♦ Daily breakfast, lunch, and early dinner. No credit cards accepted. 13 Doyers St (between Bowery and Pell St). 962.6047

14 Vietnam ★★★$ What this restaurant has saved on the decor, it has invested in the food—the menu lists about a hundred items. Start with the perfectly done Vietnamese spring rolls—filled with shrimp, pork, lemongrass, and cilantro, all wrapped in rice noodles and served with a delicious fish dipping sauce. Follow with the chicken with lemongrass. And wash it all down with Hue beer from Hue City, the ancient capital of Vietnam. ♦ Vietnamese ♦ Daily lunch and dinner. 11 Doyers St (between Bowery and Pell St). 693.0725

15 Edward Mooney House Originally built in 1789, the oldest Federal-style house in Manhattan was modified in 1971 to become a busy branch of the New York Off-Track Betting Corp., which has since moved on to larger quarters. ♦ 18 Bowery (at Doyers St)

16 Chatham Square The monument in the center of the square is the **Kim Lau Memorial,** designed by Poy G. Lee in 1962 and dedicated to Chinese-American war dead. ♦ Bounded by Bowery, Catherine St, and Park Row

17 Mariners' Temple Designed in 1842 by **Minard Lafever,** this brownstone Greek temple was originally called the **Oliver Street Church,** which served sailors based at the nearby East River piers. It is now a Baptist church serving a widely varied community. ♦ 12 Oliver St (at Henry St)

18 First Shearith Israel Cemetery Near Chatham Square, which it once covered, this is the surviving fragment of the Congregation Shearith Israel's first burial ground (there are two more), the oldest Jewish cemetery in Manhattan. The most ancient gravestone is dated 1683. Shearith Israel was founded by early Portuguese and Spanish settlers in 1654 and is now located uptown at a synagogue on Central Park West. ♦ 55 St. James Pl (between Oliver and James Sts)

19 St. James Roman Catholic Church This Greek Revival–style church built in 1837 is an interesting neighbor to the nearby **Mariners' Temple;** both were designed by **Minard Lafever.** ♦ 32 James St (between Madison St and St. James Pl). 223.0161

20 William Clark House Originally built in 1824, this house—and especially the entrance—would appear to epitomize all the elegance of the Federal style. But there is a twist: It is one of the few known to have four floors (two or three were preferred). ♦ 51 Market St (between Monroe and Madison Sts)

Manhattan measures 13.4 miles long and is only 2.3 miles across. Within the total area of the five boroughs, the longest distance between its boundaries is 35 miles, from the northeast to the southwest.

21 Nice Restaurant ★★★$ One of Chinatown's better restaurants, this place serves excellent barbecued duck and minced squab wrapped in lettuce leaves. ♦ Cantonese ♦ Daily breakfast, lunch, and dinner. 35 E Broadway (between Market and Catherine Sts). 406.9510

22 Long Shine Restaurant ★★$ The cuisine here is Fujianese, a recent import from one of China's southern provinces, and well worth trying. Don't miss the soups, particularly the savory fish *mein* soup, with shredded pork, shrimp, and Chinese cabbage. For those who want more traditional fare, there's also an extensive Cantonese menu. ♦ Fujianese/ Cantonese ♦ Daily breakfast, lunch, and dinner. No credit cards accepted. 53 E Broadway (between Market and Catherine Sts). 346.9888 ♿

23 Golden Unicorn ★★★$$ Larger and more elegant than the typical Chinatown storefront restaurant, it is popular with families who come to sample the amazing variety of dim sum. Also don't miss the tasty fried dumplings; then move on to salt-baked shrimp, and chicken with black-pepper sauce. ♦ Cantonese ♦ Daily breakfast, lunch, and dinner. 18 E Broadway (at Catherine St), Second floor. 941.0911 ♿

24 Triple 8 Palace Restaurant ★★★$$ Excellent appetizers include steamed dumplings, fresh oyster pancakes, moist and tender soy chicken and abalone, and several different vegetable soups. Hordes of workers stop by at lunch for some of the best dim sum around. ♦ Hong Kong ♦ Daily breakfast, lunch, and dinner. 88 E Broadway, Top floor (under the Manhattan Bridge). 941.8886

25 Canton ★★$$ Have the owner, Eileen, order for you at this sophisticated restaurant that attracts uptowners, including architect I.M. Pei. Special dishes on the fairly small menu include squab wrapped in lettuce. ♦ Cantonese ♦ W-Su lunch and dinner. No credit cards accepted. 45 Division St (at the Manhattan Bridge). 226.4441

26 Great Shanghai ★★$ Although you wouldn't guess it from the modern pink, gray, and neon decor, this restaurant has been here forever, and the food remains pure Chinatown. Recommended are the steamed vegetable dumplings and the prawns in ging sauce with carrots and scallions. ♦ Shangha ♦ Daily lunch and dinner. 27 Division St (between the Manhattan Bridge and Bowery) 966.7663

27 N.Y. Noodletown ★$ Ever since *The New York Times* rhapsodized about the salt-bake crabs here, it's been virtually impossible to get a seat in this place—which is not to impl that it was easy to get one before. The noodl with beef are deservedly popular, as are the various crisp roast meats—such as the pig-

and the fresh softshell crabs in season. ♦ Cantonese ♦ Daily breakfast, lunch, dinner, and late-night meals. No credit cards accepted. 28 Bowery (at Pell St). 349.0923

28 Confucius Plaza Designed in 1976 by **Horowitz & Chun** and at odds with its smaller 19th-century neighbors, this huge, chunky building solves a pressing need for more living space. It also houses a public school whose population is almost entirely first- and second-generation Chinese. ♦ Bowery (between Division St and Manhattan Bridge)

29 First Taste ★★★$$ Probably the best Hong Kong cuisine in Chinatown is served in this charming restaurant. Start with broiled eel shish kebab or cold jellyfish topped with baby squid, or chicken or beef consommé. Less adventurous types should try the soft, silky bean curd steamed with fresh scallops or the crisp salt-baked chicken with spicy ginger sauce. ♦ Hong Kong ♦ Daily lunch and dinner. 53 Bayard St (between Bowery and Elizabeth St). 962.1818 ♿

30 Oriental Garden Seafood ★★$$ Don't be surprised; the staff often seat strangers together at one table here to accommodate the crowds, which seem to be ever present. But the seafood, particularly the golden walnut prawns, is good enough to make diners forget the feeling of being packed in like sardines. ♦ Cantonese/Seafood ♦ Daily breakfast, lunch, and dinner. 14 Elizabeth St (between Bayard and Canal Sts). 619.0085 ♿

30 Lin's Sister Associates Corp. Herbs, vitamins, and various traditional medicines are carried in this drugstore. If you're feeling poorly, stop in for a detailed consultation and prescription from an herbalist, who might recommend a tea, capsules, or a poultice. ♦ Daily. 18A Elizabeth St (between Bayard and Canal Sts). 962.5417

30 Jing Fong ★★$$ Recently renovated, this place is a combination of every Chinese restaurant you've ever been to, replete with lanterns, lions on pedestals, fan-shaped windows, and dragons. The food is excellent and beautifully presented. Try the baked chicken with garlic, the paper-thin beef with Mongolian hot pot, and the baked pork chops with black beans. ♦ Cantonese ♦ Daily breakfast, lunch, and dinner. 20 Elizabeth St (at Canal St). 964.5256 ♿

31 Silver Palace ★★$$ This bustling dining room is best for dim sum. Point to what you want off the carts rolling by, and enjoy. Bills are totaled by the number of empty plates on your table. ♦ Dim sum ♦ Daily breakfast, lunch, and dinner. 50 Bowery (between Bayard and Canal Sts). 964.1204

31 Hee Seung Fung (HSF) ★$$ Long lines are common because these folks are especially welcoming to Westerners. It's easier than

usual to order dim sum here, as the restaurant offers a photographic guide to the 75 available varieties. The *harkow* (steamed shrimp dumpling) is always a winner. A full menu is offered at dinner but isn't especially recommended. ♦ Dim sum ♦ Daily breakfast, lunch, and dinner. 46 Bowery (between Bayard and Canal Sts). 374.1319

32 Manhattan Bridge The elaborate approach to the bridge from Canal Street is a shadow of its former self, but the quality still shows. Originally known as the **Court of Honor**, the bridge (illustrated on page 26)—a 1905 work by **Gustav Lindenthal**—was designed so that vehicles would pass under a triumphal arch designed by **Carrère & Hastings**. Brooklyn-bound streetcars were forced to go around the arch, and the subway was hidden underneath it. The Daniel Chester French sculptures (representing Manhattan and Brooklyn) that flanked the arch were moved to the front of the **Brooklyn Museum** in 1963. ♦ From Canal St at Bowery, Manhattan to Tillary St at Flatbush Ave, Brooklyn

33 Eldridge Street Synagogue The congregation of K'hal Adath Jeshurun Anshe Lubz built this as the first Orthodox synagogue in the area during a time when other congregations were transforming Christian churches for their own use. Constructed in grand scale in 1887 by **Herter Bros.**, the main sanctuary was an opulent room with brass chandeliers and an ark imported from Italy. The building fell into disrepair—although the congregation has never missed a Sabbath—and is currently being restored to its original splendor. Part of the building houses a center for the celebration of American Jewish history. Comedian Eddie Cantor spent his boyhood in a building across the street (he answered to the name Edward Iskowitz back then). ♦ Tu, Th, and by appointment on Su. 12 Eldridge St (between Division and Canal Sts). 219.0888

34 Harry Zarin Co. Fabric Warehouse Decorator fabrics at super prices are sold at this second-floor source—everything from opulent silk brocades to mattress ticking. This is one of the few spots in the area open on Saturday. ♦ Daily. 72 Allen St (at Grand St). 226.3492 &

34 Fishkin Women's sportswear by Adrienne Vittadini and Liz Claiborne, sweaters by Pringle, handsome boots and shoes by Via Spiga and Nickels, and silk and cashmere are sold at a 20-percent discount. ♦ M-F, Su. 314 Grand St (at Allen St). 226.6538

35 Leslie's Originals This is the place for fashionable footwear at a 30-percent (or more!) discount. Women's shoes include sandals, espadrilles, pumps, and quality leather shoes and boots, depending on the season. The men's stock includes loafers, wingtips, and sport shoes. ♦ M-F, Su. 319 Grand St (between Orchard and Allen Sts). 431.9196

36 A.W. Kaufman Luxurious lingerie from a variety of designers, including Christian Dior, Mary McFadden, and Lejaby, are packed into this narrow shop along with imports from Belgium and Switzerland. ♦ M-F, Su. 73 Orchard St (between Grand and Broome Sts). 226.1629

37 Guss Pickle Products The oldest purveyor of pickles in New York is still the best. You can get a kosher dill sour enough to make your face pucker. The sauerkraut and pickled peppers and tomatoes are terrific as well. ♦ M-Th, Su; F until 3PM. 35 Essex St (between Hester and Grand Sts). 254.4477

38 Seward Park Two blocks of tenement buildings were removed in 1900 to make way for this three-acre breathing space (named for William H. Seward, who was governor of New York, a US senator, and Lincoln's secretary of state). In its early days, the park was a gathering place for immigrants looking for daily work. The southern and western edges are the site of a regular Sunday flea market, during which elderly people sell *tchotchkes* (knickknacks). The prices are good, and the bargaining is entertaining in itself. ♦ Bounded by E Broadway and Essex St, and Canal and Hester Sts)

39 Educational Alliance Built in 1891 by **Arnold Brunner,** this is the United States' first settlement house, founded in 1889 by so-called "uptown Jews," who felt an obligation to help fellow Jews in the downtown ghetto and to stem possible anti-Semitism. It held classes to Americanize youngsters, provided exercise and bathing facilities, and gave assistance to women whose husbands had deserted them, which was common among immigrant families. Among the young people the organization served was Arthur Murray, who learned how to dance here. ♦ 197 E Broadway (at Jefferson St)

40 Ritualarium In 1904, the former **Arnold Toynbee Hall** of the Young Men's Benevolent Association was converted to a mikvah, a ritual bath for Orthodox Jewish women, who are required to attend in preparation for marriage and on a monthly basis after that. Because the Scriptures command that the water be pure, rainwater is collected in cisterns. ♦ Tours are given by appointment. For information call Mrs. Bormiko (674.5318). 313 E Broadway (at Grand St). 475.8514

41 Abrons Arts Center This performing- and visual-arts complex, built by **Prentice & Chan, Ohlhausen** in 1975, is part of the Henry Street Settlement, a social service agency that has operated on the Lower East Side since 1893. Its programs include arts workshops, professional performances, and exhibitions—all meant to help participants develop self-expression through the arts and an appreciation of the cultural diversity of New York City. The complex contains three theaters: the **Recital Hall,** the **Experimental Theater,** and the **Harry DeJur Playhouse.** ♦ 466 Grand St (between Willett and Pitt Sts). 598.0400 &

42 Bialystoker Synagogue Built in 1826 as the **Willett Street Methodist Episcopal Church,** it was purchased by the Congregation Anshei Bialystok in 1905 and is the oldest structure housing a synagogue in New York. ♦ 7 Willett St (between Grand St and Williamsburg Bridge). 475.0165

43 Williamsburg Bridge Built in 1903 by **Leffert L. Buck,** this is the second bridge to span the East River. Its construction changed Williamsburg in Brooklyn from a resort area to a new home for immigrants from the Lower East Side. The bridge (illustrated on page 26) is unusual in that there are no cables on the land side of the steel towers, robbing it of some of the soaring grace of a full suspension span. ♦ From Delancey St at Clinton St, Manhattan to Washington Plaza, Brooklyn

44 Ratner's ★$$ Its glory days far behind, this New York institution is now more a cultural, rather than a gustatory destination. It's best to soak in the *Yiddishkeit* over a bowl of soup, a plate of panfried blintzes (with a pot-cheese or potato filling), or the deep-fried pierogis. ♦ Eastern European/Jewish ♦ M-Th breakfast, lunch, and dinner; F breakfast and dinner; Sa dinner; Su breakfast and lunch. 138 Delancey St (between Suffolk and Norfolk Sts). 677.5588

45 Streit's Matzoth Company This is the only Manhattan producer of the unleavened bread used during Passover. Watch the huge sheets of matzos as they pass by the window

on conveyor belts, and buy some samples on your way out. ◆ M-F, Su. 150 Rivington St (at Suffolk St). 475.7000

46 Schapiro's House of Kosher and Sacramental Wines Take a tour of the only winery still operating in the city. Wines are also available for purchase here. ◆ Weekdays by appointment only; Su 11AM-4PM. Nominal fee. 126 Rivington St (between Norfolk and Essex Sts). 674.4404 &

47 Economy Candy Company People with a longing for old-fashioned penny candy will find it in this store, which has been selling candy of all kinds, as well as dried fruits, nuts, coffees, teas, and other delicacies, since 1937. Ask for the mail-order catalog. ◆ Daily. 108 Rivington St (between Essex and Ludlow Sts). 254.1832 &

48 Orchard Street The old pushcarts are gone, but bargain hunters still flock to this street, a seething indoor-outdoor bazaar of discount dresses, coats, shoes, linens, fabrics, and accessories. More than 300 stores line this and surrounding thoroughfares from East Houston to Canal Streets on the Lower East Side. On Sunday, many of the streets are closed to traffic, and the latest from Ralph Lauren to Christian Dior is hawked from the sidewalks. These are mostly Hong Kong–produced knock-offs. The stores carry a wide array of well-known and secondary lines of discounted fashion. This kind of shopping is not for the faint of heart, but if you go prepared for the rough and tumble of bartering and remember that not all stores take credit cards or have gracious salespeople, you can turn up some jewels among the schlock—and have fun, too. Go weekdays if you can. Sunday is insane, and many stores close early on Friday and all day Saturday. ◆ From Canal to E Houston Sts

49 Beckenstein Discounted home furnishing fabrics are sold here, though this old-time family name is best known for the enormous and excellent collection of men's fabrics across the street, including shirting of pure cotton, cashmere, mohair, and fine wools—most discounted 15 percent. ◆ M-F, Su. 130 Orchard St (between Delancey and Rivington Sts). 475.4887. Also at: 125 Orchard St (between Delancey and Rivington Sts). 475.7575 &

Giovanni da Verrazano, an Italian-born navigator sailing for France, was the first European to see New York, when he discovered New York Bay in 1524. Henry Hudson, an Englishman employed by the Dutch, reached the bay and sailed up the river now bearing his name in 1609, the same year that northern New York was explored and claimed for France by Samuel de Champlain.

50 Lower East Side Tenement Museum This small, fascinating museum is visited predominantly by the curious descendants of immigrants who fled to the US at the end of the 19th and beginning of the 20th centuries. The grim reality of the appalling hardships they faced is palpable here, re-created in an abandoned tenement. More than 300,000 Russians, escaping brutal pogroms, were crammed into a single square mile in living conditions that can only be understood after a visit to this museum, which offers changing exhibits usually relating to immigrant history and organizes two-hour Sunday walking tours through this and other history-filled ethnic neighborhoods nearby. ◆ Nominal admission. Tu-F, Su. 97 Orchard St (between Broome and Delancey Sts). 431.0233

51 Fine & Klein An extensive collection of high-end handbags, briefcases, and accessories includes the latest from Carlos Falchi, Enny and Lisette (sometimes Valentino and Givenchy, too). You'll find good discounts and gracious service at this Orchard Street institution. Upstairs, at **Lea's**, enjoy a 30-percent discount on women's clothing from such designers as Albert Nippon and Louis Feraud. ◆ M-F, Su. 119 Orchard St (between Delancey and Rivington Sts). 674.6720. Lea's: 677.7637

GISELLE SPORTSWEAR

52 Giselle Sportswear Better American sportswear for women, including warm, woolly alpaca jackets and soft leather jackets and pants are sold at 25 percent off. ◆ M-F, Su. 143 Orchard St (between Delancey and Rivington Sts). 673.1900

52 Anna Z High-fashion European clothing for women includes designs by Bill Kaiserman and Malisy Gilbert Basson at 20 percent off retail. ◆ M-F, Su. 143½ Orchard St (at Rivington St). 533.1361

52 Tobaldi European high-fashion men's clothes are discounted 20 percent. Merchandise includes tweed jackets, leather jackets, pure cotton shirts, silk ties, and bikini underwear. ◆ M-F, Su. 83 Rivington St (at Orchard St). 260.4330

53 Congregation Adath Jeshurun of Jassy Synagogue This 1903 building was also the home of the First Warsaw Congregation. Now abandoned, it still projects a rich and distinctive image with its collage of architectural styles. ♦ 58-60 Rivington St (between Allen and Eldridge Sts)

54 The Hat/El Sombrero $ You won't find the best Mexican food here, but this popular neighborhood eatery has its defenders. Try the *nachos tradicionales* (topped with beef, beans, cheese, and salsa), wash it down with a margarita, and soak in the local color. ♦ Mexican ♦ Daily breakfast, lunch, and dinner. No credit cards accepted. 108 Stanton St (at Ludlow St). 254.4188

54 The Ludlow Street Cafe ★$ This dark, bohemian cafe used to be known as a live-music hangout, not a dining spot. Since a new chef came along in 1993 and changed the menu to Cajun, the food has begun to draw as many fans as the bands. Particular favorites include blackened salmon, pickled shrimp, gumbo, and crawfish étouffée. ♦ Cajun ♦ W-Sa dinner; Su brunch and dinner. 165 Ludlow St (between Stanton and E Houston Sts). 353.0536

Puck Building

Michael Storrings

55 Katz's Delicatessen ★$ A well-known old delicatessen, this place was made even more famous by the memorable deli scene shot here for the 1989 movie *When Harry Met Sally*. Sit at a table if you're not in a hurry. For counter service, take a ticket, then pick up some sausages or a warm brisket on rye. ♦ Deli ♦ Daily breakfast, lunch, and dinner. No credit cards accepted. 205 E Houston St (at Ludlow St). 254.2246 &

56 Russ & Daughters A shopping mecca for serious connoisseurs of bagels and lox with a schmear of cream cheese, this establishment is also not bad for take-out golden smoked whitefish, unctuous sable carp, tart/crisp herring, salads, dried fruits, nuts, and other items that belong to a category of food some native New Yorkers call "appetizing." ♦ Daily. 179 E Houston St (between Orchard and Allen Sts). 475.4880 &

57 Yonah Schimmel ★$ Jewish specialties, including legendary knishes, clabbered milk (yogurt), and borscht, have been dished up in this dumpy old storefront since the turn of the century. ♦ M-F, Su. 137 E Houston St (at Forsyth St). 477.2858

58 Irreplaceable Artifacts of North America Evan Blum salvages buildings, so on any given day you're likely to find saloon bars, lighting fixtures, antique architectural ornaments, neon marquees, or stained-glass windows. There are seven floors chockablock with fascinating collectibles from Europe, Canada, South America, and the United States. ♦ Daily. 14 Second Ave (at E Houston St). 780.9700

59 Puck Building The Romanesque Revival building (pictured at left) reflects the influence of the Chicago School in its bold and vibrant use of brickwork. It was once the home of the humor magazine *Puck*, whose spirit remains in the two larger-than life statues perched on third-floor ledges at the northeast corners. The interior of this great building, constructed in 1885 to the designs of **Albert Wagner,** has been renovated as commercial condominiums for art galleries, workshops, and design offices. The opulent rooms are also rented out for weddings and other celebrations. ♦ 295 Lafayette St (at E Houston St). 274.89▮ &

60 Urban Archaeology Owner Gil Shapiro has moved his seemingly infinite collection of architectural ornaments and artifacts, display cases, lighting fixtures, and much, much more into the immense quarters of a four-story former candy factory. Interior designer Judith Stockman revamped all 50,000 square feet, a process that included sandblasting candy off the walls. Two lovely skylit areas show off cast-iron furniture and garden accessories. The stock is sold wholesale and retail. ♦ M-Sa. 285 Lafayette St (between Prince and E Houston Sts). 431.6969

61 Do Kham Sold here are clothing, jewelry, and accessories from Tibet and the Himalayas, some designed by the amiable store owner, Phelgye Kelden, a former Tibetan monk. Check out his chic fake- and genuine-fur hats. ♦ Daily. 51 Prince St (between Mulberry and Lafayette Sts). 966.2404

62 Old St. Patrick's Cathedral When the new cathedral at Fifth Avenue and 50th Street was consecrated in 1879, this became a Roman Catholic parish church serving a predominantly Irish neighborhood. Originally built by **Joseph Mangin** in 1815, it was New York's first Gothic Revival building. The church was restored in 1868 by **Henry Englebert** after its historic facade was badly altered in an 1866 fire. ♦ 264 Mulberry St (between Prince and E Houston Sts). 226.8075

63 Old St. Patrick's Convent and Girls' School Built in 1826, the beautiful Federal doorway framed with Corinthian columns makes this unusually large Federal-style building a treasure. ♦ 32 Prince St (at Mott St)

64 D & G Bakery For more than three decades this bakery has been a Little Italy landmark. Come early for the breads, which are baked fresh daily in a 100-year-old, coal-fired brick oven in a nearby basement. Those who know go for the heavenly prosciutto loaf studded with strips of meat. ♦ Daily until 2PM. 45 Spring St (between Mott and Mulberry Sts). 226.6688

65 Just Shades In stock are window shades made of string, parchment, rice paper, silk, and burlap; others can be custom-ordered. ♦ M-Tu, Th-Su. 21 Spring St (between Elizabeth and Mott Sts). 966.2757

66 Connecticut Muffin Co. A friendly staff offers fresh-baked goods at this small shop; there are even a few tables for those who want to sample their sweets. Try a banana-nut muffin or cheddar-cheese scone. ♦ Daily until 4PM. 10 Prince St (between Bowery and Elizabeth St). 925.9773 &

67 Off SoHo Suites $ The 38 suites are large and tastefully furnished, and the prices are rock bottom. What's the snag? This isn't exactly Park Avenue, and the 10 least expensive suites share a bath and kitchen. But very few others are recommended in this area east of SoHo (hence the name), with easy access to all mass transit. Most suites have color TV, marble bathtubs, air-conditioning, a gourmet eat-in kitchen, and access to a fitness center. ♦ 11 Rivington St (between Chrystie St and Bowery). 979.9808, 800/633.7646; fax 979.9801

68 Sammy's Famous Roumanian Jewish Steakhouse ★★$$$ This is the best Jewish restaurant in the city, but it's not kosher. The room is low-down and tacky, and the so-called entertainment—an electric piano and a comic who thinks he's Henny Youngman—is so bad it's good. Among the yummy dishes are chopped liver with "the works": chicken cracklings (rendered fat) with shredded black radishes and onion; and *kishke* (herb stuffing in an intestinal casing)—and those are just the appetizers. For a main course, a rib steak, a fried breaded veal chop, or boiled beef with mushroom-barley gravy will do just fine. Portions are large. To wash it down, try an egg cream, the classic New York *digestif*. ♦ Eastern European/Jewish ♦ Daily dinner; entertainment nightly. Reservations required. 157 Chrystie St (between Delancey and Rivington Sts). 673.0330

69 Mazer Store Equipment Co. Craig Claiborne, Mimi Sheraton, Lauren Bacall, and Stockard Channing come here to buy their restaurant-quality Garland stoves, which come with porcelain-coated oven walls, back, and roof. Service is what distinguishes this store from others of its kind. ♦ M-F. 207 Bowery (at Kenmare St). 674.3450

70 New York Gas Lighting Company This lighting store, one of the many concentrated in this neighborhood, takes its name from its authentic open-flame gaslights. It also offers an array of handsome fixtures including opalescent chandeliers from the Czech Republic, lamps made from antique ginger jars, and the Hunter wood ceiling fan. ♦ Daily. 145 Bowery (between Grand and Broome Sts). 226.2840 &

Restaurants/Clubs: Red		**Hotels:** Blue
Shops/ ♥ Outdoors: Green		**Sights/Culture:** Black

49

71 Green Point Bank The 1894 building designed by **McKim, Mead & White** is the former **Bowery Savings Bank.** Outside, the Roman columns attached to a Renaissance facade are somehow apropos on the edge of Little Italy. Inside, take a look at the opulent detailing. ♦ M-Th 9AM-3PM; F 9AM-6PM; Sa 9AM-noon. 130 Bowery (between Grand and Broome Sts)

72 Road to Mandalay ★★$$ In typical New York fashion, you'll find this cozy Asian restaurant right in the heart of Little Italy. Don't miss the ruby rolls (prawns and vermicelli in triangular pastry) and the grilled tiger prawns in lemongrass sauce. ♦ Thai/Burmese ♦ M-F dinner; Sa-Su lunch and dinner. 380 Broome St (between Mott and Mulberry Sts). 226.4218

73 Caffè Roma ★★$ Knowledgeable New Yorkers favor this lovely old-world bakery over all others. No redecorating was ever necessary to make this place look authentic— it just is. The cannoli, whether plain or dipped in chocolate, are perfect. ♦ Bakery/Cafe ♦ Daily. No credit cards accepted. 385 Broome St (at Mulberry St). 226.8413

73 Grotta Azzurra ★$$ The kitsch of dining in an ersatz blue cave may appeal to some, even though the food is nothing extraordinary. Chicken cacciatore is a safe bet, but avoid the seafood. Still, the portions are ample, you don't need a reservation, and it's fun. ♦ Neapolitan ♦ Daily lunch and dinner. No credit cards accepted. 387 Broome St (at Mulberry St). 226.9283

74 The Police Building A commanding presence with an imposing dome as a symbol of authority, this 1909 building by **Hoppin & Koen** was the main headquarters of the New York City Police Department for nearly 65 years. The new copper dome was crafted by French artisans brought here to restore the *Statue of Liberty*'s copper flame, and the 1988 restoration was the work of **Ehrenkranz Group & Eckstut.** The interior, by dePolo/Dunbar, has been converted into 55 cooperative apartments. ♦ 240 Centre St (between Grand and Broome Sts)

75 Italian Food Center The De Mattia family has run this one-stop shopping emporium— filled with domestic and imported Italian foodstuffs—for over 20 years, to the great delight of Italophiles. More than a dozen kinds of breads are baked on the premises daily, and the vast array of Italian cold cuts is mouthwatering. Try the New York Special hero sandwich, a fresh pizza, focaccia, *bruschetta* (toast seasoned with garlic and oil), or one of the temptingly displayed spinach or sausage rolls. If you can't wait until you get home to enjoy the delicious takeout, stop at the park bench outside and dig in. ♦ Daily. 186 Grand St (at Mulberry St). 925.2954 &

76 Benito I and Benito II ★$ The original owners of this pair of small trattorie sold out and moved to Los Angeles. The restaurants are no longer related, except by name, but either one is a good choice for a hearty low-cost meal. ♦ Neapolitan ♦ Daily lunch and dinner. No credit cards accepted. Benito I: 174 Mulberry St (between Grand and Broome Sts). 226.9171. Benito II: 163 Mulberry St (between Grand and Broome Sts). 226.9012

77 Alleva Dairy This old-fashioned cheese store has been run by the same family for over a century. Not a day goes by without a proud Alleva on hand to tend to the regular customers who come from all over the city for the mozzarella (fresh and smoked) made daily. There's also a small selection of noncheese items, including dried pasta, an excellent fresh tomato sauce packaged to go, and several types of smoked and cured meats. ♦ Daily. 188 Grand St (at Mulberry St). 226.7990 &

78 Piemonte Ravioli Company Since 1920, the same family has been churning out freshly made pasta from old family recipes in this modest-looking store that is, in fact, one of America's major suppliers. The refrigerator and counter are always stocked with pasta of all types, colors, shapes, and fillings. The filled pastas, such as ravioli and cannelloni, are favorites. Try the plump ravioli stuffed with cheese, spinach, or porcini mushrooms. ♦ Tu-Sa; Su until 3PM. 190 Grand St (between Mott and Mulberry Sts). 226.0475 &

"Something's always happening here. If you're bored in New York, it's your own fault."

Myrna Loy

78 Pearl River Chinese Products
Any Sinophile's passion for clothing and housewares can be satisfied in this store. Choose from cotton T-shirts, silk jackets, pillowcases, sheets, and bedspreads in pastel pinks, blues, and yellows embroidered with flowers and animals. For Chinese cooking, an easy-to-use wok with a wooden handle is another find. ♦ Daily. 200 Grand St (at Mott St). 966.1010 ♿

79 Ferrara $ A slick emporium, this cafe includes an extensive take-out department, featuring a wide variety of Italian pastries, cookies, and candies. The espresso bar is one of the city's more popular places for cappuccino and the like. In nice weather, the bar extends out onto the sidewalk, where a counter dispenses Italian gelati. ♦ Bakery/Cafe ♦ Daily. 195 Grand St (between Mott and Mulberry Sts). 226.6150

79 E. Rossi & Co. This old-fashioned, crowded, family-run store sells boccie balls, pasta machines, cookbooks in both Italian and English, and a variety of kitchen gadgets, such as cheese graters. ♦ Daily. 191 Grand St (at Mulberry St). 966.6640

80 Angelo's of Mulberry Street ★$$ An old Little Italy standby that is a somewhat on the touristy side, this restaurant can be counted on to churn out consistently decent meals, including *veal valdostana* (stuffed with cheese and ham) and veal parmigiana. ♦ Southern Italian ♦ Daily lunch and dinner. 146 Mulberry St (between Hester and Grand Sts). 966.1277

81 Ristorante Taormina ★$$ With its blond wood and peach furnishings, exposed brick walls, large windows, and graceful tall plants, this is not the typical Little Italy restaurant. The stuffed artichokes are excellent, and the veal entrées are also quite good, as are most items on the Neapolitan menu. Those who know something about Italian geography shouldn't be fooled by the restaurant's name, which is a town in Sicily. ♦ Neapolitan ♦ Daily lunch and dinner. 147 Mulberry St (between Hester and Grand Sts). 219.1007 ♿

82 Sal Anthony's S.P.Q.R. $$ Though the multilevel room is grand and gorgeous, what comes out of the kitchen usually isn't. Stick to such simple items as chicken with olive oil and garlic. ♦ Neapolitan ♦ Daily lunch and dinner. 133 Mulberry St (between Hester and Grand Sts). 925.3120

82 Umberto's Clam House $$ This standby is a popular landmark because famed underworld figure Joey Gallo was assassinated here, but the seafood is probably better at **Vincent's Clam Bar** (see below). ♦ Seafood ♦ Daily lunch, dinner, and late-night meals. 129 Mulberry St (at Hester St). 431.7545

83 Forzano Italian Imports Inc. Here is the place to buy a souvenir of Little Italy. Italian music is piped onto the street to lure customers inside, where they'll find a large selection of all things Italian, including records and tapes; espresso makers in every shape, size, and price; a variety of meat grinders; T-shirts celebrating the Italian heritage; and devil horns to ward off bad luck. ♦ Daily. 128 Mulberry St (at Hester St). 925.2525

83 Caffè Napoli ★$ It feels like a sidewalk cafe even inside. Take a cue from the locals, who have dessert here rather than at the more famous **Ferrara**. The cannoli is a definite star among the marvelous-looking pastries. ♦ Cafe ♦ Daily. No credit cards accepted. 191 Hester St (at Mulberry St). 226.8705

83 Puglia Restaurant ★$ Come here for generous portions of rigatoni in vodka sauce or veal parmigiana—just two of the many dishes served at this rambling restaurant. The mostly young crowd sits at communal tables and sings along with the waiters to the live music, which adds to the festive *ambiente*. ♦ Southern Italian ♦ Tu-Su lunch, dinner, and late-night meals. No credit cards accepted. 189 Hester St (between Mott and Mulberry Sts). 966.6006

84 Vincent's Clam Bar ★$ Choose the fresh seafood with a choice of hot, medium, or mild tomato sauce at this venerable neighborhood institution. Hot is for serious masochists, of which there appear to be many. An expanded menu offers a variety of meat entrées, chicken, salads, coffee, and dessert. ♦ Seafood ♦ Daily lunch, dinner, and late-night meals. 119 Mott St (at Hester St). 226.8133 ♿

84 Pho Bâng Restaurant ★$ Come here for authentic Vietnamese cooking, especially the excellent whole shrimp summer rolls. A plate of exotic lettuces and an array of sauces accompany the meal. ♦ Vietnamese ♦ Daily lunch and dinner. 117 Mott St (between Canal and Hester Sts). 966.3797. Also at: 3 Pike St (at Allen St). 233.3947; 6 Chatham Sq (at the corner of Mott St and Bowery). 587.0870

85 Wong Kee ★$ The good, fresh food offered at ridiculously low prices makes one wonder how they stay in business. Try the wonton-cabbage soup, any of the wide rice noodles, boiled skinless chicken breast, roast duck, or scrambled eggs with glazed pork. Skip the chef's suggestions. ♦ Cantonese ♦ Daily lunch and dinner. No credit cards accepted. 113 Mott St (between Canal and Hester Sts). 226.9018

85 New Chao Chow ★$ Most locals and many visitors agree this place serves up what is perhaps the best *lo soi* duck in New York. The bird is cooked in a rich sauce flavored with cinnamon, eight-star anise, and nutmeg. ♦ Northern Chinese ♦ Daily breakfast, lunch, and dinner. No credit cards accepted. 111 Mott St (between Canal and Hester Sts). 226.2590

86 Oriental Pearl ★$ Suggested items on the extensive menu at this large, dull-looking restaurant are Peking spare ribs, steamed flounder, or shrimp with walnuts. Also recommended is Peking-style chicken in a bird's nest. ♦ Cantonese ♦ Daily breakfast, lunch, and dinner. 103 Mott St (at Canal St). 219.8388 &

87 Luna ★$$ A century old, this traditional Italian restaurant feels more like an oversized kitchen than the requisite tourist stop it is. The hallway that leads to the dining room gives you a full view of the bustling kitchen. Despite, or perhaps because of, the haphazard mix of tables and booths, propped-up photographs, and occasionally gruff service, the experience feels authentic, and the food is predictably filling. ♦ Southern Italian ♦ Daily lunch, dinner, and late-night meals. No credit cards accepted. 112 Mulberry St (between Canal and Hester Sts). 226.8657

88 Il Cortile ★$$$ Bad news and good news: The lines to get in may be too long, the rooms too noisy, and the waiters too harried, but the fresh food is well prepared and the room beautifully decorated. ♦ Northern Italian ♦ Daily lunch and dinner; F-Sa late-night meals. 125 Mulberry St (between Canal and Hester Sts). 226.6060

89 Holiday Inn Downtown $$ The only hotel in Chinatown has very little Oriental detail in either the public areas or 223 guest rooms to distinguish it from any other contemporary hotel in Manhattan. Its Hong Kong–style restaurant, **Pacifica,** is very good, but with the plethora of less expensive and often more authentic restaurants within blocks of the hotel, it would be a shame to eat in. ♦ 138 Lafayette St (at Howard St). 966.8898, 800/HOLIDAY; fax 966.3933

Barbara Kirshenblatt-Gimblett
Folklorist, Tisch School of the Arts, NYU

Silvery glints in **Lower East Side** skies as pigeon flyers exercise their birds.

The elusive aroma of vanilla, rotten eggs, almonds, turpentine, and old shoes exuded by durian in **Chinatown** as the thick prickly skin splits and exposes the coveted creamy fruit.

Reading Yiddish books salvaged from Hitler's Europe at the **YIVO Institute for Jewish Research.**

Thirty varieties of local apples at the **Union Square Greenmarket** in late September.

Spotting fuzzy dice, palm crosses (during the Easter season), air freshener, magnetic saints, lucky charms, and other dashboard ornaments in parked cars.

Statue of Puck on the **Puck Building,** built in 1885.

Marks of the hand on the city—chalk lines on the asphalt for skelly and hopscotch, painted signs for shoe repair and fish shops, barber poles.

Walking Tour C of **Greenwich Village** in the *AIA Guide to New York City* on an autumn evening.

Gerry Frank
Author, *Where to Find It, Buy It, Eat It in New York*

Taking in an afternoon game at **Yankee** or **Shea Stadiums** on a warm summer day.

Looking out over the **East River** at the Manhattan skyline from **Lighthouse Park** on **Roosevelt Island.**

Visiting the **Museum of Immigration** on **Ellis Island.**

Taking a ride on one of the 388 elevators in **Rockefeller Center** (preferably to the top).

Sitting on one of the 7,674 benches in **Central Park** on a glorious spring day.

Wandering through the **Frick Collection.**

Looking down one of the open grates that expose 238 miles of subway tracks below the city streets.

Visiting the Romanesque/Byzantine-style **St. Bartholomew's Church.**

Gawking at the Fabergé eggs at the **Forbes Magazine Galleries.**

Sampling Martine's chocolates at **Bloomingdale's.**

Enjoying a leisurely and luxurious weekend at the new **Four Seasons Hotel.**

Taking in the farmer's market on Monday, Wednesday, Friday, and Saturday at **Union Square.**

Tuning in to **Joan Hamburg** for great consumer advice (WOR—710 AM radio—weekdays from 10AM to noon).

Sipping an espresso or cappuccino in **Little Italy.**

Visiting **75½ Bedford Street,** site of the city's narrowest house.

Watching a favorite episode of a favorite TV show at the **Museum of Television and Radio.**

Getting up as early as 4AM to witness the activity at the **Fulton Fish Market.**

Visiting the **Federal Hall National Memorial** (26 Wall Street), where George Washington took oath as the first US president.

Relaxing in the **Ford Foundation**'s garden atrium.

Taking the kids to see **The Cloisters.**

Taking a **Circle Line** cruise.

Visiting the **United Nations.**

Taking a boat trip on the lake in Central Park on a summer day (**Loeb Boathouse**).

Touring backstage at the **Metropolitan Opera**.

Taking a bargain ride on the **Staten Island Ferry**.

Riding through **Central Park** in a hansom cab.

Gallery hopping in **SoHo** on a Saturday afternoon.

Dancing at the **Rainbow Room**.

Attending the flea market and antiques sale on Sunday at Sixth Avenue and West 26th Street.

Exploring the towering beauty of the **Cathedral Church of St. John the Divine**.

Watching the lights on the **Statue of Liberty** while walking along the promenade at Battery Park.

Enjoying the Easter flower show at **Macy's**.

Securing a bargain ticket for a Broadway matinee at the **TKTS** booth in **Times Square**.

Watching the **Rockettes** at Radio City Music Hall.

Getting into a political discussion with a cab driver.

Browsing the **New York Is Book Country** book fair on Fifth Avenue in September.

Getting pampered at **Elizabeth Arden**.

Having one of the finest French dinners anywhere at **La Reserve**.

Visiting Theodore Roosevelt's birthplace and George Washington's headquarters (1785 Jumal Terrace).

Taking home fresh fruit and vegetables from **Grace's Marketplace**.

Sam Hall Kaplan
Los Angeles–based Design Critic and Author

Things a person born and bred in New York but living in Los Angeles likes to do when he returns to New York:

On separate weekdays, visit the **Met**, the **Whitney**, the **Guggenheim**, the **Cooper-Hewitt**, and **MoMA**.

At dusk, check out the old neighborhood, walking down **Broadway** from about West 96th Street to **Lincoln Center**, catch a concert, then stroll up **Columbus Avenue** and have a late-afternoon snack at a sidewalk cafe.

Any day, anytime, sit on the edge of the **Pulitzer Fountain** at West 59th Street and Fifth Avenue and watch the crowds go by, then join them in any direction.

Early on Saturday, wander from **Greenwich Village**, through **Washington Square Park**, SoHo, Little Italy, and **Chinatown** to the **South Street Seaport** and back again, but on different streets, noshing all the way.

On Sunday, have brunch at the **Russian Tea Room** or **Tavern on the Green**, then rent or borrow a bicycle to work off the calories exploring Central Park.

Later, especially if it is warm, pedal or walk to the **East Side** and **Carl Schurz Park**, catch a breeze and watch the boats chug by, or go to the **West Side** and **Riverside Park** at the **West 79th Street Boat Basin**.

Anne Rosenzweig
Chef and Owner, Arcadia/Vice Chairperson, 21 Club

An unusual perspective of Manhattan begins with an early-morning breakfast at **Sylvia's** (salmon cakes, grits, deep-fried slab bacon, and biscuits). This is the perfect start to a walking day.

Then a stroll through the marvelous but crumbling architecture of Harlem, especially around **Mount Morris Park**. Then to **La Marqueta**, the Spanish market under the train tracks at Park Avenue and East 116th Street. Wonderful and unearthly smells and sights—fresh baby goats, huge aloe vera plants (which soothe kitchen burns and cuts), all sorts of tropical fruits and botanicals, pigs' snouts, love elixirs mixed to order, etc. . . . Then down to the **Conservatory Garden** at Fifth Avenue and 105th Street. The gardens are completely transformed every season. In spring, huge lilac bushes create an intoxicating aroma under which one can read the Sunday papers. During the summer, they are the setting of some of the most beautiful weddings in New York.

Sitting in the upper decks of **Shea Stadium** on a hot, hot summer night just to catch a good breeze.

On the rare occasions when the city is under a deep, fresh blanket of snow—cross-country skiing in **Central Park** and getting hot roasted chestnuts afterward.

The Indian restaurants on **East Sixth Street** in summer—eating outside in back with a gang of friends on picnic tables for the cheapest sums possible.

Buying bags of flattened fortune cookies at one of the many bakeries in **Chinatown**—they're the ones that didn't make it.

Jazz cruises at night up the **Hudson River** and being able to see the skyline at twilight.

Elizabeth Tilberis
Editor-in-Chief, *Harper's Bazaar*

The view of Manhattan from the **Triborough Bridge** at dusk.

Driving down the **FDR Highway**.

Skating at **Wollman Rink**.

Eating outdoors on summer evenings as the sun sets at any restaurant with sidewalk cafes.

The shop windows at Christmastime.

The Egyptian rooms at the **Metropolitan Museum of Art**.

High tea at **Rumpelmayer's**.

Circling Manhattan at sunset before the plane lands at **La Guardia Airport**.

Chinatown for Chinese food—the children love it here.

Little League baseball on Saturday in **Central Park**.

Knicks games on Sunday at **Madison Square Garden**—and the heavenly hot dogs.

SoHo/TriBeCa

The name SoHo was coined to define the district South of **Houston Street**, not to honor the neighborhood in London. Combined with the wedge-shaped territory known as TriBeCa (the abbreviated description of Triangle Below **Canal Street**), it includes the area bounded by Houston, **Lafayette**, and **Chambers Streets** and the **Hudson River**.

In spite of soaring prices in SoHo, relatively little is modern or, for that matter, very appealing to the eye. White-on-white galleries and industrially chic buildings occupy grimy streets where 19th-century cobblestones show through the ravaged asphalt. The area was occupied by Native Americans during the 17th century, then by farms and estates spread between old New York and the outlying suburb of Greenwich Village. Houses were built here in the early part of the 19th century (the oldest one still standing, at 107 **Spring Street,** dates from 1806), and from the 1840s to 1860s this was the center of the city, boasting the major department store **Lord & Taylor,** on Grand Street, as well as the city's principal hotel, **The American House**, at Spring Street and **West Broadway.**

The architectural period referred to as American Industrial flourished in this area from 1860 to 1890. Businesses opened in prefabricated cast-iron buildings fashioned to look literally like temples of commerce. By the 1960s, light industry had moved on to new areas, and Robert Moses, the city's master planner, viewed SoHo as an industrial wasteland that he wanted to level and replace with the Lower Manhattan Expressway. When that plan was abandoned in the mid-1960s, artists looking for large, cheap studio space discovered SoHo. With the artists came avant-garde galleries, one-of-a-kind boutiques, and expensive nouvelle cuisine restaurants. The entire area was declared a Historical District in 1973. Today, SoHo is saturated with an artistic mix of original ideas and junk, sheer exuberance and exhibitionism, a funky alternative to the art world of Madison Avenue or 57th Street. (Keep in mind that many of the area's shops, restaurants, and galleries don't open until 11AM or noon and are closed on Monday and often during the month of August.)

TriBeCa, unlike SoHo, retains much of the bohemian quality that once characterized the entire complex of cast-iron architecture between Houston and Chambers Streets before it went upscale. Because this neighborhood overlaps the City Hall area, with its enormous daytime working population, it has been more successful in resisting the tide of fad enterprise. Greek coffee shops, shoe repairs, pet shops, and appliance and camera stores enliven commercial streets little changed since the 1930s. Art and commerce have, of course, transformed TriBeCa to a certain degree, but they have not overwhelmed it. With easy access to Chinatown and Lower Manhattan, it remains a unique, artistic, and ethnic New York neighborhood.

---

1 Washington Market Park Progress has reduced the former **Washington Market** to this little park. In its day the market extended up along the river from Fulton Street into this neighborhood. Even Washington Street, which once formed its spine, is now just a two-block-long thoroughfare between Murray and Chambers Streets. (Though many New York households stocked their larders with goods from the old market, it was essentially a wholesale produce exchange—now centered at Hunt's Point in the Bronx. It was also a distribution point for the imported foods that are being rediscovered in gourmet shops.) The park that remains is one of Manhattan's better play areas for young children. It is clean, safe, and, from a kid's point of view, great fun. Look for outdoor music concerts in warm weather.
♦ Bounded by Chambers and Harrison Sts and Greenwich and West Sts

2 P.S. 234 Too bad all schools aren't as well designed (some of the architectural elements seem to come straight out of a child's imagination) or as nicely sited as this one, which was built in 1988 by architect **Richard**

Dattner. Though the school is not open to the public, be sure to study the fanciful fence by artist Donna Dennis that encloses the schoolyard. ♦ 292 Greenwich St (between Warren and Chambers Sts). 233.6034

3 Cheese of All Nations If you can't find a particular type of cheese among the more than 1,000 varieties from around the world in this shop, chances are it's not imported to the US. Manhattanites come from all corners of the island for their favorite specialties. ♦ M-F. 153 Chambers St (between W Broadway and Greenwich St). 732.0752

4 Bouley ★★★★$$$$ Those in the know say a table here is the best in Manhattan. Unfortunately, for its legion of fans, the restaurant will be closed for expansion and refurbishing, with a scheduled reopening set for Spring 1997. Owner David Bouley has formed a partnership with restaurateur Warner Leroy (owner of **Tavern on the Green** and the newly purchased **Russian Tea Room**), who will help finance the new **Bouley.** The ambitious culinary endeavor will include, in addition to the restaurant, a cafe, professional cooking school, test kitchens, research center, and a retail store. Devoted followers should watch for the opening date and book a table early for Bouley's masterful French menu that changes daily. Dishes not to be missed include eggplant terrine; Maine halibut with toasted sesame seeds in tomato water; rack of lamb; medallions of venison; and roasted Maine lobster served in its own consommé with crisp asparagus, winter mint, and fresh black truffles. Any dessert will induce euphoria. ♦ French ♦ M-F lunch and dinner; Sa dinner. Reservations required weeks in advance; jacket and tie required. 165 Duane St (between Hudson and Greenwich Sts). 608.3852

5 Duane Park Cafe ★★$$$ This comfortable place offers something not often available in a New York restaurant—elbow room and relative quiet. In the pretty dining room with cherrywood accents, diners are offered a creative mix from the menus of the now-defunct **K-Paul's** and **Hubert's** (chef/owner Seiji Maeda logged time at both). Standouts include braised lamb shank with lime-coconut rice, pan-blackened scallops, and a gorgeous pear-hazelnut tart. ♦ Continental ♦ M-F lunch and dinner; Sa dinner. Reservations required. 157 Duane St (between W Broadway and Hudson St). 732.5555

6 The Odeon ★★$$ A good place to sit and schmooze over a late-night drink, this neon-lit room was the hottest spot downtown with the art crowd when it first opened in 1980. In the restaurant game, places that opened just a year ago may be considered ancient history, but this one has managed to remain on the map and stargazers still have a chance to sight the occasional celebrity. The food is generally good, but the pretentions of the kitchen and sometimes uppity staff turn off serious diners. Try the *pappardelle* (broad noodles) with chicken and chanterelle mushrooms or the grilled lamb shank with arugula and roast peppers. ♦ American/French ♦ M-Sa lunch, dinner, and late-night meals; Su brunch, dinner, and late-night meals. Reservations recommended. 145 W Broadway (at Thomas St). 233.0507 &

7 Anbar Shoe Steal Discontinued shoe styles are regularly sold at savings of up to 60 percent. Sacha London, Charles Jourdan, and Nickels labels have been discovered here among the hodgepodge of not-so-beautiful shoes. ♦ M-Sa. 60 Reade St (between Broadway and Church St). 964.4017

ROJEMARIE'J

8 Rosemarie's ★★$$$ With an attractive display of Italian plates decorating the bare brick walls, the warm and romantic ambience of this restaurant adds to the pleasures of the *nuova cucina* cooking. The ravioli filled with spinach and ricotta (available as an appetizer or main course) is exceptional, and the choice of healthy and delicious salads is extensive. The excellent menu includes shrimp and white-bean salad, osso buco, and roasted striped bass with white beans and tomatoes. Another plus: The service is outstanding. ♦ Northern Italian ♦ M-F lunch and dinner; Sa dinner. Reservations recommended. 145 Duane St (between Church St and W Broadway). 285.2610

9 American Telephone & Telegraph Long Lines Building Designed by **John Carl Warnecke & Associates** and built in 1974, this almost windowless (except for the high, squared portholes) edifice houses electronic wizardry for communications. Texturized pink Swedish granite contrasts with vertical stripes of a beige granite used for decoration. ♦ Church St (between Thomas and Worth Sts)

One man's junk is another man's treasure, and you can find outstanding examples of both along Canal Street between Broadway and Sixth Avenue. The selections range from used clothing to seemingly useless pieces of electronic equipment, plumbing supplies, and other assorted gadgets and hardware. It costs nothing to look at, and very little to buy the myriad fascinating things you see here. The street was originally a wide drainage ditch carrying polluted water from the Collect Pond (eventually filled to become the Foley Square area) over to the Hudson River. Citizen complaints about the stench and the mosquito problem led to the filling of the ditch—which the city preferred to call a canal—in 1820.

10 Knitting Factory An impressive weekly roster of performances—everything from jazz to poetry readings to the latest performance art—are held in this lively two-level venue. ♦ Cover. Shows daily; call for schedules. 74 Leonard St (between Broadway and Church St). 219.3055

11 Aux Delices des Bois Amy and Thierry Farge import mushrooms from all over the world and sell them out of this long, narrow shop. Stop in for a supply of the same mushrooms that the chefs at **China Grill** and **21** use, be it shiitake, cremini, portobello, enoki, or chanterelle. ♦ M-F. 4 Leonard St (between W Broadway and Hudson St). 334.1230

12 The Sporting Club $$ Up to nine different events can be beamed in by satellite at one time onto screens in every corner of this room straight out of a sports fanatic's dream. The main event is shown on three 10x10–foot screens above the bar. The menu is made up of aptly named dishes, such as the George Steinbrenner (a burger with a choice of two toppings) and the San Diego Chicken (with lettuce, tomato, and mayonnaise on sourdough bread). ♦ American ♦ M-Sa lunch, dinner, and late-night meals; Su brunch, dinner, and late-night meals. Reservations required for major sporting events. 99 Hudson St (between Leonard and Franklin Sts). 219.0900

Chanterelle

13 Chanterelle ★★★★$$$$ Young chef David Waltuck, acclaimed as a fresh, unspoiled genius, and his wife, Karen, have moved the dining room they established on Grand Street to this pretty space designed by **Bill Katz,** which fittingly (for SoHo) is decked out with original prints, drawings, and lithographs as well as stunning floral arrangements. The seafood sausages are justifiably renowned, as are such dishes as pepper-crusted venison with onion compote, and saddle of lamb stuffed with *merguez* (spicy lamb sausage) and topped with olive *jus.* For dessert try the warm and crispy chocolate soufflé cake, pepper-pear *tarte tatin* with pear-infused caramel sauce, or one of the famous homemade ice creams and sorbets. The prix-fixe luncheon is a bargain. ♦ French ♦ M dinner; Tu-F lunch and dinner; Sa dinner. Reservations required. 2 Harrison St (at Hudson St). 966.6960 ⟁

13 New York Mercantile Exchange Built in 1884, this is another headquarters, like the one at 628 Broadway, for the big dealers in dairy and poultry products. The main offices used to be uptown, but this great old building, closer to the actual markets, is where the action was at the turn of the century. ♦ 6 Harrison St (at Hudson St). 334.2160

14 Puffy's Tavern Retaining the atmosphere of a speakeasy, which it was during Prohibition, this pre-TriBeCa bar pulls you in from the street to have a beer, hang out, and listen to the jukebox with the after-work crowd and neighborhood regulars. ♦ M 4PM-4AM; Tu-Su noon-4AM. No credit cards accepted. 81 Hudson St (at Harrison St). 766.9159

15 A.L. Bazzini Company The city's largest dried-fruit and nut supplier, this place has been in business for more than a century. Delicious smells from nuts being dried or honey roasted fill the shop and even waft into the street. There are also a few tables at which to enjoy such homemade prepared foods as overstuffed peanut butter and jelly sandwiches (among others). ♦ Daily. 339 Greenwich St (at Jay St). 334.1280

16 Independence Plaza Built in 1975 by architects **Oppenheimer, Brady & Vogelstein** and **John Pruyn,** this 40-floor middle-income housing project is a little off the beaten path and has great views of the river. ♦ Greenwich St (between Duane and N Moore Sts)

17 Harrison Street Row Originally built in 1828 and restored in 1975 by **Oppenheimer, Brady & Vogelstein,** this row of impeccably restored Federal houses acts as an antidote to the massive apartment houses above it. ♦ 37-41 Harrison St (at Greenwich St)

18 Tribeca Grill ★★$$$ In 1990, Drew Nieporent (owner of **Montrachet**) teamed up with several celebrity partners, including actor Robert DeNiro, to open this loftlike restaurant. The menu features first-rate bistro fare, including rare seared tuna with sesame noodles, and arugula salad with *bocconcini* (mozzarella balls) and basil oil. Desserts are a must, especially the chocolate cake and banana tart. Wine lovers take note: The list is carefully chosen and well priced. ♦ American ♦ M-F lunch and dinner; Sa dinner; Su brunch and dinner. Reservations required. 375 Greenwich St (at Franklin St). 941.3900 ⟁

The New York City Council passed a bill requiring that photographic records be made of any building about to be razed. The photos become part of the municipal archives. Councilman Harry Stein, sponsor of the bill, said his only regret was that no one had thought of the idea 150 years before.

Restaurants/Clubs: Red Hotels: Blue
Shops/ 🍃 Outdoors: Green Sights/Culture: Black

19 Just Kidding The cotton children's clothing sold here, some of which is made upstairs or by artists in the neighborhood, is wonderful, but owners Margaret and Gavin Owen's most effective marketing tool may be the play area in the back. ◆ Daily. 180 Franklin St (between Hudson and Greenwich Sts). 219.0035 ♿

riverrun

RESTAURANT & BAR

19 Riverrun Cafe ★$$ Opened in 1979, this is one of TriBeCa's pioneer restaurants and remains a neighborhood staple for chicken potpie and Mom's meat loaf. It's also a comfortable place to sit, eat, and talk without feeling hassled. ◆ Continental ◆ M-F lunch and dinner; Sa-Su brunch and dinner. 176 Franklin St (between Hudson and Greenwich Sts). 966.3894

20 Nobu ★★★$$$$ The brainchild of Drew Nieporent and Robert DeNiro, this million-dollar fairy-tale forest setting features a menu that is just as dazzling. The sashimi is dressed with a sweet sesame sauce and served atop salad greens; squid "pasta" is actually strips of the seafood made to look like pasta and served with mushrooms and asparagus in a garlicky red-pepper oil. ◆ New Japanese ◆ M-Sa dinner. Reservations required. 105 Hudson St (at Franklin St). 219.0500 ♿

21 Commodities A natural foods supermarket, this place carries a large stock of organic and otherwise healthy comestibles, as well as body care products, cookbooks, and health food for pets. There's an extensive variety of flour, rice, cereal, beans, and pasta sold in bulk. ◆ Daily. 117 Hudson St (at N Moore St). 334.8330 ♿

22 White Street An eclectic range of styles reflects the history of the TriBeCa cast-iron district. There are more attractive streets nearby, but none more typical. Contrast the authentic Federal details of **No. 2,** which was originally built as a liquor store in 1809; the artful stonework of **No. 10,** which was designed by **Henry Fernbach** in 1869; and the mansard roofline of **No. 17.** The upper stories of **Nos. 8** and **10** are shorter than the lower floors—a favorite Renaissance Revival device that makes the buildings appear taller. ◆ Between Church St and W Broadway

22 SoHo Photo Gallery Here you'll find the oldest and largest cooperative gallery for photographers in the United States. ◆ Tu 6-8PM; F-Su 1-6PM. 15 White St (between Church St and W Broadway). 226.8571

22 Montrachet ★★★$$$ Former sous-chef Chris Gesualdi officially took over the kitchen in 1994 following the departure of Debra Ponzek, with a transition so seamless that even most regulars didn't notice. The popular salmon with a truffle crust, moist roast chicken, and spiced, seared tuna continue to be as sensational as ever. The extensive wine list is well chosen and the wine service knowledgeable. ◆ French ◆ M-Th dinner; F lunch and dinner; Sa dinner. Reservations recommended. 239 W Broadway (at White St). 219.2777

23 El Teddy's ★$$ Inside this three-story building topped with a life-size replica of the **Statue of Liberty**'s crown are old-fashioned booths and a neon fish tank, among other varied and unusual touches. The cooking is creative Mexican fare—goat-cheese quesadillas, etc.—and the margaritas are among the best in town. ◆ Mexican ◆ M-Th lunch and dinner; F lunch, dinner, and late-night meals; Sa dinner and late-night meals; Su dinner. 219 W Broadway (between Franklin and White Sts). 941.7070

24 Franklin Furnace Call it an alternative art space or an experimental outpost, but this is the country's largest public collection of published art works: books, periodicals, postcards, pamphlets, and cassette tapes. It also presents temporary installations using text and image. Performances by artists are sponsored by the organization and held at different locations from February to April and September to December. Call for schedule and locations. ◆ Nominal fee. Tu-Sa. 112 Franklin St (between Church St and W Broadway). 925.4671

25 Arqua ★★$$$ The poor acoustics in this pretty, peach-colored dining room with white, flying saucer–shaped light fixtures make conversation difficult. Concentrate instead on the food, especially the *pappardelle* with duck-and-mushroom sauce, gnocchi with tomatoes, and rabbit braised in white wine and herbs. ◆ Italian ◆ M-F lunch and dinner; Sa-Su dinner. Reservations recommended. 281 Church St (at White St). 334.1888

26 Let There Be Neon Founded by Rudi Stern, one of America's foremost neon artists, this gallery features clocks, chairs, windows, signs, stage sets, and interiors, all in neon. ◆ M-F. 38 White St (between Broadway and Church St). 226.4883

27 Barocco ★★$$$ No one seems to mind that they are practically sitting on the laps of their neighbors in this sparse but lively trattoria. Try the spinach ravioli filled with ricotta and Swiss chard and topped with a basil-tomato sauce, or rigatoni with pureed eggplant, peppers, and tomato. ♦ Italian ♦ M-F lunch and dinner; Sa-Su dinner. Reservations recommended. 301 Church St (at Walker St). 431.1445

28 American Renaissance ★★$$$
This dramatic dining room—with an indoor waterfall and intricately carved plaster painted aqua and gold—is the perfect setting in which to enjoy foie gras with caramelized pears; roasted Atlantic salmon glazed in vintage Port with shaved asparagus and tahini-lime dressing; and seared Arctic char (a delicate white fish) with shrimp and wild-herb and mushroom ravioli. Make sure to take a peek at the rest rooms: The women's room is a marble and mirror extravaganza with a red lizard ceiling, and the men's has TV sets positioned at eye level above the urinals. ♦ American ♦ M-F lunch and dinner; Sa dinner. Reservations recommended. 260 W Broadway (at Ericson Pl). 343.0049

29 Thai House Cafe ★$ The background Muzak is the only serious drawback at this small, unassuming, and generic-looking place. The authentic Thai food includes lemongrass soup, spicy half-duck in coconut curry, and a dish called Thai Boat (steamed seafood with Thai herbs served in a foil basket). Another plus is the friendly, helpful service. ♦ Thai ♦ M-Sa lunch and dinner. No credit cards accepted. 151 Hudson St (at Hubert St). 334.1085

30 Jan Weiss Gallery Weiss, a quantitative investment analyst–turned–art collector, shows the work of contemporary American, Australian, and European artists. ♦ Th-Sa and by appointment. 68 Laight St (at Greenwich St). 925.7313

31 Tribeca Potters Watch potters create in this working studio and gallery. All of the wares are lead-free and microwave- and dishwasher-safe. ♦ M-F; call for Saturday and Sunday hours. 443 Greenwich St (between Vestry and Desbrosses Sts) 431.7631 &

Capsouto Frères

32 Capsouto Frères ★★$$$ The menu reflects French and American styles, and there are always some specials worth sampling, as well as good desserts. Try the shrimp and scallops on a bed of pasta, duck with ginger and cassis, cassoulet, or poached salmon with vinaigrette. Be sure to save room for one of the luscious desserts, including the *tarte tatin* (upside-down apple tart). ♦ French ♦ M dinner; Tu-F lunch and dinner; Sa-Su brunch

and dinner. Reservations recommended. 451 Washington St (at Watts St). 966.4900

33 Holland Tunnel Built in 1927, this was the world's first underwater tunnel for vehicles, dipping nearly a hundred feet below the surface of the Hudson River. The tunnel is about 29 feet wide with a 12-foot ceiling. Its north tube is 8,558 feet long, and its south tube stretches 8,371 feet. Clifford M. Holland was the man who masterminded this engineering marvel, and the feat secured his name in New York—and American—history. ♦ From Canal St, Manhattan to 12th St, Jersey City

34 Triplet's Roumanian Restaurant ★$$$ As the name suggests, this place is owned and run by identical triplets, brothers who were separated at birth and reunited at age 19. Once inside, don't be misled by the decidedly un-Roumanian decor; the food is authentic. The stuffed cabbage and good professional egg creams made at your table are among the highlights. ♦ Eastern European/Jewish ♦ Tu-W lunch; Th-F lunch and dinner; Sa-Su dinner. Reservations required. 11-17 Grand St (at Sixth Ave). 925.9303

35 Moondance Diner ★$ A refurbished diner with gussied-up diner fare, this spot jibes with the creative atmosphere of the neighborhood. Soups, burgers, and sandwiches are the best bets. Barbecued chicken is moist, tender, and wonderfully sloppy. Wine prices are good and breakfasts are great. ♦ American ♦ Daily breakfast, lunch, and dinner; Th-Sa 24 hours. No credit cards accepted. 80 Sixth Ave (at Grand St). 226.1191

36 Ronald Feldman Fine Arts Inc. The gallery's eclectic and challenging stable includes American, European, and Russian artists. ♦ Tu-Sa; Monday by appointment. 31 Mercer St (between Canal and Grand Sts). 226.3232

37 Pearl River Mart This Chinese department store stocks Chinese imports, including groceries and a good selection of kimonos.

It's a great place to wander around; you almost always come away with something. ♦ Daily. 277 Canal St (at Broadway), Second and Third floors. 431.4770

38 443 Broadway In a neighborhood of iron buildings pretending to be stone, this five-story building, designed by **Griffith Thomas** in 1860, is the real thing, and it's a real beauty, once you get past the altered ground floor. ♦ Between Howard and Grand Sts

39 Amsterdam's ★$$ This always-jumping two-tier restaurant includes a long bar along one side and open rotisseries on the other. Best bets are the chicken and seafood. ♦ American ♦ Lunch and dinner. Reservations recommended. 454 Broadway (at Grand St). 925.6166

40 L'Ecole ★★$$ This place is run by students of the **French Culinary Institute.** Alain Sailhac (formerly the chef at **Le Cirque** and **Le Cygne**) is the Dean of Culinary Studies here, and Jacques Pepin (cookbook author) is the Dean of Special Events. Offerings may include fish soup and rack of lamb with Provençal herbs, along with various pâtés and terrines. Diners also get a chance to play food critic by filling out the report card that comes with the check. ♦ French ♦ M-F lunch and dinner; Sa dinner. 462 Broadway (at Grand St). 219.3300

41 478 Broadway Of all the cast-iron buildings in New York, the magazine *Architectural Record* hailed this one, built in 1874 and designed by **Richard Morris Hunt,** as the "most serious attempt to utilize the almost unlimited strength of the material." ♦ Between Grand and Broome Sts

Within 478 Broadway:

Pure Mädderlake This is an eclectic, spirited store with three identities: a florist shop specializing in fresh flowers that grow in English gardens; a home-furnishings boutique stocked with antique furniture; and a gift shop full of tabletop items, including an exclusive line of Viennese crystal that's expensive but exquisite. ♦ M-Sa. 941.7770

42 486 Broadway Built in 1883 by **Lamb & Rich,** this titanic former home of the Mechanics Bank combines Romanesque and Moorish elements in brick, stone, and terra-cotta. Look up at the mansard roof with its projecting windows and small cupolas. ♦ At Broome St

43 Haughwout Building Famous as the building that contained New York's first

elevator (a reminder of which is a small rusting sign over the door just to the left of the main entrance), this cast-iron Italian palazzo was designed by **John Gaynor** and built in 1857. The building now houses **Staples** downstairs and the **SoHo Mill Outlet** upstairs. In its former life, it was E.V. Haughwout's cut glass and silver store. ♦ 490 Broadway (at Broome St)

44 Canal Jean Co. The original home of surplus chic has much more than jeans. Shop here for the SoHo look without flattening your wallet. ♦ Daily. 504 Broadway (between Broome and Spring Sts). 226.1130

45 521-523 Broadway Nothing but this section remains of the luxurious **St. Nicholas Hotel,** which was built in 1854 and once extended along Broadway, Mercer, and Spring Streets. Its original frontage on the three streets was 750 feet. Inside, the rugs, tapestries, crystal chandeliers, and beveled mirrors made it a tourist attraction even among visitors who couldn't afford to stay there. The bridal suite, filled with satin, lace, rich rosewood, and crystal, was considered the best place to begin a happy marriage. **Long Island Fabrics,** on the ground floor of No. 521, stocks a good selection of African prints (925.4488). ♦ Between Broome and Spring Sts

45 495 Broadway Proof that hope springs eternal, this handsome brick-and-stone structure with fine iron panels, designed by **Alfred Zucker** in 1893, replaced an 1860 cast-iron building at almost the same time the district began its decline. ♦ Between Broome and Spring Sts

46 SoHo Antiques Fair and Flea Market This weekend flea market takes advantage of those who've made brunch or lunch, gallery hopping, and window shopping in SoHo part of their weekend. It's not half as big as the **Annex Antiques Fair and Flea Market,** but you might uncover a real find from dealers who prefer the smaller scale of this corner parking lot. ♦ Free. Sa-Su. Broadway and Grand St. 682.2000 ♿

47 Yohji Yamamoto Themes of recent collections by this talented Japanese designer have included turn-of-the-century Eastern Europe and haute couture with an asymmetrical twist. The prices are high, but the shop is worth a visit even if only to see the iron, rolled-steel, and bronze fixtures designed in London by Antony Donaldson. ♦ M-Sa. 103 Grand St (at Mercer St). 966.9066 ♿

48 Niall Smith Antiques This is a popular haunt for designers and collectors from all over the world in search of Neo-Classical European furniture dating from the late 18th and early 19th centuries. ♦ M-Sa. 96 Grand (between Mercer and Greene Sts). 941.7354

49 Greene Street These five cobblestoned blocks are in the heart of the SoHo Cast-Iron Historic District (designated in 1973), an area taken over by textile manufacturing and other light industry after the retail and entertainment center of the city moved north in the mid-19th century. The 50 cast-iron buildings still intact here were built between 1869 and 1895. Functionally, cast iron anticipated modern steel-frame building techniques, but decoratively, it was used to imitate styles and manners of traditional masonry construction. Designers particularly loved ornate Renaissance and Neo-Classical motifs, which they altered with a free and fantastical hand. The two outstanding buildings on this street—which are in excellent condition—are both by **J.F. Duckworth: Nos. 28-30** (1872), a magnificently mansarded representative of the Second Empire style with leafless Corinthian columns, and **Nos. 72-76** (1873), also Corinthian, but here treated in an Italianate manner with a pedimented porch and porticoes all the way up the projecting center bays. This building was built for the Gardner Colby Company, whose initials appear on the pilasters. Also noteworthy are the arched lintels and columns, with their egg-and-dart motifs, of **Nos. 114-120,** designed in 1882 as a branch of a department store; the Ionic capitals turned sideways at **Nos. 132-134, 136,** and **138** (1885); and all of the extraordinarily ornate **No. 31** (1876). Of course, not all of the buildings on Greene Street are cast iron. Several masonry buildings of the same period sport decorative ironwork as well—**Nos. 42-44** and **84-86,** for example—and one is, well, paint: The brick side wall on the corner is graced by Richard Haas's trompe l'oeil mural (1975) that mimics the cast-iron facade of the building. Many interior spaces remain intact as well. Perhaps the easiest to visit are buildings that best demonstrate the expansive qualities of a loft space and have been turned into galleries, such as the one at **No. 142.** ♦ Between Canal and W Houston Sts

50 Artists Space One of the most original and certainly one of the most successful of the alternative space galleries, this perennial springboard for new talent maintains a file of about 4,000 artists from New York State and New Jersey, which is used by collectors, curators, and architects in search of an artist who falls into a specific category: conceptual, feminist, under 35, etc. ♦ Tu-Sa. 38 Greene St (between Grand and Broome Sts.). 226.3970 ♿

51 The Drawing Center This elegant space, designed by **James Stewart Polshek** in 1986, is an important nonprofit exhibition space for unaffiliated artists, as well as for exceptional scholarly shows of works on paper from historical and contemporary periods. ♦ Tu-Sa. 35 Wooster St (between Grand and Broome Sts). 219.2166 ♿

51 Performing Garage This space is home to **The Wooster Group,** one of America's oldest experimental theater companies, founded in 1967 by director Richard Schechner. Under the direction of Elizabeth LeCompte, it redefines traditional notions of story line, thematic content, and performance structure. ♦ 33 Wooster St (between Grand and Broome Sts). 966.3651

52 La Jumelle ★$ This place must have been separated at birth from its twin (the name in French), **Lucky Strike,** just two doors down. Although owned by different people, both are charmingly frumpy bars-cum-restaurants with bistro menus written on blackboards. The clientele at both is made up of the young and the trendy. Try the duck with olives or chicken with mustard sauce. ♦ French ♦ Daily dinner and late-night meals. Reservations recommended. 55 Grand St (between Wooster St and W Broadway). 941.9651

52 Lucky Strike $$ At this very popular late-night hangout, the food is the least of the attractions. This is a place to which people come to sit, talk, and smoke, and to be seen sitting, talking, and smoking. If you must eat, try the vegetable tart or steak *frites.* ♦ French ♦ M-F lunch, dinner, and late-night meals. Sa-Su brunch, dinner, and late-night meals. 59 Grand St (between Wooster St and W Broadway). 941.0479

53 Jour et Nuit ★★$$$ The constant parade of beautiful people here may be distracting, but the food is too good to be treated merely as a prop. The chic, tightly packed dining room, where black-and-white abstract paintings hang on the walls and banquettes are covered in Native American blanket prints, offers a French menu that includes foie gras sautéed in raspberry sauce, tuna *tartare,* lobster cannelloni, and roast duck with cider sauce. The wine list is small and contains some nice choices, generally in the higher price ranges. ♦ French/Japanese ♦ M-F dinner; Sa brunch and dinner; Su brunch. Reservations required. 337 W Broadway (at Grand St). 925.5971

Prior to a regentrification in the 1970s, TriBeCa was an eyesore of abandoned warehouses and cast-iron hulls. In an area of just over 200 acres, local meatpackers have moved over to make room for a new community of some 8,000 TriBeCan actors, lawyers, and young professionals with an average income of $55,000. The median cost of a condominium loft is $450,000.

Restaurants/Clubs: Red   **Hotels:** Blue
Shops/ ♥ Outdoors: Green   **Sights/Culture:** Black

New York City in Fact. . .

Art and Architecture

AIA Guide to New York City by Norval White and Elliot Willensky (1988, Harcourt Brace Jovanovich). In this richly illustrated third edition, the authors give you an architectural insider's view of New York City's buildings and landscapes, from the familar to the off-beat. Organized by neighborhoods.

The Building of Manhattan by Donald Mackay (1987, Harper & Row). This book answers the question: "How did they build that?" Hundreds of archival photos and drawings trace the history of construction in Manhattan, from the early Dutch homes to the giant skyscrapers and the latest innovations in architecture and construction techniques.

The City Observed: New York. A Guide to the Architecture of Manhattan by Paul Goldberger (1979, Random House). Pictures and descriptions of some of the greatest urban architecture in the world.

The City That Never Was: 200 Years of Fantastic and Fascinating Plans That Might Have Changed the Face of NYC by Rebecca Reed Shanor (1988, Viking Press). Never content with leaving well enough alone, New Yorkers are constantly trying to change their fair city. Some of the stranger schemes and proposals are chronicled here, such as mooring zeppelins on the **Empire State Building** or building a moving sidewalk on **Broadway.**

The Columbia Historical Portrait of New York by John A. Kouwenhoven (1972, Harper & Row). A show-and-tell guide combining brief essays and 900 photographs accompanied by historical data.

Lost New York: Pictorial Record of Vanished NYC by Nathan Silver (1982, American Legacy Press). An illustrated history of the buildings and neighborhoods of New York.

Manhattan Architecture by Richard Berenholtz and Donald Martin Reynolds (1988, Prentice Hall Press). The diversity of Manhattan's architecture is the subject of Berenholtz's photographs and Reynolds's essays. The focus is on the big pieces: skyscrapers, bridges, and the skyline.

New York Architecture 1970-1990 by Heinrich Klotz (1989, Rizzoli). A look at some of the changes in the New York skyline during a period that saw the completion of the **Twin Towers** and the **CitiCorp Center,** as well as other smaller—but still notable— buildings.

New York Observed: Artists and Writers Look at the City, 1650 to the Present, edited by Barbara Cohen, Seymour Chwast, and Steven Heller (1988, Harry N. Abrams). New York City has long fascinated artists and writers. This collection presents some of those views over the ages.

On Broadway: A Journey Uptown Over Time by David W. Dunlap (1990, Rizzoli). Architectural and historical views and descriptions of New York from the perspective of **Broadway.**

Guidebooks

The Best Guided Walking Tours of NYC by Leslie Gourse (1989, The Globe Pequot Press). A directory and reference book for the institutions and the people to contact for a variety of specialized walking tours.

Ethnic New York: A Complete Guide to the Many Faces and Cultures of New York by Mark Leeds (1991, Passport Books). A primer on the melting pot that is New York City. The histories of different neighborhoods are coupled with a guide to restaurants, shops, museums, and, of course, festivals.

From Trout Stream to Bohemia: A Walking Guide to Greenwich Village History by Joyce Gold (1988, Old Warren Press). An illustrated history of a neighborhood that has gone from being the center of New York's urbane wealth to its fringe artistic scene, and everything in between.

From Windmills to the World Trade Center: A Walking Guide to Lower Manhattan History by Joyce Gold (1988, Old Warren Press). A guide to walking around where it all began.

Literary Neighborhoods of New York by Marcia Leisner (1989, Starrhill Press). A historical overview of the changing centers of literary and intellectual life in New York.

Manhattan's Oudoor Sculpture by Margot Gayle and Michele Cohen (1988, Prentice Hall Press). Sculptures in the parks, plazas, and squares.

New York, A Guide to the Metropolis: Walking Tours of Architecture and History by Gerard R. Wolfe (1988, McGraw-Hill). Three hundred photographs and 20 walking tours in Manhattan, **Brooklyn,** and **Queens** lead you through the history of New York by way of its architecture.

New York City Yesterday & Today: 30 Timeless Walking Adventures by Judith H. Browning (1990, Corsair Publications). This book specializes in uncommon facts, personal observations, and novel perspectives on familiar sights all over New York.

Permanent New Yorkers: A Biographical Guide to the Cemeteries by Judi Culbertson and Tom Randall (1987, Chelsea Green Publishers). A history and guide to the final resting places of well-known and some not so well-known, but nevertheless interesting, New Yorkers.

The Streets Where They Lived: A Walking Guide to the Residences of Famous New Yorkers by Stephen W. Plumb (1989, Marlor Press). Thirty-six short walking tours reveal the neighborhoods and homes of some of the best-known locals.

Other

Movie Lover's Guide to New York by Richard Alleman (1988, Harper & Row). Who did what, where, and when in the movies and in New York. A behind-the-scenes look at the romance and turmoil of the relationship between New York and film.

The New York Theatre Sourcebook by Chuck Lawliss (1981, Simon & Schuster). Although slightly dated, this reference book contains something for the novice as well as the pro, from the history of over 250 theaters to the search for cheap tickets.

The Street Book—An Encyclopedia of Manhattan's Street Names and Their Origins by Henry Moscow (1978, Fordham University Press). Just about every name that ever got to be on a street sign in New York, and why, is covered in this reference book for the truly devoted.

Under the Sidewalks of New York: The Story of the World's Great Subway Station by Brian J. Cudahy (1988, The Stephen Greene Press/Pelham Books). Everything you ever wanted to know about the oldest major subway system in the world. It covers history, technology, equipment—everything but the schedules.

You Must Remember This: An Oral History of Manhattan from the 1890s to World War II by Jeff Kisseloff (1989, Harcourt Brace Jovanovich). Not so much a history as a collection of vivid decriptions of life in New York by those who lived it. The good, the bad, the ugly, and, quite often, the funny and the touching.

ACCESS New York City Restaurants (1995, HarperCollins Publishers). The ultimate inside scoop on the city's best restaurants and fancy food shops, for gourmets and gourmands.

. . . and Fiction

The Age of Innocence by Edith Wharton, originally published 1920 (1968, Charles Scribner's Sons). An incisive but subtle attack on the mores and customs of upper-class society in turn-of-the-century New York. A richly detailed portrait of a world Wharton knew quite well, and disdained.

Catcher in the Rye by J.D. Salinger, originally published 1951 (1964, Bantam Books). This instant, if not controversial, classic, about the adolescence of Holden Caulfield, a young New Yorker who feels alienated and isolated from the world around him, has been a touchstone for a generation or two.

Diedrick Knickerbocker's History of New York by Washington Irving, originally published 1840 (1981, Sleepy Hollow). A satirical and somewhat burlesque "history" of New York, written by Irving under the pseudonym Diedrick Knickerbocker (the same narrator as in *Rip Van Winkle*).

Fourth Street East: A Novel of How It Was by Jerome Weidman (1970, Pinnacle Books). A writer well known for his Broadway plays (including "Fiorello") and for his editorial duties at *New Yorker* magazine, this autobiographical novel explores the colorful characters of the neighborhood where the author grew up.

The House of Mirth by Edith Wharton (1905, Charles Scribner's Sons). Wharton lets loose on New York society again in this novel, which is about a woman who rejects marrying for love in the hope of marrying for money. In the end, she gets neither.

This Side of Paradise by F. Scott Fitzgerald (1920, Charles Scribner's Sons). A portrait of the "Lost Generation" in its college days, and yet another battle between true love and money-lust that ends in regret and cynicism. Not a pretty picture.

Time and Again by Jack Finney (1970, Simon & Schuster). If you could go back in time and change the world, what would you do? If you have no clue, Finney offers some suggestions.

A Tree Grows in Brooklyn by Betty Smith, originally published 1943 (1968, Harper & Row). A sensitive child grows up in a rough neighborhood with a drunk but lovable father and a determined but sweet mother. Tender and moving.

Washington Square by Henry James, originally published 1880 (1990, New American Library). James grew up on Washington Square, the setting for this novel about the shy young daughter of a domineering and wealthy doctor who makes her life miserable. Made into a movie and a play titled *The Heiress*.

Children's Books

The Cricket in Times Square by George Selden (1960, Farrar, Straus & Giroux). The adventures of a cricket who spends a summer in Times Square.

Eloise by Kay Thompson (1955, Simon & Schuster). Long before *Home Alone II,* Eloise lives it up in the **Plaza Hotel.**

From the Mixed up Files of Mrs. Basil E. Frankweiler by E.L. Konigsburg (1967, Atheneum). Imagine the **Metropolitan Museum of Art** as a playground. A 12-year-old girl and her brother do as they run away and hide there.

Harriet the Spy by Louise Fitzhugh (1964, Harper & Row Junior Books). A different take on New York: Harriet is a sixth grader who wants to be a spy, so she spends part of each day "observing" the world around her.

The Little Red Lighthouse and the Great Gray Bridge by Hildegarde H. Swift (1942, Harcourt Brace Jovanovich). The story of a lighthouse on the **Hudson River** that was eventually overshadowed by the **George Washington Bridge.**

Stuart Little by E.B. White (1945, Harper & Row Junior Books). From the creator of *Charlotte's Web,* this is the story of a sophisticated and debonair mouse named Stuart Little and his adventures as he sets out in the world to find his dearest friend, a little bird. His search takes him to New York.

54 Felix ★$$$ Another player in the see-and-be-seen intersection of Grand Street and West Broadway, this place, like **Lucky Strike, La Jumelle,** and **Jour et Nuit** (see page 61), attracts a cross section of models, downtown hipsters, and trendy professionals who dine on such simple bistro fare as roast chicken and *steak frites.* The outdoor cafe is a good place to people watch. ◆ French ◆ Daily lunch and dinner. 340 W Broadway (at Grand St). 431.0021

55 Alison on Dominick Street ★★★$$$ Owner Alison Becker Hurt and chef Daniel Silverman present solid versions of the restaurant's signature hearty French food in a candlelit room that has long been considered one of the most romantic spots in town. Try the oyster stew with leeks and potatoes, sliced duck breast over lentils and cabbage with a sherry and cider-vinegar sauce, braised beef shin in red-wine sauce, roasted quail with currant couscous, seared tuna with fricassee of artichokes, plum tart, and pear cake with caramel sauce. The wine list is well chosen and not outrageously priced. ◆ French country ◆ Daily dinner. Reservations recommended. 38 Dominick St (between Varick and Hudson Sts). 727.1188

56 Bell Caffè $ The neighborhood artists who hang out here want to keep this place a secret, lest the crowds that choke the streets east of Sixth Avenue begin to encroach. The food is decent (homemade breads, soups, and vegetable pies), but the scene is more the point. The decor is eclectic and fun: an assemblage of stuff saved from the garbage dump. There's live music every night and never a cover. ◆ Cafe ◆ Daily lunch, dinner, and late-night meals. 310 Spring St (between Hudson and Greenwich Sts). 334.2355

57 Castillo Cultural Center This progressive, independent cultural center encompasses a performance space, gallery, publishing house, photo lab, and video lab. One notable performance included a live hair montage—three-dimensional environments created on top of peoples' heads. ◆ Gallery: free; Theater: admission. Gallery: M-Sa 10AM-10PM; Su noon-6PM. 500 Greenwich St (between Canal and Spring Sts). 941.5800, 941.1234 for information ⑤

58 The Ear Inn $ The building that houses this dark and dusty bar/restaurant built in 1817 has been designated a landmark. Back then, the shoreline was only five feet away from the entrance, and the joint was full of seafaring rowdies. Today, it serves a landlubbing crowd decent pub food, including burgers and sandwiches. ◆ American ◆ M-Sa lunch, dinner, and late-night meals; Su brunch, dinner, and late-night meals. 326 Spring St (between Greenwich and Washington Sts). 226.9060

59 New York City Fire Museum The Fire Department's own collection of apparatuses and memorabilia dating back to colonial times is combined here with that of the Home Insurance Co. This is the largest exhibition of its kind in the country, and if you have youngsters in tow they won't complain a bit about the long walk west when they discover this is the destination. ◆ Admission. Tu-Sa. 278 Spring St (between Varick and Hudson Sts). 691.1303 ⑤

60 Ceramica Classic Italian patterns appear on imported linens, mosaics, and earthenware—the Rafaelesco, a dragon pattern Rafael used on many of his frames, is particularly beautiful. Everything is handmade, most of it hailing from Italy. ◆ Tu-Su. 59 Thompson St (between Broome and Spring Sts). 941.1307

60 Country Cafe ★★$ SoHo doesn't lack for cozy French bistros, but there's an intimacy and friendliness about this place that puts it above the others. The delicious food is also earthy—try the wild-mushroom casserole, onion tart, Cornish hen with tarragon juice, hanger steak with shallot sauce, and the rich *tarte tatin.* There's also a good, inexpensive wine list. The only negative is the sometimes long wait on weekends. ◆ French ◆ M dinner; Tu-F lunch and dinner; Sa-Su brunch and dinner. No credit cards accepted. 69 Thompson St (between Broome and Spring Sts). No phone.

60 Classic Toys Put together your own private army, create a miniature zoo, or mount a wee Wild West show from this imaginative collection. Collectors and commercial photographers, as well as local children, shop here for tin soldiers and matchbox cars, circus sets, and stuffed dinosaurs. ◆ W-Su noon-6:30PM. 69 Thompson St (between Broome and Spring Sts). 941.9129

60 O To 60s Jewelry, furnishings, folk art, and unusual objects from 1900 through 1960 are showcased in this store. ◆ M-Sa noon-7PM. 75 Thompson St (between Broome and Spring Sts). 925.0932 ⑤

61 Il Bisonte These fine handcrafted leathergoods are known for their casual weekend style: Handbags, portfolios, luggage and accessories come straight from Florence. ◆ Daily. 72 Thompson St (between Broome and Spring Sts). 966.8773. Also at: 22 E 65th

St (between Madison and Fifth Aves). 717.4771 &

62 Think Big If you can find a use for a six-foot pencil or a wristwatch too big for King Kong, more power to you. This famous store has a whole line of outsize items that will make you feel like a Lilliputian. ♦ Daily. 390 W Broadway (between Broome and Spring Sts). 925.7300 &

62 Barolo ★★$$$ During inclement weather, the dining room here provides a sophisticated setting for excellent pasta and broiled fish dishes, but once the weather warms up the scene moves to the back garden that's decorated with cherry trees. Try the *tuna tartare, cappelletti* with calamari and broccoli, or grilled scallops with white beans. ♦ Italian ♦ M-Th, Su lunch and dinner; F-Sa lunch, dinner, and late-night meals. Reservations recommended. 398 W Broadway (between Broome and Spring Sts). 226.1102 &

63 O.K. Harris Works of Art A SoHo landmark for 20 years, this gallery is a record-setter, with more than 60 artists represented and an average of 50 exhibitions each year in its 11,000-square-foot spread. Ivan Karp, an early champion of Pop Art, is the gallery's founder and chief point man. ♦ Tu-Sa. 383 W Broadway (between Broome and Spring Sts). 431.3600

63 Portico Owner Steven Werther travels far and wide to find craftspeople who meet his meticulous standards of construction. Among the pieces he has chosen are handmade reproductions of Shaker furniture, Argentine antiques, and dishes and glassware from Italy. In the middle of the store—it's a historical landmark building that stretches all the way to Wooster Street—is a pleasant cafe setting where you can sit and relax with a cappuccino or a cup of tea (try one from the United Society of Shakers in Maine). ♦ Daily. 379 W Broadway (between Broome and Spring Sts). 941.7800. Also: Portico Bed, 139 Spring St (at Wooster St). 941-7722

63 Gemini GEL at Joni Weyl New and vintage prints from the venerable LA workshop, including editions by Ellsworth Kelly, Roy Lichtenstein, and Robert Rauschenberg, are on view. ♦ Tu-Sa. 375 W Broadway (between Broome and Spring Sts), Second floor. 219.1446 &

63 Betsy Senior Contemporary Prints Senior maintains a select inventory of contemporary prints and drawings, as well as new editions by rising stars. ♦ Tu-Sa. 375 W Broadway (between Broome and Spring Sts), Second floor. 941.0960 &

63 SoHo Emporium This haphazard gaggle of some 40 independent boutiques sells everything from furs and jewelry to crafts and crystal. Should you be in need of advice, there is even a fortune-teller. ♦ Daily. 375 W Broadway (between Broome and Spring Sts). 966.6091

64 Kenn's Broome Street Bar $ Frozen in time, this dark room looks exactly as it did 20 years ago, and the menu hasn't changed a bit either. The burgers served on pita bread, soups, and such basic sandwiches as tuna are all good. ♦ American ♦ M-F lunch, dinner, and late-night meals; Sa-Su brunch, dinner, and late-night meals. 363 W Broadway (at Broome St). 925.2086

64 The Cupping Room Cafe ★$$ Waffles with berries, giant muffins, bagels with the fixings, and a choice of terrific coffees and teas draw a fiercely loyal crowd at this cozy cafe. Be prepared to wait at brunchtime. ♦ Continental ♦ M breakfast, lunch, and dinner; Tu-F breakfast, lunch, dinner, and late-night meals; Sa brunch, dinner, and late-night meals; Su brunch and dinner. Reservations recommended for dinner. 359 W Broadway (at Broome St). 925.2898

65 59 Wooster Street Originally a warehouse, this six-story building, designed by **Alfred Zucker** in 1890, dominates the corner where it stands. Its mass is relieved by arched, iron-rimmed windows on its Broome Street facade, and by highly sculptural reliefs scattered over its surface. The seemingly random play between the rough-hewn masonry, smooth brickwork, and crenellated roofline (look hard and you'll see hand-size human faces way up top) somehow pulls the building together and gives it an oddly noble presence. It's best seen from the south side of Broome Street. ♦ At Broome St

Within 59 Wooster Street:

Brooke Alexander In luxurious quarters designed by the English architect **Max Gordon,** Carolyn and Brooke Alexander feature painting and sculpture by some of the most vigorous talents, including Jane Dickson, Yvonne Jacquette, and Tom Otterness. ♦ Tu-Sa. Second floor. 925.4338 &

66 Printed Matter Bookstore at Dia This nonprofit art center specializes in books made by artists, which means the artist has been directly involved in the conceptualization, design, and production of the work. The average price per book is $10 to $15—choose among 5,000 titles by 2,500 artists—making them one of very few bargains in the art world. ♦ Tu-Sa. 77 Wooster St (between Broome and Spring Sts). 925.0325 &

67 Brooke Alexander Editions Longtime champions of the graphic image, Brooke and Carolyn Alexander have opened a roomy, light-filled space that every print maven dreams about. Featured are American prints since 1960 by such contemporary masters as Johns, Lichtenstein, and Judd, as well as a selective inventory of works by younger artists and distinctive Europeans. ♦ Tu-Sa. 476 Broome St (between Greene and Wooster Sts), Fourth floor. 925.2070 ♿

68 SoHo 20 Gallery The gallery is a cooperative of women artists with group and individual shows. ♦ Tu-Sa. 469 Broome St (at Greene St). 226.4167

69 Craft Caravan, Inc. Traditional African handicrafts are the draw, and some interesting household items are displayed in a case up front—Beauty Pageant talc powder and Elephant Powder laundry detergent, for instance. ♦ M-F. 63 Greene St (between Broome and Spring Sts). 431.6669 ♿

69 Heller Gallery One of the most important representatives of the modern glass movement, this always interesting gallery usually has two solo shows and a monthly overview. ♦ Tu-Su. 71 Greene St (between Broome and Spring Sts). 966.5948

70 The King of Greene Street Greene Street offers a concentration of the best of SoHo's remaining cast-iron architecture, but even here this industrial palace is a stand-out. It is one of four on this street designed by **Isaac Duckworth** in 1873, and was called the "King of Greene Street" (the faded blue "Queen" is at **No. 28**). It is actually two buildings that pass as one, whose five-floor columned cast iron facade is a masterpiece of French Second Empire. ♦ 72-76 Greene St (between Broome and Spring Sts)

70 Luna d'Oro Jewelry, handicrafts, and furnishings from South and Central America are carried in this shop. ♦ Daily. 66 Greene St (between Broome and Spring Sts). 925.8225

71 Friends of Figurative Sculpture Bronze sculptures of the human figure in a variety of sizes are featured in this welcoming gallery. ♦ By appointment only. 53 Mercer St (between Grand and Broome Sts). 226.4850

72 Gourmet Garage This produce emporium offers a wide variety of goods at decent prices. Whether you're looking for a supply of crusty breads, blood oranges, portobello mushrooms, sun-dried tomatoes, calamata olives, parmigiano reggiano, English farmhouse cheddar, or one of several chutneys, you'll probably find it here. ♦ Daily. 453 Broome St (at Mercer St). 941.5850. Also at: 301 E 64th St (at Second Ave). 535.5880

73 Michael Carey American Arts & Crafts Come here for a good selection of pottery, lighting, and furniture by Gustave Stickley (1858-1942) and other period designers. ♦ Tu-Sa or by appointment. 77 Mercer St (between Broome and Spring Sts). 226.3710

73 The Enchanted Forest This bewitching shop looks like a miniature set for a fantasy adventure. Beasts, books, and handmade toys are part of the celebration. ♦ Daily. 85 Mercer St (between Broome and Spring Sts). 925.6677

74 Cascabel ★★★$$$ Geraldine Ferraro's son, John Zaccaro Jr., opened this stylishly decorated restaurant that features a hearty, robust Mediterranean menu. Two superb offerings are the chicken-and-foie-gras–stuffed *agnolotti* (half-moon–shaped ravioli) with chickpeas and leeks, and his signature dish—braised lamb shanks served with white-bean puree. End the meal with a maple crème brûlée. ♦ Mediterranean ♦ M-Sa dinner. Reservations recommended. 218 Lafayette St (between Broome and Spring Sts). 431.7300

75 Spring Street Natural ★$ The healthy menu is mostly vegetarian, although even the nonconverted should be able to find something satisfying to eat in this airy place filled with greenery. The vegetable or seafood stir-fry and the roasted chicken with honey-mustard glaze are among the best choices. ♦ American ♦ M-Th lunch and dinner; F lunch, dinner, and late-night meals; Sa brunch, dinner, and late-night meals; Su brunch and dinner. 62 Spring St (at Lafayette St). 966.0290

76 New York Open Center Each year this education center offers hundreds of workshops, courses, lectures, and performances that explore spiritual and social issues, psychology, the arts—in short, all aspects of traditional and contemporary world culture. Check out the bookstore for the latest literature on all of the above. ♦ Bookstore: daily. 83 Spring St (between Crosby St and Broadway). 219.2527

77 P.P.O.W. The adventuresome young partners, Penny Pilkington and Wendy Olsoff (hence the name), pride themselves on their preference for individuals over trends. They show David Wojnarowicz and Erika Rothenberg as well as installation work (built environments) by TODT. ♦ Tu-Sa. 532 Broadway (between Spring and Prince Sts), Third floor. 941.8642 &

78 101 Spring Street Designed by **N. Whyte** in 1871, this building displays a sensitive approach to the use of cast iron as complex ornament. The ground floor is completely unchanged. ♦ At Mercer St

79 Betina Riedel Chic yet casual women's clothes are sold in the designer's store. ♦ Daily. 113 Spring St (between Mercer and Greene Sts). 226.2350

79 Penang ★$$ This artfully designed restaurant looks a little like Walt Disney's idea of Malaysia, with a slanting straw roof suspended over the dining room, strings of white lights, and waitresses wrapped in sarongs. Try the *beef rendang* (strips cooked until tender with ground onions, chili peppers, coconut, and lemongrass) and the noodle, vegetable, and shrimp soup. ♦ Malaysian ♦ Daily lunch, dinner, and late-night meals. Reservations recommended. 109 Spring St (between Mercer and Greene Sts). 274.8883. Also at: 240 Columbus Ave (at W 71st St). 769.3988; 38-04 Prince St (between 37th Ave and Main St), Flushing, Queens. 718/321.2078

80 Jay Gorney Art This gallery is a trendy venue for contemporary painting and sculpture, with a more than ample dose of late-1980s marketing savvy. ♦ Tu-Sa. 100 Greene St (between Spring and Prince Sts). 966.4480 &

80 110 Greene Street The sign says this is "The SoHo Building," but long before anyone ever thought of calling this neighborhood SoHo, it was an annex of the **Charles Broadway Rouss Department Store** that thrived over on Broadway. It was designed by **William J. Dilthy** and built in 1908. ♦ Between Spring and Prince Sts

80 Wolfman-Gold & Good Company The contents of this boutique make a strong argument for table setting as a mode of self-expression, if not an art form. Fine china, linens, flatware, and glassware are offered here, among other accessories, and the shop's open-stock selection of restaurant china means you can mix and match to your heart's content. ♦ Daily. 116 Greene St (between Spring and Prince Sts). 431.1888

80 Buffalo Chips Bootery Choose from a fashionable line of podiatrist-approved cowboy boots with steel-reinforced arches and low, tapered heels for proper support. If you can't find a pair that you like among the 50 or so on display, they'll be glad to do a custom design. ♦ Daily. 116A Greene St (between Spring and Prince Sts). 274.0651 &

81 SoHo Kitchen and Bar ★$ Pizzas, grilled fish, and such basic pasta dishes as fettuccine with sun-dried tomatoes are the menu's mainstays. But the food takes second place to the theatrical interior designed by owner Tony Goldman—dramatic lighting, immense canvases, black ceiling, and suspended airplanes. It also boasts Manhattan's longest wine list: 96 wines and 14 brands of champagne. Oenophiles shouldn't miss the "flights of wines," a heady experience, during which anywhere from four to eight wines within a specific category are sampled in two-and-a-half-ounce portions. ♦ American ♦ M-Th, Su lunch and dinner; F-Sa lunch, dinner, and late-night meals. 103 Greene St (between Spring and Prince Sts). 925.1866

81 Barbara Gladstone Gallery Gladstone's elegant two-tiered space allows her to mount dual exhibitions from an ever-increasing stable of European and American artists. Vito Acconci, Anish Kapoor, Rosemarie Trockel, and Genny Holzer are part of her distinguished roster. ♦ Tu-Sa. 99 Greene St (between Spring and Prince Sts). 431.3334 &

81 Zona One of the very best reasons to visit SoHo, Louis Sagar's high-ceilinged, wonderfully airy space is as much a gallery as a store: Paolo Soleri's bells, garden tools, furniture of the Southwest, terra-cotta, and other well-designed earth-conscious housewares from the Great American Desert (and all over the world) are displayed with great care and imagination—qualities every store should aim for. It's worth buying something just to get it gift-wrapped. ♦ Daily. 97 Greene St (between Spring and Prince Sts). 925.6750 &

82 Platypus All sorts of upscale housewares are available here, from designer kettles and flatware by Alessi, Michael Graves, and Aldo Rossi to 18th- and 19th-century pine armoires, cupboards, and cribs. Godiva chocolates are sold as well. ♦ Daily. 126 Spring St (at Greene St). 219.3919

Restaurants/Clubs: Red   **Hotels:** Blue
Shops/♥ Outdoors: Green   **Sights/Culture:** Black

82 Peter-Roberts Antiques This upscale antiques shop specializes in American Arts and Crafts furniture and accessories. ♦ Daily. 134 Spring St (between Greene and Wooster Sts), Ground floor. 226.4777

82 Jaap Rietman Just one flight up, this is an unsurpassed source for the best books and periodicals on art, architecture, and photography. The staff is knowledgeable and the atmosphere conducive to browsing. ♦ M-Sa. 134 Spring St (between Greene and Wooster Sts), Second floor. 966.7044 &

82 Laurence Miller Gallery Rotating works by photography greats such as Helen Levitt hang in this gallery beside those of younger shutterbugs, all chosen with Miller's customary discretion. ♦ Tu-Sa. 138 Spring St (between Greene and Wooster Sts), Third floor. 226.1220

83 Manhattan Bistro ★$ In the front, the marble-topped tables and bar are great for a glass of wine and bowl of fish soup, or a cappuccino and dark-and-white chocolate mousse dessert. Farther back is a simple yet elegant dining room. Here, the best choices are homey French specialties: coq au vin, *boeuf bourguignon,* and small steaks that come with delicious skinny fries. ♦ French ♦ M-F breakfast, lunch, dinner, and late-night meals; Sa-Su brunch, dinner, and late-night meals. Reservations recommended for dinner. 129 Spring St (between Greene and Wooster Sts). 966.3459

Only a few areas remain to remind us of the once predominant Federal-style brick row house. The four-block Charlton-King-Vandam Historic District (1828-34; bounded by Sixth Avenue and Varick, and Vandam and Houston Streets) was developed primarily by John Jacob Astor. It has the city's largest concentration of these old homes and was designated a National Landmark in 1966. There is a fine example of the period in the unbroken row on the north side of Vandam Street. A larger row along Charlton's north side includes the noteworthy Nos. 37 and 39, along with four Greek Revival replacements. King Street mixes Federal with a potpourri of later styles. At the corner of King and MacDougal Streets is one of the few 19th-century storefronts left in the city.

83 The Grass Roots Garden Larry Nathanson is the green thumb behind this cornucopia of plants. ♦ Tu-Su. 131 Spring St (between Greene and Wooster Sts). 226.2662

84 Boom ★$$$ Innovative creations at this popular SoHo spot for "world cuisine" range from Senegalese *mafta* (a peanut-based vegetarian dish) to avocado blinis with lobster, Ossetra caviar, and crème fraîche. The candlelit setting is romantic. ♦ Eclectic ♦ M-W lunch and dinner; Th-F lunch, dinner, and late-night meals; Sa brunch, dinner, and late-night meals; Su brunch and dinner. 152 Spring St (between Wooster St and W Broadway). 431.3663

85 Tennessee Mountain ★$$ The smells wafting down Spring Street will whet your appetite for the food: ribs, fried chicken, and vegetarian chili. The frozen margaritas are sure to elevate your mood. ♦ American ♦ M-F lunch and dinner; Sa-Su brunch and dinner. Reservations recommended. 143 Spring St (at Wooster St). 431.3993

85 Morgane Le Fay The window at this women's clothing boutique is always austere and monochromatic. Featured inside is clothing designed by Liliana Ordas—flowing dresses, coats, capes, and skirts in a wide range of wool flannels, wool crepes, jerseys, and velvets. ♦ Daily. 151 Spring St (between Wooster St and W Broadway). 925.0144 &

85 The Irish Secret The traditional and innovative fashions by contemporary Irish designers include beautifully tailored dresses in silk, linen, cotton, and wool. ♦ Daily. 155 Spring St (between Wooster St and W Broadway). 334.6711 &

85 Kin Khao ★$$ The trendiest place around for Thai fare (the scene seems to overwhelm the food at times), this dark, cavelike spot offers decent versions of such dishes as *pla gung* (a hot-and-sour prawn salad with onions, chili, lemongrass, and basil) and *kwaytio ki mow* (sautéed spicy rice noodles with basil and tomatoes). ♦ Thai ♦ Daily dinner. 171 Spring St (at W Broadway). 966.3939

86 Detour The accent is on a European sensitivity in this collection of clothing for men. The women's collection is sold at 472 West Broadway. ♦ Daily. 425 W Broadway (between Spring and Prince Sts). 219.2692

86 Tootsi Plohound You would probably never guess that a store with a name like this sells unusual and well-made men's and women's shoes. ♦ Daily. 413 W Broadway (between Spring and Prince Sts). 925.8931 &. Also at: 137 Fifth Ave (between E 21st and E 22nd Sts). 460.8650

86 415 West Broadway There are eight galleries in this impressive six-story building with a simple cast-iron storefront. ♦ Between Spring and Prince Sts

Within 415 West Broadway:

Witkin Gallery The focus is on vintage and contemporary photography by such artists as Evelyn Hofer, George Tice, and Jerry N. Uelsmann. Also available are new, rare, and out-of-print books on photography. ♦ Tu-Sa. Fourth floor. 925.5510

86 Mary Boone A much publicized upstart among art dealers during the early 1980s heyday of neo-Expressionism, Boone has settled into the establishment with a solid roster of American and mid-career European artists. Eric Fischl, David Salle, and Ross Bleckner are among her successes. ♦ Tu-Sa. 417 W Broadway (between Spring and Prince Sts). 431.1818

86 Beau Brummel Ralph Lauren began his career designing ties for this store. Today, most of the men's clothing and accessories sold here are by European designers. ♦ Daily. 421 W Broadway (between Spring and Prince Sts). 219.2666

86 Nancy Hoffman Gallery Hoffman's generous space is the backdrop for easygoing paintings and works on paper by such Realists as Joseph Raffael and Peter Plagens, as well as oils on canvas by Rafael Ferrer and others. ♦ Tu-Sa. 429 W Broadway (between Spring and Prince Sts). 966.6676 ♿

87 Joovay Fine cotton and silk lingerie, sleepwear, and a good selection of toiletries are featured in this boutique. ♦ Daily. 436 W Broadway (between Spring and Prince Sts). 431.6386 ♿

87 420 West Broadway Two of SoHo's most prestigious galleries, **Leo Castelli** and **Sonnabend,** as well as several others, are housed in this heavy-hitter building. ♦ Between Spring and Prince Sts

Within 420 West Broadway:

Charles Cowles Gallery Contemporary painting joins sculpture and ceramics by a wide-ranging stable that includes many West Coast artists. ♦ Tu-Sa. Fifth floor. 925.3500

Leo Castelli Gallery A must-see on anyone's SoHo circuit, Castelli's extraordinary gallery features a veritable Who's Who of Abstract Expressionist and Pop artists, many of whom have shown their work with Castelli since the early 1960s. Jasper Johns, Ellsworth Kelly, and Ed Ruscha are but a few of the gallery regulars. ♦ Tu-Sa. Second floor. 431.5160

Sonnabend Gallery Ileana Sonnabend's celebrated and highly respected eye has drawn in such Americans as Robert Morris, who shares the floor with an ever-growing list of distinguished Europeans, including Jannis Kounellis, Gilbert & George, and Anne and Patrick Poirier. ♦ Tu-Sa. Third floor. 966.6160

88 Paracelso A moderately priced source for women's clothes made from natural fibers, the styles featured here—many from India—are casual and loose-fitting. ♦ Daily. 414 W Broadway (between Spring and Prince Sts). 966.4232

89 Ad Hoc Softwares Owners Julia McFarlane and Judith Auchincloss scour the marketplace for a wide range of bed and bath items, including unbleached, chemical-free linen and cotton sheets from Austria and West Germany, Italian and French waffle towels, and high-quality blankets from Europe. Also stocked are bath and beauty accessories and small gift items. ♦ Daily. 410 W Broadway (at Spring St). 925.2652 ♿

89 Spring Street Books In addition to a top-notch selection of books, this store features a good selection of newspapers, foreign magazines, and remainders. The late hours are a boon to last-minute gift shoppers. ♦ M-Th 10AM-11PM; F 10AM-midnight; Sa 10AM-1AM; Su 11AM-10PM. 169 Spring St (between W Broadway and Thompson St). 219.3033

90 Berrys ★$$ A convivial bistro, and one of SoHo's earliest culinary attractions, this dark, cozy place maintains its popularity with solid brunches and simple continental dinners, such as filet mignon in a cracked peppercorn glaze, and duck confit. The menu changes every couple of months with the seasons. ♦ Continental ♦ M-F lunch and dinner; Sa-Su brunch and dinner. Reservations recommended; reservations required for Sunday brunch. 180 Spring St (at Thompson St). 226.4394

91 Bébé Thompson These designer clothes for children include imported handmade cotton and wool outfits that will still be in style long after they have been outgrown. ♦ Daily. 98 Thompson St (between Spring and Prince Sts). 925.1122 ♿

91 Anvers Belgian designer Anne Kegels' sober designs suit busy women who need versatile clothing that can be dressed up or down for the occasion. ♦ Daily. 110 Thompson St (between Spring and Prince Sts). 219.1308

91 Peter Hermann This shop provides the finest handbags, belts, and luggage in the world, mostly from Europe. ♦ Daily. 118 Thompson St (between Spring and Prince Sts). 966.9050

92 Spring Street Garden The always charming window displays show off just a few of the exotica within—unusual varieties of tulips (the French parrot tulip is stupendous), miniature roses, and all sorts of dried flowers. Delivery within Manhattan is available. ♦ Tu-Sa. 186½ Spring St (between Thompson and Sullivan Sts). 966.2015

93 Mezzogiorno ★★$$$ This airy restaurant opens out onto the sidewalk during the warmer months. Highlights include wood-burning–oven pizzas (served at lunchtime and after 9PM) and beef carpaccio offered a variety of ways, although you can't go wrong with such pasta dishes as rigatoni with eggplant and ricotta or black linguine in a spicy tomato sauce. ♦ Italian ♦ Daily lunch, dinner, and late-night meals. No credit cards accepted. 195 Spring St (between Thompson and Sullivan Sts). 334.2112

93 Nick & Eddie ★★$$ This dependable restaurant is a local favorite; the bar starts filling up in late afternoon. The menu is solid American fare—smoked trout salad with a garlicky dressing, and grilled salmon, catfish, and tilapia (a moist, flaky fillet resembling snapper). Go elsewhere, however, for dessert. ♦ American ♦ M-F lunch and dinner; Sa-Su brunch and dinner. Reservations recommended. 203 Spring St (at Sullivan St). 219.9090

94 Blue Ribbon ★★$$$ The kitchen of this bustling spot is open until very late, which is one reason it's a favorite stop for chefs who arrive after their own shifts end. The other incentive is the eclectic menu, featuring such dishes as duck breast with orange sauce and *paella basquez* (with seafood and chicken). The desserts will transport you back to your childhood. ♦ Eclectic ♦ Tu-Su dinner and late-night meals. 97 Sullivan St (between Spring and Prince Sts). 274.0404

94 Melampo Imported Foods All sandwich shops should be like this place. Owner Alessandro Gualandi has elevated sandwich making to an art form: High-quality Italian ingredients sit atop a buttery focaccia. Among the many good choices are Allison (prosciutto, smoked mozzarella, and sweet peppers), Geppetto (*sopressata*—a mild sausage), eggplant *caponata* (cooked with onions, tomatoes, anchovies, olives, pine nuts, capers, and vinegar), and bel paese cheese, and arugula. ♦ M-Sa. 105 Sullivan (between Spring and Prince Sts). 334.9530

95 3 Degrees North $$ Richard Picasso, grandson of the famed artist, and Malaysian Princess Zerafina Idris now preside over this bustling overnight success. Stick to the simple dishes, such as green beans with *belacan* (dried-shrimp sauce) and *ching yue* (steamed whole red snapper with scallions). ♦ Malaysian ♦ Tu-F dinner and late-night meals; Sa-Su brunch, dinner, and late-night meals. Reservations recommended. 210 Spring St (at Sixth Ave). 274.0505

96 Erbe All-natural herbal products from Italy for the face, body, and hair are sold in this intimate shop. A variety of beauty services are available by appointment. ♦ Tu-Sa. 196 Prince St (at Sullivan St). 966.1445

96 Raoul's ★★$$$ This lovely old-fashioned bistro has wood floors, an Art Deco bar, leather booths, and an old stove in the middle of the room. Try the pan-seared foie gras, steak au poivre, and rare breast of duck with figs. The extensive wine list (120 selections) includes French, Italian, Spanish, American, and Australian wines. ♦ French ♦ M-Th, Su dinner; F-Sa dinner and late-night meals. Reservations recommended. 180 Prince St (between Thompson and Sullivan Sts). 966.3518

96 Hans Koch Ltd. Fine belts and handbags are featured in this shop. If nothing suits your fancy, Mr. Koch will whip up something that will. ♦ Daily. 174 Prince St (between Thompson and Sullivan Sts). 226.5385

97 Omen ★★$$ Quiet and attractive, this restaurant with exposed-brick walls, light fixtures wrapped in filmy white fabric, and gleaming dark tables has cultivated a loyal following. The namesake dish, *omen* (Japanese noodles served with a variety of toppings and flavorings), is a perfect introduction to the extensive menu, which includes a tuna steak with ginger, oysters-in-miso casserole, raw tuna with mountain yam and quail egg, yellowtail and string bean teriyaki sautéed with sake, and seafood tempura. ♦ Japanese ♦ Daily dinner. Reservations recommended. 113 Thompson St (between Spring and Prince Sts). 925.8923

97 Peter Fox Shoes All Peter Fox designs, inspired by Victorian and medieval styles, are handmade (except for the stitching of the sole to the leather) in Italy. Bridal customers have included supermodel Paulina Porizkova and model-turned-actress Phoebe Cates. ♦ Daily. 105 Thompson St (between Spring and Prince Sts). 431.6359 ♿

98 Milady ★$ This neighborhood bar is frequented by locals who come for a beer and conversation. The simple entrées include great burgers and salads. ♦ American ♦ Daily lunch and dinner. 162 Prince St (at Thompson St). 226.9340

98 Vesuvio's Bakery A SoHo landmark, this charming storefront has been selling chewy loaves of bread, breadsticks, and immediately addictive pepper biscuits since 1928. ♦ M-Sa. 160 Prince St (between W Broadway and Thompson St). 925.8248

99 The Work Space The law firm of Dolgenos Newman & Cronin maintains this contemporary art exhibition space in the same building as their offices. With the assistance of a professional curator, they show emerging and contemporary art that might not make it into a commercial gallery due to lack of mainstream marketability. ♦ Tu-Sa. 101 Wooster St (between Spring and Prince Sts). 219.2790 &

100 Comme des Garçons Japanese couturier Rei Kawakubo designs fashion-forward clothes under the Comme des Garçons label. She also designed this stark showroom to function as a dramatic setting for her exotic line—a truly minimalist experience. ♦ Daily. 116 Wooster St (between Spring and Prince Sts). 219.0661 &

100 T&K French Antiques Among the direct imports from France are copper bathtubs, ornate bird cages, and fine antique furniture. ♦ Tu-Su. 120 Wooster St (between Spring and Prince Sts). 219.2472

101 130 Prince Street Designed in 1989 by **Lee Manners & Associates,** this new "PoMo" (Post-Modern) building is home to English jewelry designer Stuart Moore's shop of sophisticated *bijoux,* plus a number of art galleries—**Lohring Augustine, Perry Rubenstein, Christine Burgin, Andrea Rosen, Petersberg, Victoria Munroe,** and **Tony Shafrazi**—each of which commissioned its own architect to design the space according to its specifications. ♦ At Wooster St

101 Stuart Moore Visit this jewelry shop if you are in the market for exceptionally well-made (expensive) jewelry in 18K gold or platinum. Custom work is the specialty, and the mark-up on gemstones exceeding $6,000 in cost is only 20 percent—a bargain, if you can afford it. ♦ Daily. 128 Prince St (between Greene and Wooster Sts). 941.1023

Until the late 1700s the western area of what is today called TriBeCa was owned by Trinity Church (Broadway and Wall Street). Its most prominent parishioners, who were probably also those with the most generous wallets, had streets named after them: (John) Chambers, (James) Duane, and (Joseph) Reade.

101 Harriet Love This is the shop that originally made antique clothes fashionable; now it's one of the best in the business of new clothing with a vintage feel. (The owner is the author of *Harriet Love's Guide to Vintage Chic.*) All of the clothes here are vintage-inspired (with the exception of the odd authentic item) mostly from the styles of the 1940s and 1950s. Vintage jewelry and alligator- and crocodile-skin bags are also in stock. ♦ Tu-Su. 126 Prince St (between Greene and Wooster Sts) 966.2280 &

101 Reinstein/Ross This is a shop devoted entirely to the exquisite jewelry created by Susan Reinstein, namely, multicolored sapphires and 22K gold, often alloyed in subtle colors, most of which she has developed herself. ♦ Tu-Su. 122 Prince St (between Greene and Wooster Sts). 226.4513 &. Also at: 29 E 73rd St (between Madison and Fifth Aves). 772.1901

agnès b.

101 agnès b. Classics for men, women, and children—such as V-necked sweaters and cotton T-shirts—are made modern with a twist by this French designer with a loyal following. ♦ Daily. 116-118 Prince St (between Greene and Wooster Sts). 925.4649 &. Also at: 1063 Madison Ave (between E 80th and E 81st Sts). 570.9333

102 David Beitzel Gallery Owner Beitzel's eye is broad-ranging, and he tends to favor emerging artists who work in highly individual idioms. ♦ Tu-Sa. 102 Prince St (at Greene St). 219.2863

102 Annina Nosei Gallery This gallery is a champion of contemporary American and international artists (who come from as far away as Argentina and Zaire). ♦ Tu-Sa. 100 Prince St (between Mercer and Greene Sts). 431.9253

102 Fanelli Cafe $ A holdover from days when this was a neighborhood of factories, this cafe has a gritty, tavernlike atmosphere. The ambience is a greater draw than the generally adequate food—except for the terrific hamburgers and fries. ♦ American ♦ Daily lunch, dinner, and late-night meals. No credit cards accepted. 94 Prince St (at Mercer St). 226.9412

Restaurants/Clubs: Red   Hotels: Blue
Shops/ 🍴 Outdoors: Green   Sights/Culture: Black

103 A Photographer's Place The shop buys and sells photographic books, antiques, and prints. ♦ Daily. 133 Mercer St (between Spring and Prince Sts). 431.9358 &

104 Zoë ★★$$$ The food keeps getting better at this stylish restaurant, where the crowd is a fairly even mix of uptown and downtown types. Don't pass up the *salmon tartare* with chili potato chips and wasabi crème fraîche, grilled loin of lamb with horseradish mashed potatoes, or grilled salmon with Moroccan spices. The marble-top bar is a lovely place to sit and sip one of the many wines available by the glass. ♦ Contemporary American ♦ M-F lunch and dinner; Sa brunch and dinner; Su brunch. Reservations recommended. 90 Prince St (between Broadway and Mercer St). 966.6722 &

105 Little Singer Building In a letter to the *Sun* in 1904, when he designed this 12-story building for the Singer Sewing Machine Co., **Ernest Flagg** said, "I believe tall buildings will shortly become unsafe. As an architect, I will never have anything to do with buildings of this kind." A year later he began work on the big Singer Building, a 41-story, 612-foot tower on Broadway at John Street, which was demolished in 1967, leaving this as a monument to what was lost. ♦ 561-563 Broadway (between Spring and Prince Sts)

106 560 Broadway This is a fine old brick structure that holds its own in a sea of cast-iron neighbors. It was remodeled to house several distinguished art galleries. ♦ At Prince St

Within 560 Broadway:

Dean & DeLuca The ultimate and original high-tech gourmet grocery is housed here in a block-long, 9,700-square-foot space. Added bonuses: a coffee/espresso bar, butcher, fish counter, and a full range of prepared take-out dishes. This place is a must for anyone passionate about food. ♦ Daily. Ground floor. 431.1691

Max Protetch Gallery The primary commercial outlet in New York for drawings by such distinguished architects as **Louis I. Kahn, Frank Lloyd Wright, Michael Graves, Aldo Rossi,** and **Rem Koolhaas,** the gallery also exhibits painting, ceramics, and sculpture. It's well worth a visit to these spacious quarters. ♦ Tu-Sa. Second floor. 966.5454 &

Salvatore Ala It's worth a trip up to this gallery that shows American, British, and European artists, with an emphasis on sculpture. ♦ Tu-Sa. Third floor. 941.1990 &

106 Duggal Downtown Professional photographers in the neighborhood come to this extension of the West 20th Street branch for their film and processing needs. It's a huge space with a continually changing photography exhibition along the right-hand wall and windows through which you can watch the technicians work. ♦ M-Sa. 560 Broadway (between Spring and Prince Sts). 941.7000. Also at: 9 W 20th St (between Fifth and Sixth Aves). 924.7777

106 Zero This is a showroom for the eponymous Italian high-tech modular display system. ♦ By appointment only. 560 Broadway (between Spring and Prince Sts). 925.3615

107 Savoy ★★$$$ This small, cozy place with a working fireplace features an eclectic menu that follows the seasons. During the winter months the menu offers such dishes as red Maine shrimp seviche with fennel, served with a salad of rice, beans, and green olives; and the signature dish, salt-crusted baked duck with walnut-pomegranate sauce. The chocolate-hazelnut ganache (iced) torte is an often-repeated standout. ♦ Continental ♦ M-Sa lunch and dinner; Su dinner. Reservations recommended. 70 Prince St (at Crosby St). 219.8570

108 280 Modern Decorative arts are this gallery's draw, with an emphasis on designer furniture from the 1920s to the 1960s. There is also a small selection of original works by the late Piero Fornasetti of Milan. ♦ M-Sa; Su by appointment. 280 Lafayette St (between Prince and E Houston Sts). 941.5825 &

108 Secondhand Rose Antiques dealer Suzanne Lipshutz (a.k.a. Secondhand Rose) fills 5,000 square feet with treasures from the late 1800s to the 1970s. Her impressive stock ranges from custom-made leather furniture to antique wallpaper and linoleum. ♦ M-F; by appointment only Saturday and Sunday. 270 Lafayette St (at Prince St). 431.7673 &

109 568-578 Broadway A boon for art lovers is the proliferation of gallery clusters in fine old Broadway buildings, making life easy for the browser, rain or shine. This dual-entry structure now houses so many galleries that it has been dubbed **The Mall** by art world locals. ♦ Between Prince and E Houston Sts

Within 568-578 Broadway:

Castelli Graphics Prints, drawings, and photographs by many of the artists represented by **Leo Castelli Gallery** (Roy Lichtenstein and Jasper Johns, for example) can be viewed, as well as works by artists from their own stable, such as Robert Cumming. ♦ Tu-Sa. 578 Broadway, Third floor. 941.9855 &

Curt Marcus Gallery Contemporary American and European artists in all mediums are exhibited here. ♦ Tu-Sa. 578 Broadway, 10th floor. 226.3200 &

109 Academy of American Poets For more than half a century this little-known academy has been the city's—and the nation's—headquarters for American poets. It sponsors an annual grant to assist American poets at all stages of their careers, and organizes a Poetry Reading Series at points around the city to further public interest and recognition. Since the society's beginning in 1934, events have centered around such literary lights as Manhattan-born Walt Whitman. Call or write for a reading schedule. ♦ M-F. 584 Broadway (between Prince and E Houston Sts), Suite 1208. 274.0343 &

109 Stark Gallery Current works by contemporary American and European artists are exhibited at this gallery, which features avant-garde abstractionists. ♦ Tu-Sa. 594 Broadway (between Prince and E Houston Sts). 925.4484 &

109 Alternative Museum Two spacious galleries house a museum founded and operated by well-known artists for unrecognized artists. Poetry readings and concerts—folk, jazz, traditional—take place, with the emphasis on the international and unusual. ♦ Donation suggested. Tu-Sa. 594 Broadway (between Prince and E Houston Sts). 966.4444 &

110 The Cockpit Recreations of the vintage goatskin and horsehair jackets preferred by daring young men in their flying machines are available here along with what the store calls "current issue." Everything to do with flying—from B-17 flight bags and shorts made from Flying Tigers briefing maps, to books, watches, patches, gloves, and boots—is here. ♦ Daily. 595 Broadway (between Prince and W Houston Sts). 925.5455, 800/354.5514 &

110 Museum for African Art This vibrant museum is one of only two in the country specializing in sub-Saharan art (the other is part of the Smithsonian). Painted wooden masks, life-size carved figures, vivid textiles, and architectural sculptures all contribute to the complex and interesting rotating exhibits mounted by founder/director Susan Vogel. Behind an 1860s cast-iron facade, **Maya Lin** designed the striking galleries, which opened in 1993. (As the **Center for African Art,** the museum was on East 68th Street for a decade before moving to these expanded quarters.) The museum gift store is an interesting stop in itself. ♦ Donation suggested. Museum: T-F. Gift store: M-F. 593 Broadway (between Prince and W Houston Sts). 966.1313 &

TheNewMuseum
OF CONTEMPORARY ART

110 The New Museum of Contemporary Art Founder/director Marcia Tucker is the force behind this unique institution. She not only shows artists who have trouble getting a foot in the museum establishment's door, but shows all aspects of their work. ♦ Donation requested. W-Su. 583 Broadway (between Prince and W Houston Sts). 219.1222 &

111 Guggenheim Museum SoHo Further enhancing this area's status as a mecca for contemporary art lovers is the new downtown branch of the uptown museum with one of the world's preeminent collections of modern and contemporary art. Within a landmark 19th-century loft building, architect **Arata Isozaki** designed the 30,000 square feet of galleries, which opened in 1992. The six-story brick structure, with its cast-iron storefronts and detailed cornice, was designed in 1881 by **Thomas Stent** for John Jacob Astor III, and in its early days housed garment manufacturers and stores. Inside, the flexible and modern exhibit spaces retain the original cast-iron columns. The **Guggenheim Museum Store** is definitely worth a visit. ♦ Donation requested. M, W-Su. Store hours: daily. 575 Broadway (at Prince St). 423.3878

At the Guggenheim Museum SoHo:

T ★$$ The airy space is whimsically decorated with chandeliers made of bronze teapots and cups, and tables of unusual colorful canisters of teas. Most items on the menu have tea as an ingredient, although some stretch the point. ♦ American ♦ M-Sa lunch and dinner; Su brunch and dinner. Reservations recommended. 142 Mercer St (at Prince St). 925.3700

111 Match ★$$ The decor is serious SoHo—wood walls, green banquettes, blown-glass light fixtures, smashed-metal sculptures—and the food is a fusion of Asian and Southwest cuisines. There's a good, fairly extensive sushi list as well, including the elegantly wrapped Match roll (shrimp, cucumber, and eel). And the sampler dessert has everything from chocolate cake to lemon tart. ♦ Fusion ♦ M-F lunch, dinner, and late-night meals; Sa-Su brunch, dinner, and late-night meals. Reservations required. 160 Mercer St (between Prince and W Houston Sts). 343.0020

112 Tansuya Corporation The Japanese word *tansu* means cabinet, and you can have one custom-made and lacquered here. They also build modern and traditional Japanese-style furniture, trays, and lacquered boxes; each piece is an original. ♦ Tu-Su. 159 Mercer St (between Prince and W Houston Sts). 966.1782

112 Distant Origin A clone of the incomparable **Zona** around the corner on Wooster Street, this shop stocks an impressive selection of Southwestern paintings, pillows, pottery, and furniture. ♦ Tu-Su. 153 Mercer St (between Prince and W Houston Sts). 941.0025

112 After the Rain The sister store of **The Enchanted Forest,** this is a grown-up's fantasy of kaleidoscopes, art glass, tapestries, and handmade jewelry. ♦ Daily. 149 Mercer St (between Prince and W Houston Sts). 431.1045 ♿

113 Jerry's ★$$ This is a bustling lunch spot for SoHo's working population, especially the gallery crowd (Jerry used to own the frame shop down the street). Fresh salads, sandwiches, and daily soups are served. The dinnertime tempo is considerably slower, but brunch can be madness. ♦ American ♦ M-F breakfast, lunch, and dinner; Sa brunch and dinner; Su brunch. 101 Prince St (between Mercer and Greene Sts). 966.9464. Also at: 302 Columbus Ave (between W 74th and W 75th Sts). 501.7500

113 Edward Thorp Gallery Owner Thorp's affinity for landscape painting with a twist is clear in the work of artist April Gornik. He also represents Deborah Butterfield, who sculpts horses out of found objects. ♦ Tu-Sa. 103 Prince St (between Mercer and Greene Sts). 431.6880

114 Phyllis Kind Gallery An eclectic collection of contemporary paintings and "outsider" art by American and international artists is shown. ♦ Tu-Sa. 136 Greene St (between Prince and W Houston Sts). 925.1200

114 John Weber A longtime art world fixture, Weber has supplemented his distinguished roster of minimal and conceptual artists, including Sol LeWitt and the estate of Robert Smithson, with some bright new—and offbeat—talent. ♦ Tu-Sa. 142 Greene St (between Prince and W Houston Sts), Third floor. 966.6115 ♿

114 Sperone Westwater The New York home to many of Italy's most innovative artists, including Mario Merz, "the three C's" (Sandro Chia, Francesco Clemente, Enzo Cucchi), and Susan Kothenberg, this gallery also boasts an impressive roster of other European and American talents. ♦ Tu-Sa. 142 Greene St (between Prince and W Houston Sts), Second floor. 431.3685. Also at: 121 Greene St (between Prince and W Houston Sts). 431.3685 ♿

114 The Pace Gallery The downtown branch of the blue-chip gallery is located in a vast space that provides a dramatic backdrop for large-scale paintings and sculpture. ♦ Tu-Sa. 142 Greene St (between Prince and W Houston Sts), Ground floor. 431.9224. Also at: 32 E 57th St (between Park and Madison Aves). 421.3292

114 Metro Pictures Along with an odd, somewhat dated assortment of painters and photographers, this gallery is home to the many-guised self-portraitist Cindy Sherman, one of the 1980s' true originals. ♦ Tu-Sa. 150 Greene St (between Prince and W Houston Sts). 925.8335 ♿

115 Back Pages Antiques An impressive collection of classic Wurlitzer jukeboxes, working slot machines, Coca-Cola vending machines, Seeburg nickelodeons, pool tables, and advertising signs is available here. If you need to furnish a party room, look no farther. ♦ M-Sa; call for Sunday hours. 125 Greene St (between Prince and W Houston Sts). 460.5998

115 Kelley and Ping ★★$ The atmosphere is pure Southeast Asian noodle shop and an open kitchen that allows a full view of the chef at work. Try *yam woosen* (clear noodles with chicken, shrimp, scallions, and red onion), Malaysian curried noodles, or lemongrass chicken. Serious cooks and kitchen dabblers may want to select ingredients to take home from the restaurant's display cases. ♦ Asian ♦ Daily lunch and dinner. 127 Greene St (between Prince and W Houston Sts). 228.1212

116 Whole Foods A full selection of every-thing you need for a sound body and soul is available here: vitamins, grains, fresh fish, organic vegetables, kosher chicken and turkeys, cosmetics, and an impressive assortment of books to tell you what you should be doing with all these things. ♦ Daily. 117 Prince St (between Greene and Wooster Sts). 982.1000

116 Dean & DeLuca Cafe ★$ Run by the people who manage the gourmet food emporium of the same name, it's a good place to come on Sunday morning to read the paper—thoughtfully provided—sip a cappuccino, and munch on pastry. The salads are good too. ♦ Cafe ♦ Daily breakfast, lunch, and early dinner. 121 Prince St (between Greene and Wooster Sts). 254.8776. Also at: 75 University Pl (at 11th St). 473.1908 &; One Rockefeller Plaza (at W 49th St). 664.1363 &

116 Prince Street Bar & Restaurant ★$ The faithful clientele come as much for the lively bar scene as for the fairly standard burgers, salads, and sandwiches. On a more interesting note, there are also Indonesian specialties, including *gado gado* salad (with peanut sauce and shrimp chips), spicy shrimp *jakarta* (jumbo shrimp with brown rice and broccoli), and beef *rendang*. ♦ Eclectic ♦ M-Sa lunch and dinner; Su brunch and dinner. 125 Prince St (at Wooster St). 228.8130

117 Paula Cooper Gallery A SoHo pioneer nearly two decades ago, owner Cooper has built a stable of remarkable winners, including Jennifer Bartlett, Jonathan Borofsky, and Elizabeth Murray. ♦ Tu-Sa. 155 Wooster St (between Prince and W Houston Sts). 674.0766 &

117 147 Wooster Street Designed in 1876 by Jarvis Morgan Slade, the arched storefront decorated with bands of fleur-de-lis and other floral motifs is all hand-carved in marble. Only the cornice is iron. ♦ Between Prince and W Houston Sts

117 Dia Center for the Arts For over 20 years, Dia (from the Greek word meaning "through") has played a vital role among art institutions both locally and internationally by producing projects in every artistic medium. Three locations (two in SoHo, the third in Chelsea) present pop, minimal, and conceptual. ♦ Donation suggested. W-Su. 141 Wooster St (between Prince and W Houston Sts). 473.8072. Also at: 393 W Broadway (between Broome and Spring Sts). 925.9397; 548 W 22nd St (between 10th and 11th Aves). 989.5912

118 Casa La Femme ★$$ SoHo's version of the Casbah, this romantic place resembles a Moroccan desert oasis at night, right down to the white tents around the banquettes for privacy. There's a decent menu including *harira* (tomato, chickpea, and lentil soup); grilled octopus; and lamb salad with dates, oranges, pine nuts, and *frisée* (curly endive). ♦ Eclectic ♦ Daily dinner. Reservations recommended. 150 Wooster St (between Prince and W Houston Sts). 505.0005 &

119 Susan P. Meisel Decorative Arts Twentieth-century decorative arts are exhibited here, including hand-painted English pottery created by Clarice Cliff between 1928 and 1938, 1950s Mexican sterling silver jewelry, and vintage watches. ♦ Tu-Sa. 133 Prince St (between Wooster St and W Broadway). 254.0137 &

119 Louis K. Meisel Owner Meisel championed the photo-realists back in the 1970s and has stuck to his convictions despite the art world's ever-changing tides. ♦ Tu-Sa. 141 Prince St (between Wooster St and W Broadway). 677.1340 &

120 SoHo Wine & Spirits Welcome to what may very well be the most civilized, not to mention the best-stocked, small wine store in town. But there is no wine snobbery in this well-organized, well-designed outlet, which also carries the world's great spirits, including the most extensive choice of single-malt Scotch whiskies in the city. ♦ M-Sa. 461 W Broadway (between Prince and W Houston Sts). 777.4332 &

120 Yoshi The latest fashions from an international set of young designers, including Faycolamor from France, Gemmakahng from New York, and Englishman Jasper Conran, are featured in this store. To top it off there's a particularly wonderful selection of *chapeaux*. ♦ Daily 11AM-8PM. 461 W Broadway (between Prince and W Houston Sts). 979.0569

120 I Tre Merli ★$$$ The exposed brick walls and high ceiling give this Italian restaurant and wine bar a quiet charm. Though the service can be inattentive, the food—especially the raw artichoke salad and the pasta—is quite good. During the summer, the tables spill out onto West Broadway. ♦ Italian ♦ M-F lunch, dinner, and late-night meals; Sa-Su brunch, dinner, and late-night meals. Reservations recommended. 463 W Broadway (between Prince and W Houston Sts). 254.8699. Also at (for lunch only): 725 Fifth Ave (between E 56th and E 57th Sts). 832.1555

121 Amici Miei ★$$$ Another SoHo venue at which to eat and be seen, this place features a wood-burning oven that turns out good pizza, focaccia, and grilled shrimp. The pastas are popular, particularly the gnocchi, spaghetti with Manila clams, and homemade black squid-ink pasta with spicy tomato sauce. ♦ Northern Italian ♦ M-F lunch and dinner; Sa-Su brunch and dinner. 475 W Broadway (at W Houston St). 533.1933

122 Can ★$$ Stylish presentations of French-Vietnamese fare are served at this attractive restaurant, designed by Japanese architect Stomu Miyacaki to resemble an art gallery. There are two levels—downstairs is the bar area, and upstairs a skylit dining room—as well as an interesting series of "water paintings," which are also the work of the architect. Try the Vietnamese pâté, barbecued beef in vine leaves, lemongrass duck, grilled stuffed squid with pork, and Vietnamese curried chicken. ♦ French/Vietnamese ♦ Daily lunch and dinner. Reservations recommended for dinner. 482 W Broadway (at W Houston St). 533.6333

122 If Boutique You can buy clothes by such popular designers as Xuly Bet, Martin Margiela, and Moschino, as well as terrific belts, shoes, and jewelry at this shop. If it's happenin', you'll find it here. ♦ Daily. 474 W Broadway (at W Houston St). 533.8660 ♿

122 Rizzoli Bookstore of SoHo Though half the space of its uptown location, this shop is worth a stop to peruse one of the best selections of fine art books, foreign magazines, and music recordings in the city. ♦ M-Th 11AM-11PM; F-Sa 11AM-midnight; Su noon-8PM. 454 W Broadway (between Prince and W Houston Sts). 674.1677. Also at: 3 World Financial Center, Winter Garden Atrium. 385.1400; 31 W 57th St (between 5th and 6th Aves). 759.2424

122 Claiborne Gallery Leslie Cozart specializes in Mexican furniture, mostly from the 19th century, plus a line of iron furniture designed by her father, Omer Claiborne. ♦ Tu-Su. 452 W Broadway (between Prince and W Houston Sts). 475.3072

123 Untitled This tiny wedge of a store sells all sorts of art and photography postcards, wrapping and note papers, calendars, and a small selection of books and periodicals. ♦ Daily. 159 Prince St (between W Broadway and Thompson St). 982.2088

124 Betsey Johnson For more than two decades, designer Johnson's fashion statements have been providing the youthful with a statement of their own. ♦ Daily. 130 Thompson St (between Prince and W Houston Sts). 420.0169. Also at: 251 E 60th St (between Third and Lexington Aves). 319.7699; 1060 Madison Ave (at E 80th St). 734.1257; 248 Columbus Ave (between W 71st and W 72nd St). 362.3364 ♿

124 Eileen Lane Antiques Scandinavian, Biedermeier, and Art Deco furniture and lighting are the specialty of this antiques shop. ♦ Daily. 150 Thompson St (between Prince and W Houston Sts). 475.2988

125 Arturo's Pizzeria ★$ Some say the crowd here is an overflow from **John's Pizzeria** a few blocks away, while others argue that this place is better. Although the quintessential-pizza-experience debate rages endlessly on, it's safe to say that both places turn out some of the city's best brick-oven, thin-crust pies. However, if you want live jazz, come here any

night after 8PM. ♦ Pizza ♦ Daily lunch, dinner, and late-night meals. 106 W Houston St (at Thompson St). 677.3820

126 Opal White Edwardian and Victorian clothing, including a wide selection of antique wedding dresses, are for sale at this shop. ♦ W-Su by appointment only. 131 Thompson St (between Prince and W Houston Sts). 677.8215

127 Depression Modern Owner Michael Smith likes to redecorate his shop, and does so every Saturday with the Moderne furniture of the 1930s and 1940s that he spends the rest of the week restoring to its original condition. ♦ W-Su. 150 Sullivan St (between Prince and W Houston Sts). 982.5699 ♿

127 Joe's Dairy Today, only about three storefronts remain of the old Italian-American enclave along Thompson and Sullivan Streets. This store, with its checkered tile floor and sweating glass cases, is one of them. *Parmigiano reggiano* is hewn from fragrant wheels, and sweet ricotta is drawn from moist, cool places. A few times a week intense acrid smoke pours from the basement door when *mozzarella afumicato* (smoked) is being made. ♦ Tu-Sa; call ahead for weekend hours. 156 Sullivan St (between Prince and W Houston Sts). 677.8780 ♿

128 Cub Room ★$$$ The bar scene is primeval, especially on weekends, but entirely another world exists in the handsome wood-and-brick dining room in the back—sophisticated and suave, but friendly. Chef Henry Meer's selections include lobster salad with mango, duck confit, baby beets, and grilled onion; roasted quail with French lentils; fillet of black bass with onion confit, mushrooms, and *pommes Anna* (potato chips layered and pressed into a scallop-shaped garnish); and the mission-fig *tarte tatin*. ♦ American ♦ M-F dinner; Sa-Su lunch and dinner. Reservations required. 131 Sullivan St (between Prince and W Houston Sts). 677.4100 ♿

FRONTIÈRE

129 Frontiere ★★$$$ Old-fashioned stone walls, a fireplace, and intimate lighting add up to an inviting experience. The food is sophisticated but earthy; try the terrine of duck made with foie gras, prunes, and Armagnac; and bowtie pasta with fresh seafood in garlic and saffron broth. ♦ French/Italian ♦ M-Sa lunch and dinner. Reservations recommended. 199 Prince St (between Sullivan and MacDougal Sts). 387.0898

Restaurants/Clubs: Red   **Hotels:** Blue
Shops/ ♥ Outdoors: Green   **Sights/Culture:** Black

PROVENCE

130 Provence ★★★$$ From its rustic wooden front painted slate-blue to its charming garden in back, Michel and Patricia Jean's Provençal bistro has a lot to recommend it: a simple but warm dining room, creamy and potent fish soup or *pissaladière* (a heady onion tart), roasted chicken in garlic, a perfectly charred crème brûlée, and, of course, French waiters. ◆ French ◆ Daily lunch and dinner. Reservations required. 38 MacDougal St (at Prince St). 475.7500

131 Brother's Bar-B-Q ★$ A funky dive loved for its down-home Southern grub, this place runs a close second to Harlem's well-known, more expensive, and somewhat more authentic **Sylvia's.** Come for heaping portions of tangy ribs, and barbecued chicken smoked over hickory wood for 10 hours. Monday is All-You-Can-Eat BBQ Night. ◆ Barbecue ◆ M-Th, Su lunch and dinner; F-Sa lunch, dinner, and late-night meals. 225 W Houston St (between Sixth Ave and Varick St). 727.2775

132 S.O.B.'s Sounds of Brazil ★★$$ Specializing in Bahian and other Brazilian food, this casual restaurant becomes a late-evening showcase for salsa, samba, reggae, and whatever else is currently being imported from the Caribbean, South America, and Africa. The *caipirinha* (a sweet and sour Brazilian cocktail) keeps them coming back. ◆ Brazilian ◆ Cover. M-Sa lunch, dinner, and late-night meals. Reservations required for dinner. 204 Varick St (at W Houston St). 243.4940

133 375 Hudson Street Say the word "advertising" and Madison Avenue naturally comes to mind. But many advertising agencies have recently relocated downtown, including Saatchi & Saatchi, the world's largest advertising agency holding company, which occupies this building. Most of its neighbors are printing companies. ◆ At W Houston St

Bests

Charles Gwathmey
Architect

A helicopter ride crossing Manhattan from river to river, from the **George Washington Bridge** to the **Verrazano-Narrows Bridge.** A boat ride around Manhattan. A run around **Central Park,** the only major outdoor space in the city.

A walk through **SoHo** and **TriBeCa, Wall Street** and **Lower Manhattan,** and **Madison** and **Fifth Avenues** from 90th Street down to 42nd Street.

The Frick Collection and **The Cloisters** are still the most civilized museums.

Stay at **Morgans** hotel.

A visit to the **International Design Center (IDC/NY)** to see the furniture showrooms and the architecture, and when in Queens, the **American Museum of the Moving Image.** Finally, see Frank Lloyd Wright's **Solomon R. Guggenheim Museum.**

Patricia Jean
Restaurant Owner, Provence

The Frick Collection. Because it feels grand and special, and I can never walk by without going in.

The **Union Square Greenmarket,** where the city and country really meet. Because it's really seasonal produce from the region. Because you can't beat the bread from **Boiceville** or the tomatoes from Long Island (no, not New Jersey).

Horseback riding in **Central Park,** ice-skating at **Rockefeller Center,** and looking up at the buildings around and feeling a sense of solitude.

Florent for onion soup and tripe at two in the morning. As close as you get to Paris without losing New York.

The food stores, especially **Dean & DeLuca** and **Jefferson Market.**

SoHo's streets before the stores and galleries open. It has the best neighborhood feeling in all New York, and it all changes after noon.

Dinner at the **River Café** at sunset because there's not a more beautiful and edifying view around!

Saturday afternoon gallery-hopping.

The flowers everywhere, but especially at the market on **West 28th Street.**

The feeling that anything is possible (it comes and goes, but I've only felt this in New York).

Merce Cunningham
Artistic Director, Merce Cunningham Dance Company

The **Union Square Greenmarket** on any market day, but particularly in the late spring through fall when the fresh produce and flowers and people are at their best. Beware the pickpockets, the signs say.

The vision of a large cruise ship through the windows of **Westbeth,** making a stately, steady progress down the **Hudson** to the open sea, when I am teaching a class of dancers. The ship's rhythm and movement is a delicious addition, however brief, to the bustle of the class, particularly in late afternoon, with the rays of the polluted sunset over New Jersey.

Being in the theater, backstage or out front, just before the curtain goes up.

Greenwich Village

Radical and old guard, quaint and glitzy, authentic and ersatz, Greenwich Village is anything but a homogenous neighborhood. Bounded by the **Hudson River, Broadway,** and **Houston and 14th Streets,** the birthplace of the bohemian spirit is home to students of **New York University (NYU),** actors in Off-Broadway theaters, jazz musicians, and an assortment of other residents who work uptown. The Village arouses fanatical loyalty in its residents, who fight among themselves about social and political issues of the day, but also fight to maintain the human scale and history of their neighborhood.

Greenwich Village's eccentric personality starts with the layout. In the 1790s, the area's country estates were sold off in lots or subdivided and developed by large landholders. Weavers, sailmakers, and craftspeople moved into rows of modest homes along streets that followed the boundaries of the old estates and travelers' paths. Later, when a grid was established for new streets in

Manhattan, it was too late to change the Village's crazy maze of thoroughfares; newly numbered streets mingled with those originally named for political personalities and affluent landowners.

New Yorkers fleeing epidemics of smallpox, yellow fever, and cholera that ravaged the city in the 1790s and early 1800s settled in Greenwich Village, which was far removed from the congested city center. Hastily built houses and hotels arose to accommodate the newcomers. **Bank Street** is named for **Wall Street** banks that opened here along with other commercial ventures during the severe epidemic of 1822.

In the 1830s, prominent families began to build town houses at **Washington Square**, which had become a public park in 1828. New York society took over **Fifth Avenue** and the side streets from **University Place** to **Sixth Avenue** (more formally known as "Avenue of the Americas"). But the fashionable Washington Square elite soon gravitated to **Gramercy Park, Madison Square,** and upper Fifth Avenue, so that by the late 1850s the Village had turned into a quiet backwater of middle-class, old-line Anglo-Dutch families. Warehouses and industrial plants proliferated along the Hudson River, and commercial development began to the east and north. But the Village always retained its residential character. In the 1880s and 1890s, Irish and Chinese immigrants moved in, while Italians populated the tenements built south of Washington Square.

Houses from all periods coexist in the Village, but only one of the many brownstones survives; they once lined Fifth Avenue from Washington Square to **Central Park** in what was called "Two Miles of Millionaires." One of the first brownstone mansions designed in the Italianate style, it was built in 1853 at 47 Fifth Avenue for Irad Hawley, president of the Pennsylvania Coal Company. The **Salmagundi Club,** the city's oldest club for art and artists (founded in 1870), moved into the brownstone in 1917, and still opens its doors for exhibitions from time to time.

As the high rollers moved out, their large houses were divided into flats and studios and their stables into homes. The cheap rents appealed to such writers as Edgar Allan Poe, Horace Greeley, Walt Whitman, Mark Twain, and

ION SQUARE/GRAMERCY/MURRAY HILL

Edna St. Vincent Millay, who at one time occupied the narrowest house in the city at 75½ **Bedford Street.** Such artists as Albert Bierstadt, Frederic Edwin Church, John Frederick Kensett, and John La Farge of the Hudson River School; Impressionists Ernest Lawson and Robert Henri; and painters William James Glackens, John French Sloan, and Edward Hopper of the early 20th-century Ashcan School moved to Greenwich Village, which established itself as the seat of bohemia in the United States before World War I.

After the war, the Village continued to be a magnet for those looking for sexual freedom, radicalism, and revolt in politics and the arts. Upton Sinclair founded the Liberal Club on **MacDougal Street;** the **Washington Square Players** (later renamed the **Theater Guild**) emerged in 1917; and the following year, the **Provincetown Players,** the company that gave Eugene O'Neill his first chance, opened in the Village (the company still puts on plays at the **Provincetown Playhouse** on MacDougal Street).

Sharing the Village's streets with bohemians in the 1930s were families who had been here for generations, white-collar workers, and Irish and Italian blue-collar workers. After World War II, the Beat generation and then the hippies in the 1960s discovered the Village, as did entrepreneurs and developers. Although residents have fought hard to keep the community the way it was, apartment houses and high-rises have made inroads. Some of the development, such as **Westbeth,** a Bell Telephone Laboratories building recycled as housing for artists, has been architecturally sensitive. One of the Village's largest landowners, Sailors' Snug Harbor, however, has been criticized for some of the decisions it has made for its 21 acres of leased land near Washington Square. In 1801, Captain Robert Richard Randall deeded this land and a small cash gift for the purpose of establishing a home for retired seamen (now located in North Carolina, and financed by the returns on the Greenwich Village holdings). Trinity Parish, the other large landowner with deeds from the same period, is usually given high marks for helping to maintain the ambience of the Village.

Today, every style of 18th- and 19th-century architecture, culture, and history intermingle in Greenwich Village, from the gracious classical houses on the north side of Washington Square, where writers Henry James and Edith Wharton lived, to converted stables in **MacDougal Alley** behind them, where in the 1900s sculptors Jo Davidson and Gertrude Vanderbilt Whitney and actor Richard Bennett occupied houses. **Judson Memorial,** a square-towered church designed in the Romanesque style by **McKim, Mead & White,** is as well known for its experimental theater productions as for its historical or architectural value. NYU now has colleges and schools at its Washington Square campus. **The New School for Social Research,** America's first university for adults, is still championing social causes and offering a dazzling variety of night-school courses. In 1970, the **New School** and **Parsons School of Design** formed a partnership that broadened the excellent curriculum of both schools.

History is everywhere—in such places as the **Minetta Tavern** on MacDougal Street, filled with photos and memorabilia from earlier days, and the **Cedar Tavern** on University Place, where Abstract Expressionists Jackson Pollock, Franz Kline, and Larry Rivers used to hang out. At the **Gansevoort Market,** the city's wholesale meat market, you can imagine what the area was like when Herman Melville worked as a customs inspector for 19 years at what was then the **Gansevoort Dock.**

1 Cafe Español $$ Spanish cuisine—chicken or lobster with garlic sauce, and paella—is served in an authentic Catalan atmosphere, dominated by a mural of Spanish villages. Dining options include a skylit room in back and a small patio outdoors in warmer weather. ♦ Spanish ♦ Daily lunch and dinner. 63 Carmine St (at Seventh Ave S). 675.3312. Also at: 172 Bleecker St (between Sullivan and MacDougal Sts). 505.0657

2 Cent' Anni ★$$$ The food can be inconsistent, but when the kitchen is performing well you can get a very good meal in this casual, friendly, Tuscan-style trattoria. The menu features an extraordinary minestrone, a few outstanding pasta dishes—try penne with sun-dried tomatoes and fettuccine with rabbit. Also good is the snapper roasted in garlic and oil, and the huge porterhouse steak. ♦ Italian ♦ M-F lunch and dinner; Sa-Su dinner. Reservations recommended. 50 Carmine St (between Bedford and Bleecker Sts). 989.9494 &

2 Tutta Pasta Ristorante ★$ An outgrowth of the store next door, this cafe serves its freshly made pasta and sauces with above-average results. Linguine with white clam sauce, gnocchi with pesto, and meat-filled tortellini in a *bolognese* sauce are especially recommended. Meat, chicken, and fish dishes are also available, but it's best to stick with the pasta and the thin-crust, brick-oven pizzas. ♦ Italian ♦ Daily lunch and dinner. 26 Carmine St (between Bedford and Bleecker Sts). 463.9653. Also at: 504 La Guardia Pl (between Houston and Bleecker Sts). 420.0652; 160 Seventh Ave (between Garfield and First Sts, Brooklyn). 718/788.9500; 8901 Third Ave (between 89th and 90th Sts, Brooklyn). 718/238.6066; 108-22 Queens Blvd (between 71st and 72nd Sts, Queens). 261.8713

"I should have been born in New York, I should have been born in the Village, that's where I belong."

John Lennon

3 House of Oldies Here is an incredible collection of rare and out-of-circulation rock 'n' roll and R&B LPs, including 10,000 rock 'n' roll 78s and over a million 45s. Additional stock is sent up from the basement via a dumbwaiter. ♦ M-Sa. 35 Carmine St (between Sixth Ave and Seventh Ave S). 243.0500

3 Church of Our Lady of Pompeii The gilded marble interior of this 1927 church designed by **Matthew Del Gaudio** convinces you this structure might have been moved intact from the hills of Italy. Some services are still conducted in Italian. ♦ 25 Carmine St (between Sixth Ave and Seventh Ave S). 989.6805

4 Marys ★$ A slanting 1820 town house is the setting for this restaurant, where such specialties as curried monkfish with blackened fennel and corn salsa top the menu. ♦ American ♦ M-F lunch and dinner; Sa dinner; Su brunch and dinner. 42 Bedford St (between Leroy St and Seventh Ave S). 741.3387

5 New York Public Library, Hudson Park Branch The original 1905 building by **Carrère & Hastings**, who also designed the main branch up on Fifth Avenue, was expanded in 1935. The library's **Early Childhood Family Center**, a facility for small children and their parents, is located here, as is the **Resource and Information Center** for parents, teachers, and caregivers; call for their special hours. ♦ M-Tu, F 1-6PM; W 10AM-6PM; Th 1-8PM. 66 Leroy St (between Seventh Ave S and Hudson St). 243.6876

6 Anglers & Writers ★$ Literary Paris of the 1930s is recaptured in this cozy, unpretentious cafe/tearoom owned by mother-and-son team Charlotte and Craig Bero. It's filled with charmingly mismatched English and Austrian china, turn-of-the-century American country furniture, and shelf after shelf of books—with an emphasis on Hemingway, Fitzgerald, and fly-fishing guides. The food is hearty and all-American; there's old-fashioned lamb stew, open-face roast turkey sandwiches, and an assortment of sensational pies. ♦ American ♦ Daily breakfast, lunch, and dinner. 420 Hudson St (at St. Luke's Pl). 675.0810

7 Village Atelier ★$$$ The farmhouse setting is an appropriate backdrop for the well-prepared American food served here. Try the roast stuffed boneless quail with montmorency cherry and brandy sauce, or fruitwood grilled tuna with spicy salsa. ♦ American ♦ M-F lunch and dinner; Sa dinner. Reservations required. 436 Hudson St (at Morton St). 989.1363 &

8 75½ Bedford Street Built in 1873, this 9.5-foot-wide building is thought to be the narrowest in the city, and was the last New York City residence of Edna St. Vincent Millay and her husband, Eugen Boissevain. **No. 77** next door, built in 1800, is the oldest house in the Village. ♦ At Commerce St

8 Cherry Lane Theater Built as a brewery in 1846, this building was converted to a 184-seat theater (founded in 1924 by Edna St. Vincent Millay) for avant-garde productions. *Godspell* had its world premiere here. ♦ 38 Commerce St (between Bedford and Barrow Sts). 989.2020

8 The Grange Hall ★$ This raucous, Generation X scene (site of the former **Blue Mill Tavern**) is popular for farm-fresh food at reasonable prices. Grazers can choose from a large variety of vegetable and grain dishes, such as warm gingered beets with raisins, available in appetizer sizes. Main courses include herb-crusted organic chicken breast with honey-glazed carrots, grilled lambsteak with rosemary red cabbage, and a platter of oven-roasted seasonal farm vegetables. ♦ American ♦ M-F lunch and dinner; Sa, Su brunch and dinner. 50 Commerce St (between Bedford and Barrow Sts). 924.5246

9 39 and 41 Commerce Street This well-preserved pair of mansard-roofed houses with a central garden dates to 1831. An apocryphal but oft-repeated tale is that they were built by a sea captain for his two unmarried daughters, who were not on speaking terms. ♦ Between Bedford and Barrow Sts

10 St. Luke-in-the-Fields James N. Wells designed this simple Federal-style building in 1822. Restored after a 1981 fire, it still has the feeling of a country church. St. Luke's School, one of the city's most highly respected Episcopal parochial schools, was established in 1945. The thrift store next door is a tad more expensive than you'd expect, but it's well stocked. ♦ 487 Hudson St (between Barrow and Christopher Sts). 924.0562

11 Grove Court Between 10 and 12 Grove Street, at the middle of what some consider to be the most authentic group of Federal-style houses in America, you can find one of the most charming and private enclaves in Manhattan. These six brick-fronted buildings were built in 1854 as houses for working men when the court was known as "Mixed Ale Alley." ♦ Between Bedford and Hudson Sts

12 Chumleys $$ A speakeasy during the 1920s, this anonymous, signless building has a convenient back door on Barrow Street that's still used by insiders. Cozy and convivial, with working fireplaces and wooden benches deeply carved with customers' initials, the place has atmosphere aplenty, but the food isn't terrific. Nevertheless, it's a great place to stop for a drink, especially if you like ghost stories. According to local legend, the long-departed Mrs. Chumley comes back and rearranges the furniture in the middle of the night.

♦ American ♦ Daily dinner. 86 Bedford St (between Barrow and Grove Sts). 675.4449

13 Pink Teacup ★$ The prices may have steadily crept up over the years, but for big eaters, a complete dinner of smothered pork chops or ribs, with soup, cabbage salad drenched in French dressing, black-eyed peas, collard greens, cornbread, and bread pudding, is a satisfying value indeed. ♦ Southern ♦ Daily breakfast, lunch, dinner, and late-night meals. No credit cards accepted. 42 Grove St (between Bedford and Bleecker Sts). 807.6755

14 Chez Michallet ★$$$ Charming and intimate, this French-style bistro is always packed with a neighborhood crowd. The classic French cooking here has been given a slight spin. Dinners include rack of lamb with rosemary red-wine sauce, and monkfish in fresh vinaigrette. The steak *frites* (with french fries) is especially good. ♦ French ♦ Daily dinner. Reservations recommended. 90 Bedford St (at Grove St). 242.8309 ♿

14 Twin Peaks In 1925, **Clifford Reed Daily** transformed this very conventional 1830 residence into a fairy-tale fantasy as a reaction against the mediocrity of Village architecture. Pseudo-Tudor details trim the stucco facing, and an unorthodox flap acts as a front cornice (there's an attic room behind it). It's not great architecture, but it *is* great fun. ♦ 102 Bedford St (between Grove and Christopher Sts)

15 Lucille Lortel Theatre Formerly the **Theatre De Lys,** this 299-seat house was a major boost to Off Broadway in the 1950s, when a revival of the Brecht-Weill classic *The Threepenny Opera* was staged here. It was later renamed for its distinguished owner Lucille Lortel, who produced *Brecht on Brecht* and John Dos Passos's *USA*. More recently, it was home to the hugely successful *Steel Magnolias* during its two-and-a-half-year run. ♦ 121 Christopher St (between Bleecker and Hudson Sts). 924.2817 ♿

15 McNulty's Tea and Coffee Company In business since 1895, this place has been quietly selling exotic coffees (from China, Sumatra, and Indonesia) long before the trend for specialty coffees began in this country. There are also more than 250 varieties of tea. ♦ Daily. 109 Christopher St (between Bleecker and Bedford Sts). 242.5351

16 Pot Belly Stove Restaurant $ In the wee hours, this place is better than most when it comes to satisfying an uncontrollable urge for a hamburger with any conceivable topping, an omelette, or a salad. ♦ American ♦ Daily 24 hours. 94 Christopher St (between Bleecker and Bedford Sts). 242.8036

17 Grove Street Cafe ★$$ A quaint, softly lit dining room, this place looks at once stylish and bohemian with exposed-brick walls and recessed lighting. Featured dishes include chicken rolled with prosciutto, mozzarella, and sun-dried tomatoes, and covered with a cognac cream sauce. It's also ideally located near all Village theaters. ♦ Continental ♦ M-Tu, Th-F lunch and dinner; W dinner; Sa-Su brunch and dinner. Reservations recommended. 53 Grove St (between Seventh Ave S and Bleecker St). 924.8299

18 Christopher Park Until the Parks Department put a sign near the entrance, everyone thought this was Sheridan Square. The confusion began when the **IRT Sheridan Square** subway stop was opened in 1918, and was compounded when Joseph Pollia's statue of the Civil War general was placed here (possibly by mistake) in 1936. ♦ Seventh Ave S (between Grove and Christopher Sts)

18 Sheridan Square Because **Christopher Park** is closer to the **Sheridan Square** subway stop, which is around the corner, Sheridan Square is at the same time one of the best-known and hardest-to-find spots in all of Greenwich Village. The community garden in the center yielded rare archaeological treasures when it was created in the early 1980s. It was the only spot in Manhattan that hadn't been disturbed since Indians lived here. ♦ W Fourth St (between Washington Pl and Seventh Ave S)

18 The Ridiculous Theatrical Company The late, great Charles Ludlam felt that farce, parody, and travesty were essential ingredients for comic drama. They still are—Ludlam's virtuosic company continues the tradition with such delights as a severely adapted *A Tale of Two Cities*. ♦ 1 Sheridan Sq (W Fourth St at Seventh Ave S). 691.2271

19 Circle Repertory Company The old **Sheridan Square Playhouse** has been the home of this theater group since it was founded by Marshall W. Mason in 1974. A permanent company of artists (which has included Judd Hirsch and William Hurt) performs new American drama, including the works of Lanford Wilson, Edward J. Moore, and Jules Feiffer. ♦ 99 Seventh Ave S (between Barrow and Grove Sts).

20 One If By Land, Two If By Sea ★★$$$$ The onetime home of Aaron Burr, this charming restaurant doesn't have a sign, which can make it a little tricky to find. Well worth the hunt, it has a large bar and working fireplace just inside the door, and the two-level interior is romantically candlelit. The food, traditionally very rich, features such dishes as beef Wellington and roasted squab with foie gras, wild mushrooms, and roasted chestnuts. ♦ Continental ♦ Daily dinner. Reservations required. 17 Barrow St (between W Fourth St and Seventh Ave S). 228.0822

21 Sweet Basil The giants of the jazz world perform here regularly. Most people come to listen to music and have a drink, but the club also offers food, including good salads and stir-fry dishes. ♦ Cover. Shows nightly at 9PM and 11PM. 88 Seventh Ave S (between Barrow and Grove Sts). 242.1785

21 Actor's Playhouse This has been one of the high spots on the Off-Broadway theater scene since it raised its first curtain in 1940. Productions have included *10% Review* and *The Good and Faithful Servant*. ♦ 100 Seventh Ave S (between Barrow and Grove Sts). 691.6226

22 Ottomanelli's Meat Market For years, the window display of stuffed rabbits and game birds here gave pause to even the least repentant of carnivores. Fortunately, this shop's reputation for very fresh game is such that there is no longer a need to advertise quite so explicitly. All the meat is cut to order and fans of the veal roast stuffed with prosciutto are legion. ♦ M-Sa. 285 Bleecker St (between Jones St and Seventh Ave S). 675.4217

23 John's Pizzeria ★★$ Arguing about the best pizza in New York is something of a local sport, and this place is always on everyone's lips. The thin-crust pies are made in a coal oven—one reason it's so good. Another is the delicious toppings—fresh mushrooms, spicy sausage, or whatever you like. The inevitable wait prolongs the anticipation, but the end result always satisfies. ♦ Italian ♦ Daily lunch and dinner. 278 Bleecker St (between Morton St and Seventh Ave S). 243.1680 ⅂. Also at: 48 W 65th St (between Central Park W and Columbus Ave). 721.7001; 408 E 64th St (between York and First Aves). 935.2895

The residents of Greenwich Village named Waverly Place after Sir Walter Scott's novel *Waverley* to honor him the year after his death.

Restaurants/Clubs: Red   **Hotels:** Blue

Shops/ ♈ Outdoors: Green   **Sights/Culture:** Black

23 Aphrodisia Whether seeking remedies or flavors, scoop your choice from among the 800 herbs and spices into a small paper bag and label it with the appropriate name and price. Those ready to turn over a new leaf could consult the wide selection of books for healthy living. ♦ Daily. 264 Bleecker St (between Sixth Ave and Seventh Ave S). 989.6440 ♿

24 Cucina Stagionale $ The best thing that can be said about this place is that the prices are low. The food is marginal, but the menu gives a twist to basic Italian fare (try the eggplant manicotti). Don't arrive hungry; there's almost always a line of people waiting for a table, bottles of wine in hand (there's no liquor license). ♦ Italian ♦ Daily lunch and dinner. No credit cards accepted. 275 Bleecker St (between Cornelia and Jones Sts). 924.2707

25 Trattoria Pesce Pasta ★★$$ Beginning with the bright red entrance and the windows displaying the catch of the day and a wide selection of antipasti, this is one of the neighborhood's more welcoming places. Start with a selection of antipasti—marinated peppers, grilled fennel, marinated white beans, mozzarella—or *pasta e fagioli* (a broth rich with beans, vegetables, and macaroni), and then move on to any of the pastas, particularly the flavorful linguine with white clam sauce. Feel free to ask the waiters what's good that day; they're friendly, accommodating, and very honest. ♦ Italian ♦ Daily lunch, dinner, and late-night meals. 262 Bleecker St (at Cornelia St). 645.2993

26 A. Zito & Sons Bakery The bread's crunchy crust and delicate inside texture lures its share of devoted customers, such as Frank Sinatra, who is pictured in a photo on the wall admiring a loaf. These breads, fresh from the oven, are easy to love; the whole wheat is especially delicious. ♦ M-Sa; Su until 1PM. 259 Bleecker St (between Cornelia and Jones Sts). 929.6139

26 Murray's Cheese Store The competitive prices, a large assortment of cheeses (90 percent are imported), and superior service keep customers coming back. Grocery items, salads, meats, and delicacies are also offered at this self-styled "mini-**Balducci's**." ♦ Daily. 257 Bleecker St (at Cornelia St). 243.3289. Also at: 198 Eighth Ave (at 20th St). 691.3948

27 Home ★★$$ In a cozy spot best described as an urban farmhouse, this neighborhood restaurant offers classic and nostalgic American cooking with a contemporary flair. Heartwarming entrées, such as peppered shoulder steak and cumin-crusted pork chops, are memorable. ♦ American ♦ M-F breakfast and dinner; Sa-Su brunch and dinner. 20 Cornelia St (between Cornelia and W Fourth Sts). 243.9579

28 Po ★★★$ Chef Mario Batali and partner Steve Crane change the menu seasonally, but whenever you visit this tiny, romantic place, you can count on such inventive, flavorful dishes as tomato ravioli filled with white beans in balsamic vinegar, or marinated brown-butter quail with a beet reduction on a salad of *frisée* (curly endive). If you're having trouble making up your mind about which Tuscan-inspired dish to select, a tasting menu is the way to go. ♦ Northern Italian ♦ Tu dinner; W-Su lunch and dinner. Reservations required. 31 Cornelia St (between Bleecker and W Fourth Sts). 645.2189

28 The Cornelia Street Café ★$ Started by artists nearly 20 years ago, this cafe, with whitewashed brick walls and glass-panel doors that open onto the quiet street of the same name, offers good roasted free-range chicken and interesting pastas, such as this fall

favorite: pumpkin ravioli with chestnut-cream sauce. Save room for one of the homemade desserts—the smooth-as-silk maple custard, for example. ♦ Bistro/Cafe ♦ M-F lunch and dinner; Sa-Su brunch and dinner. 29 Cornelia St (between Bleecker and W Fourth Sts). 989.9318 ♿

29 The Bagel ★$ The Village Breakfast—strawberry pancakes—is the big draw at this tiny restaurant and deli. It's also known for such standard deli fare as pastrami and corned beef sandwiches. ♦ American/Deli ♦ Daily breakfast, lunch, and dinner. No credit cards accepted. 170 W Fourth St (at Cornelia St). 255.0106

30 Caffè Vivaldi ★$ This Old World Village favorite always pleases with its relaxed and cozy atmosphere—it offers Manhattan a taste of turn-of-the-century Vienna, with dramatic arias playing in the background, the smell and sound of the espresso machine, and a crackling fire in the fireplace. Come here on a cold winter's day with your significant other for a light lunch or sweets. ♦ Cafe ♦ Daily. 32 Jones St (between Bleecker and W Fourth Sts). 929.9384

31 St. Joseph's Church The oldest Roman Catholic church building in Manhattan, this Greek Revival temple was built in 1834 by **John Doran**. It has a gallery inside as well as delicate crystal chandeliers and a gilded sanctuary that contrasts with the simplicity of the Greek Revival exterior. The outside wall on Washington Place is made of Manhattan schist, the extremely hard stone which

underlies the whole island. ◆ 371 Sixth Ave
(at W Washington Pl). 741.1274

32 Gus' Place ★$$ Casual and gracious,
this place specializes in Mediterranean—
predominantly Greek—fare. The *mezedes*
(a platter of assorted appetizers) is enough
to send you away satisfied and mighty happy,
but if you stopped there you'd miss Gus's
specialty—lamb shank—and that would
be a shame. ◆ Greek/Mediterranean ◆ M-Sa
lunch and dinner; Su brunch and dinner.
149 Waverly Pl (near Gay St). 645.8511 ₺

32 Gay Street Thought to be named after a
family who lived here in the mid- to late-18th
century, the block contains a well-preserved
group of Greek Revival houses on the east
side and Federal row houses on the west. **No.
14** is the location of the basement apartment
that was the setting for Ruth McKenney's play
My Sister Eileen, which later was made into
the musical *Wonderful Town.* ◆ Waverly Pl
to Christopher St

33 Oscar Wilde Memorial Bookshop This
small shop offers a tasteful selection of books
on gay and lesbian subject matter, including
literary classics, legal guides, sociology, and
periodicals. ◆ Daily. 15 Christopher St (at Gay
St). 255.8097

34 Pierre's ★$$$ The bistro's cozy
atmosphere is enhanced by a wandering
accordion player. Try the salmon puff
pastries (delicate morsels stuffed with
spinach), and for dessert, the *tarte tatin*
(apple pie baked with a caramel sauce and
served with homemade whipped cream).
The steak *pommes frites* (with fried potatoes)
is good as well. ◆ French ◆ Daily lunch and
dinner. Reservations required. No credit cards
accepted. 170 Waverly Pl (at Christopher St).
929.7194

35 Lion's Head ★$$ Local journalists, writers,
and community politicians have been known
to congregate here. The bar is the main thing;
menu selections include burgers or bangers
plus such upscale dishes as confit of duck
salad. ◆ American ◆ Daily lunch, dinner,
and late-night meals. 59 Christopher St
(at Seventh Ave S). 929.0670

36 Three Lives & Company This shop carries
a wonderful selection (particularly fiction
and specialty books) and hosts occasional
Thursday night readings. The owners are
knowledgeable and helpful. ◆ Daily 1-7PM.
154 W 10th St (between Sixth Ave and
Seventh Ave S). 741.2069

37 Crystal Gardens This shop for the
spiritually inclined offers quartz, minerals,
medicine jewelry, seminars, consultations,
and an interesting newsletter written by co-
owner Connie Barrett. ◆ Daily. 21 Greenwich
Ave (between Christopher and W 10th Sts).
727.0692

**38 New York Public Library, Jefferson
Market Branch** Frederick Clark
Withers and **Calvert Vaux** modeled this
1877 structure, built on the site of the old
Jefferson Market and originally used as
the **Third Judicial District Courthouse,**
after Mad King Ludwig II of Bavaria's castle
Neuschwanstein. It is the epitome of Victorian
Gothic, with steeply sloping roofs, gables,
pinnacles, sets of variously shaped arched
windows, and stone carvings all set off by
a rather unusual clock tower that served as
a fire lookout. After the occupants moved
out in 1945, the building sat idle until citizens
pressured the city government to find a
new user and the public library agreed to
move in. **Giorgio Cavaglieri** handled the
1967 remodeling. ◆ M-Sa. 425 Sixth Ave
(at W 10th St). 243.4334 ₺

39 Balducci's This is the grocer *ne plus ultra*
in Greenwich Village. It began humbly many
years ago as a produce stand across the
street from the present site; today this popular
family-run store is one of the grandest and
best-stocked specialty shops in New York
City. Not only is the produce still top-notch,
but the cheese selection is first-rate too,
as are the fish, meat, cold cuts, prepared
take-out dishes (try Mama's pasta—a
rich, delicious sun-dried tomato sauce over
spaghetti created by the late, beloved Mama
Balducci), and everything from the bakery
department. The shelves hold packaged
products from all over the world, but
specialize in delicacies from Italy and
France. ◆ Daily. 424 Sixth Ave (at W Ninth
St). 673.2600 ₺

40 Patchin Place Like Milligan Place around
the corner on Sixth Avenue, this cluster of
small houses constructed in 1848 by **Aaron
D. Patchin** was built as rooming houses for

waiters and other personnel from the now-departed **Brevoort Hotel** over on Fifth Avenue. It became famous in the 1920s as the home of poet e.e. cummings, among others. ♦ W 10th St (between Sixth and Greenwich Aves)

40 Sammy's Noodle Shop & Grill ★$ This smartly decorated restaurant offers Cantonese-style roast meats such as duck, pork, and soy sauce chicken, and a good selection of noodle dishes. You can also design your own dish from a selection of vegetables, meats, and different sauces. And if you're fond of Chinese pastries, stop in at the adjacent bakery. ♦ Chinese. ♦ Daily lunch and dinner. 453-461 Sixth Ave (at W 10th). 924.6688

41 Jefferson Market Devoted customers of this old-fashioned market were shocked to learn that there were plans to move it, but happy that the new location was right across the street. This space is bigger, more modern, and has wider aisles. The quality of the fresh produce, meats, cheeses, and other grocery items is as high as ever, and the longtime staff (familiar with regular customers' names) are all there. So are the famous rotisseried chickens; on Sunday nights in the summer, there is always a long line of customers at the prepared foods counter doing battle for these birds—they were a big seller even before the rotisserie craze began. ♦ Daily. 450 Sixth Avenue (at W 10th St). 533.3377 ᕼ

42 Gran Caffè Degli Artisti ★$ Ask for a table in the back, where it's dark, cozy, candlelit, and filled with funky antique furnishings. Don't bother with the Italian entrées; go straight to the iced mochaccino and one of the more decadent pastries or cakes. ♦ Cafe ♦ Daily lunch, dinner, and late-night meals. 46 Greenwich Ave (between Charles and Perry Sts). 645.4431

43 El Charro Español ★$$ A favorite local spot for earthy, garlicky Spanish food, this casual white stucco dining room offers *mariscada* (Spanish bouillabaisse); chicken with garlic and white wine; veal with onions, peppers, garlic, and sausages; shrimp grilled in the shell with lemon, garlic, and parsley; and several varieties of paella—*valenciana* (with chicken, sausage, and seafood), marinara (all seafood), and *hortelana* (vegetarian). Wash it all down with a potent margarita. ♦ Spanish ♦ Daily lunch and dinner. Reservations recommended Friday-Sunday. 4 Charles St (at Greenwich Ave). 924.5915

44 Village Vanguard This world-famous basement jazz club also features Dixieland, blues, avant-garde, and folk music. Pop singers, comedians, and poets have appeared. ♦ Cover. Shows M-Th, Su 9:30PM and 11:30PM; F-Sa 9:30PM, 11:30PM, and 1AM.

Reservations recommended. 178 Seventh Ave S (at Perry St). 255.4037

Patisserie J. Lanciani

45 Patisserie J. Lanciani ★$ Magnificent cakes, tarts, brownies, and croissants are offered in this pretty storefront cafe. In the mornings, it's a breakfast club of locals leisurely reviewing the newspaper over coffee. ♦ Cafe ♦ Daily. 271 W Fourth St (between Perry and W 11th Sts). 929.0739 ᕼ

46 Riviera Cafe $$ The people watching here is better than anything on the casual menu, which includes burgers and salads. Sip some wine and watch the ongoing parade that is Greenwich Village pass by your table. ♦ American ♦ Daily lunch, dinner, and late-night meals. 225 W Fourth St (between Christopher St and Seventh Ave S). 929.3250

47 Very Special Flowers You won't find the usual mums, gladioli, or carnations here. Instead, this florist concentrates on complicated topiary, dried-flower arrangements, and exotic bouquets made from flowers flown in daily from Holland and France. ♦ M-Sa. 204 W 10th St (between W 4th and Bleecker Sts). 206.7236

48 La Metairie ★★$$$ The Village is known for its romantic restaurants, and this rustic and candlelit place, with a white picket fence and hand-painted duck sign, is one good reason why. The menu takes on Provençal cooking—duck with orange and balsamic-vinegar sauce, and sautéed salmon with a garlic-mustard crust—with the addition of lobster risotto, or some equally unexpected dish. ♦ French ♦ Daily dinner. Reservations required. 189 W 10th (at W Fourth St). 989.0343 ᕼ

49 Pierre Deux Stop here for Provençal furniture, china, clothing, fabrics, and accessories. ♦ M-Sa. 367 Bleecker St (at Charles St). 243.7740. Also at: 870 Madison Ave (at E 71st St). 570.9343

50 Cottonwood Cafe $$ This noisy low-down Texan joint serves basic chicken-fried steak, fried chicken livers, and hefty barbecued beef ribs (mesquite-smoked Texas-style) with sides of lumpy skin-flecked mashed potatoes, cornmeal-dipped fried okra, and the obligatory cream gravy. After 10PM the place turns into a roadhouse with "original Texas" music—country-western with an overlay of Village artiness—performed at a volume loud enough to preclude anything but listening and downing great margaritas or Lone Star beer. ♦ Southern ♦ Daily lunch and dinner. 415 Bleecker St (between W 11th and Bank Sts). 924.6271

51 Biography Bookshop As the name implies, this bookstore has the best selection of biographies anywhere. Feel free to browse. ◆ Daily. 400 Bleecker St (at W 11th St). 807.8655

52 Lucy Anna Folk Art & Antique Quilts
When Karen Taber's grandmothers—Lucy and Anna—handed down their quilts to their granddaughter, they planted a seed of interest that has blossomed into this attractive shop filled with antique quilts (lots of pastels) as well as new items—such as stuffed animals—made out of quilt scraps. ◆ Tu-Su. 502 Hudson St (between Christopher and W 10th Sts). 645.9463 ᕯ

53 Taylor's This snug gourmet takeout is run by Spartan and Cindi Taylor. The onion-poppy hot dog buns—with Pommery mustard mixed into the dough—give you a good reason to eat hot dogs, and the triple-fudge brownies will throw off your calorie count for the week. ◆ Takeout ◆ Daily. 523 Hudson St (between W 10th and Charles Sts). 645.8200

53 Sazerac House ★★$$ It's worth a visit to this 30-year-old restaurant for the building alone. Part of an 18th-century farm purchased from the Earl of Abingdon, this place was fixed up in 1826 by a local carpenter who made it his home. A knowing crowd, homesick New Orleanians among them, have always come here for gumbo, jambalaya, and the perennially popular crab cakes. Lately, such brunch favorites as eggs Sazerac (scrambled eggs with ham, cream cheese, and hollandaise sauce) and *pain perdu* (French toast) are attracting a following of their own. The early prix-fixe dinner (4:30-6:30PM) is a real bargain. ◆ Cajun/Creole ◆ M-F lunch and dinner; Sa-Su brunch and dinner. Reservations recommended. 533 Hudson St (at Charles St). 989.0313

54 Caribe ★$ Although this place is not exactly original—there are a number of similar island-motif restaurant/bars like this joint offering Jamaican food and music in a junglelike setting—the food here is pretty good (try the jerk chicken or pork), and the atmosphere (West Indies meets West Village) is funky and fun. ◆ West Indian ◆ Daily lunch and dinner. 117 Perry St (at Greenwich St). 255.9191

55 Fishs Eddy This shop specializes in collecting and selling odd and interesting bits of glassware and porcelain, such as old dishes from railroad cars and remnants from extinct social clubs, hotels, or cruise ships. ◆ Daily. 551 Hudson St (between Perry and W 11th Sts). 627.3956. Also at: 889 Broadway (at E 19th St). 420.9020; 2176 Broadway (at W 77th St). 873.8819

55 White Horse Tavern Among the folks who have frequented this famous bar was the poet Dylan Thomas, who, in a particularly depressive funk, literally drank himself to death in the corner. His supposed last words: "I've had 19 straight whiskeys. I believe that's the record." The french fries are okay and the burgers are good. ◆ M-Th, Su 11AM-2AM; F, Sa 11AM-4AM. 567 Hudson St (at W 11th St). 243.9260

56 Burgundy Wine Company The finest wines of Burgundy and the Rhône are the specialty of this shop. Ask for a mail-order catalog, an informative brochure filled with vignettes about wine merchant Al Hotchkin's travels. ◆ Tu-Sa. 323 W 11th St (between Greenwich and Washington Sts). 691.9092 ᕯ

57 The Black Sheep ★★$$$ This place is the archetype of the ultimate Village restaurant—brick walls, original paintings, comfortable, and dark. The six-course dinner with limited choices is a good value; otherwise, try the crispy confit of duck leg. The wine list is excellent, and the homemade desserts, irresistible: Don't miss the banana cake with praline-butterscotch frosting. ◆ French ◆ M-Sa dinner and late-night meals; Su brunch, dinner, and late-night meals. Reservations recommended. No credit cards accepted at brunch. 342 W 11th St (at Washington St). 242.1010

In 1942, distressed by commercial publishers' lack of interest in her work, Anaïs Nin borrowed $175 and, with a friend, rented a loft at 144 MacDougal Street, purchased a used printing press, and went on to print three of her books. In 1944, in search of more professional surroundings, she moved to a larger space at 17 East 13th Street.

"In Manhattan, there are gardens on roofs, gardens outside basement apartments, and minigardens on miniterraces. How do the gardens grow? Expensively. And what do they grow? Almost anything. Apparently, even cash crops. Wildflowers have been tamed on tiny balconies, and families fed on vegetables nurtured in the alien soil bordered by sidewalks."

Ralph Caplan, writer and design consultant

58 Westbeth Built in 1897 by Bell Telephone Laboratories (then Western Electric), this was where the transistor was invented and the first TV pictures were transmitted. When Bell Labs moved to the suburbs in 1965, **Richard Meier Associates** renovated the 1900 **Cyrus Eidlitz**–designed building and turned it into a nonprofit residential building exclusively for artists of all kinds (see below). Envisioned as a center for the arts with galleries and dance and sculpture studios, it is, in fact, merely subsidized apartments for anyone who happens to be an artist. ♦ 463 West St (at Bank St)

59 Tortilla Flats $ This popular West Village dive is known for its wild times and cheap Tex-Mex eats—chicken, shrimp, or steak fajitas, *enchiladas verde* (in a green-chile salsa), and chimichangas (deep-fried chicken and refried-bean burritos)—made from natural ingredients. Monday and Tuesday are big-prize bingo nights; don't bring your mild-mannered grandma. ♦ Tex-Mex ♦ Daily lunch, dinner, and late-night meals. 767 Washington St (at W 12th St). 243.1053 ♦

60 Kelter/Malce This store has beautiful antique quilts from the early 1800s, as well as a good selection of Amish and patchwork quilts, Beacon and Pendleton blankets, Navajo weavings, folk art, and antique Christmas ornaments. ♦ M-Sa by appointment. 74 Jane St (between Greenwich and Washington Sts). 989.6760

61 Restaurant Florent ★★$$ A diner-turned-hip-bistro, this is a welcome late-night spot for those seeking a complete meal. Given the number of meatpacking plants in the neighborhood, meat entrées are, of course, specialties of the house. The *boudin noir* (blood sausage) appetizer and the steak *frites* (fried steak) are both popular. Any of the fish dishes are also worth trying. After midnight there's an all-night breakfast menu. Part of the attraction of this establishment is its stylish look: Tibor Kalman's M & Co. is responsible for the design, and to some extent the layout, of the restaurant itself. ♦ Continental ♦ Daily 24 hours. No credit cards accepted. 69 Gansevoort St (between Greenwich and Washington Sts). 989.5779 ♦

62 Gansevoort Market The city's wholesale meat district is housed in this collection of old brick buildings. The action intensifies in the early morning hours before the sun comes up, when people from restaurants all over New York converge to find the best meat to offer you for dinner. ♦ Gansevoort and W 14th Sts (between Ninth Ave and the Hudson River)

Westbeth

Michael Storrings

63 El Faro ★$$ A dark, minimally decorated den of a restaurant, this place has been around forever serving good-quality, full-flavored Spanish food. You can't go wrong with the rich and fragrant paella, seafood stew, or other fish dishes. ♦ Spanish ♦ Daily lunch and dinner. 823 Greenwich St (at Horatio St). 929.8210

64 Peanut Butter & Jane This children's clothing store stocks more than 200 brands, from basics to one-of-a-kinds by local artists, as well as toys and accessories. ♦ Daily. 617 Hudson St (between W 12th and Jane Sts). 620.7952

65 La Ripaille ★★$$ The setting, much like a French farmhouse, makes this one of the most romantic dining spots in a neighborhood full of romantic dining spots. Its Provençal-style dishes—such as breast of duck with seasonal fruit, shell steak in green peppercorn sauce, and Norwegian salmon in a light champagne velouté (sauce)—are always good. ♦ French ♦ M-Sa dinner. Reservations recommended. 605 Hudson St (between Bethune and W 12th Sts). 255.4406

66 Abingdon Square The square is named for Charlotte Warren, wife of the Earl of Abingdon and daughter of Sir Peter Warren, whose estate once covered this area. The statue at the uptown entrance, placed here in 1921, is a memorial to the American dead of World War I. ♦ Bounded by Eighth Ave, Bleecker and Hudson Sts, and W 11th and W 12th Sts

67 Casa di Pré ★$$ The honest, home-style food at this place, a fixture in the neighborhood for quite some time, is cooked with a sure, light hand. Try veal *sorrentino* (cooked in a Marsala sauce with prosciutto and mozzarella) or sole *francese* (dipped in a flour and egg batter and sautéed in lemon butter). ♦ Italian ♦ Daily lunch and dinner. Reservations recommended for three or more. 283 W 12th St (at W Fourth St). 243.7073 &

68 Corner Bistro $ If strolling around the Village has whetted your appetite for a fat, juicy burger, this neighborhood standby is the place to go. You'll have plenty of time to check out the locals in this dark, cozy pub because the indifferent staff provides extremely slow service. ♦ American ♦ Daily lunch, dinner, and late-night meals. No credit cards accepted. 331 W Fourth St (between W 12th and Jane Sts). 242.9502

69 Jane Street Seafood Cafe ★$$ Fresh and simple seafood dishes—and some surpisingly well-executed and complex ones—don't compensate for the nonchalant service found here. ♦ Seafood ♦ Daily dinner. Reservations recommended. 31 Eighth Ave (at Jane St). 242.0003

70 Nell's The doormen are less choosy these days, now that the club is less in vogue. But you might still spy hip literary types and the occasional celeb lounging on one of the cushy couches. The club's main claim to fame among younger patrons is that its owner, Nell, costarred in *The Rocky Horror Picture Show.* ♦ Cover. M-Tu, Su 10PM-3AM; W-Sa 10PM-4AM. 246 W 14th St (between Seventh and Eighth Aves). 675.1567

70 Jerry Ohlinger's Movie Material Store The collection includes innumerable posters and thousands of stills in both color and black-and-white, including some 10,000 from Disney films alone. ♦ Daily 1-7:45PM. 242 W 14th St (between Seventh and Eighth Aves). 989.0869

71 Integral Yoga Institute All aspects of yoga teaching are presented: meditation, breathing, relaxation, diet and nutrition, stress management, Hatha for pregnant women, video classes, chanting. The institute's store next door sells all kinds of macrobiotic essentials as well as natural cosmetics and remedies. Vitamins, minerals, herbs, and homeopathic remedies are for sale across the street at the **Natural Apothecary** (No. 234). ♦ M-Sa. 227 W 13th St (between Seventh and Eighth Aves). 929.0586 &

72 Cafe de Bruxelles ★$$ A sophisticated bar scene is the real attraction at this lovely spot, which has also made a name for itself as the only Belgian restaurant in the downtown area. Don't miss the rich *waterzooi* (Belgian bouillabaisse). ♦ French/Belgian ♦ Tu-Sa lunch and dinner; Su brunch and dinner. Reservations recommended. 118 Greenwich Ave (at W 13th St). 206.1830

72 Tea and Sympathy ★$ Those enamored of bangers and mash, shepherd's pie, and other English specialties flock to this cozy spot. For traditionalists, there's a Sunday dinner of roast beef and Yorkshire pudding. ♦ English ♦ M-F lunch and dinner; Sa-Su brunch and dinner. 108 Greenwich Ave (between Jane and W 13th Sts). 807.8329

They're all over New York, but rooftop water tanks seem more visible in the Village than anywhere else. Their average height above sea level is about the same as a five-story building, and any building higher than that needs to pump water to its upper floors. The tanks are made of western yellow cedar and have a life expectancy of about 30 years. The two-inch boards, which are as strong as 14 inches of concrete, are held together with steel bands around the outside, and the water inside swells the wood to a tight fit. The insulating properties of wood prevent freezing in winter and keep the water cool, if not cold, in summer.

Restaurants/Clubs: Red   **Hotels:** Blue

Shops/ 🎗 Outdoors: Green   **Sights/Culture:** Black

73 Benny's Burritos ★$ After sipping one of Benny's high-octane margaritas, you'll understand why it gets so rowdy here. Any one of the 12-inch-long burritos with a tempting choice of fillings at bargain prices is worth trying. This is the Village's *numero uno* cheap tortilla joint, so expect a line. ♦ Tex-Mex ♦ M-F lunch, dinner, and late-night meals; Sa-Su brunch, dinner, and late-night meals. No credit cards accepted. 113 Greenwich Ave (at Jane St). 727.0584. Also at: 93 Ave A (at Sixth St). 254.3286

74 Ye Waverly Inn $$ Longtime Village residents don't seem to care that the quality of the food here—chicken potpie, Southern fried chicken, and peasant meat loaf (wrapped in homemade dough)—has declined somewhat over the years. They continue to flock to this dining spot for authentic Early American charm—irregularly shaped rooms, low ceilings, rustic print wallpaper, and in winter, roaring fireplaces. Traditional Thanksgiving and Christmas dinners are served. ♦ American ♦ M-F lunch and dinner; Sa-Su brunch and dinner. 16 Bank St (at Waverly Pl). 929.4377

75 Chez Brigitte ★$ Come to this counter-only eatery for inexpensive French food. A friendly Frenchwoman named Rose, who has worked here for 25 years, has taken over the kitchen from the late Brigitte and continues to cook such homey, simple dishes as *boeuf bourguignon* and veal stew. ♦ French ♦ Daily lunch and dinner. No credit cards accepted. 77 Greenwich Ave (at W 11th St). 929.6736

76 St. Vincent's Hospital The largest Catholic hospital in the United States, built in 1977 by **Ferrer & Taylor,** this modern monstrosity is the main building and proof that not every Village community protest is successful. But the medical facility now has a physician referral service (800/999.6266), and has served the community well in every other way since it was founded by the Sisters of Charity in 1849. ♦ Seventh Ave S (between W 11th and W 12th Sts). 604.7000

77 West 14th Street Best known as a magnet for bargain-hunters, this street is also home to a number of noteworthy loft buildings. Walk on the north side of the street and look across at **Nos. 138-146** (1899), an ostentatious confection that drew on the 1893 Chicago World's Fair for its inspiration; and **Nos. 154-160** (1913), **Herman Lee Meader's** colorful glass and tile design that is literally grounded in Art Nouveau and aspiring to Art Deco. ♦ Between Sixth and Seventh Aves

Edna St. Vincent Millay gained her middle name by virtue of being born in St. Vincent's Hospital.

78 Salvation Army Centennial Memorial Temple This 1930 building by **Voorhees, Gmelin & Walker** is one of the best Art Deco extravaganzas around, with an overblown entrance and unrestrained interiors that capture the exuberance and color of the era. Not open to the public, the building houses the executive offices and programs of the Salvation Army. ♦ 120 W 14th St (between Sixth and Seventh Aves). 337.7200. &

79 Cafe Loup ★★$$ Cozy and comfortable, this French bistro serves solid fare, including grilled escargots; smoked brook trout; Colorado lamb chops in a Cabernet sauce; grilled skirt steak in shallot sauce; and grilled salmon over greens, corn salad, marinated tomato *concassé* (reduction), and *brunoise* of beets (shredded and sautéed). The eclectic and well-priced wine list includes good specials served by the glass. ♦ French ♦ M-F lunch and dinner; Sa dinner; Su lunch and dinner. Reservations recommended. 105 W 13th St (between Sixth and Seventh Aves). 255.4746 &

80 Village Community Church This abandoned gem is thought by architectural historians to be the best Greek Revival church in the city. The original design, dating to 1846 is attributed to **Samuel Thompson** and based on the Theseum in Athens. But the materials are the antithesis of the Doric model: The six huge columns and the pediment are of wood, and the walls are brick and stucco. ♦ 143 W 13th St (between Sixth and Seventh Aves)

ZINNO

81 Zinno ★$$ Occupying the ground floor of a town house, this sleek bar and restaurant offers chamber jazz and some good food. Stick to the pastas; a good choice is homemade linguine with pancetta (Italian bacon), porcini mushrooms, and tomatoes. ♦ Italian ♦ M-Sa lunch and dinner. 126 W 13th St (between Sixth and Seventh Aves). 924.5182

82 James Beard House ★★★$$$$ Majo chefs from New York and around the country do special dinners almost nightly here, which are open to members and the public. Althoug it's pricey, considering the five or six courses that are served with almost as many wines, diners get their money's worth and more. Call ahead for a schedule and membership information. ♦ Eclectic ♦ Single seating at 7PM. Reservations required. 167 W 12th St (between Sixth and Seventh Aves). 675.4984

83 Famous Ray's Pizza $ Though a number of imposters have tried to claim title to the name "Famous Ray the Pizza King," this Village institution is the only real heir to the throne, serving more than 2,000 loyal customers a day. Expect a line for pizza that's hardly as good as it used to be but is, at least, still fresh out of the oven. Ray's "Famous Slice" has *all* the toppings, but purists opt for the traditional "Red, White, and Green" (tomato sauce, mozzarella, basil, and parsley). ♦ Pizza ♦ Daily lunch, dinner, and late-night meals. No credit cards accepted. 465 Sixth Ave (at W 11th St). 243.2253

84 Butterfield House The 1962 edifice by **Mayer, Whittlesey & Glass** is an unusually sensitive apartment block. The fine seven-story, bay-windowed section on 12th Street is an in-scale counterpoint to a series of row houses. Beyond an interior courtyard, the wing on 13th Street is taller, adapting to the stronger, larger scale of that block. ♦ 37 W 12th St (between Fifth and Sixth Aves)

85 Kate's Paperie All sorts of *papier* is found here, from gift wraps and marbleized papers to printmaking and handmade papers, Noguchi paper lamps, and Samurai-inspired dolls constructed with different textures of handmade grass papers. Make your own beautiful gifts; or choose from the fine selection of journals, photo albums, and pens. Printing and engraving services are also available. ♦ M-Sa. 8 W 13th St (between Fifth and Sixth Aves). 633.0570 ₺. Also at: 561 Broadway (between Spring and Prince Sts). 941.0194

86 East West Books This is an excellent source for books on Eastern philosophy, religion, cooking, medicine, and New Age lifestyles. ♦ Daily. 78 Fifth Ave (between W 13th and W 14th Sts). 243.5994 ₺.

87 Parsons School of Design This college holds a unique place in American education. Here, art and industry were for the first time firmly linked on a large institutional level, even before Gropius and the Bauhaus school. Founded as the **Chase School** in 1896 by painter/art teacher William Merritt Chase, the institution was spurred to its current high position in the world of art and design education by the leadership of Frank Alvah Parsons. Parsons arrived in 1907 and as the school's president implemented his vision of art and directly influenced both industry and everyday life. Under his direction the school changed its name to the **New York School of Fine and Applied Arts** and added programs such as interior architecture and design, fashion design and illustration, and advertising art. In 1940, the name was changed to honor President Parsons. In 1970, the school again took an innovative step in art education, joining with the **New School for Social Research** to broaden the scope of both institutions. **Parsons** moved to a site within the **New School** campus near Washington Square in Greenwich Village. Here, nearly

7,000 full- and part-time students can utilize the city's vast cultural and professional resources. The staff is made up primarily of professionals working in New York's vibrant art and design industry. In 1977, the school added a Garment District extension, the **David Schwartz Fashion Center,** at 40th Street and Seventh Avenue. Work by students is shown from March through June at the exhibition centers at 2 West 13th Street and 66 Fifth Avenue. ♦ 66 Fifth Ave (between W 12th and W 13th Sts). 229.8910 ₺.

87 Forbes Building The heart of the Forbes publishing empire is located in this 1925 **Carrère & Hastings** building. What's best here is the **Forbes Magazine Galleries** on the main floor. The collection includes more than 500 toy boats, displayed along with Art Deco fittings from the liner *Normandie* and models of the late Malcolm Forbes's private yachts. There is a collection of 12,000 toy soldiers and 250 trophies awarded for every accomplishment from raising Leghorn chickens to surviving a working lifetime in the corporate battlefields. American history is represented in a collection of Presidential Papers, historical documents, and model rooms. But the best part, for many, is a display of 12 Fabergé Easter eggs, the world's largest private collection of these priceless objects created for the czars of Russia. Admission is limited to 900 tickets a day and is reserved for group tours and advance reservations on Thursday. ♦ Free. Tu-W, F-Sa Call to verify days and hours, as they are subject to change. 62 Fifth Ave (at W 12th St). 206.5548 ₺.

88 First Presbyterian Church Joseph C. Wells modeled this fine Gothic Revival church with an imposing tower after the one at Magdalen College at Oxford. The south transept, an 1893 addition by **McKim, Mead & White,** includes an outdoor pulpit overlooking the inviting garden. The **Church House,** which adjoins the church on the uptown side, was designed in 1960 by **Edgar Tafel** to perfectly match the 1846 building. A three-year restoration of all the wood, stained glass, and masonry was completed in the spring of 1991. ♦ 12 W 12th St (at Fifth Ave). 675.6150 ₺.

89 Gotham Bar and Grill ★★★$$$$ In this impressive, multilevel loft space—accented with massive overhead lights draped in white fabric, mustard-colored columns, and a statue

of Lady Liberty—chef Alfred Portale's dishes qualify as architectural wonders as well as palate pleasers. Try the sautéed skate wings with eggplant caviar; butternut squash risotto; seared yellowfin tuna with *pappardelle* (broad noodles) and *caponata* (a relish of eggplant, onions, tomatoes, anchovies, olives, pine nuts, capers, and vinegar cooked in olive oil); saddle of rabbit with white beans; and rack of lamb with Swiss chard. Be sure to save room for one of the devastating desserts: warm Gotham chocolate cake; vanilla and crème fraîche cheesecake with Michigan blueberries and blueberry ice cream; warm apple financier with ginger ice cream; or a caramelized banana tart. The wine list is well chosen, international in scope, and expensive. ♦ American ♦ M-F lunch and dinner; Sa-Su dinner. Reservations required. 12 E 12th St (between University Pl and Fifth Ave). 620.4020

90 Asti $$$ Enjoy the singing waiters and professional opera singers while you eat routine Southern Italian standards. Go for the fun, which begins nightly at 6:30PM, not for the food. ♦ Italian ♦ Tu-Su lunch and dinner. 13 E 12th St (between University Pl and Fifth Ave). 741.9105

91 Bowlmor Lanes The Nieuw Amsterdam Dutch introduced bowling to America, but their legacy seems to be unappreciated in Manhattan, where there are only a handful of places to play the game. This one includes a bar and grill and a pro shop. ♦ M-Th, Su 10AM-1AM; F-Sa 10AM-4AM. 110 University Pl (between E 12th and E 13th Sts). 255.8188 &

91 Japonica ★★★$$ Friendly service, spectacular specialty rolls, and an unusual assortment of sushi—baby yellowtail, giant clam, spicy smelt caviar, and baby octopus, all rolled with white or brown rice—draw diners from all over the city to this very small place. Those who are feeling experimental (and have some money to play with) should let the chef put a sushi assortment together—the artistry is extraordinary. ♦ Japanese ♦ Daily lunch and dinner. 100 University Pl (at E 12th St). 243.7752

92 Forbidden Planet This is the city's headquarters for science fiction, horror, and fantasy books, comics, and related merchandise. ♦ Daily. 821 Broadway (at E 12th St). 473.1576 &

It is rumored that during World War II a man secretly lived within the Washington Square Memorial Arch for seven months and was discovered when he hung his wash out to dry.

Restaurants/Clubs: Red   **Hotels:** Blue

Shops/ ♈ Outdoors: Green   **Sights/Culture:** Black

93 The Cast Iron Building Designed by **John Kellum** in 1868, this building was converted from the **James McCreery Dry Goods Store** into apartments by **Stephen B. Jacobs** in 1973. In a city known for outstanding cast-iron structures (particularly in the SoHo neighborhood), this is one of the most representative examples, sporting layers of Corinthian columns topped by arches. Unfortunately, the uppermost story added later is an insensitive mismatch. ♦ 67 E 11th St (at Broadway)

94 Cedar Tavern $ This barnlike restaurant and beautiful dark bar with decent hamburgers has long been a hangout for artists. ♦ American ♦ Daily lunch, dinner, and late-night meals. 82 University Pl (between E 11th and E 12th Sts). 929.9089

95 Il Cantinori ★★$$$ Country antiques from Italy set the stage for an authentic Tusca meal here. Begin with the assortment of grille vegetables, then move on to *tonno al pesto* (grilled tuna steak sliced and served with pest vinaigrette and diced tomatoes). For dessert, good luck trying to choose among the apple tart, various gelati, tiramisù, and double-layer chocolate cake. ♦ Italian ♦ Daily lunch and dinner. 32 E 10th St (between Broadway and University Pl). 673.6044

96 Knickerbocker Bar & Grill ★$$ Fascinating 19th-century artifacts and poster fill this casual yet classy bar and restaurant. T-bone steak, pork chops, and pan-roasted chicken are among the more popular dishes. But the subdued atmosphere and live jazz (Wednesday through Sunday starting at 9:45PM)—often featuring name performers—are the main draws. ♦ American ♦ Cover, drink minimum. M-F lunch and dinner; Sa dinner; Su brunch and dinner. Reservations recommended. 33 University Pl (at E Ninth S 228.8490 &

97 Rose Cafe ★★$$ Dine at the glassed-in sidewalk cafe or the sophisticated dining roo Dishes include rosemary-roasted chicken salad, an assortment of gourmet sandwiches and pizzas with ingredients such as grilled chicken and smoked salmon. More elaborate entrées to try are butternut squash ravioli in mushroom-herb sauce, grilled chicken pailla with ratatouille, and pepper-crusted loin of p with cider sauce. For dessert, have the Granny Smith apple tart. ◆ American bistro ◆ M-F lunch and dinner; Sa-Su brunch and dinner. Reservations recommended. 24 Fifth Ave (at W Ninth St). 260.4118

Marylou's

98 Marylou's ★★$$$ Skip the appetizers and soups here and go directly to the generous main courses, particularly the perfectly broiled fresh fish, of which there are usually at least a half-dozen choices. And given the graceful, traditional appointments in several dining rooms—pleasant wood-framed paintings, fireplaces, library walls—and the friendly service, this could be considered the best seafood restaurant in the Village. ◆ Seafood ◆ Daily dinner and late-night meals. Reservations recommended. 21 W Ninth St (between Fifth and Sixth Aves). 533.0012

99 Eighth Street Since the 1960s the stretch of Eighth Street between Sixth Avenue and Broadway has been the shopping district for suburban raffish types who want that Village look, whatever that may be. The selection of stores—mostly shoes and accessories—has spilled over to Broadway, where secondhand reigns. ◆ Between Broadway and Sixth Ave

100 MacDougal Alley Like Washington Mews, this is a street of converted stables, with the advantage of trees but the same disadvantage of parked cars. **No. 7**, on the north side, was built in 1899 as a studio for a stained-glass artisan. **No. 17½** was converted to a home for Gertrude Vanderbilt Whitney, founder of the **Whitney Museum**, in 1934. **No. 19**, on the south side, was built in 1901 as an automobile stable, and the 1854 stable that is **No. 21** was reconstructed in 1920 by architect **Raymond Hood**. ◆ Off MacDougal St (between Washington Sq N and W Eighth St)

101 New York Studio School of Drawing, Painting & Sculpture The **Whitney Museum** was established here in 1931. Tradition was already evident on the block, which was the heart of the Village art scene at the time. It began with the conversion of a stable at 4 West Eighth Street by **John Taylor Johnston** as a gallery for his private art collection. His friends were so impressed that they got together and founded the **Metropolitan Museum of Art** in 1870. ◆ 8 W Eighth St (between Fifth and Sixth Aves) 673.6466

102 Vince & Linda at One Fifth ★★$$ This sophisticated room, formerly **One Fifth**, still retains the porthole lights from the **SS Coronia**, and the colorful murals depicting an earlier era in New York history. Chef Anthony

Bourdain's menu is rich, assertive, and delicious. Don't miss the wild mushrooms with truffle ravioli, the steamed New England cockles and mussels, and the spicy bouillabaise. Dessert lovers will enjoy the fallen chocolate soufflé. ◆ American. ◆ M-Sa lunch; daily dinner; Su brunch. One Fifth Ave (at E 8th St). 979.1515

103 Patricia Field Trendsetting fashions are this store's forte, great for those who live by their own dress code. Unless you work in a most uncorporate job or as a bartender in an after-hours club, you probably won't get a chance to wear most of what's for sale here. Still, the music's great and the clientele colorful, and it's fun to see the latest in New York's alternative cutting-edge fashions and accessories, including outrageous wigs and makeup. Most people stop in just for the experience. ◆ Daily. 10 E Eighth St (between University Pl and Fifth Ave). 254.1699

104 Washington Mews Some of these charming little buildings behind the town houses on Washington Square North were originally stables built in the early 1900s. But those on the south side of the alley, more uniform because they were all stuccoed at the same time, date from the 1930s. Most are now used by **NYU**. Their size and quaintness contribute to the small-scale, congenial atmosphere of the neighborhood. ◆ Between University Pl and Fifth Ave (north of Washington Sq N)

105 Washington Square North At one time there were 28 of these exemplary Greek Revival row houses—home to the cream of New York society when they were built in 1831, and later the center of an artistic community. The first six constructed, **Nos. 21** to **26**, by **Martin E. Thompson**, remain intact. **Nos. 7** to **13** were gutted in the late 1930s, and the facades alone are left, fronts for an apartment complex now owned by **New York University (NYU)**. Of those demolished, **No. 1** was at one time or another the home of Edith Wharton, William Dean Howells, and Henry James, who set his novel *Washington Square* at **No. 18**, his grandmother's house; **No. 3** was where John Dos Passos wrote *Manhattan Transfer;* and **No. 8** was once the official residence of the mayor. To the west of Fifth Avenue, the mock-Federal wing of the apartment tower at Two Fifth Avenue was a compromise by the builder, **Samuel Rudin,** in response to vociferous community objection to the original plan, which had the tower directly on the square. ◆ Between University Pl and MacDougal St

106 Washington Square Hotel $ In 1961, this was called the **Hotel Earle** and was the first New York residence of Bob Dylan, who played bars and coffeehouses in the neighborhood. Today, its modest accommodations are popular with dollar-conscious graduate students and young Europeans. Nearly all 180 rooms have been renovated; ask for one overlooking Washington Square. There is no restaurant, porters, or room service, but the location is perfect if you plan to spend a lot of time in the Village. ♦ 103 Waverly Pl (at Washington Sq W). 777.9515, 800/222.0418; fax 979.8373

107 Washington Square Village life centers around this square, which is the largest public space south of 14th Street. Joggers, children, university students, and Village matrons provide the local color; flea markets and fairs occupy the grounds on weekends. The area was a marsh, a potter's field, a venue for public hangings, and a military parade ground before it was claimed as a public park in 1828. Elaborate, fashionable houses soon appeared around it, and **NYU** appropriated the east side in the late 1830s. The **Memorial Arch,** designed by **Stanford White** of **McKim, Mead & White,** was originally a wooden monument built in 1889 for the centennial celebration of George Washington's inauguration. It became so well liked that private funds were raised to rebuild it permanently in stone. The sculpture, *Washington,* on the west pier was created by Alexander Stirling Calder, father of Alexander Calder. By the 1950s the park had seriously decayed. The city transit authority was using the arch as a bus turnaround, and there was a proposal to run Fifth Avenue underneath it. Popular outrage blocked the tunnel, put a halt to the buses, and gave momentum to the movement to redesign the park—a community effort that was realized in the 1960s. The park has become haven to a variety of street types—performers, wanderers, and chess-players—but the local community has made a concerted effort to keep it safe. Weekend afternoons in warm weather still bring out a wild mix. ♦ Bounded by University Pl and MacDougal St, and W Fourth St and Waverly Pl

108 Grey Art Gallery An offbeat art gallery in a renovated building, it offers changing high-quality art and photography shows. The backdrop for exhibitions is a grid of white-painted Doric columns. ♦ Tu-Sa. 33 Washington Pl (at Washington Sq E). 998.6780 &

109 Antique Boutique The city's largest used-clothing store boasts more than 30,000 pieces, including leather motorcycle jackets, men's oversize cashmere coats, and gabardine shirts. It's not unusual to see some of New York's top designers shopping here for ideas they'll take home in their minds if not in a shopping bag. ♦ Daily. 712-714 Broadway (between W Fourth St and Washington Pl). 460.8830 &

110 Bottom Line Cabaret This small cabaret-style nightclub with a superlative sound system was the model for Boston's Paradise and LA's Roxy. Best known as the launching pad for Bruce Springsteen and Patti Smith, among others, its days as an industry showcase are long gone. But the club still continues a remarkably consistent booking policy, which includes jazz groups, comedy, drama, and assorted special presentations. The place is comfortable, clean, and efficient. A bar menu is available. Call for changing show schedules. ♦ Cover, drink minimum. 15 E Fourth St (at Mercer St). 228.7880

111 New York University (NYU) More than 15,000 full-time students study at the Washington Square campus of New York's largest private university, comprised of 14 schools, including the **Tisch School of the Arts** and the highly regarded **NYU School of Business and Public Administration.** The campus extends beyond the classroom and dormitory buildings and into the converted lofts and Greek Revival row houses common in Greenwich Village. When the old University Heights campus was sold to the **City University of New York** in 1973, the focus shifted here.

Architects **Philip Johnson** and **Richard Foster** were commissioned to make a master plan that would unify the disjointed collection of buildings and enable the campus to handle the increased activity. Their plan called for rebuilding some of the older structures, refacing the existing ones with red sandstone, and establishing design guidelines for future construction. Only three buildings were refaced before the plan was abandoned. ♦ 50 W Fourth St (bounded by Mercer St and La Guardia Pl, and West 3rd and Waverly Pl). 998.4636

Within New York University:

Elmer Holmes Bobst Library Designed by **Johnson** and **Foster** to be the architectural focal point of the university, this stolid-looking cube is 150 feet high and clad in Longmeadow redstone (in the tradition of Washington Square), with a 12-story interior atrium around which the stacks and reading rooms are organized. Chevron-like stairways with gold anodized aluminum railings give scale to the atrium, and the design of the black, gray, and white marble floor, influenced by Palladio's piazza for Venice's San Giorgio Maggiore, adds to the decorative interior detail that is the antithesis of the austere exterior. The building is not open to the public. ♦ Washington Sq S and La Guardia Pl. 998.2505. &

112 Judson Memorial Baptist Church This Romanesque church, erected in 1892 by

McKim, Mead & White, was built as a bridge between the poor to the south of the square and the rich above it, and has always had a full program of social activities. The best part is inside, where you can appreciate the fine stained-glass windows by John LaFarge. The church was named for Adinoram D. Judson, the first Baptist missionary to Burma. **Judson Hall** and the bell tower above it are now **NYU** dormitories. ♦ 55 Washington Sq S (between Thompson and Sullivan Sts). 477.0351

112 Hagop Kevorkian Center for Near Eastern Studies Designed in 1972 by **Philip Johnson** and **Richard Foster,** this huge granite building fits snugly into its corner site and is highlighted by an interesting array of angled corner windows. ♦ 50 Washington Sq S (at Sullivan St). 998.8877 &

113 Vegetarian Paradise 2 ★$ Vegetarian versions of iron steak and Peking duck are made out of bean curd, taro root, and other vegetable products. There's not a speck of meat in this restaurant, but only real die-hard carnivores will miss it. ♦ Chinese vegetarian ♦ Daily lunch and dinner. 144 W Fourth St (between MacDougal St and Sixth Ave). 260.7130

114 Blue Note Jazz Club Top jazz artists perform here nightly at 9PM and 11:30PM (and sometimes again at 1AM), and on weekends for a jazz brunch and matinee at 1PM and 3:30PM. A reasonably priced continental menu is available. Grover Washington Jr., the Modern Jazz Quartet, and Oscar Peterson all make appearances. ♦ Cover, drink minimum. Daily. Reservations recommended. 131 W Third St (between MacDougal St and Sixth Ave). 475.8592

115 Bleecker Bob's Golden Oldies The selection of records and CDs is voluminous, grouped according to genre (there's everything except classical and opera), not artist, but the knowledgeable staff knows the location of every last recording and late-night browsing is an encouraged Village tradition. You might find yourself elbow-to-elbow with old rock stars themselves. ♦ M-Th, Su noon-1AM; F-Sa noon-3AM. 118 W Third St (between MacDougal St and Sixth Ave). 475.9677 &

115 Caffè Reggio ★$ The first cafe in America, this fabulously dingy and dark place was built around 1785. It's a great spot for deep conversation or journal writing. Sip your coffee outside in nice weather. This landmark cafe appeared in the movies, *The Godfather II*

and *Serpico*. ♦ Cafe ♦ M-F until 3AM; Sa-Su until 4AM. No credit cards accepted. 119 MacDougal St (at W Third St). 475.9557

115 Players Theatre When the **Shakespeare Wright Company** first opened this 248-seat theater in 1959, they mainly performed works by the Bard. Today, they rent out the space for a variety of performance venues: music, drama, comedy, one-person shows. ♦ 115 MacDougal St (at W Third St). 254.5076

115 Minetta Tavern ★$$ The caricatures and murals behind the old oak bar and elsewhere around this Italian restaurant will take you back to the Village of the 1930s. The menu offers standard Italian fare, which is nicely prepared if not very exciting. ♦ Italian ♦ Daily lunch and dinner. 113 MacDougal St (at Minetta La). 475.3850

LA BOHÊME

116 La Bohème ★$$ With its open kitchen, floral arrangements, and dim lighting, this bistro is a cozy spot to enjoy specialties from Provence—confit of duck with orange and pear sauce, and herb-crusted grilled chicken served with mashed potatoes and caramelized garlic. Desserts include lemon tart, *marquise du chocolat* (a light chocolate mousse cake) served with orange sauce, and cold lemon soufflé topped with ice cream and raspberry sauce. In warmer months, the room opens onto Minetta Lane, a charming, quiet street—something of a rarity in noisy Manhattan. ♦ French ♦ M-Sa dinner; Su brunch and dinner. 24 Minetta La (at Sixth Ave). 473.6447

116 Minetta Lane Theatre This newer Off-Broadway theater presents revues as well as new plays in a more comfortable setting than many. Seats 378. ♦ 18 Minetta La (between Minetta St and Sixth Ave). 420.8000 &

116 1 Minetta Street DeWitt Wallace and his wife, Lila Acheson, published the first issue of the *Reader's Digest* from a basement apartment here in 1922. ♦ At Sixth Ave

---

In the 1790s, 22,000 victims of yellow fever were buried in what is now Washington Square Park. The park was later the site of a huge celebration in 1824 when 20 highwaymen were hanged from an elm in the park's northwest corner.

America's first patent was issued in New York City on 31 July 1790. It was granted to a Samuel Hopkins for a process that involved the making and purifying of potash, an ingredient used in soap. The patent was signed by President George Washington, Secretary of State Thomas Jefferson, and Attorney General Edmund Randolph.

117 Porto Rico Opened in 1907, this old-time coffee store isn't even one of the Village's oldest, but the long lines of caffeine-oholics on Saturday mornings is evidence that it's the uncontested favorite. Two reasons: the quality of the beans and the price. ♦ Daily. 201 Bleecker St (between MacDougal St and Sixth Ave). 477.5421

118 Caffè Dante ★$ Although Italian is spoken here, it's the strong coffee and the let-them-sit-as-long-as-they-want attitude that really makes this place authentic. Treat yourself to the cheesecake. ♦ Cafe ♦ M-F until 2AM; Sa-Sun until 4AM. No credit cards accepted. 79 MacDougal St (between W Houston and Bleecker Sts). 982.5275

119 Da Silvano ★$$ An uneven but quite interesting menu features central Italian fare. Start with chicken-liver *crostini* (croutons), followed by *rigatoni focaccia* (in a sauce of butter, cream, garlic, sage, rosemary, tomato, and double-smoked bacon), or one of the game dishes that include quail in a Barolo wine sauce with radicchio. The elegantly rustic rooms bring in a handsome, affluent clientele. The service is correct, and the wine list well chosen. ♦ Italian ♦ Daily lunch and dinner. Reservations recommended. 260 Sixth Ave (between W Houston and Bleecker Sts). 982.0090 &

120 Film Forum Forced to leave its Watts Street location, the art house moved here in September 1990. The intriguing new space was designed by **Stephen Tilly** and **Jay Hibbs.** The agenda is the same: independent American and foreign films and retrospectives. ♦ 209 W Houston St (between Sixth Ave and Varick St). 627.2035 &

121 Chez Jacqueline ★★$$ This popular bistro owned and run by lively Jacqueline Zini specializes in dishes from her native Provence, including one of the best fish soups in town and a delicious beef stew niçoise. The garlic-laden *brandade* (warm salt-cod puree) is a good starter. ♦ French ♦ Daily lunch and dinner. Reservations required. 72 MacDougal St (at W Houston St). 505.0727 &

121 Aggie's ★$ It looks like an LA diner, but the attitude is pure New York, and you'll find the home-style cooking hearty no matter where you're from. Aggie's friendly cats roam amid the tables to most customers' delight. ♦ American ♦ M-Sa breakfast, lunch, and dinner; Su lunch. No credit cards accepted. 146 W Houston St (at MacDougal St). 673.8994

121 Raffetto's Fresh pasta is made daily (witness the alchemy next door), and it's cut into a variety of widths before your eyes. Stuffed versions—including ravioli and tortellini—are also for sale, as are imported Italian products that will help you create first-rate dishes. ♦ Tu-Sa. 144 W Houston St (between Sullivan and MacDougal Sts). 777.1261 &

122 MacDougal-Sullivan Gardens Historic District These 24 houses date from 1844 to 1850. To attract middle-class professionals, **William Sloane Coffin** (heir to the W.J. Sloane furniture fortune) modernized them in 1920 and combined their gardens to make a midblock private park. ♦ Sullivan and MacDougal Sts (between W Houston and Bleecker Sts)

123 Sullivan Street Playhouse This 153-seat theater has long been home to the longest-running production in American history, *The Fantasticks,* which opened in May 1960. In honor of this feat, Sullivan Street along this block has been dubbed "Fantasticks' Lane" by the city. ♦ 181 Sullivan St (between W Houston and Bleecker Sts). 674.3838

124 Science Fiction Shop Although New York's sci-fi fans may miss the otherworldly atmosphere of the old shop on Bleecker Street, they're still hooked on the excellent stock of new, out-of-print, and used books and periodicals sold here. ♦ Daily. 168 Thompson St (between W Houston and Bleecker Sts). 473.3010

125 Le Figaro Café $ In the old days, this place was a Beat hangout, with underground shows downstairs. But that, as they say, is history. Today, this high-volume beanery caters to the weekend blitz of young tourists on Bleecker Street. ♦ Bistro/Cafe ♦ M-F until 2AM; Sa-Sun until 4AM. No credit cards accepted. 184 Bleecker St (at MacDougal St). 677.1100

126 Caffè Borgia ★$ This old-world coffeehouse is authentic right down to the smoke-dulled mural. It's a perfect place to spend an afternoon sipping cappuccino and reading a good book. ♦ Cafe ♦ M-F until 2AM; Sa-Sun until 4AM. 185 Bleecker St (at MacDougal St). 674.9589. Also at: 161 Princ St (between Thompson St and W Broadway). 677.1850

127 Il Mulino ★★★$$$ Behind this most unassuming facade is one of the best Italian restaurants in the Village. Only the wait at the crowded bar for a table—even with a reservation—brings it down a notch. Try any of the pastas, including *spaghetti bolognese* or *carbonara*. Follow with one of the delicious entrées: chicken braised in wine and artichokes; fillet of beef in caper sauce; rolled veal with wine, cream, and wild mushrooms; or salmon with porcini mushrooms. For dessert indulge in the sinfully delicious chocolate mousse. ♦ Italian ♦ M-F lunch and dinner; Sa dinner. Reservations required. 86 W Third St (between Thompson and Sullivan Sts). 673.3783

128 Nostalgia and All That Jazz Here's an impressive selection of vintage records with an emphasis on jazz, as well as one of New York's best selections of early radio programs and film soundtracks. ♦ Daily. 217 Thompson St (between Bleecker and W Third Sts). 420.1940 &

129 Village Chess Shop You can play chess from noon to midnight with another expert like yourself, or buy unique chess sets made from materials ranging from nuts and bolts to ivory and onyx. ♦ Daily noon-midnight. 230 Thompson St (between Bleecker and W Third Sts). 475.9580 &

129 Grand Ticino ★★$$ A neighborhood fixture since 1919, this dark little Italian restaurant will satisfy the most romantic notions of an evening out in Greenwich Village—forest-green walls and burnished wood, muted wall sconces and linen tablecloths. The food—homemade ravioli stuffed with goat cheese and arugula, and osso buco with risotto—won't disappoint, either. For a dramatic dessert, order the hot zabaglione to be flambéed at your table. The restaurant scene with Olympia Dukakis from the movie *Moonstruck* was filmed here. ♦ Northern Italian ♦ Daily lunch and dinner. 228 Thompson St (between Bleecker and W Third Sts). 777.5922

129 Stella Dallas The shop is a good source for reasonably priced men's and women's retro rags from the 1930s to 1950s, collected by a fashion stylist and a clothing designer. ♦ Daily. 218 Thompson St (between Bleecker and W Third Sts). 674.0447

129 Il Ponte Vecchio ★$$ This bustling white dining room decorated with posters is one of the old reliable Italian places in the neighborhood, and it offers a large, traditional menu. Try the calamari with marinara sauce; asparagus topped with parmesan; *spaghetti amatriciana;* rigatoni with sausage and cream; fettuccine with sun-dried tomatoes and arugula; chicken with white wine, artichokes, mushrooms, and peppers; veal parmigiana; and old-fashioned cheesecake for dessert. ♦ Italian ♦ Daily lunch and dinner. Reservations recommended. 206 Thompson St (between Bleecker and W Third Sts). 228.7701

130 Bitter End This small room has served as a springboard for numerous musical careers but now features mostly once-famous folkies and/or young hopefuls performing rock, folk, country, and occasionally comedy. ♦ Cover, drink minimum. Daily 7:30PM-4AM. 147 Bleecker St (between La Guardia Pl and Thompson St). 673.7030

130 Peculier Pub More than 250 brands of beer from 35 countries are served here to students from almost as many American colleges. ♦ M-Th, Su 4PM-2AM; F 4PM-4AM; Sa 2PM-4AM. 145 Bleecker St (between La Guardia Pl and Thompson St). 353.1327

131 Ennio & Michael ★★$$$ The hearty food is first-rate and includes stuffed artichokes, *spaghetti puttanesca* (with tomatoes, capers, and olives), and *salmon cartoccio* (oven-cooked in a bag with white wine, butter, and vegetables). End the meal with what may be the best cannoli in New York. ♦ Italian ♦ Daily lunch and dinner. 539 La Guardia Pl (at Bleecker St). 677.8577

132 University Village This 1966 high-rise housing complex is noteworthy in a city where high-rises are the norm, thanks to **I.M. Pei & Partners'** deft handling of scale, a result of the well-articulated facade. The concrete framing and recessed glass clearly define each apartment unit and provide a straightforward, unadorned exterior pattern. Because of a pinwheel apartment plan, the inner corridors are short and apartments are unusually spacious. Two towers are owned by **NYU,** the third is a co-op. A 36-foot-high sculpture in the plaza between the towers is an enlargement of a cubist piece by Picasso. **Pei & Partners** used the same exterior treatment in the **Kip's Bay** housing project (Second Avenue at West 30th Street). ♦ 100 and 110 Bleecker St (at La Guardia Pl); 505 La Guardia Pl (at Bleecker St)

133 Cable Building This 1894 **McKim, Mead & White** building was once the headquarters and powerhouse of the Broadway Cable Traction Company, which operated streetcars propelled by underground cables in the 19th century. ♦ 611 Broadway (at W Houston St)

Within the Cable Building:

Angelika Film Center Big commercial hits as well as a selection of independent and foreign films are shown in this six-screen cinema. The cafe, a good spot for reading the paper or writing in a journal, serves snacks until midnight. ♦ 995.2000

East Village

The East Village is counterculture central, where shaved heads, tattoos, and various pierced body parts are as common as is the designer-clad crowd on Madison Avenue. In this neighborhood bounded by **Broadway**, the **East River**, and **Houston** and **East 14th Streets**, many of the galleries, boutiques, clubs, and restaurants represent the cutting edge of what's next in downtown.

Believe it or not, this last bastion of Bohemia was once the grandest part of Greenwich Village. Governor Peter Stuyvesant's estate originally covered the area from the present **Fourth Avenue** to the East River and from **East Fifth** to **East 17th Streets**. He was buried beneath his chapel, now the site of **St. Mark's-in-the-Bowery Church** (built in 1799), known as much for its ministry to the disadvantaged and its far-out religious services as for its historical significance. In the 1830s, the houses of the Astors, Vanderbilts, and Delanos lined **Lafayette Street** from **Great Jones Street** to **Astor Place**. Almost nothing is left from those times except the **Old Merchants' House**

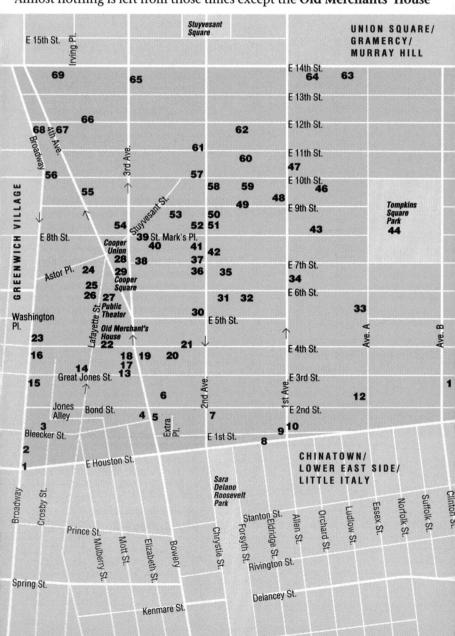

on **East Fourth Street** near Lafayette Street and the remaining homes of **Colonnade Row** (also known as "LaGrange Terrace"), where John Jacob Astor and Warren Delano, FDR's grandfather, lived.

Astor Place was once the scene of the **Vauxhall Gardens**, where people went in the summer to enjoy music and theater. It was replaced by the popular **Astor Place Opera House**, which is remembered chiefly for the 1849 riot between rival claques (hands hired to applaud a certain performer or act) of the British actor William Macready, in which 34 people were killed (or 22, depending on which account you read) before the militia brought the crowd under control. Astor Place was named for the first John Jacob Astor, who arrived from Germany in 1789 at the age of 21 with $25. Before his death at the age of 85, he had made a fortune in fur trading and Manhattan real estate.

The Astor Library, built with a bequest from John Jacob Astor, is now the home base of the **New York Shakespeare Festival** at the **Public Theater,** a multimedia, multistage enterprise where something exciting is always on the boards or on the screen. Other architectural survivors from the 1850s are the Italianate **Cooper Union,** the country's first coeducational college and the first open to all races and creeds; and **McSorley's Old Ale House,** where everyone who counts has had a glass of the special dark ale since it opened in the mid-19th century. John Sloan did a painting of it, and Brendan Behan hung out in a corner near the potbellied stove.

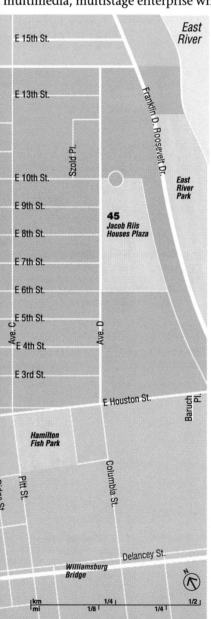

For at least 30 years, the East Village has been an enclave of counter-culture; in the 1960s, hippies crowded into Dayglo-painted "digs," spending nights with the Grateful Dead or Iron Butterfly at such clubs as the **Filmore East** and the **Electric Circus.** Though geographically connected to its gentrified western neightbor, Greenwich Village, the East Village is a younger, less manicured community. But things aren't as gritty as they once were. Even the street of the so-called "Alphabet City" (**Avenues A, B, C, and D**), once seedy and drug-infested, are now lined with restaurants and boutiques.

The East Village is more than ever a melting pot. The Italian influence is still visible in the old-fashioned *pasticcerie.* **Little India,** the stretch of **East Sixth Street** between **First** and **Second Avenues,** contains at least 20 Indian and Pakistani restaurants, with another half-dozen spilling over onto the avenues. Near Astor Place at **Cooper Square** (**Third Avenue**) and **East Seventh Street** is **Little Ukraine**—a world of Byzantine churches with onion domes, shops with Slavic music and painted eggs, and restaurants serving piroshki and stuffed cabbage. Multiethnic, yes. Flamboyant, absolutely. Happily, everyone seems to coexist peacefully in what is one of the most colorful niches of New York City today.

1 Louisiana Community Bar and Grill
★$$ The chefs at this Cajun restaurant—formerly **K-Paul's**—were all trained by Paul Prudhomme. Come for the food: blackened tuna, blackened prime rib, étouffée, jambalaya; and the music: blues, jazz, and zydeco. ◆ Cajun ◆ Daily dinner. Reservations recommended. 622 Broadway (at E Houston St). 460.9633

2 Center for Book Arts This organization offers a gallery and teaching and work space for hand-producing and publishing books, including hand bookbinding, papermaking, and letterpress printing. ◆ Gallery M-Sa. 626 Broadway (between E Houston and Bleecker Sts), Fifth floor. 460.9768

2 New York Mercantile Exchange
Herman J. Schwartzmann designed this cast-iron jungle with bamboo stems, lilies, and roses complemented with Oriental motifs in 1882. The Exchange, obviously no longer here, was once headquarters for all the big butter-and-egg men and wholesale dealers in coffee, tea, and spices. The ground floor is currently occupied by **Urban Outfitters,** clothier to many a university student. ◆ M-Sa 10AM-10PM; Su noon-8PM. 628 Broadway (between E Houston and Bleecker Sts). 475.0009

3 Bayard Condict Building The one and only **Louis Sullivan** building in New York is hidden among the industrial high-rises on Bleecker Street. The structure (formerly the **Condict Building**) was an anachronism even when it was completed in 1898, when the Renaissance Revival style that followed the 1893 Chicago World's Fair turned popular taste away from the elegant, quintessentially American designs of **Sullivan** and the Chicago School. The intricate cornice filigree and soaring vertical lines of the terracotta–clad steel piers are **Sullivan** trademarks; the six angels at the roofline were applied under client duress. ◆ 65 Bleecker St (at Crosby St)

"There are two million interesting people in New York—and only 78 in Los Angeles."

Neil Simon

"If I live in New York, it is because I choose to live here. It is the city of total intensity, the city of the moment."

Diana Vreeland

4 Bouwerie Lane Theatre In 1874, when the lower end of the Bowery was a theater district, **Henry Engelbert** built this fanciful cast-iron building as a bank. Today, it is the home of the **Jean Cocteau Repertory,** an unusual company of resident actors that often performs several works in the same week. Its presentations are usually classical plays or plays by writers better known for other literary endeavors. ◆ 330 Bowery (at Bond St). 677.0060

5 CBGB and OMFUG Long after everyone has forgotten what the initials of this Bowery dive stand for (Country, Bluegrass, Blues, and Other Music for Uplifting Gourmandisers), they will remember it as the birthplace of punk rock. Here for more than two decades (it celebrated its 20th anniversary in 1994), this long, dark bar illuminated by neon beer signs still plays host to an array of groups under a wide banner of styles. Uptowners used to go slumming here; now it attracts the suburban hard-core crowd and the nostalgic, but it still boasts some of the best acoustics in town. ◆ Cover. Daily 8PM-3AM. 315 Bowery (at Bleecker St). 982.4052

6 New York Marble Cemetery Located on the inside portion of the block (enter from an alley on Second Street), this early 1800s cemetery was one of the first built in the city and is one of the very few left in Manhattan. The burial vaults are underground, and the names of those interred are carved into marble tablets set into a perimeter wall that surrounds a small grassy area. Down the block (52-74 East Second Street) is the **New York City Marble Cemetery,** started in 1831 along the same nonsectarian lines but with aboveground vaults and handsome headstones. Genealogists can trace New York's early first families—the Scribners, Varicks, Beekmans, Van Zandts, Hoyts, and one branch of the Roosevelts—from tombstone information. Burial here is restricted to the descendants of the original vault owners, but no one has applied since 1917. ◆ Bounded by E Second and E Third Sts (between Second Ave and Bowery)

7 Anthology Film Archives Located in the **Second Avenue Courthouse** building, this center for the preservation and exhibition of film and video works holds daily screenings that are open to all. Only students, scholars, museums, and universities have access to the archives and library. ♦ Admission. Th-Su evenings; call for schedules. 32 Second Ave (at E Second St). 505.5181

8 Style Swami Colorful women's and men's African clothing designed by Alpana Bawa is showcased in this shop, along with home furnishings. ♦ Tu-Su. 70 E First St (between First and Second Aves). 254.1249

8 City Lore In a gentrified brownstone just off First Avenue, a group of serious folklorists explore New York cultural traditions through photo and tape archives, oral histories, discussion groups, music and film festivals, and concerts. ♦ Call for an appointment M-F. 72 E First St (between First and Second Aves). 529.1955

9 Boca Chica ★$ Spicy Latin music on weekends makes this funky East Village spot a must for night owls. Other days of the week aren't exactly bland either, with rivers of exotic Brazilian drinks to keep customers in jovial spirits and staples from the South American menu, such as garlicky chicken and shredded beef, which can get as hot as the music. ♦ South American ♦ M-Sa dinner; Su brunch and dinner. 13 First Ave (at E First St). 473.0108

10 ARKA This general store for the Ukrainian community stocks tapes, records, books, and newspapers, plus embroidery threads and fabrics, egg decorating kits, and more. ♦ M-Sa, early Su closing. 26 First Ave (between E First and E Second Sts). 473.3550 &

10 Lucky Cheng's ★$ At this trendy Asian spot, the waitresses in their tight silk dresses are not what they seem—it's sort of a lighthearted version of *M. Butterfly*. The food is as dramatic: miso salmon on stir-fried Chinese greens, Shanghai noodles with mixed vegetables in sesame-citrus sauce, and stir-fried noodles with scallops, mussels, and calamari in lobster sauce. ♦ Asian ♦ Daily dinner. 24 First Ave (between E First and E Second Sts). 473.0516

11 Nuyorican Poet's Cafe $ By the time this 1970s forum for young Puerto Rican poets closed in 1982, one of the founding members, the late Miguelo Pinero, had achieved international acclaim as a playwright. Back in business since 1990, the place is packed with poets and an eclectic audience. ♦ Cafe ♦ Cover. W-Sa 8PM-closing. 236 E Third St (between Aves C and B). 505.8183

12 Two Boots ★$ An East Village original, this place serves Louisiana cuisine with an Italian twist—the boots refer to the shape of both state and country. Try the pecan-crusted catfish with cilantro aioli or the barbecued-shrimp pizza. If it's home delivery you want, **Two Boots to Go** (505.5450) is right across the street. ♦ Cajun/Italian ♦ M-F lunch and dinner; Sa-Su brunch and dinner. 37 Ave A (between E Second and E Third Sts). 505.2276 &. Also at: 74 Bleecker St (at Broadway). 777.1033; 75 Greenwich Ave (at W 11th St); 514 Second St (between Seventh and Eighth Aves, Brooklyn). 718/499.3253

13 Great Jones Cafe $ Blackened fish, sweet-potato fries, gumbo, and other decent, reasonably priced eats are served in a loud and lively roadside bar atmosphere. The Blue Plate special, usually meat loaf or pork chops, is probably a lot like your Mom used to make. ♦ Cajun/American ♦ M-F dinner; Sa-Su brunch and dinner. No credit cards accepted. 54 Great Jones St (between Bowery and Lafayette St). 674.9304

14 376-380 Lafayette Street This richly ornamented yet somewhat uncomfortable warehouse is most notable because it was designed by **Henry J. Hardenbergh** in 1888, several years after he designed the **Dakota** apartments uptown on West 72nd Street. ♦ At Great Jones St

14 Time Cafe ★$$ Trendy crowds populate this spot from breakfast until late at night. They come to dine on deliciously healthy dishes that include charred yellowfin tuna salad and a free-range chicken tortilla with cilantro pesto. Within the cafe is a bilevel Moroccan club called **Fez**, which offers jazz, poetry readings, and cushy couches at night; there's a cover charge. ♦ American ♦ Daily breakfast, lunch, dinner, and late-night meals. Reservations recommended. 380 Lafayette St (at Great Jones St). 533.7000

15 Acme Bar & Grill ★$$ If you're looking for food that will stick to your ribs, you've come to the right place. The selection includes Cajun-style chicken, jambalaya, and gumbo. Don't miss the wonderful mashed potatoes with cream gravy. A ledge along one entire wall is lined with samples of every conceivable kind of hot sauce—experiment at your own risk. After dinner, head downstairs for live music; there's a cover charge. ♦ Southern ♦ M-F lunch and dinner; Sa-Su brunch and dinner. 9 Great Jones St (between Lafayette St and Broadway). 420.1934 &

Restaurants/Clubs: Red   **Hotels:** Blue
Shops/ ♥ Outdoors: Green   **Sights/Culture:** Black

Book Nooks

New York City is a book lover's paradise. Just take a look at the eight-plus pages of bookstore listings in the *Yellow Pages*. Following are some of the favorites. (Many of these are described in this book. Check the index for page numbers.)

Art and Architecture

Asia Society 725 Park Ave (at E 70th St). 288.6400

Hacker Art Books 45 W 57th St (between Fifth and Sixth Aves). 688.7600

Morton Books 989 Third Ave (at E 59th St). 421.9025

Rizzoli 31 W 57th St (between Fifth and Sixth Aves). 759.2424

Untitled 159 Prince St (between W Broadway and Thompson St). 982.2088

Urban Center Books 457 Madison Ave (between E 50th and E 51st Sts within Villard Houses). 935.3595

Foreign Language

Kinokuniya Bookstore (Japanese) 10 W 49th St (between Fifth and Sixth Aves). 765.1461

Lectorum Publications (Spanish) 137 W 14th St (between Sixth and Seventh Aves). 929.2833

Librairie de France and Librería Hispanica (French and Spanish) 610 Fifth Ave (between W 49th and W 50th Sts). 581.8810

Vanni (Italian) 30 W 12th St (between Fifth and Sixth Aves). 675.6336

General Interest

B. Dalton's, 666 Fifth Ave (at W 52nd St). 247.1740

Books & Co. 939 Madison Ave (at E 74th St). 737.1450

Burlington Bookshop 1082 Madison Ave (between E 81st and E 82nd Sts). 288.7420

Coliseum Books 1771 Broadway (at W 57th St). 757.8381

Doubleday Bookstore, 724 Fifth Ave (between W 56th and W 57th Sts). 397.0550

Gotham Book Mart and Gallery 41 W 47th St (between Fifth and Sixth Aves). 719.4448

Madison Avenue Bookshop 833 Madison Ave (at E 69th St). 535.6130

St. Mark's Books 31 Third Ave (between E Eighth and E Ninth Sts). 260.7853

Shakespeare & Co. 716 Broadway (between E 4th St and Washington Pl). 529.1330; 2259 Broadway (at W 81st St). 580.7800

Tower Books 383 Lafayette St (at E Fourth St). 228.5100

Secondhand and Out-of-Print

Academy Books and Records 10 W 18th St (between Fifth and Sixth Aves). 242.4848

Argosy Bookstore 116 E 59th St (between Lexington and Park Aves). 753.4455

Gotham Book Mart and Gallery 41 W 47th St (between Fifth and Sixth Aves). 719.4448

Gryphon Bookshop 2246 Broadway (between W 80th and W 81st Sts). 362.0706

Strand Bookstore 828 Broadway (at E 12th St). 473.1452; 159 John St (at Front St). 809.0875

Specialty

Applause Theater Books (performing arts) 211 W 71st St (between Broadway and West End Aves). 496.7511

Biography Bookstore (biographies) 400 Bleecker St (at W 11th St). 807.8655

Books of Wonder (children's) 132 Seventh Ave S (at W 18th St). 989.3270

A Different Light (gay and lesbian) 151 W 19th St (between Sixth and Seventh Aves). 989.4850

The Drama Bookshop (dramatic arts) 723 Seventh Ave (between W 48th and W 49th Sts). 944.0595

East West Books (Eastern philosophy and holistic health) 78 Fifth Ave (between W 13th and W 14th Sts). 243.5994; 568 Columbus Ave (between W 87th and W 88th Sts). 787.7552

Forbidden Planet (science fiction and comics) 821 Broadway (at E 12th St). 473.1576

Joseph Patelson Music House (classical music) 160 W 56th St (between Sixth and Seventh Aves). 582.5840

Kitchen Arts & Letters (food and wine; cookbooks) 1435 Lexington Ave (between E 93rd and E 94th Sts). 876.5550

Liberation Bookshop (African-American History; African History) 421 Lenox Ave (at W 131st St). 281.4615

Murder Ink (mysteries) 2486 Broadway (between W 92nd and W 93rd Sts). 362.8905; 1465 Second Ave (between E 76th and E 77th Sts). 517.3222; 1 Whitehall St (at Broadway). 742.7025

Mysterious Bookshop (mysteries) 129 W 56th St (between Sixth and Seventh Aves). 765.0900

New York Bound Bookshop (New York) 50 Rockefeller Plaza (between W 50th and W 51st Sts). 245.8503

Oscar Wilde Memorial Bookshop (gay and lesbian) 15 Christopher St (at Gay St). 255.8097

Paraclete (theology) 146 E 74th St (at Lexington Ave). 535.4050

A Photographer's Place (photography) 133 Mercer St (between Spring and Prince Sts). 431.9358

Revolution Books (revolutionary) 13 E 16th St (between Union Sq W and Fifth Ave). 691.3345

Three Lives & Company (literature) 154 W 10th St (between Sixth Ave and Seventh Ave S). 741.2069

Traveller's Bookstore (travel) 22 W 52nd St (between Fifth and Sixth Aves). 664.0995

16 **Tower Records** The ultimate store for the listener comprises a main building on Broadway and East Fourth Street for pop, jazz, R&B, dance, and more; a classical annex next door (on Lafayette Street); and video and electronic annexes in between. If they don't have it, chances are it's going to be tough to find. If you're a bibliophile, visit **Tower Books** down the block at 383 Lafayette Street. ♦ Daily 9AM-midnight. 692 Broadway (at E Fourth St). 505.1500. Also at: 2107 Broadway (at W 74th St). 799.2500; 725 Fifth Ave (at E 56th St). 838.8110; 1535 Third Ave (at E 86th St). 369.2500

17 **Marion's Continental Restaurant and Lounge** ★$$ This was the place to be in the 1960s, when senators, presidents, and movie stars were all regulars here. It closed in the early 1970s, but Marion's son and a business partner reopened the landmark in 1990 with much of its signature decor intact. The food is not uniformly dependable, although the Caesar salad and the steak au poivre are both good. Come for the inexpensive Vodka Gibsons, old-fashioneds, and Manhattans. ♦ Continental ♦ Daily dinner. 354 Bowery (between Great Jones and E Fourth Sts). 475.7621

18 **Bowery Bar** ★$$ A former gas station, the dining room flaunts its roots with a haute garage motif—from photos of car engines to displayed truck parts. Food is secondary here—getting the chance to furtively gawk at such celebrities as Cindy Crawford and Donna Karan is more the point. However, you can get a perfectly acceptable pan-seared salmon, roast free-range chicken, grilled lemon-ginger tuna, and for dessert, a hot fudge sundae. ♦ American ♦ M-F lunch and dinner; Sa-Su brunch and dinner. Reservations required. 358 Bowery (at E Fourth St). 475.2220

19 **Phebe's Place** During the 1960s this was a popular hangout among Off-Broadway playwrights Sam Shepard, Robert Patrick, and Leonard Melfi. Today, it continues to attract the East Village arts crowd as well as a lot of off-duty police officers. Cheap pitchers of domestic beer and burgers pull in the college students. ♦ M-F 4PM-4AM; Sa 5PM-4AM. 361 Bowery (at E Fourth St). 473.9008

20 **La Mama E.T.C.** First called **Cafe La Mama**, this theater has been in the vanguard of the Off-Broadway movement since 1962. Under the direction of Ellen Stewart, it has been instrumental in presenting both American and international experimental playwrights and directors to this country. Stewart nurtured playwrights Sam Shepard, Lanford Wilson, Ed Bullins, Tom Eyen, Israel Horovitz, and Elizabeth Swados, among others. Directors Tom O'Horgan, Marshall Mason, Wilford Leach, Andrei Serban, and Peter Brook have helped to stage many extraordinary productions here. ♦ 74A E Fourth St (between Second Ave and Bowery). 475.7710. Also at: The Annex, 66 E Fourth St (between Second Ave and Bowery). 473.8745

21 **Cucina di Pesce** ★$ A more reasonably priced good Italian seafood restaurant would be hard to find in Manhattan. Try the spinach penne with asparagus and sun-dried tomatoes in cream sauce, or the tuna steak grilled with sautéed sweet peppers, capers, olives, and onions. To accommodate the crowds, the same management opened **Frutti di Mare**, an annex across the street (84 E Fourth St, 979.2034) that serves both lunch and dinner. ♦ Italian ♦ Daily dinner. No credit cards accepted. 87 E Fourth St (between Second Ave and Bowery). 260.6800

22 **Old Merchants' House** This outstanding example of an 1830s Greek Revival town house remains intact with interiors and furnishings just the way they were when wealthy merchant Seabury Tredwell and his family lived here, thanks to Tredwell's daughter, Gertrude. Having fallen in love with an unacceptable suitor whom she was forbidden to wed, Gertude chose not to marry at all and, after her father's death, resolved to maintain the family home just as her father would have liked. Paintings, furniture, china, and books reflect their tasteful and conservative style. ♦ Admission. Th-Su 1-4PM. Call for information about group tours. 29 E Fourth St (between Bowery and Lafayette St). 777.1089

23 **Bayamo** ★$$ This is one of the better eateries on the lower Broadway strip; the menu seems a little gimmicky, but the food is consistently good. The inventive appetizers include fried or grilled chicken wings and fried wontons. Happy Hours and late nights tend to get a little crowded. If that's not your speed, maybe lunch or an early evening dinner on the balcony would be best. ♦ Cuban/Chinese ♦ Daily lunch and dinner; F-Sa late-night meals. 704 Broadway (between E Fourth St and Washington Pl). 475.5151

23 **Shakespeare & Co.** Though not related to its Paris namesake, this bookstore is a favorite among New Yorkers. ♦ M-Th, Su 10AM-11PM; F-Sa 10AM-midnight. 716 Broadway (between E Fourth St and Washington Pl). 529.1330. Also at: 2259 Broadway (at W 81st St). 580.7800

Bagels, from the Yiddish word *beygel*, are traditional Jewish rolls made from a yeast-based dough in the shape of a doughnut. Label Vishinsky, inventor of an early automatic bagel maker, claimed that the first New York bagel emerged from 15 Clinton Street in 1896.

24 Astor Place Hairstylists Considering all there is to do in New York, it may seem strange that watching haircuts has become a spectator sport on Astor Place, but look at the pictures in the window and on the walls of the far-out styles and you'll understand why. The prices are extremely low, too. (One of the signs in the window says they also do regular haircuts, but don't count on it.) ♦ Daily. 2 Astor Pl (between Fourth Ave and Broadway). 475.9854 ৬

24 Astor Wines and Spirits A large selection and generally good prices are the draws of this spacious wine shop, but sometimes the staff is less than thoroughly knowledgeable. ♦ M-Sa. 12 Astor Pl (at Lafayette St). 674.7500

25 Astor Place Theatre Across the street from the more artistically ambitious **Public Theater,** this 299-seat Off-Broadway venue has long runs *(The Foreigner)* and interesting musicals *(Tent Meeting, Middle of Nowhere)* that click with the theater crowd. ♦ 434 Lafayette St (between E Fourth St and Astor Pl). 254.4370

26 Colonnade Row The city's business and social leaders—the Astors, Vanderbilts, Delanos—once occupied the homes along this row, also known as "LaGrange Terrace." Only four of the nine built in 1833 by **Seth Greer** remain. The streetfront Corinthian colonnade was used to give the row a sense of unity and solidity. Despite designation as a New York City Landmark, these unique and historic structures remain in disrepair. ♦ 428-434 Lafayette St (between E Fourth St and Astor Pl)

Within Colonnade Row:

Indochine ★★$$ This trendy spot boasts consistently good French/Vietnamese food, which is served in a softly lit tropical-themed room that's filled with an attractive and well-dressed crowd. Try the spring rolls, the crispy duck with ginger, and the whole sea bass with lemongrass. ♦ French/Vietnamese ♦ Daily dinner. Reservations recommended. 430 Lafayette St (between E Fourth St and Astor Pl). 505.5111

Inside the doorway of the Public Theater are two white rectangular columns. "May Peace Prevail on Earth" is written on each in Japanese and English. The columns were sent to the late Joseph Papp by the Society of Prayer for World Peace, an organization that does not aim to convert lost souls, but is dedicated to planting as many peace poles as possible.

Restaurants/Clubs: Red   Hotels: Blue
Shops/ ♟ Outdoors: Green   **Sights/Culture: Black**

27 Public Theater The landmark home of the **New York Shakespeare Festival (NYSF)** has six theaters. Between **Newman** (seats 299), **Anspacher** (seats 299), **Martinson** (seats 1,650), **LuEster** (seats 135), **Susan Stein Shiva** (seats 100), and the **Little Theater** (seats 90), there's seating for over 2,500. The Romanesque Revival buildings were designed for John Jacob Astor by **Alexander Saeltzer** (south wing, 1853), **Griffin Thomas** (center, 1859), and **Thomas Stent** (north wing, 1881); originally New York City's first free library, they later served as the Hebrew Immigrant Aid Sheltering Society. These structures were on the verge of being demolished in the mid-1960s, when that dynamic man of the theater Joseph Papp came to the rescue with the **NYSF** and architect **Giorgio Cavaglieri.** Today, the **NYSF** not only manages to continually mount superb presentations but always seems to find the money needed to avert financial crises. The list of extraordinary shows that originated here and went on to Broadway includes *Hair* by Gerome Ragni and James Rado, *That Championship Season* by Jason Miller, Michael Bennett's *A Chorus Line* (which won three Pulitzers), David Rabe's *Sticks and Bones,* Caryl Churchill's *Serious Money,* and Rupert Holmes's *The Mystery of Edwin Drood.* About 25 theatrical productions are mounted each year. Film viewings were introduced in 1981. **Cavaglieri**—who also renovated the **Jefferson Market Courthouse**—did an admirable job salvaging much of the interior: Many of the theater spaces are impressive, and the entrance and lobby still include the original Corinthian colonnade. Quiktix (half-price tickets for performances) are available two hours before curtain. ♦ 425 Lafayette St (between E Fourth St and Astor Pl). 598.7150

28 Cooper Union Founded by multimillionaire Peter Cooper in 1859, this is a full-tuition-scholarship private college (illustrated at right). The inventor and industrialist, so brilliant with problems of application in the country's young iron and rail industries, spent his entire life ashamed that he'd never learned to spell or read, and the opening of this school was his attempt to help underprivileged young men and women get the education they deserved but couldn't afford. It was the first coeducational college, the first open to all races and creeds, and the first to offer free adult education courses—several are offered at night to accommodate those working in the daytime.

Architect **Frederick A. Petersen** used the rails Cooper produced in his ironworks in the college's construction (a grid of T-shaped rails was used to transmit loads to the walls). This building is considered by some to be the oldest extant building in

America framed with steel beams, and was declared a National Landmark in 1962. Two other breakthroughs in the building were the use of an elevator and the placing of vents under each of the 900 seats in the **Great Hall** auditorium—in the basement—through which fresh air was pumped. The **Great Hall** has, since the school's founding, been the scene of open expression on crucial issues of the day, from suffrage to civil rights. Abraham Lincoln delivered one of his most eloquent speeches here shortly before he was nominated as a presidential candidate. Both the NAACP and the American Red Cross were started in the building. The college still sponsors provocative lectures and many other events under its Great Hall Programs, which are open to the public. When architect **John Hejduk** gutted and renovated the building in 1974, he provided pristine classrooms, offices, and exhibition space—all with a high-modern Corbusian vocabulary. Augustus Saint-Gaudens, Adolph A. Weinman, and Leo Friedlander were graduates of the art school. More recent alumni include Milton Glaser, Alex Katz, and Seymour Chwast. Administrative offices are located at 30 Cooper Square (at E 5th St). ♦ 7 E Seventh St (at Fourth Ave). 353.4100

29 Cooper Square The statue of inventor and industrialist Peter Cooper seated in this triangular park is by Augustus Saint-Gaudens, a Cooper Union graduate. Its base is by Stanford White, who spent his boyhood in this neighborhood. Cooper was a self-made man who used the profits from a small grocery store to buy a glue factory up on 34th Street. He then invented a way to make better glue and became the biggest manufacturer in the country. Cooper invested the profits from that enterprise in Manhattan real estate and branched out to Baltimore, where he made a fortune selling land. ♦ E Seventh St (at Fourth Ave)

30 Global 33 ★$ After a long run with a Caribbean motif, the owners of the former tenant of this space—**Sugar Reef**—decided to transform it into a futuristic showcase for food and drink from all over the world. Among the international fare is couscous with fennel, orange, mint, and onion; fried zucchini polenta with roasted-pepper cream sauce; and grilled pork kabobs with Moorish seasoning. Global drinks include Brazilian *caipirinhas*, Jamaican dark and stormys, and British Pimms. ♦ International. ♦ Daily dinner and late-night meals. 93 Second Ave (between E Fifth and E Sixth Sts). 477-8427

Cooper Union

Michael Storrings

31 Back From Guatemala
The best merchandise from Central and South America and Asia, including scarves, exotic ethnic clothing, and various crafts are featured in this appealing shop. For a twist on the same theme, visit **Chrysalis** up the block at 340 East Sixth Street (533.8252); run by the same people, it focuses on contemporary ethnic jewelry, accessories, stationery, and gift items. ♦ M 1PM-10PM; Tu-Sa noon-10:30PM; Su 2PM-10:30PM. 306 E Sixth St (between First and Second Aves). 260.7010 ♿

31 Passage to India ★$ With more than 20 Indian restaurants in the area, competition is heavy, but this small spot is among the better ones. The freshly baked breads and tandoori specials are highlights. ♦ Indian ♦ Daily lunch, dinner, and late-night meals. 308 E Sixth St (between First and Second Aves). 529.5770

32 Mitali ★★$$ The running gag about the Indian restaurants on and around Sixth Street is that one central kitchen supplies them all. The cooking at this dark—even dingy—place, however, has always stood out. Try the *murgha tikka muslam* (chicken barbecued over charcoal and then cooked in a sauce of cream and almonds), or any of the tandoori meats. ♦ Indian ♦ Daily lunch and dinner. Reservations recommended. 334 E Sixth St (between First and Second Aves). 533.2508. Also at: 296 Bleecker St (at Seventh Ave). 989.1367

33 Ci Vediamo ★$ The kitschy murals of gondolas and the crooning strains of *Moon River* almost make you forget this is the cutting-edge East Village. The pastas range from good to excellent—even better when you consider what you'd be paying uptown. Try the lusty tomato-based *fettuccine alla siciliana* (with eggplant and mozzarella), but save room for the classic Italian ricotta cheesecake. ♦ Italian ♦ Daily dinner and late-night meals. No credit cards accepted. 85 Ave A (between E Fifth and E Sixth Sts). 995.5300

34 Miracle Grill ★★$$ Grilled chicken on skewers with papaya-tomatillo salsa, New York steak with chipotle (smoked jalapeño pepper) butter, and vanilla-bean flan are just a few of the inventive specialties served at this tiny and casual restaurant. Dine alfresco in the garden when the weather is fine. ♦ Southwestern ♦ M-F dinner; Sa-Su brunch and dinner. 112 First Ave (between E Sixth and E Seventh Sts). 254.2353 ♿

35 Caffè della Pace ★$ This warm and unpretentious little cafe, a few steps up from the street, has good cappuccino and a very rich tiramisù. ♦ Cafe ♦ Daily. No credit cards accepted. 48 E Seventh St (between First and Second Aves). 529.8024

36 Kiev ★$ A better buy, not to mention better borscht, would be hard to find in New York. This is one of the best of the Eastern European joints around. The cheese blintzes, pierogi (filled with cheese or potato), fried veal cutlets, and all of the soups are very satisfying. ♦ Russian ♦ Daily 24 hours. No credit cards accepted. 117 Second Ave (at E Seventh St). 674.4040 ♿

37 St. George's Ukrainian Catholic Church An old-world cathedral with modern touches, this 1977 church designed by **Apollinaire Osadea** is the anchor of a Ukrainian neighborhood of more than 1,500 people. ♦ 16-20 E Seventh St (at Second Ave). 674.1615

38 The Fragrance Shoppe Owner Lalita Kumu and her congenial staff love to get to know their customers and share their knowledge of fragrance and bodycare products. They'll introduce you to the store's own line, which includes facial and skincare products, body oils, and shampoos, and show you the products they import from other companies. ♦ Daily. 21 E Seventh St (at Cooper Sq). 254.8950 ♿

38 McSorley's Old Ale House Not so long ago, this saloon, which has been here since 1854, had a men-only policy; not surprisingly, it was among the first targets of the women's liberation movement in 1970. The current clientele, which includes women, is made up mostly of college students, but except for that, the place hasn't changed much since its early days. ♦ Daily 10AM-1AM. No credit cards accepted. 15 E Seventh St (at Cooper Sq). 473.9148

38 Surma This Ukrainian shop has Slavic cards, books, videos, and records, plus egg-decorating kits and honey. ♦ M-Sa. 11 E Seventh St (at Cooper Sq). 477.0729 ♿

39 St. Mark's Place In the 1960s, this extension of Eighth Street from the Bowery to **Tompkins Square Park** was the East Coast capital of hippiedom. The sidewalks were crowded with flower children and the smell of marijuana was everywhere. Among the shared interests of the street's denizens was the famous rock club **The Electric Circus,** which was in a former Polish social club at **No. 23.** Then, in the 1970s, the street became the punk boardwalk, and multicolored Mohawks filled the air. It is quieter these days—witness the corner of Second Avenue, where the old **St. Mark's Cinema** has been converted into co-op apartments, and retail stores have been taken over by **The Gap.** But the crowds are still colorful, proving that the street's far from dead. ♦ Ave A to Third Ave

40 St. Mark's Sounds A true music-lover's store, it doesn't have the conveyor-belt feeling of **Tower Records,** and they sell and trade used records in excellent condition. ♦ Daily 11AM-11:30PM. 20 St. Mark's Pl (between Second and Third Aves). 677.3444

40 Dojo ★$ Students of nearby **New York University** seem to depend on the food served here for their very existence. Try the chicken sukiyaki salad or the incredibly inexpensive soy burger with tahini sauce. In nice weather you can dine on the outdoor porch. ♦ Japanese/Health food ♦ Daily lunch, dinner, and late-night meals. No credit cards accepted. 24 St. Mark's Pl (between Second and Third Aves). 674.9821. Also at: 14 W Fourth St (at Mercer St). 505.8934

40 Khyber Pass ★$ A former judge of the Supreme Court in Afghanistan runs this authentic Afghan restaurant. Knowing you're in good hands, just sit back on a throw pillow and get ready to enjoy stuffed ravioli with lamb; tender, moist lamb kabobs; fresh salads with yogurt dressing; and for dessert, rice pudding topped with pistachios. ♦ Afghan ♦ Daily lunch, dinner, and late-night meals. 34 St. Mark's Pl (between Second and Third Aves). 473.0989

41 Gem Spa Smoke Shop Although the long counter has been replaced by racks of international magazines and newspapers and the owners are East Indian, this veteran shop still serves a good egg cream, the quintessential New York drink. Ask for it when you walk in; the egg cream station is a small counter at the very front. ♦ Daily 24 hours. 131 Second Ave (at St. Mark's Pl). No phone

41 B & H Dairy and Vegetarian Cuisine Restaurant ★$ Once upon a time the initials "B & H" stood for owners Bergson and Heller, and the clientele comprised the cast and crew of the Yiddish theater productions along Second Avenue. The restaurant (with its menu) has been refurbished several times since then—the vegetarian offerings being the most recent—but thank goodness the challah recipe is still the same. The French toast is heavenly. ♦ Vegetarian ♦ Daily breakfast, lunch, and dinner. 127 Second Ave (between E Seventh St and St. Mark's Pl). 505.8065

42 Orpheum Theatre This refurbished theater has been around since 1908, when it was the scene of many Yiddish theater hits. *Little Mary Sunshine* had a long run here. In recent years, it's hosted such winners as *Little Shop of Horrors,* the comedienne Sandra Bernhard's one-woman show, and *Stomp!,* the high-energy percussion performance from England. ♦ 126 Second Ave (between E Seventh and E Eighth Sts). 477.2477

43 Cafe Mogador ★$$ Moroccan cuisine is prepared here without fanfare. Lamb, beef, and *merguez* (sausage) kabobs, and several varieties of couscous follow a selection of appetizers brought to your table on an enormous tray. ♦ Middle Eastern/Moroccan ♦ Daily lunch, dinner, and late-night meals. No credit cards accepted. 101 St. Mark's Pl (between Ave A and First Ave). 677.2226

44 Tompkins Square Park The original plan for this 16-acre park called for extending it all the way east to the river. It was to be a farmers' market, and part of the plan was to cut a canal through the middle to give easy access to Long Island farmers. But the land became a parade ground instead in the 1830s. In 1874, it was the site of America's first labor demonstration, when a carpenters' union clashed with club-wielding police. Among the injured was Samuel Gompers, who later became president of the American Federation of Labor. The little Greek temple near the center covers a drinking fountain placed there by a temperance organization in 1891. The park gained its modern-day notoriety during hippiedom, when it served as the grounds for "love-ins" and "be-ins," and more recently when it was the site of a violent confrontation over real-estate speculation in the area and unsuccessful efforts to enforce a nighttime curfew. ♦ Bounded by Aves B and A, and E Seventh and E 10th Sts

45 Jacob Riis Houses Plaza The large number of people who actually use this park is a tribute to M. Paul Friedberg's careful and creative 1966 plan. Both adults and children find it a pleasant alternative to the streets, with its amphitheater, clever playground furniture, and plenty of room in which to roam. ♦ Bounded by FDR Dr and Ave D, and E Sixth and E 10th Sts

RUSSIAN &TURKISH BATHS

46 Russian & Turkish Baths The last remaining bathhouse in a neighborhood that once was full of them still gets its steam heat the old-fashioned way: Enormous boulders are heated up in the sub-basement and when they're red-hot, water is thrown on them, releasing what the owners claim is true, penetrating wet heat—not mere steam heat. And if you've never had a *platza* rub, try it. Softened oak branches are tied together in the old Russian style to form a natural loofalike scrub, soapy and tingly and very refreshing. There's also a Turkish bath (sauna). Upstairs are cots if you're overwhelmed, and a small food and drink bar. ♦ Daily 9AM-10PM (coed: M-Tu, F-Sa; women: W; men: Th, Su). 268 E 10th St (between Ave A and First Ave). 473.8806

47 DeRobertis Pastry Shop ★$ If you can get past the display counters filled with traffic-stopping cheesecakes, pies, cakes, and biscotti, you'll find a wonderfully tiled coffeehouse that hasn't changed a bit since it began serving frothy cappuccino here back in 1904. ♦ Bakery/Cafe ♦ Tu-Sa. 176 First Ave (between E 10th and E 11th Sts). 674.7137

48 Theater for the New City Now located in what used to be an indoor market, this offbeat, roots-in-the-1960s troupe has managed to keep its old ambience and point of view. The productions are hit and miss. Each of the four theaters seats between 60 and 100. ♦ 155 First Ave (between E Ninth and E 10th Sts). 254.1109 &

49 Enchantments Local and visiting witches stop here regularly for the tools of their craft: herbs, oils, tarot cards, caldrons, and ceremonial knives (used to cut air and create a sacred space), plus jewelry, books, and calendars. ♦ Daily. 341 E Ninth St (between First and Second Aves). 228.4394

The *New York World* printed the first crossword puzzle in 1913. The first comic strip serial, *The Yellow Kid*, ran in an 1896 *New York Journal*.

You've seen them in every movie about New York, from *Breakfast at Tiffany's* to *Taxi Driver*. The yellow Checker cab will forever be nostalgically associated with bygone New York City. With more than 11,000 yellow cabs, only 10 Checkers are still on the road, each having clocked an average of 500,000 miles on New York's pockmarked streets. To be lucky enough to find and flag down an available one is enough to make your day. With an ocean of leg room, two jump seats, and a taxi driver who is bound to feel like something of a national treasure, passengers sit high above the potholes and surrounding traffic. In the 1970s, as many as 5,000 Checkers cruised the streets of New York. The remaining 10 will grace New York for only a few more years, their disappearance a result of their drivers' retirements, as well as their own deterioration.

50 Veselka ★$ An amazing array of Eastern European fare—pierogi, kielbasa, blintzes, and stuffed cabbage—is turned out at bargain-basement prices in this unadorned yet cozy establishment. ♦ Ukrainian ♦ Daily 24 hours. 144 Second Ave (at E Ninth St). 228.9682

51 Ukrainian ★$ Located within the **Ukrainian National Home** community center, this place serves such wonderful Eastern European specialties as pierogi, blintzes, and stuffed cabbage. The combination platter gives a sampling of all three. ♦ Ukrainian ♦ Daily lunch and dinner. No credit cards accepted. 140 Second Ave (between St. Mark's Pl and E Ninth St). 529.5024

52 Ottendorfer Library Anna Ottendorfer, founder of the German-language newspaper *New York Staats Zeitung* , founded this terra-cotta beauty, which was built by **William Schickel** in 1884. Before becoming a branch of the **New York Public Library**, it was the **Freie Bibliothek und Lesehalle**, a German-language library and reading room. ♦ M-Sa. 135 Second Ave (between St. Mark's Pl and E Ninth St). 674.0947

53 Cloisters Cafe $ At this most delightful spot in the neighborhood for escaping the city, the inside is dark and encrusted with stained glass, while the outside is a beautiful grapevine-canopied bower. Gigantic salads, good challah French toast, and fresh fish entrées are featured. In hot weather, the yogurt ambrosia (with fresh fruits and nuts) and a glass of iced mint tea should quench your thirst. ♦ American ♦ M-F lunch, dinner, and late-night meals; Sa-Su brunch, dinner, and late-night meals. No credit cards accepted. 238 E Ninth St (between Second and Third Aves). 777.9128

53 Cafe Tabac ★★$$ This East Village eatery's menu has evolved from bistro to continental American, but food still takes a back seat to celebrity and model watching. Be forewarned—upstairs is unofficially reserved for regulars and big names. The downstairs dining room and bar are generally noisy and crowded. ♦ American ♦ Daily dinner and late-night meals. 232 E Ninth St (between Second and Third Aves). 674.7072

54 St. Mark's Bookshop This popular bookstore has recently moved, bringing its old name and loyal customers with it. It remains a good source for journals on African culture, feminist issues, socialism, and cultural theory. ♦ Daily 11AM-11:30PM. 31 Third Ave (between E Eighth and E Ninth Sts). 260.7853 ♿

55 Briscola ★★$$$ In Italy, *briscola* is a popular card game played by young and old alike. At this neighborhood find, the tables are too small to hold a full deck, but who cares about playing cards when you can feast on such authentic Sicilian specialties as artichokes with mint; tagliatelle with sausage, peas, and cream; *bucatini* (macaroni) with sardines; and swordfish carpaccio. ♦ Sicilian ♦ M-F lunch and dinner; Sa dinner. 65 Fourth Ave (between E Ninth and E 10th Sts). 254.1940

56 Grace Church The fascinating spire atop this white marble church is sited at a bend of Broadway, providing a focal point for any southern approach. **James Renwick Jr.**, won the right to design the Episcopal church in a competition. He worked with copybooks of the Pugins, the English theorists, to produce a Gothic Revival structure in 1846 that many consider to be the city's best. **Heins & LaFarge** designed an enlargement for the chancel in 1900. **Renwick**'s rectory, next door at 804 Broadway, is another marvel—a restrained foil for the more fanciful church. ♦ 800 Broadway (at E 10th St)

57 St. Mark's-in-the-Bowery Church Erected in 1799 on the site of a garden chapel on Peter Stuyvesant's estate, this church has always been held in high regard as a neighborhood church, and its stately late-Georgian style encourages this congenial attitude. As the membership grew, a Greek Revival steeple designed by **Ithiel Towne** was added in 1828, giving the church a more urban image; and a cast-iron Italianate portico was added to the entrance in 1854. This mélange does not mesh successfully, but it does reflect the parishioners' concerns about preserving the church's early history. A fire nearly destroyed the building in 1978. Architect **Herman Hassinger** took charge of the restoration, which included rebuilding the steeple according to the original design. The interior was gutted and redesigned in a simple and straightforward manner, typical of the pre- and post-Revolutionary War period. The stained-glass windows on the ground floor, newly designed by **Hassinger,** use themes similar to the original windows. The building is also home to the Poetry Project, Inc. (674.0910), Danspace (674.8112), and

Ontological Theatre (533.4650). ♦ 131 E 10th St (at 2nd Ave). 674.6377

58 2nd Avenue Deli ★$$ Ask to be seated in the **Molly Picon Room** in this very famous and popular deli where the wealth of Yiddish theater memorabilia will certainly enhance the dining experience. As for the food, try the superb chopped liver (passed out on bits of rye bread to placate the hungry crowds when lines get long on weekends), stuffed breast of veal, Romanian tenderloin steak, boiled beef, or stuffed derma. ♦ Jewish ♦ Daily breakfast, lunch, dinner, and late-night meals. 156 Second Ave (at E 10th St). 677.0606

59 Tenth Street Lounge A severe metal facade and forbidding steel doors give way to this popular neighborhood watering hole. The interior is warmed up with votive candles, a hodgepodge of overstuffed couches, and, for a curious touch of academia, school desks used as tables. ♦ Daily 5PM-3AM. 212 E 10th St (between First and Second Aves). 473.5252 ♿

60 Veniero's Pasticceria & Cafe ★$ Mirrors and chandeliers decorate this century-old bakery/cafe. But customers generally don't notice the decor; they're hypnotized by the biscotti (cookies), the creamy pastries, and the golden cheesecakes. There's also a seating area which is often crowded with tourists. ♦ Bakery/Cafe ♦ Daily. No credit cards accepted. 342 E 11th St (between First and Second Aves). 674.7264

61 Iso ★$$ At this favorite East Village destination for creative Japanese food, quarters are cramped, but the staff and customers make do in an upbeat atmosphere with fresh flowers and Keith Haring artwork. Sushi is the specialty, but cooked selections, such as chicken teriyaki and shrimp or vegetable tempura, are given the same attention. ♦ Japanese ♦ M-Sa dinner. 175 Second Ave (at E 11th St). 777.0361 ♿

"New York is a city of dreams."

Isaac Bashevis Singer

One year after New York City became the first capital under the Constitution in 1788, an official census of Manhattan's population registered 33,000. Exactly one hundred years later, the surrounding four boroughs joined Manhattan to create the world's largest city, with a population of 3 million. Today, the city is home to a whopping 7.5 million people.

62 Angelica Kitchen ★$ Named after an herb believed to bring good luck, a place like this could only exist in the East Village. The seasonal vegetarian macrobiotic menu (no dairy products or sugar) changes with the solstice and equinox. The vegetarian fare, including lentil/walnut pâté, is made with organically grown ingredients. A Zenlike setting complements the mood and provides a tranquil backdrop. ♦ Organic vegetarian ♦ Daily lunch and dinner. 300 E 12th St (between First and Second Aves). 228.2909

62 John's of Twelfth Street ★$$ This place could have been the model for every little Italian restaurant that was ever lit by candles stuck in wine bottles. It's one of the city's oldest and was once a favorite of Arturo Toscanini. The menu is red-sauce traditional; the special salad, outstanding. ♦ Italian ♦ Daily dinner. Reservations recommended. No credit cards accepted. 302 E 12th St (between First and Second Aves). 475.9531

63 Pedro Paramo ★★$ The authentic food at peso-friendly prices might fool you into thinking that you're south of the border. If you're still not convinced, just wait until the Mexican beers and excellent margaritas start flowing. Start off a traditional meal with some of the city's best guacamole, and take it from there; you can't go wrong. ♦ Mexican ♦ Daily lunch and dinner. 430 E 14th St (between Ave A and First Ave). 475.4581

64 Immaculate Conception Church Now a Roman Catholic church, this 1894 building designed by **Barney & Chapman** was originally an Episcopal mission of **Grace Church**, which included a hospital and social service facilities arranged in a cloisterlike setting punctuated by the elaborate tower. ♦ 414 E 14th St (between Ave A and First Ave). 254.0200 &

65 Kiehl's Since 1851 Located at the historical Peter Stuyvesant Pear Tree Corner, this vintage establishment produces handmade cosmetics and 118 essences (including four kinds of patchouli oil), using natural ingredients and extracts according to centuries-old formulations. The white-coated staff is extremely helpful and generous with samples. On display is an impressive collection of new and vintage motorcycles. All in all, it's an East Village must. ♦ M-Sa. 109 Third Ave (between E 13th and E 14th Sts). 475.3400

66 Footlight Records Collectors of vintage LPs rejoice! Here is the world's largest selection of film soundtracks and original Broadway cast albums as well as top vocalists (Sinatra, Crosby, Merman), jazz greats (Django Reinhardt, Bix Beiderbecke), and out-of-print records of all sorts. In most cases, you may listen before buying. ♦ Daily. 113 E 12th St (between Third and Fourth Aves). 533.1572

67 Utrecht Art & Drafting Supplies This major manufacturer of professional art and drafting supplies offers excellent prices. Mail-order catalogs are available at the store or by calling 800/223.9132. ♦ M-Sa. 111 Fourth Ave (between E 11th and E 12th Sts). 777.5353 &

68 Strand Bookstore "Miles and miles of books" is the trademark description of this epic store, and its vast collection includes thousands of review copies of new books, hundreds of coffee-table books, and tables full of mass-market and trade paperbacks, all sold at a generous discount. Antiquarian books are here, too. If you have to get lost somewhere in New York this is the best possible place. ♦ Daily. 828 Broadway (at E 12th St). 473.1452. Also at: 159 John St (at Front St). 809.0875

69 Palladium Partners Steve Rubell and Ian Schrager (of **Studio 54** and **Morgan's** fame) had a great idea—to convert the old **Academy of Music** into a dance palace. In 1985, they hired **Arata Isozaki** and Eiko Ishioko to revamp the interior. The clientele is mostly out-of-towners and the very young. ♦ Cover. F-Sa 10PM-4:30AM. 126 E 14th St (between Third and Fourth Aves). 473.7171

Bests

Ed Levine
Author, *New York Eats*

The **Second Avenue Deli** is one of the last old-time Jewish delis in New York. Have mushroom barley soup, a pastrami sandwich, and an order of fries. Then wander around the East Village and the Lower East Side. There you'll find what's left of our melting pot. Ukrainian shops coexist peacefully with Muslim meat markets, Polish bakeries, and pasta stores.

Have a meal at the **Union Square Cafe.** They're serious about food without being in the least bit pretentious. It's one of the few great restaurants in New York that treats everyone like a regular.

Go to **Madison Avenue** and window shop at the **Valentino** and the **Armani** boutiques. Don't even think about buying anything, unless you plan on taking out a second mortgage on your home.

Fairway market has a wonderful selection of produce, cheese, bread, and coffee. Next, wander up Broadway to **Zabar's** and check out the smoked fish and the cookware. Then walk over to the **Museum of Natural History** and see the dinosaurs.

Wander around **SoHo** checking out the shops and galleries. Then go to **Melampo Imported Foods** for the best focaccia sandwich you've ever eaten. Take your sandwich next door to the playground and sit at one of the booths the city has conveniently constructed for **Melampo** sandwich buyers.

Marcia Tucker
Director, The New Museum of Contemporary Art

Studio Museum in Harlem. Sunday afternoon openings; among the most exciting shows in town (plus a fabulous gift shop).

A cappuccino at **Caffè Dante.** The closest you can get to Italy in the Village.

A Sunday visit to the **Lower East Side,** particularly the shops on **Orchard Street.**

Radio City Music Hall's Easter and Christmas shows. The best kitsch anywhere in the world, destined to make you weep for the good old days.

Taking any six-year-old girl to the **Plaza** for tea. Makes you see the world somewhat differently—a little better and brighter.

The **Cowgirl Hall of Fame.** Ranks tops among eating and drinking establishments for the name alone, but the rest lives up to it. The decor provides instant respite from city overload.

Marilyn J. Appleberg
Writer, Editor, and Author of *I Love* guidebooks

The **Metropolitan Museum of Art** Friday or Saturday at 5PM for drinks on the balcony with a classical accompaniment—it's the smartest cocktail lounge in town.

Kiev's cheese blintzes, which are without a doubt the world's best.

Bay 1 at Brighton Beach for soft white sand, unpolluted water, and the sound of Russian being spoken.

Stuyvesant Street on the vernal or autumnal equinox, when the sun sets straight down the middle of this, the only *true* east-west street on Manhatttan.

2nd Avenue Deli with its multicultural countermen and the best pastrami and chopped liver.

The Alice Austin House spring and fall antiques fair on the lawn overlooking the bay.

Only in New York: events such as the Empire State Building Run Up, and the wand-breaking ceremony at Houdini's grave the afternoon of Halloween.

Barbara Cohen and Judith Stonehill
Co-owners, New York Bound Bookshop

Places for book-lovers:

Afternoon tea at **Anglers & Writers** cafe, on Hudson Street at St. Luke's Place. (Marianne Moore lived nearby and worked in the public library around the corner.)

The **New York Public Library,** with its extraordinary collection of over 6 million books spanning 88 miles of shelves.

Gansevoort Street, where Herman Melville once worked as a customs officer and where you will find authentic French bistro food 24 hours a day at **Florent.**

The **General Society Library** to see the latest books at the **Small Press Center,** or to borrow a book. The turn-of-the-century **Harvard Club** and **New York Yacht Club,** en route to the fabled **Algonquin** for tea or a cocktail and a bit of reading.

A drink at the **White Horse Tavern** on Hudson Street after work, to think of Dylan Thomas, Delmore Schwartz, Brendan Behan, and other writers who drank hour after hour there.

The **Morgan Library,** with its priceless medieval and Renaissance manuscripts, rare editions, and unique exhibitions on the book arts. Edith Wharton would have been at home in its old New York splendor.

The **Edgar Allan Poe Cottage,** a clapboard house he rented in 1846, and where he wrote *Annabel Lee.*

With breezes from the river and broad vistas, a walk along the grand **Battery** promenade evokes Melville and Whitman, especially after a summer evening reading held there by **Symphony Space.** (In the winter, we go uptown to **Symphony Space** on West 95th Street to hear actors read from literary works.)

Quiet places to read a book: the sculpture garden at the **Isamu Noguchi Museum;** the Temple of Dundur Hall at the **Metropolitan Museum;** the **Staten Island Ferry** during the quiet hours of the day.

Union Square/ Gramercy/ Murray Hill

Both Union Square, formerly known as **Stuyvesant**, and Murray Hill were named for farms, while Gramercy inherited its name from an early 19th-century housing development that lured the rich by offering them access to their own private park.

Together these three dynamic neighborhoods cover **14th to 39th Streets**, from **Sixth Avenue** to the **East River**. In recent years, publishers, ad agencies, architectural firms, photography studios, and other upscale companies running from high uptown rents have moved into these areas. Having been mostly residential since the commercial center of the city moved north in the 19th century, it is once again attracting loft dwellers lured by the neighborhood's newfound energy and a host of fashionable stores recently opened to accommodate them.

Gramercy Park, the centerpiece of the Gramercy area, was established in the 1830s by lawyer and landowner Samuel Ruggles. To make one of his tracts

more valuable, he sacrificed 42 potential building lots to create this London-style park. Then he set aside more land for a wide avenue north of the park (which he named **Lexington**, for the Revolutionary War battle) and for **Irving Place** south of it (which he named for his friend Washington Irving, who created "Father Knickerbocker," one of the symbols of New York).

The land that Ruggles owned was once part of a huge estate that belonged to Peter Stuyvesant, the last Dutch governor-general of Nieuw Amsterdam, who retired there after the British took over. His original 1651 deed noted a valley created by a creek called *Crommessie,* a combination of two Dutch words meaning "crooked little knife" (for the shape of a nearby brook). The name was eventually altered to Gramercy to fall more easily off English-speaking tongues.

Stuyvesant's name lives on in the neighborhood east of Gramercy, and in another London-style park that straddles **Second Avenue**. After the Stuyvesant family sold part of their estate to the Delanceys in 1746, it was developed into a working farm known as **Rose Hill**. It is a quiet residential area today, but through the beginning of the 20th century the notorious Gas House Gang ruled the neighborhood, averaging an estimated 30 holdups every night on **East 18th Street** alone.

The original Gas Housers' territory included another residential neighborhood, Murray Hill, which extends north from **34th** to **39th Streets**, and east from Sixth Avenue. The gang took its name from factories along the East River that produced gas to illuminate the city in the 18th century. The stretch between **23rd** and **34th Streets** is often called **Kips Bay**, after a farm established by Jacobus Kip in 1655.

By the end of the 19th century, when J. Pierpont Morgan moved to Kips Bay, a gentlemen's agreement had been established restricting the streets of Murray Hill to private houses. Until the invasion of high-rise hotels and apartments in the 1920s, it was a neighborhood of elegant mansions, many of which still stand.

Today, where gas storage tanks once sprouted east of Stuyvesant Square, thousands of people occupy middle-class apartments in the **Stuyvesant Town** and **Peter Cooper Village** rental complexes (both built in the late 1940s and attacked for being purely functional and without ornamentation), and in **Waterside** (high-rises built in 1974 on the East River between **East 25th** and **East 30th Streets**). Visible from the **FDR Drive** is **Bellevue Hospital Center,** which originated as a six-bed infirmary on the site of the present **City Hall** in a building that it shared with a poorhouse and a jail.

---

1 Union Square In 1811, when the city fathers decreed that all of Manhattan's streets should follow a rigid grid pattern, Broadway was already in place, cutting an angle from southeast to northwest. Rather than change it, they turned it to the city's advantage by creating squares wherever Broadway crossed a north-south avenue. What may have inspired them was this already existing square, which grew up around the meeting point of Broadway, the post road to Albany, and Boston Post Road, which later became Third Avenue. In the years before the Civil War, it was the heart of a fashionable residential neighborhood, surrounded by prestigious stores and theaters. When fashion moved uptown, the square became a center for labor demonstrations and rallies. It was landscaped and altered in 1936, when it was also raised a few feet above ground level to allow for the subway station under it. The pavilion at the north end, sometimes used for summer concerts, was added at the same time. The redesign also forced Broadway to make a left turn at East 17th Street and share its right-of-way with Park Avenue South before getting back on course at East 14th Street. The landscapers came back almost 50 years later to begin a multiphase renovation (phase one began in 1984) to transform the area once again. (The park had become a gloomy hangout for drug pushers and derelicts.) Among their accomplishments to date is the replacement of the magnificent **Independence Flagstaff** at the center of the park, originally donated by

Tammany Hall. The face-lift also includes new Art Deco–style subway kiosks, which flank the equestrian statue of *George Washington,* the masterpiece of sculptor John Quincy Adams Ward, which was placed there in 1856. Ward's collaborator was Henry Kirke Brown, who was responsible for the figure of *Abraham Lincoln* at the other end of the park. Nearby is a representation of the *Marquis de Lafayette,* created in 1876 by Frederic Auguste Bartholdi, who gave us the **Statue of Liberty** 10 years later. ♦ Bounded by Union Square E and and Union Square W, and E 14th and E 17th Sts

1 Union Square Greenmarket In 1976, New York City's Council on the Environment attempted to open a greenmarket in what was then a parking lot. It got off to a slow start because of the community's skepticism— a result of previously unsuccessful attempts to clean up the longtime illicit activities within the park. Today this location is the largest and arguably the most interesting of the city's greenmarkets. In addition to a huge variety of fresh (a regulation stipulates that all perishables must be sold within 24 hours of harvesting) seasonal fruits and vegetables, fish, cheese, eggs, baked goods, honey, and plants are offered. Some locals make a beeline for the fresh flowers, and at Christmastime, the freshest trees, wreaths, and garlands can be found here. ♦ M, W, F-Sa. E 17th St and Broadway. 788.7900 ♿

2 Zeckendorf Plaza There are more than 670 cooperative apartments in this 1987 building by **Davis, Brody & Associates.** Four illuminated pyramids sit atop the sprawling complex. Life here is self-contained, with such amenities as a health club and shopping facilities. At 108 East 15th is the 225-seat **Gertrude and Irving Dimson Theater,** the permanent home of the **Vineyard Theater Company.** The development is often cited as a key to the gentrification of the Union Square neighborhood. ♦ Bounded by Irving Pl and Union Sq E, and E 14th and E 15th Sts. 826.2900

3 Consolidated Edison Building This massive structure, completed in 1929 by **Henry J. Hardenbergh,** has its critics, but everyone loves its clock tower built in 1926 by **Warren & Wetmore.** It is softly lit at night, as it should be, considering that its owner is the electric company. The building, which fills nearly the whole block, replaced two structures that each had an impact on the city. Tammany Hall, which controlled City Hall for more than 100 years, was headquartered here in a large but unassuming brick building that had a spacious auditorium for public meetings, and a smaller one that became a profit center as **Tony Pastor's Music Hall,** which, in 1881, was the birthplace of American vaudeville. It was next door to a jewel box of a building known as the **Academy of Music,** the predecessor of the **Metropolitan Opera,** which in its decline became the scene of anti-Tammany rallies. In its heyday, it was the anchor for a string of the city's best restaurants, hotels, and theaters. ♦ 4 Irving Pl (at E 14th St). 460.4600 ♿

4 Con Edison Energy Museum The age of electricity, brought to New York in 1882 by Thomas Edison, is chronicled with exhibitions, artifacts, and imaginative displays that extend from the present into the future. A representation of today's New York at night is reached through a long passageway that is a tour of underground New York, complete with a passing subway. ♦ Free. Tu-Sa. 145 E 14th St (between Third Ave and Irving Pl). 460.6244 ♿

5 Stuyvesant Town There are 8,755 moderately priced rental apartments in this complex, which looks forbidding from the street (when it was built in 1947, Lewis Mumford called it "police state architecture"). The roadways within the complex are virtually free of cars. The tenants, many of whom are senior citizens and young families, live a carefree existence, thanks to good security and careful maintenance provided by the landlord, the Metropolitan Life Insurance Company. In the blocks between East 20th and East 23rd Streets, the development is known as **Peter Cooper Village,** an upscale version of this complex, with larger apartments and higher rents. ♦ Bounded by FDR Dr and First Ave, and E 14th and E 20th Sts

6 Stuyvesant Square Created in 1836 at the edge of the Gas House District (one of the city's poorest neighborhoods), this four-acre oasis, donated to the city by the Stuyvesant family, was the dividing line between rich and poor. In the center of the western half is a 1936 sculpture of *Peter Stuyvesant* by Gertrude Vanderbilt Whitney, founder of the **Whitney Museum.** ♦ Bounded by E 15th and E 17th Sts (at Second Ave)

7 Friends' Meeting House The simple, two-story Greek Revival structure, built in 1860 by **Charles T. Bunting,** reflects the peaceful nature of the Society of Friends, which holds meetings here. ♦ 15 Rutherford Pl (at E 15th St). 777.8866

8 216 East 16th Street Part of a row of striking Italianate houses built in the early

1850s, this building is still a joy to behold. The lower stories are brownstone, but brick is used on the upper floors, which, along with the wonderful windows, makes the building stand out. ♦ At Rutherford Pl

9 St. George's Episcopal Church It's easy to believe that this solid brownstone, vaguely Romanesque church was where financier J.P. Morgan attended services. Dating from 1846, it was the design of **Otto Blesch** and **Leopold Eidlitz.** ♦ E 16th St and Rutherford Pl. 475.0830

9 St. George's Chapel Built in 1911 by **Matthew Lansing Emery** and **Henry George Emery,** this Romanesque companion sits in the shadow of the massive church—most certainly one of New York's overlooked treasures. ♦ Rutherford Pl (north of the church)

10 Washington Irving High School Though originally a girls' technical high school, the school's curriculum expanded to include a full range of subjects when it moved here from Lafayette Street in 1912. The huge bust of Irving at the East 17th Street corner was created in 1885 by Friedrich Baer. ♦ 40 Irving Pl (between E 16th and E 17th Sts). 674.5000

11 Guardian Life Insurance Company In 1911, when this building was designed, there was a new architectural movement away from flat-topped buildings with cornices, which were beginning to get boring for many corporate clients. **D'Oench & Yost** responded by producing a four-story mansard roof for the top of this lavish tower. Not satisfied that it was unusual enough to become its signature, the insurance company added a huge electric sign which would soon work against them. Their name was "Germania Life," which set them apart as pariahs when World War I broke out. They solved the problem by changing their name. The 1961 extension behind the building, which adds little more than space, was designed by **Skidmore, Owings & Merrill.** ♦ 201 Park Ave S (at E 17th St). 598.8000

12 The City Bakery ★★$ Fresh ingredients from the **Union Square Greenmarket** just a half-block away are turned into tasty dishes at this bakery/cafe. Such hearty soups as lentil or potato with cumin, served with warm focaccia, are made on the premises each morning, as is the heavenly range of sweets. ♦ American ♦ M-Sa breakfast, lunch, and early dinner. 22 E 17th St (between Broadway and Fifth Ave). 366.1414 ♿.

13 Union Square Cafe ★★★★$$$ The very light, airy, modern space has rich cherry-wood floors and beige walls, wainscoted with hunter green and dotted with small brightly colored paintings. Chef Michael Romano's inventive dishes include gazpacho risotto with shrimp, cucumber, tomatoes, and peppers; and seared salmon with a peppery orange marmalade. Be sure to save room for one of the delectable desserts. ♦ American ♦ M-Sa lunch and dinner; Su dinner. Reservations required. 21 E 16th St (between Union Sq W and Fifth Ave). 243.4020

14 Coffee Shop ★$ In pleasant weather trendy "club kids" spill onto the sidewalk cafe of this slick diner with a Brazilian flair. The food includes the Sonia Braga chicken salad sandwich (rolled with papaya and cashews in a flour tortilla), and a traditional Brazilian *feijoada* (pork and bean stew) served on Saturdays. ♦ American/Brazilian ♦ Daily breakfast, lunch, dinner, and late-night meals. 29 Union Sq W (at E 16th St). 243.7969

15 Richard Stoddard Performing Arts Books Here you'll find mostly out-of-print books plus ephemera relating to the performing arts—playbills, autographs, and periodicals. ♦ M-Tu, Th-Sa. 18 E 16th St (between Union Sq W and Fifth Ave), Room 305. 645.9576 ♿

16 Steak Frites ★$$ Steak and fries are the meat and potatoes at this spot off Union Square, but there are also good soups, sandwiches, and pasta specials. Service can be spotty. ♦ Bistro ♦ Daily lunch and dinner. Reservations required. 9 E 16th St (between Union Sq W and Fifth Ave). 463.7101 ♿

16 Revolution Books Before you start your revolution, stop here for inspiration from the masters of the art. The books cover a range of political science topics, with an emphasis on the radical. ♦ Daily. 13 E 16th St (between Union Sq W and Fifth Ave). 691.3345 ♿

Tin Pan Alley, once located on West 28th Street between Broadway and Fifth Avenue, was the heart of the world-famous music publishing industry.

More than 1,200 people were killed in riots near Tudor City in 1863, caused when the rich newcomers to the area were permitted to buy draft exemptions that the poor could not afford.

17 Emporio Armani If "Emporio," rather than "Giorgio," precedes "Armani," it means that the merchandise (which includes men's and women's clothing, accessories, bath products, and leather luggage) goes for about 50 percent less than Armani's signature collections. Check for the Armani wit, such as the eagle-shaped air-conditioning unit on the ceiling, and another eagle with an antique manhole cover for an eye worked into the hundred-year-old chestnut floor. ◆ Daily. 110 Fifth Ave (at W 16th St). 727.3240 ᕼ

18 Paul Smith Rock stars and Wall Street bankers have been found here shopping for classic clothing with a twist. This is the eccentric Englishman's only US outlet—he has 45 stores in Japan and seven in London—for his handsomely made suits, sports jackets, and slacks, plus occasionally wacky play clothes. ◆ Daily. 108 Fifth Ave (at W 16th St). 627.9770

18 Joan & David This is one of three Manhattan boutiques for the exclusive lines of shoes, clothing, and accessories by wife-and-husband team Joan and David Helpern. The high-tech interior is the work of London designer Eva Jiricna. The staff is very friendly. ◆ Daily. 104 Fifth Ave (between W 15th and W 16th Sts). 233.3294. Also at: 3 World Financial Center, Winter Garden. 233.3294; 816 Madison Ave (between E 68th and E 69th Sts). 772.3970

18 Mesa Grill ★★$$$ Despite the spacious setting and high ceilings, the high noise level here eliminates any chance of intimate talk. Still, this upscale, hip Southwestern restaurant draws a crowd for chef/owner Bobby Flay's cooking. The menu includes such innovative dishes as red snapper wrapped in a blue-corn tortilla with fire-roasted poblano-chili vinaigrette, as well as shellfish and green-chili pan roast. ◆ Southwestern ◆ M-F lunch and dinner; Sa-Su brunch and dinner. 102 Fifth Ave (between W 15th and W 16th Sts). 807.7400 ᕼ

19 St. Francis Xavier Church This Baroque Roman Catholic monument to the Jesuit missionary would be right at home in his native Spain. The interior is the sort of thing American tourists go out of their way to see in Europe. ◆ 45 W 16th St (between Fifth and Sixth Aves). 627.2100

20 Flowers ★★$$$ The haute farmhouse decor with rough-hewn beams and artistic-looking lanterns suspended from the walls is where chef Marc Salonsky creates strongly flavored, savory food. Try the tuna *tartare timbale* with vine-ripened tomatoes and avocado salsa; or spicy grilled quail with cilantro, cumin, cardamom, and ginger. ◆ Eclectic ◆ M-F lunch and dinner; Sa dinner. Reservations recommended for dinner. 21 W 17th St (between Fifth and Sixth Aves). 691.8888 ᕼ

21 Siegel-Cooper & Company Originally **Siegel-Cooper Dry Goods Store,** this garish white brick and terra-cotta retail temple (fashioned by **DeLemos & Cordes** under the influence of the Chicago World's Fair of 1893) lived up to its slogan "The Big Store—A City In Itself" with 15.5 acres of space, 17 elevators, a tropical garden, and a smaller version of Daniel Chester French's monument *The Republic,* which had graced the Fair (The fountain at the base of the statue became a favorite rendezvous for New Yorkers.) The store was located in the fashionable shopping district called "Ladies' Mile," but when **Macy** and **B. Altman** moved uptown, it sold its inventory to **Gimbels** and the statue to Forest Lawn Cemetery in Los Angeles. The building was converted into a military hospital during World War I, and in recent years it has served as construction space for television scenery and home to garment manufacturing firms. ◆ Sixth Ave and W 18th St

Book-Friends Café

22 Book-Friends Cafe $ Books from the Victorian, Edwardian, and Modern eras, among other belle epoques, line this old-fashioned salon. Stop in for a sandwich, afternoon tea, or one of the "Conversations," on such subjects as Kiki's Paris, New York Literary Neighborhoods, or Sylvia Beach and the Expatriates. ◆ American ◆ M-F lunch, afternoon tea, and dinner; Sa-Su brunch, afternoon tea, and dinner. 16 W 18th St (between Fifth and Sixth Aves). 255.7407 ᕼ

23 Academy Books and Records You'll find a good selection of out-of-print, used, and rare books and records here, as well as used CDs. ◆ Daily. 10 W 18th St (between Fifth and Sixth Aves). 242.4848

24 Barnes & Noble Bookstore Originally a purveyor of textbooks with branches at most major local colleges, this store has branched out all over town (and the nation) in recent years. There are two here, the main store on the southeast corner and the **Sale Annex** across the street. You can still buy and sell textbooks, but the selection of books and records beyond that is almost overwhelming at prices that are surprisingly low. ◆ Daily. 105 Fifth Ave (at E 18th St). 807.0099. Also at other locations ᕼ

25 Daffy's Imagine three floors of designer clothes and accessories for men and women of every age group at discount prices. We're not talking Calvin and Giorgio, but those with a discerning eye will always find some good pieces. ◆ Daily. 111 Fifth Ave (at E 18th St). 529.4477. Also at: 335 Madison Ave (at E 45th St). 557.4422; 1311 Broadway (at W 34th St). 736.4477; 135 E 57th St (between Lexington and Park Aves). 557.4477 ⅄

26 America ★$$$ This was once the ultimate trendy restaurant. And though the luster has ever so slightly dimmed, it is still a great draw for the young crowd. Everything about it is big. It has 350 seats, and about as many things on the menu. But it isn't the food you come here for—it's the huge bar, where standing room is three-deep. Almost everyone drinks Rolling Rock beer or large, sweet, powerful drinks with names like "Woo-Woo" and "Russian Quaaludes." ◆ American ◆ Daily lunch and dinner. 9 E 18th St (between Broadway and Fifth Ave). 505.2110

27 Paragon This gigantic sporting goods store has an extensive sportswear collection. Its sales often have spectacular bargains. ◆ Daily. 867 Broadway (at E 18th St). 255.8036

28 MacIntyre Building This 1892 **R.H. Robertson** Romanesque office building has obviously seen better days, but it hasn't lost its pride. You can tell by the way those beasts at the corners are sticking their tongues out at you. ◆ 874 Broadway (at E 18th St)

29 Old Town Bar ★$ The popularity of this century-old tavern may be sufficient to keep it in business for another hundred years. Sit in the time-worn wooden booths and enjoy burgers, fries, and an icy mug of draft beer. ◆ American ◆ Daily lunch, dinner, and late-night meals. 45 E 18th St (between Park Ave South and Broadway). 529.6732

30 Sal Anthony's $$ The menu is basic but reliable at this casual restaurant; a huge bay window in front adds cheer to the place. Try the chicken in olive oil and garlic or the linguine with white clam sauce. During the summer, tables are set out on the sidewalk for alfresco dining. ◆ Italian ◆ Daily lunch and dinner. Reservations required. 55 Irving Pl (between E 17th and E 18th Sts). 982.9030

31 Inn at Irving Place $$$ The newest of New York's small hotels, this one is a gem, with 12 rooms handsomely appointed in Age-of-Innocence trappings in a 19th-century townhouse. Tastefully chosen period pieces might include big brass beds or oversized Victorian armoires, something until now

found often at the end of a tiring transatlantic flight. The inn's discreet albeit casual appeal extends to the lack of sign or awning or uniformed doorman. ◆ 54 Irving Pl (between E 17th and E 18th Sts). 533.4600; fax 533.4611

Within the Inn at Irving Place:

Verbena ★★★$$$ Although it won't be easy, try not to fill up on the freshly baked bread in order to save room for Diane Forley's soul satisfying menu of autumn mushrooms with angel-hair pasta in truffled mushroom broth; butternut-squash ravioli flavored with roasted oranges and sage; seared venison chop with twice-baked sweet potatoes, chestnuts, and pomegranate seeds; or succulent beer-braised ribs of beef with root vegetables and horseradish dumplings. Desserts are uniformly excellent—especially the rum-soaked savarin filled with warm bittersweet chocolate, chocolate soufflé and chocolate-chip ice cream, black plum tart, fig profiteroles, and crème brûlée with lemon verbena. ◆ American ◆ Tu-Su lunch and dinner. Reservations required. 260.5454

32 Friend of a Farmer ★$$ The country cooking and on-the-premises baking might well take you back to your grandma's kitchen. The Long Island duckling and Cajun-style chicken are always good. ◆ American ◆ Daily breakfast, lunch, and dinner. 77 Irving Pl (between E 18th and E 19th Sts). 477.2188

32 Choshi ★★$$ The fresh and well-prepared sushi and sashimi here are great buys at lunch. Choose between indoor and outdoor dining. Prix-fixe dinner menus are a terrific deal. ◆ Japanese ◆ Daily lunch and dinner. 77 Irving Pl (between E 18th and E 19th Sts). 420.1419

33 Pete's Tavern ★$$ One of several saloons that claim to be the oldest in town, this place also claims that O. Henry did some of his writing in a corner booth. If the bar was as busy then as it is now, his powers of concentration must have been incredible. The food, which runs from standard Italian specialties to hamburgers, isn't exceptional, but the atmosphere is great, and the sidewalk cafe sits on one of the city's more pleasant streets. ♦ Italian/American ♦ Daily lunch and dinner. 129 E 18th St (at Irving Pl). 473.7676

34 Police Academy and Museum In spite of what you may have seen in the movies, this academy takes its job very seriously. The building has a swimming pool and a gymnasium, as well as a museum that shows how the city's police officers came to be called New York's finest, with displays that help you understand what they've been through to earn the title. Visitors are welcome, but call first since they close when meetings are scheduled. ♦ Free. M-F 9AM-2PM. 235 E 20th St (between Second and Third Aves). 477.9753

35 Gramercy Park/Gramercy Park Historic District Established by Samuel Ruggles in 1831, this former marshland became the model of a London square ringed by proper 19th-century Neo-Classical town houses. It is the sole surviving "private park" in New York City—only surrounding residents have a key to get in—but the perimeter is well worth a stroll. Many notables have lived in this neighborhood, including James Harper, the mayor of New York City (1844), and Samuel J. Tilden, governor of New York State (1874-86), who was an unsuccessful presidential candidate; his home (at 15 Gramercy Park S) is now the **National Arts Club.** The statue in the park is of actor Edwin Booth, who lived at **No. 16** Gramercy Park South until he had the building remodeled by **Stanford White** in 1888 for **The Players Club. Numbers 34** and **36** on the east side are among the city's earliest apartment buildings, designed in 1883 by **George DaConha** and in 1905 by **James Riles,** respectively. Note the magnificent ironwork on **Nos. 3** and **4** Gramercy Park West, attributed to **Alexander Jackson Davis,** one of the city's more individualistic and energetic architects. The Gramercy Park Historic District extends in an irregular area out from the park, including all of the west and south frontages and part of the east, the park itself, and Irving Place almost to East 19th Street on the west side and to East 18th Street on the east, as well as parts of East 20th and East 21st streets west of the park. Of particular interest is the beautiful block between Irving Place and Third Avenue on East 19th Street (remodeled as a group by **Frederick J. Sterner**). ♦ Between E 20th and E 21st Sts (at Lexington Ave)

36 The Brotherhood Synagogue This austere brownstone cube was designed in 1859 by **King & Kellum** as a Friends' meeting house, and was remodeled in 1975 by **James Stewart Polshek** as a synagogue.

♦ 28 Gramercy Park S (between Third Ave and Irving Pl). 674.5750

37 National Arts Club Built in 1845 by **Calvert Vaux,** this building has housed the National Arts Club since 1906, but its colorful history began when politician Samuel J. Tilden, who gained fame by destroying the Tweed Ring, used the coup to become governor of New York. To protect himself in the topsy-turvy days of early unions and political machinery, Tilden installed steel doors at the front of this Victorian Gothic home and had a tunnel dug to East 19th Street as an escape route. ♦ 15 Gramercy Park S (at Irving Pl). 475.3424

38 The Hampden-Booth Theatre Library In 1888, founder Edwin Booth charged **The Players Club** with the task of creating "a library relating to the history of the American stage and the preservation of pictures, bills of the play, photographs, and curiosities." Small group tours and use of the library, which includes four major collections (from Edwin Booth, Walter Hampden, the **Union Square Theatre,** and William Henderson), are granted by appointment only. ♦ 16 Gramercy Park S (at Irving Pl). 228.7610

39 Patria ★★★$$$ This handsome bilevel room decorated with golden columns and earthy paintings of avocados was formerly **Positano.** The same fashionable crowd— emphasis on *crowd*—still shows up, but now they come for the exciting pan-Hispanic food of Miamian chef Douglas Rodriguez. Don't miss the Honduran seviche (a vibrant combination of tuna marinated in chilies, ginger, and coconut milk), or crispy red snapper with coconut-conch rice. Vegetarians delight in *caramiñola* (Colombian-style yucca stuffed with cheese in a mushroom broth, served with spinach). A chocolate cigar with spun-sugar matches is a whimsical and tasty conclusion to the meal. Specialty drinks, such as *mojito* (rum, sugarcane juice, lime juice, and mint), *manguini* (champagne and fresh mango juice), and the Patria colada (a variation of the piña, with passion fruit and shaved coconut) receive the same attention as the food. Everything at this place—right down to the pulsating salsa music—is part of the fun. ♦ New Spanish ♦ M-F lunch and dinner; Sa dinner. Reservations required. 250 Park Ave S (at E 20th St). 777.6211

40 Gramercy Tavern ★★$$$ The menu can be hit-and-miss, with presentations coming off more successfully than flavors. But the tuna *tartare;* eggplant Napoleon (layered with assorted vegetables and parmesan cheese); and sirloin of beef with barley, mushrooms, and horseradish are all superb and can be topped off successfully by the chocolate mousse cake with caramel sauce. The carefully chosen, reasonably priced, wine list adds to the enjoyment. ♦ American ♦ M-F lunch and dinner; Sa dinner. Reservations required. 42 E 20th St (between Park Ave S and Broadway). 477.0393 ♿

40 Theodore Roosevelt Birthplace Teddy Roosevelt was born here in 1858 and lived in a house on the site until he was a teenager. The original house was destroyed in 1916, but was faithfully reconstructed seven years later by **Theodate Pope Riddle** as a memorial to the 26th president. The National Historic Site incorporates 26 East 20th Street, once the home of Roosevelt's uncle. The restoration contains five rooms of period furniture and an extensive collection of memorabilia, including teddy bears. ♦ Nominal admission; seniors, children free. W-Su. 28 E 20th St (between Park Ave S and Broadway). 260.1616

41 Goelet Building Chicago architects developed steel-framed office buildings with highly ornamental exteriors, and in the 1880s, firms such as **McKim, Mead & White** began developing their own variations on the theme, which they called "New York Style." This is a prime example. ♦ 900 Broadway (at E 20th St)

42 Campagna ★★$$$ This faux-Tuscan trattoria decorated with white walls, country Italian antiques, and abstract paintings features a menu of fresh vegetables antipasto, six-layer lasagna, fried calamari, osso buco, and Florentine ribsteak. Desserts are more opulent here than at most Italian restaurants. ♦ Italian ♦ M-F lunch and dinner; Sa-Su dinner. 24 E 21st St (between Park Ave S and Broadway). 460.0900 ♿

43 901 Broadway Originally **Lord & Taylor Dry Goods Store,** this 1869 **James H. Giles** building displays a romantic cast-iron facade with echoes of Renaissance castle architecture as a monument to the glories of this formerly fashionable shopping neighborhood before **Lord & Taylor** moved uptown along with its neighbors **W&J Sloane** and **Arnold Constable.** Industrial tenants have occupied it ever since, and the remodeled mundane ground floor has no connection with the fanciful upper ones. ♦ At E 20th St

Perhaps the most distinguishing feature of the city's streets in the 1880s was the mass of telephone and telegraph wires overhead. After the blizzard of 1888 they were placed underground.

Only a handful of all the semiactuated signals (those chest-high buttons that pedestrians push to make the light change to green) installed on lightpoles around Manhattan actually work; most are located along 12th Avenue.

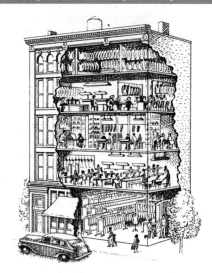

44 Saint Laurie Limited This 1869 building by **James H. Giles** was originally part of the **Lord & Taylor** emporium and has been restored for a manufacturer of quality men's and women's suits. An on-site museum demonstrates how clothing is produced, with a tour of the workrooms and exhibitions of changing styles. Custom tailoring is also available at low prices. ♦ Daily. 895 Broadway (between E 19th and E 20th Sts). 473.0100 ♿

45 ABC Carpet The original owner of this 1882 building was **W&J Sloane,** which moved uptown and became one of the city's leading furniture dealers. It specialized in carpets and rugs when it was here, and the tradition is continued by one of Sloane's former competitors. Founded in 1987, this floor-covering emporium is one of New York's more reasonably-priced sources of fine carpets of every description, from wall-to-wall carpeting to area rugs of every design, quality, and price, as well as various remnants and tile. Across the street, at **No. 881,** are six floors of merchandise, including antique and reproduction rugs and furniture, plus bed, bath, linen, and lighting departments. The floor displays are so tasteful, apartment dwellers flock here on weekends just to look for ideas. ♦ Daily. 888 Broadway (at E 19th St). 473.3000

46 Arnold Constable Dry Goods Store Building A glorious two-story mansard roof tops this skillful marriage of Empire and Italianate styles, designed by **Griffith Thomas** in 1877. Note the rare combination of marble and cast iron in the facade—the city's first use of cast-iron construction for retail space. ♦ 881-887 Broadway (at E 19th St)

Restaurants/Clubs: Red   Hotels: Blue

Shops/♥ **Outdoors:** Green   **Sights/Culture:** Black

47 News Bar ★$ A magnet for the artistic crowd from nearby ad agencies, architectural firms, and photography studios, this sleek espresso bar/newsstand was designed in a handsome minimalist style by architect **Wayne Turett.** The fresh pastries and sandwiches are great, but the espressos, cappuccinos, and steamed milks are superlative. Pull up a chair at the counter and immerse yourself in your favorite periodical, which is probably among the selection of 400 newspapers and magazines available here. ♦ Cafe ♦ Daily. 2 W 19th St (at Fifth Ave). 255.3996. Also at 366 W Broadway (at Broome St). 343.0053; 969 Third Ave (at 57th St). 319.0830 ♿

48 Magickal Child Tucked away in the deep shade cast by high loft buildings, this is a perfect setting for a store specializing in swords, daggers, candlesticks, and other supplies for your explorations into the occult. A free mail-order catalog is available. ♦ Daily. 35 W 19th St (between Fifth and Sixth Aves). 242.7182 ♿

49 Caffe Bondì ★★$$$ The bright, tiled decor, friendly and efficient staff, and delicious food make this a lovely setting for a meal or snack. Try any of the simple yet delicious pastas, which include *taglierini* (thin noodles) with tomatoes, mushrooms, and rosemary cream, or one of the Sicilian specialties. ♦ Italian ♦ Daily breakfast, lunch, and dinner. 7 W 20th St (between Fifth and Sixth Aves). 691.8136

50 Periyali ★★★$$$ The friendly staff at this comfortable taverna is unabashedly proud of its traditional Greek menu, and judging from the crowds that fill this off-the-beaten-path place, their pride is completely justified. Giant white beans with garlic sauce, charcoal-grilled octopus or shrimp, lamb chops with rosemary, anything in phyllo pastry, and fresh whole fish are all good picks. For dessert there's baklava. The white stucco walls, wooden floor, and soft Greek music complete the experience. ♦ Greek ♦ M-F lunch and dinner; Sa dinner. Reservations recommended. 35 W 20th St (between Fifth and Sixth Aves). 463.7890

51 Limelight Discotheque In better days, the **Church of the Holy Communion,** designed in 1846 by **Richard Upjohn,** had John Jacob Astor and Cornelius Vanderbilt among its parishioners. When the neighborhood died, the church died with it and, to add insult to injury, became a dance club in 1982. It is back in fashion but is most popular for private parties. ♦ Tu-Su 10PM-4AM. 660 Sixth Ave (between W 20th and W 21st Sts). 807.7850

52 Cal's ★★$$ The dining room here is reminiscent of a Parisian grand cafe with soaring ceilings. The menu is varied and well executed, featuring such dishes as oven-roasted beet and endive salad, saffron risotto primavera, and roast stuffed quail with dates and onions. Desserts too good to miss include bananas in a chocolate cookie crust, and a brownie ice-cream sandwich, which made the cover of *Chocolatier Magazine.* ♦ American ♦ M-F lunch and dinner; Sa-Su dinner. Reservations recommended. 55 W 21st St (between Fifth and Sixth Aves). 929.0740 ♿

53 Lox Around the Clock $ Few are the restaurants that can satisfy a burning desire for a good pastrami sandwich at 3AM. During the wee hours, this place caters to a young crowd (hungry from dancing at the nearby **Limelight** club, formerly a church). A full-scale deli menu is offered, with decent lox and television monitors playing music videos full blast. ♦ Deli ♦ M-W, Su until midnight; Th-Sa until 4AM. 676 Sixth Ave (at W 21st St) 691.3535

54 Lola ★$$$ Simply and attractively decorated, this restaurant serves authentically spiced and curried foods from the Caribbean, along with some familiar Italian fare. Try Lola's fried chicken or grilled snapper, and don't forget the onion rings. During weekday lunches, the private dining room becomes the less-expensive **Lola Bowla,** serving all entrées—mainly pastas and salads—in bowls. ♦ Caribbean/Italian ♦ M-F lunch and dinner; Sa dinner; Su brunch and dinner. Reservations required. 30 W 22nd St (between Fifth and Sixth Aves). 675.6700

55 Stern's Dry Goods Store This restoration of **Henry Fernbach**'s 1878 building is possibly the most sensitive of any cast-iron building in

New York. ♦ 32-36 W 23rd St (between Fifth and Sixth Aves)

56 Western Union Building A reflection of the city's Dutch origins, this building was created by **Henry J. Hardenbergh** in 1884, the same year as his **Dakota** apartment house overlooking **Central Park.** ♦ 186 Fifth Ave (at W 23rd St)

57 Flatiron Building In 1902, when **David H. Burnham** (of Chicago World's Fair fame) filled the triangular site where Broadway crosses Fifth Avenue in a most reasonable but unconventional manner—with a triangular building—he raised many eyebrows and made history. This limestone-clad Renaissance palazzo was one of the city's first skyscrapers, at 285 feet high, and it is one of **Burnham**'s best. At the juncture between traditionalism and modernism, the structure, with its articulated base and strong cornice, looks like an ocean liner in a column's clothing. Built as the **Fuller Building,** people soon dubbed it the "Flatiron" for its shape, once they stopped calling it "Burnham's Folly." ♦ 175 Fifth Ave (between E 22nd and E 23rd Sts)

Flatiron Building

Michael Storrings

58 Aja ★★★$$$ The major influences here are Asian, the undercurrents European, and the overall flavors, entirely unique. Try grilled foie gras with pears in red wine with apple celeriac puree; giant prawns and clams in a green curry, cumin, and caraway broth; or honey-roasted chicken with butternut-squash dumplings. The wine list is small but interesting, with good affordable choices from France, Italy, California, and South Africa. ♦ Fusion ♦ M-F lunch and dinner; Sa dinner. Reservations recommended. 937 Broadway (at E 22nd St). 473.8388 &

59 Alva ★★$$$ Gone are the white walls and large mural from this small, narrow restaurant which was formerly the **Chefs' Cuisiniers Club.** Today the black walls are mirrored, adorned with photos of Thomas Edison (Alva was his middle name) and illuminated by light bulbs. The earthy and flavorful fare includes duck breast in a star-anise sauce served with a poached pear stuffed with duck confit, and double-garlic roast chicken. ♦ American ♦ M-F lunch and dinner; Sa-Su dinner. Reservations recommended. 36 E 22nd St (between Park Ave S and Broadway). 228.4399 &

60 Bolo ★★$$$ This is the place where Bobby Flay, who reconceptualized Southwest cuisine at his **Mesa Grill** a few blocks away, takes on Spanish food and makes it hum. Try the warm octopus and chickpea salad with grilled tomatoes and garlic-parsley vinaigrette; and baby clams steamed in a green-onion broth. ♦ New Spanish ♦ M-F lunch and dinner; Sa dinner; Su brunch and dinner. Reservations recommended. 23 E 22nd St (between Park Ave S and Broadway). 228.2200 &

61 Calvary Church This Protestant Episcopal church, designed in 1846 by **James Renwick Jr.,** the architect of **St. Patrick's Cathedral,** once had steeples, but **Renwick** had them removed in 1860 because, some critics said, they embarrassed him. If the exterior was less than perfect, the architect made up for it with the nave, which is exquisite. The Sunday-school building on the uptown side, also a **Renwick** design, was added in 1867. ♦ 61 Gramercy Park N (at Park Ave S). 475.1216

62 C.T. ★★★★$$$ Claude Troisgros (the son of Pierre Troisgros, of the three-star Troisgros restaurant in Roanne, France) has come up with the perfect blend of French classical technique and South American spice. Try the jumbo ravioli with taro-root mousseline, white truffle oil, and mushrooms; sautéed duck foie gras with jicama, cinnamon, and star-anise sauce; and spice-rubbed skate with yams and baby artichokes in shellfish broth. Cap the meal off with the *caipirinha* (a crisp napoleon filled with cream in a lime and sugarcane sauce that's as potent as the Brazilian drink of the same name). ♦ Brazilian/French ♦ M-F lunch and dinner;

Sa dinner. Reservations required. 111 E 22nd St (between Lexington Ave and Park Ave S). 995.8500 &

63 Umeda Learn to detect the subtleties of sake at this elegant bar. Fortunately for novices, the menu offers a detailed explanation—origin, flavor, degree of dryness or sweetness—of more than 20 varieties of the rice wine. ♦ M-Sa 6-11PM. 102 E 22nd St (between Lexington Ave and Park Ave S). 505.1550

64 Russell Sage Foundation Building The foundation that set out to dispense $63 million for good works in 1906 did much of its own good work in this 1912 building by **Grosvenor Atterbury** before selling the building to Catholic Charities, which in turn sold it for development as apartments. ♦ 4 Lexington Ave (at E 22nd St).

65 Gramercy Park Hotel $$ This 1927 edifice by **Thompson & Churchill** was **Stanford White**'s last home and is a favorite of European travelers who fancy the relaxed Old-World style and sensible prices. The choice rooms face the park (guests have access), which is ringed with historic landmarks and turn-of-the-century brownstones. The 380 rooms vary (some have been renovated), so ask to see a few if you're not satisfied with yours. ♦ 2 Lexington Ave (at E 21st St). 475.4320, 800/221.4083; fax 505.0535

66 Rolf's Restaurant ★$$ New York was once famous for its German restaurants, and this is one of the very few still operating. The walls and ceilings are covered with lots of art, stained glass, and carved wood. Try the veal shank, shell steak, and excellent potato pancakes. ♦ German ♦ Daily lunch and dinner. 281 Third Ave (at E 22nd St). 473.8718

67 Asser Levy Recreational Center In 1906, right-thinking architects **Arnold W. Brunner** and **William Martin Aiken** finally used the overappropriated style of the Romans in its original manner—for baths (like Caracalla, or those of Diocletian). Until recently called the **Public Baths,** this formal structure now houses a fitness center with indoor and outdoor swimming pools; membership required. ♦ E 23rd St (at Asser Levy Pl). 447.2020

68 School of Visual Arts Working professionals teach more than 5,500 students the fundamentals of illustration, photography, video, film, animation, and other visual arts in buildings throughout the neighborhood. Frequent exhibitions in the main building on East 23rd Street are free to the public. The luminary faculty includes Milton Glaser, Eileen Hedy-Schultz, Ed Benguiat, and Sal DeVito. ♦ 209 E 23rd St (between Second and Third Aves). 679.7350 &

Restaurants/Clubs: Red   Hotels: Blue

Shops/ ♥ Outdoors: Green   **Sights/Culture:** Black

69 Samuel Weiser's Bookstore This interesting shop deals in new and used esoteric and metaphysical materials, including tarot cards, audio and video tapes, and crystals. ♦ Daily. 132 E 24th St (between Lexington Ave and Park Ave S). 777.6363

70 Live Bait $$ An extremely popular after-work destination, the bar is packed, sardine style, with a crowd downing oysters from shot glasses and sipping Rolling Rocks straight from the bottle. The menu includes chili, fried chicken, and a gumbo of andouille sausage, shrimp, and chicken, served over creole rice. ♦ Southeastern ♦ Daily lunch, dinner, and late-night meals. Reservations recommended. 14 E 23rd St (at Madison Ave). 353.2400

71 Metropolitan Life Insurance Company Originally, the 700-foot marble tower (adjacent to the main building) was decorated with 200 carved lions' heads, ornamental columns, and a copper roof. But its four-sided clock, which at 26.5 feet is 4.5 feet taller than Big Ben, hasn't changed since 1909, when the tower was built. The north building, across East 24th Street, was designed in 1932 by **Harvey Wiley Corbett** and **E. Everett Waid** and is surprisingly light for all its limestone mass. Note the sculpted quality of the polygonal setbacks, the vaulted entrances at each of the four corners, and the Italian marble lobby. This block was the site of the **Madison Square Presbyterian Church.** Completed by **Stanford White** in 1906, it was his last, and many say his finest, building ♦ 1 Madison Ave (between E 23rd and E 25th Sts). 578.2211 &

72 Madison Square What once was a swamp hunting ground, then a pauper's graveyard, is now a quiet refuge in the midst of madness The square dates from 1847, when it was a parade ground and only a small part of a proposed park that was laid out in the Randel Plan of 1811—the plan that created the city's grid street pattern. Like other squares in this part of town, it was the focus of a fashionable residential district that flourished in pre-Civil War days. After the war, the fancy **Fifth Avenue Hotel,** the **Madison Square Theater,** and the second home of **Madison Square Garden** all faced the square. This incarnation of the **Garden** will always be remembered because **Stanford White,** who designed the building, was shot and killed in its roof garden by Harry Thaw, the jealous husband who thought **White** was paying too much attention to his wife, Evelyn Nesbit. Today, the square is ringed by mostly public and commercial buildings, but manages to retain its air of serenity. ♦ Bounded by Madison and Fifth Aves, and E 23rd and E 26th Sts

73 200 Fifth Avenue This is the center of America's wholesale toy business, which extends into several nearby buildings. Its

15 floors are a dreamland for children, who, alas, are not allowed to browse. But the lobby is open to the public and not to be missed. ♦ At W 23rd St

74 Follonico ★★$$$ Veteran chef Alan Tardi, formerly of **Le Madri,** is the chef and owner of this charming trattoria. Try calamari roasted with garlic; ravioli filled with rabbit, veal, and pork in a butter and sage sauce; scallops in shellfish broth; or baked salt-crusted red snapper. Top the meal off with a sliced-apple tart baked in the wood-burning oven. The wine list is filled with unusual Italian selections that are affordably priced. ♦ Italian ♦ M-F lunch and dinner; Sa-Su dinner. Reservations recommended. 6 W 24th St (between Fifth and Sixth Aves). 691.6359

75 Serbian Orthodox Cathedral of St. Sava Built in 1855 by **Richard Upjohn** for Trinity Church, this chapel became a cathedral of the Eastern Orthodox faith in 1943. The beautiful altar and reredos inside are by **Frederick Clarke Withers.** The parish house was designed in 1860 by **Jacob Wrey Mould.** ♦ 15 W 25th St (between Broadway and Sixth Ave). 242.9240

76 Worth Monument This richly ornamented obelisk in a plot separating Broadway and Fifth Avenue marks the grave of Major General William Jenkins Worth, for whom the street in Lower Manhattan and the city of Fort Worth, Texas, were named. After fighting the Seminole in Florida, he went on to become a hero of the Mexican War in 1846. The monument was designed in 1857 by **James C. Batterson.** ♦ W 25th St and Fifth Ave

77 Annex Antiques Fair and Flea Market Commonly referred to as the "26th Street Flea Market," this is the city's original, largest, and most popular weekly antiques and flea market (though **GreenFlea** creates some competition uptown). Treasures can be found amid eclectic and fascinating trash year-round, as more than 500 vendors congregate in this parking lot in the middle of the Flower District. You'll find everything from Tiffany silver to bentwood chairs and 1950s collectibles. The **Chelsea Antiques Annex,** with an entrance at 122 West 26th Street (between Sixth and Seventh Avenues) follows the same hours. ♦ Nominal admission. Sa-Su. Sixth Ave (between W 24th and W 27th Sts). 243.5343

78 New York Life Insurance Company This 1928 Gothic masterpiece was designed by **Cass Gilbert,** the architect of the **Woolworth Building** and New York's **Federal Courthouse.** The square tower topped by a gilded pyramid—a style **Gilbert** called "American Perpendicular"—is dramatically lighted at night. Its lobby is a panorama of detail, from polychromed coffered ceilings to bronze elevator doors, and ornate grilles over the subway entrances. ♦ 45-55 Madison Ave (between E 26th and E 27th Sts). 576.7000

79 Appellate Division of the Supreme Court of the State of New York Here, in the busiest appellate court in the world, nine justices hear most appeals in civil and criminal cases arising in New York and surrounding counties. With few exceptions, their decisions are final. The building, designed by **James Brown Lord**—murals, statuary, and all—was finished in 1900 at $5,000 under budget, with a final price tag of just under $644,000. It is one of the city's treasures. Stop in and be impressed. The building is open to the public when court is not sitting. ♦ M-F. 27 Madison Ave (at E 25th St). 340.0400 ♿

80 69th Regiment Armory Designed in 1905 by **Hunt & Hunt,** this is where the infamous *Armory Show* introduced modern art to New York in 1913—the most famous work in the show was Marcel Duchamp's *Nude Descending a Staircase.* Note the gun bays overlooking Lexington Avenue, with the barrel-vaulted **Drill Hall** behind it. ♦ 68 Lexington Ave (between E 25th and E 26th Sts). 889.7249

81 La Colombe d'Or ★★★$$$ This romantic restaurant is always busy and with good reason. The food is simply delicious. Don't miss the thick *minestra* (a hearty vegetable, bean, and pasta soup with pecorino cheese), the intense fish soup, bouillabaisse, and grilled rib steak with shallot and balsamic-vinegar sauce. There's also a very carefully chosen wine list featuring wines of the Rhône Valley and nationally produced Rhône varietals. ♦ Provençal ♦ M-F lunch and dinner; Sa-Su dinner. Reservations recommended. 134 E 26th St (between Third and Lexington Aves). 689.0666

82 I Trulli ★★★$$$ Come here for a selection of wonderfully earthy dishes, such as the clay casserole of potatoes, portobello mushrooms, and herbs; baked oysters with pancetta; and ricotta dumplings with tomato sauce. For dessert, try the fruit poached in wine. In nice weather, sit in the garden out back. ◆ Italian ◆ M-F lunch and dinner; Sa dinner. Reservations recommended. 122 E 27th St (between Lexington Ave and Park Ave S). 481.7372

83 Bellevue Hospital Center Established in 1736, this municipal hospital cares for some 80,000 emergency cases per year. Its services are available to anyone, with no restrictions, including ability to pay. The medical center was a pioneer in providing ambulance service, in performing appendectomies and Caesarean sections, and in developing heart catheterization and microsurgery. It is not, as is often believed, solely a psychiatric hospital. The principal building was designed in 1939 by the prestigious architectural firm **McKim, Mead & White** and underwent subsequent additions in 1939. ◆ 462 First Ave (at E 27th St). 561.4141

84 Waterside There are 1,600 apartments in these brown towers built by **Davis, Brody & Associates** in 1974 on a platform over the East River. They are a world apart, reached by a footbridge across FDR Drive at East 25th Street, or by the riverfront esplanade to the north. The river views here are spectacular. ◆ E 25th to E 30th Sts (between the East River and FDR Dr). 725.5374

85 The Water Club ★★★$$$ Fluttering triangular flags give the entrance of this restaurant the look of a fancy yacht club. Inside the glass-enclosed, skylit former barge anchored at the river's edge, landlubbers are treated to views that are among the best in town—the cocktail lounge area opens into a terraced dining room with a panorama of the **East River**. Naturally seafood is the best choice here, and the many varieties of oysters and clams are dependably spectacular. Although the service can be harried and the noise level a bit high for intimate conversation, this place is well worth a visit. ◆ American ◆ Daily lunch and dinner. Reservations required. E 30th St and the East River (access from E 34th St). 683.3333

86 Kips Bay Plaza These twin 21-story slabs facing an inner, private park were the first exposed concrete apartment houses in New York. The complex, completed in 1965, was designed by **I.M. Pei Associates** and **S.J. Kessler.** ◆ E 30th to E 33rd Sts (between First and Second Aves)

On 21 January 1908, the first ordinance banning smoking was passed—not surprisingly, this ordinance applied to women only. New York's latest legislation went into effect in April 1995, forbidding smoking in all restaurants seating over 35 people, for both women *and* men.

87 Marchi's ★$$$ Not much has changed since this restaurant opened in 1930. The fixed menu has been the same for nearly that long: an antipasto platter, homemade lasagna, deep-fried whiting with cold string beans and beets in vinaigrette, roast veal and roast chicken with mushrooms and tossed greens, and dessert. The five generally well-prepared courses come in a relentless procession, defying even the most indomitable diner to stagger through to the final stage of fruit, cookies, and coffee. ◆ Northern Italian ◆ M-Sa dinner. Reservations recommended; jacket required. 251 E 31st St (between Second and Third Aves). 679.2494

88 Tammany Hall ★★$$ The name is Old New York (there's a lineup of black-and-white photos of the city's mayors on the wall), but the decor is modern and sleek at this fashionable tavern. To start, try the huge *terra mista* (a selection of vividly flavored salads and appetizers), steamed clams and mussels, or bruschetta of the day. Follow with the mascarpone cheesecake. ◆ Italian. ◆ Daily lunch and dinner. Reservations recommended. 393 Third Ave (at E 28th St). 696.2001

89 Manhattan Fruitier Owner Jehv Gold put together stupendous baskets filled with exotic seasonal fruits from all over the world. No matter what your needs are, he can supply the appropriate arrangement. Delivery in and around Manhattan is available. ◆ M-F. 105 E 28th St (between Lexington and Park Ave S) 686.0404

90 H. Kauffman & Sons You can have your boots custom-made here, or choose from the huge selection of riding equipment that includes anything a horse or its owner could possibly need, even gifts for your horse-owning friends who think they have everything. ◆ M-Sa. 419 Park Ave S (at E 29th St). 684.6060

90 Les Halles ★$$ A re-creation of the hangouts that once surrounded the great wholesale food market in Paris, this place has been a success since it opened in 1991. Some people patronize the butcher shop in front;

others go to the often noisy dining room in back for onion soup, garlicky sausage, steak with *pommes frites* (french fries), or cassoulet. The crowds that line up to wait for a table are mostly advertising and publishing executives who work nearby. ♦ French ♦ M-F lunch and dinner; Sa-Su brunch and dinner. Reservations recommended. 411 Park Ave S (between E 28th and E 29th Sts). 679.4111 ₺

91 Park Bistro ★★$$$ Black-and-white photos of Paris in the 1950s line the walls at this friendly bistro. Specialties include a warm potato salad topped with goat cheese and served with a small green salad; duck rillettes with celeriac and smoked duck breast; wild-mushroom ravioli in Port sauce; and fresh codfish with onion sauce and fried leeks. For dessert, try the warm chocolate torte or the thin apple tart with Armagnac. There's a good selection of mostly French wines. ♦ French ♦ M-F lunch and dinner; Sa-Su dinner. 414 Park Ave S (at E 29th St). 689.1360

92 Martha Washington $ One of the last remaining women-only hotels in the city, the establishment has an informal, homelike atmosphere and a dining room. The 450 rooms are generally small, and most share baths, but they are cheerfully decorated and some have kitchenettes. ♦ 30 E 30th St (between Park Ave S and Madison Ave). 689.1900; fax 689.0023

93 Church of the Transfiguration/The Little Church Around the Corner When actor George Holland died in 1870, a friend went to a nearby church to arrange for the funeral. "We don't accept actors here," he was told, "but there's a little church around the corner that will." They did, and the **Church of the Transfiguration**—an Episcopal church built in 1849 and later expanded—got both a new name and a new reputation among actors, some of whom, including Edwin Booth, Gertrude Lawrence, and Richard Mansfield, are memorialized among the wealth of stained glass and other artifacts inside. During World War I and in the years following, it was the scene of more wedding ceremonies than any other church in the world. ♦ 1 E 29th St (between Madison and Fifth Aves). 684.6770 ₺

94 Marble Collegiate Church This Gothic Revival church has not been changed since the day it was built in 1854 by **Samuel A. Warner.** The clock is still wound by hand every eight days, and the cane racks behind the pews are still waiting to receive your walking stick. A Dutch Reform church (the oldest denomination in the city), established here by Peter Minuit in 1628, it has served under the flags of Holland, England, and the US. The most famous minister to use its pulpit was Dr. Norman Vincent Peale, author of *The Power of Positive Thinking.* ♦ 272 Fifth Ave (at W 29th St). 686.2770

95 Hotel Wolcott $ This 300-room hotel is efficiently run and popular with the young and young-at-heart because of its near-hostel prices. The facade and lobby are turn-of-the-century, but the rooms have simple, contemporary decor meant to withstand heavy traffic: This hotel is always close to full. ♦ 4 W 31st St (between Fifth and Sixth Aves). 268.2900; fax 563.0096

96 Greeley Square Alexander Doyle's statue of *Horace Greeley,* founder of the *New York Tribune,* was donated by members of the newspaper unions—which says something about Greeley's management style. The area around the square offers the best buys in cameras and related merchandise. The site across Sixth Avenue, now the home of the **Stern's** department store, is where **Gimbels** kept its secrets safe from **Macy's,** which is only a block away on Herald Square. ♦ Bounded by Broadway and Sixth Ave, and W 32nd and W 33rd Sts

97 Stanford $ This small hotel with 130 rooms is renovating in stages. It's convenient to the **Empire State Building** and **Madison Square Garden** and shopping, and has color TVs in all rooms. ♦ 43 W 32nd St (between Fifth Ave and Broadway). 563.1480, 800/365.1114; fax 629.0043

98 Kyoto Book Center This is one of several bookstores in the neighborhood serving the Korean community. Cosmetics, too, are sold here. ♦ M-Sa. 22 W 32nd St (between Fifth Ave and Broadway). 465.0923

99 Grolier Once an exclusive hideaway for the bibliophiles of the Grolier Club, then a private home, and most recently **The Madison,** a private club, this turn-of-the-century landmark building now hosts and caters private parties. Closed to the public. ♦ 29 E 32nd St (between Madison and Fifth Aves). 679.2932

"New York had all the iridescence of the beginning of the world."

F. Scott Fitzgerald, *The Crack-up*

The small area known as Marble Hill is actually part of Manhattan. It was originally a peninsula at the northern tip of the island. The Spuyten-Duyvil Creek (Dutch for Spout-Devil), which separated Marble Hill from the mainland (the Bronx), was too narrow for ships. In 1895, the creek was filled (with dirt from the excavation of Grand Central Station), and the channel at the apex of the Harlem River was straightened and deepened. The latter action pushed Marble Hill up into the Bronx. This created a bit of an uproar, as the residents were not thrilled about losing their status as Manhattanites. They quickly drafted a successful petition to remain part of the island politically, if not physically.

100 The Empire State Building Yes, Virginia, this is the once-upon-a-time World's Tallest Building (if you count the twin towers of the **World Trade Center** as two, it now ranks fourth), famous in fact and fiction, icon of New York City, and the first place from which to study the city. It has an impressive collection of statistics: 1,250 feet to the top of the (unsuccessful) dirigible mooring mast; 102 floors; 1,860 steps; 73 elevators; 60 miles of water pipes; five acres of windows; 365,000 tons of material—and it was under construction for only 19 months. Built by **Shreve, Lamb & Harmon Associates** in 1931, during the Depression, it was known for many years as the "Empty State Building," and the owners relied on income from the **Observation Deck** to pay their taxes. Oh yes—on a good day you can see for at least 50 miles.

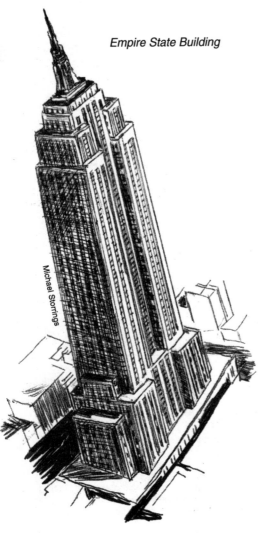

Empire State Building

Michael Storrings

The architects must be lauded for the way in which they handled the immense and potentially oppressive bulk of this building. The tower is balanced, set back from the street on a five-story (street-scale) base. The subtly modulated shaft rises at a distance, terminating in a conservatively geometric crown. The limestone and granite cladding, with its steel mullions and flush windows, is restrained, with just a touch of an Art Deco air (compared to the exuberant ornamentalism of the **Chrysler Building,** for example). This is *dignity*. Belying the fears of the general public, the tower has not yet cracked or toppled, although it does sway quite a bit in high winds, and only once has a plane crashed into it (in 1945, when a bomber broadsided the 79th floor). There have been a few suicides, and a lot of birds have been knocked out of the sky during their migrating season, one of the reasons it always stays illuminated.

The site, too, has a lively history. Between 1857 and 1893 it was the address of a pair of mansions belonging to members of the Astor family and the center of New York social life. In the early 1890s a feud erupted, and William Waldorf Astor, who had the house on West 33rd Street, moved to Europe and replaced the house with a hotel—the **Waldorf.** His aunt across the garden, Mrs. William Astor, moved within the year, and had a connecting hotel—the **Astoria**—completed by 1897. The **Waldorf** and **Astoria Hotels** immediately became a social center and operated as one hotel for many years, under the agreement that Mrs. Astor could have all connections between them closed off at any time. When the original structures were demolished in 1929, the **Waldorf-Astoria** moved uptown to Park Avenue. ♦ 350 Fifth Ave (at W 34th St)

Within The Empire State Building:

Empire State Observatories There is an open platform on all four sides of the 86th floor, well protected with heavy mesh and metal bars. A few steps above it is a glass-enclosed area with food service and a souvenir shop. An elevator takes you higher, to the all-enclosed 102nd-floor lookout, where the view, surprisingly, is slightly different. It's the quintessential not-to-be-missed way to end your evening on the town. Tickets are available on the concourse, one level below the street. ♦ Admission (combination tickets include *Skyride* admission). Daily 9:30AM-midnight; last elevator at 11:30PM. Enter on W 34th St. 736.3100 ext 73 &

Skyride You won't have to leave the building's second floor to experience some of the city's other celebrated attractions. This simulated-flight sightseeing tour guides a helicopter under, between, and over sites like the Brooklyn Bridge, the **World Trade Center,** and Coney Island's *Cyclone* roller coaster; it even crashes through the window of **FAO Schwarz**. And all this in seven minutes. ♦ Admission (combination tickets include the nonsimulated observation deck upstairs). Daily. Second floor. 564.2224

Guinness World Records Exhibit Hall
Exhibitions, dioramas, videotapes, replicas, and photographs document the achievements of humankind that possibly wouldn't have happened if there were no *Guinness Book of World Records*. ♦ Admission. Daily 9AM-9PM. Concourse level. 947.2335 ♿

101 New York Public Library, Science, Industry, and Business Branch
Scheduled to open at press time is the newest addition to the city-wide system, located on several floors of the former **B. Altman** department store. The library accommodates more than 16,000 square feet of space in this Renaissance Revival building designed in 1906 by **Trowbridge & Livingston**. The expansion is needed to relieve the overcrowded main library (on 42nd Street) of more than two million books and periodicals. ♦ M-Sa. 361 Fifth Ave (between E 34th and E 35th Sts). No phone at press time

102 Astro Gallery With a collection of minerals and gems from 47 countries, ranging from amethyst crystals to zircons, this is a paradise for collectors and a good source of fine jewelry at low prices. ♦ Daily. 185 Madison Ave (at E 34th St). 889.9000

103 Complete Traveller Bookstore This small store has an amazingly large selection of books and maps—enough to satisfy even the most jaded traveler. ♦ Daily. 199 Madison Ave (at E 35th St). 685.9007

104 Church of The Incarnation Episcopal
Built in 1864 by **Emlen T. Littel**, this modest church seems to be trying to hide the fact that it contains windows by Louis Comfort Tiffany and John LaFarge, sculpture by Daniel Chester French and Augustus Saint-Gaudens, and a Gothic-style monument designed by **Henry Hobson Richardson**. Fortunately, the church provides a folder for a self-guided tour. ♦ 209 Madison Ave (at E 35th St). 689.6350

105 Dolci On Park Caffè ★$$ You can get a satisfying meal here of linguine with sausage, penne with four cheeses, tortellini with ham, fettuccine with smoked salmon, chicken Marsala, or salmon with mushrooms and cream sauce. But far and away, the best part of a meal here is dessert. Indulge in a cannoli, chocolate eclair, mocha sponge cake, fruit tart, cheese cake, or tiramisù with a cup of espresso or cappuccino. In fair weather, sit at one of the sidewalk tables. ♦ Italian ♦ M-Sa breakfast, lunch, and dinner. 12 Park Ave (between E 34th and E 35th Sts). 686.4331 ♿

106 2 Park Avenue This better-than-average office building is particularly stunning at the top, where the basic structural pattern gives way to some jazzy, colorful Art Deco tile. **Ely Jacques Kahn** designed the building in 1927, with Leon Solon as color consultant. ♦ Between E 32nd and E 33rd Sts

106 An American Place ★★$$$ Larry Forgione, wunderkind of new American cooking, gives this cheery brasserie culinary oomph with a menu of homey, new wave dishes. Try the barbecued-duck salad over greens with a roasted-corn salsa; the roasted quail with foie gras and apple ravioli in a ham, sweet onion, and cabbage broth; or grilled duck breast with a black-pepper and molasses glaze and ginger-smashed sweet potatoes. ♦ New American ♦ M-F lunch and dinner; Sa dinner. Reservations recommended. 2 Park Ave (at E 32nd St). 684.2122

107 1 Park Avenue When Fourth Avenue below East 34th Street had its designation upgraded to "Park Avenue South," this and **2 Park Avenue** across the street kept their original addresses. Until 1925, when **York & Sawyer** built on this site, the area wasn't considered upscale. In the 19th century, it was the location of Peter Cooper's glue factory and later of barns for the livestock and horsecars of the **New York and Harlem Railroad**. ♦ Between E 32nd and E 33rd Sts

108 3 Park Avenue This brick tower structure is turned diagonally against its companions and the city. Compare this straight-up tower, built in 1976, and its stylized mansard roof with the careful, soaring composition of the **Empire State Building** two blocks away— they were designed by the same firm, **Shreve, Lamb & Harmon Associates**. A plaque on the terrace wall at East 33rd Street marks this as the site of the 71st Regiment Armory. ♦ Between E 33rd and E 34th Sts

Getting to the top is the literal object of the annual Empire State Building Run Up, a marathon race of unusual proportions. Entrants must negotiate the building's 1,575 steps. People from around the globe enter the event, held each February. Average winning time is 12 to 14 minutes, with winners and losers alike earning a splendid view from the 86th floor and an elevator ride down.

Restaurants/Clubs: Red   Hotels: Blue
Shops/ ♥ Outdoors: Green   **Sights/Culture:** Black

109 **Dumont Plaza Hotel** $$$ All the 250 rooms—be they studios or one- and two-bedroom suites—have their own kitchens. ♦ 150 E 34th St (between Third and Lexington Aves). 481.7600, 800/637.8483; fax 889.8856 ♿

110 **Nicola Paone** ★$$$ Decorated with stone designs to resemble an Italian marketplace, this place has a serious Northern Italian menu that is enlivened by such imaginative offerings as artichokes stuffed with breadcrumbs and anchovies, shrimp with basil, and smoked salmon and white wine. Good desserts include a banana and strawberry shortcake. Service is courtly and helpful, and the wine list boasts a 400-bottle selection. ♦ Italian ♦ M-F lunch and dinner; Sa dinner. Reservations recommended. 207 E 34th St (between Second and Third Aves). 889.3239

111 **St. Vartan Cathedral** This is the seat of the Armenian Orthodox Church in America, with a Romanesque design inspired by churches in Asia Minor. It was built in 1967 by **Steinman & Cain,** and its dome was re-covered in 18-karat gold leaf in 1993. ♦ 630 Second Ave (between E 34th and E 35th Sts). 686.0710

112 **El Parador** ★★$$$ Opened long before the current craze for Mexican food, this spot remains popular among Mexican food aficionados as well as those looking for a good time. Among many entrées are the chicken *parador* (marinated and steamed), grilled-sirloin fajitas, and *chilaquiles* (stewed chicken with sour cream and green-tomatillo sauce). ♦ Mexican ♦ Daily lunch and dinner. Reservations recommended. 325 E 34th St (between First and Second Aves). 679.6812

113 **Island Helicopter Sightseeing** Choose from four aerial tours of the city ♦ Daily 9AM-8PM Jan through Mar; daily 9AM-9PM Apr through Dec. E 34th St and East River. 683.4575

114 **Quark International** Discover gadgets galore, from Swiss army knives, folding bicycles, and talking translators to video camera tie clips and proton TVs. ♦ M-F; Sa by appointment. 537 Third Ave (at E 35th St). 889.1808 ♿

115 **Sniffen Court** This charming and unusually well-preserved mews of 10 carriage houses was built around the time of the Civil War (1850-60) and was designated a Historic District in 1966. ♦ 150-158 E 36th St (between Third and Lexington Aves)

116 **Shelburne Murray Hill** $$$ This all-suite hotel has a kitchen in each of the 258 rooms. ♦ 303 Lexington Ave (at E 37th St). 689.5200, 800/637.8483; fax 779.7068

117 **Doral Court Hotel** $$$ The 190 rooms here are sunny and quiet, and the staff is enthusiastic. Kitchenettes are available on request. You can visit the nearby fitness center or even have a stationary bike brought to your room. **The Courtyard Cafe and Bar** is always a pleasure. ♦ 130 E 39th St (between Lexington and Park Aves). 685.1100, 800/223.6725; fax 889.0287 ♿

117 **Doral Tuscany Hotel** $$$ The refrigerators in the 120 rooms here are stocked with refreshments, and if you run out, room service will replenish them. Leave your shoes outside your door at night and they'll be shined by morning. And when you rise and shine, you can visit the hotel's squas club and sports training institute. ♦ 120 E 39th St (between Lexington and Park Aves). 686.1600, 800/223.6725; fax 779.7822

Within the Doral Tuscany Hotel:

Time and Again ★$$$ The turn-of-the-century decor provides an extremely comfortable setting for a weekend breakfast or quiet dinner. If you're in the mood for game, order the pheasant tureen. ♦ American/French ♦ Breakfast, lunch, and dinner; breakfast and dinner only on Saturday and Sunday. Reservations recommended. 116 E 39th St (between Lexington and Park Aves). 685.8887

Rossini's

118 **Rossini's** $$$ The Hot Antipasto Rossini in champagne sauce—*clams oreganata,* shrimp scampi, and *mozzarella in carrozza* (wrapped in bread and fried)—is a specialty of this casual, friendly restaurant. An opera trio entertains on Saturday. ♦ Italian ♦ M-F lunch and dinner; Sa-Su dinner. Reservations recommended. 108 E 38th St (between Lexington and Park Aves). 683.0135

118 **Church of Our Savior** This perfect exampl of Romanesque Gothic architecture was built by **Paul C. Reilly** in 1959, a time when architects were tossing off glass boxes with the excuse that there were no craftsmen left to do this kind of work. The interior of this Roman Catholic church proves that there must have been at least a few in New York in the 1950s. ♦ 59 Park Ave (at E 38th St). 679.8166 ♿

119 **Sheraton Park Avenue** $$$ This 150-room hotel was originally the **Russell,** name for Judge Horace Russell, who once had a home on this site. An oak-paneled lobby wit book-lined shelves, spacious rooms—some with fireplaces—decorated with antiques, ar the always attentive service make it seem lik a private club or country home. ♦ 45 Park A (at E 37th St). 685.7676, 800/325.3535; fax 889.3193 ♿

The Pierpont Morgan Library

Michael Storrings

Within the Sheraton Park Avenue:

Judge's Chamber Jazz tunes are piped into the hotel's wood-paneled cocktail lounge. Light snacks are served in the evening. ♦ Daily noon-12:30AM. 685.7676

120 Doral Park Avenue Hotel $$$ Here's an Old-World–style hotel with modern touches, including access to a fitness center up the street on Park Avenue. The 188 rooms are well furnished, the atmosphere gracious and traditional. ♦ 70 Park Ave (at E 38th St). 687.7050, 800/223.6725; fax 779.0148 ♿

Within the Doral Park Avenue Hotel:

Saturnia Restaurant ★$$$ The atmosphere is warm and candlelit. In season, service extends out to a sidewalk cafe. ♦ American ♦ Daily breakfast, lunch, and dinner. Reservations recommended. 687.7050

121 Madison Towers Hotel $$ Completely modernized, this comfortable hotel offers meeting facilities and 240 rooms. A small fee gives guests access to an in-house health club with sauna and gym. Ask for a room with a view of the **Empire State Building.** ♦ 22 E 38th St (at Madison Ave). 685.3700, 800/225.4340; fax 447.0747

Within the Madison Towers Hotel:

The Whaler Bar High-beamed ceilings and a huge working fireplace make this a favorite midtown meeting place. ♦ American ♦ Daily lunch and dinner. 685.3700

122 Morgans $$$ Former discotheque owner Ian Schrager runs this trendy hotel (he also refurbished the **Royalton** and the **Paramount**), with rooms and furnishings created by French designer André Putman.

The hotel prides itself on getting you whatever you want—if the urge for sushi strikes at midnight, no problem. All 112 rooms have VCRs, stereos, blackout shades on the windows, and phones in the bedrooms and bathrooms. An extensive renovation has resulted in the addition of exercise facilties. ♦ 237 Madison Ave (between E 37th and E 38th Sts). 686.0300, 800/334.3408; fax 779.8352

123 231 Madison Avenue This 45-room freestanding brownstone mansion, built in 1852 for banker Anson Phelps Stokes, was bought by J.P. Morgan for his son in 1904. In 1944, it became the property of the Evangelical Lutheran Church, which is responsible for the architecturally sacrilegious brick addition on the East 37th Street side. It has been restored and incorporated into the **Morgan Library** and is also the new site for the museum's expanded book store. ♦ Tu-Su. At E 37th St. 685.0610

124 The Pierpont Morgan Library Financier J.P. Morgan began collecting books, manuscripts, and drawings in earnest in 1890, and eventually had to construct this magnificent small palazzo to house his treasures. It was designed in 1906 by **C.F. McKim** of **McKim, Mead & White.** The building itself is a treasure, and the 1928 annex on the Madison Avenue side complements it perfectly. Inside, Morgan's library and office have been preserved exactly as they were when he died in 1913. The collection includes more than 1,000 illuminated medieval and Renaissance manuscripts, the finest in America. It also contains the country's best examples of printed books, from Gutenberg to modern times, as well as an extensive collection of fine bookbinding. And its collection of autograph manuscripts, both literary and musical, is considered one of the best in the world. Art historian Kenneth Clark summed it all up perfectly when he said, "every object is a treasure, every item is perfect." On your way out, visit the bookshop, where you'll find wonderful books, toys, and cards. ♦ Donation requested. Tu-Su. 29 E 36th St (between Park and Madison Aves). 685.0610

Within The Pierpont Morgan Library:

Morgan Cafe ★$ A refined place indeed for the true lady's (or perfect gentleman's) lunch, this elegant skylit cafe is located near the bookshop. Sandwiches, salads, and afternoon tea are among the appropriately light and delicate offerings. ♦ Cafe ♦ Tu-Su breakfast, lunch, and afternoon tea. 29 E 36th St (at Madison Ave). 685.0008

125 Lord & Taylor This store has made a specialty of stocking clothing by American designers. Its shoe department is legendary, as is the caring quality of its sales help, which is quite a rarity these days. The department store is also justly famous for its Christmas window displays, without which the holidays in New York wouldn't be the same. The store was the first in the history of retailing to devote its window displays to anything but merchandise during the holiday season. The custom began during the unusually warm December of 1905, when customers didn't seem to feel Christmasy. The management got them into the proper mood by filling the store's windows with a snowstorm the likes of which New Yorkers hadn't seen since the

famous Blizzard of '88. If you arrive 15 minutes before the store opens in the morning, seating, free coffee (there are also three restaurants within the store), and music are provided just inside the front door. ♦ Daily. 424 Fifth Ave (between W 38th and W 39th Sts). 391.3344 ♿

126 Goldberg's Marine Distributors Most of the stores on this block sell trimmings and ribbons, but if you need a stout coil of rope, you'll find it here. New York is America's biggest seaport, but it still comes as a surprise to discover a place selling anchors, depth finders, fishing equipment (including the tournament reels that are so much more expensive in Europe), and other gear for yacht enthusiasts and sailors. It is a perfect store for the shoes and foul-weather clothes and other outfits you need if you want to look like you belong to the yacht club set. ♦ M-Sa. 12 W 37th St (between Fifth and Sixth Aves). 594.6065 ♿

127 M&J Trimming Though this well-known chockablock trimmings store looks like the kind traditionally open to the trade only, it has always been a retail-shopper's dream. Countless buttons, tassles, piping, frogs, and decorative borders will transform the most nondescript garment into an award-winner. Aspiring and professional designers come here for inspiration, resourcefully using buttons and beads for everything from jewelry to shoe decoration, kitsch to elegant. A new **M&J Decorator Collection** next door at 1014 Sixth Avenue makes the same treasure trove of braiding and trimming available for home design. ♦ M-Sa. 1008 Sixth Ave (between W 37th and W 38th Sts). 391.9072

Bests

Horace Havemeyer III
Publisher, *Metropolis, The Architecture and Design Magazine of New York*

Having lunch on weekends in the winter in **SoHo** or **Midtown** before or after visiting galleries or museums. The **MoMA** dining rooms are great for their views.

Browsing in any good bookstore. **Rizzoli's** on West 57th Street is open at night so we can drop in, often after a concert. **Doubleday** and **Brentano's** on Fifth Avenue are also favorites.

Walking almost anywhere looking at buildings and their details. Especially:

Park Avenue in the 60s, 70s, and 80s. Look at the detail in the pre-World War II buildings.

TriBeCa. Walk along **Greenwich Street** and look in at **Duane Square.** Note the continuity between the area's industrial past and residential present.

Along the waterfront looking at the rivers, river traffic, and opposite shores, such as the **Finley Walk**

along the **East River** between 72nd and 90th Streets. Going downtown from the East 80s, I always try to take the **East River Drive.**

Queen Anne–style row house. My favorites are the row of 10 houses at **146-156 East 89th Street,** the **Henderson** houses on **East End** between East 86th and East 87th Streets, and those between Amsterdam and Columbus on **West 81st Street.**

Gramercy Park, its surrounding buildings, and Park Avenue in the low 20s.

Walter Cronkite
Newscaster Emeritus, "CBS Evening News"

South Street Seaport Museum.

Staten Island Ferry. Best $1-roundtrip ride in the city. Magnificent view of **Lower Manhattan.**

Cable ride from Manhattan to **Roosevelt Island.** Exciting view of the **East River.**

Ellis Island. Where freedom began for many Americans.

ooklyn Botanic Garden. Where bonsai and
orticultural beauty abound.

acie Mansion.

J. Clarke's Bar. A saloon at the corner of East
th Street and Third Avenue in the best tradition
the old New York City saloons before they tore
wn the el.

bar's, the deli supreme. However, almost any
li in New York should be visited for its smells
d sights.

ty Hall. A magnificent example of Federal
chitecture.

e John Finley Walk along the East River near
acie Square, where you can watch the ships
ming down the river.

ndré Emmerich
wner, André Emmerich Gallery

nch midtown in the Grill Room of the Four
asons with its unequaled spa cuisine and sparkling
llow guests.

rly, pretheater dinner at Le Bernardin—the best
od in the world that stays safely within Pritikin
nits.

nday night dinner at Elaine's, the most relaxing
tting for the tensest people in the world—New
rk's intelligentsia.

opping the gentleman's quarter-mile along
adison Avenue from Chipp, Brooks Brothers,
ul Stuart, Orvis, Tripler, and on, ending at Saks
th Avenue on East 49th Street.

e antique furniture shops around Broadway below
est 13th Street.

e revived Brooklyn Museum—as the French
idebooks say, well worth the "detour" to see
spectacular exhibitions.

narbor cruise on a party boat, especially when
e ship sails close to the floodlit Statue of Liberty,
ll the grandest public sculpture in the world.

e newly installed galleries of ancient Greek and
man art at the Metropolitan Museum.

e drive into Manhattan from the north along the
enry Hudson Parkway.

nally, New York at sunset seen from my apartment,
0 feet above the avenue right behind the
ıggenheim.

bert A.M. Stern
chitect

est 67th Street between Central Park West
d Columbus Avenue. Elegant studio buildings,
ntaining dramatic double-height rooms, that
ake the block in some ways more like Paris than
ris.

e Sheep Meadow in Central Park. New York's
eat front lawn, framed by the fantastic mountain
nge of Midtown's skyscrapers.

The Promenade along Brooklyn Heights. A brilliant
urban sleight of hand, overwhelming the sight and
sound of the Brooklyn-Queens Expressway with
breathtaking views of the harbor and Lower
Manhattan.

The soaring lobby of the main branch of the Brooklyn
Public Library, where classicism and modernism
join forces to form a grand public space.

As the crowds gather for an evening of theater, the
main plaza at Lincoln Center becomes an outdoor
stage.

George Page
Host, PBS "Nature" series

The Hudson River. One of the world's greatest and
most beautiful estuaries—a natural wonder and
a highway of American history. Take the Dayliner
cruise to Bear Mountain State Park or, better still,
rent a yacht for the trip. The Circle Line cruise
around Manhattan is also recommended.

The Metropolitan Museum. Simply the world's most
glorious museum.

The Palm Court, the Oak Room, and the Oak Bar,
at The Plaza Hotel. All retain an ageless elegance
and gentility that is quintessential old New York.

Lutèce. Splurge. It's still the best restaurant in New
York, if not the world.

Under no circumstances should you visit New York
in July or August unless you enjoy walking around in
the world's largest steambath.

Florence Fabricant
Food Columnist/Cookbook Author

Manhattan from 96th Street to Wall Street—
walking, not driving as in most other cities.

Union Square—The bustle of the Greenmarket on
Monday, Wednesday, Friday, and Saturday.

Oyster Bar and Restaurant—Sitting at the counter
for oysters or pan roast.

Rainbow Room—The glamour! The view! The
setting! An incomparable experience that's
thoroughly New York.

Felissimo—Tea or a mid-afternoon snack in the
lovely fifth-floor cafe—quiet, serene.

Madison Square Garden Center—New York Knicks,
especially when they're winning.

Flushing Meadow—Tennis at the US Open in
September.

Pastrami King/Rego Park—In Queens, but the best
pastrami sandwich anywhere.

Arthur Avenue, Bronx—Old-world Little Italy.

Paley Plaza—For the waterfall.

Le Cirque—The buzz of a celebrity playpen with
great food.

Remi—Francesco's bread sticks, risottos, and the
gorgeous Venetian mural.

Chelsea

Named for the estate acquired by Captain Thomas Clarke in 1750, Chelsea was originally bounded by **West 14th** and **West 25th Streets,** and **Eighth Avenue** and the **Hudson River.** Today, the Chelsea area, which extends farther north to **West 34th Street** and east to **Sixth Avenue,** is quite a mixed bag. Clement Clarke Moore who had inherited his grandfather's land—and is best known as the author of the poem *Visit from St. Nicholas*—divided his family estate and laid out the neighborhood's original building lots in 1830, some of which he donated to the General Theological Seminary. The surrounding area was a flourishing middle-class suburb that never quite made it as a desirable address. Once the **Hudson River Railroad** opened on **11th Avenue** in 1851, it attracted breweries and slaughterhouses and their workers' shanties and tenements,

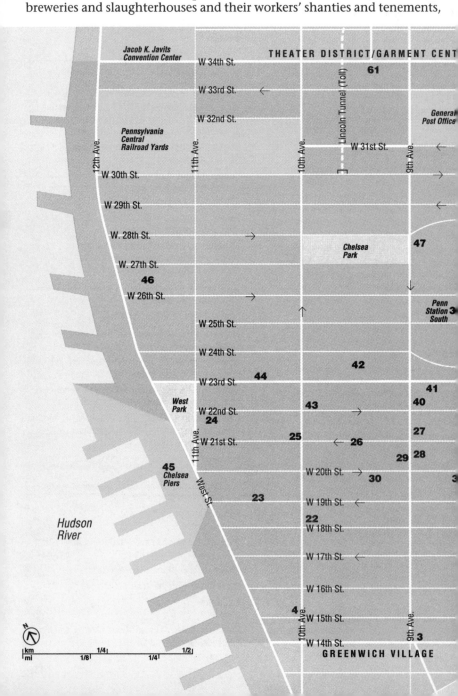

which marked the beginning of the area's aesthetic decline. In the 1870s, the remaining town house blocks were invaded by the city's first elevated railroad, on **Ninth Avenue.**

Despite its industrial image, Chelsea became a creative retail center. A flurry of theatrical activity took over **West 23rd Street** in the 1880s, but by 1892 the theater world had moved uptown, leaving behind the artists and writers who eventually departed for the newer bohemia of Greenwich Village. The funky **Hotel Chelsea,** on West 23rd Street, is a remnant of Chelsea's theatrical heyday, when actors and playwrights lodged there. In the 1960s, Andy Warhol's superstars Viva and Edie Sedgewick lived there, and his film *Chelsea Girls* documented a chapter in the renaissance of the old survivor.

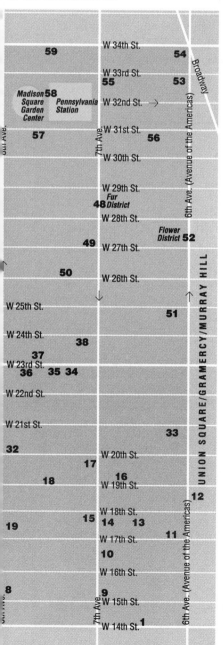

The country's motion picture industry started in Chelsea in 1905, and for a decade it flourished in old lofts and theaters used as studios. Adolph Zukor's **Famous Players Studio,** which employed Mary Pickford and John Barrymore, produced films here. But the Astoria Studios in Queens built a better facility, and eventually balmy Hollywood beckoned. The film business also moved on.

In the 1930s, new industry found quarters in the area near the piers. The 11th Avenue railroad was replaced by a less objectionable elevated train, and the Ninth Avenue line shut down. The clean sweep of 1950s and 1960s urban renewal replaced slum housing with housing projects, and renovation started on desirable Federal and Greek Revival town houses. Today, Chelsea is a pastiche of town houses, housing projects, industrial buildings, tenements, secondhand office-furniture stores, and a large number of churches.

Chelsea's retail career was also short-lived. As the gentry pursued their determined course uptown, so did fashionable stores. By the 1870s, West 23rd Street blossomed, and the blocks on Sixth Avenue south of it became known as the "Ladies' Mile." During the latter part of the century, giant dry goods stores of limestone and cast iron lined Sixth Avenue (now **Avenue of the Americas**) and **Broadway.** Many of the buildings that still stand, reminders of past retail glories, are used as lofts and offices. By the early part of the 1900s, the fashion action had moved to West 34th Street, and by the 1930s, West 23rd Street was a has-been.

But Chelsea has been discovered—again—thanks to an overflow of residents, stores, and restaurants fleeing Greenwich Village's escalating rents. In the late 1970s and 1980s, Chelsea came to be the destination of a northward immigration of Greenwich Village's gay community, with Eighth Avenue supplanting the Village's Christopher Street as the main gay thoroughfare in New York. Myriad shopping possibilities run the gamut from the ne plus ultra **Barneys** to the antiques shops on Ninth Avenue between **West 20th** and **West 22nd Streets.** The **Flower District** on the blocks between **West 27th** and **West 30th Streets** on Avenue of the Americas is dense with orchids, rare palms, and exotic bonsai, supplying wholesale and retail stores alike.

Chelsea also wears an artistic hat of late, encouraged by the arrival of SoHo's respected **Dia Center for the Arts** and a half dozen other galleries that have recently opened on West 22nd Street and neighboring blocks. One of Chelsea's—and the city's—last undesirable pockets is reinventing itself, with the newly opened **Chelsea Piers** as a massive recreational mecca.

1 **New York State Armory** The 42nd Infantry Division of the New York National Guard is headquartered in this building, designed by **Charles S. Kawecki** in 1971 to make its members feel warlike. ♦ 125 W 14th St (between Sixth and Seventh Aves).

2 **319 West 14th Street** A 20-year-old Orson Welles and his first wife, Virginia Nicholson, lived in a basement apartment here between 1935 and 1937, during which time he directed the famous all-black *Macbeth* for Harlem's **Negro Theater.** ♦ Between Eighth and Ninth Aves

3 **Old Homestead** ★★$$$$; Established in 1868, this is the oldest steak house in Manhattan, and huge steaks and prime ribs are served here the way they always have been. Those who prefer to do their own broiling or grilling can buy fresh cuts of beef (including one-inch-thick steaks) at the **Old Homestead Gourmet** shop (807.0707) next door, where a variety of gourmet items, including the *crème de la crème* of chocolates, the French Valrhona and the Belgian D'Orsay. ♦ American ♦ Daily lunch and dinner. Shop: M-Sa. Reservations recommended. 56 Ninth Ave (at W 14th St). 242.9040 &

Frank's

4 **Frank's** ★★$$$ This place has been a meat district fixture since 1912, serving some of the best steaks around to the guys who work in the business and appreciate extraordinary beef—dry aged shell steak, loin lamb chops, and a piece of filet mignon that weighs nearly a pound. Also on the menu are

such homemade pasta dishes as *fettuccine bolognese* as well as basic, good-quality desserts, including giant slabs of cheesecake. ♦ American ♦ M-F lunch and dinner; Sa dinner. Reservations recommended. 85 10th Ave (between W 15th and W 16th Sts). 243.1349

5 **El Cid** ★★$ Small and cheerful, this tapas bar with blue tablecloths and mirrored walls is an informal, fun place to come with a group to try out a range of different small plates. Don't miss the white asparagus in vinaigrette, grilled shrimp, marinated pork, or chicken in garlic sauce. And the paella should satisfy the most hungry diners. The wine list showcases good, inexpensive Spanish wines. ♦ Spanish ♦ Tu-F lunch and dinner; Sa-Su dinner. 322 W 15th St (between Eighth and Ninth Aves). 929.9332

6 **Port of New York Authority Commerce Building/Union Inland Terminal No. 1** The organization now known as the **Port Authority of New York and New Jersey** had its headquarters in this blockbuster, designed in 1932 by **Abbott, Merckt & Co.,** before moving down to the **World Trade Center.** The top floors were designed for manufacturing, but the elevators can carry a 20-ton truck to any floor. ♦ 111 Eighth Ave (between W 15th and W 16th Sts)

7 **Cajun** ★$$ The honky-tonk atmosphere and live Dixieland music (nightly at 8PM) are fun, and the creole-Cajun food, which comes in hearty portions, doesn't disappoint. ♦ Creole/Cajun ♦ M-F lunch and dinner; Sa dinner; Su brunch and dinner. Reservations recommended for five or more. 129 Eighth Ave (at W 16th St). 691.6174

Restaurants/Clubs: Red   Hotels: Blue
Shops/ ♥ Outdoors: Green   Sights/Culture: Black

8 Chelsea Trattoria ★$$ This pretty trattoria with peach walls and exposed brick is a reliable place for standard Italian fare. The osso buco (braised veal shank) and the fettuccine with artichokes, mushrooms, and tomatoes are especially recommended. ◆ Italian ◆ M-F lunch and dinner; Sa dinner. 108 Eighth Ave (between W 15th and W 16th Sts). 924.7786

9 Jensen-Lewis Two floors of creative, colorful merchandise, from sofas and beds to lamps and luggage (even bean-bag chairs), can be found here. This store is especially known for its selection of director's chairs. ◆ Daily. 89 Seventh Ave (at W 15th St). 929.4880

BARNEYS NEW YORK

10 Barneys New York This is a New York original. Name a famous designer for either men or women, and the helpful person at the front desk will direct you to their best work, from shoes to hats with every stop between. You can buy antiques, leather goods, jewelry, lingerie, or children's clothes. Downstairs, you can get your hair cut (at **Roger Thompson**) and enjoy a fancy lunch, or cappuccino, surrounded by opulence at **Le Cafe,** located on the store's lower level. Though it first opened in 1923 as a discount store for men and boys, a 1986 expansion—particularly the controversial annexation and modernization of town houses behind the original structure—has changed the store's character completely, and that of the neighborhood as well. At press time, an agreement had been struck with **Loehmann's,** the grande dame of bargain basement stores, to lease space here. ◆ Daily. Seventh Ave (at W 17th St). 929.9000. Also at: 660 Madison Ave (at E 61st St). 826.8900; 225 Liberty St (at World Financial Center). 945.1600

11 Da Umberto ★★$$$ This casual and restful trattoria specializes in Tuscan dishes, especially wild game (hare, pheasant, and venison, for example). The veal chop with cognac sauce is a favorite here, and the antipasti selections are worth a try. ◆ Italian ◆ M-Sa lunch and dinner. Reservations required. 107 W 17th St (between Sixth and Seventh Aves). 989.0303

12 Bed Bath & Beyond You'll find 80 patterns of bed linens, 132 colors and patterns of bath towels, 218 styles of place mats, as well as gadgets ranging from shelf dividers to "banana savers," all on shelves that run up to the 28-foot ceilings of this overwhelming mega-store, the flagship of the national chain. It's worth coming into the Victorian-pillared landmark, built in 1896 as the **Siegel-Cooper Dry Goods Store,** just for the experience. ◆ Daily. 620 Sixth Ave (between W 18th and W 19th Sts). 255.3550 ♿

13 Two Worlds Gallery This store is the direct importer of the antiques and unique decorative objects sold here. Paintings and custom artwork from well-known artists are also available. ◆ M-Sa. 122 W 18th St (between Sixth and Seventh Aves). 633.1668

13 Movie Star News Millions of head shots, stills, and lobby cards fill the filing cabinets in this garage space, a popular source for collectors, newspapers, magazines, and TV. Paula Klaw and her family also stock movie posters and books on theater and film. ◆ M-Sa. 134 W 18th St (between Sixth and Seventh Aves). 620.8160 ♿

13 Poster America Gallery The selection of vintage posters from 1910 to 1965, most of which are original lithographs from Europe and the US, is among the best you'll find on either side of the Atlantic. ◆ Tu-Su. 138 W 18th St (between Sixth and Seventh Aves). 206.0499

le madri

14 Le Madri ★★★$$$ Pino Luongo's stylish restaurant turns out Tuscan-style specialties for the illustrious crowds that flock here. Order roasted vegetables for the whole table and any of chef Gianni Scappin's homemade pastas, which include the delicious *agnolotti* (half-moon ravioli) filled with spinach and ricotta and served with mixed mushrooms. Osso buco and whole roasted fish are also treats. On summer weekends the restaurant hosts an "al fresco" film series; Italian movies are shown on a screen in the parking lot next door, while the crowd munches on salads, pizzas, and pastas. ◆ Italian ◆ M-Sa lunch and dinner; Su dinner. Reservations required. 168 W 18th St (at Seventh Ave). 727.8022

Most shipping these days is done by air, but the Port of New York, which handles more than 150 million tons a year, is far and away the most important seaport in America. New York Harbor is at the apex of a triangle that extends more than 100 miles to the east and south like a giant funnel.

15 Books of Wonder If there are no children in your life, this store will make you wish there were—or at least make you fondly remember when you were a child yourself. Authors and illustrators make frequent appearances to read from their books and to sign copies. There is a half-hour story hour every Sunday at 11:30AM (except between Thanksgiving and New Year's). ♦ Daily. 132 Seventh Ave (at W 18th St). 989.3270 ⑤

16 Different Light Books Having outgrown its store in Greenwich Village, and confirming the ever-growing gay community in the Chelsea neighborhood, this is undoubtedly the best bookstore of its kind in the city. It's an excellent place to find literature on a wide variety of gay- and lesbian-related topics and issues. ♦ Daily 10AM-midnight. 151 W 19th St (between Sixth and Seventh Aves). 989.4850

17 Claire ★$$ Although the atmosphere is often marred by its high-volume din, this seafood restaurant is reliable and reasonably priced. There's a hint of Florida's Key West and like the Keys, this restaurant has a predominantly gay clientele. The food, rife with sometimes fierce and often intricate flavors, has been devised by the restaurant's Thai chef; popular dishes include blackened bluefish, seared tuna steak with creole mustard sauce, and crawfish patties with cayenne-and-cilantro sauce. ♦ Seafood ♦ M-Th, Su lunch and dinner; F-Sa lunch, dinner, and late-night meals. Reservations recommended. 156 Seventh Ave (between W 19th and W 20th Sts). 255.1955

18 Bessie Shonberg Theater Operated by the **Dance Theater Workshop (DTW),** this 160-seat theater (named after the dancer, choreographer, and teacher) is one of the most active dance, mime, and poetry houses in the city and offers young performing artists a variety of support services. Famous clown/dancer/mime Bill Irwin has often played here. **DTW** also runs the picture gallery in the lobby of the theater. ♦ 219 W 19th St (between Seventh and Eighth Aves), Second floor. 924.0077

19 Cola's ★★$ Here you'll find a casual mix of Northern and Southern Italian cuisine featuring such pasta dishes as penne with goat cheese and eggplant, as well as heartier fare like pork chops in balsamic vinegar. The wine list offers many fine selections. ♦ Italian ♦ Daily dinner. 148 Eighth Ave (between W 17th and W 18th Sts). 633.8020

19 Gascogne ★★$$ Chef Pascal Condomine recreates the rich, hearty foods from the southwest region of France, including a superb fish soup, foie gras, roast duck, and an excellent cassoulet; also featured are wines from the same region. ♦ French ♦ M-F lunch and dinner; Sa dinner; Su brunch and dinner. Reservations required. 158 Eighth Ave (between W 17th and W 18th Sts). 675.6564

19 The Viceroy ★$$ Perpetually abuzz with what seems to be the entire gay male population of Chelsea, this bustling bistro serves barbecued quail salad with black-eyed peas and *frisée* (curly endive), and seared peppered tuna with stir-fried Asian greens. For dessert, don't miss the chocolate torte. Be sure to come early—by 7:30PM the place is mobbed. ♦ American ♦ M-F lunch, dinner, and late-night meals; Sa-Su brunch, dinner, and late-night meals. 160 Eighth Ave (at W 18th St). 633.8484

20 Eighteenth and Eighth ★$ The cozy—some would say cramped—dining room is decorated with dried leaves, eccentric teapots, and drawings of the male anatomy. Look for large portions of such creative comfort food as roast loin of pork stuffed with herbs; grilled leg of lamb with sun-dried tomatoes and black olives; roast chicken with lemon, garlic, and rosemary; and a very satisfying meat loaf. ♦ American ♦ Daily breakfast, lunch, and dinner. 159 Eighth Ave (at W 18th St). 242.5000

21 Man Ray ★$$ Sleek and minimalist, this Art Deco–inspired cafe serves such creative international food as black-pepper linguine with seafood, tomato, lemon, garlic, and olive oil; and grilled breast of duck with arugula and watercress in a raspberry vinaigrette. ♦ Continental ♦ M-F lunch and dinner; Sa-Su brunch and dinner. 169 Eighth Ave (between W 18th and W 19th Sts). 627.4220

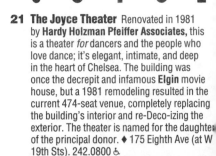

21 The Joyce Theater Renovated in 1981 by **Hardy Holzman Pfeiffer Associates,** this is a theater *for* dancers and the people who love dance; it's elegant, intimate, and deep in the heart of Chelsea. The building was once the decrepit and infamous **Elgin** movie house, but a 1981 remodeling resulted in the current 474-seat venue, completely replacing the building's interior and re-Deco-izing the exterior. The theater is named for the daughter of the principal donor. ♦ 175 Eighth Ave (at W 19th Sts). 242.0800 ⑤

The face of New York City's skyline was seriously altered during World War II, when there was a 15-story dimout limit.

La Lunchonette

22 La Lunchonette ★$$ The homey bar and open kitchen in this bistro-style restaurant seem familiar enough, but the free-range chicken with mustard, lamb sausage with sautéed apples, and panfried whole trout with wild mushrooms add interesting variations to a time-honored cuisine. ♦ French ♦ M-F lunch and dinner; Sa dinner; Su brunch and dinner. Reservations recommended. 130 10th Ave (at W 18th St). 675.0342

THE KITCHEN

23 The Kitchen This veteran institution for experimental performing and visual arts presents the works of young artists in dance, film, video, music, and performance art. Programs are scheduled most evenings and some require that tickets be purchased in advance. Call for the current performance schedule. ♦ Box office: M-F or call Ticketmaster. 512 W 19th St (between 10th and 11th Aves). 255.5793 ♿

24 Dia Center for the Arts Since branching out here in 1985 to secure additional space for its changing exhibitions, this SoHo gallery was the first to stake out a presence in Chelsea, spawning an artistic movement "uptown" that continues to flourish. Works by contemporary artists—including John Chamberlain, Walter De Marie, and John Beuys—are mounted in this four-story space. ♦ Donation suggested. Th-Sa noon-6PM; closed July-Aug. 548 W 22nd St (between 10th and Eleventh Aves). 989.5912. Also at: 141 Wooster St (between Prince and W Houston Sts). 473.8072; 393 W Broadway (between Broome and Spring Sts). 925.9397

25 Guardian Angel Church This little complex of Italian Romanesque buildings, designed in 1930 by **John Van Pelt,** surrounds what is known as the **Shrine Church of the Sea.** The name reflects the one-time presence of the busiest piers in the Port of New York, a short walk to the west. The church's Renaissance interior is even more impressive than the redbrick-and-limestone facade. The priest in charge of this Roman Catholic church is designated Chaplain of the Port, with duties that include assigning chaplains to ships based here. ♦ 193 10th Ave (at W 21st St). 929.5966

26 West 21st Street Almost all the 19th-century houses on this block follow Clement Clarke Moore's requirement of front gardens

and street trees. In its earliest years as a residential community, all of Chelsea looked much like this. The building with the unusual peaked roof on the Ninth Avenue corner was built in the 1820s by **James N. Wells** and is the oldest house in the neighborhood. ♦ Between Ninth and 10th Aves

27 Somethin' Else! There are dozens of antiques shops scattered around this neighborhood, some authentic, some dubious, all of them browsers' delights. But this one is, indeed, something else, with its collection of old toys, quilts, jewelry, and an entire wall of crystal glasses. ♦ Daily. 182 Ninth Ave (between W 21st and W 22nd Sts). 924.0006 ♿

28 Manhattan Doll House This shop has the largest collection of new and antique dolls, doll houses, and doll accessories in the city—all for sale. ♦ M-Sa. 176 Ninth Ave (between W 20th and W 21st Sts). 989.5220 ♿

29 General Theological Seminary You're welcome to enter this oasis through the library building on Ninth Avenue during public hours or, in summer, to take the free "Grand Design" tour. Land for the Episcopal Seminary was donated by Clement Clarke Moore in 1830, on the condition that the seminary should always occupy the site. The **West Building,** built in 1835, is the oldest building on campus, as well as New York's oldest example of Gothic Revival architecture. It predates **Charles C. Haight's** renovation (1883-1900), which includes all the other Gothic buildings. In the center is the **Chapel of the Good Shepherd,** with its outstanding bronze doors and 161-foot-high square bell tower. **Hoffman Hall,** at the 10th Avenue end, contains a medieval-style dining hall complete with a barrel-vaulted ceiling, walk-in fireplaces, and a gallery for musicians. The other end is dominated by the new and very much out-of-place **St. Mark's Library,** built in 1960 by **O'Connor & Kilhan,** containing some 170,000 volumes, along with one of the world's largest collections of Latin Bibles. ♦ M-F noon-2:30PM; Sa 11AM-3:30PM; closed when school is not in session and on religious holidays. 175 Ninth Ave (between W 20th and W 21st Sts). 243.5150 ♿

30 406-24 West 20th Street This row of extremely well-preserved Greek Revival houses was built by Don Alonzo Cushman, a dry goods merchant who, in 1837, developed much of Chelsea and built these as rental units. The attic windows are circled with wreaths, the doorways framed in brownstone. Even the newel posts, topped with cast-iron pineapples, are still intact. ♦ Between Ninth and 10th Aves

31 St. Peter's Episcopal Church The church and its rectory and parish hall are outgrowths of Clement Clarke Moore and James W.

Smith's 1838 plan to build them in the style of Greek temples. According to legend, the plan was changed when one of the vestrymen came back from England with tales of the Gothic buildings at Oxford. The congregation decided to switch styles, even though the foundations were already in place. The fence that surrounds this charming complex was brought here from **Trinity Church** on lower Broadway, where it had stood since 1790. Renovations are under way to replace the roof, repoint and preserve the masonry, and repair or replace all of the woodwork in the tower and window and door openings. ♦ 346 W 20th St (between Eighth and Ninth Aves). 929.2390

32 Chelsea Foods This is a gorgeously designed modern store and cafe with many interesting, but expensive, prepared and packaged foods to go. The brownies are terrific. ♦ Cafe/Takeout ♦ Daily 9AM-10PM. 198 Eighth Ave (at W 20th St). 691.3948

33 Third Cemetery of the Spanish & Portuguese Synagogue Enclosed on three sides by painted brick loft buildings, this private hideaway is the third cemetery established by the first Jewish congregation in New York; tombstones date from 1829 to 1851. The second cemetery is in Greenwich Village, the first on the Lower East Side. ♦ 98-110 W 21st St (between Sixth and Seventh Aves)

34 Hotel Chelsea $$ When the hotel was first built in 1884 by **Hubert, Pirrson & Co.,** Chelsea was the heart of the Theater District, attracting creative people just as Greenwich Village would a decade later. In its early days the hotel was home to such writers as William Dean Howells and O. Henry, and later to Thomas Wolfe, Arthur Miller, Mary McCarthy, Vladimir Nabokov, and Yevgeny Yevtushenko. Sarah Bernhardt once lived here, and this is where Dylan Thomas spent his last days. In the 1960s and 1970s, it was a favorite stopping place for visiting rock stars, who shared the atmosphere with modern classical composers George Kleinsinger and Virgil Thomson. Originally an apartment building,

it was the first in New York to have a penthouse. It was converted to a hotel in 1905. The lobby has been altered, but the stairway, best seen from the second floor, is intact. Of the 350 rooms, 225 have permanent occupants. Among the 125 available for hotel guests are rooms with kitchenettes (available upon request). At press time, sorely needed renovations were close to completion. ♦ 222 W 23rd St (between Seventh and Eighth Aves). 243.3700; fax 243.3700 ext 2171

35 Manhattan Comics & Cards Here is an extensive collection of new and old comic books and baseball cards. ♦ Daily. 228 W 23rd St (between Seventh and Eighth Aves). 243.9349

Blu

36 Blu ★★$$ The room upstairs is a twilight fantasy, with dark-green and blue walls affixed with gold stars and leaves. Downstairs, the warm and cozy cafe dispenses with the drama and some of the expense. On both levels, however, the food is inventive and satisfying. Dishes include black-pepper fettuccine with Peconic Bay scallops, sugar-snap peas, and brown garlic; and wild-mushroom dumplings with white-truffle oil. The desserts are spellbinding. ♦ Fusion ♦ M-Sa lunch and dinner; Su brunch and dinner. Reservations recommended. 254 W 23rd St (between Seventh and Eighth Aves). 989.6300

37 Unity Book Center "For books that matter" is their tagline; topics include Marxism-Leninism, socialism, African-American literature, and women's equality. ♦ M-Sa. 237 W 23rd St (between Seventh and Eighth Aves). 242.2934

38 McBurney YMCA $ One of the first social workers to deal with the problems of foreign-born New Yorkers, Robert Ross McBurney ran a Y at East 23rd Street and Fourth Avenue in the 1870s. This branch, built in 1904 by **Parish & Schroeder,** is its successor. The building contains 240 rooms (all with shared baths), a track, a gymnasium, and a rooftop sundeck. Maximum stay is 25 days. ♦ 206 W 24th St (between Seventh and Eighth Aves). 741.9226; fax 741.0012

39 Penn Station South This 12-square-block complex of 2,820 apartments was built in 1962 by **Herman Jessor** as middle-income housing for the International Ladies' Garment Workers Union. ♦ Bounded by West 23rd and West 29th Sts (between Eighth and Ninth Aves)

40 Luma ★★$$$ This restaurant caters to well-heeled and health-conscious diners. The food is not only high quality, but good for you—there's not an additive in sight. Try the seared peppered tuna with seaweed salad, pickled cucumber, and wasabi; roasted Maine codfish with vegetable confetti and ginger-soy aromatic sauce; or grilled vegetables with garlic-herb oil. The wine list includes some organic selections. ♦ American ♦ Daily dinner. Reservations recommended. 200 Ninth Ave (between W 22nd and W 23rd Sts). 633.8033

41 Negril Island Spice ★★$ This place is a downtown branch of **Island Spice** in the Theater District, with a decor that tries its best to whisk you away to the island of Jamaica, with paintings of the sea inset in the sunny yellow walls. If that doesn't quite get you there, the food definitely will. Try the codfish fritters with avocado salsa; the ginger-lime chicken; or any of the rotis. For dessert, the bread pudding in a caramelized raisin sauce is hard to resist and harder to forget. A live band plays pop reggae nightly, and there's a calypso brunch on Sundays. ♦ Jamaican ♦ M-Sa lunch and dinner; Su brunch and dinner. 362 W 23rd St (between Eighth and Ninth Aves). 807.6411 &. Also at: 402 W 44th St (between Ninth and 10th Aves). 765.1737 &

42 London Terrace Apartments This double row of buildings with a garden in the center contains 1,670 apartments. It was built in 1930 by **Farrar & Watmaugh** at the height of the Depression and stood virtually empty for several years, despite lures such as an Olympic-size swimming pool and doormen dressed as London bobbies. It is the second complex by that name on the site. The original, built in 1845, was a row of Greek Revival buildings with wide front lawns on West 23rd Street. ♦ Bounded by W 23rd and W 24th Sts (between Ninth and 10th Aves)

EMPIRE

43 Empire Diner ★$ Refurbished in 1976 by designer Carl Laanes, this 1930s-style diner has retained the trappings of the original establishment—the Art Deco aluminium-winged clock near the entrance, the baked-enamel finish outside, and the signs—everything except, of course, the grease stains and the prices. Try the omelettes with salsa or smoked mozzarella. The rest of the menu is a mixed bag, featuring chicken fajitas; a roast turkey platter; linguine with smoked salmon, watercress, and garlic; and lentil burgers. Don't miss the Cajun bread pudding with bourbon sauce for dessert. In the summertime, sit at one of the sidewalk tables for front-row viewing of the local action. ♦ American ♦ Daily 24 hours. 210 10th Ave (between W 22nd and W 23rd Sts). 243.2736

44 WPA Theater Under the impressive artistic direction of Kyle Renick, productions such as *Steel Magnolias, Little Shop of Horrors,* and *The Whales of August* have blossomed into memorable Off-Broadway hits and feature films. The theater seats 122. ♦ 519 W 23rd St (between 10th and 11th Aves). 206.0523 &

45 Chelsea Piers With city officials and enterpreneurial visionaries talking about the island's glorious future of waterfront parklands, this is the first major development whose ship has come in. The historic (and until recently abandoned) **Piers 59, 60, 61,** and **62** are scheduled to be fully in service by winter 1996, housing an ambitious $100-million sports facility with a golf driving range (**Golf Club,** 336.6400); a vast sports-fitness center (**Sports Center,** 336.6000); two outdoor regulation-size roller skating venues (**Roller Rinks,** 336.6200); twin indoor ice skating rinks (**Sky Rinks,** 336.6100); a marina (336.6600); restaurants; and **Silver Screen Studios** (336.6300), Manhattan's largest film-TV production center. Originally built in 1910 by **Warren & Wetmore,** the architects of **Grand Central Terminal,** as docks for the era's grand ocean liners, it has been refitted by **Butler Rogers Baskett** for its new role as the West Side's luxury playground. ♦ Daily. Bounded by W 17th and W 23rd Sts, and West St and the Hudson River. 336.6666

46 Starrett-Lehigh Building A pacesetter in its day, this Art Deco collection of glass, concrete, and brown brick with rounded corners was built over the yards of the **Lehigh Valley Railroad,** and had elevators powerful enough to lift fully loaded freight cars onto its upper warehouse floors. It was designed in 1931 by **Russell G.** and **Walter M. Cory** and **Yasuo Matsui.** ♦ Bounded by W 26th and W 27th Sts (between 11th and 12th Aves)

47 Church of the Holy Apostles The slate-roofed spire of this Episcopal church makes it a standout among the huge brick apartment houses all around it. Built in 1848 by **Minard LaFever** with 1858 transepts by **Richard Upjohn,** it's an unusual feature of the view to the west from the **Observation Deck** of the **Empire State Building.** ♦ 296 Ninth Ave (between W 27th and W 28th Sts). 807.6799 &

48 Fur District Yes, that man you just passed did have a silver fox cape over his arm. No, he didn't steal it, and chances are that no one will steal it from him. It's commonplace in the Fur District for thousands of dollars' worth of merchandise to be delivered in such a casual way. It's all in a day's work for the people who make and sell fur garments in this neighborhood. ♦ Bounded by Sixth and Eighth Aves, and W 27th and W 30th Sts

Restaurants/Clubs: Red   **Hotels:** Blue
Shops/♥ Outdoors: Green   **Sights/Culture:** Black

49 Fashion Institute of Technology (FIT)
If there were a competition for the ugliest block in Manhattan, the center of this complex on West 27th Street would win easily. All the buildings, built between 1958 and 1977, are by the same firm, **De Young & Moscowitz,** but obviously not by the same hand. The prestigious school, part of the **State University of New York,** was created by New York's garment industry to train young people in all aspects of the fashion business. ♦ Seventh Ave and W 27th St. 760.7673

Within the Fashion Institute of Technology:

Chelsea Cafe ★★$ This stylish room with peach walls and faux-marble columns is popular with students for the sophisticated yet affordable Italian fare offered here. ♦ Italian ♦ M-F lunch and dinner; Sa dinner. Reservations recommended. 989.3804 ⴺ

50 221 West 26th Street This building was originally an armory. It was also once the Famous Players Studio, where, in 1915, Adolph Zukor paid Mary Pickford an unprecedented $2,000 per week as one of his most famous players. ♦ Between Seventh and Eighth Aves

51 Chelsea Antiques Building If the hundreds of dealers at the weekend **Annex Antiques Fair and Flea Market** a block away don't satisfy you, this antiques cove is wonderfully convenient and considerably calmer. Twelve floors are filled with quality dealers of art, antiques, and estate treasures, from charming collectibles to serious museum pieces. ♦ Daily. 110 W 25th St (between Sixth and Seventh Aves). 929.0909 ⴺ

52 Flower District The best time to smell the flowers here is the early morning, when florists from all over the city arrive to refresh their stock. If you're in the market for a large plant or a small tree, you'll find it here on the sidewalk soaking up the sun. ♦ Sixth Ave (between W 26th and W 29th Sts)

Thaddeus Hyatt dramatically changed the sidewalks of New York in 1845, when he invented iron vault covers with glass inserts that allowed daylight to filter into building basements. Before electric lights, basement space was all but useless. Cast-iron buildings incorporated Hyatt's invention into light platforms that were raised a step or two off the sidewalk so window shoppers could indulge themselves without stopping pedestrian traffic on narrow sidewalks. The platforms usually had round, pink-tinted translucent windows on the risers of the steps to allow light into the below-ground floor. Most of them have either been removed, paved over, or turned into truck loading docks.

53 Manhattan Mall The former **A&S Plaza** was renamed following **Stern's** 1995 takeover of this former **A&S** branch (the parent company, Federated, also owns the nearby **Macy's**). Aside from the new name, not much else has changed: Eight floors of shops plus a food court will make you feel like you're in a mall in the 'burbs. **The Body Shop** (skin-care products), **Accento** (handknit sweaters), and **Moose N' Around** (clothes and accessories adorned with favorite cartoon characters) are of particular interest, but two other reasons to visit this vertical mall, designed in 1989 by Baltimore-based **RTKL Associates,** are the clean bathrooms and the **Visitors' Center** on the seventh floor; stop in if you need tourist brochures, transportation information, or assistance in getting theater tickets or making restaurant reservations. ♦ W 33rd St and Sixth Ave. 465.0500 ⴺ

54 Herald Center Built in 1985 by **Coeland, Novak, Israel & Simmon,** this shopping center, dubbed the "Tall Mall," seems to have suffered in the shadow of **Macy's** and **A&S/Stern's Plaza.** Once home to 70 stores, at present most are closed except for the food court on the eighth floor and **Toys 'R Us** and **Kids 'R Us** (first and second floors). The recent arrival of **Daffy's,** the off-price designer clothes shop on the fourth, fifth, and sixth floors should give the mall a long-awaited boost. ♦ W 34th St and Broadway. 244.2555 ⴺ

55 New York Hotel Pennsylvania $$ Originally designed in 1918 by **McKim, Mead & White,** this hotel was named for the nearby **Pennsylvania Station.** It is now the hotel closest to the **Jacob K. Javits Convention Center.** In the 1930s, it was a hot stop for the Big Bands: Glenn Miller immortalized its phone number with his "Pennsylvania 6-5000." All 1,700 rooms have recently been renovated; its **Globetrotter** restaurants serve breakfast only. ♦ 401 Seventh Ave (at W 33rd St). 736.5000, 800/223.8585; fax 502.8798

56 Schoepfer Studios Carrying on an 85-year-old family business started by his grandfather, taxidermist Jim Schoepfer stocks a zoo-full of animals, including zebras, armadillos, anteaters, birds, and fish. A sign on the door welcomes customers, not browsers; fortunately, there's a lot to see in the window display. ♦ M-F. 138 W 31st St (between Sixth and Seventh Aves). 736.6939

57 St. John the Baptist Church Designed in 1872 by **Napoleon LeBrun,** this Roman Catholic church is noted for its white marble interior. ♦ 210 W 31st St (between Seventh and Eighth Aves). 564.9070 ⴺ

58 Madison Square Garden Center
America's premier entertainment facility, designed by **Charles Luckman Associates** in 1968, hosts more than 600 events for nearly six million spectators each year. Within the center are the 20,000-seat **Arena,** the 5,600-seat **Paramount,** and the **Exposition Rotunda** with a 20-story office building. It is home to the **New York Knicks** and the **New York Rangers.** Throughout the year, the facility hosts exhibitions and trade shows; boxing; rodeos; dog, cat, and horse shows; circuses; graduations; rock concerts; tennis, track and field, and gymnastics events; and an occasional presidential convention.
♦ Seventh Ave (between W 31st and W 33rd Sts). 465.6741 ♿

Within Madison Square Garden Center:

Pennsylvania Station Make connections here for Long Island via the **Long Island Railroad** and for points north, south, and west via **Amtrak.** ♦ Bounded by W 31st and W 33rd Sts, and Seventh and Eighth Aves. Amtrak 800-USA-RAIL; Long Island Railroad 718/217.5477

59 1 Penn Plaza In 1972, **Charles Luckman Associates** designed this, the tallest of the complex of buildings that replaced the late, great **Pennsylvania Station.** ♦ 250 W 34th St (between Seventh and Eighth Aves). 239.7400 ♿

60 General Post Office The monumental stairway and columned entrance (shown at bottom) were designed by **McKim, Mead & White** in 1913. Look up for that famous inscription about rain, snow, and the gloom of night that made it the first attraction of visitors arriving by train. ♦ Daily 24 hours. Eighth Ave (between W 31st and W 33rd Sts). 967.8585

61 The Original Improvisation Although it was relocated here in 1992, this is the original, the place that marked the start on the road to stardom for talents like Richard Pryor, Robin Williams, Stiller & Meara, and Rodney Dangerfield. Light meals are served in casual surroundings. ♦ Cover, drink minimum. Shows: W-Sa. Reservations recommended. 433 W 34th St (between Ninth and 10th Aves). 582.7442 ♿

General Post Office

Michael Storrings

Theater District/ Garment Center

The Theater District and the Garment Center may well be considered the pulse of the city's economy; New Yorkers take their tourism and fashion industries very seriously. For those who love "street theater," no part of town is more entertaining than the Garment Center, which has more than a slight influence over what Atlanta, Kansas City, and Pittsburgh are wearing. Then there's **Broadway**, which has no equivalent in any other American—or foreign—city. This crucible of fashion design and theater fits in a relatively small area—**West 34th** to **West 59th Streets,** from **Sixth Avenue** (officially, **Avenue of the Americas**) to the **Hudson River.**

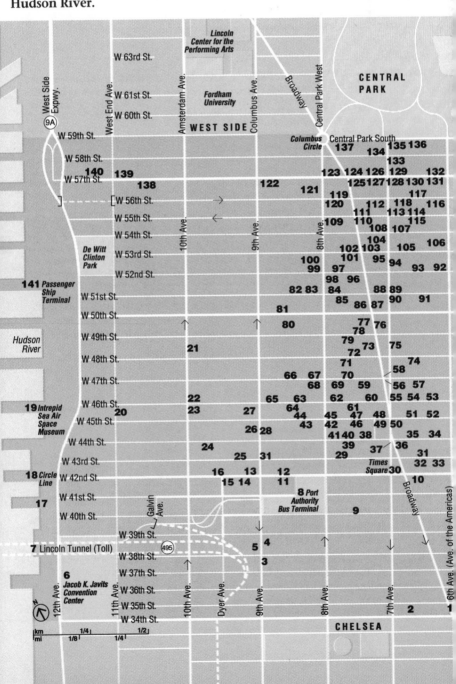

Before 1900, the garment trade was centered below East 14th Street on the Lower East Side, then home to the Eastern European Jewish community. By 1915, it had moved north along Broadway and Sixth Avenue as far as West 30th Street, replacing part of the rough-and-tumble **Tenderloin District**. The merchant princes who were establishing their fine department stores along Fifth Avenue were distressed to find garment workers mingling with their affluent customers and formed a committee to put a stop to it. The committee's solution was to order the construction of two garment workshop buildings, **Nos. 498** and **500 Seventh Avenue**, at **West 37th Street**, a comfortable distance away. Not long after the 1921 completion of the loft buildings, Seventh Avenue came to be synonymous with American fashion and New York city's "rag trade": street signs today read "Fashion Avenue." Specialists in various parts of the clothing business (apparel, accessories, jewelry, textiles, or trimming) tend to gather together; apparel showrooms, for example, are generally grouped along Seventh Avenue and Broadway, between **West 42nd** and **West 35th Streets**.

When the **Metropolitan Opera House** opened at **West 39th Street** and Broadway in 1883, the **Floradora Girls** were already packing them in at the **Casino Theater** across the street. In 1902, the first portion of **Macy's** was built at West 34th Street and Broadway where it replaced, among other buildings, **Koster & Bial's Music Hall**, where Thomas Edison first demonstrated moving pictures.

As the city's center moved uptown, the theaters followed suit. The theatrical quarter moved north across West 42nd Street in the early 1900s. Theater owners banded together in a syndicate to gain more control over the artists they booked. This gave them control over the competition that remained downtown as well, and those theatrical enterprises were effectively put out of business. The syndicate's power increased greatly in 1916, when the three **Shubert** brothers began to build new theaters in the **Times Square** area, which the subway had put within easy reach of the entire city. Other entrepreneurs joined the rush, and their legacy is still with us.

In 1876, an elevated railroad was built along **Ninth Avenue**, and thousands of immigrants, chiefly from Ireland, moved to the neighborhood from downtown. Work was plentiful in the sawmills, warehouses, stone yards, and stables along the Hudson River. Around this time, the area bordered approximately by West 30th to West 59th Streets and **Eighth** to **12th Avenues** evolved into one of America's toughest neighborhoods: **Hell's Kitchen**, named for the gang that ruled here, thriving on hoodlumism, extortion, and highway robbery. Well into the 20th century—long after gang wars in New York were officially declared over—merchants and property owners west of Eighth Avenue continued to pay "tribute" to the Hell's Kitchen Gang; they didn't have an alternative, until the gang finally disappeared. Today, although the occasional porn theater stands next to Broadway theaters and the streets are filled with the odd hustler or petty criminal, the area is a far cry from its raucous past and is chiefly inhabited by aspiring actors yearning to be near the stage.

Reformers tried to clean up the infamous Tenderloin (they called it **Satan's Circus**), which covered Fifth to Seventh Avenues from West 23rd Street to West 42nd. But the district remained the city's center of vice, as it had for nearly 50 years, until Prohibition closed its watering holes in 1920. Today, the neon-lit area surrounding Times Square (predominantly West 42nd between Seventh and Eighth Avenues and Eighth Avenue between 42nd and 44th Streets) still has its share of adult movie houses, peep shows, and other dens of iniquity, but it is undergoing radical change once again. Most recently, the Disney Company spearheaded a renewal of this area with a $40-million renovation of the 92-year-old **New Amsterdam Theater.** Other major entertainment companies that have committed to the cause include **Madame Tussaud,** London's high-tech **Wax Museum,** and American Multi-Cinemas, which had plans to create the city's largest multiplex theaters.

1 Herald Square During the 1880s and 1890s, this was the heart of the Tenderloin, an area of dance halls, bordellos, and cafes adjacent to Hell's Kitchen. New York City's theater and newspaper industries were once headquartered here. The square—which, like most of the squares in New York, is anything but—was named for the *New York Herald,* which occupied a Venetian palazzo, completed in 1921 by **McKim, Mead & White,** on the north end. Greeley Square, to the south at West 33rd Street, was named for the founder of the *New-York Tribune.* Note the **Crossland Savings Bank** by **York & Sawyer**—it has lots of columns inside and out. ♦ Bounded by Sixth Ave and Broadway, and W 34th and W 35th Sts

2 Macy's The Broadway building of this New York institution was built in 1901 by **DeLemos & Cordes;** the Seventh Avenue building was built in 1931 by **Robert D. Kohn.** Although it has always seemed to have more of everything than any other department store, it didn't have a compelling fashion image until 1974, when Ed Finkelstein, who had been president of the San Francisco store, took charge of the New York branch. Today, it is both trendy and fashionable. There is a haven for children on the fifth floor, with a vast selection of imported and domestic clothing and even a place to relax over an ice-cream soda. The ninth-floor **Corner Shop** includes a dazzling array of fine antiques. **The Cellar** turns shopping for the kitchen into a heady experience, and even includes fine food to go with the fine kitchenware (Gene Hovis creates down-home Southern specialties like buttermilk biscuits and buttermilk-fried chicken as well as a hearty lemon pound cake, macaroni and cheese, and apple pie). You can eat breakfast, lunch, and dinner, get a facial and a haircut, mail a letter, have your jewelry appraised, buy theater tickets, and convert foreign currency into dollars—without ever leaving the store. Perhaps above all else, the department store is known for its annual Thanksgiving Day Parade and its elaborate Christmas displays; try to catch both. ♦ Daily. Bounded by Broadway and Seventh Ave, and W 34th and W 35th Sts. 695.4400 ఉ

3 Hero Boy ★$ According to the Manganaro family, who established this enterprise as a satellite of their grocery store next door, the sandwich term "hero" (variously known in other parts of the country as "grinder," "po'boy," or "submarine") was coined at this stand. The Manganaros also claim to be the first to sell them by the foot. The hot meals—lasagna, baked ziti—are good too. ♦ Italian ♦ M-Sa breakfast, lunch, and dinner; Su lunch and dinner. 492 Ninth Ave (between W 37th and W 38th Sts). 947.7325 ఉ

4 Cupcake Cafe Loyal customers consider Ann and Michael Warren's cakes to be works of art. Not coincidentally, the Warrens and their team of assistants are all artists in other media—painting, sculpture, photography—who transfer those talents to a baked and frosted canvas. Even if you don't need a fanciful cake, stop by for a great muffin (especially corn), a doughnut, fruit pie, or cup of soup du jour. ♦ Daily. 522 Ninth Ave (at W 39th St). 465.1530

5 Guido's ★$$ In the rear of the **Supreme Macaroni Co.**—a store that leads you back to a time before the words "gourmet" or "nouvelle cuisine" were ever uttered—is a restaurant serving the best macaroni this side of Naples. The prices are moderate and the service straightforward. ♦ Italian ♦ M-Sa lunch and dinner. Reservations recommended. No credit cards accepted. 511 Ninth Ave (between W 38th and W 39th Sts). 564.8074 ఉ

6 Jacob K. Javits Convention Center This huge facility—made almost entirely of glass—covers 22 acres between West 34th and West Ninth Streets, making it the largest exposition hall under one roof in North America and one of the biggest buildings in the world. It has 900,000 square feet of exhibition space. The lobby, called the **Crystal Palace,** is 150 feet high. Designed by **I.M. Pei & Partners,** it was called "the center at the center of the world" when it opened in 1986, and events are already scheduled into the 21st century. Oddly enough, the building appears opaque during the day, while at night the interior lighting makes the structure glow. ♦ 655 W 34th St (between 11th and 12th Aves). 216.2000

7 Lincoln Tunnel The tunnel, which is 97 feet below the Hudson River, connects Manhattan with Weehawken, New Jersey, and more than 36 million vehicles use it every year. The 8,216-foot center tube was the first to be built. **Aymar Embury** was the architect; Ole Singstad completed the engineering in 1937. It was joined by the 7,482-foot north tube in 1945, and the 8,006-foot south tube in 1957, making it the only three-tube vehicular tunnel in the world. ♦ West 38th through W 41st Sts to Weehawken, NJ

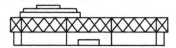

8 Port Authority Bus Terminal
Erected in 1950, the terminal was expanded in 1963 and again in 1982 by the **Port Authority Design Staff.** This is the largest and busiest bus terminal in the world, with three levels of platforms serving all of New York's long-distance bus lines and most of the commuter buses between New York and the New Jersey suburbs. A special section on the West 42nd Street side also serves all three metropolitan airports. For people who prefer driving into Manhattan but not through it, a rooftop parking garage connects directly by ramp to the Lincoln Tunnel. As in any major transportation hub, exercise caution inside the terminal, which sometimes affords temporary shelter to the homeless. Although the situation has greatly improved in recent years, be aware of your belongings at all times, and avoid isolated areas, particularly the restrooms. ♦ Daily 24 hours. Bounded by Eighth and Ninth Aves, and W 40th and W 42nd Sts. Bus info: 564.8484

9 B&J Fabrics, Inc.
This store has been at the heart of New York's Garment Center for more than 50 years. Its three floors contain 8,000 square feet of space dedicated to the finest European and American fashion fabrics, offered at discount rates. ♦ M-Sa. 263 W 40th St (between Seventh and Eighth Aves). 354.8150 ⅃

10 Hotalings News Agency
This is *the* stand in New York City for out-of-town and international newspapers and magazines. ♦ Daily. 142 W 42nd St (between Sixth Ave and Broadway). 840.1868 ⅃

11 Health Insurance Building
Better known as the original **McGraw-Hill Building,** this 35-story tower was commissioned when growth was expected in this area. Green and glorious, it still stands alone. Built in 1931 by **Hood, Godley & Fouilhoux,** it has the distinction of being the only New York building mentioned in *The International Style,* the 1932 book by **Hitchcock** and **Johnson** that codified modern architecture. In fact, this tower is not strictly glass and steel aesthetics but an individual composition with Art Deco detailing. Eminent architectural historian **Vincent Scully** called it "Proto-jukebox Modern." ♦ 330 W 42nd St (between Eighth and Ninth Aves)

D.W. Griffith's controversial landmark film, *The Birth of a Nation,* opened on 3 March 1915 at the Liberty Theater, at 234 West 42nd Street.

12 Church of the Holy Cross
Although this was built in 1870 by **Henry Englebert** as the parish church of a poor neighborhood, it has several windows and mosaics designed by Louis Comfort Tiffany. Father Francis P. Duffy, chaplain of the famous Fighting 69th Division in World War I, fought from the pulpit of this church to break up the gangs of Hell's Kitchen. He served here until his death in 1932. ♦ 329 W 42nd St (between Eighth and Ninth Aves). 246.4732 ⅃

13 West Bank Cafe ★$$
The tables at the upstairs dining room of this place are covered with butcher paper, which can be graced with an assortment of pasta dishes, such seafood specials as seared tuna steak with coriander pepper, various salads, and burgers. After dinner (or before), head downstairs to the cabaret and enjoy a musical comedy or a group of short plays. ♦ American ♦ Restaurant: M-F lunch and dinner, Sa-Su dinner; Cabaret: Tu-Sa 8PM, 10:30PM. Reservations recommended. 407 W 42nd St (at Ninth Ave). 695.6909

14 Chez Josephine ★★$$$
In 1986, the ebullient Jean Claude Baker launched this unique restaurant as a tribute to his late adoptive mother, cabaret legend Josephine Baker. Fittingly, the place has become a great hit with critics and the public alike. Featured are lobster bisque, goat-cheese ravioli, and roasted duckling with tart red cherries. Bluesy pianists and a French tap dancer add to the heady atmosphere. ♦ French ♦ M-Sa dinner. Reservations recommended. 414 W 42nd St (at Ninth Ave). 594.1925

15 Theater Row
Beginning with the former **West Side Airlines Terminal,** which now houses video recording studios and the **National Spanish Television Network,** this ambitious project, begun in 1976 by **Playwrights Horizons** (416 West 42nd Street) includes a dozen Off-Broadway theaters and a revitalized street scene that gives new life to the Lincoln Tunnel exit that cuts the block in half. Tickets for all theaters are available at Ticket Central located at **Playwrights Horizons.** ♦ Box Office: daily 1-8PM. 416 W

145

42nd St (between Ninth and 10th Aves). 279.4200

16 Manhattan Plaza These towers, built in 1977 by **David Todd & Associates,** provide subsidized housing for performing artists, whose rent in the 1,688 apartments is based on their income. Their presence pays dividends in the vitality they bring to the neighborhood. ◆ Bounded by Ninth and 10th Aves, and W 42nd and W 43rd Sts

Within Manhattan Plaza:

Good & Plenty to Go At this gourmet catering service and take-out joint (designed by Milton Glaser, Inc.), you'll find fresh breads, including sourdough onion rolls; soups; salads; hot and cold pastas; sandwiches; pizza; and such down-home favorites as bourbon-baked ham, jambalaya, crab cakes, and vegetarian chili. ◆ Daily. 410 W 43rd St (between Ninth and 10th Aves). 268.4385 ♿

Little Pie Company The aromas here are glorious and the all-natural pies are just like Mom used to make—if you were lucky. This small, bright shop offers a selection of 10 pies: Fresh fruit pies predominate in summer; sour cream–apple and pumpkin pies are highlights in fall. Pies come in regular and five-inch sizes, but at the very least, treat yourself to a slice of heaven right there at the counter. ◆ Daily. 424 W 43rd St (between Ninth and 10th Aves). 736.4780 ♿

17 World Yacht Cruises ★★$$$$ This five-yacht fleet cruises New York harbor year-round. All excursions include music, but dinner cruises also feature dancing and the romance of the port lights. Either way, the food (a four-course dinner usually featuring a salmon or beef entrée) is okay; the scenery, better. ◆ Continental ◆ Apr-Nov: M-Sa dinner, Su brunch and dinner; Dec-Mar: F-Sa dinner, Su brunch and dinner. Reservations required; jacket required for dinner. Pier 81 (W 41st St and 12th Ave). 630.8100

According to New York common law, it is acceptable to sit on a stoop and drink beer from the bottle, as long as it is in a brown paper bag. It is both illegal and a sign of low breeding to drink beer from an uncovered bottle.

Restaurants/Clubs: Red   Hotels: Blue
Shops/ ♥ Outdoors: Green   Sights/Culture: Black

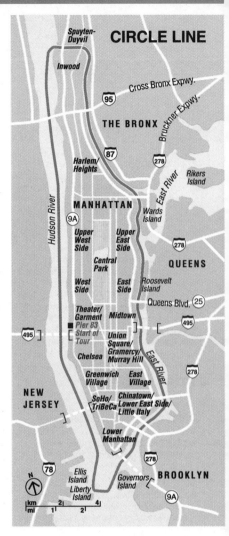

CIRCLE LINE

18 Circle Line There is simply no better way to orient yourself to Manhattan's wonders. This well-narrated tour heads down the Hudson River, past the *Statue of Liberty,* up the East River to the Harlem River, through Spuyten-Duyvil, and back down the Hudson. The eight vessels are converted World War II landing craft or Coast Guard cutters. When you get on board, try to sit on the port side (left as you face forward and head south). That way, all your views are of Manhattan. During the summer, there are 12 three-hour cruises a day starting at 9:30AM. ◆ Fee. Daily. Closed late December through March. Pier 83 (at W 42nd St and 12th Ave). 563.3200

19 Intrepid Sea Air Space Museum The veteran World War II and Vietnam War aircraft carrier *Intrepid* is now a technological and historical museum. Other than the Air and Space Museum in Washington, DC, no other institution gives such a thorough picture of the past, present, and future of warfare and technology in air, space, and sea. The tamer **Pioneers Hall** features mock-ups, antiques, and film clips of flying machines from the turn of the century through the 1930s. Insights into the future as well as contemporary exploration of the ocean and space are shown in **Technologies Hall,** along with the artifacts of 20th- and 21st-century warfare: jumbo jets, mammoth rockets, and complex weaponry. More aircraft can be inspected on the *Intrepid*'s 900-foot flight deck. The most recent acquisitions are the guided missile submarine *Growler* and the Vietnam-era destroyer *Edson*. Visitors can climb through the control bridges and command centers of the carrier, but spaces are cramped and there is often a wait. Dress warmly in winter months. ♦ Admission; under six and uniformed military free. Daily Memorial Day to Labor Day; W-Su Labor Day to Memorial Day. Pier 86 (at W 46th St and 12th Ave). 245.0072

20 Landmark Tavern ★★$$ An old waterfront tavern, this once rowdy place now offers modern-day diners a cleaner and more refined version of its 19th-century rooms, where food is still served from genuine antique sideboards. Don't miss the Irish soda bread, baked every hour. The fish-and-chips, shepherd's pie, prime rib, and hamburgers are good too. ♦ American ♦ Daily lunch and dinner. Reservations recommended. 626 11th Ave (between W 45th and W 46th Sts). 757.8595 ♿

21 Peruvian Restaurant ★$ Ignore the fluorescent lighting and Formica tables; instead concentrate on what is probably the best and most authentic Peruvian cuisine in New York: terrific baked fish with tomatoes and coriander, hearty stews, and delicious *papas asadas* (potatoes boiled in broth). The pleasant service is another plus. ♦ Peruvian ♦ Daily lunch and dinner. No credit cards accepted. 688 10th Ave (between W 48th and W 49th Sts). 581.5814

22 Mud, Sweat & Tears This is a cheerful, neat pottery studio for beginning and expert potters. The facilities include 10 Brent & Amaco electric wheels, spacious table areas, basic hand-building supplies, glazes, a kiln where firings are done frequently, and a small retail area where the potters sell their wares. ♦ M-F 11AM-8PM; Sa-Su noon-7PM. Call for information on classes. 654 10th Ave (at W 46th St). 974.9121

23 Mike's American Bar and Grill ★$ If you brave the unquestionably sleazy parade down this stretch of 10th Avenue, you'll find a cheerful, intentionally down-at-the-heels joint. Go for the grilled specials, though some faithfuls claim that Mike has the best enchiladas in Manhattan. ♦ American/Mexican ♦ M-F lunch and dinner; Sa-Su dinner. Reservations recommended. 650 10th Ave (between W 45th and W 46th Sts). 246.4115

24 The Actors Studio It was in this former Greek Orthodox church that Lee Strasberg trained such stars as Marlon Brando, Dustin Hoffman, Al Pacino, and Shelley Winters. Seats 125. ♦ 432 W 44th St (between Ninth and 10th Aves). 757.0870

24 The New Dramatists This company, which offers free readings, was founded in 1949 by a group of Broadway's most important writers and producers in an effort to encourage new playwrights; alumni include William Inge, John Guare, and Emily Mann. The nonprofit organization took occupancy of the building, formerly a Lutheran church, in 1968. ♦ 424 W 44th St (between Ninth and 10th Aves). 757.6960

25 Le Madeleine ★$$$ This casual bistro features salads, pastas, fish, and such light meat dishes as grilled chicken breast with a Pommery mustard sauce. There's also a separate skylit garden room that is always booked for brunch. ♦ French ♦ M-F lunch and dinner; Sa-Su brunch and dinner. Reservations recommended. 403 W 43rd St (between Ninth and 10th Aves). 246.2993

25 Westside Theater For more than 20 years the two theaters in this converted Episcopal church have presented award-winning productions such as *A Shayna Maidel* and *Extremities*. It seats 210 and 190. Call for performance schedule. ♦ 407 W 43rd St (between Ninth and 10th Aves). 315.2244

26 Rudy's Bar This is one of the area's few remaining neighborhood bars. Locals come for light snacks, conversation, and good drinks. ♦ Daily till 4AM. 627 Ninth Ave (between W 44th and W 45th Sts). 974.9169

26 Poseidon Greek Bakery The Fable family has been turning out paper-thin phyllo-dough pastries in this tiny shop for nearly 75 years. Try the rich, sweet baklava, spinach pies, and tempting cinnamon-and-sugar almond cookies. For those who want to make their own delicacies, the phyllo dough is for sale. ♦ Tu-Su. 629 Ninth Ave (between W 44th and W 45th Sts). 757.6173 ♿

Bali Burma

27 Bali Burma ★$ Rare are the restaurants that specialize in Balinese and Burmese cuisine. The prices are reasonable, but the food is hit-and-miss. Try the *soto ayam* (spicy chicken broth with bean sprouts, glass noodles, and chicken). ◆ Balinese/Burmese ◆ Daily lunch and dinner. 651 Ninth Ave (between W 45th and W 46th Sts). 265.9868

27 Bruno The King of Ravioli This retail shop sells a vast selection of fresh pastas and sauces, including ravioli, manicotti, cannelloni, lasagna, stuffed shells, and gnocchi, all made in a nearby factory since 1888. ◆ M-Sa. 653 Ninth Ave (between W 45th and W 46th Sts). 246.8456. Also at: 249 Eighth Avenue (between 22nd and 23rd Sts). 627.0767; 2204 Broadway (at W 78th St). 580.8150

Z E N   P A L A T E

27 Zen Palate ★★★$$ A vegetarian oasis, this place serves excellent cuisine in an upscale, minimalist setting. Try basil *moo shu* rolls (with nuts and vegetables), Zen Retreat (a squash shell stuffed with vegetables, beans, and tofu), or Dreamland (panfried spinach noodles with shiitake mushrooms and ginger). Alcoholic beverages are not served, but you can bring your own. ◆ Asian vegetarian ◆ M-Sa lunch and dinner; Su dinner. Reservations recommended. 663 Ninth Ave (at W 46th St). 582.1669 ♿. Also at: 34 Union Sq E (at E 16th St). 614.9345; 2170 Broadway (between W 76th and W 77th Sts). 501.7768 ♿

28 Film Center Building The pink and black marble in the lobby and the pattern of the orange and blue tiles on the walls helped attract some 75 motion picture distributors, who made this 1929 building by **Buchman & Kahn** their headquarters. The stores on this block rent out moviemaking equipment. ◆ 630 Ninth Ave (between W 44th and W 45th Sts). 757.6995

Jezebel

28 Jezebel ★★$$$ The nondescript exterior doesn't prepare you for the dramatic interior, which suggests nothing so much as a New Orleans bordello. Go for the smothered chicken, oxtail stew, garlic shrimp, broiled seafood platter (lobster tails, scallops, and shrimp), and shrimp creole. And don't forget the corn bread. Finish with pecan or sweet potato pie. The extensive wine list concentrates on French varieties. ◆ Soul food ◆ M-Sa dinner. Reservations required. 630 Ninth Ave (at W 45th St). 582.1045

New York City boasts 2,700 traffic signals.

29 The New York Times In 1913, less than 10 years after moving to Times Square, the *Times* had grown so much that this annex was built by **Ludlow & Peabody** around the corner on West 43rd Street. Its size was doubled in 1924. The building was expanded again in 1945, and the original tower was eventually abandoned. Most copies of the newspaper are printed in a New Jersey plant, although a substantial number come off the presses in the basement here, and the activity on Saturday evening on both the West 43rd and West 44th Street sides as delivery trucks head out with the Sunday edition, is intense. ◆ 229 W 43rd St (between Seventh and Eighth Aves). 556.1234

30 Times Square In April 1904, almost a year before the *New York Times* moved into what had been called Longacre Square, the mayor and the board of aldermen passed a resolution in April 1904, naming the area, bounded by West 42nd and West 47th Streets from Broadway to Seventh Avenue, after the newspaper. It quickly became known as "The Crossroads of the World," partly in deference to the *Times,* which certainly could claim that title. Today, it is the heart of the Theater District and the site of some of the most spectacular electric advertising signs ever created. The square is one of a series of open spaces created as Broadway crosses the straight north-south avenues, in this case Seventh Avenue. Standing at the base of the old Times tower and looking uptown, Broadway comes into the square on your left, and leaves it behind you on your right, having cut across Seventh Avenue at the intersection of West 43rd Street. ◆ Broadway and W 42rd St

30 1 Times Square When this building was under construction as headquarters for the *New York Times,* the *Times*'s arch rival, the *Herald,* grudgingly ran a story under the headline "Deepest Hole in New York a Broadway Spectacle" which said that the new *Times* tower was the most interesting engineering feat to be seen anywhere on Manhattan Island. Designed by **Eidlitz & MacKenzie,** it was completed in 1904. The newspaper's pressroom was in the tower's basement, but because the building was being built over the city's biggest subway station, the basement had to be blasted out of solid rock 55 feet down. The presses began printing the *Times* down there on 2 January 1905, after the new year had been welcomed with the dropping of a lighted ball down the flagpole on the roof. The celebration has been repeated every year since (more than 300,000 revelers rang in 1995 here, in the area from West 42nd to West 57th Street), although in 1966 the *Times* sold the building to Allied Chemical Co., which stripped it bare and refaced it with marble. It has since been sold a number of times and now houses offices. ◆ W 42nd St (between Broadway and Seventh Ave)

31 **The Town Hall** This 1921 landmark, the work of **McKim, Mead & White,** is an elegant building with excellent acoustics. Joan Sutherland made her New York debut here. Today, the hall is constantly in use for concerts and cultural events. ♦ 123 W 43rd St (between Sixth Ave and Broadway). 840.2824 &

32 **Century Cafe** ★★$$ The sophisticated dining room creates a very stylish setting for the theater crowd, including cast members of nearby shows. The menu features such outstanding dishes as seared yellowfin tuna with crushed coriander, grilled muscovy duck with roasted figs, and grilled salmon with Moroccan spices. The wine list is extensive. ♦ International ♦ M-Sa lunch and dinner. Reservations recommended. 132 W 43rd St (between Sixth Ave and Broadway). 398.1988 &

33 **National Debt Clock** In a frighteningly rapid-fire frenzy, this billboard records our national debt by the mega-second as we sink deeper into the red. In addition to displaying the ever-changing national share (whose increase, as of 1995, was $10,000 per second), it also shows the average family's share. The 1992 interest cost clocked in at $292 billion. Best not to look. ♦ Sixth Ave (between W 42nd and W 43rd Sts)

34 **Belasco** The eccentric David Belasco, whose preferred style of dress was a priest's frock, wrote and produced *Madame Butterfly* and *The Girl of the Golden West* here. Both were later adapted into operas by Giacomo Puccini. Belasco's ghost is said to continue to visit backstage. This theater, dating to 1907, was a creation of **George Keister.** ♦ 111 W 44th St (between Sixth and Seventh Aves). Telecharge 239.6200

34 **Cafe Un Deux Trois** ★$$ Crayons for doodling on the paper-covered tables provide a charming bit of bohemia for those who never venture downtown. The gimmick isn't really necessary, however, as the place delivers satisfaction with such simple but good food as scallops *provençale* and steak *frites* (with french fries). ♦ French ♦ Daily lunch and dinner. Reservations recommended. 123 W 44th St (between Sixth and Seventh Aves). 354.4148

Times Square

Michael Storrings

MILLENNIUM
BROADWAY · NEW YORK

35 Millennium Broadway $$$ This former **Hotel Macklowe** is a sleek and handsome executive-style hotel offering such business-minded amenities as two dual-line speaker phones in each of the 638 rooms, phone mail in four languages, and television access to Macktel, an interactive communication system that allows guests to preview restaurant menus, order sporting event and theater tickets, and even check out. In addition, there are a restaurant and bar, a sewing center for last-minute seam repair and button replacement, and a fitness center staffed with private trainers. At the 650-seat **Hudson Theatre,** a 1902 landmark next door, the hotel maintains a full-service auditorium and 35mm and 70mm screening facilities. ♦ 145 W 44th St (between Sixth Ave and Broadway). 768.4400, 800/934.9953; fax 789.7688 Ꮣ

36 The Manhattan Chili Company ★$ When you're in the mood for a good bowl of chili, go no farther. This place (a refugee from Greenwich Village) aims to please, offering all kinds of chili—including vegetarian and turkey—with a wide range of spiciness. ♦ Tex-Mex ♦ Daily lunch, dinner, and late-night meals. 1500 Broadway (entrance on W 43rd St). 730.8666

37 Paramount Building The bank on the corner of West 43rd Street replaced the entrance to the famous **Paramount Theater,** built in 1926 by **Rapp & Rapp.** The great glass globe on its pinnacle and the four-sided clock make the building an attraction, as does its lavish lobby. Before the theater closed in 1964, its stage had been graced by such stars as Mae West, Pola Negri, Tommy Dorsey, Bing Crosby, and, of course, Frank Sinatra. ♦ 1501 Broadway (between W 43rd and W 44th Sts)

38 Shubert It will be hard to imagine anything but *A Chorus Line* here (after 6,137 performances, the longest-running musical on

Broadway closed on 28 April 1990), but that's what they said about Katharine Hepburn in *The Philadelphia Story,* and Barbra Streisand in *I Can Get It for You Wholesale.* The theater itself was built in 1913 by **Henry B. Herts.** ♦ 225 W 44th St (between Broadway and Eighth Ave). Telecharge 239.6200 Ꮣ

38 Shubert Alley The stage doors of the **Shubert Theater** (on West 44th Street) and of the **Booth** (on West 45th) open onto this space. So does the entrance to the offices of the Shubert Organization, making this a favorite spot for Broadway hopefuls to casually stroll up and down hoping to be noticed by the right people. A gift shop, **One Shubert Alley** (M-Sa 9AM-11:30PM; Su noon-7PM), specializes in merchandise related to Broadway shows. ♦ Bounded by Seventh and Eighth Aves, and W 44th and W 45th Sts

39 Sardi's ★$$$ Practically synonymous with Theater District dining, this three-quarters-of-a-century mainstay went through a troubled couple of years before the return in 1990 of Vincent Sardi Jr, son of the founder. He brought back some old hands, and in 1994 added a new one, French chef Patrick Pinon, who spiced up the moribund menu with dishes that include a good roasted free-range chicken with garlic. Sentimental favorites, however, such as cannelloni, were retained. Once in a while, you can still spot a celebrity; otherwise, stargazers can content themselves with identifying famous customers who are immortalized in the numerous caricatures gracing the walls. ♦ Continental ♦ M-Sa lunch, dinner, and late-night meals. Reservations recommended; jacket required. 234 W 44th St (between Broadway and Eighth Ave). 221.8440

39 Helen Hayes This theater was constructed in 1912 by **Ingalls & Hoffman.** In 1965, when it was known as the **Little Theatre,** it became home to the "Merv Griffin" and "David Frost" shows. It reopened as a Broadway theater in 1974. In 1983, it was dedicated to the "First Lady" of the theater. ♦ 240 W 44th St (between Broadway and Eighth Ave). 944.9450; Ticketmaster 307.4100 Ꮣ

39 St. James At this 1927 work of **Warren & Wetmore,** Rodgers and Hammerstein's *Oklahoma!* was followed by *Where's Charley?* with Ray Bolger, which in turn was followed by, among others, *The King and I, The Pajama Game,* and *Tommy.* ♦ 246 W 44th St (between Broadway and Eighth Ave). Telecharge 239.6200 ⑂

40 Broadhurst It was here, in this 1918 work of **Herbert J. Krapp,** that Humphrey Bogart picked up his credentials as a tough guy when he appeared with Leslie Howard in *The Petrified Forest.* ♦ 235 W 44th St (between Broadway and Eighth Ave). Telecharge 239.6200

41 Majestic *The Music Man, Carousel, A Little Night Music,* and *The Wiz* helped this theater, built in 1927 by **Herbert J. Krapp,** live up to its name. *The Phantom of the Opera,* which has been playing since 26 January 1988, is carrying on the tradition. ♦ 247 W 44th St (between Broadway and Eighth Ave). Telecharge 239.6200 ⑂

42 Milford Plaza $$ Built in 1928 by **Schwartz & Gross,** this 1,300-room hotel was originally known as the **Lincoln.** It was built and first operated by the United Cigar Stores Co., which said it catered to the better element of the masses. Today, it is a Ramada property advertising itself as the "Lulla-buy of Broadway." ♦ 700 Eighth Ave (between W 44th and W 45th Sts). 869.3600, 800/221.2690; fax 944.8357

43 Martin Beck The famed Theatre Guild Studio used this 1924 house, a work of **G. Albert Lansburgh,** in the 1930s. Great performances echo from the stage, including those of the Lunts in Robert Sherwood's *Reunion in Vienna,* Katharine Cornell in *The Barretts of Wimpole Street,* and Ruth Gordon in *Hotel Universe.* In the 1950s, Arthur Miller's *The Crucible* and Tennessee Williams's *Sweet Bird of Youth* played here. In 1965, Peter Brook's incendiary production of *Marat/Sade* gave audiences a new look at documentary theater. Liz Taylor came out of Hollywood to make her Broadway debut in Lillian Hellman's *The Little Foxes.* ♦ 302 W 45th St (between Eighth and Ninth Aves). Telecharge 239.6200 ⑂

44 Triton Gallery You'll find theater posters and show cards for current and past performaces on Broadway and elsewhere in this shop that provides custom framing and mail order, too. Ask for a catalog. ♦ M-Sa. 323 W 45th St (between Eighth and Ninth Aves). 765.2472 ⑂

45 Frankie and Johnnie's ★$$$ A former speakeasy and onetime celebrity hangout for the likes of Al Jolson and Babe Ruth, this joint is still popular—some would say too much so, as it tends to get hectic and noisy. But the crowds get more than nostalgia for their money—this old Broadway chophouse can still turn out a good steak. ♦ Steak house ♦ M-Sa dinner. Reservations required. 269 W 45th St (between Broadway and Eighth Ave). 997.9494

45 Sam's ★$ A popular hangout for theater people, this place has exposed-brick walls and very reasonable prix-fixe dinners featuring ribs, shell steak, and grilled Cajun chicken. Although stars sup here occasionally, its most devoted fans are the "gypsies," members of the chorus lines. Several times a week, the staff treat late-night diners to a Broadway melody. ♦ American ♦ M-Sa lunch, dinner, and late-night meals; Su lunch and dinner. Reservations recommended. 263 W 45th St (between Broadway and Eighth Ave). 719.5416

46 Golden One of the longest-running shows in history, *Tobacco Road* (1933), played this 1927 house, another work of **Herbert J. Krapp.** *A Party with Comden and Green, At the Drop of a Hat, Beyond the Fringe,* and Victor Borge kept audiences laughing here. ♦ 252 W 45th St (between Broadway and Eighth Ave). Telecharge 239.6200 ⑂

46 Royale Actress Mae West kept house here for three years as the title character in *Diamond Lil'.* The theater was used as a radio studio by CBS from 1936 to 1940. Laurence Olivier dazzled audiences with his appearances in *The Entertainer* and *Becket. Grease,* Broadway's longest-running musical at the time, settled here during its last years. Currently playing is *An Inspector Calls.* ♦ 242 W 45th St (between Broadway and Eighth Ave). Telecharge 239.6200 ⑂

46 Plymouth *Abe Lincoln in Illinois,* with Raymond Massey, opened not long after John and Lionel Barrymore appeared here together in *The Jest.* The theater was built in 1917 by **Herbert J. Krapp.** ♦ 236 W 45th St (between Broadway and Eighth Ave). Telecharge 239.6200 ⑂

46 Booth Although this 1913 theater, created by **Henry B. Herts,** was named for Edwin Booth, Shirley Booth also made a name for herself here with Sidney Blackmer in *Come Back, Little Sheba.* ♦ 222 W 45th St (between Broadway and Eighth Ave). Telecharge 239.6200 ⑂

47 Imperial *Rosemarie* and *Oh, Kay!* set the tone for this theater, which was built by **Herbert J. Krapp** in 1923. Hit musicals have always found a home here: *Babes in Toyland, Jubilee, Leave It to Me, Annie Get Your Gun,* and the incomparable Zero Mostel performing "If I Were a Rich Man" in *Fiddler on the Roof. Les Misérables,* based on Victor Hugo's novel set in 19th-century France, is currently in its seventh year. ♦ 249 W 45th St (between Broadway and Eighth Ave). Telecharge 239.6200 ⑂

In the 1820s, a stagecoach ride from the Battery to Greenwich Village took one hour. By 1830, horse-drawn trolleys had reached 15th Street.

All the Town's a Stage: The New York Theater Scene

Center Stage: Broadway

The name "Broadway" has become synonymous with theater in America, but Broadway has many other meanings. Geographically, it is the street that runs the entire length of Manhattan. Theatrically, it is the area around **Times Square,** where most of the commercial theaters are located. Legally, it is the place where only members of theatrical trade unions can work. But most important, Broadway symbolizes the whole complex of qualities associated with the glittering world of the theater: stars, polished performances, sophisticated plays, and the all-American musical.

Known as "The Great White Way," Broadway has been the heart of American theater for over 100 years. The reasons are obvious: The audience is here. The production money is here. The best actors, directors, playwrights, designers, choreographers, and critics work here. To be accepted by Broadway is the ultimate recognition of one's talent.

Drama: New Yorkers experienced their first real season in 1753, when the **Hallam Company** of London visited. A favorite theme of dramas of that period was the triumph of native honesty and worth over foreign affectation, as seen in plays such as Royall Tyler's *The Contrast* (1787). By the 1830s, Washington Irving and Walt Whitman, in their roles as theater critics, advised that the stage offer more than just escape.

From 1850 to 1900, commercial houses featured melodramas, spectacle plays, comic operas, vaudeville, and burlesques. The most popular play of the period was *Uncle Tom's Cabin.* It was during these years that the star system was born, with Joseph Jefferson in the title role in *Rip Van Winkle,* Edwin Booth in *Hamlet,* and James O'Neill (father of Eugene) in *The Count of Monte Cristo.* John Drew, Maude Adams, Richard Mansfield, and the Barrymores made their names in various roles.

Around the time of World War I, producer Arthur Hopkins transformed Broadway by revitalizing the classics and by presenting the first modern war play, *What Price Glory?* Hopkins introduced Katharine Hepburn, Barbara Stanwyck, and Clark Gable to the stage.

Homegrown drama received a welcome stimulus with the emergence of a group of New York City playwrights who were interested in social satire, dramatic realism, and psychological expressionism. Eugene O'Neill, preoccupied with man's struggles with his own psyche and with the universe, expressed himself in such plays as *Beyond the Horizon, Anna Christie,* and *Strange Interlude.* Later writers, influenced by O'Neill, went on to create a powerful stage legacy of their own: Elmer Rice, Clifford Odets, Arthur Miller, and Tennessee Williams.

In the early 1920s, an extraordinarily successful organization, **The Theatre Guild,** brought to Broadway the works of new European dramatists, including Tolstoy, Ibsen, Strindberg, and Shaw. Many of America's best-known actors appeared in their productions: Lynn Fontanne and Alfred Lunt, Edward G. Robinson, Helen Hayes, and Ruth Gordon. Around this time, Brooks Atkinson became drama critic for *The New York Times,* and artist Al Hirschfeld began to capture the essence of the theater world with his caricatures, which still appear today.

In the 1930s and 1940s, **The Group Theater,** founded by Harold Clurman, explored and translated the theater of Stanislavski, while Lee Strasberg redefined his acting method and created **The Actors Studio** (see page 147 for graduates). The **Mercury Theater,** founded by Orson Welles and John Houseman, presented provocative works such as Marc Blitzstein's *The Cradle Will Rock.* Dramas on Broadway at the time were *Abe Lincoln in Illinois* by Robert E. Sherwood, *The Little Foxes* by Lillian Hellman, and *Our Town* by Thornton Wilder. Katharine Cornell became one of the most popular actresses in the American theater. In 1947, Elia Kazan directed two plays that exemplified American realism: *A Streetcar Named Desire* by Tennessee Williams and *Death of a Salesman* by Arthur Miller.

In the 1960s, Edward Albee's *Who's Afraid of Virginia Woolf?* deeply impressed audiences, and Eugene Ionesco's *Rhinoceros* illustrated the theater of the absurd, which dramatized an illogical and incongruous world. Political assassinations, the Vietnam War, and social problems of the 1960s and 1970s were reflected in plays such as *Hair, The Great White Hope, Streamers,* and *That Championship Season.* Many of these started Off Broadway (a trend that continues today). Many Broadway hits, such as *Fences* by August Wilson, also come from regional theaters. English productions are still popular today; the works of writers Peter Shaffer, Tom Stoppard, David Hare, Michael Frayn, and director Peter Hall are among the favorite British imports.

Comedy: Stage comedy as we know it began in the mid-1800s with the debut of the satirical play *A Glance at New York.* In 1926, *Abie's Irish Rose,* a romantic comedy, closed after a record-setting four-year run. Fine examples of literary comedy in the 1930s and 1940s included Marc Connelly's *The Green Pastures* and Philip Barry's *The Philadelphia Story.* George S. Kaufman, a master of the wisecrack, wrote (alone and with Moss Hart) a series of zany comedies such as *You Can't Take It with You* and *The Man Who Came to Dinner.* England's Noel Coward produced a string of frothy hits for the Broadway stage. The present-day king of comedy is Neil Simon, whose gift is to create hilarious situations with urbane one-liners. Harvey Fierstein, David Mamet, and John Guare have also brought often-blistering comedies to Broadway in recent years.

Musical Comedy: The American musical has traveled a long way since *The Black Crook* was presented at **Niblo's Garden** in 1866. The opening performance lasted five and a half hours, and the 100 undraped females and sexy songs proved irresistible to audiences.

Another genre of musical theater was the minstrel show, a revue with performers in blackface (later replaced by vaudeville). The first play to be called a "musical comedy" was *Evangeline* in 1874. During that time, European operettas by Offenbach, Strauss, and Gilbert and Sullivan dominated the scene. *H.M.S. Pinafore* was such wholesome entertainment that it finally brought women and children into the audience. The first great composer of operettas for the American stage was Victor Herbert; the last was Sigmund Romberg. Harrigan and Hart wrote hilarious farces about immigrant groups. Charles Hoyt's *A Trip to Chinatown* featured two hit songs, "After the Ball" and "The Bowery." George Lederer introduced the "revue" in 1894 with his *Passing Show,* which created opportunities for comedians like Weber and Fields and stars like Lillian Russell and Anna Held. Florenz Ziegfeld's *Follies* and Irving Berlin's *Music Box Revues* were the rage.

Meanwhile, George M. Cohan romanticized the American identity in shows like *Little Johnny Jones.* In the 1920s, Rodgers and Hart, George and Ira Gershwin, Cole Porter, and Oscar Hammerstein II wrote some of the most beautiful songs for the musical comedy stage. It was in Jerome Kern's *Showboat,* however, that music and lyrics were first combined with the sophisticated adult libretto. All these musicians and lyricists worked in Tin Pan Alley, where sheet music was turned out by the pound. Political satire was introduced by the Gershwins in *Of Thee I Sing* and *Strike Up the Band.* In 1935, the folk opera *Porgy and Bess,* also by the Gershwins, brought musical theater to a new plateau.

The collaboration of Rodgers and Hammerstein started with the artistic triumph of *Oklahoma!* in the 1940s. This musical was brilliantly choreographed by Agnes de Mille. *Carousel, South Pacific, The King and I,* and *The Sound of Music* also gave new meaning to the musical play. This tradition continued in the 1950s and 1960s with classics such as *Guys and Dolls* by Loesser, *My Fair Lady* by Lerner and Lowe, *West Side Story* by Bernstein and Sondheim, and *Fiddler on the Roof* by Boch and Harnick.

Musicals have dominated the Broadway stage over the last three decades. *Camelot, Funny Girl,* and *Hello, Dolly!* opened a period of romanticism. In 1967, *Hair* represented the radical psychedelic movement of the Vietnam War years. In the mid-1970s, *A Chorus Line,* directed by Michael Bennett, dazzled audiences with the energy of its dance. Almost every major director of musicals in the last 15 years has been a choreographer. An exception is producer/director Harold Prince. In recent years, his productions of *Cabaret, Sweeney Todd,* and *Evita* brought a fresh political and social viewpoint to musical theater. On the nostalgic side, *Ain't Misbehavin', 42nd Street,* and *Anything Goes* provided grand entertainment. The English musical

was the trend of the 1980s: Cameron Macintosh's *Les Misérables* and fellow Brit Andrew Lloyd Webber's *Cats* and *The Phantom of the Opera* took the city by storm; Lloyd Webber's 1990 *Aspects of Love* was not as great a success, though the much-hyped opening of his 1994 opus *Sunset Boulevard* returned him to the limelight. Macintosh's *Miss Saigon* has held its own for years, while the 1990s' trend of musical revivals successfully continues with *Damned Yankees* and *Showboat.*

Stage Left: Off Broadway and Off Off Broadway

As the whetstone for theatrical talent, the reservoir for Broadway, and the mechanism for probing the desires of an ever-changing audience, Off Broadway and Off Off Broadway have thrived in New York since the 1950s. There are currently more than 200 small theaters scattered throughout the city.

The **Provincetown Playhouse** and the **Washington Square Players** set the tone of the little-theater movement in the 1920s. Decades later, the **Circle in the Square** was the leader of the alternative dramatic scene in Greenwich Village. Geraldine Page appeared there in Tennessee Williams's *Summer and Smoke,* and Jason Robards starred in Eugene O'Neill's *The Iceman Cometh.* The Circle also helped George C. Scott, Dustin Hoffman, Cicely Tyson, and James Earl Jones establish their reputations.

The late Joseph Papp, head of the **New York Shakespeare Festival** at the **Public Theater,** was the most dynamic theater impresario in America in recent years. With his multistage Public Theater on **Astor Place,** the outdoor Shakespeare Festival at the **Delacorte Theater** in **Central Park,** and productions at **Lincoln Center's Beaumont Theater,** he nurtured artists such as writers Sam Shepard, David Rabe, and Israel Horovitz, and actors Meryl Streep and the late Raul Julia. Papp's productions that went on to Broadway include *A Chorus Line, Plenty,* and *The Mystery of Edwin Drood.*

As part of the revitalization of **West 42nd Street, Theater Row** was established several years ago between **Ninth** and **10th Avenues.** Thanks to the vision of Fred Papert, this once run-down part of the Times Square area has been transformed into an attractive addition to Off Broadway. Tenants include the **Harold Clurman Theater,** the **South Street Theater,** and **Playwrights Horizons.**

In addition, the Disney Company has entered into the redevelopment of the Times Square area with the announcement of a $40-million renovation of the **New Amsterdam Theater.**

As Off-Broadway productions moved uptown, some artists felt the need to explore subjects forbidden by the traditions of Broadway and Off Broadway, such as politics, profanity, nudity, and sexuality— creating a marvelous spirit of experimentation. The **Living Theater,** founded by Judith Malina and Julian Beck, was the most controversial of the politically oriented groups. Troupes such as **Mabou Mines, The Wooster Group,** and the **Ridiculous Theatrical Company** are alive and well today.

153

47 Music Box Composer Irving Berlin built this charming theater to accommodate his *Music Box Revue of 1921*. Also presented here were the first musical to win a Pulitzer Prize, George Gershwin's *Of Thee I Sing;* John Steinbeck's *Of Mice and Men;* Kurt Weill's last musical, *Lost in the Stars;* and Kim Stanley in *Bus Stop.* ♦ 239 W 45th St (between Broadway and Eighth Ave). Telecharge 239.6200 &

48 Marriott Marquis $$$ This hotel boasts the world's tallest atrium, through which its glass-enclosed elevators zip up and down, serving 47 floors and almost 2,000 rooms! It has a Broadway theater on the third floor, New York's largest ballroom, and its highest lobby (reached by a chain of escalators passing through floor after quiet floor of meeting rooms). The two on-site gyms have Nautilus, sauna, Jacuzzi, and a trainer, if you need a push. Valet parking, concierge, and several restaurants and lounges are also available in this 1985 creation of **John Portman.** ♦ 1535 Broadway (at W 45th St). 398.1900, 800/228.9290; fax 704.8930 &

Within the Marriott Marquis:

Marquis New York's youngest Broadway theater is operated by the famed Nederlanders. Many expected it to suffer from its somewhat untheatrical surroundings—and the bad press caused by the demolition of several old theaters to make way for it. The ill will seems to have been forgotten, however, during the almost four-year run of the theater's first production, *Me and My Girl.* ♦ 307.4100

The View ★$$$$ Except for one at the old World's Fair site in Queens, this is New York's only revolving restaurant. It has a limited view, as do the revolving lounges above it, but when the turntable takes you past **Rockefeller Center** and the skyline to the east and uptown, you'll be glad you took a ride in that glass elevator. ♦ Continental ♦ Tu-Sa dinner; Su lunch and dinner. Reservations required. No sneakers or jeans. 704.8900

49 Minskoff In 1973, Debbie Reynolds opened this house with a revival of *Irene.* Capacious and modern, it houses the bigger and more technically extravagant productions such as the current *Sunset Boulevard* by Andrew Lloyd Weber that opened in November 1994. ♦ 200 W 45th St (at Broadway). 869.0550; Ticketmaster 307.4100 &

50 Roundabout Theatre This theater was built in 1928 by **Thompson, Holmes & Converse.** Under the leadership of producing director Todd Haimes, the Roundabout has won recognition as one of the city's finest theatrical organizations. It remains committed to producing classics by the world's greatest playwrights at affordable prices—Ibsen's *Ghosts,* Pirandello's *Enrico 4,* Carson

McCullers's *Member of the Wedding.* ♦ 1530 Broadway (at W 45th St). 869.8400 &

50 Xanadu Look no farther for New York–inspired kitsch. The store's young Afghani owner is a passionate fan of New York, and it shows in his 2,000-item inventory, which includes everything from King Kong pens to the **Statue of Liberty** in six sizes and three colors. **Yankees** jackets, subway-token keychains? It's all here and more. ♦ M-Th 9AM-11PM; F-Sa 9AM-midnight; Su 10AM-11PM. 1528 Broadway (at W 45th St). 768.2202 &

51 Lyceum Producer Daniel Frohman built this theater in 1903. Now a city landmark, it is the oldest New York house still used for legitimate productions. It opened with *The Proud Prince.* In 1947, Judy Holliday and Paul Douglas wise-cracked through *Born Yesterday.* The **A.P.A.-Phoenix Repertory** made this home base for several seasons, and in 1980, *Morning's at Seven* by Paul Osborn was revived here. A lyric, Neo-Baroque structure with banded columns and undulating marquee, it was the first theater designed by **Herts & Tallant,** undisputed kings of theater architecture. Frohman was such a theater fan that he had his apartment above the theater fitted with a trapdoor through which he could see the stage. ♦ 149 W 45th St (between Sixth and Seventh Aves). Telecharge 239.6200 &

51 Hamburger Harry's ★$ In addition to the 16 varieties of major-league burgers served at this casual grill, the mesquite-grilled seafood and steaks lure connoisseurs of the rare and well done. A Mexican accent adds color to the menu—the Ha-Ha Burger comes freighted with chilies, guacamole, *salsa verde,* and cheddar cheese. ♦ American ♦ Daily lunch and dinner. 145 W 45th St (between Sixth and Seventh Aves). 840.2756. Also at: 157 Chambers St (between Hudson and Greenwich Sts). 267.4446

52 Cabana Carioca ★★$$ Count on seriously large servings of Brazilian food including suckling pig, steak dishes, and *feijoada,* a traditional Brazilian Sunday afternoon dish of black beans and pork, served here every day. If you really want to get into the spirit, try a potent *caipirinha* (a drink made from a sugarcane-derived spirit, crushed lemon, ice, and sugar). ♦ Brazilian ♦ Daily lunch and dinner. 123 W 45th St (between Sixth and Seventh Aves). 581.8088

52 47th Street Photo Old New York reigns supreme at this outpost of the famous West 47th Street branch. You'll find the same frenzied atmosphere and an equally frenzied, impatient (though knowledgeable) staff, so come knowing what you want and don't expect to bargain. Both stores stock the same merchandise. ♦ M-Th, Su. 115 W 45th St (between Sixth and Seventh Aves). 921.1287. Also at: 67 W. 47th St (between Fifth and Sixth Aves). 921.1287 &

53 American Place This theater was founded with the intention of providing a forum for living American playwrights. It opened originally at **St. Clement's Church** in 1964 with two memorable plays: Robert Lowell's *Old Glory* and William Alfred's *Hogan's Goat*. In 1971, a brand new theater with a modified thrust stage was built, adding another dimension to the quality productions. ♦ 111 W 46th St (between Sixth and Seventh Aves). 840.3074 &

54 Actor's Equity Building This is the union for all stage actors in America—from the virtually unknown to the most famous. It was founded in 1913 by 112 actors to protect the rights and establish good working conditions for professional stage performers and stage managers. If you're into stargazing, keep your eyes peeled. ♦ 165 W 46th St (between Sixth and Seventh Aves)

55 I. Miller Building Almost hidden behind advertising signs, on the facade of the building, are sculptures of great women of the theater: Marilyn Miller, Rosa Ponselle, Ethel Barrymore, and Mary Pickford, none of whom would have thought of appearing on stage in anything but I. Miller shoes. The figures are by A. Stirling Calder, whose son, Alexander Calder, invented the mobile. The shoe store is gone, but the ladies are still here, at least for now. ♦ W 46th St (at Seventh Ave)

56 Duffy Square World War I chaplain of the Fighting 69th, Father Francis P. Duffy served as pastor of nearby **Holy Cross Church** and is honored in this triangle with a 1937 sculpture by Charles Keck at West 46th Street. He shares the honor with a 1959 statue, by George Lober, of *George M. Cohan,* the actor/producer/writer who wrote "Give My Regards to Broadway," among hundreds of other songs. ♦ Bounded by Seventh Ave and Broadway, and W 46th and W 47th Sts

56 TKTS The Theater Development Fund, housed in this 1973 work of **Mayers & Schiff,** sells tickets to Broadway and Off-Broadway shows and **Lincoln Center** productions; tickets are sold at half-price (plus a service charge) for performances on the day of sale. Tickets are not available for every show, but a board tells you what is on sale. A better selection is sometimes available close to curtain time, when producers release unused house seats, and during bad weather, when fewer people venture out. Also try Monday and Tuesday evenings, when most theaters alternate closing. ♦ Tickets go on sale 10AM for matinees, 3PM for evening performances. No credit cards or personal checks accepted. W 47th St (between Seventh Ave and Broadway). 768.1818 &. Also at: 2 World Trade Center (between Liberty and Vesey Sts). Same phone number &

56 Palace Theater "Playing the Palace" was the dream of every vaudeville performer from the theater's 1913 opening well into the 1930s. The advent of movies brought hard times, but the theater was renovated and reopened as a showcase for big musicals in 1966. *Sweet Charity, Applause, La Cage aux Folles,* and *The Will Rogers Follies* were among its long-running hits; its newest arrival, Disney's *Beauty and the Beast,* is the most extravagant and expensive musical production to ever be mounted on Broadway. ♦ 1564 Broadway (between W 46th and W 47th Sts). 730.8200; Ticketmaster 307.4100 &

56 Doubletree Guest Suites $$$ This modern 460-suite hotel is within easy walking distance of **Rockefeller Center,** Fifth Avenue shopping, **Lincoln Center,** and Broadway theaters. ♦ 1568 Broadway (between W 46th and W 47th Sts). 719.1600, 800/362.2779; fax 921.5212 &

57 Portland Square Hotel $ This was once home to James Cagney, Lila Lee, and John Boles. Today, the renovated budget-priced hotel features 136 attractive rooms. ♦ 132 W 47th St (between Sixth and Seventh Aves). 382.0600, 800/388.8988; fax 382.0684 &

58 Renaissance New York $$$ Opened in 1992, this post-modern structure by **Steven Jacobs** features 305 rooms, including 10 one-bedroom suites, in the heart of Times Square. Guests are offered richly furnished accommodations that include such amenities as three telephones in each room, call waiting, fax ports, voice mail, and VCR. There's also the added benefit of a 24-hour concierge service which will secure theater tickets in no time. The top three **Club Floors** offer additional personal services. ♦ 714 Seventh Ave (between W 47th and W 48th Sts). 765.7676, 800/228.9898; fax 765.1962 &

Macy's, which claims to be "The World's Largest Store," boasts over two million square feet of floor space.

Seventy-five percent of New York City's restaurants change hands or close before they are five years old.

Restaurants/Clubs: Red   **Hotels:** Blue

Shops/ Outdoors: Green   **Sights/Culture:** Black

Within the Renaissance New York:

![Windows on Broadway RESTAURANT · BAR logo]

Windows on Broadway ★★$$$
This sleek, Art Deco–inspired bistro affords panoramic views of the bustling city below in an intimate setting. Chef Ben Cottrel captures Southern Italian flavors in a range of dishes including parfait of artichoke, crab and grilled vegetables; pepper-crusted filet mignon with gorgonzola and wine sauce; and veal saltimbocca with sage and prosciutto. Leave room for the tiramisù. The vintage wine list is not only good but affordable. ♦ Italian ♦ Daily for breakfast, lunch, and dinner. 261.5200

59 The Edison Hotel $ Except for certain aspects of the lobby, a recent renovation has left few vestiges of this 1931 hotel's Art Deco heritage intact. The 1,000 rooms are nice but sometimes nondescript in their contemporary decor. The hotel is popular with large groups, but rooms are often available, and it's well located for those who want to stay in the very heart of the Theater District. Don't miss breakfast in the well-known coffee shop, a longtime hangout for theater people. ♦ 228 W 47th St (between Broadway and Eighth Aves). 840.5000, 800/637.7070; fax 596.6850 &

60 Lunt-Fontanne Both Mary Martin and Theodore Bikel appeared here in *The Sound of Music,* and Marlene Dietrich performed here alone not long afterward. The theater, a work of **Carrère & Hastings**, dates to 1910. ♦ 205 W 46th St (between Broadway and Eighth Ave). 575.9200; Ticketmaster 307.4100 &

61 Richard Rodgers This is where Gwen Verdon appeared in *Damn Yankees, Redhead,* and *New Girl in Town.* It is also where Olsen & Johnson began the long-running *Hellzapoppin'.* Formerly the **46th Street Theater,** built in 1925 by **Herbert J. Krapp,** it was dedicated to Richard Rodgers in March 1990. ♦ 226 W 46th St (between Broadway and Eighth Ave). 221.1211; Ticketmaster 307.4100 &

62 Paramount Hotel $$$ This venture from hotelier Ian Schraeger and French designer Philippe Starck is more affordably priced than its sister, the **Royalton.** The 610-room hotel, in a building erected in 1928 by **Thomas V. Lamb,** is reminiscent of the set for a movie, with a large gray staircase that looks as though it could lead up to a spaceship but goes only as far as the mezzanine, where food is served. Elevators are illuminated in

different colors: purple and orange, for example; and the bathrooms in the smallish rooms (the less expensive rooms can be downright tiny) contain some futuristic Starck designs like silver cone-shaped sinks and lamps that resemble stethoscopes. Amenities include fitness and business centers; VCRs and fresh flowers in every room; and a **Dean & DeLuca** gourmet shop. Even if you prefer to put down your suitcases in a more conservative setting, stop in for a peek or rest with a drink at the popular **Whiskey** bar. ♦ 235 W 46th St (between Broadway and Eighth Ave). 764.5500, 800/224.7474; fax 354.5237

Within the Paramount Hotel:

The Mezzanine ★★$$$ Though you'll be able to watch the comings and goings of people down in the lobby from this perch, the food will make a bid for your attention too. The varied menu ranges from light grilled-chicken and wild-mushroom salad to the more substantial mustard-glazed salmon fillet and roast loin of lamb in a red-wine sauce. It's also a good place to come for dessert—the banana splits and ice-cream sodas are great. ♦ American ♦ Daily breakfast lunch, and dinner. 764.5500

Since 1906

63 Barbetta ★★$$$ This romantic old-timer boasts a beautiful garden and wonderful truffles, sniffed out by dogs in Tuscany. The menu changes seasonally but may include such dishes as *farfalle ai pisellini* (butterfly pasta with young peas), roast rack of lamb with braising greens, and *bistecca alla fiorentina* (Florentine-style steak). Desserts are tempting: baked fresh fruits and bittersweet chocolate mousse are tops. ♦ Northern Italian ♦ M-Sa lunch and dinner. Reservations recommended. 321 W 46th St (between Eighth and Ninth Aves). 246.9171

64 Orso ★$$$ It's easy to relax at this Norther Italian bistro serving pasta, seafood, veal, and wonderful pizzas—try the pie topped with roasted peppers, sun-dried vegetables, provolone, and sage. The handsome marble bar is an inviting place to unwind either befor or after the theater. ♦ Italian ♦ Daily lunch an dinner. Reservations recommended. 322 W 46th St (between Eighth and Ninth Aves). 489.7212

64 Joe Allen ★$$ Here is an opportunity to gaze upon posters of failed Broadway shows handsome waiters, a stagestruck clientele, and occasionally the stars themselves. A blackboard menu lists the simple fare, but food is not really the point at this place. If you must have nourishment, try a salad, hamburger, bowl of chili, or grilled fish. ♦ American ♦ Daily lunch and dinner. 326 W 46th St (between Eighth and Ninth Aves). 581.6464

65 Becco ★$$ The Bastianich family, who own the felicitous **Felidia** restaurant on the East Side, are also the proprietors of this informal spot on Restaurant Row. A wide variety of flavorful Italian dishes, such as wild-mushroom risotto and roast suckling pig, are featured. The prix-fixe lunch and daily menus are both good values. ♦ Italian ♦ M-Sa lunch and dinner; Su dinner. 355 W 46th St (between Eighth and Ninth Aves). 397.7597

65 Lattanzi ★$$$ Enjoy a taste of the Roman Jewish Quarter in a casual atmosphere. Baby artichokes sautéed in olive oil, homemade pastas, and grilled fish are all made to order. ♦ Italian ♦ M-F lunch and dinner; Sa dinner. Reservations recommended. 361 W 46th St (between Eighth and Ninth Aves). 315.0980

65 Hour Glass Tavern $ Like it or not, the hourglass above the table gives customers exactly 60 minutes to savor the reasonably priced, three-course prix-fixe dinner, featuring such entrées as spicy blackened shrimp and homemade lamb sausage. Young Broadway hopefuls are well represented among the clientele. ♦ American ♦ M-F lunch and dinner; Sa-Su dinner. No credit cards accepted. 373 W 46th St (between Eighth and Ninth Aves). 265.2060 &

66 Koyote Kate's $$ If you've got a hankering for honky-tonking, this is the place. The Tex-Mex menu here includes a good 10-ounce burger and jalapeño shrimp (the peppers are stuffed with whole shrimp, breaded, and deep fried). Dip these in sour cream to put out the fire, or better yet, order a frozen margarita or two and go hog wild. Live country-western music is performed every night except Wednesday, when the blues reigns supreme. ♦ Tex-Mex ♦ M-F lunch and dinner; Sa-Su dinner and late-night meals. 307 W 47th St (between Eighth and Ninth Aves). 956.1091

67 B. Smith's ★$$$ With its sleek, contemporary decor, this dining spot is one of the more popular restaurants in the Theater District. The entrées are creatively presented and include shrimp scampi and filet mignon; sweet potato–pecan pie and profiteroles are favorite desserts. ♦ Continental ♦ Daily lunch and dinner. Reservations recommended. 771 Eighth Ave (at W 47th St). 247.2222

68 Acropolis $ A very plain taverna, this place is good to know about if you're in the market for affordable but authentic Greek food—souvlaki, moussaka, stuffed grape leaves, and spinach pie. ♦ Greek ♦ Tu-Su lunch and dinner. 767 Eighth Ave (at W 47th St). 581.2733

69 Brooks Atkinson The former **Mansfield,** designed by **Herbert J. Krapp** in 1926, was renamed in 1960 in honor of the *Times* critic. *Come Blow Your Horn,* the first in a series of Neil Simon comedy hits, opened here. Charles Grodin and Ellen Burstyn performed here for three years in *Same Time Next Year.* ♦ 256 W 47th St (between Broadway and Eighth Ave). 719.4099; Ticketmaster 307.4100 &

69 Pierre au Tunnel ★★$$$ A good Theater District standby, this place serves excellent bistro fare, especially such Old World specialties as *tripes à la mode de Caen* (calf intestines in a consommé with white wine, apple brandy, potatoes, carrots, and white turnips) and *tête de veau vinaigrette* (calf brains, tongue, and cheek in a thick mustard vinaigrette with capers). ♦ French ♦ M-Sa lunch and dinner. Reservations required. 250 W 47th St (between Broadway and Eighth Ave). 575.1220

70 Barrymore One of the great artists of her era, Ethel Barrymore opened this theater (designed by **Herbert J. Krapp**) in 1928 in *Kingdom of God.* The stage has seen the start of many illustrious careers: Fred Astaire danced his way to stardom in Cole Porter's *The Gay Divorce* (filmed as *The Gay Divorcée*); Walter Huston introduced the haunting standard "September Song" in *Knickerbocker Holiday;* and Marlon Brando first achieved prominence when he costarred with Jessica Tandy in *A Streetcar Named Desire.* ♦ 243 W 47th St (between Broadway and Eighth Ave). Telecharge 239.6200 &

71 Pong Sri ★$$ Manhattan has become nearly saturated with Thai restaurants, but this one has long received high marks for being among the most authentic. Dishes include lobster stir-fry with basil leaf and chili paste, whole deep-fried red snapper with a hot and spicy sauce, and assorted vegetables with bean curd in red curry and coconut milk. ♦ Thai ♦ Daily lunch and dinner. 244 W 48th St (between Broadway and Eighth Ave). 582.3392. Also at: 106 Bayard St (between Baxter and Canal Sts). 349.3132

71 Longacre In the 1930s, **The Group Theater** premiered three Clifford Odets plays: *Waiting for Lefty, Paradise Lost,* and *Till the Day I Die.*

157

Julie Harris appeared in *The Lark* and *Little Moon of Alban*. In 1960, theater of the absurd invaded Broadway with the brilliant Zero Mostel in *Rhinoceros* by Eugene Ionesco. In 1980, *Children of a Lesser God* won a Tony. The 1913 building is the work of **Henry B. Herts.** ♦ 220 W 48th St (between Broadway and Eighth Ave). Telecharge 239.6200 &

72 Walter Kerr It took precisely 66 days for the Shubert Organization and eminent theater designer **Herbert J. Krapp** to build the former **Ritz Theatre** in 1921. It opened with Clare Eames in John Drinkwater's *Mary Stuart* and left audiences spellbound in 1924 with Sutton Vane's eerie *Outward Bound,* starring Alfred Lunt and Leslie Howard. After years of being used for live radio and TV broadcasts, the theater underwent restoration and returned to legitimacy in 1971 with the rock opera *Soon.* Heavily restored again in 1983, the house easily ranks as one of Broadway's most beautiful theaters and authentically executed restorations, a showcase of Italian Renaissance detail. Until recently, it was home of Tony Kushner's unqualified hit *Angels in America,* a two-part AIDS epic (*Millennium Approaches* and *Perestroika*) that many claim brought integrity back to Broadway drama. ♦ 219 W 48th St (between Broadway and Eighth Ave). Telecharge 239.6200 &

73 Holiday Inn Crowne Plaza $$$ The arrival of the ultracontemporary chain's crown jewel in 1989 gave a major boost to the ongoing effort to revamp the Times Square area. The 770 rooms are ideally situated for sightseeing and theatergoing. For a view of Broadway, book a room on the east side; to see the Hudson River, book the west side. Indulge in one of the popular restaurants—**Broadway Grill, Samplings,** or **The Balcony**—and work off those calories at the pool or fitness center. ♦ 1605 Broadway (between W 48th and W 49th Sts). 977.4000, 800/HOLIDAY; fax 333.7393 &

74 Cort Many fine plays have opened on this stage, including *The Swan, Merton of the Movies, Charley's Aunt,* and *Lady Windermere's Fan.* But one of the most poignant was *The Diary of Anne Frank,* by famed Hollywood writers Frances and Albert Hackett, which won a Pulitzer in 1955. The theme of children living under political oppression returned here in the 1980s with *Sarafina!* In 1990, *The Grapes of Wrath* took the Tony for best play. ♦ 138 W 48th St (between Sixth and Seventh Aves). Telecharge 239.6200 &

74 Sam Ash Music Store For decades this block of West 48th Street has been a musician's mecca. Orchestral and rock 'n' roll musicians—from those struggling at the bottom of the heap to those celebrating at the top of the charts—come here for state-of-the-

art supplies and equipment. Wander in just to see who's buying. ♦ M-Sa. 160 W 48th St (between Sixth and Seventh Aves). 719.2661 &

75 Drama Bookshop Established in 1923, this is one of the city's most comprehensive sources of books on the dramatic arts (the **Library of Performing Arts at Lincoln Center** is another). Subject areas include domestic and foreign theater, performers, music, dance, makeup, lighting, props, staging, even puppetry and magic. ♦ Daily. 723 Seventh Ave (between W 48th and W 49th Sts). 944.0595 &

76 Caroline's Comedy Club This upscale venue is a major stop on the comedy club circuit for up-and-coming talent. Jerry Seinfeld, Jay Leno, and Billy Crystal all cut their teeth here. Dinner is served, but you can just order drinks. ♦ Cover; drink minimum. Shows M-Th, Su 8PM; F-Sa 8PM, 10:30PM. Reservations required. 1626 Broadway (between W 49th and W 50th Sts). 757.4100 &

77 The Brill Building At the turn of the century, publishers of popular songs were all located on 28th Street west of Broadway. The noise of pianos and raspy-voiced song pluggers gave the name "Tin Pan Alley" to the street. When the action moved uptown, the publishers moved to this building and brought the name with them. The bust of the young man over the door is a memorial to the son of the building's original owner, who died just before construction began. ♦ 1619 Broadway (between W 49th and W 50th Sts)

Within The Brill Building:

Colony Records An institution for recordings and sheet music for soundtracks, shows, and jazz, this is a fun stop for post-theater browsing. ♦ Daily 9:30AM-1AM. 265.2050 &

78 Ambassador Built in 1921, this is another work of **Herbert J. Krapp.** In 1939, Imogene Coca, Alfred Drake, and Danny Kaye began their careers here in the *Strawhat Review.* ♦ 215 W 49th St (between Broadway and Eighth Ave). 735.0500; Telecharge 239.6200

79 Eugene O'Neill This 1925 work of **Herbert J. Krapp** was the site of Arthur Miller's first major success, *All My Sons,* which opened here in 1947 with Ed Begley and Arthur Kennedy. The revival of *Grease* currently has the audience rockin'. ♦ 230 W 49th St (between Broadway and Eighth Ave). Telecharge 239.6200 &

80 Worldwide Plaza Changes in zoning laws encouraged the construction of this mixed-use complex of residences and offices on the site of the second **Madison Square Garden** (1925-66). The apartment towers were designed by **Frank Williams;** the office tower by **Skidmore, Owings & Merrill.** Both were built in 1989 in a slow but successful attempt to bring commercial activity to this area of

Eighth Avenue. Commercial occupants include Ogilvy & Mather and Polygram Records. ♦ Bounded by Eighth and Ninth Aves, and W 49th and W 50th Sts

81 Chez Napoléon ★★$$$ Tucked away at the edge of the Theater District is this casual bistro where such classic French dishes as onion soup, escargots, steak au poivre, and *choucroute garni* (sauerkraut garnished with potatoes and pork) top the menu. A hearty bouillabaisse is offered on Friday and Saturday nights. ♦ French ♦ M-F lunch and dinner; Sa dinner. Reservations required. 365 W 50th St (between Eighth and Ninth Aves). 265.6980

82 Café Des Sports ★$ Although regular customers would no doubt prefer that this dining spot remain one of New York's better-kept secrets, the staff ensures that all newcomers are warmly welcomed. The menu features such traditional French dishes as roast breast of chicken and grilled steak. ♦ French ♦ M-F lunch and dinner; Sa-Su dinner. 329 W 51st St (between Eighth and Ninth Aves). 974.9052

83 Rene Pujol ★★$$ A truly old-fashioned bistro, this town-house dining room is filled with French country atmosphere and decor, including exposed-brick walls and pottery on display. Try the lobster bisque, roast breast of duck, grilled steak, or rack of lamb. The crème brûlée and any of the soufflés are highly recommended, as is the good, reasonably priced wine list. ♦ French ♦ M-F lunch and dinner; Sa dinner. Reservations recommended. 321 W 51st St (between Eighth and Ninth Aves). 246.3023

84 Les Pyrénées ★$$$ The working fireplace at this casual country restaurant makes it a cozy spot, especially in winter. Recommended dishes include rack of lamb, escargots, cassoulet, grilled Dover sole, thin apple tart, and chocolate mousse. ♦ French ♦ M-Sa lunch and dinner; Su dinner. Reservations recommended. 251 W 51st St (between Broadway and Eighth Ave). 246.0044

85 Gershwin Formerly the **Uris Theater,** the present structure was built in 1972 by **Ralph Alswang.** Today it is the proud venue of the lavish revival of the well-loved musical *Showboat,* which now spans four generations (directed by Hal Prince). ♦ 222 W 51st St (between Broadway and Eighth Ave). 586.6510; Ticketmaster 307.4100 ♿

86 Circle in the Square In the past three decades, this theater company has produced more than 100 plays—many in its original house in Greenwich Village—and has earned a national reputation for excellence. In 1972, directors Theodore Mann and Paul Libin built the present arena stage in response to what they saw as a need for classic theater on Broadway. In recent years, *Present Laughter* with George C. Scott, *The Caine Mutiny Court Martial* with John Rubinstein, and *A Streetcar Named Desire* with Blythe Danner achieved critical acclaim. ♦ 1633 Broadway (between W 50th and W 51st Sts). Telecharge 239.6200 ♿

87 Winter Garden This beautiful theater, designed by **W.A. Swasey,** opened with Al Jolson in 1911. The Shuberts produced 12 annual editions of their revue *The Passing Show.* Fanny Brice, Bob Hope, and Josephine Baker were featured in the *Ziegfeld Follies.* Other hit musicals were *Plain and Fancy, West Side Story, Funny Girl,* and, currently, those fabulous felines in *Cats,* who have been performing here since 1982! ♦ 1634 Broadway (between W 50th and W 51st Sts). Telecharge 239.6200 ♿

88 Sheraton Manhattan $$$ A heated indoor swimming pool, a sun deck, and a gym furnished with modern exercise equipment are features of this conveniently located hotel, the handsome result of a major overhaul that included the 660 rooms completed in 1992. Rates are slightly more expensive here than across the street. Children stay free if no extra bed is required. ♦ 790 Seventh Ave (between W 51st and W 52nd Sts). 581.3300, 800/325.3535; fax 315.4265 ♿

89 Equitable Center A huge mural created by Roy Lichtenstein for this 1985 building by **Edward Larrabee** brings you in off the street. When you get inside there are other works of art to be seen, the most striking of which are the murals in the corridor to the left, which were painted in 1930 by Thomas Hart Benton and moved here from the **New School for Social Research.** Also off the building's lobby are the **Equitable Gallery** and the **Brooklyn Museum Shop.** ♦ Gallery and shop: M-Sa. 787 Seventh Ave (between W 51st and W 52nd Sts). 554.4818

Restaurants/Clubs: Red Hotels: Blue
Shops/♥ Outdoors: Green Sights/Culture: Black

Within the Equitable Center:

LE BERNARDIN

Le Bernardin ★★★★$$$$ The death of owner Gilbert Le Coze stunned the food world in 1994, but this esteemed seafood dining spot—which he opened in 1986—continues apace under the supervision of his sister Maguy. Try the seared Atlantic salmon with olives and sun-dried tomatoes; pan-roasted yellowtail snapper atop balsamic-glazed artichokes with foie gras and truffle sauce; or crispy Chinese spiced red snapper with cèpes, aged Port and Jerez vinegar reduction. Desserts are devastating. There's a well-chosen wine list. ♦ French/Seafood ♦ M-F lunch and dinner; Sa dinner. Reservations required. 155 W 51st St (between Sixth and Seventh Aves). 489.1515

Palio ★★$$$$ Named for a horse-racing festival in the Italian town of Siena, this place is worth a visit if only to see the stunning interior designed by **Skidmore, Owings & Merrill.** The lovely table appointments are by Vignelli Associates, and a wraparound Sandro Chia mural dominates the ground-floor bar, where the Bellinis (an apéritif of peach nectar and champagne) are a delight. The second-floor dining room delivers luxury in every detail. The menu contains such treats as risotto with lobster and fillet of beef with a shallot and mustard sauce, but overall, the food doesn't live up to the grandeur of the surroundings. ♦ Italian ♦ M-F lunch and dinner; Sa dinner. Reservations required; jacket and tie recommended, even at the bar. 151 W 51st St (between Sixth and Seventh Aves). 245.4850

At the corner of Washington Place and Greene Street, a plaque commemorates the deaths of 146 people in a fire at the Triangle Shirtwaist Company. The victims were predominantly Jewish and Italian immigrant women. When the fire broke out, the workers were unable to escape because the owners locked them in the building during shifts, a common practice. The fire brought attention to the despicable conditions of employment in the sweatshop industry, and the state enacted many reforms in the fire code and workplace safety regulations. The owners of the Triangle Shirtwaist Company were acquitted of any responsibility for the deaths in a court of law.

90 Michelangelo $$$ Some of the space of the old **Taft Hotel** has gotten a new lease on life in the form of this 178-room marble and crystal palace that belongs to the Star Italian chain of hotels—hence its name and the large number of Italian guests. Amenities include 24-hour room service, a concierge, a complimentary 24-hour fitness center, and access (for a fee) to a health club across the street. The larger-than-average rooms have TVs enclosed within hand-inlaid armoires (there are smaller TVs in the bathrooms). Valet parking is available. Another plus: The management *likes* children. ♦ 152 W 51st St (at Seventh Ave). 765.1900, 800/237.0990; fax 541.6604 &

91 Cité ★★★$$$ Designed to resemble a grand Parisian cafe, this elegant restaurant is filled with artifacts imported from that city: floral-pattern Art Deco grillwork from the original Au Bon Marché department store and intricate crystal chandeliers from an old Parisian cinema. For a truly Parisian experience, order a fine roast prime rib or filet mignon au poivre. For more casual tastes, the less expensive, but equally excellent, bistro is right next door. ♦ French ♦ Daily lunch and dinner. Reservations recommended. 120 W 51st St (between Sixth and Seventh Aves). 956.7100

92 Looking Toward the Avenue Installed in 1989, artist Jim Dine's three enormous bronze *Venuses* (ranging in height from 14 to 23 feet) are a humanizing presence amid the impersonal towers that surround them. ♦ 1301 Sixth Ave (between W 52nd and W 53rd Sts)

Ben Benson's
STEAK HOUSE

93 Ben Benson's Steakhouse ★★$$$$ Housed in a relatively new building, this classic-style New York restaurant serves massive portions of meat—including T-bones, aged sirloins, and triple-cut lamb chops—that few will be able to finish in one sitting. If you have any room left for dessert, try the cheesecake or bread pudding with bourbon sauce. ♦ American ♦ M-F lunch and dinner; Sa-Su dinner. Reservations recommended. 123 W 52nd St (between Sixth and Seventh Aves). 581.8888

94 Sheraton New York Hotel & Towers $$$ This efficient, modern hotel has excellent convention facilities for the mainly corporate clientele. The 1,700 rooms and public areas were completely restored in 1992; the original building, by **Morris Lapidus & Associates,** dates to 1962. Guests have use of the indoor swimming pool across the street at the pricier **Sheraton Manhattan.** There are several restaurants and lounges, and room service is available until 1AM. ♦ 811 Seventh Ave (between W 52nd and W 53rd Sts). 581.1000, 800/325.3535; fax 841.6496 ♿

95 Martini's ★★$$ Come here for very good grilled fish, including charred tuna with green mango, tomato, and spring onion sauce, and fabulous desserts—try the sinful lemon tart. And be sure to order the namesake drink, a martini, which comes in a designer glass. ♦ American/Mediterranean ♦ Daily lunch and dinner. Reservations recommended. 810 Seventh Ave (at W 53rd St). 767.1717

96 Novotel $$$ Part of a respected French chain, the hotel begins on the seventh floor of this 1984 building by **Gruzen & Partners,** and many of its 474 rooms and suites look down into the heart of Times Square. Room service runs until midnight. ♦ 226 W 52nd St (between Broadway and Eighth Ave). 315.0100, 800/221.3185; fax 765.5369

Within Novotel:

Cafe Nicole ★$$$ This restaurant and wine bar has a seventh-floor view of the Theater District. You'll find jazzy piano entertainment on the terrace at dinner. Steamed salmon and roast duck are sure bets. ♦ French/American ♦ Daily breakfast, lunch, and dinner. Reservations recommended. 315.0100

Gallagher's

96 Gallagher's Steak House ★★$$$$ Even confirmed carnivores may flinch as they pass the glass-walled meat locker (also visible from the street) filled with raw slabs of beef. But it's been there since the restaurant opened in 1927, and like many other aspects of the place, it hasn't changed a bit. The steaks are big and satisfying. ♦ Steak house ♦ Daily lunch and dinner. Reservations recommended. 228 W 52nd St (between Broadway and Eighth Ave). 245.5336

97 Roseland The legendary ballroom, which opened in 1919, still plays host to big bands

and aspiring Fred Astaires and Ginger Rogerses (as well as rock, salsa, and world music bands), although only two days a week now—Thursday, when there is a DJ, and Sunday, when there is live music. ♦ Admission. Th, Su 2:30-11PM. 239 W 52nd St (between Broadway and Eighth Ave). 247.0200 ♿

97 Virginia Formerly called the **ANTA,** it was built in 1925 by **Howard Crane** for the **Theatre Guild.** Pat Hingle and Christopher Plummer starred here in Archibald MacLeish's *J.B.,* which won the Pulitzer Prize in 1959. Sir Thomas More was brilliantly played by Paul Scofield in Robert Bolt's *A Man for All Seasons* in 1961. *No Place To Be Somebody* moved here from the **Public Theater** after its author, Charles Gordone, won the Pulitzer in 1969. ♦ 245 W 52nd St (between Broadway and Eighth Ave). Telecharge 239.6200 ♿

98 Neil Simon When this theater was erected in 1927 by **Herbert J. Krapp,** Fred and Adele Astaire were in the first production, George and Ira Gershwin's *Funny Face.* A more recent hit was *Annie,* which arrived here exactly 50 years later. ♦ 250 W 52nd St (between Broadway and Eighth Ave). 757.8646; Ticketmaster 307.4100 ♿

98 Russian Samovar ★$$ Featured on the menu here are the staples and specialties of Slavic cooking: blini with caviar, grilled fish, and lamb. A four-course prix-fixe dinner keeps the regular customers coming back, who enjoy in the bargain the Russian decor and nightly music. ♦ Russian ♦ M dinner; Tu-Sa lunch and dinner; Su dinner. Reservations recommended. 256 W 52nd St (between Broadway and Eighth Ave). 757.0168

99 King Crab ★$$ Spacious it's not, but this pretty seafood restaurant is charming, with gaslit lamps and a gracious staff. The daily specials feature whatever the morning trip to the **Fulton Fish Market** has netted. Don't pass up the soft-shell crabs (if available). ♦ Seafood ♦ M-F lunch and dinner; Sa-Su dinner. Reservations recommended. 871 Eighth Ave (at W 52nd St). 765.4393 ♿

100 Bangkok Cuisine ★★$$ The food is excellent, and among the best dishes are the seafood soups spiced with pepper and lemongrass, any of the satays, *mee krob* (crispy noodles tossed with pork, shrimp, and bean sprouts), chicken *masaman* (with coconut milk, peanuts, avocado, and curry), and baked fish smothered with hot spices. It's crowded in the early evening but becomes increasingly peaceful as the night wears on. ♦ Thai ♦ M-Sa lunch and dinner; Su dinner. Reservations recommended. 885 Eighth Ave (between W 52nd and W 53rd Sts). 581.6370 ♿

101 Broadway Ethel Merman filled this theater with sound and ticket-holders as the star of

161

Gypsy. Built in 1924 by **Eugene DeRosa,** this is also where Barbra Streisand performed in *Funny Girl,* and where Yul Brynner gave his final performance in *The King and I. Miss Saigon* opened here on 11 April 1991 and is still going strong. ♦ 1681 Broadway (between W 52nd and W 53rd Sts). Telecharge 239.6200 ⅙

102 Ed Sullivan This landmark theater, which was built by **Herbert J. Krapp** in 1927 and is full of Gothic details inside and out, has showcased vaudeville, music hall, stage shows, radio, and TV. It was a casino-style nightclub in the 1930s, then became the broadcast home of the Fred Allen radio show, and, from 1948 to 1971, "The Ed Sullivan Show." Under its vaulted cathedral ceiling, American audiences got their first look at the Beatles, Elvis Presley, and Rudolf Nureyev. **CBS** bought and completely restored the theater in 1993; it is now home to the ever-popular David Letterman's "Late Show." ♦ 1697 Broadway (between W 53rd and W 54th Sts)

103 Au Cafe ★$ This is an idea whose time has certainly come: a coffee bar with a variety of sandwiches, salads, soups, pastas, burgers, and pastries. It's an ideal place to relax with your thoughts or a newspaper. The spacious palm-lined outdoor seating area far from the street is delightful in nice weather. ♦ American ♦ Daily breakfast, lunch, and dinner. 1700 Broadway (at W 53rd St). 757.2233

104 Stage Delicatessen $$ The once-great spot for Damon Runyon characters is now in high disrepute among New Yorkers. The pastrami is fair, and like all the rest of the sandwiches, way overpriced. ♦ Deli ♦ Daily breakfast, lunch, dinner, and late-night meals. 834 Seventh Ave (between W 53rd and W 54th Sts). 245.7850

105 Remi ★★★$$$ Fresh antipasti, Venetian-style ravioli filled with fresh tuna and crispy ginger in a light tomato sauce, and a selection of grilled meats and fish please the palate here. The desserts are worth the splurge, especially the *cioccolatissima* (a warm chocolate soufflé cake with a cappuccino parfait) and the *zabaglione sarah venezia* (broiled zabaglione with fruit and vanilla ice cream). For those who like grappa, there are 45 varieties offered. ♦ Italian ♦ M-F lunch and dinner; Sa-Su dinner. Reservations recommended. 145 W 53rd St (between Sixth and Seventh Aves). 581.4242

106 New York Hilton and Towers $$$ The quintessential luxury convention hotel in town is this tower of more than 2,000 well-

appointed rooms, each with a small private bar, and offering services for businesspeople such as quick checkout, a copy center, rental pocket beeper phones, and a multilingual staff. **Executive Tower** rooms offer a refrigerator, radio alarm, electric shoe polisher, and a free copy of *USA Today* with breakfast. A battery of restaurants and cocktail lounges includes **Sports Bar** and **Grill 53,** a fine restaurant. ♦ 1335 Sixth Ave (between W 53rd and W 54th Sts). 586.7000, 800/HILTONS; fax 315.1374 ⅙

107 Rhiga Royal Hotel $$$$ All rooms are spacious in this 54-story 214-room luxury hotel, though 30 suites define indulgence. There are great views; amenities include VCRs and two independent phone lines. Most rooms have computer and facsimile ports. Chef John Halligan prepares continental nouvelle cuisine in **The Halcyon,** and there is 24-hour room service. ♦ 151 W 54th St (between Sixth and Seventh Aves). 307.5000, 800/937.5454; fax 765.6530 ⅙

108 Carnegie Delicatessen ★★$$ Indulge yourself at *the* classic kosher-style deli, a New York legend that became famous for sandwiches named after other New York legends. The menu may seem a bit pricey at first, but wait until you see the size of the sandwiches—massive affairs that inevitably provide enough to share or cart home. Leave room, if you can, for the cheesecake. The downside: Getting people in and out—not providing gracious service or comfort—is the goal here, and after so many years it's become an honored tradition. The deli made a star appearance in Woody Allen's *Broadway Danny Rose.* ♦ Deli ♦ Daily breakfast, lunch, dinner, and late-night meals. No credit cards accepted. 854 Seventh Ave (between W 54th and W 55th Sts). 757.2245

109 Siam Inn ★$ Spicy, authentic fare is offered in the humdrum dining room of this noisy and fashionable Thai restaurant. Fish and seafood dishes are best. ♦ Thai ♦ M-F lunch and dinner; Sa-Su dinner. 916 Eighth Ave (between W 54th and W 55th Sts). 974.9583

110 Broadway Diner ★$ This upscale, 1950s-style diner, with lots of tables and counter seats, features a wide variety of good daily specials—including salads, steaks, and fish. ♦ American ♦ Daily breakfast, lunch, dinner, and late-night meals. No credit cards accepted. 1726 Broadway (at W 55th St). 765.0909. Also at: 590 Lexington Ave (at 52nd St). 486.8838 &

111 MONY Tower When built in 1950 by **Shreve, Lamb & Harmon,** this was the headquarters of the insurance company known as Mutual of New York, which has since become MONY Financial Services.

The mast on top of the tower is all about change of another kind: If the light on top is green, look for fair weather; orange means clouds are coming, and flashing orange signals rain; when it flashes white, expect snow; and if the lights on the mast itself are rising, so will the temperature, and when they descend, it is going to get cold. ♦ 1740 Broadway (between W 55th and W 56th Sts)

112 Park Central $$ When the 1920s roared, a lot of the sound and fury echoed through these halls, which were a meeting place for bootleggers and small-time gangsters. The ghosts have all been exorcised, and the 1927 hotel by **Groneburg & Leuchtag** has a new lease on life. You'll find a lovely on-site bistro, **Nicole,** plus a lounge, a drugstore, a newsstand, and a barbershop. The 1,200 reasonably-priced rooms attract groups and airline crews. ♦ 870 Seventh Ave (between W 55th and W 56th Sts). 247.8000, 800/843.6664; fax 484.3374 &

113 Hotel Wellington $ This 1930s gem is often overlooked, even though it has 700 rooms, a coffee shop, a restaurant, and a cocktail lounge. A renovation of all rooms was completed in early 1993, making this even more of a find. ♦ 871 Seventh Ave (between W 55th and W 56th Sts). 247.3900, 800/652.1212; fax 581.1719 &

Christer's

114 Christer's ★★★$$$ After garnering rave reviews during his tenure as chef at the nearby **Aquavit,** Swedish-born Christer Larsson opened his own restaurant in 1993. The rustic decor of split logs and plaid-covered banquettes centers around a stone fireplace; a number of fish paintings grace the walls. The food, American with Scandinavian leanings, highlights fresh fish and seafood; don't miss the gravlax; house-smoked Serrano salmon with black beans, corn, avocado, and tomatillo salsa; or salmon

barbecued on an oak board with bacon and tamales. Desserts include a chocolate cake with an almond crust and peach sauce, the Apple Leaf (apples baked in phyllo dough topped with vanilla ice cream), and a lingonberry compote with chocolate ice cream. For refreshment try the aquavit, a clear-colored liqueur flavored with caraway seeds. ♦ American/Scandinavian ♦ M-F lunch and dinner; Sa dinner. Reservations recommended. 145 W 55th St (between Sixth and Seventh Aves). 974.7224

114 City Center Theater This somewhat unlikely Moorish emporium was built as a Shriners' temple in 1924 by **H.P. Knowles** and converted to a theater in 1943. It was the home of the **New York City Opera** and the **New York City Ballet** before they moved to **Lincoln Center.** Splendidly renovated, the 2,731-seat theater has raking and improved sightlines, so audiences no longer have to strain their necks to see. Regular performers include the **Alvin Ailey, Martha Graham,** and **Merce Cunningham** dance companies. ♦ Box office noon-8PM. 131 W 55th St (between Sixth and Seventh Aves). 581.7907 &

115 Castellano ★$$$ The peach-colored dining room is a re-creation of Harry's Bar in Venice, and the food is authentic Venetian fare, although a few dishes from other regions make an appearance. Try the green-and-white fettuccine with cream and ham or any of the grilled fish entrées. ♦ Italian ♦ M-F lunch and dinner; Sa-Su dinner. Reservations required. 138 W 55th St (between Sixth and Seventh Aves). 664.1975

115 Gorham Hotel $$$ First opened in 1929, this 120-room hotel was renovated to the tune of $16 million in 1993. It's a lovely and convenient Midtown choice for visitors and particularly families, since contemporary-style rooms are large and come with a compact although fully equipped kitchenette—and there's no charge for children under 16. If you've opted for one of the 45 suites, you can look forward to a whirlpool bath at the end of a long day. ♦ 136 W 55th St (between Sixth and Seventh Aves). 245.1800, 800/735.0710; fax 582.8332 &

116 Corrado ★$$$ The *tortellini in brodo* (tortellini in broth) are as good as they are in Bologna; the pasta is homemade; the sauces light and skillfully spiced; and the desserts worth waiting for, especially the flavorful ice creams. Next door is the **Corrado Kitchen,** a popular take-out place. ♦ Italian ♦ M-F lunch and dinner; Sa-Su dinner. Corrado Kitchen: daily. Reservations recommended. 1373 Sixth Ave (between W 55th and W 56th Sts). 333.3133

116 Ellen's Stardust Diner $ The burgers here won't win any culinary awards, but they're delivered to the shake, rattle, and roll of vintage 1950s music. Be prepared to wait. ♦ American ♦ Daily breakfast, lunch, dinner, and late-night meals. 1377 Sixth Ave (at W 56th St). 307.7575 &

117 The Mysterious Bookshop If you want to know *whodunit,* the amazingly well-informed staff here won't spoil the fun by telling you, but they will guide you to the exact book that you're looking for. There are thousands of mystery books, both new and out-of-print, in this two-level shop. ♦ M-Sa. 129 W 56th St (between Sixth and Seventh Aves). 765.0900

118 Joseph Patelson Music House Musicians, from beginners to world-renowned maestros, have been coming to this former carriage house for their music needs (sheet music and books, orchestral and opera scores) ever since it opened in 1920. With the widest selection of music (mostly classical, with some jazz, pop, and Broadway) in New York, it's no surprise that this shop receives orders from as far away as Japan. ♦ M-Sa 160 W 56th St (between Sixth and Seventh Aves). 582.5840 &

119 Lee's Studio Sleek, contemporary lighting fixtures and table and floor lamps like those you'd expect to find in Milan or at the **Museum of Modern Art,** as well as a selective choice of chairs, sofas, and accessories, fill this shop. ♦ Daily. 1755 Broadway (at W 56th St). 581.4400. Also at: 1069 Third Ave (at E 63rd St). 371.1122 &

120 India Pavilion ★$ Come here for the best curries and chicken *tikka* (marinated in yogurt and cooked dry—a boneless tandoori) in the neighborhood, and save yourself a trip downtown to Little India on East Sixth Street. ♦ Indian ♦ M-F lunch and dinner; Sa-Su dinner. 240 W 56th St (between Broadway and Eighth Ave). 243.8175 &

121 Hearst Magazine Building Architect **Joseph Urban**'s bizarre 1928 concoction is reminiscent of the Viennese Secession, with strange obelisks standing on a heavy base and rising over the roof of the six-story pile. Apparently, this was intended to be the plinth for another seven stories; it would have remained a folly nonetheless. The building is not open to the public. ♦ 959 Eighth Ave (between W 56th and W 57th Sts). 649.2000

122 Parc Vendome Apartments This was one of the sites considered for a second **Metropolitan Opera House.** The scheme died when opera patrons were told that a skyscraper would be built to help support it. "We don't need that kind of help," they sniffed and took their money elsewhere. The 570-unit apartment house, a 1931 creation of **Henry Mandel,** contains a private dining room, a gymnasium and pool, a music room, and terraced gardens. ♦ 340 W 57th St (between Eighth and Ninth Aves). 247.6990

123 Coliseum Books Here you'll find a huge mix of both general interest and scholarly books: academic, trade, and mass-market paperbacks; sports; how-to books; scholarly journals; and oversize paper and hardcover remainders. Computer reference, a helpful staff, and late hours are also pluses. ♦ M 8AM-10PM; Tu-Th 8AM-11PM; F 8AM-11:30PM; Sa 10AM-11:30PM; Su noon-8PM. 1771 Broadway (at W 57th St). 757.8381

124 Hard Rock Cafe $$ The tail end of a 1958 Cadillac is the marquee of this mecca for young tourists. Inside, check out the guitar-shaped bar and rock memorabilia that includes dozens of gold records of old and new artists, Jimi Hendrix's guitar, and lots of good memories of The Beatles and Rolling Stones. The sandwiches and burgers are decent. Requisite **Hard Rock** T-shirts and sweatshirts are for sale in the gift shop next door. ♦ American ♦ Daily lunch, dinner, and late-night meals. 221 W 57th St (between Seventh Ave and Broadway). 459.9320

124 Art Students League The three central panels on this French Renaissance palace represent the Fine Arts Society, the Architectural League, and the Art Students League, all of which originally shared this facility and made it the scene of nearly every important exhibition at the turn of the century. Dating to 1892, this is a work of **Henry J. Hardenbergh.** ♦ 215 W 57th St (between Seventh Ave and Broadway). 247.4510

125 Lee's Art Shop, Inc. "The Department Store for Artists" is appropriately located directly across the street from the **Art Students League.** The extensive materials department attracts artists and architects, and the pens, stationery, and picture frames make great gifts. ♦ Daily. 220 W 57th St (between Seventh Ave and Broadway). 247.0110 &

Restaurants/Clubs: Red   **Hotels:** Blue
Shops/ ❦ Outdoors: Green   **Sights/Culture:** Black

126 The Osborne Except for the removal of its front porch and the addition of retail stores, this wonderful apartment building has hardly changed since it was built by **James E. Ware** in 1885. Unfortunately not open to the public, the opulent lobby was designed by Louis Comfort Tiffany. ♦ 205 W 57th St (at Seventh Ave)

126 Cafe Europa ★$ Bright and pretty, with dreamy trompe l'oeil ceilings, this cafe is a convenient spot to have a sandwich or such hot dishes as pizza and pasta. Try the muffins, tarts, and cakes accompanied by full-flavored coffees. ♦ Cafe/Takeout ♦ Daily breakfast, lunch, dinner, and late-night meals. 205 W 57th St (at Seventh Ave). 977.4030 &

127 Trattoria Dell'Arte ★★$$$ According to the proud management of this colorful restaurant opposite **Carnegie Hall,** the world's largest antipasto bar resides here. Choose from the impressive assortment, which includes sun-dried tomatoes, roasted fennel, fresh mozzarella, various seasonal vegetables, and a separate seafood bar with lobster, shrimp and scallop salad, calamari, and smoked salmon. The casual Italian menu also features delicate thin-crust pizzas. ♦ Italian ♦ Daily lunch and dinner. Reservations required for dinners before and after Carnegie Hall performances. 900 Seventh Ave (between W 56th and W 57th Sts). 245.9800 &

128 Carnegie Hall This landmark (shown below) was built in 1891 by **William B. Tuthill; William Morris Hunt** and **Dankmar Adler** served as consultants. Peter Ilyich Tchaikovsky conducted at the opening concert, and during the next 70 years, the **New York Philharmonic** played here under such greats as Gustav Mahler, Bruno Walter, Arturo Toscanini, Leopold Stokowski, and Leonard Bernstein. Considered to have acoustics matched by few others in the world, the hall has attracted all of the 20th century's great musicians, and not just the classical variety; W.C. Handy brought his blues here in 1928, and was followed by Count Basie, Duke Ellington, Benny Goodman, and others. When it was announced in the 1950s that the **New York Philharmonic** would be moving to **Lincoln Center,** the landmark was put up for sale. Violinist Isaac Stern and a group of concerned music lovers waged a successful campaign to save it. Their efforts eventually resulted in a restoration, completed in 1986 by **James Stewart Polshek and Partners,** which rendered it as glorious visually as it is acoustically. The corridors are lined with scores and other memorabilia of the artists and composers who have added to the hall's greatness. The space above the auditorium contains studios and apartments favored by musicians and artists. Another part of the space is occupied by the **Weill Recital Hall,** used by soloists and small chamber groups. In the spring of 1991, **The Rose Museum at Carnegie Hall** took over yet another part of the building. ♦ Free. Tours M-Tu, Th-F 11:30AM, 2PM, and 3PM. Museum: M-Tu, Th-Su 11AM-4:30PM. 154 W 57th St (at Seventh Ave). 247.7800 &

Michael Storrings

Carnegie Hall

128 The Russian Tea Room ★★$$$
Definitely 1995's most talked about restaurant takeover, this New York City dining landmark is scheduled to reopen in late 1996 after an elaborate renovation. New owner Warner Leroy has committed to keeping the whimsical ambience for which the **Tea Room** has long been known. The added surprise is the celebrated arrival of executive chef David Bouley—well known for the success of his own downtown restaurant—who will create a contemporary Russian menu. Happily, the blini and caviar will remain. ◆ Russian ◆ Daily lunch and dinner. Reservations required; jacket and tie recommended. 150 W 57th St (between Sixth and Seventh Aves). 265.0947

129 Uncle Sam's Umbrella Shop This shop has been protecting New Yorkers from the elements for more than 120 years with umbrellas in all different sizes, shapes, and prices, and repairs while you wait. All of the umbrellas for the musical *My Fair Lady* were made here. ◆ M-Sa. 161 W 57th St (between Sixth and Seventh Aves). 582.1977 ♿

130 Planet Hollywood ★$$ This mecca of movie memorabilia with an interior created by the set designer of the original *Batman* film is owned (though not managed) by the omnipotent trio of Sylvester Stallone, Bruce Willis, and Arnold Schwarzenegger. A hot new eatery that is forever loud, packed, and fun, it almost always demands a wait (no reservations are taken). On weekends it may seem that everyone is "Romper Room" age; the crowd is the same mixed-age group as at the equally trendy **Hard Rock Cafe** down the block. The pizza and burger selections are good, but everyone leaves room for the apple strudel, especially Arnold: It's made from his mother's secret recipe. A gift shop next door will supply you with souvenirs for the friend who has everything. ◆ American ◆ Daily lunch, dinner, and late-night meals. 140 W 57th St (between Sixth and Seventh Aves). 333.7827

130 Poli Fabrics Fine fabrics at fair prices are well labeled with the price, fiber content, and, often, the name of a designer who has used it: Carolyn Roehm or Ellen Tracy, for example. ◆ M-Sa. 132 W 57th St (between Sixth and Seventh Aves). 245.7750

131 Le Parker Meridien $$$$ Its main entrance is on West 56th Street, but they've included an attractive corridor leading to the other side, which gives it a more uptown address. When making a reservation, ask for an odd-numbered room above the 26th floor, and you'll be rewarded with a wonderful view of **Central Park.** The 42-story hotel has 700 rooms, two restaurants (**Le Patio** turns out a sumptuous buffet breakfast; Japanese-American **Shin's** is the more elegant of the two), a rooftop swimming pool with a jogging track, and racquetball and squash courts. The 24-hour room service has a European flair, as does everything else about the hotel. ◆ 118 W 57th St (between Sixth and Seventh Aves). 245.5000, 800/543.4300; fax 307.1776 ♿

132 Salisbury Hotel $$ Most of the 320 large rooms here have serving pantries and individual safes. Guests are served a complimentary continental breakfast, and an ice cream shop is open during the summer. Floor-by-floor renovation began in early 1995. ◆ 123 W 57th St (between Sixth and Seventh Aves). 246.1300, 800/223.0680; fax 977.7752 ♿

132 Steinway Hall Look through the concave window into the showroom of this prestigious piano company, housed, appropriately, in a domed hall with a huge crystal chandelier. The 12-story building, built in 1925, with a three-story Greek temple on the roof, also includes a recital salon. The relief of *Apollo* over the central arch is by Leo Lentelli; the building is by **Warren & Wetmore.** ◆ Daily. 109 W 57th St (between Sixth and Seventh Aves). 246.1100

133 Alwyn Court The terra-cotta dragons and other decorations that cover every inch of this 1909 apartment house by **Harde and Short** are in the style of the great art patron of the Renaissance, Francis I. His symbol, a crowned salamander, is prominently displayed above the entrance at the West 58th Street corner. Although it is not open to the public, almost no one ever passes by without stopping for a lingering look. ◆ 180 W 58th St (at Seventh Ave)

133 Petrossian ★★★$$$$ Many varieties of precious roe are offered at this high-class, Art Deco–influenced marble and mink-trimmed room, with ornate gilded statuettes and enlarged etchings of Erté drawings. Sample the sevruga, ossetra, and beluga, the foie gras terrine, or the sampling of salmon—marinated, smoked, and spiced. These appetizers can be made into a meal in and of themselves, but if you can press on to the main course, you most certainly should. Chef Joseph Pace's innovative and delicious dishes include roasted lobster with fricassee of winter vegetables, potato puree, and mushroom truffle sauce; and roasted black sea bass with French lentils, fried oysters, and bittersweet meat glaze. Desserts are similarly hard to pass up. The wine list is excellent and the very best Champagnes can be ordered by the glass. There's a sublime prix-fixe brunch and surprisingly affordable prix-fixe lunch and dinner. Take-home delicacies are available in the adjoining retail shop. ♦ Continental ♦ M-F lunch and dinner; Sa-Su brunch. Reservations required; jacket required. 182 W 58th St (at Seventh Ave). 245.2214

134 Freed of London Best known to beginning and professional ballet dancers for their handmade shoes from England and Spain, the store also sells tap, ballroom, and theatrical shoes, plus dancewear. ♦ M-Sa. 922 Seventh Ave (at W 58th St). 489.1055

135 The New York Athletic Club This 22-story building, designed by **York & Sawyer** in 1930, houses handball and squash courts as well as other exercise facilities, including a swimming pool. The club itself was founded in 1868 and has sent winning teams to many Olympic Games. There are guest rooms, but visitors who want to begin their day running in **Central Park** are not permitted to go through the lobby in jogging outfits. ♦ Daily for members only: M-F 6:30AM-9PM; Sa 9AM-7PM; Su 10AM-6PM. 180 Central Park S (at Seventh Ave). 247.5100

135 Essex House $$$ After a two-year renovation completed in fall 1991, the only remaining parts of the original 1930 grand hotel by **Frank Grand** are the exterior walls and bronze Art Deco elevator doors. Still, the Art Deco details of the facade and the artful use of setbacks make it one of Manhattan's more pleasing towers. The hotel now boasts a small spa facility with exercise room, massage, facials, and body wraps. There are two restaurants, both overseen by famed chef Christian Delouvrier—the gourmet dining room **Les Célébrités,** and the more casual **Cafe Botanica.** Plans for a Japanese restaurant are on the boards, a reminder of the hotel's new owner, the prestigious NIKKO chain of hotels. A third of the 600 rooms have **Central Park** views. ♦ 160 Central Park S (between Sixth and Seventh Aves). 247.0300, 800/NIKKO-US; fax 315.1839 &

Within the Essex House:

Les Célébrités ★★★$$$$ The setting here exudes wealth and power, with ornate gold-leaf columns, dark red banquettes, and glistening black walls dotted with paintings done by celebrity amateurs. Chef Christian

Delouvrier's signature foie gras burger, between Granny Smith apple rings, is delicious as well as impressive for the sheer amount of foie gras on the plate. Regulars tend to stick to meat and poultry dishes; try the roasted rack and saddle of lamb, roast squab, or duck with orange-honey glaze and fig puree (if you don't mind sweet sauces). ♦ French ♦ Tu-Sa dinner. Reservations required; jacket required. 247.0300

136 Hampshire House A hotel converted to elite cooperative apartments, this building, a work of **Caughey & Evans,** has a peaked roof of copper that has turned a marvelous shade of green, one of the highlights of the skyline bordering **Central Park.** Its lobby is a joy; when the cornerstone was put in place, it was filled with the best books and music of 1931. ♦ 150 Central Park S (between Sixth and Seventh Aves)

136 Ritz-Carlton $$$$ Until its 1982 refurbishing by **Parrish-Hadley,** which included the charming bow to another era of putting awnings over the windows, this was known as the **Navarro.** The new owner also owns the Boston Ritz, among other properties that follow the tradition of the great César Ritz, who changed British tradition when he opened a hotel in London in 1898. The design of the 214-room hotel is in the style of English manor houses. Amenities include 24-hour room service, robes, twice-daily housekeeping, turndown service, refrigerators upon request, and no fewer than three phones in every room. ♦ 112 Central Park S (between Sixth and Seventh Aves). 757.1900, 800/241.3333; fax 757.9620 &

Within the Ritz-Carlton:

Fantino ★★$$$ The name means jockey in Italian, and in its previous incarnation this restaurant was known as the **Jockey Club.** Today, the hunter-green walls and paintings of horses have been replaced by a soft peach color in the dining room, with chandeliers and delicately lit 19th-century oil paintings. Try the house-smoked sea bass and eggplant with Tuscan white beans and basil olive oil, ravioli of fresh wild mushrooms flavored with white truffles, and pan-roasted lamb chops covered in an oregano-pecorino crust and Vernaccia wine. ♦ Italian ♦ M-Sa dinner. Reservations recommended; jacket required. 664.7700

New York Bay is really a tidal estuary and the world's southernmost fjord.

Before the Ninth Avenue El was pushed uptown in 1879, the only "rapid" means of transportation on the Upper West Side were the Eighth Avenue horse car line and a stage coach on the Bloomingdale Road (now Broadway).

137 Gainsborough Studios In 1908, Charles W. Buckham designed this apartment building—now one of the oldest in the city—as an artists' cooperative. It is worth passing by for a look at the frieze by **Isadore Konti** across the second floor—a festival procession with a bust of Gainsborough at the center. In addition, the building has one of the best facades; this one was just restored in 1992. ♦ 222 Central Park S (between Seventh Ave and Broadway)

137 San Domenico ★★★★$$$$ After captivating the palates of international food critics for 18 years in a suburb of Bologna, Gianluigi Morino transplanted his labor of love to New York in 1988, and began dazzling food critics here. Today, the same standards are maintained under the watchful eye of present owner Tony May. The decor—marble bar, terra-cotta floor imported from Florence, and smooth, ocher-tinted stucco walls applied by artisans from Rome—is lovely, although perhaps a little subdued compared to the theatrical settings that have come recently into vogue. All the dazzle you need, however, will arrive in the form of chef Theo Schoenegger's sublime cooking. Don't miss the meltingly rich soft egg yolk–filled ravioli with truffle butter; it's a taste experience that you'll remember for years. The sensational and affordable prix-fixe dinner is a great deal for those who don't mind eating early. ♦ Italian ♦ M-F lunch and dinner; Sa-Su dinner. Reservations required; jacket required. 240 Central Park S (between Seventh Ave and Broadway). 265.5959 &

138 CBS Broadcast Center Currently operating as a TV production center and the headquarters of "CBS News," this was originally the headquarters of a dairy, and **CBS** old-timers still refer to it as the "Cowbarn." ♦ 524 W 57th St (between 10th and 11th Aves). 975.4321

139 The YIVO Institute for Jewish Research (Yidisher Visnschaftlekher Institut) This organization has just moved crosstown from its Fifth Avenue location, which had been its home since 1955. Covering all aspects of Jewish life, it has the world's largest collections of books, letters, and manuscripts in Yiddish, some dating back to 1600; its extensive library is open for browsing. ♦ M-Th. 555 W 57th St (at 11th Ave), Suite 1100. 246.6080

140 Copacabana In the 1940s and 1950s, you could be thrilled here by the **Copa Girls** and entertained by such personalities as Sammy Davis Jr. and Jerry Vale. Although nightclub shows like those are a thing of the past, this club is still a bright spot on Tuesday night, when Latin music is the lure, and Friday and Saturday nights, when the Latin beat is augmented by an upstairs disco. Shows usually begin around 10:30PM. The rest of the time it is used for private parties. In 1993, the club moved here from the East Side. ♦ Cover. Tu 6PM-3AM; F 9:30PM-4AM; Sa 10:30PM-4AM. 617 W 57th St (between 11th and 12th Aves). 582.2672

141 Passenger Ship Terminal The last of the great ocean liners (also known as the "Cunard Queens"), the SS *France* and the USS *United States,* used piers in this neighborhood. But before this terminal complex was finished in 1976, except for the *QE2,* only cruise ships called here regularly. Most arrive Saturday morning and leave the same afternoon. The facility is used at other times as exhibition space. ♦ 711 12th Ave (between W 48th and W 55th Sts). 246.5451

David N. Dinkins assumed the city's highest office in 1990 as the city's first black mayor. He was defeated in 1994 after one term by current Mayor Rudolph Giuliani.

The name for Broadway was taken from the Dutch *Breede Wegh,* but began as an Indian trail known as the *Weekquaesgeek Trail.* Its origin explains why, as one of New York City's major thoroughfares, it is the only one that twists and crosses over other avenues before reaching as far north as Yonkers. Wherever it crosses over a north-south avenue at an angle (Union Square, Duffy Square, Sheridan Square, etc.), the city's urban planners created triangular or square "squares."

Bests

Corky Pollan
"Best Bets" Editor, *New York* magazine

The Frick Collection—this is probably on everyone's list of favorites, but where else in New York can you view some of the greatest works of art without having to jockey for position?

The **Seal Pond** at the renovated **Central Park Zoo.**

Lunch at the **Post House** for old-world elegance and service.

Tea at the **Mayfair** for soothing teas, delectable sandwiches, and comforting sofas.

The **Conservatory Garden** any spring day.

The **Museum of the City of New York** for its enchanting collection of antique and vintage dolls, doll houses, and toys.

Lower Broadway on a Saturday or Sunday to catch the hottest and trendiest fashion looks.

Rizzoli, even when you're not looking for a book.

Drinks at the **Top of the Tower** at the **Beekman Tower Hotel** at sunset—one of the city's most romantic spots.

Helen Gurley Brown
Editor, *Cosmopolitan* magazine

All visitors to New York would enjoy a lunch or dinner at the **Russian Tea Room.** Obviously there are hundreds (maybe more) of fabulous restaurants in New York City, but this one to me captures the warmth, glamour, and charm of our metropolis.

Once in a while you will see a movie star seated close to you at a table. If you don't, the food is still worth a visit. It was the first restaurant someone took *me* to when I arrived in New York 30 years ago, and it's better than ever.

Other things to do in New York City: Walk the entire length of **East** and **West 57th Street**—that street, to me, as much as **Madison Avenue** and **Fifth** and **Park,** epitomizes our city. A visit to the top of **Rockefeller Center** is always a thriller—**Rainbow and Stars** is the best nightclub in the world, with wonderful entertainers (Rosemary Clooney, Tony Bennett, etc.) in an intimate atmosphere.

Another best restaurant is **Elaine's.** Again, civilians can rub shoulders—well almost—with the famous and the food is great.

Beverly Sills
Diva/Former Director of the New York City Opera

The **New York City Opera.**

The best restaurants in the world.

The greatest theater district in the world.

Brooklyn, where I was born.

As it enters its record 15th year on Broadway, *Cats* has gone through 25, 545 makeup brushes, over a ton of yak hair, 21,030 wig caps, 288 Siamese cat swords—plus 172,250 aspirin, 705 pounds of coffee, and 14,976 ice packs.

Midtown

A sense of power pervades Midtown, the heart of Manhattan. Giant high-rises stand shoulder to shoulder, creating solid walls of concrete and glass that seem to stretch to the sky. Each weekday morning on the crowded sidewalks below, briefcase-toting people in business suits and well-shined shoes race to their offices with definite purpose, emerging at midday—to head for power lunches at some of the finest restaurants in the city or to grab a sandwich from a corner deli—and again in the evening, to jump in a cab for a night on the

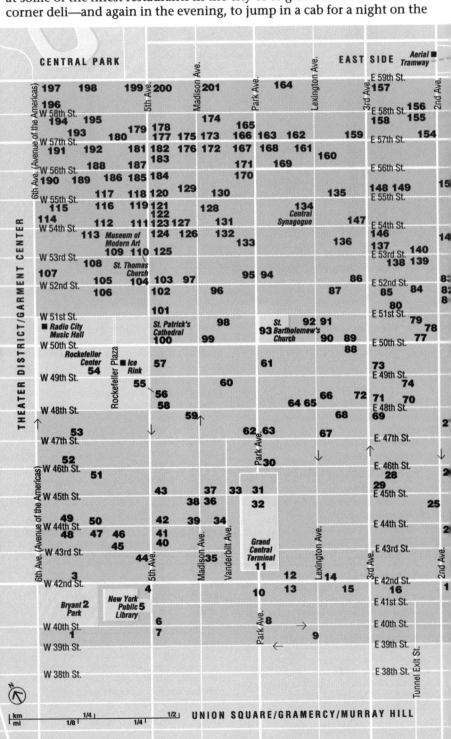

town or to hurry home, only to begin the cycle again bright and early the next morning.

Midtown's weighty importance begins with a concentration of office buildings around **Grand Central Terminal**, touches on **Rockefeller Center** to the west, encompasses the headquarters of the **United Nations** to the east, and extends to the border of **Central Park** to the north. On **Fifth Avenue**, the tote of choice is more often a classy shopping bag than a briefcase. The street is home to some of the world's most exclusive stores, including **Saks**, Henri Bendel, Cartier, Tiffany, and **Bergdorf Goodman**. Also within Midtown's boundaries (roughly **40th** and **59th Streets, Sixth Avenue**, and the **East River**) are world-class hotels (**The Plaza**, the **Waldorf-Astoria, The Pierre, The St. Regis**), the many art galleries of **East** and **West 57th Street**, and the incomparable **Museum of Modern Art**.

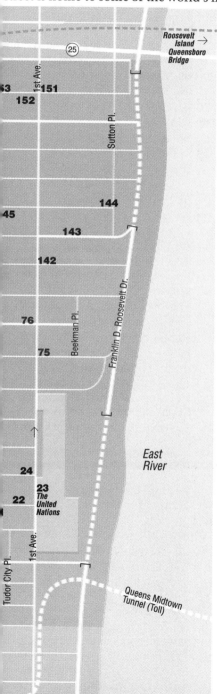

It's a good bet that 90 percent of the people who jam Midtown's streets live elsewhere. But the area is actually a great place to live. The possibilities include the huge **Tudor City** complex overlooking the UN; **Turtle Bay**, with its blocks of brownstone houses in the 50s east of **Third Avenue**; and dozens of pre-war apartment buildings standing proud throughout. **Beekman Place**, two blocks of town houses on **East 49th to East 51st Streets** between **First Avenue** and the East River, is a hidden treasure. **Sutton Place**, a longer residential street above **East 50th Street** along the river, was part of a plan for English-style houses for the well-to-do developed in 1875 by Effingham B. Sutton. Morgans, Vanderbilts, and Phippses, among other notables, lived here.

But it wasn't always that way. When Sutton Place was built, it was in wild territory overlooking what was then called **Blackwell's Island** (now **Roosevelt Island**) in the East River, where the city maintained an almshouse, workhouse, prison, and insane asylum. Although there was a horsecar line running along **Second Avenue** between Fulton and 129th Streets, Sutton's riverfront property was a long way from the mainstream. The neighborhood didn't become "acceptable" until J.P. Morgan's daughter moved here in 1921.

171

Before then, society generally stayed west of **Park Avenue**. In fact, in the 19th century anyone who suggested that **Fourth Avenue** would one day be called Park Avenue would have been laughed out of the city. In 1832, a railroad line was built in the center of the dirt road, and steam trains huffed and puffed their way in and out of New York past squatters' shacks with goats in the front yards and pigs out back.

Little by little roofs were constructed over the tracks, but it wasn't until the present **Grand Central Terminal** was designed in 1903 that anything was done about covering the railroad yards that had grown up between **Madison** and **Lexington Avenues** from **East 42nd** to **East 45th Streets**. When the UN moved into the area in 1947, the cattle pens disappeared and **Midtown East** became a neighborhood in its own right. Luxurious tulip beds in the spring and illuminated Christmas trees in the winter now cover the meridians where those train tracks once ran down Park Avenue.

From the day Fifth Avenue was first established in 1837, the rich and famous began to arrive. Railroad tycoon Jay Gould was one of the first. He built a mansion at **47th Street** and Fifth Avenue and began taking important friends like Russell Sage, Morton F. Plant, and William H. Vanderbilt to business dinners at the nearby **Windsor Hotel**.

By the late 1800s, Vanderbilt had built three mansions on the west side of Fifth Avenue at 51st Street. His son, William K. Vanderbilt, built a fourth palace a few doors uptown. Another son, Cornelius II, tried to upstage them with an even grander house at **58th Street**. In their quest to outdo one another, they ended once and for all the idea of the traditional New York row house with a brownstone front. Who would have thought of living anywhere but on Fifth Avenue in the blocks between 40th and 59th Streets?

Mrs. Astor, that's who. When her husband's nephew, William Waldorf Astor, built a hotel (**The Waldorf**) next to her house on Fifth Avenue at West 33rd Street, she retaliated by tearing down the house and building another hotel next to his (**The Astoria**). Then she built a Renaissance *palazzo* for herself at Fifth Avenue and **East 65th Street**. After her inaugural ball there in 1896, "Millionaire's Row," as Fifth Avenue was called, began moving uptown. (Both of the hotels where eventually destroyed to make room for the **Empire State Building**, and the **Waldorf-Astoria** reopened in its present site at Park Avenue and East 49th Street.)

Only a few reminders of the 19th-century mansions remain on Fifth Avenue, including the one that houses **Cartier** at **East 52nd Street**, which, according to one story, Morton F. Plant traded to Pierre Cartier for a string of pearls. But many of the fine public buildings survive. Houses of worship include such landmarks as **St. Thomas Church**, **St. Patrick's Cathedral**, the Romanesque **St. Bartholomew's Church**, and the vaguely Moorish **Central Synagogue**— the oldest building in the city in continuous use as a synagogue. Secular monuments also remain, such as the vast **New York Public Library** and, of course, **Grand Central Terminal**, which was saved after a long, citizen's battle spearheaded by the late Jacqueline Onassis.

Except for **St. Bartholomew's Church**, the **Waldorf-Astoria Hotel**, and a few more holdouts, today Park Avenue north of **Grand Central Terminal** is wall-to-wall office buildings, including important examples of the "glass box" genre built in the 1950s: the seminal **Seagram Building** by **Ludwig Mies van der Rohe** and **Philip Johnson**, and the **Lever House** by **Skidmore, Owings &**

Merrill. On Park Avenue north of East 57th Street, things turn decidedly residential.

Impressive office buildings and complexes on the other avenues range from the 19 buildings that comprise the Art Deco–period **Rockefeller Center** to the contemporary **Olympic Tower, Citicorp, Sony Plaza,** and **IBM** buildings. Madison Avenue above East 50th Street has seen an office-building boom, but it's Third Avenue in the 20-block strip from **39th Street** to 59th Street that has had the real mega-office building explosion.

Unexpected pockets of distinctive apartment buildings and town houses continue to cling to the side streets of Midtown (**West 54th Street** near the **Museum of Modern Art,** for example). In combination with small parks such as **Greenacre** and **Paley,** they bring greenery and human scale to what might seem at first glance to be a solid concentration of masonry. Nevertheless, despite the relief the parks provide Midtown will always be the place where New York puts all its strength and energies on display.

1 American-Standard Building Originally known as the **American Radiator Building,** this 1923 tower was **Raymond Hood**'s first major project in New York City (he had just won the *Chicago Tribune* commission). He later had his hand in the McGraw-Hill, Daily News, and **Rockefeller Center** buildings. This 21-story midblock high-rise is a stylized variation of the *Tribune* design, with Gothic details tempered by Art Deco lines. Hood used black brick so that the window holes would fade into the sculpted mass and the gold ornamented top would be that much more spectacular. When lit, it has been compared to a glowing coal. The plumbing showroom in the lobby is not part of the original design. ♦ 40 W 40th St (between Fifth and Sixth Aves)

2 Bryant Park The only park in the city designed like a formal garden was named for the poet William Cullen Bryant, a prime mover in the campaign to establish **Central Park** and a champion of the Hudson River School of painters, which established the fashion for wild, naturalistic parks. Before becoming a park, the land was a potter's field, and in 1853 it was the site of America's first **World's Fair,** held in a magnificent domed pavilion of iron and glass known as the **Crystal Palace.** The building stood here until 1858, when it burned to the ground. After the ruins were cleared, the space was used as a parade ground for troops getting ready to defend the Union in the Civil War. When the war was over, it was dedicated as a public park.

In 1934, as the result of a competition to aid unemployed architects, the park was redesigned by **Lusby Simpson,** whose plan was executed under the direction of urban planner Robert Moses. In the Depression years, the area was a gathering spot for the unemployed, and in the 1960s it became a retail space for marijuana peddlers. In 1980, the Bryant Park Restoration Corporation (Hanna/Olin Ltd.) began a massive restoration program, and today the park is a safer, handsomer, and friendlier spot, with new landscaping and lighting, restored monuments, footpaths and benches, food service, and a host of public events. Glamor arrived with the recent decision to stage "Seventh on Sixth," a biannual fashion show where more than 50 American designers present their new lines for the season under big white tents (for press and trade only). A $4.2-million glass and steel pavilion designed by **Hardy Holzman Pfeiffer Associates** houses the **Bryant Park Grill** and the more informal **B.P. Cafe,** which serves seasonal American fare. ♦ Sixth Ave (between W 40th and W 42nd Sts)

Within Bryant Park:

Music & Dance Tickets Booth Stop here for same-day half-price tickets for music and dance performances in all five boroughs. Also available are full-price advance tickets for TicketMaster sports and entertainment events. ♦ Tu-Su noon-2PM, 3-7PM. 382.2323

One of the waiting rooms in Grand Central Station was once known as the "Kissing Gallery" because it was there that travelers who had come long distances were met and kissed by kin and loved ones.

Jacob Walton, the owner of the Gracie Mansion area in 1770, was loyal to the King of England. When the Revolution began, he built a tunnel leading to the East River so he could escape to a waiting ship if necessary. The tunnel wasn't discovered until 1913.

3 W.R. Grace Building Some people actually like this sloping, ski-jump, wind-loading building, but it is generally considered a poor interruption of the street wall. Designed in 1974 by **Skidmore, Owings & Merrill,** it has a barren little plaza on the corner of **West 43rd Street** and Sixth Avenue—an alleged public amenity in exchange for which the developers were allowed extra floors. The architects built an identical structure for a different client at 9 West 57th Street at the same time. ♦ 43 W 42nd St (between Fifth and Sixth Aves)

4 Nat Sherman's The tobacconist to the stars, his specialty is the pure tobacco cigarette wrapped in brown or in such trendy colors as shocking pink, turquoise, or scarlet. He also stocks cigars and Dunhill lighters. ♦ M-Sa. 500 Fifth Ave (at W 42nd St). 246.5500

5 New York Public Library Treat your soul to one of New York's greatest experiences, the sight of the front of this library's **Center for the Humanities,** designed in 1911 at a cost of $9 million by **Carrère & Hastings.** The familiar lions, *Patience* and *Fortitude,* are the work of Edward Clark Potter. But there is much more to see: the bases of the 95-foot-high, tapered steel flagposts (by Thomas Hastings) on the terrace; the lampposts; the balustrades; the urns; the sculpture high above by Paul Bartlett, George G. Barnard, and John Donnelly; and the fountains in front, both by Frederick MacMonnies (the one on the right represents *Truth,* the other *Beauty*). The library was built with the resources of two privately funded libraries, combined in 1895 with the infusion of a $2-million bequest by New York Governor Samuel J. Tilden. John Jacob Astor's library, the first general reference library in the New World, was enhanced by James Lenox's collection of literature, history, and theology. (In 1891, Andrew Carnegie donated $52 million for the establishment of 80 more branches in the New York Public Library system.) This grand building is completely dedicated to research, and none of its more than six million books or 17 million documents can be checked out; so vast is the collection that the original four floors of stacks beneath the building and behind the reading rooms have been supplemented by a new space underneath **Bryant Park,** which can hold up to 92 miles of stacks.

Considered one of the largest research collections in the world, it remains one of the finest examples of Beaux Arts architecture. The main lobby, **Astor Hall,** contains the information desk, the bookshop, and an exhibition area. Marble from floor to ceiling, the hall is lavishly decorated with carved garlands, ribbons, and rosettes. The room directly behind **Astor Hall** is the **Gottesman Exhibition Hall,** which has the most beautiful ceiling in the city. The hall's changing exhibitions are thematic, covering a variety of subjects such as urban history, architecture, and photography. The exhibitions are based on materials drawn from the library's own holdings, demonstrating the richness of the research collections.

W. R. Grace Building

Michael Storrings

Grand Central Terminal

Michael Storrings

The **Third Floor Hall** and the rooms it serves are rich with carved wood panels and vaulted ceilings. The murals, by Edward Lanning, were executed as part of a WPA project. The library's art collection, including paintings by Gilbert Stuart, Sir Joshua Reynolds, and Rembrandt Peale, is displayed in the **Edna B. Salomon Room.** Directly across the hall is **Room 315,** the catalogue room, where you can request books. **Room 315** leads into the **Main Reading Room,** 51 feet high and one-and-a-half blocks long. The room is divided in half by the facilities for delivering books, but the ceiling soars above it all with paintings of blue skies and white clouds and carved scrolls.

The library has been undergoing extensive restoration since 1986 by such design firms as **Davis, Brody & Associates.** One beautifully restored room is the **Celeste Bartos Forum,** distinguished by its 30-foot-high glass dome which rests on steel pillars adorned with Corinthian ornamentation. It is used for lectures, concerts, films, and special events. Free tours meet at the front desk; call ahead for schedule. ♦ Main Reading Room: M-Sa. Tours: M-Sa 11AM, 2PM. Fifth Ave (between W 40th and W 42nd Sts). 661.7220, 930.0800

6 **Quality Inn by Journey's End Hotel** $$$ Ten of this hotel's 189 rooms are specially designed for disabled guests. Priced at the low end of this category, amenities include complimentary morning coffee and newspaper, in-room movies, and laundry and dry-cleaning services. ♦ 3 E 40th St (at Fifth Ave). 447.1500, 800/221.2222; fax 213.0972 ♿

7 **New York Public Library, Mid-Manhattan Branch** This branch, redesigned in 1981 by **Giorgio Cavaglieri,** once housed **Arnold Constable,** the department store that provided trousseaux for fashionable brides in the 1890s (you can see pictures of the brides in the library's collection of microfilm editions of old newspapers.) This library has the largest circulating collection of any of the branch libraries. The ground floor includes a branch of the **Metropolitan Museum**

of Art gift shop. Free tours meet at the ground-floor information desk. ♦ Collections: M-Sa. Tours: M, W, F 2:30PM. 455 Fifth Ave (at E 40th St). 340.0833 ♿

8 **101 Park Avenue** Designed in 1983 by **Eli Attia & Associates,** this speculative tower of black glass rises, angled and tucked, above a granite plaza on an awkward corner. Its slick outline and sheer height, which may be fun from the inside, are somewhat disturbing from the outside. ♦ At E 40th St

9 **New York Astrology Center** The country's largest source of astrology books, healing books, and Tarot cards can be found here. The center also offers computerized and one-on-one horoscope interpretations. ♦ M-Sa. 350 Lexington Ave (between E 39th and E 40th Sts). 947.3603

10 **Philip Morris Headquarters** Ulrich **Frazen & Associates'** light gray granite-clad building, designed in 1983, is a glass box hiding behind a postmodernist/historicist appliqué of Palladian patterns. The main facade, rather oddly, faces the Park Avenue viaduct. The enclosed garden and lobby of the building contains an espresso bar, a gift shop featuring contemporary Native American art, a chocolate shop, a magazine stand, and the **Whitney Midtown,** a satellite exhibition space of the **Whitney Museum of Modern Art.** The museum showcases a permanent sculpture exhibition in a vast, high-ceilinged area, while a smaller, more intimate space houses changing exhibitions of 19th- and 20th-century American art, sometimes relating to Midtown life (paintings by the Ashcan School depicting New York street life, for instance). Gallery talks take place Monday, Wednesday, and Friday at 1PM. The site was originally the home of the **Art Moderne Airlines Building** (built in 1940 by **John B. Peterkin**). ♦ Museum: free. M-F. 120 Park Ave (between E 41st and E 42nd Sts). 878.2550 ♿

11 **Grand Central Terminal** This extraordinary complex (illustrated above) may appear tarnished today, but it is a true jewel

nonetheless (long-awaited and extensive renovations are under way). In 1913, **Reed & Stem**'s designs for the new terminal to replace the **New York Central and Hudson River Railroads' Grand Central Station** were chosen in a competition that included submissions by **Daniel Burnham** and **McKim, Mead & White**. The firm of **Warren & Wetmore** was hired as the associate architect and was largely responsible for the design of the elaborate public structure. **Reed & Stem** and railroad engineer William Wilgus devised the still-efficient multilayered organization of the immense amount of traffic that flows through the terminal: trains (on two levels), subways, cars, and people.

The main, southern facade of the terminal is dominated by Jules Coutan's sculptures of Mercury, Hercules, and Minerva *(Glory of Commerce, Moral Energy, and Mental Energy)*. At the center of the facade is a bronze figure of Commodore Cornelius Vanderbilt, founder of the railroad. The building's other major facade fronts Vanderbilt Avenue and what was a genteel residential neighborhood to the west; the tenements to the east were disregarded. In building the terminal, 32 miles of new tracks were laid, 18,000 tons of steel were used, and 2.8 million cubic yards of earth were excavated.

The inner workings of the terminal are organized around the impressive **Main Concourse.** When entered by way of the arcades from Lexington Avenue, the soaring vault is particularly striking. But the space may be better appreciated as a whole from the marble stairs or the **Cafe** at the Vanderbilt Avenue end. The hall is 160 feet wide, 470 feet long, and 150 feet high at its apogee—larger than the nave of Notre-Dame in Paris. The ceiling, a plaster vault suspended from steel trusses, is decorated with a zodiac representing the constellations of the winter sky. Designed by Paul Helleu, the 2,500 stars used to be lit. They are painted backward—"as God would see it," painter Whitney Warren is reported to have remarked. The floors of the **Main Concourse** are Tennessee marble and the trim is Italian Bottocino marble. The great arched windows are 60 feet tall and 33 feet wide; recently cleaned, they now let in massive amounts of light that augment the artifical light from enormous egg-shaped chandeliers.

The terminal was the centerpiece of a gigantic real-estate development that included eight hotels and 17 office buildings by 1934. When the railroad was forced to electrify, engineer Wilgus realized that if the trains were run underground and the tracks covered over, the air rights could be leased to developers. Thus Park Avenue was born. **Metro North** operates from here; all **Amtrak** service has slowly been relocated to **Penn Station.** Tours are conducted by

the Municipal Art Society for a small fee (883.0009); they meet at the Chemical Bank in the Main Concourse on Wednesday at 12:30PM. ♦ E 42nd St and Park Ave. Train information: 532.4900

Within Grand Central Terminal:

Oyster Bar and Restaurant ★★$$$ Located in the lower level of **Grand Central Station,** this place offers nicely prepared and absolutely fresh seafood, including, of course, a large variety of oysters. For a full meal, take a table in the main dining room, but for a quick bite, try the counter bar next to the dining room, or the slightly more sedate bar through the swinging doors. Due to the tiled, vaulted ceilings, however, the lunch-hour crowd generates megadecibels. ♦ Seafood ♦ M-F lunch and dinner. Reservations recommended. Grand Central Station, Lower level, 42nd St and Park Ave. 490.6650 &

Transit Museum Gift Shop The perfect way to while away a minute or an hour between trains, this modern gift shop celebrates something most Americans and certainly most Manhattanites take for granted: transportation. A host of subway and train-related souvenirs are handsomely displayed beneath a contemporary mural by Brian Cronin. ♦ M-F; Sa mornings. 682.7572

12 Grand Hyatt Hotel $$$ The 1934 **Warren & Wetmore**–designed **Commodore Hotel** was remodeled in 1980 by **Gruzen & Partners,** and is now a bustling commercial hotel reminiscent of Las Vegas with waterfalls and a soaring atrium. Glamorous dining and watering holes are visible from the lobby, including the **Crystal Fountain** and **Sun Garden Restaurant,** which is cantilevered over East 42nd Street. **Trumpets** serves its signature nouvelle American cuisine. The 1,400 rooms are attractive, although some are small, and the hotel is affiliated with a nearby health club, which guests can use for a moderate fee. ♦ E 42nd St (between Lexington and Park Aves). 883.1234, 800/223.1234; fax 697.3772 &

New York traffic engineers have not taken on the project of installing Walk/Don't Walk lights (a.k.a. "ped" lights) on Park Avenue between East 46th and East 56th Streets because of what lies barely eight inches below: the tunnels in and out of Grand Central Station.

Restaurants/Clubs: Red	Hotels: Blue
Shops/♥ Outdoors: Green	Sights/Culture: Black

13 Home Savings of America Resembling a Roman basilica, the main banking room is 160 feet long, 65 feet high, and definitely worth a visit. The walls are limestone and sandstone, and the mosaic floors are French and Italian marble. The building was designed in 1923 by **York & Sawyer.** ♦ 110 E 42nd St (between Lexington and Park Aves). 953.8330

13 Chanin Building The headquarters of the Chanin real-estate empire is an Art Deco triumph built in 1929 by **Sloan & Robertson.** At the third-floor level is an exuberant terra-cotta frieze. The detailing of the lobby is extraordinary, particularly the convector grilles and elevator doors. ♦ 122 E 42nd St (between Lexington and Park Aves). 697.2200

14 Chrysler Building Built by **William Van Alen** in 1929 for the Chrysler Automobile Company, this tower (illustrated at right), which many consider the ne plus ultra of skyscrapers, is an Art Deco monument. The building has many car-oriented decorative elements: abstract friezes depicting automobiles, flared gargoyles at the fourth setback resembling 1929 radiator hood ornaments, and the soaring spire modeled after a radiator grille. The lobby, decorated with African marble and once used as a car showroom, is another Deco treasure. Use the Lexington Avenue entrance and look up at the representation of the building on the ceiling of the lobby, and be sure to peek into an elevator cab. The lighting of the spire at night—with specially fitted lamps inside the triangular windows—was an idea of **Van Alen**'s that was rediscovered and first implemented in 1981. The edifice was briefly the tallest building in the world until surpassed by the **Empire State Building** in 1929. ♦ 405 Lexington Ave (at E 42nd St)

15 Mobil Building The self-cleaning stainless-steel skin on this monolith is 37 thousandths of an inch thick—self-cleaning because the creased panels create wind patterns that scour them. The building was designed by **Harrison & Abramovitz** in 1955. ♦ 150 E 42nd St (between Third and Lexington Aves)

16 New York Helmsley Hotel $$$$ If you are looking for the **Harley Hotel,** this is it. Harry and Leona Helmsley, despite recent financial dificulties, are still the present owners. They have maintained the old-fashioned service in this 788-room property and room service is available around the clock. Other niceties include **Harry's New York Bar** for drinks and **Mindy's Restaurant** for elegant dining. ♦ 212 E 42nd St (between Second and Third Aves). 490.8900, 800/221.4982; fax 986.4792 ♿

16 Daily News Building New York's most successful tabloid relocated in 1995 to larger quarters at 450 West 33rd St. (at Tenth Avenue). Employees wax nostalgic at leaving this clean, purely vertical, undecorated plastic mass that was designed in 1930 by **Howells & Hood,** the pair responsible for the Chicago Tribune Tower (in all its Gothic wonder). The stringent composition even has a flat top—a bold step in 1930. The building tells its own story in the frieze over the entrance and in the lobby, where a globe is the center of an interplanetary geography lesson. (When the globe was first unveiled, it was spinning the wrong way.) The 1958 addition on Second Avenue, by **Harrison & Abramovitz,** is not up to the original. ♦ 220 E 42nd St (between Second and Third Aves)

Michael Storrings

Chrysler Building

17 The Tudor $$$ This renovated property (once notorious for having the smallest rooms in the city) boasts 303 expanded rooms, each with a marble bathroom, trouser press, two-line telephones, and fax and PC ports. Within the hotel are a restaurant, a bar and lounge, meeting rooms, conference and banquet facilities, a business center, and a small health club facility. ♦ 304 E 42nd St (between First and Second Aves). 986.8800, 800/879.8836; fax 986.1758 ♿

18 Tudor City Soaring over East 42nd Street, this Gothic development on its own street was built in 1925 by the **Fred F. French Company** and **H. Douglas Ives**. It comprises 11 apartment buildings, a hotel, shops, a restaurant, a church, and a park. The complex's orientation toward the city seems ill-considered today, but when this enclave was planned, the East River shore below was a wasteland of breweries, slaughterhouses, glue factories, and gasworks. At the turn of the century, the bluff, known as Corcoran's Roost, was the hideout of the infamous Paddy Corcoran and the Rag Gang. Now it provides a good vista of the nearby **UN**. ♦ Bounded by First and Second Aves, and E 40th and E 43rd Sts

19 Ford Foundation Building This 1967 design by **Kevin Roche** and **John Dinkeloo & Associates** is probably the oldest and certainly the richest and least hermetic re-creation of a jungle in New York City. Though the building is small with a rather typical entrance on East 43rd Street, the East 42nd Street side is much more extroverted. It appears as if a container had been opened, leaving the black piers barely restraining an overflowing glass and Cor-Ten steel box of offices that contains a luxuriant park inside a 12-story atrium. Although economically foolhardy and somewhat noisy, this building is handsome and very definitely not to be missed. ♦ 320 E 43rd St (between First and Second Aves). 573.5000 ♿

20 Sichuan Palace ★★$$$ The Chinese menu here is one of the most interesting in the city and popular with **United Nations** delegates. During lunch regulars tend to get preferential service, so if you want more evenhanded treatment, come at dinnertime. Lobster *kew,* chicken with mixed mushrooms, lemon chicken, ginger-and-scallion shrimp, scallops with peppercorn sauce, and crispy fish are all good choices. ♦ Chinese ♦ Daily lunch and dinner. Reservations required for lunch, recommended for dinner. 310 E 44th St (between First and Second Aves). 972.7377

Articles for sale in the United Nations gift shop are duty-free because the UN is not officially in any country. The gift shop offers items from every member nation.

21 UNICEF House Newly renovated, the exhibitions here illustrate the international children's operation in action, highlighting the importance and potential of global cooperation between all races. **The Danny Kaye Center**, housed in the same building, runs *Within Our Reach,* a film about the challenges that face children all over the world. The center's retail shop has an extensive collection of UNICEF cards and gifts. ♦ Free. M-F. 3 UN Plaza (between First and Second Aves). 326.7000

22 United Nations Plaza This combination office building, apartment house, and hotel with a striking glass-curtain wall was designed by **Kevin Roche** and **John Dinkeloo & Associates** in 1976. It was so successful that it was duplicated in 2 UN Plaza, adjoining it to the west, in 1980. ♦ E 44th St (between First and Second Aves)

Within 1 United Nations Plaza:

United Nations Plaza Park Hyatt $$$$ Beginning on the 28th floor of 1 UN Plaza, this contemporary hotel includes 428 rooms, a lounge and restaurant, and a swimming pool and health club with a dazzling view. Complimentary limousine service to Wall Street, the Garment District, and theaters is also available, though the majority of diplomat guests need only stroll across the street for their day's business appointments. ♦ 758.1234, 800/228.9000; fax 702.5051 ♿

Within the United Nations Plaza Park Hyatt:

Ambassador Grill Restaurant ★$$$ New chef Matthew Mitnitsky is revitalizing this old-fashioned mirrored dining room within the **Park Hyatt Hotel** with dishes such as roasted corn and crab timbale, grilled prawns with mushroom linguine and soy-wasabi dressing, and roulade of chicken on parmesan-herb orzo with baby asparagus. ♦ American ♦ M-Sa lunch and dinner; Su brunch and dinner. Reservations recommended. 702.5014

23 The United Nations (UN) This complex (illustrated top right) was designed in 1952 by an international committee of 12 globally renowned architects that included **Le Corbusier** of France, **Oscar Niemeyer** of Brazil, and **Sven Markelius** of Sweden; the committee was headed by American **Wallace K. Harrison**. The site—once the actual Turtle Bay where the Saw Kill ran into the East River—was a run-down area with slaughterhouses, light industry, and a railroad barge landing when John D. Rockefeller Jr. donated the money to purchase the land for the project. The complex, an enclave apart from the city (it is considered international and not American territory) and in formal contrast to it, has had tremendous influence on its surroundings as well as on the direction of architecture.

United Nations

Michael Storrings

Housing the staff bureaucracy, the 39-story **Secretariat** was New York's first building with all-glass walls (these are suspended between side slabs of Vermont marble), and is the only example that approaches the tower-in-the-park urban ideal of the 1940s. (To make way for the **UN** building, the city diverted the traffic on First Avenue into a tunnel under UN Plaza and created a small landscaped park, **Dag Hammarskjold Plaza.**) Measuring 544 feet high and 72 feet wide, this anonymously faced building is a remarkable sight seen broadside from East 43rd Street, where it was set in deliberate opposition to the city grid. The General Assembly meets in the limestone-clad, flared white building to the north under the dome.

Visitors enter through the north side of the **General Assembly Building** at East 45th Street. Outside, flags of all 184 member nations fly in alphabetical order at equal height, the same order in which delegates are seated in the General Assembly. More than a million visitors come here every year to see the physical presence of this forum of nations,

but also in search of the elusive spirit of peace it symbolizes. Taking a tour is a good idea if you want to explore more than the grounds (don't miss the gardens) and the Chagall stained-glass windows in the lobby of the **General Assembly Building.** But don't expect to witness more than real estate if the General Assembly isn't in session (regular sessions are from the third Tuesday in September through mid-December).

The United Nations has a peace garden that boasts more than 1,000 rose bushes.

New York is the only American city to house an American embassy, the United States Mission, located across the street from the United Nations.

Between March and August of 1946, 26 sessions of the United Nations Security Council were held in the Hunter College gymnasium in the Bronx. Other locations used included a building on the East River and another in Lake Success on Long Island.

Tours, conducted by young people from around the world, steer large groups through the elegant **Assembly Hall** (note the Léger paintings on the walls); the **Secretariat Building**; and the **Conference Building,** which houses media, support systems, and meeting rooms, including the **Security Council Chamber** (donated by Norway), the **Trusteeship Council Chamber** (donated by Denmark), and the **Economic and Social Council Chamber** (donated by Sweden). But you can find out more about how the organization actually functions by witnessing the public part of the UN's business as it takes place in the **General Assembly.** Tours of the General Assembly end at the basement **UN Gift Shop,** a great souvenir source with interesting hand-crafted gifts representing all 184 member nations. Special events in 1995-1996 are scheduled to celebrate the 50th anniversary of the signing of the UN Charter. ♦ Admission. Tours daily 9:15AM-4:45PM. E 45th St and First Ave. General information: 963.1234; group tours: 963.4440; tours: 963.7713; gift shop: 963.7700

Within The United Nations:

Delegates' Dining Room ★★$$$
The **UN** dining room is open to the public for lunch during the week. It offers a very good international luncheon buffet with a choice of 22 dishes, in addition to an à la carte menu that includes asparagus with lemon vinaigrette, lobster salad, and barbecued salmon. Try the chocolate terrine or frozen-raspberry soufflé for dessert. Wines of a specific nation are also offered monthly. The view of the East River is the best of any restaurant in Manhattan. ♦ Continental ♦ M-F lunch. Reservations required; jacket required. UN Conference Building (E 45th St at First Ave). 963.7625

24 International Education Information Center The information center is for foreign nationals interested in studying in the United States, and US nationals who wish to study abroad. Staffed primarily by volunteers, the center provides guidebooks, brochures, and university catalogs, as well as materials describing scholarships, internships, and teaching opportunities. ♦ Tu-Th. 809 UN Plaza (between E 45th and E 46th Sts). 984.5413

25 Palm ★★$$$$ This venerable dining room (opened in 1926) serves huge prime cuts and addictive cottage-fried potatoes. The serious carnivores who come here don't seem to mind the close and chaotic premises, the long wait for a table, or the surly, often rushed service. Across the street is its younger sibling (only 20 years old), **Palm Too** (697.5198); it has sawdust on the floor unlike the original. ♦ Steak house ♦ M-F lunch and dinner; Sa dinner. Reservations required. 837 Second Ave (between E 44th and E 45th Sts). 687.2953

26 Captain's Table ★$$$ Come here for superb fresh fish offered in a variety of preparations—halibut with aioli, grilled red snapper, and breaded shrimp with hot peppers and mozzarella, for example. There's also a separate market section where you can buy fresh fish to take home. ♦ Seafood ♦ M-F lunch and dinner; Sa dinner. Reservations recommended. 860 Second Ave (at E 46th St). 697.9538

Studio Shoo-Ins: How to Get TV Tickets

New York is headquarters for a variety of major TV shows and talk shows that the public can attend without charge. Although most tickets must be obtained in advance, many programs offer standby seats (policies vary, so call ahead). Lines for standby seats often form hours in advance, particularly when well-known guests are booked.

The following addresses for written ticket requests do not always reflect the location of the studio or the place where standby tickets are distributed. Audience members must be 18 or older. Request tickets by postcard unless otherwise indicated, and specify which show you want to see and the number of seats.

Asking for a certain day or week is discouraged. But if you will only be visiting New York for a short time and you send in your request a few months in advance, most studios will try to accommodate you, usually permitting two to four tickets per postcard. Even if you don't stipulate a specific date, it can take a few months to receive tickets for the more popular shows.

Rolando Corujo

Geraldo (CBS)
CBS
524 W 57th St
New York, NY 10019
212/265.1283

Tapings take place Tuesday through Thursday
at 1PM and 3PM. For ticket requests for up to
10 people, call the above number or send a letter
with a stamped, self-addressed envelope; expect
a one-month wait. Standby tickets are sometimes
available at 530 West 57th Street, one hour before
taping.

Late Night with Conan O'Brian (NBC)
NBC
30 Rockefeller Plaza
New York, NY 10112
212/644.3056

David Letterman's successor accepts postcards
requesting no more than two tickets and will not
accommodate specific dates. The show is taped
Monday to Friday at 5:30PM; a limited number of
standby tickets (one per person) are distributed at
9AM in NBC's main lobby; entry isn't guaranteed.

The Late Show with David Letterman (CBS)
Dave Letterman Tickets
1697 Broadway
New York, NY 10019
212/975.2476

"The Late Show," taped Monday through Friday
at 5:30PM, is one of the hottest tickets in town—
expect a three- to four-month wait. One hundred
standby tickets are distributed weekdays at noon,
though the line forms as early as 9AM on days
when important guests are scheduled. Two tickets
are allotted for each postcard.

Live with Regis and Kathie Lee (ABC)
"Live" Tickets
Ansonia Station
PO Box 777
New York, NY 10023
212/456.3537

This talk show broadcasts Monday through Friday
at 9AM. Request up to four tickets per postcard,
but be prepared to wait—about eight to 10 months.
Standby tickets are available after ticket-holders
are seated each weekday; the line usually starts
forming around 7:30AM at the studio, 7 Lincoln
Square (at West 67th Street and Columbus
Avenue).

The Rush Limbaugh Show (Independent)
Unitel Studios, 515 W 57th St
New York, NY 10019
212/397.7367

The show is taped Monday through Thursday
at 5:30PM. Tickets can only be requested by
phone: Call Monday to Thursday from 10AM to
1PM. There is usually a three-month wait, although
tickets from last-minute cancellations are often
available by phone.

Sally Jessy Raphael (NBC)
"Sally Jessy Raphael" Tickets
PO Box 1400
Radio City Station
New York, NY 10101
212/582.1722

Tapings are scheduled Monday through Thursday
at 11AM. Each request can yield up to six tickets,
with a usual two- to three-month wait. For standby,
show up at 10AM at the studio at 515 West 57th
Street.

Saturday Night Live (NBC)
"Saturday Night Live" Tickets
NBC
30 Rockefeller Plaza
New York, NY 10112
212/664.3056

A ticket lottery is held each year at the end of
August; only postcards (two tickets each) sent
in August will be accepted. Since the majority
of each audience fills up with network associates,
advertisers, and their families and friends, few
seats make it to the lottery. Winners are seated
on Saturday at 8PM for a dress rehearsal and
11:30PM for the live taping. On Saturday morning,
50 standby tickets for each of these seatings are
distributed at 9:15AM at NBC at the 49th Street
entrance of Rockefeller Plaza. One person is
admitted per ticket, although holding a ticket does
not guarantee admission. Fans have been known to
camp out overnight for tickets when a popular host
is scheduled.

Other popular shows taped in New York City

Gordon Elliot Show (Fox)
524 W 57th St
New York, NY 10019
212/975.8540

Shows are taped Wednesday through Friday at noon
and 3PM.

Jon Stewart Show
226 W 26th St, Fourth floor
New York, NY 10001
212/807.5300

Shows are taped Monday through Friday from 6 to
7PM.

Montel Williams (Fox)
356 W 58th St
New York, NY 10019
212/560.3003

Shows are taped Thursday and Friday at 10AM,
1PM, and 3PM.

Ricki Lake Show
401 Fifth Ave, Fifth floor
New York, NY 10016
212/889.7091

Shows are taped Monday through Friday at
scheduled times.

27 Annabelle ★$$$ Fusion is the cooking style here, where Parisian chef Jean-Christophe Michel creates such enticing dishes as smoked salmon mounded over bean sprouts, sautéed foie gras with caramelized pears, wild striped bass with Cabernet sauce, and medaillons of lamb with eggplant caviar. ♦ French ♦ M-F lunch; M-Sa dinner. Reservations recommended. 890 Second Ave (between E 47th and E 48th Sts). 486.2560

28 Sparks ★★$$$$ As at the other great steak houses, excellent cuts of beef and fresh seafood are cooked to order here. But what makes this place different is the exceptional wine list—the extraordinary selection and fair prices make it a must for oenophiles. ♦ Steak house ♦ M-F lunch and dinner; Sa dinner. Reservations required. 210 E 46th St (between Second and Third Aves). 687.4855

29 Pen & Pencil ★$$$$ A gracious, wood-paneled old-timer, this place served beef downstairs and gin upstairs during Prohibition, and got its name from the artists, journalists, and writers who showed up for both. Today, the restaurant feels a bit stuffy and old-fashioned, but the capable kitchen still turns out adequate meals of steak, rack of lamb, and chicken paillard. ♦ Steak house ♦ M-F lunch and dinner; Sa-Su dinner. 205 E 45th St (between Second and Third Aves). 682.8660

an American Restaurant

30 Colors ★$$$ The menu flies the colors of many nations with its internationally inspired offerings, including such specialties as lobster *tartare* with tarragon and endive, saffron soup with clams and sea scallops, braised veal shank, baked salmon with a pepper crust, and curried grilled swordfish— although these dishes tend to sound better than they taste. The wine list is extensive and features some Swiss varieties, as well as American and French labels. ♦ Continental ♦ M-F lunch and dinner, Sa dinner. Reservations recommended. 237 Park Ave (entrance on E 46th St). 661.2000

31 The Helmsley Building Designed in 1929 by **Warren & Wetmore,** this fanciful tower was originally the **New York Central Building,** then **New York General.** An example of creative, sensitive urban design, it was a lively addition to the architects' own **Grand Central Terminal** and the hotels that surrounded it. Built above two levels of railroad tracks, it essentially "floats" on its foundations—those inside feel nary a vibration. The gold-leafed building is worth a special viewing at night. Pause to appreciate the distinct separation of automobile and pedestrian traffic in the street-level arcades, and stop for a look at the wonderful Rococo lobby. ♦ 230 Park Ave (between E 45th and E 46th Sts)

Within The Helmsley Building:

Snaps ★★$$ Modern and yellow with brown hanging sculptures and yellow-and-brown drapes, this dining room bustles at lunchtime and is just slightly more subdued at dinner. Try the blini tart (three levels of blini, smoked salmon, Matjes herring, and salty fish roe); one of the open-faced sandwiches, particularly gravlax with mustard sauce; or salmon burger with beet-horseradish crème fraîche. A nicely priced prix-fixe dinner is offered all evening. ♦ Scandinavian ♦ M-F breakfast, lunch, and dinner; Sa dinner. Reservations recommended. 949.7878

32 Metropolitan Life Building Formerly the **Pan Am Building,** this 59-story monolith set indelicately between the **Helmsley Building** and **Grand Central Terminal** started in 1963 as a purely speculative venture and became the largest commercial office building ever built, with 2.4 million square feet. Art in the lobby includes a mural by Josef Albers and a space sculpture by Richard Lippold. The shape of the tower is supposedly derived from an airplane wing section. The architects were **Emery Roth & Associates, Pietro Belluschi,** and **Walter Gropius.** Bauhaus founder and High Modernist, Gropius could have done better. ♦ 200 Park Ave (between E 44th and E 45th Sts)

Within the Metropolitan Life Building:

TROPICA
Bar and Seafood House

Tropica ★★$$$ At lunchtime, it's a capacity crowd with a corresponding noise level. At night, though, the hubbub recedes and chef Fred Sabo shows off creative seafood preparations to an appreciative audience. Try crab cakes with mustard beurre blanc; barbecued shrimp with Szechuan peppercorns; conch chowder; and grilled red snapper with cashew-basmati rice, avocado, and tropical fruit chutney. ♦ Regional American/Tropical ♦ M-F lunch and dinner. Ground level. 867.6767 ♿

Cafe Centro ★★$$$ This $5-million brasserie with marble inlay floors, gold-leaf columns, and etched Lalique-style chandeliers is reminiscent of the grand cafes in European train stations. Try the roast chicken cooked to perfection in one of the rotisseries enclosed within the massive stone fireplace near the entrance. It's the only place in New York to get an Amberly—a French brew made from whiskey malt instead of the usual barley and hops. ♦ American/French ♦ M-F lunch and dinner; Sa dinner. Reservations recommended. Ground level. 818.1222 ♿

Metropolitan Life Building

Michael Storrings

33 Takesushi ★★$$$$ The long lines during lunch attest to the fact that this is one of the more popular sushi bars in the city; come after 5:30PM to avoid the crowd. ♦ Japanese ♦ M-F lunch and dinner; Sa dinner. Reservations required. 71 Vanderbilt Ave (at E 45th St). 867.5120

34 The Yale Club In a neighborhood crowded with clubs waving the old school tie, this one boasts easy access to trains headed to New Haven for the over-nostalgic. The building was designed in 1913 by **James Gamble Rogers.** Only Yalies are allowed in; a handful of rooms are available for their overnight use. ♦ 50 Vanderbilt Ave (between E 44th and E 45th Sts). 661.2070

35 Worth & Worth Hat lovers know top quality when they see it, and it doesn't get any better in the city. The staff is knowledgeable, patient, and friendly, and the merchandise ranges from classic to cutting-edge. ♦ M-Sa. 331 Madison Ave (between E 42nd and E 43rd Sts). 867.6058 ♿

36 Orvis Fishing equipment and gear, a wide selection of books on such topics as fly-fishing, trout streams, and duck decoys, and outdoor clothing and accessories that complement the country way of life are sold. ♦ M-Sa. 355 Madison Ave (entrance on E 45th St). 697.3133

37 The Roosevelt Hotel $$ Built in 1924 by **George M. Post,** this old hotel was prestigious when railroads were the main form of transportation and the location near **Grand Central** was highly valued. Popular with those doing business nearby, its newly renovated 1,031-soundproof rooms have received a much-needed facelift. The staff is multilingual. A bar and a lobby lounge are located within the hotel. ♦ 45 E 45th St (at Madison Ave). 661.9600, 800/223.1870; fax 687.5064

38 Paul Stuart Classic, well-made clothing for the conservative gentleman (and -woman) is the specialty. Look for jackets and suits in herringbone, Shetland, and tweed; handknit sweaters in alpaca, cashmere, and Shetland wool; and shirts of Sea Island cotton. Women have a reasonable niche to themselves on the mezzanine level, where there are tailored skirted suits, Shetland sweaters, and cotton shirts. If you're not the one shopping, a 17th-century Flemish tapestry and comfortable leather chairs make waiting quite pleasant. ♦ Daily. E 45th St (at Madison Ave). 682.0320 ♿

Restaurants/Clubs: Red	**Hotels:** Blue
Shops/ ♥ Outdoors: Green	**Sights/Culture:** Black

39 Brooks Brothers The home of the Ivy League look—the natural-shoulder sack suit, worn with an oxford cloth shirt and silk rep tie—this store is an American institution. Founded in 1818, it is the country's oldest menswear shop, and continues to offer traditional, conservative clothing. Some styles have become classics, such as the trench coats, Shetland sweaters, oxford cloth shirts, and bathrobes of soft wool and cotton. Boys can choose from shirts, slacks, and sweaters; and women will find a feminine version of all the above on the fifth floor. ♦ M-Sa. 346 Madison Ave (at E 44th St). 682.8800 ♿

40 Zen Oriental Bookstore Most of the books and magazines are in Japanese. Those in English cover Buddhism and Zen, Japanese language, history, society, and literature, Japanese and Zen cooking, origami, and bonsai. There's even a guide to job hunting in Japan. ♦ M-Sa. 521 Fifth Ave (between E 43rd and E 44th Sts). 697.0840 ♿

41 Chikubu ★★★$$$ This plainly decorated restaurant caters to a mostly Japanese clientele and is a good place for the delicate dishes of Kyoto. Specialties include *akabeko-ju* (rice with thin slices of grilled beef and broiled baby flounder) and *omakase* (a tasting menu of seven to eight courses). ♦ Japanese ♦ M-F lunch and dinner; Sa dinner. Reservations recommended. 12 E 44th St (between Madison and Fifth Aves). 818.0715

42 J. Press This clothier has been dressing Ivy League men in well-made classics and calico patchwork shorts and slacks since 1902. ♦ M-Sa. 7 E 44th St (between Madison and Fifth Aves). 687.7642 ♿

43 Fred F. French Building The colorful glazed tiles in the tower call out from across the street. Answer the call; the lobby is a stunner. The building was designed in 1927 by **Fred F. French Company** and **H. Douglas Ives.** ♦ 551 Fifth Ave (at E 45th St)

Within the Fred F. French Building:

Morton's of Chicago ★★★$$$ With all of the wonderful steak houses in New York, especially in this part of town, the sad truth is that this arrival from Chicago tops them all. The extra-thick, extra-aged, extra-tender porterhouse led *New York Magazine* in 1994 to name this the best place for steak, a title shared with Brooklyn's historic **Peter Luger's.** The chicken and seafood dishes are just as delicious. ♦ Steak house ♦ M-F lunch and dinner; Sa-Su dinner. Reservations recommended. Entrance on E 45th St. 972.3315

44 Chemical Bank This 1954 edifice was the first bank to depart from the tradition of rock-solid architecture, and just to make sure potential customers would recognize it as a bank, architects **Skidmore, Owings & Merrill**

put the safe in the window. ♦ 510 Fifth Ave (at W 43rd St). 997.0770 ♿

45 Century Association McKim, Mead & White designed this 1891 Palladian clubhouse for men of achievement in arts and letters (**McKim** and **Mead** were members), which is not open to the public. The large window above the entrance was originally a loggia. ♦ 7 W 43rd St (between Fifth and Sixth Aves). 944.0090

46 Mansfield $$ With 131 rooms, this is the largest and the newest of the Gotham Hospitality Group (The **Shoreham,** the **Franklin,** and the **Wales**), which guarantees that their small hotels are big on style. A few steps off Fifth Avenue and an easy stroll to most Broadway theaters, location is an important draw but so is the recent top-to-toe renovation. ♦ 12 W 44th St (between Fifth and Sixth Aves). 944.6050; fax 764.4477

47 General Society Library of Mechanics and Tradesmen More than 140,000 books of fiction, nonfiction, and history are stocked in this private library. The comfortable, elegant surroundings are worth the low membership fee. Within the library are the **Small Press Center,** a nonprofit facility exhibiting books by independent publishers, and the *John M. Mossman Collection of Locks,* where 375 different locks—antique padlocks, powder-proof key locks, and friction locks—are on display. ♦ M-F; closed July. 20 W 44th St (between Fifth and Sixth Aves). 840.1840

48 Hotel Royalton $$$$ This hotel's block-long lobby is the setting for an ultra-dramatic space (cognac mahogany and green-gray slate) by French designer Philippe Starck. The front desk is discreetly tucked away, as is the bar, patterned after Hemingway's favorite at the Paris Ritz. The **Round Bar** is forever full of networking hipsters, and the 167 rooms, many with working fireplaces, are on the cutting edge of modern design and comfort. Amenities include daily newspaper delivery, Kiehl shampoos and bathcubes, and valet parking. The original structure, built in 1898 by **Ehrick Rossiter,** was renovated in 1988 by **Gruzen, Samton, Steinglass.** ♦ 44 W 44th St (between Fifth and Sixth Aves). 869.4400, 800/635.9013; fax 869.8965 ♿

Within the Hotel Royalton:

Restaurant 44 ★★$$$ Philippe Starck's minimalist decor—beige walls, furniture with clean modern lines, a hanging horizontal mirror—is just one of the draws at this dining room. Another is the American nouvelle cuisine created by chef Geoffrey Zakarian. Try the chamomile-cured salmon with *frisée* (curly endive) and pepper crisps, the preserved duck leg on warm spinach salad, the roasted quail with cheese- and mushroom-laced orzo, the striped bass with warm fennel, and the rare duck breast. Top the meal off with the lemon tart or Valrhona chocolate soufflé. ♦ American ♦ M-F breakfast, lunch, and dinner; Sa-Su brunch and dinner. Reservations required. 944.8844

49 The Algonquin Hotel $$$ Built in 1902 by **Goldwyn Starrett,** this hotel was a gathering place for literary types even before the famous Round Table of such writers as Alexander Woollcott, Robert Benchley, and Dorothy Parker began meeting regularly in the **Rose Room.** What the Round Table members had in common, besides their razor-sharp wit, was that they were contributors to *The New Yorker,* whose offices at 25 West 43rd Street conveniently open into the hotel at West 44th Street. Few nearby places are as comfortable as the hotel's lobby, where you can summon a cocktail with the ringing of a bell. Guests find all the comforts and friendliness of a country inn here. (Of the 165 rooms, visiting writers favor Room 306, a suite whose walls are adorned with *Playbill* magazine covers.) ♦ 59 W 44th St (between Fifth and Sixth Aves). 840.6800, 800/548.0345; fax 944.1419 &

Within The Algonquin Hotel:

Oak and Rose Rooms ★$$$ The dark paneling in the **Oak Room** contrasts with the brighter **Rose Room.** But the menu is the same in both, and the quality doesn't vary. The plate-size apple pancake topped with tart lingonberries is a perfect after-theater snack. **The Oak Room** provides supper club entertainment after 8PM from Tuesday through Saturday. ♦ American ♦ Daily breakfast, lunch, and dinner. Reservations recommended. 840.6800

49 The New York Yacht Club This unusually fanciful, sculptured work was the creation of **Warren & Wetmore** in 1899. The highlight of the eccentric facade are the sailing-ship sterns in the three window bays, complete with ocean waves and dolphins. The setback above the cornice used to be a pergola. This was the home of **The America's Cup** from 1857 to 1983, when it was lost to Australia (San Diego reclaimed it in 1987). ♦ 37 W 44th St (between Fifth and Sixth Aves). 382.1000

50 The Harvard Club The interior of this 1894 Georgian-style building by **McKim, Mead & White** is much more impressive than its facade indicates. If you're not a **Harvard** alum, go around the block and see it through the magnificent window in back. If you are a

club member, 60 rooms are available for your use. ♦ 27 W 44th St (between Fifth and Sixth Aves). 840.6600

51 Via Brasil ★★$$ This is the best place to sample *feijoada,* the national dish, a hearty, delicious stew of black beans, sausage, beef, bacon, and pork served on rice that's perfect on a blustery winter day. Or you might want to try one of the lighter grilled meat or poultry dishes, such as *frango ma brasa* (char-broiled breast of chicken). Down your meal with a *caipirinha,* the potent national drink made of rumlike *cachaça,* fresh lime juice, sugar, and ice. Diners are regaled with live music all evening, Wednesday through Saturday, and there's no cover charge. ♦ Brazilian ♦ Daily lunch and dinner. Reservations recommended. 34 W 46th St (between Fifth and Sixth Aves). 997.1158

52 Wentworth $ This modest, renovated Art Deco hotel has 195 comfortable rooms with color TVs, air-conditioning, and all the modern amenities (though no restaurant). Gem-loving guests will like the location next door to the **Jewelry Exchange,** where 60 dealers offer treasures like those sold in the nearby **Diamond Center** on West 47th Street. ♦ 59 W 46th St (between Fifth and Sixth Aves). 719.2300, 800/223.1900; fax 768.3477 &

53 Gotham Book Mart & Gallery Founded by Frances Steloff in 1920, this bookstore has long been a mecca for New York City's literati; Theodore Dreiser, Eugene O'Neill, George Gershwin, and Charlie Chaplin all shopped here. Today, this New York equivalent to Paris's Shakespeare & Company is a bibliophile's heaven: a messy hodgepodge of books, mostly literature (especially 20th century), poetry, drama, art, and literary journals as well as small press and used and rare books. In the upstairs gallery, you'll find changing art exhibitions, including a summer show of vintage postcards from the extensive collection of the store's owner, Andy Brown. ♦ M-F, Su. 41 W 47th St (between Fifth and Sixth Aves). 719.4448

New York City hosts the consulates or missions of 125 nations.

Since 1931, the Rockefeller Center Christmas tree has been one of New York City's most beloved traditions. Today, the chosen tree is decorated with more than 27,000 7½-watt, multicolored bulbs on five miles of wire. It takes 15 to 20 people and an 80-ton crane to erect and move the tree. Since 1971, all trees have been recycled: The mulch is used for trails at a Boy Scout camp in New Jersey.

Rockefeller Center

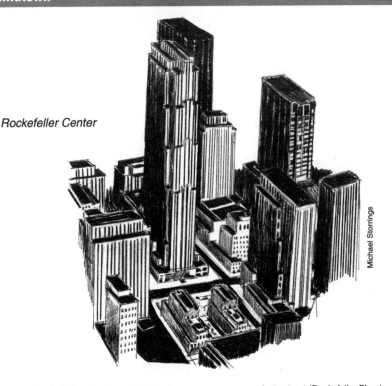

Michael Storrings

54 Rockefeller Center This is the largest privately owned business and entertainment complex in the world, with 19 buildings covering 21 acres (see above). It all began in 1928 when John D. Rockefeller Jr. secured leases on land in the area to provide a setting for the **Metropolitan Opera House,** which was going to move here from the Garment Center. The Great Depression changed the opera's plans and left the philanthropist with a long-term lease on 11.7 acres of Midtown Manhattan. He decided to develop it himself, and demolition of 228 buildings to make way for the project began in May 1931. The last of Rockefeller's original 14 buildings, the **Paramount Publishing Building** at 1230 Sixth Avenue, was opened in April 1940. Construction started again in 1957, when Marilyn Monroe detonated the first charge of dynamite to begin excavation for the **Time & Life Building,** designed by **Harrison & Abramovitz,** at 1271 Sixth Avenue. Since then, the building at 1211 Sixth Avenue and the **McGraw-Hill Building** at 1251 Sixth Avenue, also by **Harrison & Abramovitz,** have been added along Sixth Avenue.

The original complex was designed by **Associated Architects,** a committee made up of **Reinhard & Hoffmeister; Corbett, Harrison and MacMurray;** and **Hood and Fouilhoux.** At its head, representing the Rockefeller interests, was John R. Todd of Todd, Robertson & Todd Engineering Corp. Their ideas included a north-south, midblock private street (Rockefeller Plaza) between West 48th and West 51st Streets, underground pedestrian and shopping passageways connecting all the buildings, and off-street freight delivery 30 feet underground, capable of handling a thousand trucks a day. The art that enhances the lobbies and exteriors is the work of 30 of the finest artists of the century. The crown jewel of the original **Rockefeller Center** complex is the 70-story **GE Building** (formerly the **RCA Building**), at 1256 Avenue of the Americas. Todd told the architects that no desk anywhere in the building should be more than 30 feet from a window. They obliged him by placing all the rentable space no farther than 28 feet from natural light. About one quarter of the available space has been left open—unusual for an urban development—and much of it has been landscaped. The complex's gardeners are kept busy with more than 20,000 flowering plants that are moved periodically, as well as two acres of formal gardens on the rooftop. A complete description of the buildings can be found in a walking tour guide available free at the information desk in the lobby at 30 Rockefeller Plaza. A free exhibition chronicling the history of the center through photographs, models, an 11-minute video presentation, and period memorabilia is located on the concourse level of 30 Rockefeller Plaza. ♦ Bounded by Fifth and Sixth Aves, and W 48th and W 51st Sts. 632.3975

At Rockefeller Center:

Radio City Music Hall Since 1932, this Art Deco palace has maintained a tradition of spectacular entertainment. When it opened as a variety house operated by entrepreneur Roxy Rothafel, it was the largest theater in the world and included such features as a 50-foot turntable on the 110-foot stage, sections of which changed level, 75 rows of fly lines for scenery, a network of microphones, six motor-operated light bridges, a cyclorama 117 feet by 75 feet, and a host of other controls and effects. The scale was overwhelming. "What are those mice doing on stage?" someone asked on opening night. "Those aren't mice, those are horses," his neighbor replied.

The opening of the hall in December 1932 drew such celebrities as Charlie Chaplin, Clark Gable, Amelia Earhart, and Arturo Toscanini. The premiere performance had 75 stellar acts, including Ray Bolger, **The Wallendas,** and the **Roxyettes** (later known as the **Rockettes**).

The hall was soon turned into a movie house with stage shows, featuring the **Rockettes,** the **Corps de Ballet,** the **Symphony Orchestra,** and a variety of guest artists. The premiere feature film was Frank Capra's *The Bitter Tea of General Yen* with Barbara Stanwyck. From 1933 until 1979, more than 650 features debuted here, including *King Kong, It Happened One Night, Jezebel, Top Hat, Snow White and the Seven Dwarfs, An American in Paris,* and *Mister Roberts.* In 1979, a new format was introduced. Musical spectaculars, special film showings, and pop personalities in concert are the current bill of fare, with major names such as Frank Sinatra, Bette Midler, and Stevie Wonder performing to sold-out audiences. The 57 **Rockettes** still make an annual appearance during the traditional Christmas and Easter shows (35 or so will appear on stage at any one time). Since the theater's opening night on 27 December 1932, nearly 2,000 **Rockettes** have high-kicked their way across the 144-foot stage.

The 5,882-seat hall was awarded landmark status and completely restored in 1979. The public areas, designed largely by **Donald Deskey,** are grand: A plush foyer rises 50 feet, overlooked by a sweeping stair and three mezzanine levels lined with gold mirrors and topped by a gold-leaf ceiling. The restrooms retain much of their fine Deco detailing—tilework, trim, and fixtures—although most of the original art is gone. (A painting by Stuart Davis that once hung in a men's room is now at the **Museum of Modern Art.**) The auditorium is a plaster vault of overlapping semicircles lit from the inside edge in a rainbow of colors provides sunsets and sunrises as the lights go down and up.

♦ Tours: fee. Tours: M-Sa 10AM-5PM; Su 11AM-5PM. 1250 Ave of the Americas (between W 50th and W 51st Sts). 247.4777

NBC Studio Tours Tours of the radio and television facilities of the **National Broadcasting Co.** are offered. Depending on shooting schedules, you might visit the "Donohue" or "Saturday Night Live" sets. Children under six are not admitted. If you don't want to wait in line, walk over to West 49th and Rockefeller Plaza and see if you can catch sight of Katie Kouric and Bryant Gumbel who do the "Today Show," live from their street level picture-window studio. ♦ Admission. Daily. 30 Rockefeller Plaza (between W 49th and W 50th Sts). 664.4000 ♿

The Rink at Rockefeller Center The summertime outdoor restaurant (see the **American Festival Cafe**) becomes an ice-skating rink every October, staying slick and smooth right through April. Ice skates can be rented at the rink. ♦ Admission; additional fee for skate rental. Daily. Call for changing sessions. Lower Plaza. 757.5730

Librairie de France and Librería Hispanica (French and European Publications) This bookstore provides one of the best—albeit expensive—selections of books in French and in English about France, with a smaller offering of Spanish books. ♦ M-Sa. 610 Fifth Ave (between W 49th and W 50th Sts). 581.8810 ♿

Teuscher Chocolates of Switzerland Selling some of the city's best (and most expensive) chocolate bonbons, the window displays here are whimsical and change with the season. ♦ M-Sa. 620 Fifth Ave (between W 49th and W 50th Sts). 246.4416 ♿

Metropolitan Museum of Art Gift Shop At three floors and 6,000 square feet, this is the largest of the museum's nine gift shop outposts. The merchandise, for the most part inspired by the museum's permanent collections and special exhibitions, includes prints and posters, stationery, jewelry, tabletop accessories, sculpture reproductions, and educational gifts for children. Especially popular are the museum's signature items, which include *William,* a reproduction of the 12th-dynasty Egyptian hippo (the **Met**'s unofficial mascot); and Venus earrings, one black and one white teardrop, worn by the goddess in Rubens's *Venus Before the Mirror.* ♦ Daily. 15 W 49th St (between Fifth and Sixth Aves) 332.1380

The Sea Grill

The SeaGrill ★★★$$$$ Fresh seafood is served in a lush setting of cherrywood and rich fabrics. A favorite is the Baltimore crab cakes served with a stone-ground mustard and scallion sauce, and the buttery salmon with a dijon-mustard and roasted-shallot sauce. Nonfish dishes are available too. Try one of the delectable desserts, including chocolate steamed pudding with Valrhona chocolate sauce. ♦ Seafood ♦ M-F lunch and dinner; Sa dinner. Reservations required. 19 W 49th St (at Rockefeller Plaza). 246.9201 ⑅

American Festival Cafe
at Rockefeller Plaza

American Festival Cafe ★$$$ The modern wood booths and minimal decor at this eatery are enhanced by the view through the glass wall that overlooks the skating rink, making this an atmospheric, if expensive, place to stop for a lunchtime burger, Cobb salad, or excellent crab cakes. The dinner menu offers a large and very good prime rib, and various poultry and fish dishes. A good selection of microbrewery beers is featured, but skip dessert. ♦ American ♦ M-F breakfast, lunch, and dinner; Sa-Su brunch and dinner. 20 W 50th St (at Rockefeller Plaza). 246.6699 ⑅

Dean & DeLuca Cafe ★$ The latest in **Dean & DeLuca**'s growing chain of Italian gourmet takeouts/restaurants, this airy cafe is a welcome, convenient place to stop for either a full lunch or afternoon tea. ♦ Italian/Takeout ♦ Daily breakfast, lunch, and early dinner. 9 Rockefeller Plaza (at W 49th St). 664.1363 ⑅. Also at: 121 Prince St (between Wooster and Greene Sts). 254.8776; 75 University Pl (at 11th St). 473.1908 ⑅

THE RAINBOW ROOM

The Rainbow Room ★★★$$$$ When this place reopened in 1987 after two years of restoration, *The New York Times* described it

as "a room that wants to be filled with people in formal dress and the sounds of Gershwin and Cole Porter." The redesign (architecture by **Hardy Holzman Pfeiffer Associates;** graphic design by Milton Glaser) was supervised by restaurateur Joseph Baum of **The Four Seasons, Windows on the World,** and **Aurora** fame. The results make this place—even without the view—a romantic place for dining and dancing. Start with a Kir Royale (Champagne and cassis), which is made at the table, and a cold seafood platter. For a real splurge, try the trio of caviars on wafers of potato puree. Then move on to grilled swordfish in red wine and marrow sauce, roast guinea hen with potato *galette* (a flat cake) and sweet garlic sauce, or soft-shell crabs in season. A stunning place for visitors, it's also a good escape for New Yorkers craving relief from the city's often oppressive rat race. The view is at its best from the bar on the south side. There's a $20 cover charge for the **Rainbow Room Orchestra,** which plays nightly from 7:30 to 11PM. ♦ Continental ♦ Tu-Su dinner. Reservations required; jacket and tie required. 30 Rockefeller Plaza (between W 49th and W 50th St), 65th floor. 632.5000

New York Bound Bookshop More than 3,000 books (new and out-of-print) on both the city and the state—from guidebooks to literature, architecture, city planning, performing arts, and politics—fill the shelves of this shop. Maps, photographs, and prints are sold as well. Linger awhile—chairs are provided for your comfort. ♦ M-Sa. 50 Rockefeller Plaza (between W 50th and W 51st Sts). 245.8503

55 **La Réserve** ★★★$$$$ Handsome and spacious with peach fabric banquettes, mirrors, and a mural of the sea, this is the right place for a romantic dinner. The classic French menu features *cassolette d'escargots niçoise* (casserole of snails with tomatoes and black olives); marinated lamb fillet; saddle of rabbit with wine sauce; and sliced duck breast with cabbage, honey, and balsamic vinegar. The chocolate basket filled with chocolate mousse and raspberries is an absolute must. ♦ French ♦ M-F lunch and dinner; Sa dinner. Reservations required. 4 W 49th St (at Fifth Ave). 247.2993

56 **The Goelet Building** Ignore the ground-floor shops in this crisp, early-modern structure, built in 1932 by **E.H. Faile & Co.** But do stop in the elevator lobby: The highly ornamented space is a hidden Art Deco gem all the way to the paneling of the elevator cabs. Note the lighting in the pilasters and cornices. ♦ 608 Fifth Ave (at W 49th St)

57 **Saks Fifth Avenue** Fashionable and always in good taste, this New York institution has another asset few other stores can offer:

service. Great designer collections throughout the store will please any woman's sense of style, and the men's department is legendary. The selection for children is heaven-on-earth for parents and grandparents who enjoy seeing the little ones turned out in style. The small luxury selection of candies, liqueur cakes, and chocolates includes beautiful truffles from Joseph Schmidt and decadent chocolate- and caramel-covered apples from Mrs. Prindables. The airy *Cafe SFA* on the 8th floor is a great spot for lunch, particularly if you come early and secure a window table overlooking **St. Patrick's Cathedral** or **Rockefeller Center.** If it's Christmas time, the window displays are a must-see. ♦ Daily. 611 Fifth Ave (between E 49th and E 50th Sts). 753.4000 ♿

58 Hatsuhana ★★★$$$ Sushi lovers give this bar top ratings for the freshest sushi, creatively rolled. Sit at a table or at the counter, but definitely try to find a spot where you can watch the sushi chef in action. In addition to the raw stuff, good tempura and some skewered grilled dishes are available. A la carte items tend to add up quickly, so if you're on a budget, the prix-fixe lunch menu is a good buy. ♦ Japanese ♦ M-F lunch and dinner; Sa dinner. Reservations recommended. 17 E 48th St (between Madison and Fifth Aves). 355.3345

59 Crouch & Fitzgerald This store is an old New York institution for luggage, handbags, and business cases. ♦ M-Sa. 400 Madison Ave (at E 48th St). 755.5888 ♿

60 Dolce ★$$$ The lighting in this apricot-colored dining room is so vivid it might well be a stage set. Come here for decent pastas, including chicken, spinach, and artichoke ravioli with tomato-garlic sauce; *penne bolognese;* simple pizzas; and such fish dishes as pan-seared salmon with lemon-caper crust. ♦ Italian ♦ M-F lunch and dinner; Sa dinner. Reservations recommended. 60 E 49th St (between Park and Madison Aves). 692.9292 ♿

61 Waldorf-Astoria Hotel $$$$ The incomparable grande dame has been home to permanent guests such as the Duchess of Windsor and the American representative to the **UN,** as well as temporary guests like King

Faisal of Saudi Arabia and every US president (including Clinton) since 1931. It was moved here when the **Empire State Building** rose on its former site on lower Fifth Avenue. Taking up nearly the entire block between Park and Lexington Avenues and East 49th and East 50th Streets, it has almost 1,215 spacious guestrooms and, together with the adjacent and slightly more expensive **Waldorf Towers** with 118 guest rooms and 77 suites, it is now administered by the Hilton hotel chain. Designed by **Schultze & Weaver,** the building is considered by many to be the best on this stretch of Park Avenue. The base is in proper relation to the surrounding buildings, while the unique twin towers are still noteworthy additions to the skyline.

The hotel epitomized the good life of New York in the 1930s, carrying on in the tradition of its fashionable predecessor at West 34th Street and Fifth Avenue. (The hotel's tony guests often arrived underground in their private railway cars on a specially constructed spur off the tracks under Park Avenue.) The luxurious Art Deco interiors have suffered some mistreatment and neglect over the years—the burled walnut elevator cabs, for example, were lined with brocade—but have been meticulously restored. Of particular interest are the Louis Rigel murals in the lobby and the *Wheel of Life* mosaic in the floor of the lobby. Decent fare can be had at the **Bull and Bear** and the pretty **Peacock Alley.** ♦ 301 Park Ave (between E 49th and E 50th Sts). 355.3000, 800/445.8667; fax 872.7272 ♿

Within the Waldorf-Astoria Hotel:

Inagiku Japanese Restaurant ★★ $$$$ When Emperor Hirohito stayed at the **Waldorf,** he felt right at home in the hostelry's Japanese restaurant. The menu features sushi, sashimi, tempura, and teriyaki in a setting that would be considered among the nicest and plushest in Tokyo—gold lamé, black lacquer, and rich red velvet. The sushi is top quality—particularly the roe and yellowtail. ♦ Japanese ♦ M-F lunch and dinner; Sa-Su dinner. Reservations required; jacket required. 111 E 49th St (between Park and Lexington Aves). 355.0440

Jack Dempsey's 14-room apartment at 145 Central Park West included a huge kitchen where the fighter practiced his favorite hobby—cooking.

The task of cleaning Rockefeller Center's rentable area of 15,000,000 square feet is equivalent to cleaning almost 11,000 six-room apartments. Some 65,000 people work in Rockefeller-owned or -operated buildings daily, and approximately 175,000 visit each day for business or pleasure, giving it a daily population of 240,000. Only 60 cities in the US exceed this total.

62 Chemical Bank World Corporate Headquarters This 53-story monster was built in 1960 by **Skidmore, Owings & Merrill** for Union Carbide, which has since moved to the suburbs. Railroad yards under the building made it necessary to begin the elevator shafts on the second floor, which is why the ground-floor lobby looks forgotten. ♦ 270 Park Ave (between E 47th and E 48th Sts). 270.6000

63 ChemCort at Chemical Bank World Headquarters The plants and mini-waterfalls in this greenhouse lobby have a soothing effect. **Emery Roth & Sons** designed the main building in 1962; **Haines Lundberg Wachler** executed the **ChemCort** addition in 1982. ♦ 277 Park Ave (between E 47th and E 48th Sts)

64 Hotel Inter-Continental New York $$$ Once known as the **Barclay,** this 692-room hotel designed by **Cross & Cross** in 1927 was the most luxurious of the hotels built by the **New York Central Railroad.** Now part of the Inter-Continental chain, it's as prestigious as ever, with special amenities to make life easier for visiting businesspeople (24-hour room service, concierge, valet service, and health spa). The "Barclay" name lives on in the **Barclay Restaurant** and in the gracious **Barclay Terrace** overlooking the lobby; the name of the clubby bar off the lobby was changed to **Bar One Eleven.** American and Continental cuisine is featured in the restaurant; the **Terrace** specializes in afternoon tea. Both recommend reservations. ♦ 111 E 48th St (between Lexington and Park Aves). 755.5900, 800/327.0200; fax 644.0079 ♿

65 Caswell-Massey Established in 1752 and considered to be America's oldest chemist and perfumer, the shop has been called everything from "the Disneyland of drugstores" to "a beauty browser's paradise." The historic flagship store (there are more than 30), here since 1926, no longer boasts the soda fountain where Bogart and Bacall were once regulars. But it's still worth the trip to pick up any of the nostalgically packaged bath items and toiletries. ♦ Daily. 518 Lexington Ave (at E 48th St). 755.2254. Also at: South Street Seaport (between Water and Front Sts). 608.5401; 225 Liberty St (at the World Financial Center). 945.2630

66 New York Marriott East Side $$$ Originally the **Shelton,** a club/hotel for men, this 34-story tower designed by **Arthur**

Loomis Harmon in 1924 was the first major building to reflect the 1916 zoning regulations. Its set-back massing is admirable, and the design became particularly famous as the winner of architectural awards and as the subject of many paintings by Georgia O'Keeffe. The hotel's 655 renovated rooms have character but are sometimes cramped. Within the hotel are a coffee shop, the **Shelton Grill** for more serious dining, and the **Champion Sports Bar.** ♦ 525 Lexington Ave (between E 48th and E 49th Sts). 755.4000, 800/228.9290; fax 751.3440 ♿

67 Roger Smith Hotel $$$$ The **Winthrop's** long-term renovation program is finally complete. All of the 163 rooms and suites have been redecorated and the lobby has been redone with mahogany and free-form bronze sculptures by hotel president/artist James Knowles. Rooms come with their own coffeemakers, and most rooms on the **Concierge Floor** have granite bathrooms with Jacuzzis and hair dryers. ♦ 501 Lexington Ave (at E 47th St). 755.1400, 800/455.0277; fax 319.9130 ♿

68 Helmsley Middletowne $$$ Part of the Helmsley chain, this 192-room hotel offers predominantly junior and large suites, some with kitchenettes, terraces, and fireplaces. ♦ 148 E 48th St (between Third and Lexington Aves). 755.3000, 800/221.4982; fax 832.0261 ♿

69 767 Third Avenue This squeaky-clean curved office tower designed in 1981 by **Fox & Fowle** is high-tech, clothed in brick and wood instead of aluminum and steel. The chessboard on the side wall of the building next door was provided by the developer, Melvyn Kauffman, so that guests would have something to look at. A new move is made on the board each week; ask the concierge at No 767 for the bulletin and a short description of how to play the game. ♦ At E 48th St

70 Turtle Bay Gardens When planning began for the **UN** complex just east of here, these blocks were slated for demolition. Cooler heads prevailed, and this little development, dating from 1870 and remodeled in 1920 by architect **Clarence Dean,** was saved. The development, not open to the public, was created for Mrs. Walton Martin, who bought a back-to-back row of 10 houses on each street then ripped out all the walls and fences behind them to create a common garden. She left a 12-foot strip down the middle for a path, at the center of which she installed a fountain copied from the Villa Medici in Rome. She redesigned the 20 houses so that their living rooms faced the private garden rather than the street and began attracting such tenants as Tyrone Power and Leopold Stokowski. Katharine Hepburn still lives here. ♦ 227-247

E 48th St and 226-246 E 49th St (between Second and Third Aves)

71 Lescaze Residence Glass blocks, stucco, and industrial-pipe railings replaced the original brownstone front of this town house when modernist architect **Paul Lescaze** converted it to his combination office/residence in 1934. **Lescaze** is well known as the co-designer of Philadelphia's extraordinary PSFS Building with **George Howe.** He also participated in the design of **1 New York Plaza** overlooking the harbor, and the **Municipal Courthouse** at 111 Centre Street. ◆ 211 E 48th St (between Second and Third Aves)

72 780 Third Avenue This 50-story tower is clad in brick, but the cross patterns are the structure showing through—a sort of dressed version of Chicago's John Hancock Tower. A plaza on three sides is a relief in a crowded area. **Raul de Armas** was the partner in charge of the 1983 **Skidmore, Owings & Merrill** design. ◆ Between E 48th and E 49th Sts

73 Smith & Wollensky ★★$$$ Young corporate types favor this meat palace above all others. The decor is dramatic and the upstairs dining room has three skylights. The steaks and prime ribs are sure to please; such basic desserts as Austrian strudel don't disappoint either. The restaurant boasts an extraordinary American wine list. ◆ American ◆ M-F lunch and dinner; Sa-Su dinner. Reservations required. 797 Third Ave (at E 49th St). 753.1530

74 Chin Chin ★★$$$ Chinese cooking takes an innovative turn in this handsome, sophisticated restaurant with beige walls and recessed lighting. Try the country-style chicken with spinach, crispy sea bass, steamed salmon with black-bean sauce, or sautéed leg of lamb with leeks. ◆ Cantonese ◆ Daily lunch and dinner. 216 E 49th St (between Second and Third Aves). 888.4555

75 Beekman Tower Hotel $$$ Originally called the **Panhellenic Hotel,** catering to women belonging to Greek-letter sororities, this is now an all-suite hotel (there are 171) catering to **UN** visitors looking for reasonably priced accommodations with fully equipped kitchens. **John Mead Howells** designed the building in 1928. For a wonderful view of the East River, have a drink in the **Top of the Tower.** ◆ 3 Mitchell Pl (E 49th St and First Ave). 355.7300, 800/637.8483; fax 753.9366

76 Wylie's ★$$ Rib fans don't often agree, so it's not surprising that some call this the best while others consider it the worst rib joint in town. Despite the controversy, it's always crowded with a satiated-looking crowd of happy habitués. Specialties include juicy beef or pork ribs, and moist barbecued chicken with a side of onion rings—which call out for the restaurant's tasty hallmark dipping sauce. ◆ Barbecue ◆ Daily lunch, dinner, and late-night meals. 891 First Ave (between E 50th and E 51st Sts). 751.0700

77 Lutèce ★★★$$$$ For over thirty years, Andre Soltner's elegant bastion of Alsatian cooking has been tops on every critic's list of special French restaurants, so it struck fear into hearts of loyalists when Soltner sold the restaurant in 1994 to the Ark Corporation. Eberhard Mueller is the man now running the kitchen's daily operations. How that will change Soltner's trademark dishes—truffle with foie gras in croissant, mousse of duckling with juniper berries, trout in cream sauce, lobster ravioli, medaillons of veal with morels, and frozen raspberry soufflé—is something that food mavens are watching carefully. More worrisome still is Ark's reported intention to start opening **Lutèce** clones elsewhere. ◆ French ◆ M, Sa dinner; Tu-F lunch and dinner. Reservations required. 249 E 50th St (between Second and Third Aves). 752.2225

78 Zarela ★★$$ This place, decorated with antique Mexican masks, colorful paper cutouts, and very bright fabrics, maintains an ongoing party atmosphere. Don't miss the fresh margaritas and Zarela's famous red snapper hash. ◆ Mexican ◆ M-F lunch and dinner; Sa-Su dinner. Reservations required. 953 Second Ave (between E 50th and E 51st Sts). 644.6740

79 Pickwick Arms Hotel $ The 370 redecorated rooms (100 less expensive rooms share baths) in this hotel are popular for their Midtown location; other pluses are a roof garden, a cocktail lounge, and a gourmet deli. ◆ 230 E 51st St (between Second and Third Aves). 355.0300, 800/PICKWICK; fax 755.5729 &

80 Greenacre Park Another "vest pocket park," this one is slightly larger and more elaborate than its cousin, **Paley Park.** Designed in 1971 by **Sasaki, Dawson, DeMay Associates,** it was a gift to the city by Mrs. Jean Mauze, daughter of John D. Rockefeller Jr. ♦ 217-221 E 51st St (between Second and Third Aves)

81 Artichoke Consistently fresh and delicious salads, as well as a small selection of meats, cheeses, packaged goods, breads, cakes, and pastries are stocked in this immaculate store. ♦ M-Sa. 968 Second Ave (between E 51st and E 52nd Sts). 753.2030

82 Fu's ★★$$$ Decorated in a contemporary style in shades of gray, pink, and burgundy, this is a popular spot for gourmet Chinese food. Order the Grand Marnier shrimp (it's not on the menu but regulars know to ask for it), lemon chicken, crispy orange beef, or panfried flounder. A faithful and high-powered clientele was cultivated and pampered by former hostess Gloria Chu and they miss her, which is why the restaurant still invites her back for special occasions. ♦ Chinese ♦ Daily lunch and dinner. Reservations recommended. 972 Second Ave (between E 51st and E 52nd Sts). 517.9670

83 Eamonn Doran $$ An Irish pub gone Continental, this place has too much carpeting, comfort, and Muzak for James Joyce fans. But rugby players and other assorted real and would-be Irish folk carouse here and take advantage of the extensive list of imported beers. ♦ Irish ♦ Daily lunch, dinner, and late-night meals. 998 Second Ave (at E 52nd St). 752.8088

84 242 East 52nd Street Like the **Lescaze Residence,** this 1950 **Philip Johnson** design is a quintessentially modern composition in a row house lot. Commissioned by John D. Rockefeller Jr. as a guesthouse for the **Museum of Modern Art,** it was also used at one time by **Johnson** as a New York City pied-à-terre. The base is Wrightian brick, the top Miesian steel and glass, and the whole composition is almost Oriental in its simplicity and mystery. ♦ Between Second and Third Aves

85 Bridge Kitchenware Corp. Pros like Craig Claiborne and Julia Child pick up their copper pots, knife sets, and pastry tubes at this exceptional store, which stocks every utensil you could possibly need, no matter how obscure. ♦ M-Sa. 214 E 52nd St (between Second and Third Aves). 688.4220

86 Nippon ★★$$$$ One of the first restaurants to introduce sushi and sashimi to New Yorkers, this gracious place maintains its overall high quality and continues to offer dishes unfamiliar to Western palates—*ususuzukuri* (marinated fluke in very thin slices) and *hanazukuri* (marinated raw beef). There are also excellent versions of more familiar dishes, such as *shabu shabu* (beef and vegetables cooked at the table in a hot pot of soy broth) and tempura. ♦ Japanese ♦ M-F lunch and dinner; Sa dinner. Reservations recommended. 155 E 52nd St (between Third and Lexington Aves). 758.0226

87 Rand McNally Map and Travel Center The well-stocked book department also has travel videos, road maps, wall maps, globes, travel games, map puzzles, beachballs, pillows, and geography games. Call 800/234.0679 for 24-hour mail-order service. ♦ M-Sa. 150 E 52nd St (between Third and Lexington Aves). 758.7488 &

88 San Carlos Hotel $$ Most of the 146 comfortably furnished rooms here have kitchenettes. ♦ 150 E 50th St (between Third and Lexington Aves). 755.1800, 800/722.2012; fax 688.9778

89 Tatou $$$ Opulent and slightly decadent-looking, this 1930s opera house sports lamps attached to Mephistophelian heads, a giant chandelier that looks borrowed from the set of *Phantom of the Opera,* statues and paintings of cherubs, and faux-antique windows set against yellow brocade walls; a band performs nightly—if only the food were as captivating as the setting. Stick to simpler dishes such as parfait of tuna and salmon *tartare* with osetra and salmon caviar, tea-smoked chicken salad, and linguine with grilled portobello mushrooms. ♦ Continental ♦ M-F lunch and dinner; Sa dinner. Reservations recommended. 151 E 50th St (between Third and Lexington Aves). 753.1144

St. Bartholomew's Church

Michael Storrings

90 The Beverly $$$ Most of the 200 accommodations are suites or junior suites with kitchenettes in this homey and comfy hotel. **Kaufman Pharmacy** within the hotel is one of the few left in New York open 24 hours a day (but its prices are exorbitant). Decent steak can be had at **Kenny's Steak and Seafood House.** ♦ 125 E 50th St (at Lexington Ave). 753.2700, 800/223.0945; fax 753.2700 &

91 Loews New York Hotel $$$ **Morris Lapidus** and **Harle & Liebman**'s 1961 plastic modern design for this hotel is nonetheless cheery and comfortable inside. The lodging offers 726 rooms as well as an in-hotel garage, barbershop, beauty salon, and jewelry shop. There is also a coffee shop and the **Lexington Avenue Grill** for breakfast and dinner. ♦ 569 Lexington Ave (at E 51st St). 752.7000, 800/223.0888; fax 758.6311

92 General Electric Building This 51-story tower was designed in 1931 by **Cross & Cross** to harmonize with the Byzantine lines of **St. Bartholomew's Church,** and is still best seen with the church at its feet. But it's a beauty from any angle, lavishly decorated with what may have been intended to be stylized lightning bolts in honor of its first tenant, the Radio Company of America, which moved soon after to the new **Rockefeller Center.** Take a peek at the lobby. ♦ 570 Lexington Ave (at E 51st St)

93 St. Bartholomew's Church This richly detailed Byzantine landmark (shown above) with a charming little garden is a breath of fresh air on a high-rise–lined block. But it has been the object of a long-running battle between preservationists and church fathers, who want to sell off the **Community House** for commercial development (the plans were eventually nixed). The portico was a Vanderbilt-financed, **Stanford White** –designed addition (1903) to a church by **James Renwick.** In 1919, **Bertram Goodhue** inherited the portico and designed the church—a confabulation handled with style. The site was a Schaefer brewery in the 1860s. ♦ Park Ave (between E 50th and E 51st Sts). 751.1616 &

94 Seagram Building The ultimate representation of pure modernist reason, this classically proportioned and exquisitely detailed 1958 bronze, glass, and steel box by **Ludwig Mies van der Rohe** and **Philip Johnson** is the one everybody copied (see Sixth Avenue and other parts of Park Avenue)—but it's still the best. The immutable object is a vestigial column set back on a plaza that was an innovative relief when it was conceived. ♦ 375 Park Ave (between E 52nd and E 53rd Sts)

Restaurants/Clubs: Red   Hotels: Blue

Shops/ 🍴 Outdoors: Green   **Sights/Culture: Black**

Within the Seagram Building:

The Four Seasons ★★★★$$$$
Two dining rooms coexist here at one of New York's hottest eating places. **The Bar Room Grill** is power central at midday, when the top echelon of New York's publishing world gathers to exchange notes and gossip. Featured in this casual space later in the day is the new "Grill at Night," offering true fine-dining bargains—an under-$40 three-course meal, including coffee. The **Pool Room** next door, a more formal spot, has been going strong since 1958 and features such dishes as oxtail ravioli with sage, pumpkin bisque with cinnamon, carpaccio of tuna and salmon with ginger, foie gras with figs, and sea bass in an herb crust. ♦ Continental ♦ M-F lunch and dinner; Sa dinner. Reservations required; jacket and tie required. 99 E 52nd St (between Park and Lexington Aves). 754.9494

Brasserie ★$$$ One of the first restaurants to serve New York's round-the-clock needs, this place is scheduled to reopen by the end of the year after undergoing extensive renovations. The menu remains basic, hearty French fare—French onion soup, Caesar's salad, snails in garlic-herb butter, crab cakes, vegetable terrine, *choucroute* (sauerkraut cooked with goose fat, onions, juniper berries, and white wine), and duck confit with stewed beans and tomatoes. ♦ French/American ♦ Daily 24 hours. Reservations recommended. 100 E 53rd St (between Lexington and Park Aves). 751.4840

95 Racquet and Tennis Club A somewhat uninspired Florentine palazzo, this 1918 **McKim, Mead & White** design is an appropriate foil for the **Seagram Building** across the street. Hard (and shameful) to believe as we approach the 21st century, but "men only" partake in tennis, squash, racquets (an English game similar to squash but faster), and swimming. ♦ Members only. M-F 7AM-11PM. 370 Park Ave (between E 52nd and E 53rd Sts). 753.9700

96 Fresco ★★$$ Colors abound on the ocher walls with complex floral displays and bold paintings by SoHo artists. It is also the setting for rich, robust flavors: Try spaghettini with clams, garlic, basil, and roasted tomatoes; baked penne with pancetta (Italian unsmoked bacon), parmesan, and cream; ravioli stuffed with duck, portobello mushrooms, and sage; lemon thyme baby rack of lamb; and grilled veal chop. The cinnamon ice-cream sandwich makes a perfect ending. ♦ Italian ♦ M-F lunch and dinner; Sa dinner. Reservations

recommended. 34 E 52nd St (between Park and Madison Aves). 935.3434 ♿

97 Omni Berkshire Place $$$ The old **Berkshire** has become one of the city's best European-style hotels, known for its personal service. Its 1995 $50-million renovation has added new life to the 396 generously proportioned rooms, which now boast faxes, two phone lines, and sitting areas; 44 spacious suites offer even more amenities. **Kokachin** serves a fine seafood menu with Mediterranean and Pacific influences. The face-lift also produced a new health club and fitness center. ♦ 21 E 52nd St (at Madison Ave). 753.5800, 800-THE-OMNI; fax 755.2317

Within the Omni Berkshire Place:

Kokachin ★★$$$ This is quickly becoming a popular destination thanks to chef Elka Gilmore's distinctive Asian-influenced cuisine. Choose from among such unusual but appealing pairings as mussels with curry rice paper; foie gras with green papaya salad; crispy quail with spicy greens in a mango vinaigrette; and taro-wrapped lobster with cèpes and chestnuts. Main courses are equally inventive, including marinated sturgeon with pickled plums and griddled rice cakes, and miso marinated cod with eggplant and tomato ginger sauce. ♦ Asian/Seafood ♦ Daily lunch and dinner. Reservations recommended. 355.9300 ♿

98 Sushisay ★★$$$ The name means fresh sushi and that's exactly what you'll get at this branch of the Tokyo original, complete with white walls and shoji screens. At lunchtime it's filled with Japanese businessmen, so don't count on getting a seat at the sushi bar. ♦ Japanese ♦ M-F lunch and dinner; Sa dinner. Reservations required. 38 E 51st St (between Park and Madison Aves). 755.1780

98 Tse Yang ★★$$$ Like the original Tse Yang in Paris, this stateside outpost offers outstanding Beijing cuisine and European-style service in a stunning setting of black mirrors, rich wood paneling, and hammered copper and brass appointments. Try the crab-leg salad, tea-smoked salmon, hot-and-sour soup, orange beef (served cold), and pickled cabbage. For dessert have the caramelized apples for two. ♦ Chinese/French ♦ Daily lunch and dinner. Reservations required; jacket required. 34 E 51st St (between Park and Madison Aves). 688.5447

99 The New York Palace Hotel $$$$
"Queen" Leona Helmsley once stood guard over this 55-story glass tower (inches shorter than the **Four Seasons Hotel,** New York's tallest), designed in 1980 by **Emery Roth & Sons. The Palace** looms over the restored

110-year-old **Villard Houses,** parts of which are incorporated into the hotel's public rooms, resulting in an uneasy but interesting marriage. The bars and dining rooms in the old section are opulent—even excessively so—with the ornate woodwork, marble, frescoes, and fireplaces from the Gilded Age all intact. The main dining room, **Le Trianon,** is tricked out as New York's answer to Versailles, but the **Gold Room,** with a vaulted ceiling and a harpist playing from a musician's balcony is, with all its ostentatiousness, a splendid spot for high tea (held every day of the year, including Christmas, from 2PM to 5PM). **Harry's New York Bar** is slickly contemporary, unlike the more atmospheric, paneled upstairs bar. The 963 guestrooms are spacious, comfortably—if overly—decorated, and thoughtfully appointed. In 1994, the royal family of Brunei (a.k.a. the Amedeo Corp.) purchased the hotel (which had become a major liability after Helmsley was sentenced to prison for tax evasion in 1989) to the tune of $202 million. At press time, it was learned that Sirio Maccioni would be relocating his **Le Cirque** to this location with a scheduled opening in late 1996. ◆ 455 Madison Ave (at E 50th St). 888.7000, 800/NYPALAC; fax 303.6000

99 The Villard Houses This collection of six houses (illustrated above) was designed in 1884 by **McKim, Mead & White** to resemble a single Italian palazzo at the request of the original owner, publisher Henry Villard. They were later owned by the Archdiocese of New York, which sold them to Harry Helmsley. In a precedent-setting arrangement, Helmsley incorporated two of the landmark houses into his **Palace Hotel** and restored the interiors to their turn-of-the-century rococo splendor—although you might wonder if they ever looked as new as they do now. ◆ 451-455 Madison Ave (between E 50th and E 51st Sts)

Within The Villard Houses:

Urban Center The Municipal Art Society, Parks Council, Architectural League of New York, and the New York Chapter of the **American Institute of Architects** share the north wing of **The Villard Houses,** where they frequently host exhibitions that are open to the public. The Information Exchange, a service project of the Municipal Art Society that helps find answers to questions about New York City, "the built city," is also here. The service will, for example, field queries about the history of **Central Park** or how to clean brownstones and repair old plasterwork. ◆ M-F 10AM-1PM. 935.3960

Urban Center Books As you would expect, the emphasis is on books, periodicals, and journals about architecture, historic preservation, and urban design. ◆ M-Sa. 457 Madison Ave (between E 51st and E 50th Sts). 935.3595 &

Sky Books International Originally a mail-order business run by a former RAF flight instructor, this shop has the world's largest collection of books and magazines on military history and aviation. ◆ M-Sa. 48 E 50th St (between Park and Madison Aves). 688.5086

100 St. Patrick's Cathedral Now dwarfed by its surroundings—particularly by the **Rockefeller Center**—this church was considered too far out of town when **James Renwick Jr.** built it in the 1880s. (**Charles T. Matthews** added **Lady Chapel** in 1906.) The 11th-largest church in the world, the structure is a finely detailed and well-proportioned but not very strict adaptation of its French-Gothic predecessors. There are no flying buttresses, for example, but there are pinnacles. The spires rise to 330 feet, and the rose window above the center portal is 26 feet in diameter. More than half of the 70 stained-glass windows were made in Chartres and Nantes. **Renwick** also designed the high altar, presided over by John Cardinal O'Connor. ◆ Fifth Ave (between E 50th and E 51st Sts). 753.2261 &

101 Olympic Tower This black glass box full of exclusive apartments was designed in 1976 by **Skidmore, Owings & Merrill.** The hospitable interior arcade is complete with a waterfall and a refreshment stand, plus a foreign currency exchange office. Reflections of **St. Patrick's** are a nice bonus. ◆ 645 Fifth Ave (at E 51st St)

Cartier

102 Cartier Lovely baubles for the body and the home, mostly at astronomical prices, are this shop's stock in trade. The originator of the tank watch is always coming up with original designs, and there are all those rings of diamonds, emeralds, and pearls. Don't miss "Les Musts," the more affordable boutique collection of gifts, such as cigarette lighters. Once the residence of businessman Morton F. Plant, the Renaissance palazzo-style building is a rare survivor of the days when Fifth Avenue was lined with the private homes of such people as William Vanderbilt, who lived diagonally across the street. **Robert W. Gibson** designed the building in 1905; **William Welles Bosworth** supervised the conversion to a store in 1917. Note the detailing of the entrance and centralized composition on East 52nd Street. ♦ M-F; Sa June-August. 2 E 52nd St (at Fifth Ave). 753.0111 &

LA GRENOUILLE

103 La Grenouille ★★$$$$ The annual budget for flowers here is close to $100,000, and the fresh daily arrangements show it. Mirrors sparkle everywhere, and the lighting is nearly perfect, making the "beautiful people" who frequent this place look even more beautiful. There are wonderful traditional dishes on the menu such as Dover sole, rack of lamb, cheese soufflé, but be prepared to spend big time if you want a good wine to go with them. ♦ French ♦ Tu-Sa lunch and dinner; closed mid-July–August. Reservations required; jacket and tie required. 3 E 52nd St (at Fifth Ave). 752.1495

104 B. Dalton Bookseller The flagship store of the Dalton chain is organized by subject and arranged by author with hardcover, paperback, and backlist included in each section. Computer software is downstairs. ♦ Daily. 666 Fifth Ave (at W 52nd St). 247.1740. Also at: 396 Sixth Ave (at W 8th St). 674.8780

104 Top of the Sixes $$$$ Only out-of-towners who don't know any better come here for dinner. But it's a great place for a frozen strawberry daiquiri and a heart-stopping sunset or nighttime view of Midtown in all its illuminated glory—39 floors above it all. ♦ New American ♦ M-Sa lunch and dinner. 666 W Fifth Ave (at 52nd St). 757.6662

105 21 Club ★★$$$$ Although traditionalists will want to try the lunch of champions—the "21" burger or chicken hash—the food has gotten more inventive since Michael Lomonaco took over the kitchen in 1989. Innovations include quail salad with truffle oil, crab cakes with horseradish cream, black bean soup, creamy polenta with wild-mushroom pan roast, peppered seared tuna with seared tomatoes. The wine list represents a cellar of 40,000 bottles, with excellent choices at all price levels. This was one of Jackie O's favorite lunch spots when she was an editor at Doubleday. ♦ Continental ♦ M-Sa lunch and dinner. Reservations required; jacket and tie required. 21 W 52nd St (between Fifth and Sixth Aves). 582.7200

105 Museum of Television and Radio Originally called the **Museum of Brodcasting**, this gallery was founded in 1965 by the late William S. Paley, the founder of **CBS**. Only the winners air here, such as a Hitchcock retrospective or a tribute to Henry Fonda or Barbra Streisand. You can choose from TV and radio programs from the museum's vast archives—everything from Edward R. Murrow to "Mr. Ed"—and screen or listen for hours if you wish. The entire permanent collection consists of more than 60,000 recordings (from commercials to documentaries). In 1991, the museum (illustrated at right) moved from its longtime home next to **Paley Plaza** on East 53rd Street into this $55-million, 17-story building designed by **John Burgee Architects** that more than doubled the museum's size and added two theaters, a screening room, a gallery space, an expanded library with computer access to catalogs, and a museum shop. Docent-led tours are usually held at 12:30PM on Tuesday. ♦ Admission. Tu-Su. 25 W 52nd St (between Fifth and Sixth Aves). 621.6600

105 Hines Building In 1986, while designing this building, architect **Kevin Roche** was also working on plans for the new zoo in **Central Park.** The zoo has covered walkways supported by columns with sliced edges, an effect called chamfering. **Roche** and co-architect **John Dinkeloo & Associates** used the same idea here and put the building on similar columns. In 1989, with the support of neighboring cultural institutions, including the **American Craft Museum** and the **Museum of Television and Radio,** the occupants established the ground-floor **Lobby Gallery,** a nonprofit exhibition space that mounts about 12 shows a year. ♦ 31 W 52nd St (between Fifth and Sixth Aves). 767.2666 &

106 Traveller's Bookstore Owner Diana Wells doesn't stock every book in print on a certain destination. Instead, she reads (and uses, if possible) all of the available books and sells only the very best. Stop in for guidebooks and related fiction and nonfiction, phrase books, practical maps from all over the world, and sound advice from the congenial and knowledgeable staff. An extensive mail-order catalog is available. ♦ M-F; Sa-Su 11AM-5PM. 22 W 52nd St, Lobby (between Fifth and Sixth Aves). 664.0995; 800/755.8728

106 Bombay Palace ★$$ The crisp and light Indian breads, such as nan stuffed with cashew nuts and dried fruits, are delightful, the curries mild, and the tandoori chicken properly moist and tender at this pleasant, subtly lit Indian restaurant with friendly service. Try the lamb *nilgiri* (in mint and coriander sauce), followed by mango ice cream. ♦ Indian ♦ Daily lunch and dinner. 30 W 52nd St (between Fifth and Sixth Aves). 541.7777

Museum of Television and Radio

Michael Storrings

106 Cesarina ★$$$
Owned and run by the proprietors of Italy's legendary Villa d'Este Hotel, this airy, elegant restaurant has an efficient and friendly staff eager to make suggestions about the carefully prepared risottos or pastas. The veal cutlet Milanese and osso buco are as delicious as the simple fish specialties that change depending on the market's catch of the day. ♦ Northern Italian ♦ M-F lunch and dinner. Reservations recommended for lunch. 36 W 52nd St (between Fifth and Sixth Aves). 582.6900

107 CBS Building This is **Eero Saarinen's** only high-rise building, although he didn't live to see its completion in 1965. Known as "Black Rock," the dark gray granite mass is removed from the street, and its surface is given depth by triangular columns. With the top the same as the bottom, the tower is the image of mystery (even the entrances are hard to identify)—a replica of the monolith from *2001* right on Sixth Avenue. ♦ 51 W 52nd St (between Fifth and Sixth Aves)

Within the CBS Building:

China Grill ★★$$$ Although this place is not related to Wolfgang Puck's Santa Monica landmark, **Chinois on Main**, the cooking—an amalgam of Asian, French, and California influences—is similar. However, the owners here—**Chinois** expatriates—can lay claim to the real thing. The food is inventive and delicious; try the grilled salmon on a bed of Asian greens, grilled rosemary scallops atop beet risotto, Australian lamb with a quinoa salad and mandarin orange sauce, or crispy duck with caramelized black-vinegar sauce. Dishes are served family style, making it fun to share. ♦ New Asian ♦ M-F lunch and dinner; Sa-Su dinner. Reservations required. 333.7788 &

108 The MoMA Design Store Design-sensitive merchandise is inspired by the **Museum of Modern Art** collections across the street, including educational toys (Colorforms, kaleidoscopes, architectural blocks), furniture (designs by **Frank Lloyd Wright** and Charles Eames, plus a reproduction of the famous butterfly chair by Antonio Bonet, Jorge Farrari, and Juan Kurchen), housewares, desk accessories, and great gift ideas. ♦ Daily. 44 W 53rd St (between Fifth and Sixth Aves). 767.1050

108 American Craft Museum The appreciation of American crafts has grown in recent years, partly due to an interest in things that are not machine-made and partly due to the pioneering of the American Crafts Council and its New York City museum, built in 1986 by **Fox & Fowle Architects.** Works in glass, fiber, wood, clay, metal, and paper by America's most talented craftspeople, either from the museum's collection (from 1900 to the present) or from changing loan exhibitions, are displayed. Sometimes the shows are amusing, sometimes serious, but the level of taste is always high. ♦ Admission. Tu-Su. 40 W 53rd St (between Fifth and Sixth Aves). 956.6047 &

108 New York Public Library, Donnell Library Center When he died in 1896, textile merchant Ezekiel Donnell left his estate to the New York Public Library to establish a place where young people could spend their evenings away from demoralizing influences. Thanks to Donnell's legacy, this library has one of the best collections of children's literature in the United States. ♦ Each department has its own hours; call for specific times. Main floor: daily. 20 W 53rd St (between Fifth and Sixth Aves). 621.0618

109 Museum Tower This prestigious apartment building, designed in 1983 by **Cesar Pelli & Associates,** was built to raise funds for the **Museum of Modern Art** next door. ♦ 15 W 53rd St (between Fifth and Sixth Aves)

109 Museum of Modern Art (MoMA)
When this museum was founded in 1929, a few days after the big stock market crash, the idea of a museum dedicated to the understanding and enjoyment of contemporary visual arts was novel. Founders Abby Aldrich Rockefeller (wife of John D. Jr.), Lillie P. Bliss, and Mrs. Cornelius J. Sullivan were joined by other collectors and philanthropists in the venture, and the collections have grown through the largesse of the early benefactors and others.

The original sleek white horizontal building with its marble veneer and tile-and-glass facade was designed in 1939 by **Philip L. Goodwin** and **Edward Durell Stone** in the International Style—a striking statement by an innovative institution, practicing what it preached in a row of brownstones. There was (briefly) a plan to cut a street through the two blocks from **Rockefeller Center** leading directly to the museum (the Rockefellers controlled the land in the vicinity). **Philip Johnson**'s 1951 and 1964 additions, black glass wings to the east and west, not only expanded the gallery space and improved the **Sculpture Garden** (designed in 1953 by **Johnson** and **Zion & Breen**), but were an effective frame for the original front. The tower and addition by **Cesar Pelli** in 1984 replaced **Johnson**'s west wing; **Pelli** also replaced the garden facade with a glassed-in **Garden Court** full of escalators. The then-controversial condominium tower rising above the base of the museum wing is an important source of income for the museum, though it is criticized by those who appreciated the sunny garden and low-rise side streets. The tower's cladding consists of 11 shades of glass. The expansion doubled the space available for loan shows and for the permanent collection.

One of the institution's most important contributions to the art world is its embracing of disciplines previously considered unworthy of museum status, resulting in a collection that is not only strong in 20th-century painting and sculpture, but also photography, film, theater, music, industrial design, and architecture. When the museum's first director, Alfred H. Barr Jr., espoused this multidepartmental concept in 1929, the idea of including practical as well as fine art was considered radical. At first the museum displayed only 19th-century paintings, but soon began a slow and steady implementation of Barr's idea. Today, **MoMA** also includes a publishing house, movie theater, and film department.

The museum is strongest in art of the first half of the century—Impressionists, Cubists, and Realists such as Picasso, Matisse, Miró, and Hopper—but it also has good examples of post–World War II Abstract Expressionists through Conceptualists, including de Kooning, Rothko, Lichtenstein, di Suvero, and LeWitt. The photography galleries are worth seeing, as are the galleries of architecture and design, where you will find such 20th-century classics as Thonet bentwood chairs, Tiffany glass, Bauhaus textiles, and Marcel Breuer furniture. Among the most important paintings in the collection are van Gogh's *Starry Night,* Mondrian's *Broadway Boogie Woogie,* Matisse's *Dance,* Picasso's *Les Demoiselles d'Avignon,* Andrew Wyeth's *Christina's World,* and Jackson Pollock's *One (Number 31, 1950).* With its newfound spaciousness, the unrivaled multidepartmental museum has truly fulfilled Barr's dream. The lower level holds the **Roy and Niuta Titus Theaters,** showing off the Department of Film, the largest international collection of its kind. The ground floor leads to temporary exhibitions and the **Abby Aldrich Rockefeller Sculpture Garden.** Stretching across the second floor is the **Painting and Sculpture Collection,** with separate rooms allotted to Picasso and Matisse, among others. The **Drawing Collection** on the third floor has its own exhibition space. Acquisitions include Max Pechstein's *Reclining Nude with Cat* and Picasso's 1913 *Head.* The *Prints and Illustrated Books* collection owns a 1968 etching by Picasso, the first of a series of 347 intaglio prints, and the only self-portrait of him as an old man. The *Architecture and Design Collection* on the fourth floor features two designs for houses by **Frank Lloyd Wright** and a Mindset Computer. ♦ Admission; members and children under 16 accompanied by an adult free; voluntary contribution Thurs and Fri evenings. M-Tu, Th-Su. 11 W 53rd St (between Fifth and Sixth Aves). 708.9480; film schedule 708.9490 ♿

Heroes have been honored with parades along lower Broadway since Colonial times. President Theodore Roosevelt was the first to be showered with ticker tape, as part of his welcome home from an African safari in 1910. Flags flew and paper cascaded from every window of every building, except one: The building at 26 Broadway, across from Bowling Green, didn't even raise a flag that day. It was the home of John D. Rockefeller whose Standard Oil was involved in an antitrust suit instigated by the old "Rough Rider" himself. These days the tons of ticker tape that once filled the air have been replaced by shredded computer printouts.

Restaurants/Clubs: Red   **Hotels:** Blue

Shops/ 🍴 Outdoors: Green   **Sights/Culture:** Black

Within the Museum of Modern Art:

The Sculpture Garden One of the most pleasant outdoor spaces in the city, the garden has sculpture by Rodin, Renoir, Miró, Matisse, and Picasso, among others. Weather permitting, it's open the same hours as the museum and holds a variety of concerts in the summer. The **Garden Cafe** overlooks the garden and offers a variety of snacks and light meals. ♦ 708.9480

The MoMA Bookstore Be sure to peruse the bookstore's extensive assortment of books, posters, and cards relating to the museum's collection. **The MoMA Design Store** is located across the street. ♦ M-Sa. 708.9480

Sette MoMA ★$$$ The dining room is cool and contemporary, fitted with art from the museum's permanent collection, and in nice weather tables are set on the outdoor terrace, which has a lovely view of the sculpture garden. Best bets include the simple grilled vegetable plate, and sautéed loin of lamb with juniper berries. During museum hours, enter through the museum; after 5PM use the entrance on W 54th Street. ♦ Italian ♦ M dinner; Tu, Th-Sa lunch and dinner; W, Su lunch. Reservations recommended. 11 W 53rd St (between Fifth and Sixth Aves). 708.9710 ♿

110 St. Thomas Church Cram Goodhue & Ferguson designed this picturesque French Gothic edifice (illustrated below right) on a tight corner in 1914. You have to wonder why a second tower wasn't included; the single one is rather awkward in an otherwise symmetrical composition. A dollar sign next to the "true lover's knot" over the Bride's Door is presumably a sculptor's comment on the social standing of the congregation. The Episcopal church's world-renowned boys' choir celebrated its 75th anniversary in 1994; it makes the services here a memorable experience from October through May. Call in advance for a schedule. ♦ 1 W 53rd St (at Fifth Ave). 757.7013 ♿

111 University Club Considered by many to be the finest work of **Charles Follen McKim** (of **McKim, Mead & White**), this 1899 building is an original composition with a bow to a half-dozen Italian palaces. When it was built, in the days before air-conditioning, it had striped awnings in the windows, which made the pink marble exterior even more interesting. The interior is just as lavish. For decades, this private club set the style for all the others that followed for decades. Despite its name, it is not linked with any particular university and only recently has accepted female members. ♦ 1 W 54th St (at Fifth Ave). 247.2100

112 Aquavit ★★★$$$$ Although Nelson Rockefeller once lived in this town house, he probably wouldn't recognize the eight-story atrium, complete with birch trees and a copper waterfall, that is the main dining room of this lovely, modern restaurant. Try smoked salmon with wasabi crème fraîche and radish sprouts, salmon sashimi with lime and lemon juice and warm sesame oil, foie gras with apples and cabbage, spice-grilled salmon with caraway-scented artichoke broth, rare beef in beer and beef *jus,* and sweet mustard-glazed Arctic char. Be sure to save room for the rich chocolate cake or gingersnap ice-cream sandwich. And don't forget to try the liquor that gives this place its name—a vodkalike spirit often flavored with anise, caraway, fennel, or orange peel. ♦ Scandinavian ♦ M-F lunch and dinner; Sa dinner. Reservations recommended; jacket requested. 13 W 54th St (between Fifth and Sixth Aves). 307.7311

112 Rockefeller Apartments When John D. Rockefeller Jr. was assembling the site for **Rockefeller Center,** he lived on this block. By the end of 1929 he owned 15 of the block's houses, having joined his neighbors, most of whom were members of his family, in protecting the street from commercial use. But he wasn't above a little commercialism himself, and hired **Harrison & Fouilhoux** to design this building in 1936, a few months before he moved over to Park Avenue. Its bay-windowed towers overlook the garden of the **Museum of Modern Art.** ♦ 17 W 54th St (between Fifth and Sixth Aves)

St. Thomas Church

Michael Storrings

113 Suarez High-end designer bags—most of them European and all top-of-the-line—at 20 percent (and more) below standard retail are the specialty of this well-stocked boutique. Fendi, Chanel, Ferragamo, Desmo—they're all here. ♦ M-Sa. 26 W 54th St (between Fifth and Sixth Aves). 315.5614

113 Hotel Dorset $$$ This attractive, unassuming hotel has a very loyal following and a prime location—next door to the **Museum of Modern Art.** A renovation completed the summer of 1994 refurbished all 319 rooms. The bar and cafe are jovial and popular, while the **Dorset Dining Room** is more proper. ♦ 30 W 54th St (between Fifth and Sixth Aves). 247.7300, 800/227.2348; fax 581.0153 &

Within the Hotel Dorset:

Park Cafe ★★$$$ Bay scallops in cream sauce with white wine and wonderful cold appetizers are some of the always delicious choices. The room is large, bright, and comfortable. ♦ Continental ♦ Daily lunch and dinner. Reservations required. 247.7300

114 Warwick Hotel $$$ Rich in history, this 1926 apartment hotel was publishing magnate William Randolph Hearst's dream as his elegant residential retreat for his Hollywood friends. At a cost of over $5 million, this building, designed by **George P. Post and Sons** and **Emery Roth,** was considered one of the two tallest apartment hotels in the world. It's still quite impressive with its graceful towers. Following a major renovation, all 424 spacious guest rooms boast brocade decor, marble bathrooms, two-line phones, and voice mail. The **Ciao Europa** is a lively spot with outdoor tables in warm weather. ♦ 65 W 54th St (at Sixth Ave). 247.2700, 800/522.5634; fax 957.8915

115 Allegria ★$$ If the weather allows outdoor dining and you stick to the simpler dishes—there are a variety of good pizzas and pastas—you're likely to experience "happiness," as this popular Italian restaurant's name translates. Especially good are rigatoni with eggplant, pasta with seafood, and a number of chicken dishes that include a grilled version topped with artichokes and fresh tomatoes. ♦ Italian ♦ Daily lunch and dinner. 66 W 55th St (between Fifth and Sixth Aves). 956.7755 &

116 La Côte Basque ★★★$$$$ Considered by many to be one of the top restaurants in New York, this place was founded by Henri Soule and is now the domain of owner Jean Jacques Rachou. The presentation of lobster terrine (a combination of shellfish, green beans, tomato, shredded carrots, and *céleri rémoulade*—a mustard-flavored mayonnaise-type sauce with shredded celery root) is stunning and sure to please. The wine list is one of New York's most extensive. The restaurant recently moved here from the other side of Fifth Avenue, and Rachou brought with him a beloved vestige from the ultra-elegant dining room—the *St. Jean de Luz at La Côte Basque* mural. ♦ French ♦ M-F lunch and dinner; Sa dinner. Reservations required; jacket and tie required. 60 W 55 St (between Fifth and Sixth Aves). 688.6525

116 J.P. French Bakery Croissant lovers take note: This shop may have the best croissants in town, as well as a panoply of excellent French breads—from *ficelle* (a thin baguette) to large, round loaves—all baked on the premises. ♦ Daily. 54 W 55th St (between Fifth and Sixth Aves). 765.7575

116 La Bonne Soupe ★$ Soups, omelettes, a variety of chopped beef dishes, and daily French specials such as *filet au poivre* are good at this popular longstanding bistro. ♦ French ♦ Daily lunch and dinner. 48 W 55th St (between Fifth and Sixth Aves). 586.7650

116 Michael's ★★$$ Sleek and airy, this is a popular place with Midtown business types for healthy breakfasts and lunches. Michael's signature dish is warm grilled chicken on a bed of goat cheese, grilled peppers, red onions, vine-ripened tomatoes, and baby greens, covered in jalapeño-and-cilantro–seasoned olive oil. Service, however, can be snooty and condescending to nonregulars. ♦ American/California ♦ M-F breakfast, lunch, and dinner; Sa dinner. 24 W 55th St (between Fifth and Sixth Aves). 767.0555

117 La Fondue $ Swiss chocolate and cheese fondues, steaks, seafood, and such pasta dishes as spinach cannelloni are featured here along with chocolate mousse and other standard desserts. All are served in the warm, casual atmosphere of a European cellar. ♦ Swiss ♦ Daily lunch, dinner, and late-night meals. 43 W 55th St (between Fifth and Sixth Aves). 581.0820 &

117 Menchanko-tei ★$ Japanese businessmen frequent this cozy noodle emporium for hearty soups filled with a variety of ingredients. As authentic a noodle shop as can be found in Midtown, this place is great to duck into for a steamy broth. ♦ Japanese ♦ M lunch, dinner, and late-night meals; Tu-Su breakfast, lunch, dinner, and late-night meals. 39 W 55th St (between Fifth and Sixth Aves). 247.1585 &

117 La Caravelle ★★★$$$$ Classic French cuisine gets a modern spin here without loosing a bit of European finesse. Specialties include "French lasagna" (shrimps and scallops tucked inside thin layers of pasta), crispy duck with cranberries, rack of lamb in a clay crust with wild mushrooms, and grilled Dover sole with mustard sauce. Owners Rita and Andre Jammet also happen to be among the friendliest and most charming hosts in New York. ◆ French ◆ M-F lunch and dinner; Sa dinner. Reservations required; jacket and tie required. 33 W 55th St (between Fifth and Sixth Aves). 586.4252 ₺

117 Shoreham Hotel $$ Most of the hotels in this neighborhood are far grander than this. But the 84-room hostelry's 1994 make-over brought the Moderne decor up several notches on the luxury scale. This plus its excellent location make it a favorite among denizens of the fashion world. Amenities include a complimentary breakfast and a CD library. ◆ 33 W 55th St (between Fifth and Sixth Aves). 247.6700, 800/553.3347; fax 765.9741

118 Fifth Avenue Presbyterian Church When society moved uptown, this church, which had been at 19th Street since 1855, moved with it to this 1875 building designed by **Carl Pfeiffer.** Future president Theodore Roosevelt was one of the original parishioners, along with the Auchinclosses, Livingstons, and Walcotts. It was called the most influential congregation in New York. ◆ 7 W 55th St (at Fifth Ave). 247.0490

THE PENINSULA
NEW YORK

119 The Peninsula New York $$$$ This hotel was built in 1905 by **Hiss & Weeks** and for many years, as the **Gotham Hotel,** was a favorite stopping place for movie stars. Then it briefly became **Maxim's** and was completely restored in the Belle Epoque tradition of the original Maxim's in Paris. The latest and most successful incarnation reflects the "Peninsula" style. The 242 oversize rooms are outfitted with marble baths and Art Nouveau decor. Services range from newspaper delivery to 24-hour room service, and the hotel includes two lounges (including the **Gotham Lounge**), two restaurants (including **Bistro d'Adrienne**), and complimentary access to the well-known tri-level fitness center and spa with a glass-enclosed rooftop swimming pool. ◆ 700 Fifth Ave (at W 55th St). 247.2200, 800/262.9467; fax 903.3943 ₺

Within The Peninsula New York:

Adrienne

Adrienne ★★$$$ This dining room is inspired by elaborate, Belle Epoque–style mirrors and etched flower-petal lights. The food is French with a mix of other European influences and more than just a pinch of creole flavors. Try the crawfish and foie gras with angel-hair vegetables (a thin julienne) and cinnamon-apple compote, or the pan-seared duck breast with rosemary Chambord vinaigrette. ◆ Continental ◆ M, Su lunch; Tu-Sa lunch and dinner. Reservations required; jacket and tie required. 247.2200

Pen-Top Bar and Terrace $ The beautiful view of the Manhattan skyline from this glass-enclosed bar at the top of the hotel can't be beat. ◆ American ◆ M-Sa 5PM-midnight. 700 Fifth Ave (at W 55th St), 23rd floor. 247.2200

120 Christian Dior Boutique Reminiscent of Dior's Paris headquarters at 30 Avenue Montaigne, the luxurious 4,500-square-foot space is large enough to display Gianfranco Ferre's complete haute couture and ready-to-wear collections. ◆ M-Sa. 703 Fifth Ave (at E 55th St). 223.4646

121 The St. Regis Sheraton $$$$ When **Trowbridge & Livingston** built the **St. Regis** for John Jacob Astor in 1904, Astor said he wanted the finest hotel in the world, a place where guests would feel as comfortable as they did in a gracious private home. Today, this is the only hotel in New York that offers 24-hour butler service. A three-year, $100-million renovation, completed by **Brennan, Beer Gorman** in 1991, produced one of New York's most elegant hotels—a jewel in the crown of ITT Sheraton's Luxury Collection. The capacity has actually been lowered, from more than 500 rooms to 322, 86 of them suites. The spectacular landmark exterior remains, with its stone garlands and flowers and its slate mansard roof. But now it's complemented inside by state-of-the-art technology, computerized phones, and other comforts. The hotel contains the **Astor Court,** which serves light meals and tea, and the **King Cole Bar and Lounge.** ◆ 2 E 55th St (at Fifth Ave). 753.4500, 800/759.7550; fax 787.3447 ₺

Within The St. Regis Sheraton:

Lespinasse ★★★$$$$ This formal dining room brings forth images of Louis XVI grandeur, with pink satin chairs and gilt-framed oil paintings. As prepared by Gray Kunz, originator of East-West fusion, the food is another story. Each spunky bite is shaded with many different tastes—some brilliant, some less so. Try the sautéed foie gras with lentil salad, risotto with wild mushrooms, steamed black bass scented with kafir and bell pepper, roasted lobster ragout, or seared rack of lamb with eggplant tart. The wine list offers a well-chosen selection in a variety of price ranges. ♦ Fusion ♦ M-Sa breakfast, lunch, and dinner; Su breakfast. Reservations required; jacket required. 339.6719

122 Takashimaya Japan's largest retail conglomerate launched a unique venture in 1993 when it opened this elegant 20-story building designed by New York architect **John Burgee.** A distinctive array of East-meets-West design-sensitive products are sold on the third through fifth floors, ranging from home furnishings and fashion accessories to table and bed linens, specialty gifts, and objets d'art. The ground floor consists of a 4,500-square-foot gallery as well as a multilevel atrium, used as an exhibition space for contemporary Asian and American art and artisanal crafts. ♦ M-Sa. 693 Fifth Ave (between E 54th and E 55th Sts). 350.0115 &

Within Takashimaya:

Tea Box Cafe ★$ This soothing beige cafe in the store's basement is the perfect place for escaping the bustle of Midtown. Try one of the 40 varieties of tea, including apricot, lemongrass, and *hoiji-cha* (a woodsmoked green tea), and a delicate sandwich—shrimp or cucumber on pressed rice, smoked salmon, or chicken with wasabi. ♦ Japanese tearoom ♦ M-Sa lunch and afternoon tea. 350.0100 &

123 Elizabeth Arden Salon The famous red door leads to a world apart, filled with designer fashions, lingerie, and sportswear and a salon that has made pampering a fine art. The salon offers exercise facilities, massages, facials, hair styling, and more, all calculated to make you look and feel terrific. ♦ Daily. 691 Fifth Ave (between E 54th and E 55th Sts). 546.0200 &

123 Façonnable Replicating the Façonnable store on Rue Royale in Paris, this shop has already become a destination for well-heeled and well-dressed professional men who like the grouping of items by color and pattern. Choose from more than 7,000 ties and shirts in some 200 patterns. ♦ Daily. 689 Fifth Ave (at E 54th St). 319.0111 &

Directly after the Revolution, New York City had a short career as the capital of the young United States. George Washington was inaugurated in Lower Manhattan.

In 1826, Elisha Otis demonstrated his "safety holster" (or elevator-braking device) at America's first World's Fair, held at the Crystal Palace in New York City. His invention cleared the way for the construction of tall buildings.

124 Indonesian Pavilion This is one of the few remaining buildings from the time when 54th Street east and west of Fifth Avenue was called "The Art Gallery of New York Streets." It was designed in 1900 by **McKim, Mead & White** and built by W.E.D. Stokes, who sold it to William H. Moore, a founder of the United States Steel and American Can companies. Note the massive balcony and strong cornices—evidence of **Charles Follen McKim**'s interest in Renaissance architecture. It has recently been converted into the New York branch of the *Banco di Napoli.* ♦ 4 E 54th St (at Fifth Ave)

124 Gucci A staff that ranges from very pleasant to simply cool sells shoes and leather goods for men and women, exquisitely crafted by the generations-old Florentine family. Recently infused with a fresh breath of contemporary style, leather goods are now joined by suits, topcoats, dresses, ties, and scarves. The famed red and green stripe and internationally recognized double-linked Gs are omnipresent on handbags, boots, and luggage. ♦ M-Sa. 685 Fifth Ave (at E 54th St). 826.2600 &

124 Fortunoff You would never expect to find a reasonably priced jewelry and silver store on Fifth Avenue, but here is one (complete with a glitzy facade) that offers good prices on strings of pearls, gold chains, hammered silver pitchers, urns, chalices, sterling silver, and silver plate flatware by Oneida and Towle, Reed & Barton, and stainless-steel flatware by Fraser and Dansk. The sales help is refreshingly courteous. ♦ M-Sa. 681 Fifth Ave (between E 53rd and E 54th Sts). 758.6660 &

125 The Museum Company With the city's major (and sometimes minor) museums now offering handsomely-stocked gift stores that are as much a draw as the permanent art collections, this store one-ups them with a vast selection of items, all of which have been inspired by the great art collections of museums around the world. The two-floor shop's stock in trade includes such global treasures as boxed notes and greeting cards, coffee-table books, frames, jewelry, and journals. ♦ M-Sa. 673 Fifth Ave (at E 53rd St). 758.0976

125 Samuel Paley Plaza Named for the father of its benefactor, the late William S. Paley of **CBS,** this park is a spare, very welcome anomaly in the densest part of town. Good furniture and a wonderful waterfall provide the perfect spot to steal a moment's peace. The park was designed in 1967 by landscape architects Zion & Breen and consulting architect **Albert Preston Moore.** Just a few storefronts east on this side of the street is another tiny outdoor seating area, worth a visit to see the large graffiti-covered slabs from the Berlin Wall. ♦ E 53rd St (between Madison and Fifth Aves)

125 Seryna ★★$$$ Avoid the frenzied crowds at lunch and visit this handsome restaurant for dinner, when it becomes sedate and you can really enjoy the excellent steaks cooked on a hot stone at your table and served with garlic-soy and chili sauces. There's also excellent *shabu shabu*, and an array of fresh fish, including poached salmon, stuffed Dover sole, and eel teriyaki. The sushi and sashimi are also very fresh.
♦ Japanese ♦ M-F lunch and dinner; Sa dinner. Reservations recommended. 11 E 53rd St (between Madison and Fifth Aves). 980.9393

126 San Pietro ★★$$$ Sister restaurant to the Upper East Side's **Sistina,** this place features dishes from Italy's Amalfi Coast. Try the chickpea pasta with pesto, shrimp with peppers and herbs, black sea bass braised with fennel and red wine, or monkfish with aioli-pepper marinade. The sunny yellow setting, with jars of olives and sun-dried tomatoes, manages to feel simultaneously elegant and homey. ♦ Neapolitan ♦ M-Sa lunch and dinner. Reservations required; jacket and tie required. 18 E 54th St (between Madison and Fifth Aves). 753.9015 ♿

127 Bice ★★$$$ The long, curved white-marble bar, multilevel seating, bright lighting, and exquisite flower arrangements create a luxurious setting. The food can be a bit uneven, but among the more reliable main courses are roast rack of veal with new potatoes, baby chicken, and such grilled fish dishes as salmon, swordfish, or sole. ♦ Italian ♦ Daily lunch and dinner. Reservations recommended. 7 E 54th St (between Madison and Fifth Aves). 688.1999

128 Morrell & Company, The Wine Emporium A playground for oenophiles, this large, well-organized store carries practically every worthwhile label, including many direct imports. Service is knowledgeable but occasionally impatient. ♦ M-Sa. 535 Madison Ave (between E 54th and E 55th Sts). 688.9370 ♿

129 The Sony Building and Sony Plaza Known as the **AT&T Headquarters** until 1992, this pinkish granite building designed by **Philip Johnson** and **John Burgee** in 1984 continues to be recognized by its top, often referred to as "Chippendale" in style. At its base, the glass-enclosed building is a cross between a technology museum and an amusement park, open and free to the public. An authentic 1925 French mail plane hangs from the ceiling along with other props and klieg lights to create the impression of being backstage. On the main concourse you can spend hours in *Sony Style*, a hands-on interactive electronics boutique; *Sony Signatures*, licensed merchandise with familiar faces and logos on everything from T-shirts to baseball caps; and the most popular of them all, *Sony Wonder Technology Lab*, where you can design your own video, re-edit videos by rock's megastars, or operate a sonogram. Recuperate from it all at the enticing *Baked From Scratch*. The building's profile is one of the more recognizable elements in Manhattan's urban fabric.
♦ Free. 550 Madison Ave (between E 55th and E 56th Sts). Info 833.8830

130 Friars Club This is the private club for actors who invented the famous roasts, in which members poke fun at celebrity guests. The building is not open to the public.
♦ 57 E 55th St (between Park and Madison Aves). 751.7272

131 Oceana ★★★$$$$ When Rick Moonen, formerly of **The Water Club,** took charge of this kitchen already known for fine seafood, he proceeded to bring it up another level. Now diners in the pretty pastel room can experience such extraordinary dishes as oven-steamed spaghetti squash with vegetables and tomato *concassé* (reduction), crab cake with chipotle sauce, house-cured salmon gravlax with spicy black-bean cakes and cilantro crème fraîche, and grilled salmon paillard with asparagus in ginger-soy vinaigrette. ♦ Seafood ♦ M-F lunch and dinner; Sa dinner. Reservations required; jacket required. 55 E 54th St (between Park and Madison Aves). 759.5941

131 Bill's Gay Nineties ★$$ The sirloin steak special at this saloon is named for Diamond Jim Brady, who would be right at home here. A pianist plays in the dining room, where such American fare as salads, roast chicken, and grilled fish are served. ♦ American ♦ M-F lunch and dinner; Sa dinner. 57 E 54th St (between Park and Madison Aves). 355.0243

132 Hotel Elysée $$$ Tallulah Bankhead used to be a regular here, as was Tennessee Williams. Recently and handsomely renovated, the hotel still retains its Old-World atmosphere in spite of the modern buildings rising around it. Each of the 99 rooms has its own personality, and most go by names as well as numbers. ♦ 60 E 54th St (between Park and Madison Aves). 753.1066, 800/535.9733; fax 980.9278 ♿

Restaurants/Clubs: Red   **Hotels:** Blue

Shops/ ❦ Outdoors: Green   **Sights/Culture:** Black

Within the Hotel Elysée:

Monkey Bar ★★★$$$ The crowds inside the bar are so thick that it's sometimes impossible to see the whimsical monkey murals in this drop-dead-glamorous dining room. Try the *brandade* (a salt cod, olive oil, garlic, milk, and cream puree) ravioli. ♦ American ♦ M-F lunch and dinner; Sa dinner. Reservations required. 838.2600

133 Lever House **Gordon Bunschaft** was the partner in charge of this 1952 **Skidmore, Owings & Merrill** design. The first glass wall on Park Avenue, built when Charles Luckman was president of Lever Brothers, has, after a long battle, been awarded landmark status and saved from possible destruction or disfigurement. The articulate building displays the tenets of orthodox Corbusian Modernism: It is raised from the ground on columns, it has a roof garden, and there is a free facade on the outside and free plan on the inside. With the **Seagram Building** across the street, this is a landmark corner that changed the face of the city. ♦ 390 Park Ave (between E 53rd and E 54th Sts)

134 Central Synagogue This 1872 Moorish Revival building designed by **Henry Fernbach** is the oldest continuously used synagogue in the city. The onion domes on the 222-foot towers and the brightly stenciled interior add a bit of fancy to the mottled brownstone facade. ♦ 652 Lexington Ave (at E 55th St). 838.5122 &

135 Shun Lee Palace ★★★$$$$ Owner Michael Tong recently collaborated with designer Adam Tihany to renovate this landmark Chinese restaurant. The result includes blue-suede walls with gold-leaf panels, chandeliers of frosted glass, and mahogany cases displaying treasures of past dynasties. Try the unfortunately named dish *Ants Climb on Tree* (a combination of beef, Chinese broccoli, and cellophane noodles), steamed dumplings, orange beef, or whole poached sea bass with brown-bean sauce. ♦ Chinese ♦ Daily lunch and dinner. Reservations required. 155 E 55th St (between Third and Lexington Aves). 371.8844. Also at: 43 W 65th St (between Central Park W and Broadway). 595.8895

New York City post offices once used underground pneumatic tubes to rush mail between branches at speeds four times faster than could be reached via the streets.

Appointed in 1911, Samuel Battle was New York's first black police officer. He was promoted to lieutenant and later became a member of the Parole Commission.

136 Citicorp Center Designed in 1978 by **Hugh Stubbins & Associates,** the rakish angle of the building's top was planned as a solar collector but is now nothing more than a vent for the cooling system, which provides a steamy effect for the night lighting. Also under the roof is a 400-ton computer-operated Tuned Mass Damper (TMD or "earthquake machine" to most of us). They don't expect an earthquake any time soon, but the building (shown below) is cantilevered on 145-foot columns that allow it to sway in the wind. Those 10-story-high stilts also make it possible for the structure to be the world's only skyscraper with skylights; they brighten its sunken floors, where free concerts and other programs take place in the center of a gaggle of shops and restaurants. ♦ 153 E 53rd St (between Third and Lexington Aves). 559.1000

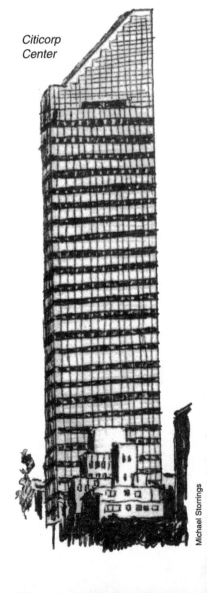

Citicorp Center

Michael Storrings

Within Citicorp Center:

St. Peter's Lutheran Church This church is a major reason for the engineering and formal antics of **Citicorp Center**'s design: The church refused to sell its air rights to Citicorp unless the bank agreed to build a new church clearly distinct from the tower with the skyscraper perched on 10-story stilts above it. In contrast to the high-tech tower, the church is granite, with wooden furnishings and interior detailing by Massimo and Lella Vignelli. Within the church, the **Erol Beaker Chapel** was created by sculptor Louise Nevelson. Watch for jazz vespers every Sunday at 5PM (the church is known as the city's jazz ministry). But the interior is well worth a look at any time. ♦ 619 Lexington Ave (at E 54th St). 935.2200 &

York Theatre Company at St. Peter's Church Two productions began in this excellent 165-seat space in the basement of **Citicorp Center** and went on to Broadway: *Tintypes* and *The Elephant Man*. ♦ 935.5820 &

The Market at Citicorp Center
Accessible from the sunken plaza at the corner of East 53rd Street and Lexington Avenue, this international bazaar offers three levels of dining as well as culinary and housewares shopping. Slate floors and an all-glass front add a homogeneity to the potpourri of shops. Midtown office workers fill up the tables, where you can bring food from the shops and restaurants at lunch or just sit and read a newspaper. Semi-regular free entertainment enlivens the atrium (check the posted list of scheduled events): weeknight cabaret and pop concerts at 6PM, Saturday night jazz at 8PM, Sunday classical concerts at noon, and often Saturday programs for kids at 11AM. ♦ Concert information: 559.1700

Nyborg-Nelson ★★$ The Scandinavian specialties served at this restaurant/take-out shop include gravlax, marinated herring, stuffed cabbage, and such sandwiches as Black Forest ham and brie, which the office workers from upstairs often take out. Table service is also available. ♦ Scandinavian ♦ M-Sa lunch and early dinner. Lobby level. 223.0700

37 **Fisher & Levy** Caterers Chip Fisher (of **Mr. Chips** Upper East Side ice-cream parlor fame) and Doug Levy are the owners of this decidedly upscale food store that also does a huge catering and delivery business. For breakfast, try the homemade doughnuts and **Petrossian** smoked-salmon platters; for lunch, order the California-style pizza. ♦ M-F. 875 Third Ave (at E 53rd St), Concourse level. 832.3880

38 **Solera** ★★$$ Tapas and other Spanish delicacies top the list in this stylishly redesigned town house. Specialties include empanadas (meat patties), grilled shrimp with garlic, pheasant and guinea hen terrine with morels, grilled salmon over vegetable puree with stuffed eggplant, roasted duck breast with lemon, and spiced peach and rhubarb compote. ♦ Spanish ♦ M-F lunch and dinner; Sa dinner. Reservations recommended. 216 E 53rd St (between Second and Third Aves). 644.1166

139 **Quest Book Shop of the New York Theosophical Society** The stated purpose of the society is: "To form a nucleus of the Universal Brotherhood of Humanity, without distinction of race, creed, sex, caste, or color. To encourage the study of Comparative Religion, Philosophy, and science. To investigate unexplained laws of Nature and the powers latent in man." ♦ M-Sa. 240 E 53rd St (between Second and Third Aves). 758.5521 &

140 **Il Nido** ★★$$$$ Excellent, if pricey, Italian food is served in this rustic dining room with timber beams and mirrors that are made to look like farmhouse windows. Try *malfatti* (irregularly shaped pasta squares filled with spinach and cheese), *linguine alla amatriciana* (in tomato sauce with onions and prosciutto), tortellini with four cheeses, baked red snapper with clams, and braised chicken in a white-wine sauce with mushrooms and tomato. ♦ Italian ♦ M-F lunch and dinner; Sa dinner. Reservations required; jacket and tie required. 251 E 53rd St (between Second and Third Aves). 753.8450

141 **La Mangeoire** ★★$$$ The atmosphere of this warm, rustic Provençal spot complements the piquant spices and sunny flavors of the dishes, which include *pissaladière* (an onion, anchovy, and olive tart) and penne with tomato, olive puree, and basil sauce. ♦ French ♦ M-F lunch and dinner; Sa-Su dinner. Reservations recommended. 1008 Second Ave (between E 53rd and E 54th Sts). 759.7086

142 **Le Perigord** ★★★$$$ A favorite haunt of **UN** ambassadors, this formal but cozy French restaurant has been around for about 30 years and may seem, in contrast to newer places, somewhat dated. But the room, with its pink banquettes, is still pretty, and owner George Briguet is a charming host. Try the foie gras in apple-and-truffle sauce; chateaubriand; frog's legs; or herb-stuffed quail with truffle sauce. Save room for one of the extraordinary soufflés. ♦ French ♦ M-F lunch and dinner; Sa-Su dinner. Reservations required; jacket and tie required. 405 E 52nd St (at First Ave). 755.6244

143 **River House** This 26-story, twin-towered, limestone and gray brick cooperative, built in 1931 by **Bottomley, Wagner & Whitee,** has always been one of the most exclusive apartment buildings in the city (when there was a dock on the river, only the best yachts used it). The lower floors house the **River Club,** which includes squash and tennis courts, a pool, and a ballroom. The building is not open to the public. ♦ 435 E 53rd St (between the East River and First Ave)

144 Sutton Place and Sutton Place South
Until colonized by Vanderbilts and Morgans moving from Fifth Avenue in the early 1920s, this elegant end of York Avenue was a run-down area. The town houses and apartment buildings are by such architects as **Mott Schmidt, Rosario Candela, Delano & Aldrich,** and **Cross & Cross.** Visit the park at the end of East 55th Street and the terrace on East 57th Street for views of the river and the Queensboro Bridge. Also peek in from East 58th Street, where Riverview Terrace, one of New York's last private streets, runs along the river lined with five ivy-covered brownstones. The secretary-general of the **United Nations** lives at **Nos. 1 to 3.** ♦ E 54th to E 59th Sts

145 54th Street Recreation Center
These turn-of-the-century enclosed public bathhouses built by **Werner & Windolph** in 1906 now offer an indoor running track, gymnasium facilities, and an indoor swimming pool open all year. ♦ M-F 3PM-10PM; Sa 10AM-5PM. 348 E 54th St (between First and Second Aves). 397.3154

146 Vong ★★★$$$ Superchef Jean-Georges Vongerichten (of **JoJo** and **Lipstick Cafe**) weighs in with his wonderful interpretation of Thai/French cuisine in an elegant Eastern-influenced space. Try sautéed duck foie gras with ginger sauce and mango, raw tuna, and vegetables in rice paper with dipping sauce; lobster with Thai herbs; and roasted baby chicken marinated with lemongrass and herbs. ♦ Thai/French ♦ M-F lunch and dinner; Sa dinner. 200 E 54th St (at Third Ave). 486.9592

146 Lipstick Cafe ★★$ In his "spare time," Jean-Georges Vongerichten (of **JoJo** and **Vong**) throws a tasty bone to hungry Midtown workers on a dining budget. Delicious homemade soups, salads, and sandwiches are served to go or stay. The baked goods are a real treat. ♦ American ♦ M-F breakfast and lunch. 885 Third Ave (at E 54th St). 486.8664 ♿

147 900 Third Avenue The aluminum section at the base of this brick-clad tower and the silhouette of the greenhouse at the top are a reference to the neighboring **Citicorp Center** across East 54th Street. It was built in 1983, five years after **Citicorp,** by **Cesar Pelli & Associates** with **Rafael Vinoly.** ♦ At E 54th S

148 P.J. Clarke's ★$$ There are few better places than this to witness rambunctious young professionals of Midtown getting slowly pickled during cocktail hour. Mysteriously, the hamburgers are famous, although habitués come here looking to meet, not eat, meat. ♦ American ♦ Daily lunch dinner, and late-night meals. 915 Third Ave (at E 55th St). 759.1650

149 Michael's Pub ★$$$ Well-known jazz singers and instrumentalists, including Mel Torme, perform nightly at Gil Wiest's restaurant, and on Monday nights when he's in town, Woody Allen puts in an appearance with his clarinet to play a few sets ♦ American ♦ M-F lunch and dinner; Sa dinne Reservations recommended. 211 E 55th St (between Second and Third Aves). 758.2272

150 The Manhattan Art & Antiques Center
More than a hundred dealers spread their quality wares over three large floors at Manhattan's specialized antiques "mall." One-stop shopping offers every imaginable item from affordable to exorbitant, from tiny pillboxes to magnificent chandeliers. The variety is extensive and prices are competitive. ♦ Daily. 1050 Second Ave (between E 55th and E 56th Sts). 355.4400 ♿

151 March ★★★$$$ Tucked away in a fin-de-siècle town house, this romantic restaurant is fitted with elegant banquettes and tapestries on the walls. The menu is eclectic (all dinners are prix-fixe); five-spice salmon with mushrooms and rack of lamb with a sweet mustard and herb crust are among some of the best entrées. Save room for desserts like crispy pancakes with vanilla ice cream, mango, and berries; Valrhona chocolate cake; or poached pear cake with lemon curd and spiced cranberry sauce. Another plus is the affordable wine list. ♦ American ♦ M-Sa prix-fixe dinner. Reservations recommended. 405 E 58th St (between Sutton Pl and First Ave). 838.9393

152 Rosa Mexicano ★★$$$ Forget about tacos and enchiladas; you won't miss them because in their stead are complex regional dishes—platters of fresh seafood, *carnitas* (barbecued pork), shrimp in mustard-chili vinaigrette, and chicken wrapped in parchment. The frozen margaritas aren't bad, either. ♦ Mexican ♦ Daily dinner. Reservations recommended. 1063 First Ave (at E 58th St). 753.7407

153 Café Nicholson ★$$$ Dining at this intimate, romantic hideaway is a theatrical experience. The fanciful decor, which include ornate hand-painted 19th-century tiles, is ri with antiques—furniture, paintings, and pottery. The eccentric owner opens the restaurant when he feels like it, so be sure to call in advance. On arrival, you may be asked whether you want the vanilla or chocolate soufflé. If you decline both, you may experience a slight chill in the air. ◆ French ◆ Tu-Sa dinner. Reservations required. 323 E 58th St (between First and Second Aves). 355.6769

154 Iris Brown's Victorian Doll and Miniature Shop For 25 years Brown has been specializing in dolls and dollhouses, miniature furniture and toys, and Christmas ornaments of the Victorian era. ◆ M-Sa. 253 E 57th St (between Second and Third Aves). 593.2882

154 Les Sans Culottes ★$$$ Each meal at this rustic bistro with dark wood beams begins with an overflowing basket of charcuterie. Pace yourself, because most of the food is just as rich. Dinners (all are prix-fixe) include such dishes as baby rack of lamb, shell steak, chicken with tangerine sauce, and duck with sherry sauce. ◆ French ◆ M-Sa lunch and dinner; Su dinner. Reservations recommended. 1085 Second Ave (between E 57th and E 58th Sts). 838.6660. Also at: 347 W 46th St (between Eighth and Ninth Aves). 247.4284

155 Bruno ★$$$ This sophisticated Italian restaurant has smooth service and a smart-looking modern dining room, but alas, an inconsistent menu. Among the hits are homemade fettuccine with portobello mushrooms, Cognac, and parmesan; grilled veal chop; marinated grilled jumbo shrimp with baby artichoke hearts; and sea bass with leeks and tomatoes. ◆ Italian ◆ M-F lunch and dinner; Sa dinner. Reservations recommended. 240 E 58th St (between Second and Third Aves). 688.4191

156 Felidia ★★$$$$ Owners Felix and Lidia Bastianich preside over their rustic brick and Tuscan-tiled namesake, which features such specialties from Lidia's native Istria (near Trieste) as *stinco di vitello* (roast veal shank sautéed in its own juices). Pastas are especially good, particularly the *pappardelle* (broad noodles) with porcini. ◆ Italian ◆ M-F lunch and dinner; Sa dinner. Reservations required; jacket required. 243 E 58th St (between Second and Third Aves). 758.1479

156 Silk Surplus Those in the know shop here and at the annex at 223 East 58th Street for generous discounts on Scalamandre and other luxurious fabrics used for upholstery, tablecloths, draperies, wallpapers, and trimmings. ◆ M-Sa. 235 E 58th St (between Second and Third Aves). 753.6511

157 Norton Books Books and periodicals on architecture, gardening, and interior design are the specialty of this small shop. ◆ M-Sa. 989 Third Ave (at E 59th St). 421.9025

158 Dawat ★★★$$$ Actress and cookbook author Madhur Jaffrey is the guiding spirit behind this sophisticated Indian restaurant, considered one of the best in town. Try *baghari jhinga* (shrimp with garlic, mustard seeds, and curry leaves) or vegetarian stew flavored with tamarind. ◆ Indian ◆ M-F lunch and dinner; Sa dinner. Reservations recommended. 210 E 58th St (between Second and Third Aves). 355.7555

159 Royal Athena Galleries Ancient, European, Oriental, pre-Columbian, and tribal works of art are sold here. Each object is labeled and has a price tag, but the staff enjoys answering questions from browsers as well as from serious collectors. ◆ M-Sa. 153 E 57th St (between Third and Lexington Aves). 355.2034 ౸

159 Nesle, Inc. Albert Nesle has combed the great houses of India, London, and Paris, and features the greatest collection of chandeliers, mirrors, and thrones in the city. ◆ M-F. 151 E 57th St (between Third and Lexington Aves). 755.0515 ౸

159 Le Colonial ★★$$ A glamorized Vietnamese bistro with white, black, and brown shutters and potted palms, this place has been packing them in since the day it opened in 1993. Choice dishes include spring rolls, ginger-marinated roast duck with tamarind dipping sauce, and crispy fried noodles with stir-fried vegetables. ◆ Vietnamese ◆ Daily lunch and dinner. Reservations required. 149 E 57th St (between Third and Lexington Aves). 752.0808

159 Hammacher Schlemmer Unintentionally one of the funniest stores in the city, it carries gadgetry to the limits of credibility with such items as a solar-powered ventilated golf cap, an electronic one-armed-bandit home casino, and an interactive talking chess game. On the practical side, it was the first store to introduce the steam iron, electric razor, and pressure cooker. The mail-order catalog is a kick, too. ◆ M-Sa. 147 E 57th St (between Third and Lexington Aves). 421.9000 ౸

160 The Fitzpatrick Manhattan Hotel $$$ One of the few hotels in this part of Midtown—and just two blocks from Bloomingdale's—this is the only US representation of a small Irish chain. A welcome attention to detail, 92 tastefully furnished rooms and public areas, marbled whirlpool baths, a smiling top-hatted bellman, and Irish-inspired hospitality make this a veritable oasis in the chaos of Midtown Manhattan. **Fitzers** serves an Irish grill including corned beef and cabbage. ♦ 687 Lexington Ave (between E 56th and E 57th Sts). 355.0100, 800/367.7701; fax 355.1371 ♿

161 Allerton Hotel for Women $ This hotel has a homelike atmosphere in a good location. Not all the 400 rooms have air-conditioning and only 70 have private baths, but there is a sunroof and a restaurant. ♦ 130 E 57th St (at Lexington Ave). 753.8841

162 The Gazebo Hundreds of old and new quilts fill this airy shop, which also features baskets, charming white wicker indoor and outdoor furniture, appliquéd and patchwork pillows, and unusually wide (11 feet) rag rugs. New quilts are produced to the store's specifications with American fabrics in Haiti. Both quilts and rugs can be custom-made. ♦ Daily. 127 E 57th St (between Lexington and Park Aves). 832.7077

162 The Galleria This midblock tower, designed in 1975 chiefly by **David Kenneth Specter** and **Philip Birnbaum,** comprises luxury apartments above a health club, retail facilities, and a public through-block arcade. Also worthwhile is the individualistic silhouette created by a multigreenhouse quadriplex (considered one of Manhattan's most expensive apartments) custom-built for philanthropist Stewart Mott. Apparently Mott had such a passion for fresh milk that he wanted to keep cows on the roof, and the building's board turned him down. ♦ 117 E 57th St (between Lexington and Park Aves)

163 Mitsukoshi ★★★$$$$ Follow the lead of Japanese businessmen and come here for perfect sushi and sashimi in a comfortable setting—dignified beige walls and subdued lighting. The private Tatami rooms are even more elegant. Try the grilled fish of the day, smoked eel, tempura, or one of the bento boxes during lunch. ♦ Japanese ♦ M-F lunch and dinner. Reservations recommended. 461 Park Ave (at E 57th St). 935.6444

163 Ritz Tower Emery Roth and **Carrère & Hastings** built this 42-story tower in 1925 as part of the Hearst apartment-hotel chain. Its stepped spire is still a distinctive mark in the skyline. ♦ 465 Park Ave (at E 57th St)

164 Argosy Book Store Few places in the United States have a better selection of historical pictures: photographs, posters, playbills, maps, engravings, lithographs, etchings, and woodcuts. ♦ M-Sa. 116 E 59th St (between Lexington and Park Aves). 753.4455

165 Helene Arpels The pampered feet of Jacqueline de Ribes and Marie-Helene de Rothschild are among those sporting Helene Arpels designs. Shoes for both men and women can be custom-decorated with hand embroidery, bead appliqué, stone studding, or exotic leathers. ♦ M-Sa. 470 Park Ave (between E 57th and E 58th Sts). 755.1623

166 Four Seasons Hotel $$$$ The tallest in town, this 52-story (plus tower) world-class hotel was designed by **I.M. Pei.** The sparse limestone lobby with its 33-foot onyx ceiling and serene public areas has been compared to a soaring marble mausoleum, cool and Zen-like in its simplicity. But the 367 elegant and spacious (600-square-foot) rooms are considerably cozier and warmer, with Art Deco–influenced decor and wonderful views of the city and **Central Park.** Services befitting such a deluxe operation include 24-hour concierge, well-equipped fitness facilities, an executive business center, and the lobby's busy **5757,** a contemporary American grill/restaurant serving breakfast, lunch, and dinner. If you're not content with your room's 120-square-foot bathroom, look into the heart-stopping $4,000-a-night Presidential Suite. ♦ 57 E 57th St (between Park and Madison Aves). 758.5700, 800/332.3442; fax 758.5711 ♿

166 Louis Vuitton Luggage and leather accessories with the familiar LV signature fill the store. The designer's new collection of leather goods in solid, bright colors presents a more contemporary look. ♦ M-Sa. 49 E 57th St (between Park and Madison Aves). 371.6111 ♿

166 Prada Milano The supple leather and industrial-nylon handbags and knapsacks sold here have become the accessories of choice for global customers who zealously follow this generations-old Milanese institution. Third-generation Miuccia Prada is responsible for the contemporary fashions displayed throughout the store, from shoes to separates. ♦ M-Sa. 45 E 57th St (between Park and Madison Aves). 308.2332

167 Buccellati Silver Italy's most opulent handcrafted silver, including flatware, is sold in this store. ♦ M-Sa. 46 E 57th St (between Park and Madison Aves). 308.2507

167 Sherle Wagner International Film stars, industrialists, and kings and queens are among the clientele of this purveyor of the most luxurious bathtubs, toilets, and sinks, including tubs of rose quartz, counters of tigereye, bidets of marble, and gold-plated basins. ♦ M-F. 60 E 57th St (between Park and Madison Aves). 758.3300 &

168 Le Chantilly ★★★$$$$ Young, creative chef David Ruggerio has infused the predictably classic cuisine with sunny new flavors, as is evident in such dishes as braised salmon in Moroccan spices and pan-seared lamb chop with eggplant tartlet, essence of tomato, and virgin olive oil. Vegetarians take note: There is an imaginative tasting menu available. The extensive wine list features top-quality red Bordeaux, and is generally expensive. ♦ French ♦ M-Sa lunch and dinner; Su dinner. Reservations recommended; jacket required. 106 E 57th St (between Lexington and Park Aves). 751.2931 &

168 Universal Pictures Building This 1947 building by **Kahn & Jacobs** is noteworthy as the first office building on this previously residential section of Park Avenue and as the first to be built to the "wedding cake" outline of the then-current zoning regulations. It is perhaps the best example of pre–glass-curtain wall design. Compare it to its 1972 counterpart across the street at 450 Park Avenue. ♦ 445 Park Ave (between E 56th and E 57th Sts)

169 Lombardy $$$ Built in 1927 by **Henry Mandell,** this residential hotel has transient suites and studios, each with a different decor and all with serving pantries and refrigerators. About a third of the accommodations are secured by long-term residents who call this home. ♦ 111 E 56th St (between Lexington

and Park Aves). 753.8600, 800/223.5254; fax 754.5683 &

170 Mercedes-Benz Showroom One of New York City's rare works by **Frank Lloyd Wright,** this 1955 design is a curious exercise in glass, ramp, plants, and fancy cars in a too-tight space. ♦ M-Sa 430 Park Ave (at E 56th St). 629.1666

171 The Drake Swissôtel $$$ Built by **Emery Roth** in 1927, this hotel was purchased by real-estate entrepreneur William Zeckendorf in the 1960s and became the home of the city's first discotheque, **Shepheards.** It was restored in 1980 and again in 1995 by the Swissôtel chain to its original elegance, and is now more a setting for chamber music than rock. The **Drake Bar** serves fresh seafood and grilled dishes with a Swiss flair. Amenities include refrigerators in all 615 rooms, 24-hour room service, concierge, and parking facilities. ♦ 440 Park Ave (at E 56th St). 421.0900, 800/372.5369; fax 688.8053

172 The Pace Gallery Among the heaviest of the city's heavy hitters, this gallery represents a formidable roster of artists and artists' estates, including Jim Dine, Chuck Close, Louise Nevelson, Mark Rothko, and Lucas Samaras. Housed in the same building are the gallery's many offspring—**Pace Prints, Pace Master Prints, Pace Primitive Art,** and **Pace/MacGill** for 20th-century photography. ♦ Tu-Sa. 32 E 57th St (between Park and Madison Aves). 421.3292. Also at: 142 Greene St (between Prince and W Houston Sts). 431.9224 &

172 Guy Laroche The city's only outpost for the ready-to-wear collection of this French label carries everything from silk camisoles to full-length ball gowns. ♦ M-Sa. 36 E 57th St (between Park and Madison Aves). 759.2301

173 Fuller Building The identification over the entrance of this black-and-white Art Deco tower, designed in 1929 by **Walker & Gillette,** is graced by a pair of figures by sculptor Elie Nadelman. The building is home to many art galleries, including **Marisa del Re, André Emmerich,** and **Susan Sheehan.** ♦ 41 E 57th St (at Madison Ave)

173 Ronin Gallery This is the place to see Japanese art, including woodblock prints, ivory netsuke, and metalwork from the 17th through 20th centuries. The gallery offers free appraisals of Japanese art. ♦ M-Sa. 605 Madison Ave (between E 57th and E 58th Sts). 688.0188

173 Maxwell Davidson Gallery This seasoned dealer, relocated from SoHo, hosts a variety of artists, with an emphasis on Realism. ♦ Tu-Sa. 41 E 57th St (at Madison Ave). 759.7555

Restaurants/Clubs: Red	Hotels: Blue
Shops/♥ Outdoors: Green	**Sights/Culture: Black**

174 Coming or Going ★★$$$ Romantic is the best way to describe this charming restaurant. It may also be the only place in the area with its own herb garden. Try yellowfin tuna *tartare* with seasoned cucumber and black-olive vinaigrette. ♦ American ♦ M-Sa lunch and dinner. Reservations recommended. 38 E 58th (between Park and Madison Aves). 980.5858

175 James II Galleries Edwardian and Victorian jewelry, Spode pottery, ironstone, majolica, brass, silver plate, and Art Nouveau and Art Deco silver are featured. ♦ M-Sa. 11 E 57th St (between Madison and Fifth Aves). 355.7040

175 Hermes Saddlery, scarves, and silk shirts are sold at this quintessentially Parisian original. Home of the Hermes tie, the foolproof gift for the boss who has everything. ♦ M-Sa. 11 E 57th St (between Madison and Fifth Aves), Ground floor. 751.3181

175 Chanel This world-class boutique was scheduled to open at press time in this more spacious location. It showcases the increasingly popular Chanel fashions and accessories. The scent of Coco remains, but it is Karl "the Kaiser" Lagerfeld who now calls the sartorial shots from his Paris atelier. ♦ Daily. 15 E 57th St (at Fifth Ave). 355.5050 &

176 IBM Building This 43-story green granite building, designed in 1982 by **Edward Larrabee Barnes,** rises dramatically over a high atrium containing tables and chairs for relaxing and lots of bamboo to take your mind off Midtown's hectic pace. That water rushing by outside the East 56th Street entrance is a horizontal fountain designed by Michael Helzer. Recently purchased by a multinational corporation, the building's future and possible change of name are uncertain. ♦ 590 Madison Ave (between E 56th and E 57th Sts)

177 Burberrys A recent redesign of the store mirrors the rejuvenated image this store hopes to project. Their classic raincoat has always possessed an incomparable style, but now the rest of the clothes for men and women—including hats, coats, jackets, trousers, and skirts—are striving to appeal to a less staid generation. ♦ Daily. 9 E 57th St (at Fifth Ave). 371.5010 &

177 Warner Brothers Studio Store Smack in the middle of a tony enclave of luxury stores and sky-high real estate is this three-story Hollywood-inspired shopping center that resembles a high-tech back lot, with TV screens playing old Warner Brothers movies. The gift-shop area is filled with watches, address books, posters, ties, mugs, and more. But if you're not in the mood to buy any of the 3,000 items (much of it apparel), just come for the experience. ♦ Daily. 1 E 57th St (at Fifth Ave). 754.0300 &

178 David McKee Gallery This small but very smart gallery boasts an impressive list of youngish artists like sculptor Martin Puryear and painters Sean Scully and Jake Berthot, as well as the estate of the influential Philip Guston. ♦ Tu-Sa. 745 Fifth Ave (between E 57th and E 58th Sts). 688.5951

178 Forum Twentieth-century figurative American paintings and sculpture by names such as William Beckman and Gregory Gillespie are featured in this gallery. ♦ Tu-Sa. 745 Fifth Ave (between E 57th and E 58th Sts). 355.4545

178 Bergdorf Goodman Men According to department store's chairman, Ira Neimark, this store is "for the sort of men who dine at the best restaurants, stay at the best hotels, and join the best clubs." What do these men wear? Shirts from Turnbull & Asser and Charvet; suits from Zegna and Brioni, Luciana Barbera, and St. Andrews; sportswear from Willis & Geiger. The couture also leans toward the cutting edge with names like Romeo Gigli and Dolce & Gabbana. ♦ M-Sa. 745 Fifth Ave (between E 57th and E 58th Sts). 753.7300 &

179 Bergdorf Goodman The most luxurious of the city's legendary department stores (although there is some moderately priced merchandise), the idea that living well is the best revenge reigns, partly because of the architecture (high ceilings, delicate moldings, arched windows) and partly because of the wares. It was the first store to promote the designers of Milan with a vengeance. And all the merchandise bears the stamp of luxury, whether it's the impeccable clothing by Donna Karan and Calvin Klein, the iridescent jewelry of Ted Muehling, the aromatic scents from London's Penhaligon, delicate candies from Manon Chocolates, or glove-leather bags by Paloma Picasso. There is also a top-of-the-line beauty salon **(Frederic Fekkai)** and a cafe. ♦ M-Sa. 754 Fifth Ave (between W 57th and W 58th Sts). 753.7300 &

179 Van Cleef & Arpels When the late Shah of Iran needed a tiara made for his Empress Farah, he came here. The boutique department, where jewelry ranges from moderate to expensive, is actually in **Bergdorf**'s main store next door, while gemstones that cost more are sold here. Jewelry can be custom-designed. Estate jewelry is also bought and sold. The guard is formidable, but the salespeople at least deign to acknowledge customers who make it past him. ♦ M-Sa. 744 Fifth Ave (at W 57th St). 644.9500 &

180 9 West 57th Street Designed in 1974 by **Skidmore, Owings & Merrill,** the best feature of this black glass swoop—built at the same time and by the same designers as the **W.R. Grace Building** on 42nd Street—is its address: The big red "9" is by graphic designer Ivan Chermayeff. ◆ Between Fifth and Sixth Aves

181 The Crown Building At 26 stories, this was once the tallest building on Fifth Avenue above 42nd Street. Originally called the **Heckscher Building,** it was designed by **Warren & Wetmore** and built in 1922 as a wholesale center for women's fashions. In 1929, the **Museum of Modern Art** opened its first gallery here. The gold leaf on the facade and tower is recent, as is the lighting of this entire intersection. ◆ 730 Fifth Ave (between W 56th and W 57th Sts)

Within The Crown Building:

Bulgari Elegantly nestled on the corner of one of the world's most expensive–per–commercial-square-foot intersections is this temple to the Rome-based jeweler of the privileged. Bold mountings offset the precious stones of vibrant colors for which this generations-old house is renowned. The intricate workmanship of some pieces is often an engineering and artisanal feat. ◆ M-Sa. 315.9000

182 Tiffany & Co. Built in 1940 by **Cross & Cross,** this store has become so famous for quality and style that many of its well-designed wares have become classics: the all-purpose wineglass and Wedgwood china, to name just a couple. Given as gifts, these items are further enhanced by the cachet of the signature light-blue box. In addition to table appointments, the store also boasts a selection of fine jewelry, gems, stationery items, crystal, clocks, and watches in all price ranges. Salespeople are friendly and helpful. The window displays are worth going out of your way to see—especially at Christmas. ◆ M-Sa. 727 Fifth Ave (at E 57th St). 755.8000

William Marcy "Boss" Tweed began his political career in 1848 as the organizer of the Americus Volunteer Fire Company, whose unusually large fire engine was painted with the head of a tiger. The fire company was associated with Tammany Hall (the Democratic political machine), and it was an easy step from one to the other. By 1853 Tweed had become a congressman; by 1867 he was powerful enough to overthrow Reform mayor Fernando Wood and put his own man, George Opdyke, in charge at City Hall. In 1868, he became Grand Sachem of Tammany Hall, which gave him backroom control over the state as well as the city. Attacks by cartoonist Thomas Nast in *Harper's Weekly* led to his downfall in 1873. He was convicted, but jumped bail and slipped away to Spain, where he was captured by police who recognized him from the Nast cartoons. He died in prison three years later.

183 Trump Tower Donald Trump, the developer whose name this building bears, currently lives here in a triplex. Offices fill the lower floors, along with a glitzy six-story atrium replete with a vertical waterfall along a soaring pink granite wall. Its image as a home base for exclusive stores such as **Ferragamo, Cartier,** and **Harry Winston** has been slightly tempered by the arrival of less elitist retailers like **Coach** and **Tower Records.** Cafes and restaurants are on the sunken ground level. Built in 1983, the tower was designed by **Der Scutt** of **Swanke, Hayden, Connell & Partners.** ◆ Daily. 725 Fifth Ave (at E 56th St). 832.2000 &

184 Steuben More like a museum than a store, engraved sculptures featuring Chinese calligraphy, animals, or even a forest of spreading pine are showcased here. All are displayed in backlit glass cases in a gray-walled sanctuary. The State Department buys its gifts for heads of state here, and the hoi polloi find crystal in the shape of dolphins, elephants, and hippopotamuses. ◆ M-Sa. 717 Fifth Ave (at E 56th St). 752.1441, 800/424.4240

185 Henri Bendel The windows are among the most imaginative in New York, but don't stop there. Shopping here is an experience no one should miss. This exclusive store is filled with unique merchandise, including tabletop wares by Frank McIntosh, and it's still fun to kick up your heels and announce you just got those stunning shoes at **Bendel's** (be sure to say *Ben-dls*, as the natives do). The second floor's **Petite Cafe** and **Salon de The** are pricey but delightful. ◆ Daily. 712 Fifth Ave (between W 55th and W 56th Sts). 247.1100

185 Harry Winston, Inc. The father of this world-famous seller of diamonds owned a little jewelry store on Columbus Avenue, but Harry went into business for himself while he was still a teenager and eventually established what may be the most intimidating diamond salon in the city. It is the only store on Fifth Avenue that processes diamonds from rough stones to finished jewelry. ◆ M-Sa. 718 Fifth Ave (at W 56th St). 245.2000

FELISSIMO

186 Felissimo ★★$ Located within a turn-of-the-century town house built by **Warren & Wetmore** in 1901, this landmark building is the setting for a fourth-floor tearoom in the elegant store of the same name. Providing an oasis of calm in frenzied Midtown, the beige walls, natural wood, and gentle New Age background music here make this an ideal place to linger—even over a lone cup of tea.

211

The 27 types of tea, including orange-ginger-mint and mango-Ceylon, are served in Japanese cast-iron pots and go nicely with homemade scones, particularly the spicy ginger heart-shaped variety. There are also pasta dishes, including bowties with chicken, red peppers, and broccoli in a sun-dried tomato–soy vinaigrette. ♦ American ♦ M-Sa breakfast, lunch, and afternoon tea. Reservations recommended. 10 W 56th St (between Fifth and Sixth Aves). 956.4438 &

186 L'Ermitage ★★$$ The cream-colored walls are hung with 19th-century Russian paintings, the lighting is subdued, and the menu reflects both the French and Russian nationals in the kitchen. Don't miss the *pelmeni* (nicely spiced Siberian meat dumplings served with just a touch of sour cream), blini with caviar, and marinated lamb. Finish the meal off with a warm fruit tart, particularly if it's plum. ♦ Russian/French ♦ M-F lunch and dinner; Sa dinner. Reservations recommended. 40 West 56th St (between Fifth and Sixth Aves). 581.0777 &

187 Grace Borgenicht Milton Avery and other masters of 20th-century art and promising newcomers are shown here. ♦ Tu-Sa. 724 Fifth Ave (at W 56th St), Eighth floor. 247.2111 &

187 Virginia Zabriskie American and European painting, sculpture, and photography of the 20th century are shown in this quality gallery. Zabriskie represents the estates of such modern masters as Archipenko, Zorach, and Kunioshi. ♦ Tu-Sa. 724 Fifth Ave (at W 56th St), 12th floor. 307.7430 &

187 OMO Norma Kamali Kamali is the designer who put many American women into high-fashion sweatshirt dresses, blouses, slit skirts, and cocoon wraps. The bottom floor carries shoes, less expensive cottons and lycra knits, and swimsuits, while the upstairs floor has one-of-a-kind eveningwear. Kamali is also known for her outerwear, particularly her talent for making down coats and jackets look fashionable. ♦ M-Sa. 11 W 56th St (between Fifth and Sixth Aves). 957.9797 &

187 Doubleday This respected bookstore keeps a high profile of new releases in fiction and nonfiction, backlist books, and trade and mass market paperbacks on four well-arranged floors. Especially good for cookbooks, art, and applied art, they'll ship anywhere in the world. ♦ Daily. 724 - Fifth Ave (between W 56th and W 57th Sts). 397.0550

187 Kennedy Galleries Works by American artists from the 18th century on, including John Singleton Copley, Edward Hopper, Georgia O'Keeffe, and John Marin, are shown at this newly relocated gallery, founded in 1874. Its catalogs are wonderful, too. ♦ Tu-Sa. 730 Fifth Ave (between W 56th and W 57th Sts), Second floor. 541.9600 &

188 Kiiroi Hana ★★$$ The simple but carefully selected Japanese menu offers dishes besides sushi, including bacon-wrapped filet mignon, *negimaki* (steak wrapped around scallions), salmon teriyaki, and noodle dishes. For an extra treat, sit at the sushi bar and watch the deft assembly behind the counter, but be prepared for a manic lunchtime scene as everyone arrives and scrambles for seats seemingly all at once. ♦ Japanese ♦ M-Sa lunch and dinner; Su dinner. Reservations recommended for dinner. 23 W 56th St (between Fifth and Sixth Aves). 582.7499

189 Darbar Indian Restaurant ★★★$$$ This is easily one of the best and loveliest Indian dining spots in town. The decor is authentic and beautiful—full of tasteful tapestries and brass appointments; the fabric-covered walls are decorated with copper hangings. Downstairs are several quiet little corner tables, separated by screens that offer complete privacy. The staff is friendly and helpful, and the kitchen thoroughly professional. To start, try the delightful *pakoras* (fried spinach fritters) and move on to *josh vindaloo* (lamb stew cooked with potatoes in a hot curry sauce) or *murgh tikka masala* (chicken in a mild, creamy tomato sauce). ♦ Indian ♦ M-F lunch and dinner; Sa-Su dinner. Reservations recommended. 44 W 56th St (between Fifth and Sixth Aves). 432.7227

190 Harley Davidson Cafe ★$$ Welcome to Harleywood. Located in the formerly staid American Savings Bank building, the cafe seats up to 300 (in nice weather, 100 more can be accommodated in what is Midtown's largest outdoor seating area). Inside, Harleys dangle from the ceiling in an atmosphere that's somewhere between Mardi Gras and mayhem. The menu features blackened chicken, burgers, sandwiches, and Mississippi mud pie. ♦ American ♦ Daily lunch, dinner, and late-night meals. 1370 Sixth Ave (at W 56th St). 245.6000 &

191 Frumkin/Adams Gallery The blue-ribbon stable of contemporary artists includes Jack Beal, Robert Arneson, and Luis Cruz Azaceta.

♦ Tu-Sa. 50 W 57th St (between Fifth and Sixth Aves), Second floor. 757.6655 &

191 Marlborough Gallery One of New York's old-line establishments represents some of the most important names in European and American art, including Larry Rivers, Fernando Botero, Red Grooms, and Magdalena Abakanowicz. ♦ M-Sa. 40 W 57th St (between Fifth and Sixth Aves), Second floor. 541.4900 &

192 J.N. Bartfield Galleries & Books Nineteenth-century American and European art, including works by Remington, Russell, and other masters of the American West, are displayed here, along with elegantly bound antiquarian books by famous authors such as Shakespeare and Dickens. ♦ M-F mid-October–May; M-Sa June to mid-October. 30 W 57th St (between Fifth and Sixth Aves), Third floor. 245.8890 &

192 Galerie St. Etienne This import from Vienna features works by Austrian and German Expressionists as well as European and American folk art. ♦ Tu-Sa. 24 W 57th St (between Fifth and Sixth Aves), Eighth floor. 245.6734 &

192 William H. Schab Gallery Master prints and drawings by such artists as Delacroix, Dürer, Piranesi, and Rembrandt are showcased. ♦ Tu-Sa. 24 W 57th St (between Fifth and Sixth Aves). 974.0337 &

192 Marian Goodman Gallery The gallery's stark but generous space is devoted to a host of weighty imported talents, including the German painter Anselm Kiefer and British sculptor Tony Cragg. Don't miss the gallery's new space, where **Multiples,** the print-publishing arm, displays its wares. ♦ M-Sa. 24 W 57th St (between Fifth and Sixth Aves), Fourth floor. 977.7160 &

192 Susan Bennis/Warren Edwards The designers of this collection of shoes for men and women use such exotic skins as baby crocodile, ostrich, and emu. Styles include sexy hot-weather sandals, tasseled loafers, evening pumps of lace and *peau de soie* for women, patent leather for men, and boots in unusual materials and colors. ♦ Daily. 22 W 57th St (between Fifth and Sixth Aves). 755.4197 &

192 Blum Helman Gallery This unusually large space features contemporary American painting and sculpture. ♦ Tu-Sa. 20 W 57th St (between Fifth and Sixth Aves), Second floor. 245.2888 &

193 Rizzoli Bookstore The ultimate bookstore, it is reminiscent of an oak-paneled library in an opulent Italian villa, with classical music playing (records are for sale) and a hushed, unhurried atmosphere. Known for foreign-language, travel, art, architecture, and design books, the store also has an outstanding

foreign and domestic general interest and design periodical department. The building dates from the turn of the century, and was restored in 1985 by **Hardy Holzman Pfeiffer Associates.** ♦ Daily. 31 W 57th St (between Fifth and Sixth Aves). 759.2424. Also at: 454 W Broadway (between Prince and W Houston Sts). 674.1616; 3 World Financial Center (at Vesey St). 385.1400

193 Brewster Gallery The graphics at this gallery are by such important European artists as Picasso, Miró, and Chagall. ♦ Tu-Sa. 41 W 57th St (between Fifth and Sixth Aves), Third floor. 980.1975 &

193 Hacker Art Books This store features in- and out-of-print art books and reprints, plus some excellent bargains on the literature of the visual arts. ♦ M-Sa. 45 W 57th St (between Fifth and Sixth Aves). 688.7600 &

194 Jean Lafitte ★★$$$ This cozy Parisian-style neighborhood bistro in the heart of Manhattan is no flash in the pan—it's been around for years, thanks to a reliably good menu and loads of charm. Onion soup—perfect on a wintery day—and the authentic *choucroute* come highly recommended. Also try the rack of lamb with roasted garlic, chicken grilled with rosemary, and roast duck with grapes. ♦ French ♦ M-F lunch and dinner; Sa-Su dinner. 68 W 58th St (between Fifth and Sixth Aves). 751.2323

195 Wyndham Hotel $$ This remarkably comfortable hotel is a favorite with stars appearing on Broadway, many of whom, such as Peter Falk, Hume Cronyn, and the late Ingrid Bergman, could easily have afforded to stay at the **Plaza.** Some stars, planning for a long Broadway run, have been known to arrive with their own furniture. Although there are over 200 rooms, the atmosphere is that of a small, charming hotel. ♦ 42 W 58th St (between Fifth and Sixth Aves). 753.3500, 800.257.1111; fax 754.5638 &

196 The Manhattan Ocean Club ★★★$$$ The excellent seafood here reflects an often overlooked fact—New York is still a port, with easy access to the treasures of the sea. Try appetizers of seared tuna with lattice potatoes and *salsa verde,* or baked oysters with morel cream; follow with grilled swordfish with cream of lentil curry, salmon with tandoori spices, or red snapper with rosemary crust. The owner's personal collection of more than a dozen Picasso ceramics is on display. The wine list is extensive, well chosen, and well priced. ♦ Seafood ♦ M-F lunch and dinner; Sa-Su dinner. Reservations recommended; jacket and tie requested. 57 W 58th St (between Fifth and Sixth Aves). 371.7777

197 St. Moritz on the Park $$$ Designed in 1931 by **Emery Roth & Sons,** this park-side hotel has 680 small but comfortable rooms. Parkview and the less-expensive Avenue-view rooms have been renovated. Not yet renovated and facing a courtyard are a number of the least expensive rooms available. Niceties include room service, a newsstand, and a gift shop. ♦ 50 Central Park S (at Sixth Ave). 755.5800, 800/221.4774; fax 751.2952 ♿

Within the St. Moritz on the Park:

Rumpelmayer's $$ A recent renovation stripped down the faded grandeur of this deluxe ice-cream parlor so that it now looks like one of the many overpriced coffee shops of the faux Deco variety. But it's still *the* place to go for a fabulously rich hot chocolate. The restaurant of the **St. Moritz** hotel, it also has a full menu of appetizers, entrées, snacks, and desserts, including New Wave Chicken (strips of lemon-pepper chicken served with Caesar's salad), crab cakes with sweet-potato fries and a mixed green salad, the famous Rumpelmayer's club sandwich, and the Banana Royale (with five kinds of ice cream, any number of toppings, whipped cream and a cherry). ♦ Continental ♦ M-F breakfast, lunch, dinner, and late-night meals; Sa-Su brunch, dinner, and late-night meals. 50 Central Park S (at Sixth Ave). 755.5800

By the 1800s, Yorkville had become a haven for middle-class Germans, although the majority of Manhattan Germans still lived on the Lower East Side in an area around Tompkins Square Park called "Kleindeutschland." By the turn of the century, many German families were leaving the southern part of the island to resettle in Yorkville in order to avoid the waves of immigrants from Eastern Europe and Italy. The single greatest event that originally brought New York Germans to Yorkville was the *General Slocum* disaster of 1904. This excursion steamer was filled with passengers, mostly women and children from Kleindeutschland. It burned and sank in the East River, killing more than a thousand people. The men of these families, who had not been on board because they could not get away from work that day, found their empty homes unbearable. They moved to Yorkville to help them forget.

198 Mickey Mantle's ★$$ Sports fans of all ages love this place. They get to watch the day's big game or memorable moments of the late New York Yankee hero on huge video screens, and study the restaurant's collection of uniforms and memorabilia. The basic American fare—gigantic burgers, ribs, and hot-fudge sundaes. ♦ American ♦ Daily lunch and dinner. 42 Central Park S (between Fifth and Sixth Aves). 688.7777

198 Helmsley Park Lane Hotel $$$ A relative newcomer to the neighborhood, the arches at the top of this 46-story building designed by **Emery Roth & Sons** in 1971 add interest to the block. Harry and Leona Helmsley (of tax-evasion fame), who own several hotels and a lot of real estate in Manhattan, once picked this as their own home address. Today it's undergoing a long-term renovation, with half of its 640 rooms finished at press time. Marble and chandeliers abound, and the multilingual staff is eager to please. ♦ 36 Central Park S (between Fifth and Sixth Aves). 371.4000, 800/221.4982; fax 319.9065

199 Grand Army Plaza One of the city's few formal pedestrian spaces, the plaza (dissected by **Central Park South**) acts as both a forecourt to the **Plaza Hotel** to the south and as an entrance terrace to **Central Park** to the north. Although the wall of the square has been weakened by the **GM Building,** the center has held strong, solidly anchored by the circular Pulitzer Memorial Fountain, built with funds provided in Joseph Pulitzer's will and designed by **Carrère & Hastings.** The sculpture on top is by Karl Bitter, and the equestrian statue of General William Tecumseh Sherman (by Augustus Saint-Gaudens) was displayed at the **World Exhibition** in Paris in 1900 and was erected here in 1903. Tradition still survives in the horse-drawn carriages that congregate here. They were the limousines of another era, and in the 1930s, Hollywood loved to send romancing couples off in them for jaunts in **Central Park.** You can still take a romantic ride through the park in a carriage, many with top-hatted drivers. ♦ Fifth Ave (between W 58th and W 60th Sts)

199 The Plaza Hotel $$$ This hotel is a legend in its own time, a landmark that has hosted Teddy Roosevelt, the Beatles, and F. Scott Fitzgerald and his wife, Zelda (who, it's rumored, danced nude in the fountain out front). Solomon R. Guggenheim lived for years in the State Suite surrounded by

Restaurants/Clubs: Red   **Hotels:** Blue

Shops/ ♟ **Outdoors:** Green   **Sights/Culture:** Black fabulous paintings, and **Frank Lloyd Wright** made the grande dame his New York headquarters.

This stylish Edwardian/French pile dating from 1907 is considered one of architect **Henry J. Hardenbergh**'s masterpieces (he also did the **Dakota** apartments). **Warren & Wetmore** oversaw the 1921 addition. Located on a unique site with two sides of the building equally exposed, the dignified hotel has survived many years as the center of high social activity. The decor, size, and location of the 804 rooms vary wildly (resultantly in price as well: from \$\$\$ to \$\$\$\$). Many of the lovely high-ceilinged ones are still in top condition, but some face air shafts. Request an outside room— or better still, a park view. The 24-hour room service remains, and so do the flags outside representing countries of important foreign guests. Donald Trump bought the hotel in 1988; his now ex-wife, Ivana, oversaw a major renovation and hired several of New York's top hotel personnel, but she has since left. **The Oak Bar and Restaurant** is still in its original (woody, elegant, and comfortable) condition; the **Oyster Bar** still opens sparkling fresh clams and oysters to order; and the venerable, paneled **Edwardian**

Room is still a fashionable spot for dining and dancing. The fabled **Palm Court** in the lobby is fine and festive, particularly as a choice for high tea. The trendy **Gauguin** tropical restaurant and club is located where the old **Trader Vic's** used to be, and is more popular for tropical drinks than its less than authentic menu. ♦ Fifth Ave (between W 58h St and W 59th Sts). 546.5493, 800/759.3000; fax 546.5324 &

200 **FAO Schwarz** Because this is the best-stocked toy store in the United States, some parents never bring their kids here; the sight of so many toys can turn children into monsters of greed. The inexhaustible stock includes Madame Alexander dolls, Steiff stuffed animals, LGB electric trains, outdoor swings, magic tricks, video games, and hundreds of other amusements. At Christmastime you may have to wait in line just to go inside. This is *Babes in Toyland.* ♦ Daily. 767 Fifth Ave (between E 58th and E 59th Sts). 644.9400 &

201 **Baccarat** Newly expanded and more luxurious than ever, this is where to come for world-famous crystal, Limoges china, plus fine glassware and silver. ♦ M-Sa. 625 Madison Ave (at E 59th St). 826.4100, 800/777.0100

Bests

Henry Wolf
Photographer

Taking a cab up **Park Avenue** at 2AM, making 15 blocks on one light, easy.

Jim McMullen's—a lively, congenial place to eat and look at models, politicians, yuppies, and Wall Streeters and taste good, reasonable food. Chicken potpie, mashed potatoes, and chocolate brownies.

Joan Juliet Buck
Novelist/Film Critic/Journalist

The **West 27th Street Flea Market** for relics from the 1920s.

E.A.T. on Madison Avenue for the deep-fried baby artichokes.

The **Fifth Avenue** bus all the way downtown.

Strand Bookstore, because you don't know what you don't know till you find it here, usually from the top of a ladder and slightly out of reach, definitely out of print.

Weekend lunch at **Petaluma** because it's bright and the *quattro stagioni* pizza is perfect.

Ballet lessons at any reliable ballet school.

The **Russian Samovar** because it's Roman Kaplan's Moscow—poets, dancing dervishes, jazzmen from Kiev.

Fred Ferretti
Columnist, *Gourmet* magazine

A bowl of fresh and thick barley soup with mushrooms in **Ratner's Dairy Restaurant** on the Lower East Side. With onion rolls.

The cooking, on any day, in the very best of the city's French restaurants—**Lutèce, La Reserve,** and **Montrachet.**

Some of the best Italian cooking, in a place overrun by Italian restaurants, in, of all places, **Le Cirque,** where Sirio Maccioni is teaching his bright young French chefs the niceties of *la cucina rustica.*

There is nothing better than a hot dog, boiled on a street cart, served with a lot of mustard and a bit of sauerkraut, and eaten while sitting with *General Sherman* at the entrance to **Central Park.**

The 100-year-old Spanish tiles, the Tiffany lamp, the marble statuary, the lure of the city's most romantic restaurant, **Café Nicholson.**

Breakfast, lunch, or dinner, provided they have slabs of that rough country pâté, at **Café des Artistes,** just outside Central Park's western border.

The upper right-field stands of **Yankee Stadium** on a hot Sunday afternoon with a cold beer, hoping that Don Mattingly will hit one near you.

The best steak in the city at **Sparks** steak house, with a selection from what may well be New York's best list of American wines.

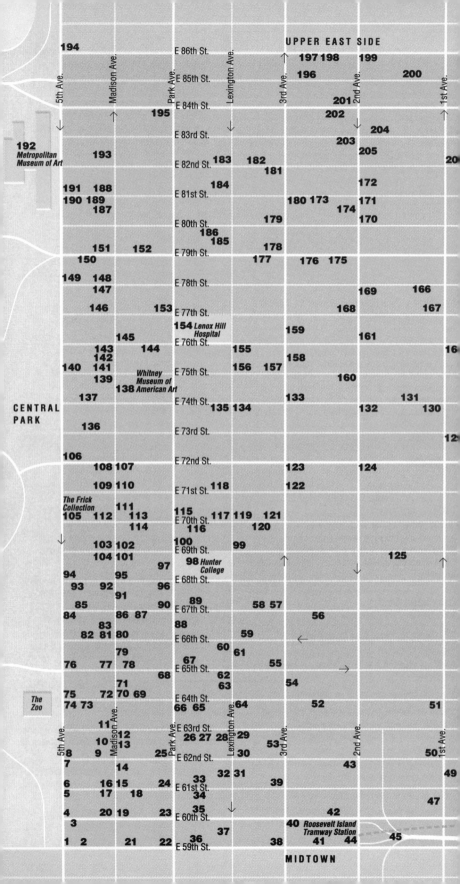

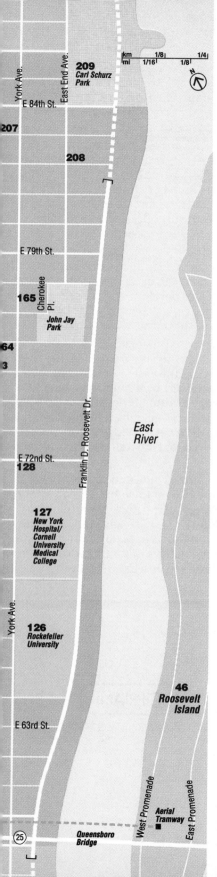

East Side

In the 1920s, *The New York Times* described the East Side as "a string of pearls: Each pearl is a double block of millionaires, and **Madison Avenue** is the string." Like everything else about New York, the East Side has been altered by time. But there are few places in the city where memory is as intact as in the blocks bounded by **East 59th** and **East 86th Streets**, and **Fifth Avenue** and the **East River**.

Until the close of the Civil War, this was the part of New York where the fashionable gathered to escape city summers—the counterpart of today's Hamptons on Long Island's South Shore. At the end of the 18th century, a necklace of mansions in parklike settings followed the shore of the East River all the way to Harlem. The **Boston Post Road**, now **Third Avenue**, made access to the city below Canal Street convenient, and summer residents with lots of leisure time traveled downtown on steamboats. By the late 1860s, the old summer houses were converted to year-round use for pioneering commuters, and, a few years later, the coming of elevated railroads on **Second** and Third Avenues opened the area to working-class people.

The improved transportation brought summer fun-seekers as well. The area bounded by **East 66th** and **East 75th Streets** from Third Avenue to the East River became **Jones's Wood**. It included such attractions as a beer garden, a bathhouse, an athletic club, and a block-long coliseum for indoor entertainment.

High society became firmly ensconced on the East Side when Caroline Schermerhorn Astor built a mansion on Fifth Avenue at **East 65th Street** in 1896. (She had been forced uptown from Fifth Avenue at 34th Street when her nephew built the **Waldorf Hotel** next door to her house. She would later build her own, the **Astoria Hotel**; both were relocated to the present **Park Avenue** site of the **Waldorf-Astoria Hotel** when the **Empire State**

Building went up in their stead.) Her presence here was only part of the draw for people such as the Fiskes, the Havemeyers, the Armours, and jeweler Charles Tiffany. Just as important was the completion of **Central Park** (providing a verdant buffer on the west) and the railroad that ran down what is now Park Avenue, which kept the riffraff in their place to the east.

Society had its heyday on the East Side between 1895 and the outbreak of World War I. The state of American architecture was superb at the time, and the super rich had the financial resources to hire the best. Technology was very much in vogue then, and it was a rare four-story house that didn't have at least one elevator. Nearly every house had an elaborate intercom system, and all installed dumbwaiters, usually electrically operated, to make life simpler for the servants.

But the showplace was the bathroom—no New York house had indoor plumbing until the **Croton Aqueduct** began operating in 1842. Until the turn of the century, the style had been to bathe in dark, wood-paneled rooms designed to conceal their use. As the East Side developed after 1895, elaborate ceramic fixtures, imported tiles, gold-plated pipes, and showers that sprayed water in several directions at once were considered absolute necessities.

Up until 1900, any family sharing a house with other families (except servants, of course) was labeled déclassé. But when the barrier fell, the "best of the best" apartment buildings appeared on the East Side, especially along Park Avenue, which after 1915 became what one contemporary called "a mass production of millionaires." The huge apartment houses created a kind of leveling effect among the wealthy, as well as a guarantee that this would remain *their* kind of neighborhood. They didn't even budge during the Great Depression, when armies of the unemployed took up residence across the way in **Central Park.**

The 1960s brought construction of uninspiring white and yellow brick apartment houses to the area; many of the elegant town houses had already been broken up into multiple-unit dwellings years before. Nevertheless, an air of privileged—often luxurious—lifestyle still prevails. And at the very mention of a stroll to the East Side, one still thinks of Madison Avenue and its roster of exclusive galleries and fashion boutiqes brimming with European designer labels. The neighborhood continues to be what it has been for nearly a century: New York City's elite enclave.

1 Sherry-Netherland Hotel $$$$
One of the grandes dames rimming **Central Park,** this hotel, designed in 1927 by **Schultze & Weaver** and built by Louis Sherry of ice cream fame, was once the centerpiece of an elegant trio, sitting between **The Pierre** and the **Savoy-Plaza** (whose site now hosts the **General Motors** tower). Its high-peaked roof sports gargoyles and chimneys like a Loire Valley confection. On the walls lining the entrance are panels rescued from a Vanderbilt mansion by **Richard Morris Hunt.** The 65-room hotel reopened in 1993 after a two-year total renovation that cost $18 million. Service is continental luxury class, and the rooms are large, many with park views. ◆ 781 Fifth Ave (at E 59th St). 355.2800, 800/247.4377; fax 319.4306

Within the Sherry-Netherland Hotel:

Harry Cipriani ★★$$$$ If you can't get to Venice to experience the original **Harry's Bar,** this spin-off comes pretty close. *Bellinis* (made from peach nectar and dry Prosecco wine) are specialties of the house, as are the pastas. Try cannelloni and ravioli with fillings that change daily, tagliatelle with vegetables and smoked chicken, or baked angel hair with ham and béchamel sauce. ◆ Northern Italian ◆ Daily breakfast, lunch, and dinner.

Reservations recommended; jacket required. 753.5566

IL TOSCANACCIO

2 Il Toscanaccio ★★★$$ The name means "naughty Tuscan" and that's the spirit restaurateur Pino Luongo (owner of **Coco Pazzo, Le Madri,** and **Mad. 61**) is trying to achieve with this redo of the space formerly occupied by his formal **Amarcord.** The food is earthy: Don't miss the antipasto; baby octopus stewed in a spicy tomato sauce; bowtie pasta with spring vegetables, herbs, tomato, and parmigiana; and homemade linguine with scallops, clams, mussels, and calamari. Desserts are many and each one remarkable. ◆ Tuscan ◆ M-Sa lunch and dinner; Su dinner. Reservations recommended. 7 E 59th St (between Madison and Fifth Aves). 935.3535

3 The Harmonie Club In 1852, wealthy German Jews, excluded from most other men's clubs, formed the *Harmonie Gesellschaft,* which was described at the time as "the most homelike of all clubs" because its members made it a practice to bring along their wives. Today, the home of this private club is located in a 1906 building designed by **McKim, Mead & White.** The building is not open to the public. ◆ 4 E 60th St (between Madison and Fifth Aves). 355.7400

4 Metropolitan Club Also designed by **McKim, Mead & White** in 1894, this is a good example of **Stanford White** in an enthusiastic mood. Note particularly the extravagant, colonnaded carriage entrance behind the gates of the château. An addition was built in 1912 by **Ogden Codman.** The association was organized by J.P. Morgan for his friends who were not accepted at other clubs. ◆ 1 E 60th St (at Fifth Ave). 838.7400

5 The Pierre $$$$ Designed in 1930 by **Schultze & Weaver,** the architects of the **Sherry-Netherland,** this is another of the grand old European-style hotels with many permanent guests and a loyal following of the rich and the powerful. A stretched mansard roof clothed in weathered bronze at the top of the tower gives the structure a distinctive silhouette; it and the **Sherry** next door make a romantic couple. It is a wee bit intimidating, perhaps, with all those limos in front and the miles of mural-lined lobby, but the hotel offers the kind of luxury one could get used to: 202 enormous rooms (with good **Central Park** views from the upper floors) and vast bathrooms; 24-hour room service; an attentive, multilingual staff; twice-daily maid service; complimentary shoe shine; even an unpacking service. Afternoon tea is served daily in the **Rotunda.** ◆ 2 E 61st St (at Fifth Ave). 838.8000, 800/743.7734; fax 826.0319. &

Metropolitan Club

Michael Storrings

Within The Pierre Hotel:

Cafe Pierre ★★★$$$ This sophisticated dining room may be mistaken for a French chateau with its tones of pale yellow and gray, imported silks, and ceiling murals. But the elegance doesn't rest there. Indulge in an equally classic menu of risotto with wild mushrooms, asparagus, truffles, and chervil, and roasted rack of lamb in herb crust with sautéed artichokes. Also appealing are the tempting desserts, including white-and-dark chocolate terrine with ginger chips and caramelized orange sauce. There's a fine wine list. ♦ Continental ♦ Daily for breakfast, lunch, and dinner; dinner dancing Th-Sa. 940.8185

6 800 Fifth Avenue Until her death in 1977, Mrs. Marcellus Hartley Dodge, a niece of John D. Rockefeller Jr., lived here with her famous collection of stray dogs in a five-story brick mansion that was a mate to the nearby **Knickerbocker Club.** In 1978, **Ulrich Frazen & Associates** moved in, promising a tasteful building that would be a credit to the neighborhood. This 33-story building is how the promise was kept. The zoning law forced them to build a three-story wall along Fifth Avenue. Unfortunately, it isn't high enough to hide the building behind it. ♦ At E 61st St

7 The Knickerbocker Club In the 1860s, some members of the **Union Club** proposed that its membership be restricted to men descended from the colonial families of New York, known as the Knickerbockers. When their suggestion was rejected, they started their own club. But one of its most influential founders was August Belmont, a German immigrant. Today, the club is located in this 1914 building by **Delano & Aldrich,** which is not open to the public. ♦ 2 E 62nd St (at Fifth Ave). 838.6700

8 810 Fifth Avenue Former residents of this 13-story limestone building designed in 1926 by **J.E.R. Carpenter** include William Randolph Hearst and Mrs. Hamilton Fish, one of the last of the grandes dames of New York society. Before he moved to the White House in 1969, Richard M. Nixon lived here. His neighbor on the top floor was Nelson Rockefeller, who had New York's only fully equipped bomb shelter. The building is not open to the public. ♦ At E 62nd St

9 Arcadia ★★★$$$$ Chef/owner Anne Rosenzweig made culinary headlines ten years ago as the first woman to storm the hithertofore male bastion of the city's top-rated restaurants. Her cooking remains impressive to this day; signature dishes on the seasonal menu include corn cakes with crème fraîche and caviar, chimney-smoked lobster with tarragon butter, grilled salmon with red grapefruit and rhubarb vinaigrette, and a chocolate bread pudding swimming in a brandy-custard sauce. ♦ American ♦ M-Sa

lunch and dinner. Reservations required; jacket and tie required. 21 E 62nd St (between Madison and Fifth Aves). 223.2900

10 Addison on Madison Subdued yet interesting men's shirts of fine French cotton are offered in appealing, gentle stripes and checks, with a few bolder stripes. Sleeves come short, regular, and extra long. ♦ M-Sa. 698 Madison Ave (between E 62nd and E 63rd Sts). 308.2660. Also at: 725 Fifth Ave (between E 56th and E 57th Sts). 752.2300 ♿

10 Nello ★★$$$ Whether the cuisine or people watching is the greater attraction here is debatable, but on this stretch of Madison Avenue, the latter usually wins. The food, however, is fine and includes *tagliolini* (thin noodles) with smoked salmon, tomatoes, and cream; and red snapper in tomato sauce with capers and olives. ♦ Italian ♦ Daily lunch and dinner. Reservations recommended. 696 Madison Ave (between E 62nd and E 63rd Sts). 980.9099

LE RELAIS

11 Le Relais ★★$$$ Models, soap-opera stars, and other beautiful trendies while away evenings here eating such simply prepared French food as poached salmon and steak *frites* (with french fries) when not otherwise occupied with the "view." No surprise: The outdoor cafe is popular during the warmer months. ♦ French ♦ Daily lunch and dinner. Reservations required. 712 Madison Ave (at E 63rd St). 751.5108

11 Laura Ashley Home Furnishings Ashley is the Welsh designer who put nosegays and sprigs of flowers on pure cotton, and created an empire by whipping up the fabric into sweet Victorian dresses, petticoats, nightgowns, peasant skirts, and little girls' dresses. Here her signature prints are available on furniture, in fabric by the roll, in wallpaper, and in home accessories. ♦ M-Sa. 714 Madison Ave (between E 63rd and E 64th Sts). 735.5000. Also at: (clothing) 21 E 57th St (between Madison and Fifth Aves). 752.7300; (clothing and furnishings) 398 Columbus Ave (at W 79th St). 496.5110

THE LOWELL

12 The Lowell $$$$ White-glove treatment is the norm in this small, charming hotel. Many of the 65 rooms and suites in the 1926 building by **Henry S. Churchill** have serving pantries and wood-burning fireplaces, and some can accommodate formal board meetings. Room service meals arrive on a silver tray, or, if you prefer company, the second-floor dining room is both cheerful and serene. One of New York City's very best. ♦ 28 E 63rd St (between Park and Madison Aves). 838.1400, 800/221.4444; fax 319.4230

Within The Lowell:

POST THE HOUSE

The Post House ★★★$$$$ Many New York steak houses are strictly for red meat eaters, but this gracious establishment in the intimate **Lowell Hotel** has a softer touch—subdued lighting, peach walls, 18th-century American folk portraits, and models of ship hulls. The menu offers crab cakes and lemon-pepper chicken in addition to some of the best beef in the city. The extensive, well-priced wine list is one of New York's best. ♦ American ♦ M-F lunch and dinner; Sa-Su dinner. Reservations required. 28 E 63rd St (between Park and Madison Aves). 935.2888

13 Margo Feiden Galleries The specialty here is the work of caricaturist Al Hirschfeld, who has been capturing the essence of famous faces for *The New York Times* since the 1920s. The trick is to find all the "Ninas" in each drawing. Hirschfeld hides his daughter's name within folds of clothing, pompadours, wherever. One clue: The number of times "Nina" appears is indicated next to his sign-off. Original pen and ink drawings, limited editions, etchings, and lithographs are shown. ♦ Daily. 699 Madison Ave (between E 62nd and E 63rd Sts). 677.5330

14 Julie: Artisans' Gallery Clothes conceived as art to wear: Julia Hill's jackets of hand-painted silk, Linda Mendelson's scarves and coats knitted in geometrical patterns, and many other flights of fancy. ♦ M-Sa. 687 Madison Ave (between E 61st and E 62nd Sts). 688.2345 &

14 Georg Jensen/Royal Copenhagen Silver, including flatware and exquisite jewelry, is featured here: sleek, gleaming bangles and cuffs, Art Nouveau pins shaped like leaves and trimmed with precious stones. This is also a good source for crystal glassware and the entire collection of Royal Copenhagen china. ♦ Daily. 683 Madison Ave (between E 61st and E 62nd Sts). 759.6457 &

5 Sherry Lehman One of the top wine merchants in the country, this place may have the most extensive retail inventory in the world. The store specializes in French, California, and Italian wines, but also stocks German, Spanish, and kosher labels. Catalogues are published five times a year—one each season and an extra issue at Christmas—and the staff offers courteous, expert advice. It's also a handsome store for browsing. ♦ M-Sa. 679 Madison Ave (at E 61st St). 838.7500

16 Le Bistrot de Maxim's ★$$$ An homage to the Belle Epoque original, this downstairs cafe—formerly **L'Omnibus de Maxim's**—specializes in French-Asian fusion cuisine. The menu changes every few weeks and offers mushroom and escargot wontons with garlic-herb butter; spicy grilled gulf shrimp with a sauce of tamarind and yellow peppers; and fillet of grilled salmon on a bed of spinach with Chinese black-bean sauce. ♦ Fusion ♦ Tu-Sa lunch and dinner. Reservations required. 21 E 61st St (at Madison Ave). 980.6988

17 Barneys This nine-story, 230,000-square-foot fashion temple designed by minimalist architect **Peter Marino** opened to much hoopla in 1993, three years—and $100 million—after the Pressman family decided to bring their downtown clothing mecca for men and women to Midtown. The largest specialty store to be built in Manhattan since the Depression, it's light and airy, with large stretches of loftlike space. The women's side measures more than twice the size of its quarters in the flagship store in Chelsea. ♦ Daily. 660 Madison Ave (at E 61st St). 826.8900. Also at: Seventh Ave (at W 17th St). 929.9000; 2 World Financial Center (West St, between Vesey and Liberty Sts). 945.1600 &

Within Barneys:

mad. 61

Mad. 61 ★★$$$ Centered around a marble mosaic pool, this restaurant tempts hungry shoppers with its trademark rich and rustic Italian cuisine, featuring such dishes as fettuccine with wild mushrooms and truffle oil and loin of rabbit roasted with fennel and pancetta. Surrounding the dining room are a wine bar (the extensive list offers a choice of 160) and an Italian espresso bar. ♦ Italian ♦ Daily breakfast, lunch, and dinner. Reservations required. 10 E 61st St (at Madison Ave). 833.2200 &

18 Aureole ★★★$$$$ This is one of the most charming dining rooms in town. Chef Charlie Palmer's complex, architectural food is also among the most admired. Try the terrine of natural foie gras with pressed duck confit or applewood-grilled salmon with basil-braised artichokes. The desserts are spectacular and the handmade chocolates, complimentary with dinner, also make a splendid finish. ♦ Continental ♦ M-F lunch and dinner; Sa dinner. Reservations required. 34 E 61st St (between Park and Madison Aves). 319.1660

19 Boyd's Madison Avenue Legions of well-known women, including Cher and the late Jackie Onassis, have come here to choose from a vast, international collection of feather powder puffs, rouges, combs, hairbrushes, and toothbrushes. ♦ Daily. 655 Madison Ave (at E 60th St). 838.6558 ὅ

20 Calvin Klein The trend-setting designs of one of America's timeless fashion icons can be seen here at Madison Avenue's latest mega-store. The 22,000-square-foot retail space, built in 1928 to house the **Morgan Guaranty Bank,** now offers shoppers his distinctive collection, accessories, and home furnishings. ♦ M-Sa. 654 Madison Ave (at E 60th St). 292.9000

21 Kaplan's $$ Large, clean, and modern, this delicatessen offers fair prices and better-than-average salads, along with such sandwiches as corned beef and pastrami and soups; the service is attentive. ♦ Deli ♦ Daily breakfast, lunch, and dinner. 59 E 59th St (between Park and Madison Aves). 755.5959

22 Caviarteria ★★$$$$ This caviar and champagne bar has an on-site retail store with a huge variety of fish roe—offered at very good prices because it's the largest caviar importer in the country—pâtés, chocolates, and other delicacies. But for more immediate gratification, take a seat in the cafe and have a caviar platter. ♦ International/Caviar ♦ M-Sa breakfast and lunch; Su brunch. 502 Park Ave (at E 59th St). 759.7410

22 Christie's The New York headquarters of the famous London auction house specializes in old masters, Impressionists, 19th- and 20th-century European and American art, and 22 other areas of art including antiques and Chinese art. Tickets, available without charge a week or two before an auction, are required for evening auctions. Previews of items to be auctioned are held five days prior to the auction itself, and catalogs are available. ♦ Open to the public only during viewings before scheduled auctions. Call first. Call 546.1007 for schedule. 502 Park Ave (at E 59th St). 546.1000 ὅ

23 Christ Church Built in 1932 by **Ralph Adams Cram,** this is an interesting limestone-and-brick Methodist church. One of the best ecclesiastical structures of the 1930s, it was designed to look hundreds of years old. ♦ 520 Park Ave (at E 60th St). 838.3036

23 The Grolier Club Named for the 16th-century bibliophile Jean Grolier, this Georgian structure, designed by **Bertram G. Goodhue** in 1917, houses a collection of fine bookbindings and a specialized library open only to scholars

and researchers. Regularly changing exhibitions display books, prints, and rare manuscripts. ♦ Free. M-Sa. 47 E 60th St (between Park and Madison Aves). 838.6690

24 The Regency $$$$ This elegant hotel is the scene of some of New York's most important power breakfasts, at which the city's movers and shakers get together to start their business day. Guests can take advantage of 24-hour room service for their breakfast, but it isn't as exciting. Other advantages include a well-equipped fitness center and a large, multilingual staff. The 393-room hotel is furnished with French antiques, which give it a feeling of luxury uncommon in newer buildings. ♦ 540 Park Ave (at E 61st St). 759.4100, 800/23LOEWS; fax 826.5674 ὅ

25 The Colony Club The building, which houses an exclusive club for society women, presents a solid, Neo-Georgian, Federal redbrick face, settled on a limestone base. It was designed in 1924 by **Delano & Aldrich** and is not open to the public. ♦ 564 Park Ave (at E 62nd St). 838.4200

26 Park Avenue Cafe ★★★$$$ This whimsical stylish room with blond wood and an American flag mural is a relaxed setting for chef David Burke's creative combinations. Try the tuna and salmon *tartare*, lobster dumplings, crabmeat ravioli in a seafood broth, and baby lamb chops wrapped in pastry. Finish off with the chocolate-caramel cake with caramel ice cream. ♦ American ♦ M-F lunch and dinner; Sa dinner; Su brunch and dinner. Reservations required. 100 E 63rd St (between Lexington and Park Aves). 644.1900

27 Society of Illustrators Built in 1875, this museum of American illustration features changing exhibitions of advertising art, book illustration, editorial art, and other contemporary work. ♦ Free. M-Sa. 128 E 63rd St (between Lexington and Park Aves). 838.2560 ὅ

28 Saint-Remy Produits de Provence Pale, muted floral and paisley fabrics are sold here, mainly by the yard (but can be ordered made up into napkins, lamp shades, and place mats). ♦ M-Sa. 818 Lexington Ave (between 62nd and E 63rd Sts). 486.2018 ὅ

One of the more colorful inmates at Roosevelt Island's New York City Lunatic Asylum was Mae West, who was locked up there for 10 days in 1926 and fined $500. She had been appearing locally in a lewd play called *Sex* that raised one too many eyebrows. Upon her request, she was permitted to wear her silk undergarments beneath her prison uniform.

29 The Barbizon Hotel $$$ Its richly detailed brickwork and fine interiors have made this former residence for women—actresses Candice Bergen, Gene Tierney, and Grace Kelly stayed here at various times—one of the East Side's better-known buildings; it was designed in 1927 by **Murgatroyd & Ogden.** Until 1981—when it was converted to a hotel open to both sexes, with interiors by Milton Glaser—its upper floors were off-limits to men. But the rooftop arcades framed skyline views that were made famous by photographer Samuel Gottscho. The view also inspired painter Georgia O'Keeffe. Among its amenities are 12 tower suites, a multilingual staff, a cafe (**Cafe Barbizon**), and an oak-paneled meeting room with a pipe organ, stained-glass windows, and a fireplace. The Morgan's Hotel Groups (**Morgan's, The Royalton, The Paramount**) purchased this fine old hotel in the fall of 1988 but it is now operating independently. The completion of restorations in 1994 resulted in the addition of **Alexis,** a new upscale French restaurant, and a new fitness center . ♦ 140 E 63rd St (at Lexington Ave). 838.5700, 800/223.1020; fax 223.3287 ♿

30 Tender Buttons Featured here are millions and millions of buttons, new and antique, made of brass, stoneware, taqua nut, Lucite, wood, abalone, seashell, agate, plastic, silver—you name it. ♦ M-Sa. 143 E 62nd St (between Third and Lexington Aves). 758.7004

31 New York Doll Hospital Even if your doll isn't sick, don't miss this experience. They buy and sell antique dolls and toys here, but what makes it so much fun is the collection of spare parts. ♦ M-Sa. 787 Lexington Ave (between E 61st and E 62nd Sts), Second floor. 838.7527

32 Brio ★$$ This attractive, wood-paneled trattoria is almost always full. The hearty polenta with porcini or aromatic pesto-laden fusilli are two reasons to return again and again. ♦ Italian ♦ Daily lunch, dinner, and late-night meals. Reservations recommended. 786 Lexington Ave (between E 61st and E 62nd Sts). 980.2300

33 Il Valletto ★$$$ If the owner, Nanni, is around when you visit, let him order for you. If not, here are some suggestions: *bruschetta* (toast seasoned with garlic and oil), tender baked clams, eggplant *siciliana* (with light ricotta and spinach), and linguine with delicate, tender clams in a light white sauce. For dessert, try the baked pear with zabaglione or fresh fruit salad. ♦ Italian ♦ M-F lunch and dinner; Sa dinner. Reservations required; jacket required. 133 E 61st St (between Lexington and Park Aves). 838.3939

34 Mme. Romaine de Lyon ★★$$ With more than 500 kinds of omelettes to choose from, it's safe to say that this is New York's ultimate place for the proverbial broken-egg dish. The setting is charming and comfortable, and the staff is friendly. ♦ French ♦ M-Sa lunch and dinner; Su lunch. Reservations recommended. 132 E 61st St (between Lexington and Park Aves). 759.5200

34 The Pillowry Owner/designer Marjorie Lawrence sells kilims and Oriental rugs and makes pillows from antique rugs and textiles collected from all over the world. ♦ M-F. 132 E 61st St (between Lexington and Park Aves), Second floor. 308.1630

35 Le Veau d'Or ★$$$ Longtime East Siders still flock to this great old bistro for such well-prepared, basic French fare as steak au poivre. The service is unpretentious and efficient. ♦ French ♦ M-Sa lunch and dinner. Reservations recommended. 129 E 60th St (between Lexington and Park Aves). 838.8133

36 The Lighthouse This is the newly relocated headquarters of the New York Association for the Blind. The on-site gift shop, staffed by volunteers, sells items made by blind persons, and all proceeds benefit the blind. ♦ Hours vary; call ahead. 111 E 59th (between Lexington and Park Aves). 821.9200 ♿

37 The Original Levi's Store An icon in the annals of American fashion, the Levi's jean is here in every model, size, color, and interpretation imaginable. This spacious store is always filled with foreign shoppers having a field day. ♦ Daily. 750 Lexington Ave (between E 59th and E 60th Sts). 826.5957 ♿ Also at: 1492 Third Ave (at E 84th St). 249.5045 ♿; 3 E 57th St (between Madison and Fifth Aves). 838.2188

38 Bloomingdale's This store is show business. It caters to those who like to buy their clothes, food, and sofas in an atmosphere that is a cross between a designer showcase and a Middle Eastern suk. Once you get beyond the smiling models who threaten to squirt perfume at you, and TV screens showing endless tapes of designer fashion shows, you'll find the children's department, with layettes, strollers, Oshkosh overalls, and hand-knit sweaters. For women, there is slinky knitwear by Missoni, seductive knits by Sonia Rykiel, the American chic of Ralph Lauren, and the luxe of Yves Saint Laurent. For men, there are clothes by Donna Karan, Calvin Klein, and Armani. The sixth-floor **Main Course** is a cornucopia of kitchenware and gadgets. Descamps has a boutique in the linen department. There is a shop devoted solely to Petrossian caviar. If it's all too much for you, special shopping services are extensive. ♦ Daily. 1000 Third Ave (at E 59th St). 705.2000

Restaurants/Clubs: Red   **Hotels:** Blue
Shops/ ♦ Outdoors: Green   **Sights/Culture:** Black

Within Bloomingdale's:

Le Train Bleu ★$$ A re-creation of the dining car on the famous **Orient Express,** this welcome resting ground in **Bloomingdale's** for worn-out shoppers has a spectacular view of the Queensboro Bridge and the **Roosevelt Island Tramway.** The food—such as Cajun shrimp and pasta salad, fettuccine with tomatoes and gorgonzola, and grilled chicken over Caesar salad—takes second place. ♦ Continental ♦ M-F lunch and afternoon tea; Sa lunch; Su brunch. Reservations recommended. Sixth floor. 705.2100

39 Trump Plaza You can easily pass this 1987 building by **Philip Birnbaum & Associates.** It is another attempt to immortalize the name of developer Donald Trump. It's not open to the public, but don't pass up the waterfall or the open space to the left of the entrance that make it so pleasant. ♦ 167 E 61st St (at Third Ave)

39 Matthew's ★★★$$$ Named one of *Food and Wine Magazine*'s chefs of the year in 1994, Matthew Kenney now pushes the limits of American cuisine. Try *ahi* (Hawaiian tuna) *tartare* with green-olive *tapenade* (a thick paste made from capers, anchovies, olives, olive oil, and lemon juice); and marinated shrimp and yam salad with avocado, lime, and sweet onion. Rustic yet elegant, the setting is perfect for the beautiful crowd who gravitate to this fashionable place. ♦ American ♦ M-Sa lunch and dinner; Su brunch and dinner. 1030 Third Ave (at E 61st St). 838.4343 &

40 Yellowfingers ★★$$ A perfect place to recover after a splurge at **Bloomingdale's,** this spot's open kitchen turns out generous salads, sandwiches (all served on thick focaccia), plentiful burgers, and a hearty entrée called *fa'vecchai* (a pizza-like dough baked with toppings that include grilled mushrooms, braised onions, olives, and eggplant). ♦ American/Italian ♦ M-Sa breakfast, lunch, and dinner; Su brunch and dinner. 200 E 60th St (at Third Ave). 751.8615

40 Contrapunto ★★$$$ This modern glassed-in room is a dependable spot for good pasta, including fresh squares filled with lobster, scallops, fresh fennel, and leeks in a lemon-cream sauce; and delicate angel-hair pasta with littleneck clams. There are also decent desserts. ♦ American/Italian ♦ Daily lunch and dinner. 200 E 60th St (at Third Ave), Second floor. 751.8615

ARIZONA 206

40 Arizona 206 ★★★$$$ Authentically ensconced in lots of adobe, bare wood, and desert flowers, this cavelike place is pleasing to the eyes, but hard on the ears—it gets terribly loud. The crowds are in attendance for such imaginative Southwestern fare as wild striped bass in a roasted tomatillo broth; barbecued pork tamales with corn and chili sauce; and skate salad with corn-mushroom salsa. Chocoholics will love the Arizona chocolate plate—warm chocolate cake and chocolate ice cream covered in mint and raspberry cream. ♦ Southwestern ♦ Daily lunch and dinner. Reservations recommended. 206 E 60th St (between Second and Third Aves). 838.0440

41 Galleria Hugo Owner Hugo Ramirez is a master of restoration of 19th-century antique lighting. His work (all done by hand) can be found in **Gracie Mansion,** city museums, and historic homes around the country. ♦ By appointment only. 233 E 59th St (between Second and Third Aves. 750.6877. Also at: 304 E 76th St (between First and Second Aves). 288.8444; 341 E 76th St (between First and Second Aves). 288.844

42 Serendipity ★$$ The over-the-top Victorianesque decorations; fine, simple food—shepherd's pie, barbecued-chicken casserole—and decadent desserts, including the famed frozen hot chocolate, have made this a busy attraction since it opened in 1954 ♦ American ♦ Daily lunch, dinner, and late-night meals. 225 E 60th St (between Second and Third Aves). 838.3531

43 Pushbottom for Kids This shop carries outfits for children by the famous purveyor of quality sweaters. The little fashion plate in your family will turn everyone's head in one of **Pushbottom**'s crocheted bow ties. ♦ M-Sa 252 E 62nd St (between Second and Third Aves). 888.3336

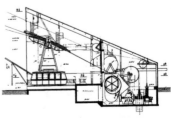

44 Roosevelt Island Tramway Station The Swiss-made tram (see diagram), designed i▸

1976 by Prentice & Chan, Ohlhausen, would be more at home on a snow-covered mountain. It takes you across the East River's West Channel at 16mph and provides wonderful views of the East Side and the Queensboro Bridge. ◆ Nominal charge. M-Th, Su 6AM-2AM; F-Sa 6AM-3:30AM. Second Ave (between E 59th and E 60th Sts). 832.4543 &

45 Queensboro Bridge Designed by engineer Gustav Lindenthal and built in 1909 by **Palmer & Hornbostel**, the distinctive triple span of this bridge (illustrated on page 26) is the image of a machine, an intricate web of steel that speaks of power, if not finesse. Referred to by most locals, including Simon and Garfunkel, as the "59th St. Bridge."
◆ From E 59th St and Second Ave, Manhattan, to Queens Plaza, Queens

46 Roosevelt Island This island is separated from Manhattan by 300 yards and more than a few decibels, but politically it is very much a part of it. The community, built in the 1970s, is accessible from Manhattan by tramway and subway, and from Queens by a small bridge at 36th Avenue, Queens Plaza. The master plan for a series of U-shaped housing projects facing the river was designed by **Philip Johnson** and **John Burgee**. Only the southern section was built, and it's taller and denser than they recommended. Until the 1970s, when rental agents needed a name change, it was known as **Welfare Island** because of its many hospitals and sanitariums. Before 1921, it was **Blackwell's Island**, named for the family that farmed it for two centuries. A prison was built in 1828, and over the next several years, a workhouse, an almshouse, and an insane asylum were added. A century later those institutions were swept away and hospitals were substituted. The present city has reminders of each of the island's former lives. The ruin at the southern end was the **Smallpox Hospital**, designed in 1856 by **James Renwick Jr.** Just above it are the remains of the 1859 **City Hospital**, and under the Queensboro Bridge is **Goldwater Memorial Hospital**. Not far from the tramway station is the **Blackwell Farmhouse** (1796-1804). Nearby are the **Eastwood Apartments**, built for low- and middle-income tenants in 1976 by **Sert, Jackson & Associates**. On the Manhattan side are **Rivercross Apartments**, built in 1975 by **Johansen & Bhavnani**, for people who can afford to pay more. There are two more luxury complexes: **Westview**, built in 1976 by **Sert, Jackson & Associates**, and **Island House**, built in 1975 by **Johansen & Bhavnani**, which has a glassed-in swimming pool overlooking Manhattan.

Cars are not allowed on the island except in the garage complex known as **Motorgate**. Garbage is removed through vacuum tubes to the **AVAC (Automated Vacuum Collection) Building**—where it is sorted, sanitized, and packed for removal. Near this monument to a "Brave New World" is the **Chapel of the Good Shepherd**, originally built in 1889 by **Frederick Clarke Withers** and restored by **Giorgio Cavaglieri** in 1976, now used as a recreation center. Landmarks at the northern end include the **Octagon Tower**, an 1839 building by **Alexander Jackson Davis**, all that's left of the **New York City Lunatic Asylum**, and a 50-foot stone lighthouse designed in 1872 by **James Renwick Jr.** (According to an inscription on the lighthouse, it was built by John McCarthy, an asylum inmate who busied himself by building a fort to defend himself against the British but was persuaded to replace it with a more attractive lighthouse instead.) The hospital at the uptown end of the island is the 1952 **Bird S. Coler Hospital for the Chronically Ill**. A complex of 1,104 apartments, **Northtown II** was completed by Starrett Housing in 1989. Currently, plans are under way for 15-acre **Octagon Park**, just south of the **Coler Hospital**, and **Southtown**, a complex of 2,000 mixed-income apartments. Transportation on the island is provided by bus, but probably the best way to enjoy it is by walking on its riverside promenades. ◆ East River

47 Darrow's Fun Antiques This is a place for grownups to become children: toy soldiers; cigar store Indians; antique windup monkeys, dogs, and bears; movie star memorabilia; and even the occasional funhouse mirror. ◆ M-Sa. 1101 First Ave (between E 60th and E 61st Sts). 838.0730

47 Chicago City Limits Established in New York in 1980, this is one of the oldest, and probably the only self-sustaining, comedy improvisation groups in the city. It was formed in Chicago in 1977 by George Todisco and actors participating in workshops at that city's renowned **Second City**. It then moved to Manhattan's Theater Row, then the **Jan Hus Church**, before moving here. ◆ Shows: W-Th 8:30PM; F-Sa 8PM, 10:30PM. 1105 First Ave (at E 61st St). 888.LAFF

48 Abigail Adams Smith Museum The daughter of John Quincy Adams, for whom this 1799 house-museum is named, never even slept here. But she and her husband, Colonel William Smith, did own the land it was built on. They bought 23 choice acres on the bank of the East River in 1786 with the idea of building a country estate called "Mt. Vernon" (Colonel Smith served under George Washington). Because of financial reverses, they sold the estate in 1799. The stone stable that is now the museum was remodeled as an inn in the 1820s, then used as a private dwelling until the neighborhood fell on hard times. The Colonial Dames of America rescued it in 1924, furnished it in the style of the Federal period, planted an 18th-century garden, and opened the house as a museum.

225

Colonial Dames members, well versed in the contents of the house (but not necessarily about antiques or the history of the period), show visitors the nine rooms filled with delicate Aubusson rugs, graceful Sheraton chests, a framed letter from George Washington, a mannequin wearing a simple summer dress that Abigail had made for herself (she had indeed fallen on hard times), and unexpected touches such as a cardroom set up with a game of loo. ◆ Admission. M-F, Su. 421 E 61st St (between York and First Aves). 838.6878

49 Dangerfield's This club, which showcases new and established comic talent, is owned and operated by well-known comedian Rodney Dangerfield. It has a typical Las Vegas/Atlantic City atmosphere and caters to out-of-town convention goers and suburbanites. ◆ Cover. Shows: M-Th 9PM and 12:30AM; F 9PM, 11:15PM; Sa 8PM, 10:30PM, 12:30AM; Su 9PM and 12:30AM. 1118 First Ave (between E 61st and E 62nd Sts). 593.1650

50 Il Vagabondo ★$$ Robust Italian cooking, mostly Southern style, is one of the draws at this noisy, good-humored neighborhood trattoria. But the main reason to come here is to watch people play boccie at the city's only indoor court (ask for a courtside table). Specialties include homemade gnocchi, tuna steak, a fragrant veal stew, and fillet of sole. ◆ Italian ◆ M-F lunch and dinner; Sa-Su dinner. 351 E 62nd St (between First and Second Aves). 832.9221

51 Manhattan Cafe ★$$$ Come here for traditional steak-house fare in a comfortable, posh setting. There are also decent veal and pasta dishes in all the usual varieties. ◆ American ◆ M-F lunch, dinner, and late-night meals; Sa dinner and late-night meals; Su brunch, dinner, and late-night meals. Reservations recommended. 1161 First Ave (at E 64th St). 888.6556

52 Jackson Hole ★$ Delicious, juicy hamburgers approaching the size of Wyoming are the specialty of this restaurant. Any (or several) of the 12 available toppings can be requested to adorn the seven-ounce burgers; a side order of onion rings or french fries is an integral part of the experience. ◆ Hamburgers ◆ Daily lunch, dinner, and late-night meals. 232 E 64th St (between Second and Third Aves). 371.7187. Also at: 521 Third Ave (at E 35th St). 679.3264; 1270 Madison Ave (at E 91st St). 427.2820 &; 517 Columbus Ave (at W 85th St). 362.5177

53 Carol Rollo/Riding High You'll find bold, luxurious—and expensive—clothing for men and women, including designs from Jean Paul Gaultier, Chloe, and Sitbon. ◆ M-Sa. 1044 Third Ave (between E 62nd and E 63rd Sts). 832.7927

54 New York Women's Exchange Established in 1878 to help women support themselves without sacrificing their pride, this is an excellent source of handmade children's articles, lingerie, and gifts. ◆ M-Sa. 1095 Third Ave (between E 64th and E 65th Sts). 753.2330 &

55 The Sign of The Dove ★★★$$$$ In this restaurant, which is one of the most romantic settings in the city, chef Andrew D'Amico takes inspiration from Italy for butternut-squash and parmesan ravioli with butter and sage, from Thailand for seared tuna with green chilies and coriander, and from Morocco for spiced salmon. Finish the meal with one of the delectable desserts, including chocolate-espresso pudding. The savory bread comes from the restaurant's bakery, **Ecce Panis** (see below). A cafe menu is also available for those who want simpler fare at a lower price. ◆ American ◆ M dinner; Tu-F lunch and dinner; Sa-Su brunch and dinner. Reservations recommended; jacket required. 1110 Third Ave (at E 65th St). 861.8080

Ecce Panis

55 Ecce Panis Here the crusty sourdough loaves, focaccia, and biscotti (Italian cookies) are sublime. And if you've run out of coffee to serve with them, it's on sale here too. ◆ Daily. 1260 Madison Ave (at E 90th St). 348.0040. Also at: 1120 Third Ave (between E 65th and E 66th Sts). 535.2099

56 Solow Houses Developer Sheldon Solow, who built the innovative office building at 9 West 57th Street in 1983, created these 11 houses (designed by **Attia & Perkins**), the first new town house row in the city since the end of the 19th century. The granite facade, which binds them together between flat and slightly bowed fronts, barely articulates each individual house. The front is fortresslike, hiding luxurious interiors. ◆ 222-242 E 67th St (between Second and Third Aves)

Rockefeller University, at York Avenue in the east sixties, has the lowest teacher-pupil ratio of any university in the United States.

57 Soleil ★★$$ Gone are the dark carpets and Cantonese cuisine of **Fortune Garden,** the former denizen; in their place are bright yellow walls and a Mediterranean menu. Start with grilled portobello mushrooms served with arugula and tomato, and move on to any of the pasta dishes, including rigatoni with tomatoes, prosciutto, and basil, or vegetable lasagna. ♦ Mediterranean ♦ M-Sa lunch and dinner; Su brunch and dinner. Reservations required. 1160 Third Ave (between E 67th and E 68th Sts). 717.1177 ♿

57 Janovic Plaza This is just one of several outlets of the most thorough paint store in the city. It offers not only 8,000 colors and finishes but fabrics from design houses such as Schumacher, as well as bed-and-bath linens. ♦ Daily. 1150 Third Ave (at E 67th St). 772.1400 ♿

58 Park East Synagogue Designed in 1890 by **Schneider & Herter,** this Moorish extravaganza has a more sedate Victorian interior. ♦ 163 E 67th St (between Third and Lexington Aves). 737.6900

59 131-135 East 66th Street The two apartment blocks, designed in 1905 by **Charles Adams Platt,** are most noted for dignified grandeur and Mannerist porticoes. ♦ Between Third and Lexington Aves

60 Cosmopolitan Club Cast-iron balconies give a New Orleans flavor to this 1932 Greek Revival building, designed by **Thomas Harlan Ellett.** It is the headquarters of a prestigious women's club for those interested in the arts and sciences. ♦ 122 E 66th St (between Lexington and Park Aves). 734.5950

60 The Forgotten Woman This unfortunately named store offers handsome designer clothing for the larger woman (sizes 14 to 24). There are tailored suits, pure cashmere sweaters, cocktail dresses, and leather skirts. The service is exceptionally good. ♦ Daily. 888 Lexington Ave (at E 66th St). 535.8848 ♿

61 Church of St. Vincent Ferrer When New York's Roman Catholic elite make wedding plans, **St. Patrick's Cathedral** is their first choice. If the cathedral is booked, this is where they turn. It was designed by **Bertram G. Goodhue** in 1923. ♦ 686 Lexington Ave (between E 65th and E 66th Sts). 744.2080

62 Ségires à Solanée Classic Provençal designs—hand-painted wood furniture, iron furniture, faience from Moustiers-Sainte-Marie, and linen place mats and napkins abound in this sunny shop. ♦ M-Sa. 866 Lexington Ave (at E 65th St). 439.6109 ♿

62 Lex ★$$$ A sophisticated hangout for the well heeled, this subdued spot has cream-colored walls dotted with colorful Sonia Delaunay fashion illustrations, flattering light, and a menu full of upscale comfort food. Try the lobster, crabmeat, avocado, and *frisée* (curly endive) salad, wild mushroom pan roast, roast chicken tarragon, and crab cakes with horseradish-mustard sauce. The desserts tend to be overly sweet, and although the wine list features off-year vintages, there's nothing "off" about the prices. ♦ American ♦ M-F lunch and dinner; Sa dinner. Reservations required. 133 E 65th St (between Lexington and Park Aves). 744.2533

63 Fletcher Morgan Provisions ★$ The food, by caterer-to-the-fashion-industry chef Herve Rossano, includes roast chicken with tarragon and tomato, mustard, and vinegar sauce; duck prosciutto with green lentils and walnut oil; lamb *tajine* (a Moroccan stew); and Thai beef salad. For dessert, try the *tarte tatin* (an upside-down apple tart). In good weather, the food can be enjoyed in a back garden, bedecked with flowers, trees, and a flowing fountain. The shelves are stocked with gourmet food gifts. ♦ French ♦ M-Sa breakfast, lunch, and early dinner; Su breakfast and lunch. 864 Lexington Ave (between E 64th and E 65th Sts). 288.6764

64 JoJo ★★★$$$ Hailed as a creative genius and forerunner in the movement to replace cream- and butter-based sauces with more healthful infused oils and vegetable juices, chef Jean-Georges Vongerichten (also co-owner of **Vong**) offers interpretations of bistro fare, including shrimp in carrot juice with Thai lime leaves; chicken roasted with ginger, green olives, and coriander juice; foie gras with quince puree; and for dessert, a spectacular chocolate cake. The wine list spotlights good French wines, some at affordable prices. ♦ French ♦ M-F lunch and dinner; Sa dinner. Reservations recommended. 160 E 64th St (between Third and Lexington Aves). 223.5656

64 Toscana ★★$$ The food seems to get better and better at this sleek, sophisticated Italian cafe with subdued lighting and terra-cotta tiles. Tuscan dishes are featured: bean soup, broiled veal chop with thyme, and such homemade pastas as ricotta-stuffed ravioli. ♦ Italian ♦ M-F lunch and dinner; Sa-Su brunch and dinner. Reservations recom-mended. 843 Lexington Ave (at E 64th St). 517.2288

65 Edward Durell Stone House Designed by **Edward Durell Stone** in 1956, the concrete grillwork covering the facade of the late architect's home is similar to the screen he used in his design for the American Embassy in New Delhi two years earlier. ♦ 130 E 64th St (between Lexington and Park Aves)

66 Central Presbyterian Church To build this former Baptist church, which was designed by **Henry C. Pelton** and **Allen & Collens** in 1922, John D. Rockefeller Jr., matched every contribution, dollar for dollar; he also taught Bible classes here. In 1930, the congregation moved to **Riverside Church,** also largely funded by Rockefeller. ♦ 593 Park Ave (at E 64th St). 838.0808

67 China House Gallery/China Institute in America This gift of publisher Henry R. Luce, the son of missionaries to China, reflects his lifelong interest in Sino-American cultural and political exchange. Along with changing exhibitions on Chinese fine arts and folk traditions, the institute, housed in a 1905 building by **Charles A. Platt,** conducts educational programs. ♦ Donation suggested. Daily. 125 E 65th St (between Lexington and Park Aves). 744.8181

68 Mayfair Hotel $$$$ Originally an apartment house designed by **J.E.R. Carpenter** in 1925, it was converted to a small European-style hotel in 1934—one of the few in the city with 24-hour staffed elevator service. The lobby exudes an air of old money with its mellow marble and antique mahogany. Of the 200 elegantly renovated rooms and suites, many include a sitting area, a working fireplace, and a butler's pantry. Guests are offered an array of soaps, terry robes, and an umbrella on rainy days. ♦ 610 Park Ave (at E 65th St). 288.0800, 800/223.0542; fax 737.0538

69 Hotel Plaza Athénée $$$$ Formerly the **Alrae Apartments,** designed by **George F. Pelham** in 1927, this intimate, ultraclassy hotel is modeled after the famous Paris original. Its moderate size (153 spacious rooms and 36 suites) and residential location attract guests, such as the Princess of Wales, in search of serenity rather than the hustle of Midtown. The lobby is a combination of French period furnishings, Italian marble floors, and hand-painted mural tapestry walls. Amenities include 24-hour concierge

and room service, kitchenettes, in-room safes (the hotel itself is extremely secure, with only one entrance), and fax machines available upon request. Each of the four duplex penthouse suites includes a terrace and solarium. ♦ 37 E 64th St (between Park and Madison Aves). 734.9100, 800/447.8800; fax 772.0958 ♿

Within the Hotel Plaza Athénée:

Le Regence ★★★★$$$$ This glittery Louis XIV–style restaurant in a color scheme of aquamarine and shell is bedecked with mirrors, chandeliers, and a ceiling mural of a cloudy sky. Not surprisingly, it excels in all categories: The service is impeccable and the food top flight. Consult the à la carte menu or choose between two elaborate prix-fixe meals. Duck-liver salad, Mediterranean seafood soup, and Dover sole are frequently offered. Come on Sundays for a sensational brunch. ♦ French ♦ M-Sa breakfast, lunch, and dinner; Su brunch and dinner. Reservations required; jacket and tie required. 606.4647

70 Boutique Descamps A French company devoted to the luxury of bed and bath, this store carries plush toweling and robes, cotton sheets in delicate prints, and down comforters and pillows. ♦ M-Sa. 723 Madison Ave (at E 64th St). 355.2522 ♿

71 Walter Steiger This women's shoe salon features the newest silhouettes from Europe by one of the leading designers. ♦ M-Sa. 739 Madison Ave (between E 64th and E 65th Sts). 570.1212 ♿. Also at: 417 Park Ave (at E 55th St). (826.7171)

72 Chase Manhattan Bank A brick wall to the left of this Georgian bank, designed by **Morrel Smith** in 1932, conceals a colonial garden—a rarity on this busy street. ♦ 726 Madison Ave (at E 64th St)

72 Wildenstein & Co. In 1932, **Horace Trumbauer** designed the building housing this gallery, which is known for the depth of its collections of old and contemporary paintings and objets d'art. Exhibitions often rival museum shows. ♦ M-F. 19 E 64th St (between Madison and Fifth Aves). 879.0500 ♿

73 Emilio Pucci This boutique for the Italian designer is in a house that was once owned by Consuela Vanderbilt Smith, daughter of William K. Vanderbilt. It was built in 1882 by **Theodore Weston,** with a 1920 facade by **Mott B. Schmidt.** Pucci, whose designs became popular in the 1950s, passed away in 1992. ♦ M-Sa. 24 E 64th St (between Madison and Fifth Aves). 752.4777

74 Berwind Mansion This Venetian Renaissance mansion was the home of coal magnate Edwin J. Berwind, who was the sole supplier of coal for America's warships. Today, the building, which was designed in

1896 by **N.C. Melton,** contains cooperative apartments. ♦ 2 E 64th St (at Fifth Ave)

74 820 Fifth Avenue Designed in 1916 by **Starrett & Van Vleck,** this is one of the earliest luxury apartment buildings on Fifth Avenue. Among its first tenants was New York's governor Al Smith. ♦ At E 64th St

75 India House This unusually wide (65 feet) mansion, designed by **Warren & Wetmore** in 1903, would be right at home on the streets of Paris. It was built for banker Marshall Orme Wilson, whose wife was Carrie Astor, daughter of the Mrs. Astor who lived around the corner. It is now owned by the government of India. ♦ 3 E 64th St (at Fifth Ave)

76 Temple Emanu-El Designed by **Robert D. Kohn, Charles Butler,** and **Clarence Stein** in 1929, this impressive gray limestone edifice on the site of a mansion belonging to Caroline Schermerhorn Astor is the temple of the oldest Reform congregation in New York. Resembling only the nave of a cathedral, the structure has masonry-bearing walls. In style, it is Romanesque with Eastern influences; these are repeated on the interior with Byzantine ornaments. The hall is 77 feet wide, 150 feet long, and 403 feet high; it seats 2,500—more than **St. Patrick's Cathedral.** ♦ 1 E 65th St (at Fifth Ave). 744.1400 ♿

77 Cambridge Chemists Any top-of-the-line European product can be found here, including Cyclax of London, Innoxa, Roc, and Vichy. ♦ M-Sa. 21 E 65th St (at Madison Ave). 734.5678 ♿

78 Ferrier ★$$ Good bistro cooking is offered in the beige back room: Try the coq au vin, roasted salmon in a fennel and Champagne sauce, confit of duck marinated and cooked in a red-wine sauce, and roasted monkfish with sautéed spinach. ♦ French ♦ M-F lunch and dinner; Sa-Su brunch and dinner. Reservations recommended. 29 E 65th St (between Park and Madison Aves). 772.9000

78 Sarah Delano Roosevelt Memorial House In 1908, when her son, Franklin, was married, Sarah Delano Roosevelt commissioned **Charles A. Platt** to design this pair of houses; one was for herself, the other for the newlyweds. The houses are identical, with a common entrance. Several of their rooms were connected by folding doors to make them larger when necessary, as well as to give interior access between the two houses. It was in the fourth-floor front bedroom of the house on the right that Roosevelt went through his long recovery from polio in 1921-22. The future president's mother wanted him to go to their estate in Hyde Park, New York, but his wife, Eleanor, persuaded him to stay in the city. She felt he had a future in politics and needed to be

closer to the centers of power, even though he was bedridden. Her decision doomed her to live under the thumb of her mother-in-law, not one of her favorite people. The buildings are now a community center for **Hunter College** students. ♦ 45-47 E 65th St (between Park and Madison Aves)

78 American Federation of the Arts (AFA) Located in a 1910 building that was designed by **Trowbridge & Livingston,** this organization provides traveling exhibitions for small museums around the country. The interior of the building, designed by **Edward Durell Stone** in 1960 and now devoted to office space, is richly detailed. ♦ 41 E 65th St (between Park and Madison Aves). 988.7700

79 LS Collection Elegant high-design housewares, such as leather desk accessories by Arte Cuoio, sterling silver desk accessories and vases from Zucchi & Pampaloni, and perfume bottles from Canadian sculptor Max Leser are found here. ♦ M-Sa. 765 Madison Ave (between E 65th and E 66th Sts). 472.3355 ♿

80 45 East 66th Street Designed in 1900 by **Harde & Short,** this building displays a lacy pastry exuberance at an even higher level than the **Alwyn Court Apartments** (at West 58th and Seventh Avenue) designed by the same firm. Note the Elizabethan and Flemish Gothic detailing and the sensuous ease of the round tower on the corner. ♦ At Madison Ave

81 North Beach Leather Whether they prefer trendy or classic styles, male and female leather aficionados will find all manner of leather jeans, jackets, shirts, overblouses, coats, bras, hot pants, and dresses. ♦ Daily. 772 Madison Ave (at E 66th St). 772.0707

82 The Lotos Club Designed by **Richard H. Hunt** in 1900, this was once the home of William J. Schieffelin, head of a wholesale drug firm and a crusader for civil rights at the end of the 19th century. The rusticated limestone base supports a redbrick midsection and a double-story mansard roof. A vigorous Second Empire composite on the verge of being excessive, it is now headquarters of an organization of artists, musicians, actors, and journalists. ♦ 5 E 66th St (between Madison and Fifth Aves). 737.7100

83 Emanuel Ungaro Here is the new location for this French designer's pret-a-porter collection for women, including his opulently printed, jewel-toned fabrics—paisleys, stripes, florals, and checks. The shop also sells such accessories as boots, shoes, belts, and shawls. ♦ M-Sa. 792 Madison Ave (between E 67th and E 66th Sts). 249.4090 ♿

Restaurants/Clubs: Red   **Hotels:** Blue
Shops/ ♥ Outdoors: Green   **Sights/Culture:** Black

84 4 East 67th Street This is an ornate Beaux Arts mansion, built for banker Henri P. Wertheim in 1902 and designed by **John H. Duncan.** It is now the residence of the Consul General of Japan. ♦ Between Madison and Fifth Aves

85 13 and 15 East 67th Street This is a curious pair, particularly in contrast to the Modernist red-granite face at **No. 17.** No. 13, designed in 1921 by **Harry Allan Jacobs,** is an Italian Renaissance concoction that was built for theatrical producer Martin Beck. No. 15, a 1904 building by **Ernest Flagg,** now the **Regency Whist Club,** was the **Cortland Field Bishop House.** Concocted of stone and restrained ironwork, this rather Parisian house was designed by the man who did **Scribner's Bookstore.** ♦ Between Madison and Fifth Aves

86 Montenapoleone Fabulously silky and embroidered Italian and French lingerie is sold here. ♦ M-Sa. 789 Madison Ave (between E 66th and E 67th Sts). 535.2660 Ꮸ

malo

86 Malo If you have to ask how much these sumptuous cashmere items for men and women cost, you'd best not enter. This is the company's first American boutique, featuring their remarkably lightweight—if heavy-priced—items of ultimate luxury. ♦ M-Sa. 791 Madison Ave (at E 67th St). 717.1766 Ꮸ

87 Gallery of Wearable Art Everything here makes a statement. Whether it is a statement you'd care to make is something you'll have to decide. In addition to daily—though hardly quotidian—clothes, there's a unique collection of wedding gowns and bridal accessories. ♦ Tu-Sa. 34 E 67th St (between Park and Madison Aves). 425.5379 Ꮸ

88 Seventh Regiment Armory Designed by **Charles W. Clinton** in 1880, this is a crenellated, almost cartoonish fort in an otherwise very proper neighborhood. The interiors were furnished and detailed by Louis Comfort Tiffany. The hall is immense: 187 feet by 290 feet. It is the site of the annual **Winter Antiques Fair** and other huge events. ♦ E 66th to E 67th Sts (between Lexington and Park Aves). 744.4107 Ꮸ

89 115 East 67th Street Designed in 1932 by **Andrew J. Thomas,** this building is a happy place with owls, squirrels, and other animals in the decorative panels and huge arched entry. ♦ Between Lexington and Park Aves

90 660 Park Avenue Architect **Philip Sawyer,** of **York & Sawyer,** carved a reputation for himself as a designer of banks, but his work on the rustication of this handsome 1927 apartment building is worthy of any of them. ♦ At E 67th St

91 Frette This sleek Italian shop features extravagant linens for bed and table, including piqué bedspreads, linen sheets, and damask tablecloths. ♦ M-Sa. 799 Madison Ave (between E 67th and E 68th Sts). 988.5221 Ꮸ

91 Thomas K. Woodard At the city's premier shop for high-quality antique and early 20th-century quilts, you'll find sizes ranging from crib to king. Designs include stars, postage stamps, and "drunkard's path." ♦ M-Sa. 799 Madison Ave (between E 67th and E 68th Sts), Second floor. 988.2906

91 Cerutti This may be the most useful children's clothing store in the city, due to its broad and well-chosen range. There are the practical, the perky, and the extravagant (hand-knit sweaters and leggings sets from Italy). ♦ M-Sa. 807 Madison Ave (between E 67th and E 68th Sts). 737.7540 Ꮸ

92 Joseph Tricot The latest knits from London are here—some simple, some romantic, all representing the world of street chic. Also for sale are hats and leather bags. ♦ M-Sa. 804 Madison Ave (between E 67th and E 68th Sts). 570.0077 Ꮸ

92 Billy Martin's Western Wear Yes, it's the late Billy Martin who used to pace the dugout at **Yankee Stadium.** This one-stop source of cowboy boots, fancy belts, and other expensive duds will make you look at home on the range. ♦ Daily. 812 Madison Ave (at E 68th St). 861.3100 Ꮸ

93 6, 8, and 10 East 68th Street These three houses, designed by **John H. Duncan** in 1900, were bought by financier Otto Kuhn, of Kuhn, Loeb & Co., in 1916, and altered in 1919 with a French Renaissance limestone facade designed by **Harry Allan Jacobs.** ♦ Between Madison and Fifth Aves

94 9 East 68th Street Designed in 1906 by **Heins & LaFarge,** this was formerly the **George T. Bliss House.** Four giant columns hold up nothing but that little balcony and a brave front to the world. Remarkably out of scale, the house is noteworthy because it is engaging and not overly pretentious. ♦ Between Madison and Fifth Aves

95 MaxMara One of the avenue's latest Italian arrivals, this upscale women's clothing company purchased this six-story building and tastefully restored it to the tune of $1 million. Designed and built in 1882 in the Neo-Greco style with Federal elements, the first two floors provide elegant retail space for the well-known manufacturer's stylish collections. ◆ M-Sa. 813 Madison Ave (at E 68th St). 879.6100

95 Giorgio Armani Boutique The Italian designer's complete avant-garde ready-to-wear and couture lines for men and women are now under one roof. ◆ M-Sa. 815 Madison Ave (at E 68th St). 988.9191 &

95 Bogner You expect slick, well-made active sportswear from this Austrian manufacturer of ski clothing. The surprise is the line of leisurewear for men and women—jackets, coats, sweaters, pants, skirts, and shoes. ◆ M-Sa. 821 Madison Ave (between E 68th and E 69th Sts). 472.0266

95 Valentino In this hushed and lavish setting, you can see the ready-to-wear collection of Valentino, including classic pants, beautifully shaped jackets, and luxurious dresses for day and night. ◆ M-Sa. 825 Madison Ave (between E 68th and E 69th Sts). 772.6969

96 Council on Foreign Relations This building, designed in 1920 by **Delano & Aldrich,** was built by **Harold I. Pratt,** son of Charles Pratt, a partner of John D. Rockefeller Jr. and founder of Brooklyn's **Pratt Institute.** The present owner is an organization that promotes interest in foreign relations and publishes the influential magazine *Foreign Affairs.* ◆ 58 E 68th St (at Park Ave). 734.0400

97 Americas Society In the late 1940s and early 1950s, this was the **Soviet Delegation to the United Nations,** which made this corner the scene of almost continuous anti-Communist demonstrations. Before the Russians arrived, it was the home of banker Percy Rivington Pyne. The building, designed in 1909 by **McKim, Mead & White,** now houses a gallery specializing in Central, South, and North American art. ◆ Tu-Su noon-6PM. 680 Park Ave (at E 68th St). 249.8950 &

97 680-690 Park Avenue A lively but not exceptional collection of brick and limestone Neo-Georgian buildings, this ensemble is special because it is the only full block of town houses surviving on Park Avenue. No. 680: **Center for Inter-American Relations,** formerly the **Soviet Delegation to the UN,** originally the **Percy Pyne House,** was designed in 1909 by **McKim, Mead & White; No. 684: Spanish Institute,** the house of Pyne's son-in-law, Oliver D. Filey, was built in Pyne's garden in 1926, by **McKim, Mead & White; No. 686: Istituto Italiano di Cultura,** formerly the **William Sloane House,** was designed in 1918 by **Delano & Aldrich; No. 690: Italian Consulate,** originally the **Henry P. Davidson House,** was designed in 1917 by **Walker & Gillette.** ◆ Between E 68th and E 69th Sts

98 Hunter College Founded in 1870 as a school for training teachers, this is one of the colleges of the **City University of New York.** Today, the school emphasizes such practical disciplines as science, premed and nursing, and education. The **Hunter College Theater** (772.4000), in the main building, is used for lectures, political forums, and music and dance programs. ◆ E 68th to E 69th Sts (between Lexington and Park Aves). 772.4000 &

99 S. Wyler An excellent source of 18th- and 19th-century English sterling silver, Victorian and old Sheffield plates, as well as antique porcelain, this shop is more than a century old. ◆ M-Sa 941 Lexington Ave (at E 69th St). 879.9848

100 The Union Club Designed in 1932 by **Delano & Aldrich,** this limestone and granite structure is a rather dry palazzo composition (compare with the **University** or **Metropolitan Clubs**) and, no doubt, looks the way you would expect the oldest men's club in New York City to look. The building is not open to the public. ◆ 101 E 69th St (at Park Ave). 734.5400

101 TSE Cashmere Manhattan's fashion newcomer opened an impressive minimalist 3,000 square feet space to showcase its cashmere collection. Recently expanded to include silk and fine-gauged wool, this spacious modern setting is the perfect backdrop for the natural and pure hues and lines of the designer collection. ◆ M-Sa. 827 Madison Ave (at E 69th St). 472.7790

When the first burials took place in St. Paul's and Trinity churchyards, they provided employment for gentlemen licensed by the city as Inviters to Funerals. Dressed in somber black, with long black streamers attached to their stovepipe hats, they marched in pairs from house to house extolling the virtues of the recently deceased. As they walked through the streets, one tolled a bell and the other pounded the pavement with a long black pole. They served as masters of ceremonies at the funeral itself, and their fee was determined by the turnout. At the gravesite the 12 pallbearers were given souvenir spoons engraved with figures of the 12 apostles, which were usually so badly cast they were known as monkey spoons. Female relatives were given a mourning brooch or ring, which had a compartment containing strands of the deceased's hair. (If they were burying a bald man, it was the hair of his nearest male relative.) Spoons, brooches, and rings were all sold by the Inviters, who also earned a fee for supervising the party that followed every funeral. The quality of the wine served was a tribute in itself, and many people stored away the best they could afford to be used at their own funerals. When a person became mortally ill, a different pair of licensed professionals, known as Comforters of the Sick, were hired by relatives to spend as many hours as were needed reading Scriptures, singing hymns, and otherwise preparing the doomed soul for an easy entry into Heaven.

102 Pratesi One of the more sybaritic bed-and-bath shops in town, sheets of linen, silk, and Egyptian cotton, as well as comforters filled with goose down or cashmere and covered in silk, are sold here. ◆ M-Sa. 829 Madison Ave (at E 69th St). 288.2315 ♿

102 Madison Avenue Bookshop It looks deceptively small, but the two no-nonsense floors are packed with a wide range of literary criticism, art, current fiction, and cookbooks. It stocks the full line of every major publisher, including a lot of first novels. ◆ M-Sa. 833 Madison Ave (at E 69th St). 535.6130 ♿

102 Maraolo Italian-made shoes for men, women, and children can be found here at reasonable prices, considering the style, location, and the quality. If you're looking for a bargain, two locations serve as outlets for overstocked items and discontinued styles (131 West 72nd Street, between Columbus and Amsterdam Aveunes, 787.6550; and 316 East 59th Street, at First Ave, 319.6582). ◆ Daily. 835 Madison Ave (between E 69th and E 70th Sts). 628.5080. Also at: 782 Lexington Ave (between E 60th and E 61st St) 832.8182; 1321 Third Ave (between E 75th and E 76th Sts). 535.6225

103 Minna Rosenblatt An enchanting collection of Tiffany lamps and other glass antiques are offered here. ◆ M-Sa. 844 Madison Ave (between E 69th and E 70th Sts). 288.0250 ♿

103 Missoni The whole store is devoted to the Missoni signature Italian knits on what is becoming "European Designers' Row." The recognizable blend of subtle color combinations and patterns is worked up in all kinds of dashing sportswear for men and women. ◆ M-Sa. 836 Madison Ave (at E 69th St). 517.9339 ♿

103 The Westbury Hotel $$$$ There is a Westbury in London with an American flavor, but its American counterpart is decidedly British. Amenities include 24-hour room service, in-room safes, PC and fax ports, same-day valet service, and a multilingual staff. The Chippendale furniture and 17th-century Belgian tapestries in the lobby are genuine. All of its large 235 rooms and suites are handsomely decorated. ◆ 15 E 69th St (at Madison Ave). 535.2000, 800/225.5843; fax 535.5058 ♿

Within The Westbury Hotel:

The Polo ★★$$$ Given the dignified setting, chef Kerry Heffernan's food is appropriately complex; however, some of it works, some doesn't. Try the sautéed foie gras with banyuls vinegar (made with tiny, red, very tart berries); grilled Louisiana shrimp with artichokes, haricots verts, and orange-tarragon vinaigrette; or sautéed Canadian salmon with mustard sauce. ◆ American/French ◆ M-Sa breakfast, lunch, and dinner; Su brunch and dinner. Reservations recommended; jacket required. 840 Madison Ave (between E 69th and E 70th Sts). 439.4835 ♿

104 MacKenzie-Childs Madison Avenue's newest purveyor of high-end home accessories is no place for the minimalist-minded. Designed and decorated with objets such as lamps, boxes, and frames that are hand-painted with spots, checks, stripes, and flowers, this charming three-level store is supplied by artisan workshops in upstate New York. Hand-painted dinnerware in myriad designs and mix-and-match possibilities is a particular strength. ◆ M-Sa. 824 Madison Ave (at E 69th St). 570.6050

104 D. Porthault This shop can weave tablecloths that will go the entire length of a ballroom, sheets to fit the beds of private airplanes, and duvet covers of fine linen. Queen Elizabeth II has slept on **Porthault** sheets. ◆ M-Sa. 18 E 69th St (at Madison Ave). 688.1660

105 The Frick Collection When the old Lenox Library was torn down, Henry Clay Frick, chairman of the Carnegie Steel Corp., bought the site, wanting a place to display his art. He had **Thomas Hastings** design the Beaux Arts house in 1914—one of the last great mansions on Fifth Avenue—with apartments for the family and reception rooms for the art. In his will, Frick decreed that his wife could continue living there until her death, at which time it would be renovated and expanded as a museum (illustrated at right). **John Russell Pope,** who later designed the National Gallery in Washington, DC, designed in 1935 what is now the museum. He is responsible for its unique character, especially the glass-covered courtyard, a rewarding retreat from city anxieties if ever there was one. The east wing was added in 1977, designed by **John Barrington Bayley** and **Harry Van Dyke;** the great landscape architect Russell Page designed the garden.

Visiting here is like being asked into the sumptuous private home of a collector who bought only the crème de la crème of the old masters. Treasures here include Rembrandt's *The Polish Rider,* Van Dyck's *Virgin and Child with Saints, and Donor,* Bellini's *Saint Francis in the Desert,* Titian's *Man in a Red Cap,* El Greco's *Saint Jerome,* Piero della Francesca's *Saint Simon the Apostle,* and a whole room of Fragonard. There are occasional free lectures and chamber music concerts. (Call or write for ticket information.) Absolutely worth a visit. ◆ Admission. Tu-Su. Children under 10 not admitted. 1 E 70th St (at Fifth Ave). 288.0700 ♿

The Frick Collection

Michael Storrings

106 Lycee Français The French school now occupies two French Renaissance mansions: **No. 7,** designed in 1899 by **Flagg & Chambers,** was the **Oliver Gould Jennings House; No. 9,** created in 1896 by **Carrère & Hastings,** was the **Henry T. Sloane House.** ♦ 7 and 9 E 72nd St (between Madison and Fifth Aves). 861.9400

107 Polo–Ralph Lauren If you like the Polo look, you'll love the exquisite wonderland Ralph Lauren has created here. Designed in 1898 by **Kimball & Thompson,** the French Renaissance building was commissioned by Gertrude Rhinelander Waldo, a descendant of one of New York's most influential families. She lived here for a few months, but preferred to live across the street with her sister. She offered it to her son, but he preferred to live elsewhere too, and the house stood empty until it was sold in a foreclosure in 1920. Before Lauren moved in, it was the **Philips Auction Gallery.** Now it overflows with his designs for outerwear, sportswear, separates, and accessories for men, women, and children and an opulent home design section as well. It's well worth a visit even if you don't buy anything. ♦ M-Sa. 867 Madison Ave (at E 72nd St). 606.2100 ♿

108 Polo Sport–Ralph Lauren Ralph Lauren has extended his fashion emporium across the street to this modern 10,000-square-foot activewear shop. There's a boutique featuring Lauren's Double RL division of weathered classics: jeans, motorcycle jackets, flannel shirts, and the like. ♦ M-Sa. 888 Madison Ave (at E 72nd St). 434.8000 ♿

109 Pierre Deux The French family Demery has spent 300 years creating richly colored paisley and floral fabrics that are quintessentially Provençal, and they sell their best designs— the **Souleiado** line—to this shop. ♦ M-Sa. 870 Madison Ave (at E 71st St). 570.9343.

Also at: 369 Bleecker St (at Charles St). 243.7740

110 St. James Episcopal Church Originally designed in 1884 by **R.H. Robertson,** this church was established on the East Side before the invasion of the millionaires, but its future was secured when families such as the Schermerhorns, the Rhinelanders, and the Astors became members of its vestry. In 1924, the church was rebuilt by **Ralph Adams Cram;** the steeple was added by **Richard Kimball** in 1950. ♦ 865 Madison Ave (at E 71st St). 288.4100

111 Yves Saint Laurent–Rive Gauche Neighboring stores combine to offer the entire Saint Laurent line for men and women. Together, they have the city's largest variety of his collections, including hats, umbrellas, shirts, slacks, dresses, suits, and ball gowns. ♦ M-Sa. 855-859 Madison Ave (between E 70th and E 71st Sts). 988.3821 ♿

112 Hirschl & Adler Top-quality shows of 18th-, 19th-, and 20th-century American and European art appear here. Also featured are American prints and contemporary paintings and sculpture. ♦ Tu-Sa. 21 E 70th St (between Madison and Fifth Aves). 535.8810 ♿

112 Knoedler Gallery The oldest New York–based art gallery, founded in 1846, handles contemporary greats such as Richard Diebenkorn, Nancy Graves, Robert Motherwell, Frank Stella, and Robert Rauschenberg. Located in a 1910 building by **Thornton Chad,** this gallery is always worth checking out. ♦ Tu-Sa. 19 E 70th St (between Madison and Fifth Aves). 794.0550

113 45 East 70th Street Originally the home of investment banker Arthur S. Lehman, this nondescript town house was designed by **Aymar Embury II** in 1929. His wife was the former Adele Lewisohn, a philanthropist and champion tennis player. It is now the home of Estee Lauder. ♦ Between Park and Madison Aves

114 46 East 70th Street This ornate Neo-Jacobean house, designed in 1912 by **Frederick Sterner,** was built for Stephen C. Clark, whose family owned the Singer Sewing Machine Co. Parts of his extensive art collection are in the **Metropolitan Museum of Art.** Among his many interests was baseball—he founded the Baseball Hall of Fame at Cooperstown, New York. The former residence is now the **Lowell Thomas Building of the Explorers Club.** ♦ Between Park and Madison Aves

115 The Asia Society The permanent collection of Asian art assembled by John D. Rockefeller III between 1951 and 1979 was moved in 1981 to this building designed by **Edward Larrabee Barnes.** It is known for its outstanding Southeast Asian and Indian sculpture, Chinese ceramics and bronzes, and Japanese ceramics and wood sculptures. Other galleries in this serene albeit extravagant building feature changing exhibits ranging from Chinese snuff bottles to Islamic books from the collection of Prince Aga Kahn. The society also sponsors lectures here on Asian arts and adventures, as well as films and performances. A large bookstore is well stocked with books, periodicals, and prints from or about Asia. ♦ Admission; free Thursday after 6PM. Tu-Su. Tours: Tu-Sa 12:30PM; Su 2:30PM. 725 Park Ave (at E 70th St). 288.6400 &

115 Visiting Nurse Service of New York This organization is located in a Tudor Revival mansion, designed in 1921 by **Walker & Gillette,** that was once home to Thomas W. Lamont, chairman of J.P. Morgan & Co. ♦ 107 E 70th St (between Lexington and Park Aves). 794.9200

116 124 East 70th Street Built for financier Edward A. Norman in 1941 by **William Lescaze,** this International-style house was cited by the **Museum of Modern Art** for its innovative design. ♦ Between Lexington and Park Aves

117 123 East 70th Street Designer **Samuel Trowbridge,** whose works include the **St. Regis Hotel** and other Beaux Arts gems, built this house for himself in 1903. ♦ Between Lexington and Park Aves

117 Paul Mellon House This French Provincial town house, right at home in New York, was built for the industrialist and art collector

in 1965 by **H. Page Cross.** ♦ 125 E 70th St (between Lexington and Park Aves)

118 131 East 71st Street America's first interior decorator, Elsie de Wolfe, lived here and used the house as a showcase for her talents. The house was built in 1867, but she designed the present facade in 1910 with **Ogden Codman Jr.** ♦ Between Lexington and Park Aves

119 Sette Mezzo ★★$$$ A simple whitewashed cafe, this is a local favorite for such pasta dishes as rigatoni with sausage, artichokes, and tomato and ravioli with mixed vegetables and saffron. Note: Service can sometimes be a bit sloppy—regulars often get better treatment, and the room can get noisy. ♦ Italian ♦ Daily lunch and dinner. Reservations recommended. No credit cards accepted. 969 Lexington Ave (between E 70th and E 71st Sts). 472.0400

120 The Lenox School This Tudor house, built in 1907 by **Edward P. Casey** for Stephen H. Brown, governor of the New York Stock Exchange, was considered one of the area's showplaces before it was converted to a school in 1932. ♦ 154 E 70th St (between Third and Lexington Aves)

121 Gracious Home The ultimate neighborhood hardware store: TVs, woks, umbrellas, dishwashers, typewriters, radiator covers, mason jars, and all the expected basics. At the store across the street (No. 1217), you will find a complete bath shop—everything from sinks and faucets to shower curtains and bath mats. ♦ Daily. 1220 Third Ave (at E 70th St). 517.6300

122 Grace's Marketplace It's no coincidence that this gourmet market resembles **Balducci's;** Grace is the daughter of that downtown institution's founding family. Similarly, this place has glorious produce, cheeses, breads, prepared foods, and cakes of the highest quality. But there's also a salad bar here and spectacular fresh pasta in colors seen only on tropical fish. ♦ Daily. 1237 Third Ave (at E 71st St). 737.0600

123 Evergreen Antiques Scandinavian country furniture and accessories as well as continental and Biedermeier furniture are available here. ♦ M-Sa. 1249 Third Ave (at E 72nd St). 744.5664

124 Cafe Greco ★$$ Lively and flower-filled, this restaurant offers cuisines that touch upon the Mediterranean's various shores; French, Italian, Spanish, and Moroccan dishes all find their way onto a menu that includes grilled octopus and penne with black olives, tomatoes, and capers. ♦ Continental ♦ Daily lunch and dinner. 1390 Second Ave (between E 71st and E 72nd Sts). 737.4300

125 First Reformed Hungarian Church Hungarian-born architect **Emery Roth** gave us a taste of the old country in 1915 when he designed this ornamented white stucco church topped by an 80-foot, conical-roofed bell tower. ♦ 344 E 69th St (between First and Second Aves). 734.5252

126 Rockefeller University This collection of buildings was originally known as the **Rockefeller Institute for Medical Research.** This lovely site, which was a summer estate of the Schermerhorn family, was acquired in 1901; the first building, **Founder's Hall,** opened in 1903 as a laboratory. Most striking are the gray hemisphere of **Caspary Auditorium,** built in 1957, and the **President's House,** built in 1958, both by **Harrison & Abramovitz.** It's worth a visit. Ask the guard for permission to enter, and while you're here, stroll toward the river for a look at the gardens. ♦ E 64th to E 68th Sts (between FDR Dr and York Ave). 327.8000

127 New York Hospital/Cornell University Medical College What appears to be a singular, almost solid, well-balanced mass is actually 15 buildings, designed in 1932 by **Coolidge, Shepley, Bullfinch & Abbott.** The strong vertical lines are offset by Gothic arches. ♦ 525 E 68th St (between FDR Dr and York Ave). 746.5454

128 Sotheby's The London-based Sotheby's is the largest and oldest fine-arts auctioneer in the world. With its original Madison Avenue headquarters closed, it has relocated here in a larger but less personal space, where there is a full round of important sales, exhibitions, and free seminars. Admission to the more important auctions is by ticket only, but all viewings are open to the public. ♦ Open for viewings before scheduled auctions. Call ahead for schedule. 1334 York Ave (at E 72nd St). 606.7000 &

129 Petaluma ★$$$ Fallen from the fickle graces of the chic and trendy, this eclectic cafe still attracts a decent crowd. The food—which includes *spaghetti primavera;* baby chicken in a light mustard sauce; and swordfish with tomatoes, capers, and olives—is fine. And dessert fans shouldn't miss the fabulous Belgian chocolate cake. ♦ Italian ♦ Daily lunch and dinner. Reservations required. 1356 First Ave (at E 73rd St). 772.8800

130 Cafe Crocodile ★★$$ The fresh, earthy foods of the Mediterranean—be they of Greek, French, Italian, or North African origin—are variously featured here on a menu that changes monthly. Owner/chef Andree Abramoff's love of cooking comes through in every dish; Moroccan couscous, seared tuna with ginger, and duck confit are all highly recommended. ♦ Mediterranean ♦ M-Sa dinner. Reservations recommended. 354 E 74th St (between First and Second Aves). 249.6619

131 Jan Hus Church This 1914 Presbyterian church was founded by the Czech community, whose presence in the neighborhood led it to be known as Little Bohemia in the 1920s and 1930s. The parsonage is furnished to resemble a Czech peasant's house. ♦ 351 E 74th St (between First and Second Aves). 288.6743

132 AccScentiques Decorative and fragrant accents for the home—tapestry and moiré pillows, hand-painted boxes and mirrors, a bamboo desk and chair, sachets, dried flowers, and potpourri. ♦ Tu by appointment only; W-Su. 1418 Second Ave (at E 74th St). 288.3289 &

133 Mezzaluna ★$$ This tiny restaurant is quite popular among East Siders for pizzas baked in a wood-burning oven, as well as carpaccio, salads, and pasta specials. Pumpkin *tortelloni* (large tortellini) is among the favorites. ♦ Italian ♦ Daily lunch, dinner, and late-night meals. 1295 Third Ave (between E 74th and E 75th Sts). 535.9600 &

134 Paraclete Theological (mainly Christian) works are this bookstore's specialty. ♦ Tu-Sa. 146 E 74th St (at Lexington Ave). 535.4050 &

135 Vivolo ★$$ Reasonably priced and therefore crowded, this trattoria features standard, well-prepared dishes that include *capellini primavera;* fettuccine with pesto; chicken with tomatoes and mushrooms; and chicken with lemon, butter, and spinach. For dessert, try the zabaglione and ricotta cheesecake. ♦ Italian ♦ M-Sa lunch and dinner. Reservations required. 140 E 74th St (at Lexington Ave). 737.3533. Also at: 222 E 58th St (between Second and Third Aves). 308.0112

136 La Maison du Chocolat From the acclaimed Parisian chocolatier Robert Linxe comes a shop for the true connoisseur. Of course, these delicacies that are among the best chocolates in the world don't come cheap. ♦ M-Sa. 25 E 73rd St (between Madison and Fifth Aves). 744.7117

137 Coco Pazzo ★★$$$$ Still the most popular hit in Pino Luongo's empire (which includes **Mad. 61, Il Toscanaccio,** and **Le Madri**), this place continues to pack them in. The menu is well prepared—seafood risotto, grilled calamari, and homemade penne with veal and sage. The desserts, including warm cinnamon-chocolate pudding with caramel sauce and warm apple tart, are impossible to resist. The Italian wine list is fairly esoteric and generally expensive. ♦ Italian ♦ Daily lunch and dinner. Reservations recommended. 23 E 74th St (between Madison and Fifth Aves). 794.0205

138 Books & Co. This is a general bookstore with the focus on literature, literary periodicals, and the complete works of many major writers. The leather sofa in the philosophy section is a welcome retreat for weary shoppers and museumgoers. ♦ Daily. 939 Madison Ave (at E 74th St). 737.1450

138 Whitney Museum of American Art
Sculptor Gertrude Vanderbilt Whitney founded this museum in 1931 to support young artists and increase awareness of American art. The nucleus of its collection was 600 of the works she owned by Thomas Hart Benton, George Bellows, Maurice Prendergast, Edward Hopper, John Sloan, and other American artists of the era. The present building (shown at right), designed by **Marcel Breuer** with **Hamilton Smith** in 1966, is the museum's third home. Like the **Guggenheim,** the structure is more sculpture than building. A dark, rectilinear, Brutalist mass steps out toward the street, almost threatening those who want to enter. Only the drawbridge entrance seems protective. The museum, perched on the corner, is isolated from its surroundings by sidewalls. You can peer down into the sunken sculpture garden and see through to parts of the lobby. But otherwise, the interior's workings are a mystery, guarded by angled trapezoidal windows that refuse to look you in the eye.

The vast gallery spaces are surprisingly flexible, and can be quite appropriate for a variety of types of art—an important quality for a museum dedicated to temporary exhibitions of contemporary art. A recently approved $13.5-million expansion is expected to be completed by 1997. The permanent collection, which has been increased to 10,000 pieces through gifts and acquisitions, includes works by Alexander Calder, Louise Nevelson, Georgia O'Keeffe, Robert Rauschenberg, Ad Reinhardt, and Jasper Johns, among others, and a portion of it is always on display. Special exhibitions often concentrate on the output of a single artist. It could be video art of the 1980s Nam June Paik, or Realist of the 1930s Edward Hopper. The museum's regular invitational *Biennial,* which critics often pan, is a mixed bag of what's going on across the country. The museum has an aggressively independent series for American film and video artists and makes adventurous forays into the performing arts. For information on these and gallery lectures, check the information desk. The restaurant overlooking the sculpture garden is a pleasant place for refreshments and light meals. The museum operates two branches, including one at Champion International Corp. in Stamford, Connecticut, and one at the **Philip Morris Building** (Park Ave and 42nd St). David Ross was appointed director in 1991. ♦ Admission; free Th 6-8PM. W-Su. Madison Ave and E 75th St. 570.3676 ♿

Within the Whitney Museum of American Art:

Sarabeth's at the Whitney ★★$$ This branch of the **Sarabeth's** restaurant family is the perfect place to relax. Try the lemon linguine with vegetable sauce or choose from a selection of hearty soups and sandwiches. Try one of the famous desserts—perhaps Budapest cake or chocolate mousse cake. ♦ American ♦ Tu-F lunch; Sa-Su brunch. 945 Madison Ave (at E 75th St). 570.3670. Also at: 1295 Madison Ave (between E 92nd and E 93rd Sts). 410.7335; 423 Amsterdam Ave (between W 80th and W 81st Sts). 496.6280

Whitney Museum of American Art

Michael Storrings

139 The Chocolate Soup Charming children's clothes and accessories are crammed into this minuscule store. The most renowned item is the Danish Superbag, an imported schoolbag that's as popular with adults as with children. Great sales. ◆ M-Sa. 946 Madison Ave (between E 74th and E 75th Sts). 861.2210

140 Harkness House This 1905 building by **Hale & Rogers** was built for Edward S. Harkness, son of a Standard Oil Company founder. It is now headquarters of the Commonwealth Fund, a philanthropic foundation. ◆ 1 E 75th St (at Fifth Ave). 535.0400

141 Givenchy For women who want their haute couture brought to their doorsteps, this boutique sends fitters from the House of Givenchy in Paris to New York each spring and fall to measure their local clients. For others, there are blouses, skirts, sweaters, coats, suits, ball gowns, and hats from both ready-to-wear and couture adaptations, which feature the same styles as in the couture collection but in less expensive fabrics. ◆ M-Sa. 954 Madison Ave (at E 75th St). 772.1040

141 Delorenzo Top-drawer furniture of the Art Deco era, sometimes including pieces by such imminent designers as Emile Rouhlmann, Jean Dunand, and Pierre Chareau, is available here. ◆ M-Sa. 958 Madison Ave (at E 75th St). 249.7575

142 Time Will Tell More than 1,000 antique watches and timepieces by such prestigious manufacturers as Rolex and Tiffany fill this specialty store. Pocket watches from the 1800s join more "modern" pieces from the turn of the century, a variety of Art Deco models, and even some of the early Mickey Mouse numbers. A full repair service is available. ◆ M-Sa. 962 Madison Ave (between E 75th and E 76th Sts). 861.2663 &

143 The Surrey $$$ This small apartment-hotel, part of the Manhattan East group, has 130 large and tastefully decorated rooms. The room service is from **Restaurant Daniel,** a favorite spot of the staff of the nearby **Whitney Museum** and other art-world movers and shakers. ◆ 20 E 76th St (between Madison and Fifth Aves). 288.3700, 800/637.8483; fax 628.1549 &

Restaurants/Clubs: Red   **Hotels:** Blue
Shops/ ⓣ Outdoors: Green   **Sights/Culture:** Black

Within The Surrey:

Restaurant Daniel ★★★★$$$$ New York's hottest four-star restaurant is the domain of master-chef Daniel Boulud, whose menu changes frequently; favorites include foie gras with quince, Maine Peekytoe crab salad, quail salad, bay scallops with porcini mushrooms, steamed skate in lobster broth, nine-herb ravioli, and smoked-salmon Napoleon. Go ahead and give in to the desserts—particularly the gratin of chocolate and the baked red-wine tart. ◆ French ◆ M, Sa dinner; Tu-F lunch and dinner. Reservations required; jacket required. 288.0033 &

144 William Secord Gallery William Secord, former director of the Dog Museum (now located in St. Louis), operates this gallery devoted to man's best friend. Exhibitions may also include cats and barnyard animals. ◆ M-Sa. 52 E 76th St (between Park and Madison Aves), Third floor. 249.0075

145 Carlyle Hotel $$$$ At 38 stories, this hotel, designed in 1929 by **Bien & Prince,** soars above the East Side. Decorous charm and easy elegance pervade the 180 guestrooms and public premises; it is always at the top of someone's list of best New York City hotels, and is one of the few hotels tolerated by those who are used to the grand European style. For them, the **Tower** apartments seem to fill the bill for short stays or as permanent residences. Pianist Bobby Short has made the **Cafe Carlyle** famous, but his frequent substitutes are popular, too. The more relaxed and less expensive **Bemelmans Bar,** named for illustrator Ludwig Bemelmans, who painted the murals here, features jazz singer/pianist Barbara Carroll. The **Gallery** is recommended for people watching at tea time. The **Carlyle Restaurant** serves an elegant dinner. ◆ 35 E 76th St (at Madison Ave). 744.1600, 800/227.5737; fax 717.4682 &

146 The Mark $$$$ This elegant and intimate luxury hotel boasts rooms with original 18th-century Piranesi prints, feather pillows, VCRs, marble bathrooms, terry cloth robes, and heated towel racks. Many of the 180 rooms and suites have their own kitchens. ◆ 25 E 77th St (between Madison and Fifth Aves). 744.4300, 800/843.6275; fax 744.4586 &

Within The Mark:

Mark's ★★$$$$ The menu changes monthly, as does the selection of vintage wines offered by the glass, but the inventive and vibrant complexity of chef Erik Maillard's cooking is constant. Good choices are the Maine Peekytoe crab salad with tangerine-and-lime dressing, and fricassee of calamari with braised cabbage and Guinness stout and cream sauce. The desserts are quite rich. ◆ French ◆ M-Sa breakfast, lunch, and dinner; Su brunch and dinner. Reservations recommended. 879.1864

147 Sant Ambroeus ★★$$$ This Milanese institution is known on both sides of the Atlantic for elegant Italian fare, topped off with the best cappuccino or espresso around. Try the mixed seafood antipasto, risotto with arugula and tomatoes, shrimp with mustard sauce, and grilled salmon. The pastries look terrific, but stick to simpler confections, such as mocha cake and chocolate mousse. ♦ Italian ♦ M-Sa lunch and dinner; Su lunch. Reservations recommended. 1000 Madison Ave (between E 77th and E 78th Sts). 570.2211

148 Stuyvesant Fish House Designed by **McKim, Mead & White** in 1898, this Renaissance palace was once the scene of the city's most lavish parties. It was owned by Stuyvesant Fish, who was president of the Illinois Central Railroad. He and his wife, Marion, were prominent social leaders. ♦ 25 E 78th St (at Madison Ave)

149 James B. Duke House A copy of an 18th-century château in Bordeaux, this mansion, designed in 1912 by **Horace Trumbauer,** was built for the founder of the American Tobacco Company. It was given to **New York University** in 1959 by Duke's widow and her daughter, Doris (who, along with Barbara Hutton, was known as a "poor little rich girl" in the 1930s), and is now **NYU's Institute of Fine Arts.** Many of the original furnishings are still here, including a Gainsborough portrait in the main hall. ♦ 1 E 78th St (at Fifth Ave). 772.5800

149 French Embassy Created in 1906 by **McKim, Mead & White,** this Italian Renaissance mansion, built for financier Payne Whitney, is typical of upper Fifth Avenue at the turn of the century, before the arrival of massive apartment houses. ♦ 972 Fifth Ave (between E 78th and E 79th Sts). 439.1400

150 Acquavella One of the uptown heavy hitters, this gallery shows 19th- and 20th-century European masters and postwar American and European artists. ♦ M-F. 18 E 79th St (between Madison and Fifth Aves). 734.6300

150 Salander-O'Reilly Galleries Twentieth-century Modernist American painters of the Stieglitz group (Alfred Maurer, Arthur Dove, Stuart Davis) as well as bold, contemporary ones (Susan Roth, Dan Christensen, John Greifen) are shown here. ♦ Tu-Sa. 20 E 79th St (between Madison and Fifth Aves). 879.6606

151 Hanae Mori A striking balance of stucco front and off-center chrome cylinder, this slightly mysterious 1969 storefront is **Hans Hollein**'s first work in Manhattan. Inside is the retail outlet for the designer's sophisticated, Japanese-influenced women's clothing. ♦ M-Sa. 27 E 79th St (between Madison and Fifth Aves). 472.2352 &

152 New York Society Library Often confused with the **New York Historical Library,** this is New York City's oldest circulating library, founded in 1754 by a civic-minded group who believed that the availability of books would help the city to prosper. Housed since 1937 in a handsome Italianate town house built in 1917 by **Trowbridge & Livingston,** today it is a local landmark boasting a collection of more than 200,000 volumes, as well as first editions and rare books and manuscripts. The library's particular strengths are in English and American literature, biography, history, art history, travel and exploration, and works relating to the Big Apple. There is also a children's section. ♦ M-Sa. 53 E 79th St (between Park and Madison Aves). 288.6900

153 870 Park Avenue This 1898 town house has been completely remodeled. The tripartite division of the facade alludes to that era's tradition and the scale of the surrounding buildings. In terms of styling, this is the next step after Modernism (see the **Lescaze Residence** and **112 East 64th Street**), and it holds its own. This structure was designed in 1976 by **Robert A.M. Stern** and **John S. Hagmann.** ♦ At E 77th St

154 Lenox Hill Hospital A compound of modern buildings extends from the hospital's nucleus, the **Uris Pavilion,** built in 1975 by **Rogers, Butler, Burgun & Bradbury.** Ranked as one of the city's—and the nation's—best, this hospital is a forerunner in obstetrical and neonatal care (its **Prenatal Testing Center** is one of the most comprehensive in the country); cardiology (the first balloon angioplasty in the country was performed here in 1978); and sports medicine (the **Nicholas Institute of Sports Medicine and Athletic Trauma** was the first such hospital-based center in the US). ♦ Bounded by Lexington and Park Aves, and E 76th and E 77th Sts. 439.2345

155 St. Jean Baptiste Church This Roman Catholic church, designed by **Nicholas Serracino** in 1913, was founded by French Canadians in the area. It is a little overwrought, but charming. Among its best features is the French-style organ, one of the finest in any New York church. ♦ Lexington Ave and E 76th St. 288.5082

156 Mortimer's ★$$$ This unpretentious tavern serves simple food. At the bar sit captains of industry and fashionable women. Safe bets from the menu include Caesar salad, steak *frites* (with french fries), and roast chicken. ♦ Continental ♦ Daily lunch and dinner. Reservations required. 1057 Lexington Ave (at E 75th St). 517.6400

157 Bonté The specialties here are extravagantly decorated cakes with exquisite marzipan and spun-sugar work, although there is hardly a pastry or cake that isn't divine. This patisserie also makes croissants and brioches, fruit tarts, and some of the best eclairs in Manhattan. ◆ M-Sa. 1316 Third Ave (between E 75th and E 76th Sts). 535.2360

158 La Piazzetta di Quisisana ★$$$ Named for a small square in front of Capri's Quisisana hotel, this cozy trattoria—with apricot walls, terra-cotta details, and Italian pottery—features the food of that Italian isle. Try penne with shrimp, red beans, and fresh tomatoes; one of the fresh fish dishes grilled in a wood-burning oven; or roasted baby chicken with rosemary and garlic. ◆ Italian ◆ Daily lunch, dinner, and late-night meals. Reservations recommended. 1319 Third Ave (between E 75th and E 76th Sts). 879.5000

Jim McMullen

159 Jim McMullen ★$$ At this handsome, modern tavern—an enduring scene for singles and networking—the experience is greater than the sum total of the food. Still, it is possible to get a good meal; try the sesame-crusted salmon with tomato vinaigrette or roasted chicken with a ginger glaze. There are also a number of highly potable wines by the glass. ◆ American ◆ M-Sa lunch and dinner; Su brunch and dinner. Reservations recommended. 1341 Third Ave (between E 76th and E 77th Sts). 861.4700

160 Baraonda ★★$$$ The cheery, whimsical room is fitted with primary-color lanterns, caricatures on the walls, and streamers. Late at night there's even dancing on the tables. Before running completely amok, line your stomach with a good, simple plate of pasta, such as *tagliolini* (thin noodles) with tomato and basil. ◆ Northern Italian ◆ Daily lunch and dinner. Reservations required. 1439 Second Ave (at E 75th St). 288.8555

160 Pamir ★$$ The latest ethnic invasion is exotic Afghan cuisine. Try the skewered-meat dishes—lamb and chicken—served with moist rice pilaf and side dishes of yogurt and sautéed eggplant. ◆ Afghan ◆ Tu-Su dinner. Reservations recommended. 1437 Second Ave (between E 74th and E 75th Sts). 734.3791

161 Il Monello ★★$$$ Those who like a little razzle-dazzle with their meal will enjoy the way most dishes are given finishing touches in the dining room; otherwise, the food is simple and reliable. Try breast of chicken with

onion, tomato, and basil sauce; and red snapper with a pine-nut crust and balsamic sauce. The in-depth Italian wine list is not only laudable, it's applaudable. ◆ Italian ◆ Daily lunch and dinner. Reservations required. 1460 Second Ave (between E 76th and E 77th Sts). 535.9310 &

162 Voulez Vous ★★$$$ With a glass front, this French bistro looks slicker than most, but the food couldn't be more traditional. Try coq au vin, cassoulet, filet mignon au poivre, or duck confit; and for dessert, sample one of the heavenly homemade fruit tarts. ◆ French ◆ M-Sa lunch and dinner; Su brunch and dinner. Reservations required. 1462 First Ave (at E 76th St). 249.1776

163 The Red Tulip ★$$ The bright dining room in back of the dimly lit bar is gaily decorated with old, hand-painted pottery, wooden shelves, and cabinets. The ample portions of rich goulash soup, sour cream and double-smoked bacon, Hungarian sausage, braised veal shank with vegetables, stuffed cabbage, and delicate spaetzle are made from fresh ingredients and are full of rich cooked-in flavors. ◆ Hungarian ◆ W-Su dinner. Reservations recommended. 439 E 75th St (between York and First Aves). 734.4893

164 Frederic York Avenue Patisserie The inventive chef Frederic Piepenburg fills his shop with an interesting array of pastries, including oregano croissants, brioches, and reduced-calorie apple tarts. He also does low fat "diabetic baking" with low or no sugar. ◆ M-F 7AM-9PM; Sa-Su 8AM-7PM. 1431 York Ave (at E 76th St). 628.5576

165 Cherokee Apartments Built as model housing for the working class, these apartments are distinguished by the amount of light and air admitted by large casements and balconies—an unusual commodity in the days of "dumbbell" tenements; these were designed in 1909 by **Henry Atterbury Smith**. ◆ Between E 77th and E 78th Sts, and Cherokee Pl and York Ave

166 Rigo Hungarian Pastry The strudels, cakes, tortes, and other attractions here are legendary. Try the caramel-topped *dobos* torte (rich layers of sponge cake and chocolate buttercream, topped with a hard caramel glaze). ◆ Daily. 318 E 78th St (between First and Second Aves). 988.0052

167 Maruzzella ★$$ The wood-burning oven and simple stucco interior here radiate a cheery charm. Chef Giovanni Pinato does wonders with ravioli stuffed with spinach and cheese. Then there are the pizzas—perfect crusts topped with creamy mozzarella, ham, sausages, and vegetables. ◆ Italian ◆ Daily lunch and dinner. 1479 First Ave (at E 77th St). 988.8877

coconut grill

168 Coconut Grill ★$ The social scene is usually in high gear at this attractive, deep-yellow and royal-blue spot. The food is respectable, particularly such homemade pastas as rigatoni with smoked mozzarella, eggplant, and plum tomatoes; and basil linguine with shrimp, scallops, mussels, and clams in a spicy tomato sauce. ♦ American ♦ M-Sa lunch and dinner; Su brunch and dinner. 1481 Second Ave (at E 77th St). 772.6262

169 Caffe Bianco ★$ The pastas, salads, chicken dishes, and such sandwiches as fresh mozzarella and tomato are fine, but desserts like the Valencia orange cake and chocolate truffle cake are sublime. The cappuccinos are pretty terrific too. In summer, the tables spill out onto the sidewalk—just like in Italy. ♦ Italian ♦ M-Th, Su lunch and dinner; F-Sa lunch, dinner, and late-night meals. No credit cards accepted. 1486 Second Ave (between E 77th and E 78th Sts). 988.2655

169 Lusardi's ★★$$$ This is one of several informal, clublike uptown trattorias that attract a sleek, affluent crowd. The food here, however, is more reliable than at other places, and the service is more attentive. Try calamari with tomato sauce, sun-dried–tomato ravioli, pasta with white truffles (in season), and chicken with artichokes and sausage. ♦ Italian ♦ M-F lunch and dinner; Sa-Su dinner. Reservations recommended. 1494 Second Ave (between E 77th and E 78th Sts). 249.2020

170 Istanbul Kebap ★★$ Although there's no decor to speak of in this small Turkish restaurant, the excellent kabobs and rich honey-soaked desserts are so good you won't notice. Also worth trying are the stuffed grape leaves, eggplant dishes, *yogurtlu kebab* (a casserole of chopped lamb, onions, yogurt, paprika, and tomato), and broiled fish, all of which are as authentic as they are cheap. ♦ Turkish ♦ Daily dinner. 303 E 80th St (between First and Second Aves). 517.6880

171 Pig Heaven ★$$ Go ahead and pig out on the Cantonese suckling pig and any of the lighter-than-air steamed dumplings. Other recommended dishes include scallion pancakes and lobster with ginger. ♦ Chinese ♦ M-Th, Su lunch and dinner; F-Sa lunch, dinner, and late-night meals. Reservations recommended weekends. 1540 Second Ave (between E 80th and E 81st Sts). 744.4333

171 Divino Ristorante ★$$ Service and pasta are the high points of this unpretentious favorite of Italian expatriates. Specialties include good fettuccine with four cheeses, linguine with baby clams, breaded veal chop Milanese, and shrimp scampi. Top it all off with a wonderful cappuccino. ♦ Italian ♦ Daily dinner. Reservations required. 1556 Second Ave (between E 80th and E 81st Sts). 861.1096

172 The Comic Strip A showcase club for stand-up comics and singers. Eddie Murphy, Jerry Seinfeld, and Paul Reiser started here, and sometimes a big name will drop by. ♦ Cover, minimum. Shows: M-Th 9PM; F 8:30PM, 10:45PM; Sa 8PM, 10:30PM, 12:30AM; Su 8:30PM. 1568 Second Ave (between E 81st and E 82nd Sts). 861.9386

173 Etats-Unis ★★$$$ The Rapp family has no professional culinary training, so the success of the ever-changing, highly personal menu is all the more impressive (based upon sheer natural talent). You never know what you're going to get on any given evening—it could be arugula and beet salad with goat cheese, roasted sea bass with coriander, or grilled veal rib with a tuna and caper sauce. ♦ American/Eclectic ♦ M-Sa dinner. Reservations recommended. 242 E 81st St (between Second and Third Aves). 517.8826

174 Sistina ★★$$$ Owned by brothers Giuseppe, Gerardo, Antonio, and Cosimo Bruno, this restaurant serves a pleasing mix of Northern and Southern Italian dishes. Try *pappardelle* (broad noodles) in veal sauce with mushrooms and tomatoes, grilled chicken with arugula salad, and sea scallops in a tarragon broth. For dessert, don't miss the almond cake with chocolate and vanilla sauces. ♦ Italian ♦ Daily dinner. Reservations required. 1555 Second Ave (between E 80th and E 81st Sts). 861.7660

175 Border Cafe $ Fajitas, nachos, chilies, chicken wings, and of course, frozen margaritas are the main draw here. Late in the evening, especially on weekends, this place becomes a crowded bar scene. ♦ Southwestern ♦ M-F dinner; Sa-Su brunch and dinner. Reservations recommended. 244 E 79th St (between Second and Third Aves). 535.4347

The oldest independent secondary school in the country is the Collegiate School on the Upper West Side (378 West End Avenue).

Among the famous New Yorkers who have called the serene St. Luke's Place home are Mayor Jimmy Walker, Sherwood Anderson, Marianne Moore, and Theodore Dreiser.

176 New York Public Library, Yorkville Branch This rather academic Neo-Classical building, designed in 1902 by **James Brown Lord,** is the earliest of what are known as the "Carnegie Libraries." There are 65 of these small branch libraries throughout the city, established by a donation from Andrew Carnegie. Later ones, similar in style, were designed by **Lord** and other distinguished architects such as **McKim, Mead & White, Carrère & Hastings,** and **Babb, Cook & Willard.** ♦ M-Sa. 222 E 79th St (between Second and Third Aves). 744.5824

Trois Jean

177 Trois Jean ★★★$$$ The three Jeans of the name refer to owner Jean-Luc Andriot, chef Jean-Louis Dumonet, and the late pastry chef Jean-Marc Burillier (ably succeeded by Bernard Chenivese). Together, they run one of the finest bistros in New York, turning out earthy, delicious food in a candlelit environment. Among the many good choices are risotto with wild mushrooms and truffle oil, and sautéed sweetbreads and artichokes with cumin served on mixed greens with fried leeks. ♦ French ♦ Daily lunch, afternoon tea, and dinner. Reservations recommended. 154 E 79th St (between Third and Lexington Aves). 988.4858

178 Parma ★$$$ It's no longer as popular as some of the newer places, but the kitchen has maintained its standards. Pastas and main courses, including linguine with clam sauce, ravioli with ricotta and spinach, osso buco, and veal chops are well prepared, but dessert is not a strong suit. ♦ Italian ♦ Daily dinner. Reservations recommended. 1404 Third Ave (at E 79th St). 535.3520

179 Tirami Sù ★★$ Whimsically decorated with gold sun and moon masks and mythical figures on the walls, this crowded cafe seems determined to offer its fashionable customers a good time. On the menu are excellent homemade pastas with strong zesty sauces, pizzas with classic and unusual toppings, and authentic Italian desserts served with excellent espresso. ♦ Italian ♦ Daily lunch and dinner. 1410 Third Ave (at E 80th St). 988.9780

180 Samalita's Tortilla Factory ★$ Within this small, bright, yellow and blue room with Mexican silver lamps, colorful tiles, and wicker chairs, diners are treated to fresh-tasting Mexican and Cal-Mex fare. Wash it all down with a Corona, Pacifico, or Negro Modello. ♦ Mexican ♦ Daily lunch and dinner. 1429 Third Ave (at E 81st St). 737.5070 &

181 Cafe Metairie ★$$ With rustic wood beams, authentic French country decor, and a fireplace, this bistro can't be beat for charm. The food, however, can be hit-and-miss. Safe choices include a good cassoulet, and tender steak au poivre with thin *frites.* For dessert, there are excellent fruit tarts and crème caramel. ♦ French ♦ M-F lunch and dinner; Sa dinner; Su brunch and dinner. 1442 Third Ave (at E 82nd St). 988.1800

181 Le Refuge ★★$$$ The ever-changing menu is prepared with carefully chosen fresh ingredients, all cooked and seasoned with a sure hand. Fish dishes are particularly delectable, and some consider the bouillabaisse here the best in town. When it's available, don't miss the quail stuffed with morel mousse. ♦ French ♦ M-F lunch and dinner; Sa-Su brunch and dinner. Reservations recommended. 166 E 82nd St (between Third and Lexington Aves). 861.4505

182 Girasole ★$$$ A local, conservative crowd of East Siders favors this dependable, noisy Italian restaurant located on the ground floor of a brownstone. Poultry and game dishes—such as chicken sautéed with lemon, and grilled organic Cornish hens with peppercorns—are best. ♦ Italian ♦ Daily lunch and dinner. Reservations required. 151 E 82nd St (between Third and Lexington Aves). 772.6690

183 Big City Kite Co., Inc. More than 150 kinds of kites are sold here. They come in a variety of shapes, including tigers, teddy bears, sailboats, sharks, dragons, and bats. They will also guide you to nearby kite flights. ♦ M-Sa. 1210 Lexington Ave (at E 82nd St). 472.2623

184 Rosenthal Wine Merchant Here you'll find unique wines from California and Europe (particularly burgundies). ♦ M-Sa. 1200 Lexington Ave (between E 81st and E 82nd Sts). 249.6650 &

185 Tiny Doll House All the teeny, tiny furniture and accessories it takes to make a doll's home, including mini Degas paintings, handmade English houses, and furniture, are here under one roof. If you think you can make something better yourself, all the supplies you need are available. ♦ M-Sa. 1146 Lexington Ave (between E 79th and E 80th Sts). 744.3719 &

186 Junior League of The City of New York One of a trio of perfect neighbors, this sophisticated 1928 Regency-style mansion by **Mott B. Schmidt** was built for Vincent Astor. The other two are **Schmidt**'s Georgian house for Clarence Dillon (1930) at 124 East 80th Street, and the Federal-style **George Whitney House** (1930) at 120 East 80th Street, by

Cross & Cross. ♦ 130 E 80th St (between Lexington and Park Aves). 288.6220

187 **E.A.T.** ★★$$$ Owned by Eli Zabar (of **Zabar's** fame), this informal eatery makes all its breads with a sourdough starter, including the famous *ficelle* (a super-crusty loaf that's 22 inches long with a diameter barely larger than a silver dollar). Popular picks from the menu are linguine with broccoli rabe, the Three-Salad Plate (choose three from a list of 12 salads), lamb sandwich, crab cakes, pot roast, and grilled chicken. For dessert try the chocolate cake or raspberry tart. ♦ American ♦ Daily breakfast, lunch, and dinner. 1064 Madison Ave (between E 80th and E 81st Sts). 772.0022

188 **Frank E. Campbell Funeral Chapel** In this building, possibly the most prestigious funeral chapel in the world, we have said farewell to Elizabeth Arden, James Cagney, Jack Dempsey, Tommy Dorsey, Judy Garland, Howard Johnson, Robert F. Kennedy, John Lennon, J.C. Penney, Damon Runyon, Arturo Toscanini, Mae West, and Tennessee Williams, to name-drop just a few. ♦ 1076 Madison Ave (at E 81st St). 288.3500 &

188 **Burlington Book Shop** This neighborly bookstore, a fixture for the last 50 years, is run by Jane Trichter. Upstairs is the out-of-print department. Downstairs is **Burlington Antique Toys,** a dusty basement shop full of antique and vintage racing cars, tin soldiers, wooden boats, and more. ♦ Daily. The hours downstairs vary but are usually M-Sa. 1082 Madison Ave (between E 81st and E 82nd Sts). 288.7420

189 **Parioli Romanissimo** ★★★$$$$ Located in a charming town house, this dining room is sedately decorated with beige walls and beige print fabric window shades and seat cushions. The delicate egg pasta and risotto with porcini (among others) are divine, and the entrées, including baked sea bass with tarragon sauce and baby chicken roasted with black truffles, are impeccable. For dessert, have the tiramisù or zabaglione. The wine list is extensive, well chosen, and expensive. ♦ Italian ♦ M-Sa dinner. Reservations required well in advance; jacket and tie required. 24 E 81st St (between Madison and Fifth Aves). 288.2391

190 **The Stanhope Hotel** $$$$ Created in 1926 by **Rosario Candela,** this hotel is strategically located across the street from the **Metropolitan Museum of Art** and **Central Park.** The septuagenarian has been freshened up without great disturbance to its gentility. The 148 rooms (nearly all suites), decorated in the French style, have such amenities as in-room safes and multiple telephones. Room service and valet service are available 24 hours, and limousine service is provided to **Lincoln Center** and the Theater District. Rooms facing the museum and the park are particularly choice. **Le Salon** and the **Dining Room** are favorite escapes from museum overload. ♦ 995 Fifth Ave (at E 81st St). 288.5800, 800/828.1123; fax 517.0088

Metropolitan Museum of Art

Michael Storrings

191 998 Fifth Avenue This 1912 apartment building in the guise of an Italian Renaissance palazzo was built by **McKim, Mead & White** when the bulk of society lived in mansions up and down the avenue. The largest apartment here has 25 rooms; it was originally leased by Murray Guggenheim. ♦ At E 81st St

191 1001 Fifth Avenue Designed in 1978 by **Philip Birnbaum,** this average apartment tower has been upgraded with a limestone facade by **Philip Johnson** and **John Burgee.** Half-round ornamental molding relates horizontally to the neighboring 998 Fifth Avenue, while the mullions struggle for a vertical emphasis, pointing at the mansard-shaped cut-out roof. ♦ Between E 81st and E 82nd Sts

192 Metropolitan Museum of Art The first, original section was built in 1880 by **Calvert Vaux** and **Jacob Wrey Mould.** Additions and renovations were as follows: southwest wing 1888, **Theodore Weston;** north wing 1894, **Arthur Tuckerman;** central facade 1902, **Richard Morris Hunt, Richard Howland Hunt,** and **George B. Post;** Fifth Avenue wings 1906, **McKim, Mead & White;** stairs, pool, **Lehman Wing,** and **Great Hall** renovations 1970, **Kevin Roche, John Dinkeloo & Associates;** later additions 1975-87, **Kevin Roche, John Dinkeloo & Associates; Andre Meyer Gallery** renovation 1993, **David Harvey, Gary Tinterow,** and **Philippe de Montebello** with **Alvin Holm** and **Kevin Roche.** Ten years after the first section was finished at the edge of **Central Park,** Frederick Law Olmsted, the park's designer, said he regretted having allowed it to be built there. He should see it now. The museum (pictured at left) has grown to 1.4 million square feet of floor space (more than 32 acres), with some 3.3 million works of art, making it the largest art museum in the Western Hemisphere. It seems to be expanding and getting better every day (much of this growth must be credited to director **Philipe de Montebello**). Founded in 1870 by a group of art-collecting financiers and industrialists who were on the art committee of New York's **Union League Club,** the museum's original collection consisted of 174 paintings, mostly Dutch and Flemish, and a gift of antiquities from General di Cesnola, the former US consul to Cyprus.

The more recent additions, including the **Lila Acheson Wallace Wing** (20th-century art) with its beautiful roof garden, provide a dramatic contrast of high-tech glass curtain walls to the solid limestone Beaux Arts front. The interiors are spectacular, too, contrasting but not fighting with **Richard Morris Hunt**'s equally spectacular **Great Hall,** just inside the main entrance.

The list of benefactors who have swelled the museum's holdings over the years reads like a *Who's Who* of the city's First Families—Morgan, Rockefeller, Altman, Marquand, Hearn, Bache, Lehman. The push to house the collection in style has produced the **Sackler Wing** (1979) for the *Raymond R. Sackler Far East Art* collection; the entire Egyptian **Temple of Dendur** (1978), given to the people of the United States for their support in saving monuments threatened by the construction of the Aswan High Dam; the **Egyptian Galleries** (1983) for the museum's world-class permanent collection; the impressive **Michael C. Rockefeller Wing** (1982) for the art of Africa, the Americas, and the Pacific Islands; the **Douglas Dillon Galleries of Chinese Painting** (1983) and the **Astor Chinese Garden Court** (1980), with a reception hall from the home of a 16th-century scholar; an expanded and dramatically redesigned **American Wing** (1980); and the **Lehman Wing** (1975), which displays its collection of paintings, drawings, and decorative objects in rooms re-created from the original Lehman town house on West 54th Street. Don't miss the beautifully renovated **Andre Meyer Galleries** (1993), where you'll see the premier collection of 19th-century European paintings and sculpture in the world, rivaling the Musée d'Orsay in Paris.

The permanent collection (about a third of which can be displayed at any one time) is expanding in every department. The museum already has the most comprehensive collection of American art in the world, and excels in Egyptian, Greek and Roman, and European art, including arms and armor, ranging from medieval times to the 20th century. The list of priceless art and artifacts within these walls is almost impossible to comprehend.

The **Costume Institute** displays its 35,000 articles of clothing in stylish themes, with special temporary blockbuster exhibits you won't want to miss.

The information desk in the center of the **Great Hall** has floor plans and a helpful staff to direct you. The staff also has information about concerts and lectures in the museum's **Grace Rainey Rogers Auditorium** and will help you arrange for a guided tour, available in several languages. At the north end of the **Great Hall,** tape-recorded tours of most of the exhibits are available for rental. Just off the **Great Hall** is the justly famous and recently expanded book and gift shop.

The museum restaurant is a hectic, cafeteria-style arrangement with tables around a pool. A little-known resource is weekend brunch in the elegant upstairs dining room, which, during the week, is only open to sponsors.

The Iris and B. Gerald Cantor Roof Garden, a lovely open-air sculpture garden with grand views from the roof of the museum, is open early May through late October and sells coffee, wine, and soft drinks.

The Friday and Saturday evening hours have added a touch of civility and grace to the busy city scene. Many of the museum's guests take advantage of the tranquil twilight hours, when, beginning at 5PM, a string quartet serenades from the **Great Hall** balcony, where a bar and candlelit tables are set up for relaxation. Evening educational offerings—art lectures and documentaries—coincide with the concerts in the **Grace Rainey Rogers Auditorium.** ♦ Admission. Tu-Su. Fifth Ave and E 82nd St. 535.7710, 879.5500 ♿

193 William Greenberg Jr. Desserts Other bakeries may turn out fancier-looking cakes, but pound for pound, none can match the all-American classics here. Bundt cakes with a slick chocolate icing, pound cakes, brownies, chocolate-chip cookies—all find their richest, most definitive expression here and are utterly delicious. Those who like their pleasures sweetened with guilt can ruminate for a while about the massive amounts of butter and sugar it takes to makes things taste this good. ♦ M-Sa; Su 10AM-4PM. 1100 Madison Ave (between E 82nd and E 83rd Sts). 744.0304. Also at: 518 Third Ave (between E 34th and E 35th Sts). 686.3344

194 The Serge Sabarsky Foundation Since 1955, this historical landmark building was home to **The YIVO Institute for Jewish Research.** The nonprofit organization purchased it in 1994 and in the spring of 1995 began work on its new incarnation as a museum of Austrian and German Expressionist art. They have chosen a handsome location in one of the last great Fifth Avenue mansions, designed by **Carrère & Hastings.** ♦ 1048 Fifth Ave (at E 86th St). 535.6700

195 Church of St. Ignatius Loyola The overscaled Vignoia facade on Park Avenue was designed by **Ditmars & Schickel** in 1898. Its flat limestone late-Renaissance style looks very comfortable here—and it's a welcome change from all that Gothic. ♦ 980 Park Ave (at E 84th St). 288.3588 ♿

196 Apex Fitness Club Fitness facilities around the city have turned into urban country clubs, and this is one of the hottest. In addition to standard long-term membership, single-visit coupons are available. ♦ Daily. 205 E 85th St (between Second and Third Aves). 737.8377

197 ManAlive You think clubs with male go-go dancers are only in the suburbs? Not so at the relocated, former **Chippendale's,** whose chiseled hunks are still titillating the ladies. The fervor of the 1980s is over, but out-of-towners still come here to check out the boys.

♦ Cover. Shows: F-Sa 8PM. You must arrive 45 minutes in advance. 210 E 86th St (between Second and Third Aves). 935.6060

198 Kleine Konditorei ★$$ The wood-paneled and burgundy dining room, fitted with chandeliers and small-shaded table lamps, is reminiscent of the 1950s. Sauerbraten, Wiener schnitzel, roast goose, and *natur schnitzel* (plain, panfried veal cutlet) are the specialties in this old-fashioned restaurant, along with potato pancakes and pastries. It's definitely not for the calorie conscious. ♦ German ♦ Daily lunch and dinner. 234 E 86th St (between Second and Third Aves). 737.7130 ♿

198 Elk Candy Company Moist, chocolate-covered marzipan and other tempting treats, such as almond bark, butter crunch, and chocolate turtles, are for sale in this sweet little hole-in-the-wall. ♦ Daily. 240 E 86th St (between Second and Third Aves). 650.1177

199 Schaller & Weber This incredible store is filled from floor to ceiling with cold cuts. Liverwursts, salamis, bolognas, and other savories are piled on counters, packed into display cases, and hung from the walls and ceilings. ♦ M-Sa. 1654 Second Ave (between E 85th and E 86th Sts). 879.3047

199 Estia ★★$$$ Here you'll find fresh and always satisfying Greek food in a typical, noisy taverna setting. The Greek antipasto for two, which includes fish roe, eggplant salad, *tzatziki* (yogurt, garlic, and dill), stuffed grape leaves, and pickled octopus, is a good introduction to a hearty meal, as is the fried zucchini, which comes with a wondrous almond-garlic sauce for dipping. ♦ Greek ♦ Tu-Sa dinner. Reservations required on weekends. 308 E 86th St (between First and Second Aves). 628.9100 ♿

200 Paola's ★★$$$ Proprietor and chef Paola Marraccino (who also owns **Maison Caribe** next door) turns out excellent pasta (especially tortellini), hearty soups, good veal and chicken dishes (particularly chicken with sausage), and creamy cheesecake at this delightful Northern Italian restaurant. The atmosphere is romantic and intimate, but the acoustics could be better—when crowded, it's a bit noisy. At press time, the restaurant opened just for dinner, serving lunch only to small parties that booked in advance. However, plans are in the works to open for lunch soon, so call for more information. ♦ Italian ♦ Daily dinner. Reservations recommended. 347 E 85th St (between First and Second Aves). 794.1890

201 Elio's ★★$$$ Wall Streeters and bankers mix with media types and celebs at this trendy neighborhood eatery, a spin-off of the ever-popular **Elaine's.** It's always crowded and noisy, and the food is always good. Order one of the specials, which seem to inspire the kitchen even more than the regular menu does. But the pasta dishes and veal chops are also good picks. ♦ Italian ♦ Daily dinner. Reservations required. 1621 Second Ave (between E 84th and E 85th Sts). 772.2242 ♿

202 Azzurro ★★$$ In a neighborhood filled with formula Italian trattorias, this casual family-run Sicilian establishment offers delicious homemade pastas. Try the penne with eggplant in tomato sauce, gnocchi with pesto, and ravioli with porcini sauce. There are also such grilled dishes as chicken paillard and sirloin with a black-peppercorn cream sauce. ♦ Italian ♦ Daily dinner. Reservations recommended. 245 E 84th St (between Second and Third Aves). 517.7068

Erminia

203 Erminia ★★$$$ The crowning achievements here are the lushly sauced *pappardelle* tossed with artichokes, tomato, sausage, and porcini, and the excellent Tuscan lamb grilled over a wood fire. There are also a number of other roasted dishes, including veal chops. The romantic candlelight atmosphere makes this restaurant a popular place, so be sure to reserve a couple of days in advance. ♦ Italian ♦ M-Sa dinner. Reservations required. 250 E 83rd St (between Second and Third Aves). 879.4284

204 Trastevere ★★$$$ Its name refers to the artists' neighborhood in Rome, but this Italian kitchen didn't become glatt kosher until it was mistakenly listed as such in a local restaurant guide—it turned out there was quite a demand. Dietary laws notwithstanding (all the food served here is glatt kosher), this place features tasty Italian dishes everyone can enjoy. Try carpaccio (without parmesan), *capellini primavera,* polenta with mushrooms, *veal alla Romana* (sautéed with artichokes), chicken with Marsala and mushrooms, and veal chops with tomato salad. ♦ Italian ♦ M-Th, Sa-Su dinner. Reservations required. 309 E 83rd St (between First and Second Aves). 734.6343

205 Mocca Hungarian ★$ Treat yourself to hearty Hungarian home cooking that will please your purse as well as your palate. The portions are more than generous at prices that are improbably low. As you might expect, the Wiener schnitzel, stuffed cabbage, and strudel are the best picks. ♦ Hungarian ♦ Daily dinner. No credit cards accepted. 1588 Second Ave (between E 82nd and E 83rd Sts). 734.6470 ♿

206 Primavera ★★$$$$ One of the great watering holes for the older, distinguished smart set, the food is similarly dignified and usually of good quality. Try the chicken breast with Champagne sauce, pasta with truffles, or green and white pasta with peas and ham. ♦ Italian ♦ Daily dinner. Reservations required; jacket and tie required. 1578 First Ave (at E 82nd St). 861.8608

207 Wilkinson's 1573 Seafood Cafe ★★$$$ The interior of this little gem of a restaurant is relaxed and intimate, with pastel-colored murals adorning the bare-brick walls. Try such creatively prepared seafood dishes as grilled John Dory (a white fish found in the Pacific, also known as St. Peter's fish) with Thai ginger broth, and pan-seared, spice-coated tuna. ♦ Seafood ♦ Daily dinner. Reservations recommended. 1573 York Ave (at E 83rd St). 535.5454

208 Sirabella ★★$$ Perpetually packed, this place makes fresh pasta *in casa.* Taste the difference it makes in such standard dishes as linguine with clam sauce. On cold winter nights the rich textured soups are a must, as are the crisp calamari. The osso buco is delectable, and the vegetables—cooked escarole, for example—are redolent of garlic and olive oil. ♦ Italian ♦ Daily lunch and dinner. Reservations recommended. 72 East End Ave (between E 82nd and E 83rd Sts). 988.6557

209 Carl Schurz Park Situated on land acquired by the city in 1891, the park was named in 1911 for the German immigrant who served as a general during the Civil War, was a senator from Missouri and secretary of the interior under President Hayes, and went on to become editor of the *New York Evening Post* and *Harper's Weekly.* The park, which was remodeled in 1938 by Harvey Stevenson and Cameron Clark, is a delightful edge to the neighborhood of Yorkville. It is not very large, but its distinct sections and the varied topography make a walk here rewarding. The promenade along the East River above FDR Drive is named for John Finley, a former editor of *The New York Times* and an enthusiastic walker. **Gracie Mansion,** the residence of the mayor of New York City, occupies the center of the north end of the park.

Across the river is Astoria, Queens; spanning the river are the Triborough Bridge and Hell Gate railroad trestle; also visible are Ward's Island and Randall's Island; the yellow building is **Manhattan State Mental Hospital,** and the little island that looks like an elephant's head is known as Mill Rock. This point of the river is a treacherous confluence of currents from the Harlem River, Long Island Sound, and the harbor—hence the name "Hell Gate." ♦ East End Ave (between E 84th and E 90th Sts)

Restaurants/Clubs: Red | **Hotels:** Blue
Shops/ ♥ Outdoors: Green | **Sights/Culture:** Black

Upper East Side

The upscale and largely residential Upper East Side, which is bounded by **East 86th** and **East 110th Streets**, and **Fifth Avenue** and the **East River,** has a heavy concentration of town houses, deluxe apartment buildings, elitist hotels, and elegant mansions, interspersed with churches, museums, restaurants, gourmet take-out stores, and its fair share of tenements and neglect. It is a mixed bag, where one of the city's most prestigious zip codes abuts one of the worst as you head north toward **Spanish Harlem.**

Most of the great mansions of **Park** and Fifth Avenues and the cross streets between them, the first constructions in this part of New York, were built between 1900 and 1920, when the classical tradition was in flower—they all exhibit Neo-Georgian, Neo-Federal, Neo-French, or Neo-Italian Renaissance styling. The original owners, families such as the Whitneys, the Astors, the Straights, the Dillons, the Dukes, the Mellons, the Pulitzers, and the Harknesses, all moved here from downtown. It was an era of lavish balls and of "the 400" (so named because Mrs. William Astor could accommodate only 400 of her closest friends comfortably at one time).

Construction of apartment houses and hotels began in 1881 and ended in 1932. Almost all the churches were erected between 1890 and 1920. Although

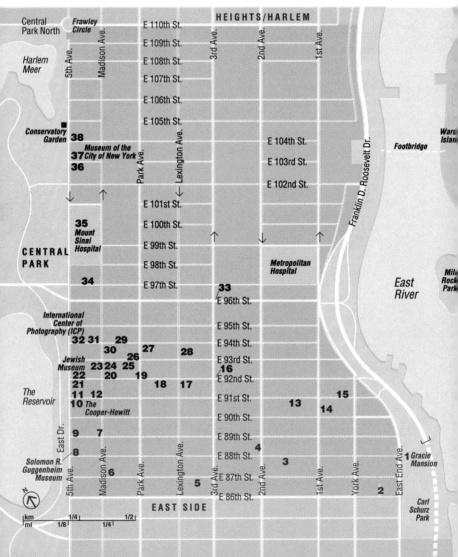

there are still isolated blocks of row houses that date from the late 1860s to 1880s, as well as a few colonial relics and some contemporary buildings, the look, especially in the western part of the district, is generally more uniform than elsewhere in the city. The reason for the relatively late start in populating this area is that, except for the German village of **Yorkville** nestled along its western border, this was all open country. When work started on **Central Park** in 1857, the neighborhood consisted mainly of farms and squatters' shanties, and pigs grubbed on Fifth Avenue. Even after the park opened in 1863, steam trains chugging along Park Avenue made this an undesirable residential neighborhood. But in 1907, when the **New York Central Railroad** electrified the trains and covered the Park Avenue tracks, the Upper East Side became an attractive place for the well-to-do to live.

Fifth Avenue facing **Central Park** is New York City's "street of parades," and the most elegant of the avenues. A few new buildings have been slipped into the otherwise unbroken frontage that progresses up Fifth Avenue north of **Grand Army Plaza** at **West 58th Street. Museum Mile** begins at the heroic **Metropolitan Museum of Art** on the park side of Fifth Avenue and ends with the **Museum of the City of New York** at **103rd Street.** In between are the **International Center of Photography,** the **Cooper-Hewitt Museum,** the **Solomon R. Guggenheim Museum,** and the **Jewish Museum.** The vertical palace on **East 92nd Street** that was the former home of Marjorie Merriwether Post is only one of the numerous outstanding apartment buildings and town houses in the neighborhood.

Among the many churches on the Upper East Side are the **Episcopal Church of the Holy Trinity** and **St. Christopher Home and Parsonage** at **East 88th Street,** which form a Neo-Gothic grouping around a courtyard built on land donated by Serena Rhinelander that had been in her family since 1798.

Madison Avenue has become largely a street of important art galleries, jewelry stores, antiques shops, clothing boutiques, and restaurants. Although the Saturday afternoon stroll is still a diversion for East Siders, Madison Avenue above East 86th Street now seems sedate compared to SoHo with its newer galleries and boutiques, or Columbus Avenue with its trendy shops.

Park Avenue, with its landscaped center island (covered with thousands of tulips in the springtime and a forest of evergreen trees in the winter months) and legions of dignified apartment houses and old mansions (most of which are now occupied by foreign cultural missions or clubs), is still an address to conjure with.

Lexington Avenue is a Madison Avenue without the cachet—and often without the quality. Shops, restaurants, and singles bars line **Third, Second,** and **First Avenues,** and, farther north, more high-rise "people boxes" border these thoroughfares. The side streets are a mix of tenements—some gentrified, some not—and modest town houses. A pocket neighborhood around Madison Avenue in the East nineties called **Carnegie Hill** has become an increasingly attractive magnet for young couples choosing to raise families in Manhattan.

Yorkville, which extends from the East River to Lexington Avenue, from **East 77th** to **East 96th Streets,** continued to receive immigrants from Germany over the first half of the 20th century, but the ethnic heart is shrinking. At one time, East 86th Street was filled with German restaurants, beer gardens, and grocery, pastry, and dry goods stores. Now, although there still are inexpensive chain stores and fried chicken and pizza parlors, a new Eastern European presence can be felt, and only a few of the old restaurants, groceries, and record stores remain. Amidst it all sits **Gracie Mansion,** the official mayoral residence since the 1942 term of Fiorello La Guardia and present home to Mayor Rudolph Giuliani.

In the Market for a van Gogh? Try New York's Museum Gift Shops

No trip to a New York City museum is complete without a stop at its gift shop. Gone are the days when posters and art books related to the museum's collection were the sole merchandise. Museum shops now emblazon their logos and most famous works of art on everything from T-shirts to toothbrushes. Gift shops generally operate during museum hours, although some may be open on days when the museum is closed. Several have additional outlets throughout the city.

The Asia Society (725 Park Ave, at E 70th St, 288.6400) The accent in this well-stocked museum store is on books pertaining to the arts of the major and minor Asian cultures, including travel guides, cookbooks, and volumes on history, the performing arts, languages, philosophy, and religion. A smaller inside room displays a carefully edited selection of crafts and some antiques from such countries as Indonesia, Nepal, Thailand, and India.

Brooklyn Museum (200 Eastern Pkwy, at Washington Ave, Prospect Heights, Brooklyn, 718/638.5000) Contemporary and antique crafts, jewelry, and objects from around the world make this museum shop seem more like a visit to the **United Nations Gift Shop.** Representative of the international scope and diversity of the museum's collections, the global merchandising unfortunately overshadows the art books and reproductions from the museum's collections. But it's a great place to browse and, unlike other museum shops, often offers discounts. A branch is located at the **Equitable Building,** 787 Seventh Ave, between E 51st and E 52nd Sts, 554.4888.

The Cooper-Hewitt (2 E 91st St, between Madison and Fifth Aves, 860.6878) The small gift shop at the Smithsonian Institution's **National Museum of Design,** housed in the lovely music room of the former Andrew Carnegie mansion, is filled with a generous, design-oriented collection of objects for the desk, dining room, coffee table, and even the bath (handsomely packaged soaps and designer toothbrushes). A book and postcard selection vies with salt and pepper shakers and flower vases for shelf space, most reflective of the design sensibility of the museum.

Metropolitan Museum of Art (Fifth Ave and E 82nd St, 879.5500) The city's star museum store has grown to nearly 19,000 square feet on two floors and is a proud homage to the **Metropolitan**'s unrivaled collections and visiting exhibitions. Downstairs is a huge book selection and jewelry store (jewelry accounts for nearly one-third of the 1,600 items the museum reproduces), and a cornucopia of silver, glass, porcelain, and statues from different centuries and cultures. Upstairs are rugs, the bridal registry, and prints on consignment from contemporary artists. A mail-order catalog is available. Additional branches are located in **Rockefeller Plaza,** the **Public Library** at 445 Fifth Avenue, **Macy's Herald Square,** and **The Cloisters.**

Museum of American Folk Art (62 W 50th St, between Fifth and Sixth Aves, 247.5611) The museum's focus on American crafts and early Americana is reflected in the gift shop, with how-to books on everything from quilt-making and stenciling to basket-weaving. This store is particularly charming at Christmastime, when scores of handmade tree ornaments and tabletop decorations made by American craftspeople are sold. The **Museum of American Folk Art** is three blocks away on West 53rd Street. A branch is located at 66 Columbus Ave, between W 65th and W 66th Sts, 496.2966.

Museum of Modern Art (MoMA; 11 W 53rd St, between Fifth and Sixth Aves, 708.9700) The museum now boasts two gift shops: the **MoMA Design Store,** an off-site gift shop just across the street (44 W 53rd St, between Fifth and Sixth Aves, 767.1050); and the original gift shop off the museum's lobby, now dedicated exclusively to books, magazines, posters, and cards. The extensive selection at the **Design Store** includes everything to furnish your office, home, and garden, from table-top conversation pieces to such design-collection classics as Charles Eames chairs and Alvar Aalto tables.

Solomon R. Guggenheim Museum (1071 Fifth Ave, at E 89th St, 423.3615) In addition to books, postcards, and posters, the shop has a small selection of hand-crafted jewelry and scarves not related to the museum's collections. The only way into the **Guggenheim**'s new branch museum in **SoHo** (575 Broadway, at Prince St, 423.3876) is through its museum store, where merchandise is much the same as in the parent institution.

Whitney Museum of American Art (945 Madison Ave, at E 75th St, 570.3614) As in the **Museum of Modern Art,** the **Whitney**'s on-site bookstore outgrew its limited space; hence the opening of the adjacent **Store Next Door** (943 Madison Ave, between E 75th and E 74th Sts, 606.0200). The museum's lobby shop offers a small but well-focused selection of catalogs and books, while the **Store Next Door** carries design-conscious lifestyle collections that feature everything from Shaker-influenced objects to handmade ceramics and birdhouses.

1 Gracie Mansion The site was known to the Dutch as "Hoek Van Hoorm"; when the British captured it during the Revolutionary War, the shelling destroyed the farmhouse that was there. The kernel of the present house was built in 1799 by Scottish-born merchant Archibald Gracie as a country retreat. Acquired by the city in 1887, it served, among its many uses, as the first home of the **Museum of the City of New York,** a refreshment stand, and a storehouse. In 1942, at the urging of Parks Commissioner Robert Moses, Fiorello La Guardia accepted it as the mayor's official residence. (The 98 men who preceded him in the office had lived in their own homes.) In 1966, an addition to the house was designed by **Mott B. Schmidt.** Currently it is the home of Mayor Rudolph Giuliani. The **Gracie Mansion Conservancy** has restored the mansion to something better than its former glory, and conducts tours and special programs there. ♦ Voluntary contribution. Tours by appointment only W 10AM, 11AM, 1PM, 2PM mid-Mar to mid-Nov. East End Ave and E 88th St. 570.4751 &

2 Henderson Place These 24 Queen Anne houses were commissioned by John C. Henderson, a fur importer and hat manufacturer, and designed by **Lamb & Rich** in 1882 as a self-contained community with river views. Symmetrical compositions tie the numerous pieces together below an enthusiastic profusion of turrets, parapets, and dormers. There are rumors in the neighborhood that some of these houses are haunted. The ghosts may be looking for the eight houses from the group that were demolished to allow for a yellow apartment block. ♦ Off East End Ave (between E 86th and E 87th Sts)

3 Church of the Holy Trinity Built in 1897 by **Barney & Chapman,** this picturesque gold, brown, and red Victorian church modestly slipped into this side street encloses a charming garden. The sleek tower with its fanciful Gothic crown is rather nice, too. ♦ 316 E 88th St (between First and Second Aves). 289.4100

New York is the only major city in the country that has an official residence for its mayor (Gracie Mansion).

The section of Fifth Avenue currently named Museum Mile used to be called Millionaire's Row. The introduction of income tax, however, had such an impact on the wealthy that this high-falutin name soon fell away.

4 Elaine's ★$$$ Those whose idea of a good time is watching celebrities eat steamed mussels should be in heaven here. It's a kind of club for media celebrities, gossips, and literary types they don't necessarily come here for the food, although the *spaghetti bolognese* and grilled veal chops are decent. ♦ Italian ♦ Daily lunch, dinner, and late-night meals. Reservations required. 1703 Second Ave (between E 88th and E 89th Sts). 534.8103

5 The Franklin Hotel $$ Built in 1931, this refurbished 53-room hotel offers high style for the price. The rooms are small but nicely decorated, the service is good, and the buffet breakfast is complimentary. East Side residents often book rooms for their guests here. ♦ 164 E 87th St (between Third and Lexington Aves). 369.1000, 800/600.8787; fax 369.8000

6 Au Chat Botté Expensive charm pervades this newly relocated shop, which sells baby furniture—cribs, chairs, chests of drawers, clothes racks, and bumper guards—as well as children's clothes. ♦ M-Sa. 1192 Madison Ave (at E 87th St). 772.6474 &

7 Art & Tapisserie The young students from the prestigious private schools in the neighborhood are a captive audience for the personalized toys, toy chests, children's books, and frames sold here. ♦ M-Sa. 1242 Madison Ave (at E 89th St). 722.3222 &

8 Solomon R. Guggenheim Museum When Solomon R. Guggenheim wanted a museum that would "foster an appreciation of art by acquainting museum visitors with significant painting and sculpture of our time," he founded this repository, which has remained a testament to his personal taste. Guggenheim collected old masters at first, but in the 1920s he began acquiring the avant-garde work of painters such as Delaunay, Kandinsky, and Léger. Soon his apartment at **The Plaza** was bursting at the seams (the old masters were relegated to his wife's bedroom), and he began to look for other quarters for his burgeoning collection. During two sojourns in rented space, his new museum began to buy more of everything by both established and new talent. Finally, the need for a permanent home was realized in a building (shown on page 250) designed in 1959 by **Frank Lloyd Wright.**

The museum is one of the architect's fantasies, first dreamed of in the mid-1940s. It is an extraordinary structure: A massive concrete spiral sits atop one end of a low horizontal base, expanding as it ascends, dominating not only its plinth and a counterweight block of offices at the other end, but the site itself and the blocks around it.

Restaurants/Clubs: Red   **Hotels:** Blue
Shops/♀ Outdoors: Green   **Sights/Culture:** Black

Solomon R. Guggenheim Museum

The display of art was clearly not **Wright**'s main concern, however. The essence of architecture for the sake of architecture, the **Guggenheim** seems to evoke an opinion from most people who visit—some positive, many negative. To make matters worse, the first addition, built in 1968 by **Taliesin Associates,** was not up to snuff. That firm, **Wright**'s successors and keepers-of-the-flame, never had the touch of the Master, who had personally handled all the details of the construction of the original building, right down to the Fifth Avenue sidewalk.

Construction of a second addition, by **Gwathmey Siegel & Associates,** was completed in 1992. Although it doubles the museum's gallery space and visitors have increased, controversy continues over its questionable aesthetics.

Dean & DeLuca is the museum cafe, where you'll find their trademark uncompromising quality, unique selections, and innovative combinations. There is often live music scheduled for weekend evenings in the lobby, making this a particularly appealing pre-dinner destination. ♦ Admission; voluntary contribution Friday 6-8PM. M-W, F-Su. Cafe: M-W, Su 8AM-7PM; Th 8AM-3PM; F-Sa 8AM-9PM. Museum shop: daily. Fifth Ave and E 88th St. Museum: 360.3500. Shop: 423.3615. Cafe: 423.3657. Annex: 575 Broadway (at Prince St). 423.3500

9 National Academy of Design Since its founding in 1825 by Samuel F.B. Morse, painter and inventor of the telegraph, this academy has been an artist-run museum, a fine-arts school, and an honorary organization of artists. Headquartered in a town house that was remodeled in 1915 by **Ogden Codman Jr.,** and located around the corner from its **School of Fine Arts,** it is the second-oldest museum school in the country. In addition to an annual exhibition (alternately open to member artists and all artists), the academy presents special exhibitions of art and architecture. Painters, sculptors, watercolorists, graphic artists, and architects number among its members today. ♦ Admission. W-Th, Sa-Su noon-5PM; F noon-8PM. 1083 Fifth Ave (at E 89th St). 369.4880 &

10 The Cooper-Hewitt After an extensive $20-million renovation to its galleries, the museum (slated to reopen September 1996) is the perfect setting for the **Smithsonian Institution**'s **National Museum of Design.** This splendidly decorated mansion designed in 1903 by **Babb, Cook & Willard** was built on the northern fringe of the well-heeled stretch of Fifth Avenue mansions for industrialist Andrew Carnegie, who requested "the most modest, plainest, and most roomy house in New York City." The rather standard Renaissance-Georgian mix of red brick and limestone trim on a rusticated base is most noteworthy for the fact that it is freestanding in quite an expansive garden. The richly ornamented rooms of the sumptuous mansion, which was renovated in 1977 by **Hardy Holzman Pfeiffer Associates,** sometimes compete with the exhibitions; the conservatory is particularly pleasant. Also notice the very low door to what was once the library at the west end—Carnegie was a short man, and this was his private room.

The permanent collection—based on the collections of the Cooper and Hewitt families and now under the stewardship of museum director Diane Pilgrim—encompasses textiles dating back 3,000 years, jewelry, furniture, wallpaper, and metal-, glass-, and earthenware. It also includes the single largest group of architectural drawings in this country. The library is a design student's reference paradise of picture collections, auction catalogs, and 17th- and 18th-century architecture books. Lectures, symposia, summer concerts, and classes for school groups take place on a regular basis. A gift shop in the **Louis XV Music Room** sells design objects, catalogs, postcards, and museum publications. ◆ Admission; free Tuesday 5-9PM. Tu 10AM-9PM; W-Sa 10AM-5PM; Su noon-5PM. 2 E 91st St (between Madison and Fifth Aves). 860.6868 &

11 The Convent of the Sacred Heart Originally built in 1918 by **C.P.H. Gilbert** and **J. Armstrong Stenhouse,** this extravagant Italian palazzo was one of the largest private houses built in New York City, and the last on "Millionaire's Row." It was the home of Otto Kahn, a banker, philanthropist, and art patron. Now it's a private school for girls. ◆ 1 E 91st St (at Fifth Ave). 722.4745

12 Mrs. James A. Burden House When Vanderbilt heiress Adele Sloane married James A. Burden, heir to a steel fortune, they moved into this freestanding mansion, which was built in 1902 by **Warren & Wetmore.** The spiral staircase under a stained-glass skylight is one of the city's grandest, and was called the "stairway to heaven." Not surprisingly, it is a favorite rental location for wedding receptions. ◆ 7 E 91st St (between Madison and Fifth Aves)

12 Mrs. John Henry Hammond House When Hammond saw the plans for this house, designed in 1906 by **Carrère & Hastings,** he said that this gift from his wife's family made him feel "like a kept man." He moved in anyway, along with a staff of 16 full-time servants. The couple's musicales were legendary. Benny Goodman came here frequently in the 1930s to play Mozart's clarinet works. ◆ 9 E 91st St (between Madison and Fifth Aves)

13 Playhouse 91 Plays that relate to the Jewish experience are given standard to excellent treatment here by the **Jewish Repertory Theatre,** which stages revivals (of Chekhov, Neil Simon), originals (*Crossing Delancey* premiered here), and musicals. ◆ 316 E 91st St (between First and Second Aves). 831.2000

14 El Pollo ★★$ What this tiny storefront lacks in atmosphere, it more than makes up for with its chicken served with a side order of fried plantains. Wash it all down with an Inca Kola and top it off with an exotic pudding made of raisins, cinnamon, and quinoa. ◆ Peruvian ◆ Daily lunch and dinner. No credit cards accepted. 1746 First Ave (between E 90th and E 91st Sts). 996.7810

The Cooper-Hewitt

Michael Storrings

★ THE ★
VINEGAR FACTORY

15 Vinegar Factory Located in an old mustard-and-vinegar factory, this timely brainchild of **E.A.T.**'s owner Eli Zabar recycles unsold prepared foods in a most delicious way. Eli's famous focaccia is twice as good made into parmesan toast; dried-out loaves of brioche become a scrumptious bread pudding. Foods in their first incarnations are available, too. There's also a full range of fresh produce and homemade pâtés. At press time, there were plans to offer brunch on the balcony above the selling floor. ♦ Daily. 431 E 91st St (between York and First Aves). 987.0885

16 Yura and Company ★★$ One of the neighborhood's best cafes, this place has excellent bouillabaisse, braised stuffed chicken breast with wild-mushroom ragout, and osso buco. Some of this gourmet fare is also available for takeout. ♦ American/French ♦ Daily breakfast, lunch, and dinner. 1650 Third Ave (at E 92nd St). 860.8060 &

17 92nd Street Y This branch of the **Young Men's/Women's Hebrew Association** is one of the city's cultural landmarks. Under music director Gerard Schwartz, its **Kaufman Concert Hall** has become New York's best place to hear chamber music and recitals. Such groups as the **Guarneri, Cleveland,** and **Tokyo Quartets** are regulars here. The renowned **Poetry Center** has offered readings by every major poet in the world since its founding in 1939, and the tradition continues with such writers as Saul Bellow, Joseph Brodsky, and Isaac Bashevis Singer. The **American Jewish Theater** is sponsored by the organization, as are lectures, seminars, and workshops, and even unusual tours of the city. ♦ 1395 Lexington Ave (at E 92nd St). 427.6000 &

17 De Hirsch Residence $ Because of its affiliation with the well-known cultural and community center next door, this lodging tends to attract an interesting international crowd as compared to what you'd expect to find at a **Y.** Men and women are accommodated in 300 dorm-style rooms on separate floors with shared bathrooms and kitchens, or in simple private rooms for shorter stays (limited coed accommodations for couples do exist). Guests receive discounted admission to the cultural center's events. There is a three-night minimum stay requirement and a maximum stay of one year with special monthly rates; applications are needed in advance for long-term stay. ♦ 1395 Lexington Ave (at E 92nd St). 427.6000, 800.858.4692; fax 415.5578 &

18 120 and 122 East 92nd Street Because fire laws made the construction of wooden houses illegal in the 1860s, there are very few of them in Manhattan. This pair (and the frame houses at 160 East 92nd Street and 128 East 93rd Street), built in 1850, are a reminder of what this neighborhood was like in the mid-19th century. ♦ Between Lexington and Park Aves

19 Night Presence IV The intentionally rusty steel sculpture is by the late Louise Nevelson. The view down the avenue from here is picture-perfect. ♦ Park Ave and E 92nd St

20 Busby's ★$$ The white dining room is large and airy but plainly decorated, a spare setting for the all-American, California-influenced menu that includes roasted goat cheese wrapped in roasted eggplant, and grilled swordfish with caramelized shallots, as well as burgers. ♦ American ♦ M-Sa lunch and dinner; Su brunch and dinner. Reservations recommended. 45 E 92nd St (at Madison Ave). 360.7373

20 Wales Hotel $$ This small, moderately priced European-style hotel is ideally located if you plan to spend a lot of time on Museum Mile, shopping on Madison, or jogging every morning in **Central Park.** All of the 90 rooms have been tastefully renovated, but ask for a large, bright room or you may end up with the opposite. ♦ 1295 Madison Ave (between E 92nd and E 93rd Sts). 876.6000, 800/428.5252; fax 860.7000

20 Sarabeth's Kitchen ★★$$ Many a New Yorker has stood in line here for a weekend brunch of gourmet comfort foods: homemade waffles and pancakes served with fresh fruit, hot porridge, and warm-from-the-oven muffins (no reservations accepted for brunch). ♦ American ♦ M-F breakfast, lunch, and dinner; Sa-Su brunch and dinner. Reservations recommended for dinner. 1295 Madison Ave (between E 92nd and E 93rd Sts). 410.7335. Also at: 423 Amsterdam Ave (between W 80th and W 81st Sts). 496.6280; the Whitney Museum, Madison and E 75th St. 570.3670

21 1107 Fifth Avenue Built in 1925 by **Rouse & Goldstone**, this was a perfectly ordinary apartment building except for a few anomalies on the facade—evidence of an era past. Marjorie Merriwether Post (at the time married to stockbroker E.F. Hutton) purchased a 54-room apartment here. The Palladian window near the top center of the facade opened onto the main foyer of this apartment. ♦ At E 92nd St

---

Restaurants/Clubs: Red   Hotels: Blue
Shops/♥ Outdoors: Green   Sights/Culture: Black

ewish Museum

22 Jewish Museum This renovated museum (illustrated above) holds the country's largest collection of Judaica. Besides permanent and rotating exhibits, it has classrooms, a delightful kosher cafe, and an attractive book and gift shop. Designed by **C.P.H. Gilbert** in 1908, the French Renaissance mansion was the home of financier Felix M. Warburg. Two annexes have been added: the first, in 1963, is by **Samuel Glazer,** and the second, finished in 1993, is by **Kevin Roche.** ♦ Admission; free Tu 5-8PM. M, W-Th, Su 11AM-5:45PM; Tu 11AM-8PM. 1109 Fifth Ave (at E 92nd St). 423.3230

23 Bistro du Nord ★★$$ This cozy little bistro serves haute versions of dishes you'd expect to find in this kind of place—smoked salmon from **Petrossian** downtown, and baby rack of lamb with ratatouille. Steak *frites* and roasted codfish are among the more basic fare, but the high quality of their preparations renders them special. ♦ French ♦ M-Sa lunch and dinner; Su brunch and dinner. Reservations required. 1312 Madison Ave (at E 93rd St). 289.0997

24 Corner Bookstore Featuring a wide selection of books, over a third of them for children, this store has an atmosphere conducive to browsing. Works on literature, art, and architecture are well represented.

♦ Daily. 1313 Madison Ave (at E 93rd St). 831.3554 &

24 Island ★$$$ You might expect to find this sort of place on the West Side—a room full of young people wolfing down good, if slightly overpriced, pasta and dishes from the grill, including chicken paillard and pepper-roasted tuna. There's also a good hearty braised lamb shank. ♦ Continental ♦ M-F lunch and dinner; Sa-Su brunch and dinner. Reservations recommended. 1305 Madison Ave (between E 92nd and E 93rd Sts). 996.1200 &

25 Smithers Alcoholism Center This former home of showman Billy Rose was the last of the large, great mansions to be built in New York. It is in the delicate style of the 18th-century Scottish brothers **Lambert** and **Nicholas Adam,** who created most of the best houses in Edinburgh and London. This one, however, was designed in 1932 by **Walker & Gillette.** ♦ 56 E 93rd St (between Park and Madison Aves). 369.9566

25 60 East 93rd Street After Mrs. William K. Vanderbilt divorced her husband, she leased an apartment on Park Avenue, only to discover that her ex-husband had one in the same building. She broke the lease and had **John Russell Pope** build this beautiful French Renaissance mansion in 1930. ♦ Between Park and Madison Aves

253

26 Synod of Bishops of the Russian Orthodox Church Outside Russia Built in 1917 for Francis F. Palmer and renovated in 1928 by **Delano & Aldrich** for banker George F. Baker, this unusually large Georgian mansion has remained virtually unchanged, except for the introduction of exquisite Russian icons. A small cathedral occupies the former ballroom. ♦ 75 E 93rd St (between Park and Madison Aves). 534.1601

27 1185 Park Avenue Designed in 1929 by **Schwartz & Gross,** this is the only East Side version of the full-block courtyard apartment house typified by the **Belnord, Astor Court,** and **Apthorp** across town. The Gothicized entrance adds needed levity to the otherwise traditional composition. ♦ Between E 93rd and E 94th Sts

28 Kitchen Arts & Letters Books on low-fat cooking, regional American cooking, cooking with flowers, and cooking on boats, along with more traditional cookbooks—approximately 9,000 in all, covering every aspect of food and wine—are displayed in this unique store. Paintings and photographs of food, and reproductions of tin biscuit boxes and other culinary memorabilia are on sale as well. ♦ M-Sa; summer hours are irregular, call first. 1435 Lexington Ave (between E 93rd and E 94th Sts). 876.5550

29 Squadron A and Eighth Regiment Armory/Hunter High School When the armory—a distinctly businesslike fortress built in 1895 by **John Rochester Thomas**—was on the verge of being torn down, community protest saved at least the facade on Madison Avenue. The school's architects, **Morris Ketchum, Jr. & Associates,** did a marvelous task in 1971 of using it as both a backdrop to the playground and as a formal inspiration for the new building. ♦ Bounded by E 94th and E 95th Sts (between Park and Madison Aves)

30 Dollhouse Antics Here you'll find all the necessary Lilliputian accessories for dollhouse decorating: playpens, paint easels, overstuffed sofas, sterling silver knives and forks, copper pots and pans, and hundreds of other minute items. Houses can be custom-ordered and even wired for electricity. ♦ M-Sa. 1343 Madison Ave (at E 94th St). 876.2288

31 Saranac ★$ This small American restaurant has the feel of a lodge in the Adirondacks, belying its uptown Manhattan location. The menu offers such dishes as corn chowder, chicken potpie, pan-seared salmon with lemon-brown butter, and Maryland crab cakes, all of which are well prepared. ♦ American ♦ M-F lunch and dinner; Sa-Su brunch and dinner. 1350 Madison Ave (between E 94th and E 95th Sts). 289.9600

32 International Center of Photography (ICP) Here you'll find the only museum in New York City—and perhaps the world—devoted entirely to photography. Designed in 1914 by **Delano & Aldrich,**, the building is an ebullient and hospitable home for practitioners of the art, where the best and the brightest are given shows and encouragement. Every inch of the Georgian town house it occupies is used in the service of photography: four galleries for revolving shows; workshops and photo labs; a screening room; and a gallery for the permanent collection, which includes works by 20th-century photographers W. Eugene Smith and Henri Cartier-Bresson, among others. A gift shop sells books, catalogs, posters, and, of course, picture postcards. The center maintains additional gallery space at 1133 Sixth Avenue. ♦ Admission; voluntary contribution Tuesday 6PM-8PM. Tu 11AM-8PM; W-Su 11AM-6PM. 1130 Fifth Ave (at E 94th St). 860.1777. Also at: 1133 Sixth Ave (at W 43rd St). 768.4680 &

33 Islamic Center of New York A computer was used to ensure that this mosque faces Mecca, as Islamic law requires. Built in 199_ by **Skidmore, Owings & Merrill,** it is New York's first major mosque, and is intended as the spiritual home of the city's 400,000 Moslems and to serve diplomats from Islamic countries. ♦ 1711 Third Ave (at E 96th St). 722.5234

34 Russian Orthodox Cathedral of St. Nicholas Built in 1901-02, this church is unusual because, set above the polychrome Victorian body, there are five onion domes. ♦ 15 E 97th St (between Madison and Fifth Aves). 289.1915

35 Mount Sinai Hospital The most recent construction project, completed in 1992 by **Cobb Freed & Partners,** includes three hospital towers in one grand pavilion. These facilities replace 10 older buildings—some dating as far back as 1904—all of which ha_

been demolished. Also of architectural interest is the **Annenburg Building,** a 436-foot Cor-Ten steel box that gets its color from a coating of rust that protects the steel from further corrosion. ♦ Bounded by E 98th and E 101st Sts (between Madison and Fifth Aves). 241.6500 &

36 **New York Academy of Medicine** Built in 1926 by **York & Sawyer,** this charming combination of Byzantine and Romanesque architecture contains one of the most important medical libraries in the country. The collection includes 4,000 cookbooks, a gift of Dr. Margaret Barclay Wilson, who believed that good nutrition was the key to good health. ♦ M-F. 2 E 103rd St (at Fifth Ave). 876.8200

MUSEUM OF

MC

THE CITY OF

NY

NEW YORK

37 **Museum of the City of New York**
The story of New York City is told through historical paintings, Currier & Ives prints, period rooms, costumes, Duncan Phyfe furniture, Tiffany silver, ship models, and wonderful toys and dolls, all handsomely displayed in a roomy Neo-Georgian building. The structure, red brick with white trim, designed by **Joseph Freedlander** in 1932, was built for the museum after it moved from **Gracie Mansion.** Puppet shows are staged for children, concerts and lectures for adults. ♦ Donation suggested. W-Sa; Su 1PM-5PM. 1220 Fifth Ave (between E 103rd and E 104th Sts). 534.1672

38 **El Museo del Barrio** This culture center and showcase for the historic and contemporary arts of Latin America (especially Puerto Rico) began as a neighborhood museum in an East Harlem classroom. Video, painting, sculpture, photography, theater, and film are featured. Permanent collections include pre-Columbian art and hand-carved wooden saints, one of the culture's most important art forms. ♦ Donation suggested. W-Su 11AM-5PM. 1230 Fifth Ave (between E 104th and E 105th Sts). 831.7272

Bests

George Lang
Consultant and Author/Owner of Café des Artistes

Remi—I have rarely eaten Italian food as good as that served in this place, even in the Mother Country. Chef **Francesco Antonucci's** dishes—like the roasted quail wrapped in bacon and served with warm lentil salad—remind me that a good chef is like a good fairy who dispenses happiness. Even the most knowledgeable Italian wine connoisseur will find surprises on the reasonably priced wine list.

Park Bistro—When I stepped through the lace-lined door into the packed, noisy 65-seat restaurant with its plain wood floors, banquettes, posters, and photos of France, it was almost like being in Paris. One of my favorite dishes is lamb shank braised for seven hours with bits of dried apricots, currants, vegetables, and wild mushrooms.

Carmine's—I think Carmine's reflects the post-Reagan–era yearning for an America where the tables had four legs, the light source was not halogen, and the pasta of choice was spaghetti. My recommendations, based on serious soul- and stomach-searching: fried calamari, rigatoni with broccoli, or chicken Contadina.

Jimmy Breslin
Writer, *Newsday*

Sit at night on **Shore Road** and watch the *Queen Elizabeth II* slide under the **Verrazano-Narrows Bridge.** The ship at first seems to be part of another shore. Then you see it moving so quickly.

Coming from **Queens** to Manhattan at night over the **Queensboro Bridge.**

Living anywhere on the water in **Brooklyn Heights, Williamsburg, Long Island City,** or up on the hill in **Maspeth** and **Middle Village** in Queens and looking over at Manhattan. The people in Manhattan can only see Queens with its Pepsi-Cola signs. The smart people live in Queens and get a view that is unique in the world, even to photos, for the most sophisticated camera people don't know where these neighborhoods are.

The May Wave in the **Ramble** at **Central Park** and in the **Bird Sanctuary** at **Jamaica Bay.** The flocks come north again and on 10 May the same birds are in the same places. For decades the same type of bird is in the same spot, in the **Ramble** or at the bird sanctuary. So many types that even the best books cannot have them all cataloged. They are en route to Canada and as far as the North Pole.

Third Avenue and **East 42nd Street** and all the sidewalks in every direction at 5PM. Crowds of such size that it is hard to think that one place can hold them.

CENTRAL PARK

Map continues on next page

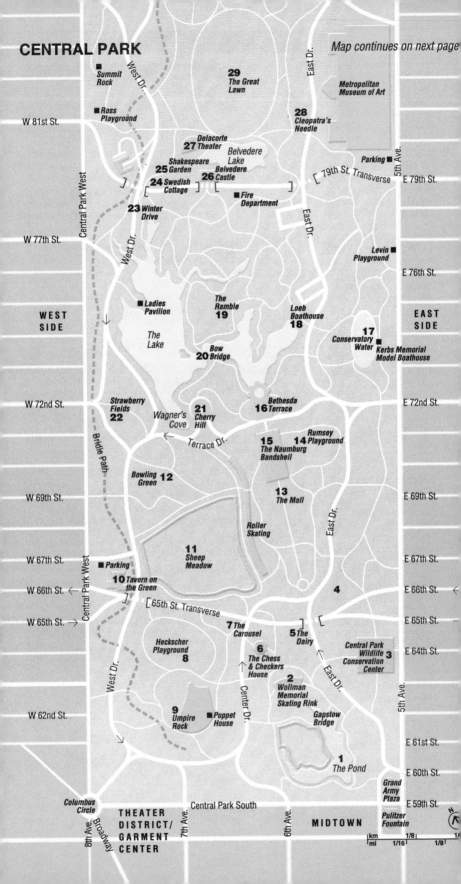

■ Summit Rock

West Dr.

East Dr.

29
The Great Lawn

Metropolitan
Museum of Art

■ Ross Playground

W 81st St.

28
Cleopatra's Needle

27 Delacorte Theater

Belvedere Lake

Parking ■

5th Ave.

E 79th St.

[79th St. Transverse]

25 Shakespeare Garden

26 Belvedere Castle

24 Swedish Cottage

■ Fire Department

23 Winter Drive

Central Park West

West Dr.

W 77th St.

Levin Playground ■

E 76th St.

WEST SIDE

■ Ladies Pavilion

19
The Ramble

18
Loeb Boathouse

EAST SIDE

The Lake

17
Conservatory Water

Kerbs Memorial Model Boathouse

20 Bow Bridge

East Dr.

W 72nd St.

Strawberry Fields **22**

Wagner's Cove

21 Cherry Hill

16 Bethesda Terrace

E 72nd St.

Terrace Dr.

15 The Naumburg Bandshell

14 Rumsey Playground

Bridle Path

12 Bowling Green

13
The Mall

East Dr.

W 69th St.

E 69th St.

Roller Skating

11
Sheep Meadow

W 67th St.

E 67th St.

Central Park West

■ Parking

10 Tavern on the Green

4

E 66th St.

W 66th St.

[65th St. Transverse]

E 65th St.

W 65th St.

7 The Carousel

5 The Dairy

Heckscher Playground **8**

6
The Chess & Checkers House

Central Park Wildlife Conservation Center **3**

E 64th St.

Center Dr.

2
Wollman Memorial Skating Rink

West Dr.

9 Umpire Rock

■ Puppet House

Gapstow Bridge

W 62nd St.

E 61st St.

1
The Pond

E 60th St.

Columbus Circle

8th Ave.

Broadway

7th Ave.

Central Park South

6th Ave.

Grand Army Plaza

E 59th St.

THEATER DISTRICT/ GARMENT CENTER

MIDTOWN

Pulitzer Fountain

N

km
mi   1/16   1/8   1/8

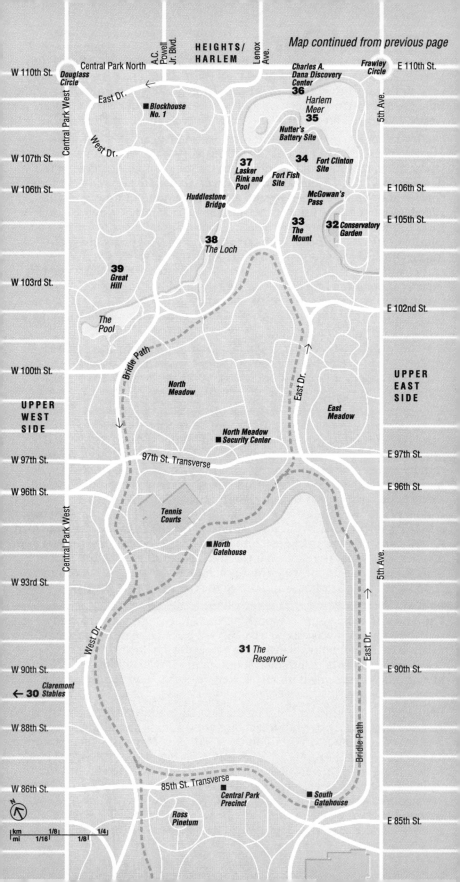

W 110th St.

Central Park North

A.C. Powell Jr. Blvd.

HEIGHTS/ HARLEM

Lenox Ave.

Frawley Circle

E 110th St.

Douglass Circle

East Dr.

■ *Blockhouse No. 1*

Charles A. Dana Discovery Center

36

Harlem Meer

35

5th Ave.

West Dr.

Nutter's Battery Site

W 107th St.

W 106th St.

E 106th St.

37 *Lasker Rink and Pool*

34 *Fort Clinton Site*

Fort Fish Site

Huddlestone Bridge

McGowan's Pass

E 105th St.

33 *The Mount*

32 *Conservatory Garden*

38 *The Loch*

39 *Great Hill*

E 102nd St.

The Pool

Bridle Path

W 103rd St.

W 100th St.

East Dr.

North Meadow

UPPER WEST SIDE

East Meadow

UPPER EAST SIDE

■ *North Meadow Security Center*

W 97th St.

97th St. Transverse

E 97th St.

W 96th St.

E 96th St.

Central Park West

Tennis Courts

■ *North Gatehouse*

5th Ave.

W 93rd St.

East Dr.

W 90th St.

West Dr.

31 *The Reservoir*

E 90th St.

← **30** *Claremont Stables*

W 88th St.

W 86th St.

Bridle Path

85th St. Transverse

■ *South Gatehouse*

Central Park Precinct

N

Ross Pinetum

E 85th St.

km mi

1/8   1/16   1/8   1/4

Central Park

"This different and many smiling presence" is how Henry James once referred to **Central Park**, bounded by **Central Park South** and **West 110th Streets**, **Fifth Avenue**, and **Central Park West**. The completely man-made park, unlike any other urban park in the United States, certainly elicits smiles from the more than 14 million people who wander through it every year. Nearly 250 species are sighted here, with the best birding at **The Ramble.**

Not long after work began to clear the site on 12 August 1857, a friend suggested to journalist Frederick Law Olmsted, whose avocation was landscaping, that he should compete for the job of superintendent of the new **Central Park.** He quickly found backers in newspaper editors Horace Greeley and William Cullen Bryant, and when writer Washington Irving added his name to the list, Olmsted got the job. Later that same year, the Parks Commission announced a design competition for the new park, and Olmsted's friend, landscape architect Calvert Vaux, suggested they join forces. Olmsted—concerned that the commissioners might consider his participation a conflict of interest—wasn't interested at first. But when his superiors convinced him otherwise, he accepted Vaux's proposal, and the two men went to work.

On 28 April 1858, after Olmsted and Vaux submitted what they called their "Greensward" plan, Olmsted wrote: "Every foot of the Park's surface, every tree and bush, as well as every arch, roadway, and walk, has been placed where it is with a purpose." In the years since, buildings and monuments have been added, and playgrounds, roads, even parking lots have been constructed. But the original purpose is still well served.

The groundswell of support for the park had begun in 1844 when William Cullen Bryant warned that commerce was devouring Manhattan inch by inch. He pointed out that there were still unoccupied parts of the island, but that "while we are discussing the subject, the advancing population of the city is sweeping over them and covering them from our reach." By the mayoral election of 1851, Bryant and others had moved the cause forward to the point where it was the only issue both candidates could agree on. The winner of the race, Ambrose C. Kingsland, immediately recommended buying a 153-acre tract known as "Jones's Wood," between the **East River** and **Third Avenue**, from **East 66th** to **East 75th Streets**. His proposal was attacked from all sides: Park supporters argued it was too small; influential businessmen objected to giving up the waterfront property to any purpose but commerce. In 1853, the state legislature authorized the city to buy the larger and much more central present site. The price tag was $5 million.

The land was no bargain. A swampy pesthole filled with pig farms and squatters' shacks, it was used as a garbage dump and served as a prime location for bone-boiling plants. After surveying it, Olmsted called it a "pestilential spot where miasmatic odors taint every breath of air." But he succeeded in turning it into what New Yorkers today proudly call the "lungs of the city."

Actual work began in 1857, and by the time the park was considered finished 16 years later, nearly five million cubic yards of stone and dirt had been rearranged and almost five million trees planted. Before construction started, 42 species of trees grew on the site; by the time it was completed, 402 kinds of deciduous trees thrived, along with 230 species of evergreens and 815 varieties of shrubs. There were also 58 miles of pedestrian walks, 6.5 miles of roads, and a bridle path 4.5 miles long. A reservoir was created in 1862, covering 106 acres, and a sprawling lake occupied another 22 acres. A series of smaller lakes and ponds was also created and some 62 miles of pipe installed to carry off unwanted water. In those days, earthmovers consisted of gangs of men with picks and shovels and teams of horses pulling wagonloads of dirt.

Olmsted was single-minded about what he wanted, and as superintendent of construction, he usually, but not always, got his way. He opposed buildings on park grounds not related to the park itself: "Reservoirs and museums are not part of the park, but deductions from it," he said. The **Metropolitan Museum of Art** hasn't stopped deducting from the park since Calvert Vaux designed the original building in 1880. Olmsted was also testy about monuments: "The Park is not a place for sepulchral memorials. The beautiful cemeteries in the vicinity of the city offer abundant opportunities to commemorate the virtues of those who are passing away." Today, there are more than 80 monuments in **Central Park**. Frederick Law Olmsted may well be turning over in his grave (which, by the way, is not in the park).

Fortunately, **Central Park** is alive and well in spite of countless schemes to "improve" it. In 1918, someone in all seriousness suggested digging trenches in the **North Meadow** to give people an idea of what the doughboys were going through "over there." A year later, plans were submitted for an airport near **Tavern on the Green**, which was then a sheepfold. There have been several proposals to use some of the space for housing projects, and plans for underground parking garages have been coming and going since the 1920s. Not only have the **Parks Department** and the **Central Park Conservancy** resisted encroachment, they've been working for a decade or more to restore the park to what it once was. The result is that one of the best things about New York is getting better every day.

Note: Although city officials claim that the park is safer due to increased patrol efforts, it is wise to avoid walking or jogging here at night; and even during daylight hours, be cautious, and don't wander into densely wooded areas.

Michael Storrings

The Dairy

CENTRAL PARK WILDLIFE CONSERVATION CENTER

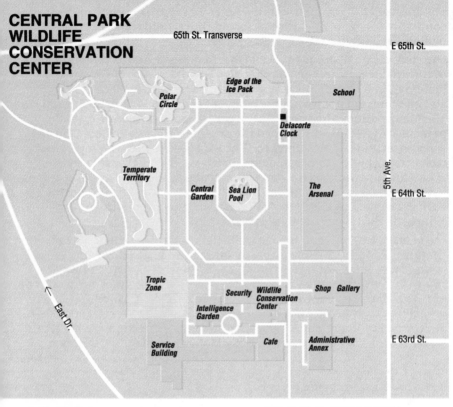

1 **The Pond** A shot of the reflection of the nearby buildings, especially **The Plaza Hotel**, in this crescent-shaped haven for ducks and other waterfowl may be among the best pictures you'll take home. The view is from the Gapstow Bridge, which crosses the northern end. The water pocket was created to reflect the rocks in what is now a bird sanctuary on its western shore, and a favorite lunch spot for nearby office workers. From the time the park opened until 1924, swan boats like the ones still used in the Boston Garden dodged real swans here. The Pond was reduced to about half its original size in 1951 when the **Wollman Memorial Skating Rink** was built. ◆ Between W 59th and W 62nd Sts (near Fifth Ave)

2 **Wollman Memorial Skating Rink** The original rink lasted less than 30 years, and when the city attempted to rebuild it, the project became mired in so much red tape that it began to look as though it might take another 30 years to replace it. In 1986, real estate and casino tycoon Donald Trump took it upon himself to do the job—without the regulations the city imposes on itself—and finished it in record time. Trump occasionally appears here on winter weekends to accept the warm thanks of the skaters. Though an encroachment on the park, it is a hugely popular one, and space on the ice is usually at a premium. Ice-skating is generally from October to April, with roller-skating at other times. ◆ Admission; skate rental. M 10AM-

5PM; Tu-Th, Su 10AM-9:30PM (classes offered W-Th 6-7:30PM); F-Sa 10AM-11PM. W 63rd St (off East Dr). 517.4800

3 **The Arsenal** The 10 acres of land around this building were a park before **Central Park** was even a dream. Designed by **Martin E. Thompson** and completed in 1851, its original use as a storehouse for arms and ammunition accounts for the iconography of cannons and rifles around the Fifth Avenue entrance. It became the citywide headquarters of the **Parks and Recreation Department** in 1934, following use as a police precinct, a weather bureau, a menagerie, and the first home of the **American Museum of Natural History**. A third-floor gallery contains, among other exhibits, the original Greensward plan, whose results are all around you. ◆ Free. M-F. E 64th St and Fifth Ave. 360.8141 &

The first New York City Marathon took place in 1970, when 127 runners circled Central Park four times. The meager $1,000 budget left no room for extravagance: To save money, post-race sodas were purchased in Greenwich Village and lugged uptown, where soda was more expensive. In 1994, 25,000 people from all corners of the globe participated, with thousands of applicants turned away.

Restaurants/Clubs: Red   **Hotels:** Blue
Shops/ ❦ Outdoors: Green   **Sights/Culture:** Black

3 Central Park Wildlife Conservation Center This 5.5 acre complex is home to some 450 animals representing more than a hundred species. Opened in 1988 at the cost of $35 million, the zoo it replaced had elephants, antelopes, and other animals too large for such cramped quarters; they were given to other zoos with more hospitable facilities. The bears and sea lions have been given new, more natural homes here, and two flocks of penguins cavort under a simulated ice pack in a pool with glass walls that allow you to watch their underwater antics. Monkeys swing in trees in a reproduction of an African environment, bats fly through their own naturalistic cave, and alligators swim in the most comfortable swamp north of the Okefenokee. The center encompasses three climatic zones: tropic, temperate, and polar. A cafeteria and a gift shop at the southern edge are accessible without entering the grounds. The zoo was designed by **Kevin Roche** and **John Dinkeloo Associates.** Free one-hour tours are given daily at 2:30PM; weekends 10:30AM and 2:30PM. ♦ Admission. Daily. E 64th St and Fifth Ave. 861.6030

4 Balto One of the most popular monuments in the park, this 1925 bronze portrait by Frederick G.R. Roth represents the husky who led his team of dogs from Anchorage to Nome (a thousand miles) to deliver serum to stem a diphtheria epidemic. ♦ W 66th St and East Dr

5 The Dairy When this Gothic building (illustrated on page 259) was constructed in 1870, fresh milk was a relative luxury. The park's planners, following European models, added milkmaids and a herd of cows to enhance the sylvan setting and to provide children with a healthy treat. After the turn of the century, the cows were sent off to the country, the milkmaids retired, and the building became a storehouse. In 1981, it was restored and its wooden porch replaced and painted in Victorian colors. It is now the park's central **Visitors' Center,** with an information desk and exhibitions. Weekend walking tours, led by the Urban Park Rangers, usually leave from here or from the **Dana Discovery Center.** ♦ Visitor Center: Tu-Th, Sa-Su 11AM-5PM; F 1PM-5PM. W 65th St (west of the Zoo). Urban Park Rangers (tour information) 427.4040; special events 360.1333

6 The Chess & Checkers House A gift of financier Bernard Baruch in 1952, this mecca for checkers-playing retirees sits on top of a rock known as the *Kinderberg* (Children's Mountain), named for a rustic summerhouse that once stood here as a retreat for children. ♦ W 64th St (southwest of the Dairy)

7 The Carousel There has been a merry-go-round here since 1871. The original was powered by real horses that walked a treadmill in an underground pit. The present one, built

in 1908 at Coney Island, was moved here in 1951. Its 58 horses were hand-carved by Stein & Goldstein, considered the best woodcarvers of their day. Don't just stand there—climb up and go for the ride of your life. ♦ Nominal admission. Daily. W 65th St Transverse and Center Dr. 879.0244

8 Heckscher Playground The original park plan didn't include sports facilities, but this was one of three loosely connected areas for children who had secured the proper permits to play games like baseball and croquet. In the 1920s, adults wanted to get into the game and pressured the city into building them five softball diamonds with backstops and bleachers. At about the same time, the former meadow was converted into an asphalt-covered playground to give the kids something to do while the adults were running bases. It was the first formal playground in the park. The softball fields are available by permit only, and are used by teams from corporations, Broadway shows, and other groups. Call 794.6567 to see who's playing today; for a permit for your own team, call 408.0209 or 397.3100. ♦ W 63rd St (between Center and West Drs)

9 Umpire Rock Central Park is laced with rocky outcrops like this one, left behind some 20,000 years ago by the Laurentian Glacier. The boulder on top is called an erratic, and was carried down with the ice from the Far North. The tracks on the face of the rock, called striations, were formed by the scraping of large stones embedded in the glacier as it moved southeast across Manhattan. Most of the rocky outcrops in the park are a type of mica-rich shale called Manhattan schist. About 400 million years ago, they formed the base of a mountain chain about as high as the present-day Rocky Mountains. The rocks were already here when the park was built, of course, but Olmsted exposed many that had previously been below the surface. Most experts agree that the erratic on Umpire Rock was moved here by Olmsted's construction crews. But many of the erratics in the park were left where the glacier had deposited them. ♦ W 62nd St (overlooking ballfields)

TAVERN ON THE GREEN

10 Tavern on the Green ★★$$$$ Designed by **Jacob Wrey Mould,** the building housing this lovely dining spot was erected in 1870 by Boss Tweed and his corrupt Tammany Hall city government over the strenuous objection of Frederick Law Olmsted, landscape architect and designer of **Central Park.** Originally called the **Sheepfold,** the structure housed the herd of Southdown sheep that grazed in **Central Park's Sheep Meadow** until 1934, when they were exiled to **Prospect Park** in Brooklyn. The **Sheepfold** then became a restaurant, and was completely redesigned in 1976 by **Paul K.Y. Chen** and **Warner LeRoy.** The outdoor garden is a wonderful place to spend a summer evening and from November through May is spectacularly lit by twinkling lights in the trees; lanterns provide light the remainder of the year. But any season the **Crystal Room,** dripping with chandeliers, is an unforgettable experience, especially for Sunday brunch. ◆ American ◆ M-F lunch and dinner; Sa-Su brunch and dinner. Reservations required. W 67th St (at Central Park W). 873.3200

11 Sheep Meadow The original park design called for a meadow here to enhance the view from the gentle hill to the north. The 15-acre hill was resodded in 1980 after concerts and other crowd-pleasing events had reduced it to hardpan. On the first warm day of the year, New Yorkers flock here for picnicking, sunbathing, and quiet recreation. The view from the hill with the city skyline in the background is in some ways more breathtaking than the park's architects ever envisioned. ◆ 1 April-30 Oct: Tu-F, Su 11AM-5PM; Sa 1-5PM. Closed November through April unless there are at least six inches of snow. W 67th St and West Dr

12 Bowling Green Lawn bowling and croquet were first played here in the 1920s. The folks who play here today take their games very seriously, which explains why the greens are so well maintained. You can get a permit to join them by calling. ◆ Games start at 1PM and 1:30PM Tu-Sa 1 May-1 Nov. W 70th St and West Dr. 360.8133

12 Mineral Springs The concession stand overlooking **Sheep Meadow** also houses a comfort station. It replaced the **Mineral Springs Pavilion,** built in 1868 by a mineral water company that used it to dispense some 30 varieties of water. ◆ Daily Apr-Nov. W 70th St and West Dr

13 The Mall This formal promenade was largely the work of Ignaz Anton Pilat, a plant expert who worked with Olmsted and Vaux on the overall design of the park. He deviated from the romantic naturalism of the plan by planting a double row of elm trees along the length of the promenade, but in the process created a reminder of what country roads and New England villages were like a century ago. The walkway was placed on a northwest angle to provide a sightline directly to a high outcropping above 79th Street known as **Vista Rock.** Vaux designed a miniature castle for the top of the rock to create an impression of greater distance. The bandshell in the northeast corner was designed in 1923 by **William G. Tachau** and donated by Elkan Naumburg, who presented concerts here for many years. It replaced an 1862 cast-iron bandstand that included a sky-blue cupola dotted with gold-leaf stars. The current bandshell, which now sits vacant, was used

for *Summer Stage* concerts and special events until recently; they're now held at **Rumsey Field** near the playground. ◆ Between W 66th and W 72nd Sts (off East Dr)

14 Rumsey Playground A 1938 sculpture of *Mother Goose* by Frederick G.R. Roth and Walter Beretta provides a welcome to this walk-up playground with a wisteria-covered pergola at its western edge. Its location at the top of a hill and a less-than-inviting design make it unattractive to parents of small children. A recent decline in the number of children living near the park has reduced the use of all the park's playgrounds. This one is used primarily as an athletic field for nearby private schools. It was built on the site of the **Central Park Casino,** a cottage originally designed as a ladies' house of refreshment. In the 1920s, it was turned into a restaurant, designed by **Joseph Urban,** which became the most popular place in town for the likes of Gentleman Jimmy Walker, whose basic rule of life was that the only real sin was to go to bed on the same day that you got up. ◆ W 71st St and East Dr

15 The Naumburg Bandshell Until recently, the bandshell was a vital summertime center for jazz, folk dance, and theatrical performances. These events now take place at **Rumsey Field** near the playground (360.2756). ◆ W 72nd St and the Mall

16 Bethesda Terrace Located between the Lake and the Mall, this terrace has always been considered the heart of **Central Park.** It was named for a pool in Jerusalem that the Gospel of St. John says was given healing powers by the annual visitation of an angel. The *Angel of the Waters,* Emma Stebbins's statue on top of the magnificent fountain (shown at right), re-creates the event. It was unveiled in 1873, but the terrace itself had opened in 1861. The basic design is the work of Calvert Vaux. But the arcade ceiling, tile floors, and elaborate friezes and other ornamentation are by **Jacob Wrey Mould,** whose early background was in Islamic architecture—which explains why the terrace is so much like a courtyard in a Spanish palace. ◆ W 72nd St and Terrace Dr

---

If you get lost in the park, find the nearest lamppost. The first two numbers signify the nearest numbered (east-west) street.

"In its influence as an educator, as a place of agreeable resort, as a source of scientific interest, and in its effect upon the health, happiness, and comfort of our people may be found its chief value."

Frederick Law Olmsted,
Report of the Commissioners of Central Park,
1870

17 Conservatory Water The name for this pond comes from a conservatory that was never built. The space is occupied by the **Kerbs Memorial Model Boathouse,** designed by **Aymar Embury II** in 1954. It houses model yachts that race on the pond every Saturday in the summer. At the north end is José de Creeft's fanciful *Alice in Wonderland* group, given to the park in 1960 by publisher George Delacorte. At the western edge is George Lober's 1956 bronze statue of *Hans Christian Andersen,* a gift of the Danish people. During the summer, a storyteller appears here every Saturday at 11AM. A small snack bar with outdoor tables overlooks the water on the east side. ♦ Between W 73rd and W 75th Sts (off Fifth Ave)

18 Loeb Boathouse Built in 1954, this is the third boathouse on the lake. It was tucked away here in the northeast corner so it wouldn't spoil lake views. Besides rowboat and bicycle rentals, there is also an authentic Venetian gondola that holds six people. The Venetians gave a gondola to the park in 1862, but for lack of a gondolier, it rotted away. This one, a more recent gift, includes the services of an expert to pole it around the lake. Bicycle rentals are also available (call 861.4137 for information). ♦ Fee for gondola rides. Rowboat rentals: Daily. Gondola rides: M-F 5PM-10PM; Sa-Su 3PM-10PM Mar-Oct. Reservations required. W 74th St and East Dr. 517.2233

Within Loeb Boathouse:

Boathouse Cafe ★$$$ Sit on the out-door terrace in good weather and take in the peaceful view of the lake. The light fare includes perfectly acceptable pasta dishes, grilled chicken, and swordfish. After 7PM, a trolley at 72nd Street and Fifth Avenue will take you right to the restaurant. ♦ Northern Italian ♦ Daily lunch and dinner Mar-Nov. E 74th St (at East Dr). 517.2233

Bethesda Fountain

Michael Storrings

19 The Ramble This 37-acre wooded section of the park was conceived as a wild garden preserve for native plants and was also intended as a foreground for **Vista Rock** as viewed from the Mall. The garden has seen better days, but it is still a wild place, with a brook meandering through and tumbling over several small waterfalls, and it's a perfect place for bird-watching. One of the winding paths led to a man-made cave at the edge of the lake, but the cave was walled up in the 1920s. There are few better places to get away from it all. Because this little forest can be relatively deserted, it may be best to share its pleasures with a friend. ♦ From W 74th to W 79th Sts (between East and West Drs)

20 Bow Bridge Calvert Vaux designed most of the park's bridges, and no two are alike. This one, crossing the narrowest part of the lake, is considered one of the most beautiful. When the cast-iron bridge was put in place, it was supposedly set on cannonballs to allow for expansion caused by temperature changes. But when it was restored in 1974, no cannonballs were found. ♦ W 74th St (between Cherry Hill and the Ramble)

21 Cherry Hill Designed as a vantage point with a view of the Mall, the lake, Bethesda Terrace, and the Ramble, this spot also provided a turnaround for carriages and a fountain for watering the horses. It was converted into a parking lot in 1934 but restored with 8,500 new trees and shrubs and 23,000 square feet of new sod in 1981. ♦ Terrace Dr (west of Bethesda Terrace)

22 Strawberry Fields This is a teardrop-shaped memorial grove, rehabilitated and maintained with funds provided by Yoko Ono in memory of her late husband, John Lennon. The former Beatle was assassinated in front of the **Dakota** apartment house, which overlooks this tranquil spot. ♦ W 72nd St and Central Park W

23 Winter Drive Evergreens were originally planted in all parts of the park to provide color in the winter months, but the heaviest concentration is here, where 19th-century gay blades entered the park for ice-skating. When the ice on the lake was hard enough, a red ball was hoisted on the flagpole above **Belvedere Castle,** and horsecars on Broadway carried the message downtown by displaying special flags. The parks commissioners estimated that as many as 80,000 people a day crowded the 20-acre frozen lake during the 1850s. The **Arthur Ross Pinetum,** added in 1971 at the north end of the **Great Lawn,** enhances the original plantings with unusual species of conifers from all over the world. ♦ West Dr (between W 77th and W 100th Sts)

Restaurants/Clubs: Red   **Hotels:** Blue
Shops/ ♟ Outdoors: Green   **Sights/Culture:** Black

24 Swedish Cottage Moved here from Philadelphia after the 1876 Centennial Exposition, this building was used as a comfort station until Swedish-Americans mounted a protest. After many years, it was converted into a marionette theater in 1973. ♦ Admission. General public: shows at Sa noon and 3PM; Tu-F 10AM and noon. Hours may vary, so it's best to call ahead. Reservations required. 79th St Transverse and West Dr. 988.9093

25 Shakespeare Garden In this lovely secluded garden, you'll find a series of pathways, pools, and cascades among trees and plants mentioned in the works of William Shakespeare. ♦ W 80th St and West Dr

26 Belvedere Castle A scaled-down version of a Scottish castle (pictured below) was placed here to become part of the view. Its interior is just as impressive. The building houses a National Weather Service station and the **Central Park Learning Center.** ♦ W-Su 11AM-4PM. 79th St Transverse (between East and West Drs). 772.0210

27 Delacorte Theatre A 1960 addition to the park provides a modern home for the late Joseph Papp's **New York Shakespeare Festival.** Obtaining one of the 2,000 tickets (which are given out to the general public only on the day of the performance) is a summer ritual that begins when would-be audience members queue up for tickets distributed at 1PM for that evening's performance. The line starts to form early, but with good friends and a picnic, it can be a pleasant experience. Tickets can also be picked up at the **Public Theater** (425 Lafayette St, between E Fourth St and Astor Pl) from 1-3PM only, on the day of the performance. Two Shakespeare plays are chosen for performance each summer. ♦ Free performances. Tu-Su at 8PM late June to early Sept. W 80th St and West Dr. 861.7277 ⑃

28 Cleopatra's Needle The Khedive of Egypt gave this obelisk to New York in 1881 and presented its mate to Queen Victoria, who had it placed on the Thames Embankment in London. When the 200-ton granite shaft was delivered to New York, it was placed in a special cradle and rolled here from the Hudson River on cannonballs. Because it had stood for many centuries in front of a temple once believed to have been built by Cleopatra, New Yorkers immediately dubbed it Cleopatra's Needle. It was, however, built by Egypt's King Thotmes III in 1600 BC. The hieroglyphics on its sides had survived for 3,500 years, but New York's air pollution has rendered them unreadable in fewer than a hundred. Movie producer Cecil B. De Mille thoughtfully provided plaques translating the tales they told of Thotmes III, Rameses II, and Osorkon I. ♦ W 82nd St and East Dr

29 The Great Lawn The largest field in the park was formerly a rectangular reservoir that was drained just in time to provide a location for a Depression-inspired collection of squatters' shacks known as a Hooverville. By 1936 it was cleared again, and the oval-shaped lawn, with Belvedere Lake at the south end and two playgrounds to the north, was fenced off to create a cooling patch of green. It didn't stay that way long. It is now surrounded by ball fields with their backstops where the lawn should be, and overuse has almost completely eliminated the grass; it is now being reseeded. In 1980, Elton John drew 300,000 people here for a concert; Simon & Garfunkel attracted 500,000 a year later; in 1982, an antinuclear rally brought out 750,000; and in 1993, Pavarotti sang before an audience of 500,000. The **New York Philharmonic** and the **Metropolitan Opera** give several free performances here every summer, each of which attracts about 100,000 people who bring blankets and picnic dinners. ♦ Bounded by East and West Drs, and W 80th and W 85th Sts

30 Claremont Stables Though not actually in the park, the stables are very much a part of it. Riders experienced with English saddles rent horses here and enjoy **Central Park** from its bridle path. ♦ M-F 6:30AM-10PM; Sa-Su 6:30AM-5PM. Reservations required. 175 W 89th St (between Columbus and Amsterdam Aves). 724.5100 or 724.5101

31 The Reservoir Designed as part of the Croton Water System in 1862, this billion-gallon reservoir actively fed the city's thirst until 1994 when it was pulled out of service. Covering nearly 107 acres, it is better known for the soft-surface track that encircles it, providing a perfect amenity for serious runners—one of whom was the late Jacqueline Kennedy Onassis, after whom the reservoir has been unofficially renamed. Once around is 1.58 miles. ♦ Between Fifth Ave and Central Park W (from W 86th to W 96th Sts)

Belvedere Castle

Michael Storrings

32 Conservatory Garden A park nursery was replaced in 1899 by a glass conservatory, which was removed in 1934 to create this series of gardens. It remains one of **Central Park**'s best-kept secrets, even though its presence is announced by an elaborate iron gate that once stood in front of the Cornelius Vanderbilt II mansion. The roofs of the buildings set into the hillside overlook three formal gardens, one of which is planted with seasonal flowers, another with perennials, and a third with grass surrounded by yew hedges and flowering trees and featuring a wisteria-covered pergola. Each is enhanced by a fountain. ♦ Free. Daily 8AM-dusk. E 105th St and Fifth Ave. 860.1382

33 The Mount When General Washington's army was retreating through Manhattan in 1776, the British were held at bay here from a small fortress overlooking McGowan's Pass. The Mount was named for a tavern on top of the hill, which in 1846 became, of all things, a convent. The sisters moved out when the park was created, and the building was converted back into a tavern. It was one of the city's better restaurants in the late 19th century, but was demolished on orders of Mayor John Purroy Mitchel in 1917. ♦ W 105th St and East Dr

34 The Forts During the War of 1812, three forts were built on the future park site to fend off an anticipated British attack. None was actually used, but their now-barren sites are marked with plaques and are waiting for a history buff to re-create them. A little farther to the north, an 1814 blockhouse, the oldest structure in the park, is also waiting for renovation. These days, its thick walls, laced with gunports, look into groves of trees. But when they were placed there, men inside could spot an enemy miles away. None ever came, and few people climb the hill to see the site today. ♦ Between W 106th and W 108th Sts (off East Dr)

35 Harlem Meer The park's original northern boundary was at 106th Street until 1863, when it was extended another four blocks northward, at which time this 11-acre lake was created. It uses the Dutch word for lake, although it hardly qualified as a lake or a meer for a long time. In 1941, the **Parks Department** altered its shoreline to eliminate the natural coves and inlets the original designers had placed there, and the whole thing was rimmed and lined with concrete. Fortunately, this once beautiful corner of the park, desperately in need of loving care, has now been restored to its natural appearance. With a new playground just opened, work is also underway to rebuild the boathouse, create a discovery center for children, and build an esplanade for small concerts at 110th Street. ♦ E 110th St and Fifth Ave

36 Charles A. Dana Discovery Center This is the newest of the park's visitors' centers, opened in 1993, with exhibits and programs on environmental issues for all ages. Some of the park tours led by the Urban Park Rangers leave from here. ♦ Tu-Su. E 110th St and the Harlem Meer. 860.1370 ♿

37 Lasker Rink and Pool Built in 1964, this shallow swimming pool doubles as an ice-skating rink from Thanksgiving through March. It gets considerably less traffic than the downtown **Wollman Rink,** even though it costs less to use. It was built at the mouth of the stream that feeds Harlem Meer. ♦ Free. Pool: Daily 11AM-7PM July-Sept. Ice-skating: M-Th, Su 10AM-9:30PM; F-Sa 10AM-11PM Thanksgiving-Mar. W 107th St and Lenox Ave. 534.7639

38 The Loch This natural pond, undisturbed by the original designers, has been left alone to the point of being silted almost out of existence. A brook leading from the north end forms a small waterfall near the Huddleston Bridge, which carries the East Drive over it. ♦ Between W 103rd and W 105th Sts (off East Dr)

39 Great Hill The mansion of the Bogardus family that once stood on the crest of this 134-foot hill was home to Frederick Law Olmsted during the park's construction. He considered replacing it with a lookout tower because of the view, not only of the park, but of the Hudson River to the west. The view is gone and so is the charm of the hill, which, although recently resodded and replanted, remains capped with asphalt. ♦ W 103rd St and Central Park W

There are 22 playgrounds, 26 ball fields, and 30 tennis courts in Central Park.

Before construction on Central Park began in 1856, Fifth Avenue from 59th to 120th streets was called "Squatters' Sovereignty," where poor people lived in shacks made of wooden planks and flattened tin cans. When construction on the park started, the poor were evicted and soon the area housed the city's richest and most powerful people.

Particularly evident from Central Park are a flurry of twin-towered buildings on Central Park West. Landmark luxury apartment complexes that are a favorite element in New York City's distinctive skyline, they were built from 1929 to 1931 during the peak of the Art Deco period when zoning laws allowed taller buildings if setbacks and towers were used. That period's prolific architect, the eminent Emery Roth, designed the San Remo at 145 Central Park West as well as the Eldorado at 300 Central Park West and Oliver Cromwell at West 72nd Street. The Art-Deco gem at 55 Central Park West was featured in the film *Ghostbusters.*

West Side

Bisected by Broadway and its casual jumble of bookstores, delis, theaters, and restaurants, Manhattan's West Side is more relaxed and laid-back than its fashionable East Side counterpart across **Central Park.** The area was first settled by Eastern European Jews and other immigrants from the Lower East Side in the early part of the century. Today, this vibrant neighborhood, bounded by the **Hudson River, Central Park,** and **West 59th** and **West 86th Streets,** is characterized by in-line skaters zipping past patrons at sidewalk cafes, young mothers pushing baby carriages, and well-dressed crowds pouring in and out of the concert halls and restaurants. Highlights include **Lincoln Center for the Performing Arts,** the ever-changing mix of clothing stores and sidewalk

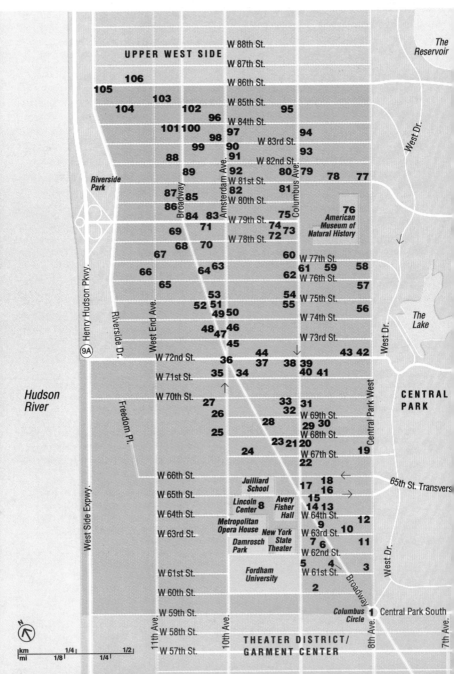

cafes on **Columbus Avenue** and **Broadway,** and numerous architecturally noteworthy buildings.

Riverside Drive, along the neighborhood's western edge, was originally a street of upper-middle-class town houses, and although it had spectacular river views, it lacked the cachet of Fifth Avenue, where "the 400" (Mrs. William Astor's most intimate circle, so called because her home could only accommodate that number) were erecting their palazzi and châteaux. Riverside Drive only had a few grand mansions, like the one Charles Schwab built in 1906 at **West 73rd Street** (now an apartment house). Many of the private homes were replaced in the 1920s by the 15-story apartment buildings of today, their faces sometimes curving to follow the shape of the street.

Some argue that **Central Park West,** skirting the neighborhood's eastern edge, is finer than Fifth Avenue, which borders the other side of the park, because the buildings are more distinguished and the street wider. Most of the buildings on Central Park West were originally built as apartments rather than houses, including the wonderfully chateau-like **Dakota** (the city's first luxury apartment house, built in 1884 by the same architect who would later design the **Plaza Hotel**) at **West 72nd Street,** and the Art Deco **Century** (built in 1931) at 25 Central Park West. A number of twin-towered Art-Deco apartment buildings, most notably the **San Remo** and **Eldorado,** make Central Park West's skyline unique.

The park blocks—the numbered streets between Central Park West and Columbus Avenue—contain interesting collections of brownstones and apartments. Particularly noteworthy are the six buildings with artists' studios on **West 67th Street,** including the **Hotel des Artistes** (home of the **Café des Artistes**), whose plush apartments have been home to many well-known artists, actors, and writers, among them Isadora Duncan, Noel Coward, and Fannie Hurst.

West End Avenue—once lined with Romanesque and Queen Anne–style row houses and now with apartment houses—was supposed to be the West Side's commercial street, while Broadway was slated to be the residential area; hence the avenue's generous width and the mall in the center. But the reverse happened, and Broadway became—and has remained—the neighborhood's "Main Street."

---

1 Columbus Circle This traffic circle (today a real runaround for pedestrians) was built after the commissioners of **Central Park** were empowered to develop the West Side from West 55th to West 155th Streets in 1887. Around the edges are the Moorish white block of the **New York City Department of Cultural Affairs,** designed in 1962 by **Edward Durell Stone** and originally built by A&P heir Huntington Hartford for his abortive **Gallery of Modern Art;** and the grayish lump of the **Coliseum,** designed in 1956 by **Leon & Lionel Levy**— all in all a dismal landscape in a difficult space that planners have been trying to solve for years. One bright note is the announcement to transform the **Gulf + Western Building** tower into the luxurious **Trump International Hotel and Tower,** which is scheduled to be completed in 1998. ♦ Central Park S and Central Park W

At Columbus Circle:

Visitors Information Center Stop by the offices of the **New York Convention and Visitors Bureau** for brochures about attractions and lists of restaurants, shops, and hotels. Warning: Only organizations that are members of the bureau are listed. The center also has coupons for half-priced tickets to Broadway shows and information regarding free tickets to TV shows. ♦ M-F; Sa-Su and holidays 10AM-3PM. 2 Columbus Cir (between Broadway and Eighth Ave). 397.8222

2 Gabriel's ★★$$$ Come here for arguably the best homemade pasta, risotto, grilled dishes, and desserts in the **Lincoln Center** area. Among the offerings is a good red-wine *pappardelle* (broad noodles) with braised squab, carrots, and rosemary; owner Gabriel Aiello is also a great source for wine and food recommendations. Don't be surprised to see

Dan Rather or Diane Sawyer sitting at the next table. ♦ Northern Italian ♦ M-Sa lunch and dinner. Reservations recommended. 11 W 60th St (between Broadway and Columbus Ave). 956.4600

3 Mayflower $$$ Well-located for **Lincoln Center,** this hotel offers 377 roomy accommodations, all with color TVs and most with serving pantries. Ongoing renovations (scheduled for completion by late 1996) include the refurbishing of rooms, and a new fitness center. **The Conservatory Restaurant** serves breakfast, lunch, and dinner, plus an after-theater supper, often with classical music; it's a popular spot for Sunday brunch. ♦ 15 Central Park W (at W 61st St). 265.0060, 800/223.4164; fax 265.5098

4 Bible House/American Bible Society This society tries to make the Holy Scripture available in every language on earth. Its headquarters has a gallery for exhibitions from its collection of rare and unusual bibles, which includes pages from the *Gutenberg Bible.* ♦ Free. M-F. 1865 Broadway (at W 61st St). 408.1200

5 45 Columbus Avenue Designed by **Jardine, Hill & Murdock** in 1930, this 27-story building was originally the **Columbus Circle Automatic Garage.** It is a tremendous Art Deco sampler: All the walls are embellished with ornament. ♦ Between W 61st and W 62nd Sts

6 The Ballet Shop This favorite shop of balletomanes specializes in dance publications—in- and out-of-print—and records, videos, and souvenirs. ♦ Daily. 1887 Broadway (between W 62nd and W 63rd Sts). 581.7990

7 The Radisson Empire Hotel $$ A $70-million renovation, completed in 1992, has brought the 375 rooms into the electronic age: Each is equipped with a cassette and CD player, a VCR, and a two-line telephone. Other highlights are the corporate lounge, the new **West 63rd St. Steakhouse,** and its proximity to **Lincoln Center.** ♦ 44 W 63rd St (between Broadway and Columbus Ave). 265.7400, 800/333.3333; fax 315.0349 ♦

Within The Radisson Empire Hotel:

West 63rd Street Steakhouse ★★★$$$ The simple name belies the richness of the experience you're sure to have at this restaurant. First, the sumptuous setting:

mahogany paneling, elaborately draped windows, handsome table lamps, and Australian aboriginal art. Then there's the food which, made up mostly of prime cuts of beef—including a 24-ounce T-bone—is outstanding, enhanced by excellent red-wine shallot, herb butter, or Chardonnay-lemon sauce. The wine list is well chosen and affordable. ♦ Steak house ♦ M-Sa breakfast and dinner; Su breakfast. Reservations recommended. 246.6363 ♦

7 Iridium $$ Modern, amorphic shapes, undulating walls, gilt surfaces, and deep burnished woods create a surrealistic environment that looks to be inspired by Dr. Seuss—inside and out. That's one of the reasons to come here; another is the convenient location across the street from **Lincoln Center.** There's also a Sunday brunch with a live jazz trio; and a changing roster of jazz musicians play downstairs nightly from 9:30PM to midnight (the cover charge depends on the act). As to the food, stick to simpler items, such as grilled lemon-pepper salmon or one of the burgers. The wine list features a range of good, decently priced wines. ♦ American ♦ M-Sa lunch and dinner; Su jazz brunch and dinner. 44 W 63rd St (at Columbus Ave). 582.2121

8 Lincoln Center for the Performing Arts Robert Moses, urban planner and New York powerbroker, initiated the idea of a center for the city's major performing arts institutions in the 1950s, and this conglomeration of travertine halls came slowly into existence. Massed on a plaza above the street, the buildings have been called an Acropolis, but the arrangement around the fountain is actually a static version of Michelangelo's Capitoline Hill in Rome. Although the main theaters all take their formal cues from images of classical architecture, critics claim they never really come together as a whole, and remain, at best, individual *tours de trite.* Although **Wallace K. Harrison** coordinated the project and designed the master plan, individual architects designed the buildings in the 1960s. ♦ W 65th St and Broadway. 875.5000

At Lincoln Center for the Performing Arts:

Avery Fisher Hall Standing opposite the **State Theater,** this building was designed in 1966 by **Max Abramovitz.** Originally **Philharmonic Hall,** it has been reconstructed several times in the hopes of improving the sound, and a final touch-up in 1992 turned it into an acoustic gem. The stabile in the foyer is by Richard Lippold. **The New York Philharmonic** is in residence here from September through May. Music director Kurt Masur is the latest in an illustrious line that has included Zubin Mehta, the late Leonard Bernstein, Arturo Toscanini, and

Leopold Stokowski. The informal *Mostly Mozart* concerts are held in July and August; *Great Performances* concerts are held September through May. Both are presentations of Lincoln Center Productions. **The Philharmonic's** *Young People's Concerts* have been letting kids in on the motives behind the music since 1898; performances take place four times a year. Don't miss the orchestra's regularly scheduled open rehearsals, which usually occur on Thursday morning at 9:45AM. ♦ Broadway and W 65th St. 875.5030 ♿

Within Avery Fisher Hall:

Panevino ★$$ This is a pleasant place for dinner, a pastry and coffee, or just drinks. During the summer, this cafe in the lobby of **Avery Fisher Hall** spills out onto the plaza. For dinner, try carpaccio, linguine with seafood, grilled chicken paillard with balsamic vinegar, or grilled salmon with lentils and herbs. ♦ Italian ♦ M-Sa dinner. Reservations recommended. 132 W 65th St (at Columbus Ave). 874.7000

Metropolitan Opera House Home to the **Metropolitan Opera Company**, the plaza's magnificent centerpiece (designed by **Wallace K. Harrison**) opened in 1966 with Samuel Barber's *Anthony and Cleopatra*. Behind the thin, 10-story colonnade and sheer glass walls, two wonderful murals by Marc Chagall beam out onto the plaza. The interior is filled with a red-carpeted lobby, a dramatic staircase lit by exquisite Austrian crystal chandeliers, and an equally plush auditorium. The opera season, from mid-September to April, leaves the stage available for visiting performers and companies, including the **American Ballet Theater,** during the rest of the year. ♦ Broadway and W 65th St. 362.6000 ♿

Within Metropolitan Opera House:

Metropolitan Opera Shop Imaginative opera- and music-related gifts and clothing are sold, most of them exclusive to this shop. Pick up hard-to-find books, records, posters, and libretti, with proceeds going to the **Metropolitan Opera.** ♦ M-Sa 10AM-second intermission (usually 9:30PM); Su noon-6PM. Next to the Met box office. 580.4090

To create Lincoln Center—six buildings devoted to theater, music, and dance in an area of 14 acres—it was necessary to demolish 188 buildings and relocate 1,600 people. These were the very slums in which Leonard Bernstein set his famous American musical *West Side Story*. He would later be instrumental in the development and creative organization of Lincoln Center.

Restaurants/Clubs: Red   Hotels: Blue
Shops/♥ Outdoors: Green   Sights/Culture: Black

New York State Theater Located on the plaza's south side, this theater was designed in 1964 by **Philip Johnson** and **Richard Foster.** At the culmination of a series of increasingly grand entrance spaces is a striking four-story foyer with balconies at every level, a pair of large white marble sculptures by Elie Nadelman, and a gold-leaf ceiling. The rich red and gold auditorium was designed for both ballet and musical theater. From 1964 to 1968, under the artistic directorship of Richard Rodgers of the **Music Theater of Lincoln Center,** revivals of musical classics were staged here. Now it's home to the **New York City Ballet** and the **New York City Opera.** In March 1989, conductor Christopher Keene took over the opera company's direction from former opera star Beverly Sills, who assumed the position in 1979. The ballet's season is usually late November through February and April through June. The annually sold-out *Nutcracker* season runs the entire month of December. The opera performs from July through November. Note the diamond-shaped floodlights surrounding the building. ♦ Ballet: late Nov-Feb; Apr-June. Opera July-Nov. W 63rd St and Columbus Ave. 870.5570 ♿

Guggenheim Bandshell South of the **Met,** within **Damrosch Park** (site of the annual *Big Apple Circus*), the bandshell is a beautiful space for free concerts. It was designed by **The Eggars Partnership** in 1969 and seats 2,500. ♦ SW corner of Lincoln Center. 875.5000

Vivian Beaumont Theater North of the **Met,** behind a tree-studded plaza and reflecting pool (with a sculpture by Henry Moore), this theater was designed by **Eero Saarinen & Associates** and first opened in 1965. It has had its share of trouble since the **Repertory Company of Lincoln Center** opened here under the direction of Robert Whitehead and Elia Kazan with Arthur Miller's apologia *After the Fall.* After several mediocre productions, there was a change of leadership. The new team, Jules Irving and Herbert Blau of the **Actor's Workshop** in San Francisco, produced some fine plays, including Bertolt Brecht's *Galileo,* Heinar Kipphardt's *In the Matter of J. Robert Oppenheimer,* and a revival of Tennessee Williams's *A Streetcar Named Desire.* The theater, however, was losing money, and after eight years, impresario Joseph Papp took over. His **New York Shakespeare Festival** at **Lincoln Center** presented many innovative productions here and at the **Mitzi E. Newhouse,** including David Rabe's *Streamers,* Brecht's *Threepenny Opera,* Miguel Pinero's *Short Eyes,* and Anton Chekov's *The Cherry Orchard* (directed by André Serban). After continued deficits and power struggles, however, Papp left in 1977.

The **Beaumont** was dark for three years, until director Richmond Crinkley formed a group of famous entertainment-world personalities to chart a new course for the theater, including writer/actor/director Woody Allen, playwright Edward Albee, and directors Robin Phillips, Ellis Rabb, and Liviu Ciulei. At press time, the theater was undergoing a $4.7-million renovation and scheduled to reopen late 1997. ♦ 150 W 65th St (at Broadway). 239.6277 &

Mitzi E. Newhouse Theater Directly below the **Beaumont,** this smaller theater is for experimental and workshop productions, such as Mike Nichols's controversial *Waiting for Godot* starring Steve Martin, Robin Williams, and Bill Irwin. The 334-seat theater itself was designed by **Eero Saarinen & Associates** and opened in 1965. ♦ 150 W 65th St (at Broadway). 239.6277

Juilliard School Located across a large terrace/bridge over West 66th Street is one of the nation's most acclaimed performing arts schools, founded in 1905 by Augustus D. Juilliard. Enrollment is limited to fewer than a thousand, making acceptance in itself a career achievement for gifted students of music, dance, and drama. The building, a Modernist contrast to **Lincoln Center**'s classicism, was designed by **Pietro Belluschi** with **Eduardo Catalano** and **Westerman & Miller,** and opened in 1968. Theaters: **Juilliard Theater** (seats 933); **Drama Theater** (seats 206); **C. Michael Paul Recital Hall** (seats 278). ♦ 60 Lincoln Center Plaza (W 65th St and Broadway). 799.5000

Alice Tully Recital Hall South of **Juilliard,** entered from Broadway, this recital hall is the most intimate and best of the auditoriums at **Lincoln Center.** Designed for chamber music and recitals by **Pietro Belluschi** in 1969, it is the home of the **Chamber Music Society of Lincoln Center** from October through May. Students of the **Juilliard School** perform here, too. Films from around the world are shown every late September and October at the **New York International Film Festival.** ♦ 1941 Broadway (at W 66th St). 875.5050. Film Society: 875.5610 &

New York Public Library/Library and Museum of the Performing Arts The two galleries at this popular library branch were part of the 1965 creation of **Skidmore, Owings & Merrill.** They exhibit costume and set designs, music scores, and other tools and tricks of the trade, as well as art. The 212-seat **Bruno Walter Auditorium** presents showcase productions and music recitals. In addition to the most extensive collection of books on the performing arts in the city, the library is equipped with state-of-the-art audio equipment and a vast collection of recordings.

A convenient entrance is in Lincoln Plaza next to the **Vivian Beaumont Theater.** ♦ M, Th noon-8PM; T-W, F-Sa noon-6PM. Lincoln Center Plaza, 111 Amsterdam Ave (at W 65th St). 870.1630 &

Lincoln Center Guided Tours Take a tour to see the physical plant, hear the legends and history, and peek at whatever else is going on, perhaps a rehearsal of **The Philharmonic** or *Rigoletto.* Another plus: the expertise and enthusiasm of the tour guides, who are often performers themselves. Backstage tours of the **Met** are also conducted by knowledgeable guides and provide a behind-the-scene look at the opera scene. ♦ Fee. Hourly tours are offered daily; schedule varies, so call ahead. Main Concourse (accessible through the lobby of the Met). 769.7020 &

Performing Arts Gift Shop Records, music boxes, jewelry, clothing, and toys, all tuned into the performing arts, are sold here. Many items, such as the composer signature mugs and a belt with a music staff brass buckle, are designed for and sold exclusively at **Lincoln Center.** ♦ Daily. Main Concourse. 580.4356 &

Lincoln Center Poster Gallery This is the sales outlet for specially commissioned **Lincoln Center** prints and posters by such artists as Josef Albers, Marc Chagall, Robert Indiana, and Andy Warhol. ♦ M-Sa. Main Concourse. 580.4673 &

Samuel B. & David Rose Building Tenants on the first 10 floors of this tower, designed by **Davis, Brody & Associates** and completed in 1990, include the Riverside branch of the **New York Public Library,** the **Walter Reade Theater,** the Film Society of **Lincoln Center,** and Lincoln Center, Inc. offices. Floors 12 to 29 are dormitories for students at **Juilliard** and the **School of American Ballet.** In order to finance construction of this building **Lincoln Center** sold $50 million worth of air rights to the developers of the neighboring condominiums at 3 Lincoln Plaza. ♦ 165 W 65th St (between Broadway and Amsterdam Ave)

9 Fiorello's ★$$$ The location across from **Lincoln Center** is only one reason tables continue to fill up here, and fill up they do. Pre-theater, the place is a madhouse, but after 8PM, the wood-paneled room, decorated with burgundy banquettes and Mark Kostabi paintings, is a calm place where you can sample the antipasto bar; such pastas as lamb *bolognese* and linguine with clams, calamari, and mussels; and main courses that include clay-pot–roasted chicken with rosemary, roasted bass with olives and sun-dried tomatoes, and lamb osso buco. ♦ Italian ♦ M-F lunch and dinner; Sa-Su brunch and dinner. Reservations required. 1900 Broadway (at W 63rd St). 595.5330

10 West Side YMCA $ In 1966, the city planned to raze this building—designed by **Dwight James Baum** and built in 1930— to clear the entire block up to Central Park West for a **Lincoln Center** mall. Plans fell through when the **YMCA** refused to sell out. This hostelry offers 550 single and double rooms to both men and women. In addition to a popular sports/fitness center, it has a family and youth services department. ♦ 5 W 63rd St (between Central Park W and Broadway). 787.4400, 800/FIT.YMCA; fax 580.0441 ♿

11 Century Apartments Brother of the **Majestic (No. 115,** designed in 1930), this is the southernmost pair of the sets of twin towers designed by the office of **Irwin S. Chanin** that make the skyline of Central Park West so distinctive. The structure was built in 1931, when Jacques Delamarre was the director of **Chanin**'s office. The apartment house occupies the site of the resoundingly unsuccessful (but magnificent) **Century Theater,** a 1909 building by **Carrère & Hastings,** which first failed as a national theater, then as an opera house, and finally as a Ziegfeld vaudeville theater. ♦ 25 Central Park W (between W 62nd and W 63rd Sts). 265.1608

12 New York Society for Ethical Culture It's refreshing to find this example of Art Nouveau in New York. **Robert D. Kohn,** who was also the architect of **Temple Emanu-El,** was the president of the society at the time he designed this building in 1910. ♦ 2 W 64th St (at Central Park W). 874.5210

13 Picholine ★★★$$$ The sunny foods of the Mediterranean, especially Provence, are what make this restaurant so appealing. Don't miss the grilled octopus with fennel, potato, and lemon-pepper vinaigrette; or the carpaccio of tuna with vegetables *escabèche* (marinated in lemon juice) and *tapenade aioli* (an olive-based mayonnaise). ♦ Mediterranean ♦ M dinner; Tu-Sa lunch and dinner. 35 W 64th St (between Central Park W and Broadway). 724.8585

O'NEALS'

13 O'Neals' ★★$$$ Fans of the old **O'Neals' Balloon** will be glad to see it has relocated just a block away in the space formerly occupied by the **Ginger Man.** The menu is straight-forward and offers predictably decent fare ranging from hamburgers and Chicago-style ribs to tarragon chicken. The dining room is visibly calmer after 8PM, when the crowds empty out to catch the curtain at **Lincoln Center.** ♦ American ♦ Daily lunch, dinner, and late-night meals. 49 W 64th St (between Central Park W and Broadway). 787.4663

14 The Saloon $$ The service in this cavernous dining room and street cafe is as erratic as the food on the enormous snack and dinner menu; the many offerings include crab cakes, quesadillas, angel-hair pasta with prosciutto, and various pizzas. **The Saloon Grill** (874.2082) next door serves the same food in a slightly calmer atmosphere. ♦ Continental ♦ M-F lunch and dinner; Sa-Su brunch and dinner. Reservations recommended. 1920 Broadway (at W 64th St). 874.1500 ♿

14 World Gym If you've taken advantage of one too many New York restaurants, this popular bodybuilding gym offers mini memberships by the day, week, or month. This is serious stuff, obvious from the pumped-up late-night worka-holics who take advantage of the 24-hour schedule. ♦ M-F open 24 hours, Sa-Su 7AM-9PM. 1926 Broadway (between W 64th and W 65th Sts), Second floor. 874.0942. ♿

15 Sfuzzi ★★$$ Dramatic decor and fun food are served in this lively trattoria. The bar is packed before and after the theater with smart, young trendy types sipping frozen Sfuzzis—a combination of fresh peach nectar, champagne, and peach schnapps. Specialties include veal scallopini with asparagus, parmesan gnocchi and lemon-sage sauce; and salmon with crisp potatoes, green beans, and basil-citrus sauce. ♦ Italian ♦ Daily lunch and dinner. Reservations recommended. 58 W 65th St (between Central Park W and Broadway). 873.3700. Also at: 2 World Financial Center (between Liberty and Vesey Sts), Winter Garden Atrium. 385.8080

16 Shun Lee Dynasty ★$$$ Long a favorite of the **Lincoln Center** crowd, its kitchen does many regional Chinese cuisines justice. Try the steamed dumplings, beggar's chicken (baked in clay), or prawns in black-bean sauce. The vast dining room is dramatic—black banquettes and brightly colored dragon lanterns—though it's not as fancy as the prices. In the second dining room is the lower-priced **Shun Lee Cafe,** featuring dim sum. ♦ Chinese ♦ Daily lunch and dinner. Reservations required. 43 W 65th St (between Central Park W and Broadway). 595.8895. Also at: 155 E 55th St (between Third and Lexington Aves). 371.8844

17 Museum of American Folk Art/Eva and Morris Feld Gallery at Lincoln Square The best of American folk art from the 18th century to the present, including paintings, sculpture, textiles, furniture, and decorative arts, is displayed here. The museum holds regular lectures and workshops and has an adjacent gift shop that's worth a visit. ♦ Voluntary contribution. Tu-Su. 2 Lincoln Sq (Columbus Ave between W 65th and W 66th Sts). 977.7298; gift shop 496.2966 &

18 First Battery Armory, New York National Guard Today, **ABC**'s TV studios hide behind this fortress facade, designed in 1901 by **Horgan & Slattery** and altered in 1978 by **Kohn Pederson Fox.** ♦ 56 W 66th St (between Central Park W and Broadway)

19 Hotel des Artistes An early studio building designed by **George Mort Pollard** in 1913 specifically for artists—duplexes with double-height main spaces—this is now one of the more lavish co-ops around. It has always attracted noteworthy tenants, among them Isadora Duncan, Alexander Woollcott, Norman Rockwell, Noel Coward, and Howard Chandler Christy. ♦ 1 W 67th St (between Central Park W and Columbus Ave). 362.6700

Within the Hotel des Artistes:

Café des Artistes ★★★$$$ The West Side's most charming and romantic restaurant was originally, as the name suggests, intended for artists. Light streams through the leaded-glass windows by day, and the murals of ethereal female nudes, painted in 1934 by Howard Chandler Christy, are wonderful. Regular dishes you shouldn't miss include the salmon four ways (smoked, poached, gravlax, and *tartare*), duck confit, and rack of lamb with basil crust. Save room for the Great Dessert Plate—it could possibly exceed your sweetest dreams. The famous weekend brunch is a must. ♦ French ♦ M-F lunch and dinner; Sa-Su brunch and dinner. Reservations required; jacket and tie required after 5PM. 877.3500 &

20 Vince & Eddie's ★★★$$ Locals pack this rustic-looking, intimate room—especially before a **Lincoln Center** performance—for chef Scott Campbell's earthy but elegantly prepared dishes. The menu changes seasonally, but such standout dishes as braised lamb shank with Michigan cherry sauce and pan-roasted chicken with spinach and lentils are available all year. Vegetable purees, including turnip and pumpkin, may sound humble but are silky and rich and not to be missed. ♦ American ♦ M-Sa lunch and dinner; Su brunch and dinner. Reservations recommended. 70 W 68th St (between Central Park W and Columbus Ave). 721.0068

20 67 Wine & Spirits The extensive selection of wines and spirits in this store is well known for its diversity, fair prices, and knowledgable staff. ♦ M-Sa. 179 Columbus Ave (at W 68th St). 724.6767

21 Reebok Sports Club/NY This six-level, mega-club is the latest and most extravagant of urban country clubs. Over 140,000 square feet of tracks, courts, sun decks, pools, and locker rooms are outfitted with $55 million worth of state-of-the-art equipment. Membership is steep, but where else in town will you find a 45-foot rockclimbing wall or a downhill-skiing simulator? ♦ Daily. 174 Columbus Ave (at W 68th St). 362.6800

22 American Broadcasting Company Facilities (ABC) Fortunately, these two buildings don't intrude on this quiet, low-scale street: 30 West 67th Street, the technical center, is set back respectfully, and the limestone, tan brick, and glass are in harmony with the surroundings. In 1979, architects **Kohn Pederson Fox** used a lot of glass to create an inviting lobby for the local television studios at 7 Lincoln Square; an open atrium with a flying staircase on the top three floors is illuminated at night. ♦ 30 W 67th St and 7 Lincoln Sq (between Central Park W and Broadway)

23 Sony Theaters Lincoln Square The new multiplex flagship of this Japanese-owned chain is a show in itself, although one seen by some area residents as a threat to the neighborhood's tranquillity. Each of the 10 screening rooms is reminiscent of old-time movie palaces. But the centerpiece of the lavish complex, opened in late 1994, is the 3-D Imax theater with an eight-story–high screen (the largest in the US); reclining chairs and a sleek wraparound headset guarantee virtual immersion. ♦ Daily. Broadway and W 68th St. 336.5000 &

24 Merkin Concert Hall Concert series are held here, including ensemble programs and contemporary and chamber music. The 457-seat hall is located in the **Abraham Goodman House.** ♦ 129 W 67th St (between Broadway and Amsterdam Ave). 362.8719 &

25 Sweetwater's One of the few remaining cabaret rooms in town, this club occasionally forays into R&B and jazz. It's known for consistently solid bookings, some big-name singers and groups, and a savvy and appreciative audience. ♦ Cover, minimum. Daily; no shows Sunday. Call for performance schedule. Reservations recommended. 170 Amsterdam Ave (at W 68th St). 873.4100 &

26 Lincoln Square Synagogue Designed in 1970 by **Hausman & Rosenberg,** this is a mannered, curved building with fins and rectangular block attached, all clad in travertine, à la neighboring **Lincoln Center.** It's one of Manhattan's most popular Orthodox synagogues. ♦ 200 Amsterdam Ave (at W 69th St). 874.6100

27 Cafe Luxembourg ★★$$$ A people watcher's Art Deco brasserie, this cafe is affiliated with TriBeCa's trendy **Odeon.** The zinc-topped bar here draws a stylish, international crowd, and the menu is a mélange of French, Italian, and regional American offerings. Try marinated octopus; lemon risotto with fresh asparagus and parmesan; or Provençal vegetable tart. Top it off with profiteroles and mint-chip ice cream. ♦ French ♦ M-F lunch, dinner, and late-night meals; Sa-Su brunch, dinner, and late-night meals. Reservations recommended. 200 W 70th St (between Amsterdam and West End Aves). 873.7411

28 Christ and St. Stephen's Church This charming country church, built in 1880 to the designs of **William H. Day** and altered in 1897 by **J.D. Fouguet,** is holding up well in the big city. ♦ 120 W 69th St (between Columbus Ave and Broadway). 787.2755

La Boîte en Bois

29 La Boîte en Bois ★★$$$ A few steps down and far from the madding crowd on Columbus Avenue, this charming French bistro with a country atmosphere and Provençal menu offers fine fish soup, roast chicken with herbs, and roast salmon glazed with honey mustard. ♦ French ♦ Daily dinner. Reservations recommended. No credit cards accepted. 75 W 68th St (between Central Park W and Columbus Ave). 874.2705

30 Santa Fe ★$$ This refurbished town-house dining room is painted in flattering soft desert tones and fitted with fine Southwestern arts and crafts. It's a very pleasant place to dine on such Southwestern fare as seviche, shrimp in a green tomatillo sauce, and crab cakes in a smoked tomato-and-chile sauce. ♦ Southwestern ♦ Daily lunch and dinner. Reservations recommended. 72 W 69th St (between Central Park W and Columbus Ave). 724.0822

31 World Cafe ★$$ The all-encompassing menu in this beige eatery with ceiling fans spans the globe from East to West. The Indian spiced yogurt-avocado dip is interesting, as is the grilled tuna in a carrot-ginger glaze. But the most successful item on the menu might well be the humble hamburger, given a jolt here with chipotle barbecue sauce. ♦ Continental ♦ M-F lunch and dinner; Sa-Su brunch and dinner. Reservations recommended. 201 Columbus Ave (at W 69th St). 799.8090

32 Rikyu ★$$ Predating the invasion of trendy spots along Columbus Avenue, this popular restaurant is a favorite with locals and the **Lincoln Center** crowd for good traditional dishes and fresh sushi. Other pluses: the tatami rooms and reasonable prices. ♦ Japanese ♦ Daily lunch and dinner. Reservations recommended. 210 Columbus Ave (between W 69th and W 70th Sts). 799.7847

33 Soutine A tiny bake shop with the feel of a French *boulangerie,* this place is a neighborhood favorite. Try the *pain au chocolat* (a chocolate-filled croissant) and bread knots filled with cheddar cheese. ♦ M-Sa; Su until 3PM. 106 W 70th St (between Columbus Ave and Broadway). 496.1450

34 The Dorilton When this Beaux Arts masterpiece, designed by **Janes & Leo,** was completed in 1902, critic Montgomery Schuyler was so displeased with its design that he wrote the following in *Architectural Record:* "The incendiary qualities of the edifice may be referred, first to violence of color, then to violence of scale, then to violence of 'thingness,' to the multiplicity and importunity of the details." When the Landmarks Preservation Commission granted this apartment building its landmark status in 1974, they described it as "exceptionally handsome." ♦ 171 W 71st St (at Broadway)

35 Applause Theater Books For thespians, this is a good place to find an obscure play or movie scenario. Books on other performing arts are also sold. ♦ Daily. 211 W 71st St (between Broadway and West End Ave). 496.7511

36 Sherman Square Another one of those places where Broadway crosses the city grid to form a bow tie, not a square, this one is occupied by an **IRT Subway Control House,** which was designed by **Heins & LaFarge** in 1904. This is one of two surviving ornate entrances to the original **IRT** subway line (the other is at the **Battery Park Control House** in Lower Manhattan). Note the stylish detailing of the Neo-Dutch, somewhat Baroque shed. ♦ W 72nd St (bounded by Broadway and Amsterdam Ave)

36 Gray's Papaya $ Nowhere else does a dollar buy so much. A cast of characters frequents this super-cheap round-the-clock hot dog stand that claims its "tube steaks" are "tastier than filet mignon" and its papaya drink is "a definite aid to digestion." Unless you've got a cast iron stomach, you'll need all the help you can get. The fruit-flavored refreshments are definitely worth a stop here. ♦ Hot dogs ♦ Daily 24 hours. 2090 Broadway (at W 72nd St). 799.0243

37 Acker-Merrall-Condit Experts on Burgundy, these established liquor merchants boast a reputation for good service. The store design is nice, too. ♦ M-Sa. 160 W 72nd St (between Columbus Ave and Broadway). 787.1700 &

37 Fine & Schapiro ★$$ This long-established classic kosher delicatessen makes one nostalgic for the days before cholesterol counts. There's a salt-free corner on the menu, but if you need to consult it, you're probably in the wrong place. ♦ Jewish deli ♦ Daily lunch and dinner. 138 W 72nd St (between Columbus Ave and Broadway). 877.2874

37 Blades West Rent a pair of rollerblades and protective gear, then set off for a day of blading in the park. The blades—as well as ice skates, skateboards, snowboards, helmets, and accessories—are also for sale. ♦ Daily. 120 W 72nd St (at Columbus Ave). 787.3911. Blades East at: 160 E 86th St (between Third and Lexington Aves). 996.1644

38 To Boot New York This West Side landmark specializes in cowboy boots but also stocks the best in other types of men's and women's footwear—casual, business, and formal. Handwoven ties and scarves are also available. ♦ Daily. 256 Columbus Ave (at W 72nd St). 724.8249

39 Charivari 72 This is one of five locations for the Weiser family emporium, known since 1967 for its intriguing mix of expensive fashion-forward and evening clothes for men and women. Selections range from leather coats and hand-knit sweaters to evening dresses. ♦ Daily. 257 Columbus Ave (at W 72nd St). 787.7272. Also at: 18 W 57th St (between Fifth and Sixth Aves). 333.4040; 1009 Madison Ave (at E 78th St). 650.0070

40 Harry's Burrito Junction ★$ If **Lincoln Center** tickets have busted your budget, or if you happen to be in the market for some great nachos, this is the place. A young crowd that fills the three-level space decorated with memorabilia from the 1960s seems to have a special fondness for the foot-long bay burrito, oozing with black beans and shredded beef. ♦ Mexican ♦ M-F lunch and dinner; Sa-Su brunch and dinner. 241 Columbus Ave (at W 71st St). 580.9494

41 Fishin Eddie ★★$$$ Courtesy of the folks behind **Vince & Eddie's** (see above), this restaurant specializing in seafood is ideal for a pre- or post-**Lincoln Center** meal. The yellow-and-chartreuse color scheme, however, and the nautical props (including buoys) suggest nothing so much as the inside of a fish tank, an interesting setting for a high-quality fish dinner. Try grilled black bass with thyme pesto, cioppino (a seafood stew in a spicy red broth), grouper sautéed with arugula and tomato sauce, or perfectly steamed lobster. For dessert there's an excellent lemon tart; the chocolate-walnut cake and apple-oat tart are also recommended. ♦ Seafood ♦ Daily dinner. Reservations recommended. 73 W 71st St (between Central Park W and Columbus Ave). 874.3474

41 Café La Fortuna ★$ A mainstay of the neighborhood for years—and one of the late John Lennon's hangouts—this pleasant, unassuming cafe serves excellent Italian coffees and a array of traditional Italian pastries and other sweets. Sandwiches, antipasti, and salads are also available. ♦ Cafe ♦ Daily lunch, dinner, and late-night meals. No credit cards accepted. 69 W 71st St (between Central Park W and Columbus Ave). 724.5846

Dakota Apartments

Michael Storrings

42 Dakota Apartments Built in 1884, this was one of the first luxury apartment houses in the city (along with the **Osborne** on West 57th Street and **34 Gramercy Park East**). The building (pictured above) was christened when someone remarked to its owner, Edward Clark, president of the Singer Sewing Company, that it was so far out of town, "it might as well be in Dakota Territory." Clark, not without a sense of humor, went on to instruct the architect, **Henry J. Hardenbergh,** to embellish the building with symbols of the Wild West; arrowheads, sheaves of wheat, and ears of corn appear in bas-relief on the building's interior and exterior facades. (**Hardenbergh** later designed **The Plaza Hotel.**) The apartment building is a highly original masonry mass with echoes of Romanesque and German Renaissance architecture. Recent cleaning has revealed the rich creamy brown stone of the facade. Victorian details and miscellaneous pieces sprout at every turn—turrets, gables, oriels, dormers, and pinnacles. The top three floors, once servants' quarters and a playroom and gymnasium for children, are now some of the most prized apartments in Manhattan. The building has gained notoriety not only as the setting for the film *Rosemary's Baby* but also as the home of Boris Karloff, Judy Garland, Lauren Bacall, Leonard Bernstein, Rex Reed, Roberta Flack, Yoko Ono and John Lennon, and Kim Basinger. ♦ 1 W 72nd St (at Central Park W)

43 Dallas BBQ $ The barbecued ribs and chicken are well seasoned, tender, and juicy. But the big draw for many of the neighborhood fans of this large, informal, and noisy restaurant is the huge loaf of greasy onion rings. ♦ Barbecue ♦ M-Th, Su lunch and dinner; F-Sa lunch, dinner, and late-night meals. 27 W 72nd St (between Central Park W and Columbus Ave). 873.2004. Also at: 1265 Third Ave (at E 73rd St). 772.9393; 21 University Pl (at E Eighth St). 674.4450; 132 Second Ave (at St Mark's Pl). 777.5574

44 Eclair $$ The traditional midafternoon *kaffee und kuchen* (coffee and cake) is wonderful—try the *schwarzwalder kirsch torte* (a flat, dense Viennese torte with a chocolate or raspberry filling) or linzer torte. There is also a scattershot menu to choose from, featuring substantial specialties such as Wiener schnitzel, sauerbraten, and yankee pot roast, along with lighter fare—broiled fish dishes, vegetarian plates, and sandwiches. ♦ Cafe ♦ Daily breakfast, lunch, and dinner. 141 W 72nd St (between Columbus Ave and Broadway). 873.7700

45 Star Magic If you're in the market for crystals, New Age–inspired accessories, and trinkets for the astral traveler, stop by this shop. ♦ Daily. 275 Amsterdam Ave (at W 73rd St). 769.2020. Also at: 745 Broadway (at Astor Pl). 228.7770; 1296 Lexington Ave (at E 85th St). 988.0300 ♿

46 Vinnie's Pizza ★$ At this neighborhood favorite, the thin-crusted pizza is loaded with cheese and super-fresh toppings. The parlor itself wouldn't win any design awards, so get your pie to go. ♦ Pizza ♦ Daily lunch and dinner. 285 Amsterdam Ave (between W 73rd and W 74th Sts). 874.4382

47 Apple Bank ★ A Florentine palazzo seems like an appropriate model for a bank. This one, designed in 1928 by the masters **York & Sawyer** (who also designed the **Federal Reserve Bank of New York**), skillfully contains a proper rectangular banking hall within the trapezoidal building necessary on the site. ♦ 2100 Broadway (between W 73rd and W 74th Sts). 472.4545 ♿

48 Ansonia Hotel Designed by **Graves & Duboy** and built in 1904, this Belle Epoque masterpiece, bristling with ornament, balconies, towers, and dormers, is one of the great apartment buildings in New York. (As with the **Hotel des Artistes,** this was never a hotel at all; the appellation is from the French *hôtel de ville,* meaning town hall.) The thick walls and floors required for fireproofing have made the 16-story cooperative apartment building a favorite of musicians. Among those who have lived here are Enrico Caruso, Arturo Toscanini, Florenz Ziegfeld, Sol Hurok, Theodore Dreiser, and George Herman (Babe) Ruth. ♦ 2109 Broadway (between W 73rd and W 74th Sts). 724.2600

48 Tower Records Along with **Tower Video,** these sister stores to the larger downtown branch are the West Side's most complete resource for audio and video home entertainment. ♦ Tower Records and Tower Video: daily 9AM–midnight. Tower Records: 1107 Broadway (between W 73rd and W 74th Sts). 799.2500. Tower Video: 1977 Broadway (at W 67th St). 496.2500. Also at: Trump Tower, 725 Fifth Ave (at E 56th St). 838.8118 ♿

49 Josie's ★★$ This place offers food that is appropriately health-conscious: The grains and produce are organic, the water is filtered, and all dishes are dairy-free. The creative cuisine features such dishes as ginger-grilled calamari with pineapple–red pepper salsa, and sweet-potato ravioli with gulf shrimp, sweet corn, and roasted peppers in white wine–and–leek sauce. There are some unrepentently sinful desserts, including lemon-ribbon ice-cream pie. ♦ American ♦ Daily dinner. Reservations required. 300 Amsterdam Ave (at W 74th St). 769.1212 ♿

50 Freddie and Pepper's Gourmet Pizza ★$ This popular no-frills pizza place makes a good tomato base for its myriad toppings. Try the unusual seafood smorgasbord pie. ♦ Pizza ♦ Daily lunch and dinner. No credit cards accepted. 303 Amsterdam Ave (between W 74th and W 75th Sts). 799.2378

50 Shark Bar ★$ Within a swanky setting—dark, split-level, candlelit—is a beautiful and well-dressed crowd, including more than a few models and music industry types. Among the inventive appetizers that shouldn't be missed is the soul roll (pastry filled with vegetables, chicken, and rice). Otherwise, skip the Cajun side of the menu and stick to classic soul food dishes—barbecued ribs, fried chicken, and collard greens. ♦ Soul food/Cajun ♦ M-Tu dinner; W-F lunch and dinner; Sa-Su brunch and dinner. Reservations recommended. 307 Amsterdam Ave (between W 74th and W 75th Sts). 874.8500

51 China Club This fun dance bar with a young, energetic crowd features electrifying contemporary sounds. Regulars live for the Monday night scene when entertainers and sports celebrities stop by. ♦ Cover. M, W-Sa 10PM-3AM or 4AM. 2130 Broadway (at W 75th St). 877.1166

51 Beacon Theatre Special films, dance groups, and foreign performing arts groups, as well as mainstream soul and rock artists, are featured in this 2,700-seat theater. Some say the magnificent interior by **Walter Ahlschlager** is second only to **Radio City**'s. ♦ 2124 Broadway (at W 75th St). 496.7070

52 Fairway Residents swear by this all-purpose market, which has the best produce, freshest cheese, and good prices. Best times to shop: early morning or after 8PM. ♦ Daily 7AM-midnight. 2127 Broadway (between W 74th and W 75th Sts). 595.1888

52 Citarella This retail fish store and raw seafood bar is ideal for a quick stand-up snack before a show at the **Beacon Theatre.** The elaborate fish-sculpture displays take the art of window dressing to new heights. Not in the mood for fish? Then try the prime cuts of meat, homemade pasta, and appetizers. ♦ Daily. 2135 Broadway (at W 75th St). 874.0383

Restaurants/Clubs: Red   **Hotels:** Blue
Shops/ 🍴 Outdoors: Green   **Sights/Culture:** Black

53 Ernie's $$; Recently reopened after a long renovation, this barnlike restaurant now has a fresh, airy look with its light-wood floor, white walls, and spotlights. The menu is basically the same, though shorter, and such favorites as angel-hair pasta with lobster, Caesar salad, grilled chicken, and death by chocolate were retained. But this place has always been more about chatting with friends than about food. ♦ Italian ♦ M-Th lunch and dinner; F lunch, dinner, and late-night meals; Sa brunch, dinner, and late-night meals; Su brunch and dinner. Reservations recommended. 2150 Broadway (at W 75th St). 496.1588

54 Mughlai $$ For Indian food that never errs on the too-spicy side, this is the place. The tandoori here is best, and the mango chutney served with the curry is quite good. Desserts are uninspired, except for the highly recommended rice pudding with rosewater. ♦ Indian ♦ M-F dinner; Sa-Su brunch and dinner. Reservations recommended. 320 Columbus Ave (at W 75th St). 724.6363

55 Pappardella $$ This is a popular destination for pasta and *secondi piatti* (second, or main, dishes) with a Tuscan accent. Try a thin-crusted pizza with a glass of Chianti, ravioli with mushrooms, or *bistecca fiorentina* (grilled T-bone steak marinated in olive oil, rosemary, and a touch of garlic, served with sautéed vegetables), and relish the escape from the bustle of Columbus Avenue. ♦ Italian ♦ Daily lunch and dinner. Reservations recommended. 316 Columbus Ave (at W 75th St). 595.7996

56 San Remo In contrast to the streamlined **Century** and **Majestic** apartments by **Irwin S. Chanin, Emory Roth**'s twin towers, constructed in 1930, are capped with Roman temples surmounted by finials. ♦ 145-146 Central Park W (between W 74th and W 75th Sts)

57 Central Park West/76th Street Historic District This district, designated a historic area in 1973, comprises the blocks on Central Park West between West 75th and West 77th Streets and about half of West 76th Street. It includes a variety of row houses built at the turn of the century; the Neo-Grecian **Nos. 21-31** by **George M. Walgrove** are the earliest, and the Baroque **Nos. 8-10** by **John H. Duncan** are the most recent. Of interest as well are the **Kenilworth** apartment building (151 Central Park West), designed in 1908 by **Townsend, Steinle & Haskell,** noteworthy for its convex mansard roof and highly ornamented limestone, and the Oxfordish **Universalist Church of New York** (West 76th Street and Central Park West), designed in 1898 by **William A. Potter.** Also included in the designated area is **44 West 77th Street,** designed in 1909 by **Harde & Short,** a Gothic-style building used as artists' studios; much of the ornament was removed in 1944. ♦ Central Park W (between W 75th and W 77th Sts)

58 New-York Historical Society The society is housed in a fine Neo-Classical French building, the central portion of which was designed by **York & Sawyer** in 1908, with unimaginative 1938 additions by **Walker & Gillette.** Inside, the collection is rich with such Americana as wall-to-wall silver, rare maps, antique toys, splendid carriages, portraits by Gilbert Stuart and Benjamin West, watercolors by John James Audubon, and landscapes by again-popular Frederic Church and the rest of the Hudson River boys. The society also has stunning 17th-, 18th-, and 19th-century furniture arranged in chronological order. Changing shows touch on cast-iron stoves, American bands, or early women's magazines. The society's library is one of the major reference libraries of American history in this country. If you're wondering about the hyphen in "New-York Historical Society," it's a point of pride for the museum: When it was founded in 1804, everybody spelled New York that way. ♦ Admission. Call for hours. 170 Central Park W (between W 76th and W 77th Sts). 873.3400 ♿

59 Scaletta ★★$$$ A large dinner menu, fast and efficient service, and excellent pasta and antipasto (especially the prosciutto) are highlights of this lovely Northern Italian restaurant. Also try the specials of the day, which might include risotto with wild mushrooms, and veal *sorrentino* (sautéed with eggplant and mozzarella). Desserts are of the rich Italian variety, and the espresso is good too. ♦ Northern Italian ♦ Daily dinner. 50 W 77th St (between Central Park W and Columbus Ave). 769.9191

MUSEUM ♦ CAFE

60 Museum Cafe $$ Its location just across the street from the **American Museum of Natural History** and the **Hayden Planetarium** makes this place a convenient stop. Another plus is that the restaurant stays open all night on Thanksgiving Eve, when the **Macy's** Thanksgiving Day Parade floats are inflated out front. Best bets here are the Grecian chicken salad or one of the gargantuan bowls of pasta. The interior is a dull, restful pink with wood trim; it's better to sit at a table in the enclosed sidewalk cafe. ♦ American ♦ M-F lunch and dinner; Sa-Su brunch and dinner. 366 Columbus Ave (at W 77th St). 799.0150

61 Isabella ★$$ Well liked for its simple, pleasant decor and inviting sidewalk cafe, this place offers such homemade pasta as cheese-and-herb ravioli in tomato sauce, and grilled dishes, including veal chops and chicken, all of which are good. ♦ Italian ♦ M-F lunch and dinner; Sa-Su brunch and dinner. 359 Columbus Ave (at W 77th St). 724.2100

61 Kenneth Cole Shoes and accessories by the witty, self-promoting designer are sold in this shop. Copies of his print ads, which address the political and social issues of the moment—one suggests that customers buy one less pair of shoes and, instead, donate the money to AIDS research—are displayed along the right-hand wall as you enter. ♦ Daily. 353 Columbus Ave (between W 76th and W 77th Sts). 873.2061. Also at: 95 Fifth Ave (at E 17th St). 675.2550

61 Putumayo Fashions from developing countries around the world—Thailand, Peru, Guatemala—are here in vivid, eye-appealing colors. Create complete outfits of chiffonlike skirts and crisp linen blouses and shirts, or use one piece, such as the classic llama sweaters, to match any wardrobe. ♦ Daily. 341 Columbus Ave (between W 76th and W 77th Sts). 595.3441. Also at: 147 Spring St (between Wooster St and W Broadway). 966.4458

Congregation Shearith Israel at West 70th Street is the oldest Jewish congregation in the United States. The first house of worship was built in 1730 by descendants of 23 men, women, and children who arrived from Nieuw Amsterdam in 1654. It was moved uptown three times until the current synagogue at West 70th Street was built in 1897.

GreenFlea

62 GreenFlea/IS 44 Market If you can't make the trek down to the larger weekend flea market at West 26th Street and Sixth Avenue, you'll fare well here, though the pickings aren't as extensive. The emphasis is on new, used, and vintage clothing and accessories, with a nice mix of antiques, collectibles, and furniture. ♦ Free. Su. Columbus Ave and W 76th St. 721.0900

63 Equinox Fitness Club Ideal for visitors, this cutting-edge mega-gym opens its doors for one-time-use admission. A huge success since its 1991 debut, this gym is as famous for its social scene as for its unsurpassed fitness programs. A killer 10-week program is available for those who plan to stay on in New York. ♦ M-Th 5:30AM-11PM; F 6AM-10PM; Sa-Su 8AM-9PM. 344 Amsterdam Ave (between W 76th and W 77th Sts). 721.4200

64 Promenade Theatre New plays and revivals of lesser-known plays by established playwrights are featured at this intimate 399-seat theater, often with big-name stars returning to the boards to hone their craft. ♦ 2162 Broadway (between W 76th and W 77th Sts). 580.1313

65 Milburn Hotel $ Handsome prewar apartment buildings are common in this residential area, and the **Milburn** was one of them until a recent multimillion-dollar refurbishing converted it to a gracious 70-suite hotel. All the traditionally furnished rooms have fully equipped kitchens with microwaves, making this a good choice for families and long-term visitors. ♦ 242 W 76th St (between Broadway and West End Ave). 362.1006, 800/833.9622; fax 721.5476

66 343-357 West End Avenue Built in 1891 and designed by **Lamb & Rich,** this complete block-front on West End and around both corners is a lively, well-ordered collection typical of Victorian town houses, and the only West Side block without high-rises between West End Avenue and Riverside Drive. (Rumor has it that Mayor Jimmy Walker's mistress lived at West 76th Street and Broadway and the block was supposedly zoned to protect his river view.) The variety of shapes and materials—gables, bays, dormers, and limestone, red, and tan brick—is clearly under control, resulting in a stylish, humorous energy with no dissonance. ♦ Between W 76th and W 77th Sts

67 West End Collegiate Church and School The school, established by the Dutch in 1637, is housed in a copy of the market building in Haarlem, Holland. Designed in 1893 by **Robert W. Gibson,** this is a particularly good example of Dutch detailing; note the stepped gables and the use of long bricks. ♦ 368 West End Ave (between W 77th and W 78th Sts). 787.1566 &

68 La Caridad $ Expect a wait at this popular and inexpensive Cuban/Chinese beanery where such standards as roast pork and shredded beef are the standouts. ♦ Cuban/Chinese ♦ Daily lunch and dinner. No credit cards accepted. 2199 Broadway (at W 78th St). 874.2780

69 Apthorp Apartments Designed by **Clinton & Russell** and built in 1908, this is the best of the three big West Side courtyard buildings (the **Belnord** on West 86th Street and **Astor Court** on Broadway between West 89th and West 90th Streets are the others). The ornate ironwork here is especially wonderful. It was built by William Waldorf Astor, who owned much of the land in the area, and was named for the man who had owned the site in 1763. ♦ 2101-2119 Broadway (between W 78th and W 79th Sts)

70 Stand-Up NY Up-and-coming and established merchants of the one-liner play this comedy club. ♦ Cover, minimum. Shows: M-Th, Su 9PM; F 9PM, 11:30PM; Sa 7:30PM, 9:30PM, 11:30PM. Reservations required. 236 W 78th St (between Amsterdam Ave and Broadway). 595.0850 &

71 Two Two Two ★★★$$$$ This skylit town-house restaurant has detailed oak paneling, classic oil paintings, and an ornate crystal chandelier, all of which set the tone for the exquisite menu that includes fresh white and black truffles served on homemade gnocchi simmered in gorgonzola, white truffle butter, cream sauce, and wild mushrooms. For those with room left for dessert, try the excellent maple crème brûlée or fresh fruit sorbets. There are two wine lists, one American and one French, both full of exceptional (and expensive) selections. ♦ Continental ♦ Daily dinner. Reservations recommended. 222 W 79th St (between Amsterdam Ave and Broadway). 799.0400 &

71 Eastern Seafood Company ★$ The decor at this simple seafood house consists of brown vinyl booths and green-and-white checkered tablecloths. The food isn't fancy

either, but when it tastes this good, it doesn't have to be. Get the littleneck clams on the half shell, steamed mussels, grilled swordfish with sweet-apple salsa, or seared tuna steak in a red-wine sauce. There's also an adjoining retail market for fresh fish. ♦ Seafood ♦ M-Sa lunch and dinner; Su brunch and dinner. 212 W 79th St (between Amsterdam Ave and Broadway). 595.5007

72 21-131 West 78th Street Built in 1886 by Raphael Gustavino, an Italian mason famous for his vaults (see the **Oyster Bar** at **Grand Central Terminal**), these six red and white houses are unified by their symmetrical arrangement and cheery details. ♦ Between Columbus and Amsterdam Aves

73 Alice Underground Climb down into this large basement store for an eclectic mix of inexpensive, wearable separates and outerwear for men and women, much of it unisex fashion, from the 1950s to the 1970s. ♦ Daily. 380 Columbus Ave (between W 78th and W 79th Sts). 724.6682. Also at: 481 Broadway (at Broome St). 431.9067

73 Only Hearts Silky lingerie, sweet-smelling sachets, jewelry, books about hearts and kissing, and heart-shaped waffle irons and fly swatters are sold in this pretty shop for the shameless romantic. ♦ Daily. 386 Columbus Ave (between W 78th and W 79th Sts). 724.5608 &

74 Bag One Arts Named after the interviews that John Lennon and Yoko Ono gave from the inside of a black bag, this gallery sells limited-edition graphics by the ex-Beatle. ♦ By appointment only. 110 W 79th St (between Columbus and Amsterdam Aves). 595.5537 &

75 Laura Ashley Floral patterns, frilly trim, and classic understatement are the Laura Ashley trademark. Home furnishings and fashions are also available. It's as if Louisa May Alcott had gone into retailing a century later. ♦ Daily. 398 Columbus Ave (at W 79th St). 496.5110. Also at: (home furnishings) 714 Madison Ave (between E 63rd and E 64th Sts). 735.5000; (clothing) 21 E 57th St (between Madison and Fifth Aves). 752.7300

76 American Museum of Natural History This preeminent scientific research institution is one of the top cultural draws in New York City. Its collections—more than 34 million artifacts and specimens—constitute a priceless record of life, illuminating millions of years of evolution from the birth of the planet through the present day.

Built in 1872 in the middle of a landscape of goats and squatters, the original building (designed by **Jacob Wrey Mould** and **Calvert Vaux**) can now be glimpsed only from Columbus Avenue. The body of the museum (built in 1899 by **J.C. Cady & Co.** and **Cady, Berg & See,** with later additions by **Charles**

Vos and **Trowbridge & Livingston**), an example of Romanesque Revival at its grandest, can best be admired from West 77th Street. The building itself is nothing if not a piecemeal reflection of changing tastes in style. In between the turreted extensions, a massive carriage entrance passes under a sweeping flight of stairs: The heavy red-brown brick and granite add to the medieval aura and positive strength typified by the seven-arch colonnade. That welcoming entrance is now ignored, and the main facade of the museum has been shifted to the recently renovated **Theodore Roosevelt Memorial** facing Central Park West—a Beaux Arts triumphal arch and terrace designed by **John Russell Pope** in 1936. On top of the four giant Ionic columns are statues of explorers *Boone, Audubon,* and *Lewis and Clark* (these and the attic frieze are by James Earle Fraser; the animal relief is by James L. Clark). Behind this facade is intimidating **Memorial Hall.**

The museum is widely recognized as having the greatest collection of fossil vertebrates in the world. The dinosaur and fossil halls reopened in 1995 as part of an extensive ongoing $45-million remodeling that will restructure the entire fourth floor, adding six exhibition halls to tell the story of the evolution of vertebrates. Barosaurus, the world's tallest freestanding dinosaur exhibit, stands majestically in the **Theodore Roosevelt Hall.** The museum is returning the halls to their original splendor—expanding exhibition spaces, revealing architectural details that include grand arches and columns, and providing panoramic views of **Central Park.**

The **Wallace Wing,** housing two new fossil halls, displays an extraordinary assemblage of fossil mammals, including saber-toothed cats, woolly mammoths, giant sloths, and bizarre reptilelike creatures with three-foot sails on their backs. An interactive computer system allows visitors to explore different locations and time periods and the animals that inhabited them. Of the four exhibitions under construction, two dinosaur halls opened in the 1995 and showcase Tyrannosaurus rex and Apatosaurus, dramatically remounted to reflect new scientific thinking, along with Triceratops, a duck-billed dinosaur mummy, and dozens more. The final two halls, plus an orientation center and a hall of primitive vertebrates, is set to open in the spring of 1996. **The Hall of Human Biology and Evolution,** the newest permanent exhibit, examines the heritage we share with other living things and traces the patterns of human evolution using the latest multimedia technology and exhibit techniques. *The New York Times* predicted the hall will be "the most popular museum exhibition New York City has seen."

The museum has an ongoing program of lectures, films, plays, workshops, and concerts. Free Museum Highlights Tours assemble at the second-floor information desk approximately every hour. Two gift shops, one just for children, offer Mexican and Indian crafts, microscopes, puppets, books, petrified wood, and other surprises. There are three restaurants: the **Whale's Lair** (cocktails and snacks), the **Garden Cafe** (lunch and dinner in a greenhouse setting), and **Dinersaurus** (cafeteria). Limited paid parking is available in the museum lot, on West 81st Street. ◆ Suggested admission. M-Th, Su; F-Sa 10AM-8:45PM. Central Park W and 79th St. 769.5000

American Museum of Natural History

Michael Storrings

Hayden Planetarium

Michael Storrings

At the American Museum of Natural History:

Nature Max Theater Super-spectacular films are shown daily on a four-story-high screen that puts you right into the action. ♦ Admission. Call for schedule. 769.5000 &

76 Hayden Planetarium The copper dome on the brick box outside is an obvious reflection of the spaces inside, which house astronomy exhibitions such as the *Hall of the Sun,* the *Laserium,* and *Astronomia.* The **Sky Theater** auditorium is 75 feet in diameter and 48 feet to the top of the dome, and hosts the famous *Sky Shows* that keep you in touch with what the heavens are up to. Imbedded into the concrete in front of the planetarium is Michele Oka Doner's *Celestial Plaza,* a sculpture comprising 300 cast bronze pieces that represent astronomical bodies. Renovations are scheduled to begin in 1997. Admission charge covers museum. ♦ Admission. Call for schedule. Central Park W and W 81st St). 769.5920 &

77 The Beresford On a street of twin-towered landmarks, this deluxe 1939 apartment building designed by **Emery Roth** distinguishes itself by having three rather squat Baroque turrets that give it a double silhouette from two directions. Famous residents have included poet Sara Teasdale, underworld crime leader Meyer Lansky, Margaret Mead, and Rock Hudson. Tennis great John McEnroe and newscaster Peter Jennings are among the current residents. ♦ 211 Central Park W (at W 81st St). 787.2100

78 Excelsior $ In a classy block across the street from the grounds of the **American**

Museum of Natural History, this budget hotel caters to the convention crowd. The majority of the 150 guestquarters are one-bedroom suites. ♦ 45 W 81st St (between Central Park W and Columbus Ave). 362.9200, 800/368.4575; fax 721.2994

79 Charivari Workshop One of five stores in the Weiser family–owned chain featuring the latest inspirations from such designers as Dolce & Gabbana, Paul Smith, and Katharine Hamnett. ♦ Daily. 441 Columbus Ave (between W 81st and W 82nd Sts). 496.8700. Also at: 18 W 57th St (between Fifth and Sixth Aves). 333.4040; 1001 Madison Ave (between E 57th and E 58th Sts). 650.0078; 58 W 72nd St (at Columbus Ave). 787.7272; 201 W 79th St (at Amsterdam Ave). 799.8650 &

79 Maxilla & Mandible When they say you can find anything in this city, they mean it. This shop specializes in selling all types of bones. Definitely worth a visit. ♦ Daily. 451 Columbus Ave (between W 81st and W 82nd Sts). 724.6173

80 Penny Whistle Toys The Pustefix teddy bear out front is forever blowing bubbles to get your attention. If he could talk, he'd tell you all about the quality classics inside: board games, stuffed animals, dolls, cars, indoor gyms, table soccer games, rattles for infants, and—surprise—no electronic video games! The shop is owned by Meredith Brokaw—yes, she's Tom's wife. ♦ Daily. 448 Columbus Ave (between W 81st and W 82nd Sts). 873.9090. Also at: 1283 Madison Ave (between E 91st and E 92nd Sts). 369.3868

80 Greenstones & Cie European clothing for children, including brightly colored French sportswear from Petit Boy and Maugin and dressy duds from Italy's Mona Lisa, are sold. Happily, nothing is so extravagant that it's unwearable. ♦ Daily. 442 Columbus Ave (between W 81st and W 82nd Sts). 580.4322. Also at: 1184 Madison Ave (between E 86th and E 87th Sts). 427.1665

81 Pizzeria Uno $ The deep-dish, Chicago-style pizza at this chain outpost is a decent pie. This place also happens to be one of the very few near the **American Museum of Natural History** that is appropriate for children—the express lunch is ready in five minutes. ♦ Pizza ♦ Daily lunch, dinner, and late-night meals. 432 Columbus Ave (at W 81st St). 595.4700. Also at: South Street Seaport. 791.7999; 391 Sixth Ave (between Waverly Pl and W 8th St). 242.5230

82 Sarabeth's Kitchen ★★$$ One of the better—and busier—brunch spots in the neighborhood, this place serves pancakes and waffles with fresh fruit that are simply delicious. In winter, Sarabeth's hot porridge is something of a miracle cure. If you don't feel like waiting in line for weekend brunch, try any meal during the week. Don't miss the lemon linguine with a rich, spicy vegetarian sauce of tomato, eggplant, onion, pepper, olives, and basil. For dessert, try the Budapest cake (a buttery cinnamon bundt cake). ♦ American ♦ M-F breakfast, lunch, and dinner; Sa-Su brunch and dinner. Reservations accepted for dinner only. 423 Amsterdam Ave (between W 80th and W 81st Sts). 496.6280. Also at: 1295 Madison Ave (between E 92nd and E 93rd Sts). 410.7355; the Whitney Museum, 945 Madison Ave (at E 75th St). 570.3670

83 Baci ★$$ Zippy but uneven Sicilian fare is served in this upbeat, handsome candlelit dining room. Pasta dishes are the best bets here, particularly the gnocchi with pesto, and rigatoni with cauliflower, raisins, pine nuts, and tomato sauce. ♦ Italian ♦ Daily lunch and dinner. No credit cards accepted. 412 Amsterdam Ave (between W 79th and W 80th Sts). 496.1550

83 Dublin House Tap Room At night, the area's younger, newer residents take over this former workingman's retreat, and the place gets very lively indeed. The brilliant neon harp over the door beckons you to have a lager, and the separate back room makes you wish you'd invited the whole team. ♦ M-Sa 8AM-4AM; Su noon-4AM. 225 W 79th St (between Amsterdam Ave and Broadway). 874.9528

84 Filene's Basement This longtime Boston tradition came first to New York via Queens, and now another store on Broadway. Known for selling perfect and slightly damaged clothing and shoes for men and women from the country's best department stores at bargain prices, this store gave rise to the expression "bargain basement." ♦ Daily. 2222 Broadway (at W 79th St). 875.0161 &

85 VideoTown Laundrette Come here to make copies, rent videos or a mailbox, send or receive a fax, soak up some rays in the tanning salon and, oh yes, do your laundry. ♦ Daily 7AM-midnight. 217 W 80th St (at Broadway). 721.1706 &

85 Gryphon Book Shop Used and rare books are sold at decent prices. Look for general humanities plus theater, performing arts, and children's books, especially the *Oz* series by L. Frank Baum. ♦ Daily 10AM-midnight. 2246 Broadway (between W 80th and W 81st Sts). 362.0706

86 H&H Bagels West It turns out 60,000 bagels a day, some of which are shipped as far as London! Count on getting one fresh from the oven around the clock. This also happens to be one of the last Manhattan bastions of the "baker's dozen" (buy 12, get 13). While you're at it, check out the section of kosher and nonkosher deli products. ♦ Daily 24 hours. 2239 Broadway (at W 80th St). 595.8003, 800/692.2435 &. Also at: 639 W 46th St (at 12th Ave). 261.8000 &

87 Zabar's This food bazaar is like no other in the world. Evolved from a small Jewish deli, it's now a giant grocery and housewares store. On weekends, a long line forms for the Western Nova Salmon (if you're lucky, the counter help will pass you a slice to nosh on). ♦ Daily. 2245 Broadway (at W 80th St). 787.2000 &

Adjacent to Zabar's:

Zabar's Cafe ★$ Cappuccino as good as any that can be found on the West Side is served in the neighborhood's most undistinguished interior. Try a warm knish or pastry with your coffee for a superlative afternoon delight. An espresso may be just the restorative you need after a shopping trip to **Zabar's**. ♦ Cafe/Takeout ♦ Daily. 787.2000

Restaurants/Clubs: Red   **Hotels:** Blue

Shops/♥ Outdoors: Green   **Sights/Culture:** Black

88 Barnes & Noble Though this mega-bookstore chain has more than 900 stores around the country, including the **B. Dalton, Doubleday,** and **Scribner's** chains, no branch has opened to such hype and acclaim as this one. One of 110 "superstores" throughout the US—this vast two-story space has late hours that encourage the neighborhood's singles to cruise in an intelligent environment, and an interior designed to look like a library, with varnished wood, brass lighting fixtures, and Shaker-style chairs and tables where you can sit and read for hours. ♦ M-Th, Su 9AM-11PM; F-Sa 9AM-midnight. 2289 Broadway (at W 82nd St). 362.8835. Also at other locations ᕷ

Within Barnes & Noble:

Barnes & Noble Cafe $ One of the singles bars of the 1990s (*New York Magazine* recently listed this particular place as one of "Fifteen Ways to Meet Your Lover"), this cafe offers decent espresso and a sedate, literary atmosphere. ♦ Cafe ♦ Daily. 2289 Broadway (at W 82nd St). 362.8835. Also at: 4 Astor Pl (between Broadway and Lafayette St). 420.1332; 675 Sixth Ave (between 21st and 22nd Sts). 727.1227; Citicorp Center, 160 E 54th St (between Third and Lexington Aves). 750.8033

89 The Yarn Co. In addition to being one of the best sources for yarn and expert knitting instruction in the city, this is one of the most pleasant yarn shops, boasting an oversize wooden farm table and chairs in the center of the room and an abundant stock of high-quality yarns. ♦ Tu-Sa. 2274 Broadway (between W 81st and W 82nd Sts), Second floor. 787.7878

90 Bath Island An oasis for stressed-out New Yorkers in search of biodegradable beauty and bath products—shampoo, essential perfume oils, and bubble bath. You can't miss the store; every morning they scent the sidewalk with hot sudsy water and one of the 75 available perfume oils. ♦ Daily. 469 Amsterdam Ave (between W 82nd and W 83rd Sts). 787.9415

91 Shoofly You may want to only admire, not buy, the adorable children's shoes and accessories here, as many cost more than parents spend on their *own* shopping sprees. The European shoes are displayed on low shelves that children can reach (gulp!), and the hats, either from Europe or made by local artisans, are each hung on a different-shaped hook, ranging from a dinosaur to a crab to a corn cob. ♦ Daily. 465 Amsterdam Ave (between W 82nd and W 83rd Sts). 580.4390

91 Avventura Gorgeous hand-painted pottery imported from all over the world, particularly Italy, is on display at this handsome store. The one-of-a-kind platters, bowls, and plates are absolute knockouts. ♦ M-Th, Su; F until sunset. 463 Amsterdam Ave (between W 82nd and W 83rd Sts). 769.2510

Silk Road Palace

92 The Silk Road Palace ★$ The name of this small restaurant is a tad overstated (in fact, the place is anything but palatial), but the crowd forever outside waiting for a table is proof that the management is on to something with its combination of good, reasonably priced Chinese food and friendly service. ♦ Hunan/Szechuan ♦ M-Th, Su lunch and dinner; F-Sa lunch, dinner, and late-night meals. 447B Amsterdam Ave (between W 81st and W 82nd Sts). 580.6294

92 Louie's Westside Cafe ★$$ Grand yet casual, this cafe with peach walls, subdued lighting, and French rattan chairs offers a basic but well-prepared American menu, with something for everyone. Try the crab cakes, spinach linguine with turkey *bolognese,* herb-roasted chicken, hanger steak, lamb chops with Tuscan white-bean stew, or *pasta primavera.* For dessert, have the mocha torte, chocolate velvet cake, or carrot cake. Brunch may be the best meal to have here; try the pecan waffles or Southwestern style eggs. ♦ American ♦ M-F breakfast, lunch, and dinner; Sa-Su brunch and dinner. Reservations recommended. 441 Amsterdam Ave (at W 81st St). 877.1900 ᕷ

FUJIYAMA MAMA

93 Fujiyama Mama ★$$ Not your ordinary Japanese restaurant, this place has loud rock music and waitresses dressed in traditional kimonos. The menu has some interesting offerings, especially the *yakitori* (broiled dishes), but gives dishes strange, incomprehensible names: Chicken teriyaki, for some reason, is called "Chicken the Chicken," and sirloin with vegetables in a curry sauce is "Agony and Ecstasy." ♦ Japanese ♦ Daily dinner. Reservations recommended. 467 Columbus Ave (between W 82nd and W 83rd Sts). 769.1144

94 Isola ★$$ The apricot and yellow walls, covered with wave and fish stencils, evoke an Italian island feeling. Good picks from the menu include delicious thin-crusted pizzas, and pasta with sardines, pine nuts, fennel, and raisins. ♦ Italian ♦ Daily lunch and dinner. 485 Columbus Ave (between W 83rd and W 84th Sts). 362.7400 &

94 Handblock For those who like the exotic look of handblocked fabrics, this is an oasis. The owners have asked their suppliers in India to make traditional patterns as well as totally untraditional ones, such as checks and Provençal-inspired florals, and to whip them up into pillowcases, duvet covers, tablecloths, placemats, and pillow shams. The fabrics themselves are not stocked. ♦ Daily. 487 Columbus Ave (between W 83rd and W 84th Sts). 799.4342 &

95 Down & Quilt Shop Reasonably priced quilts and down comforters are this store's specialty. ♦ Daily. 518 Columbus Ave (at W 85th St). 496.8980

96 Harriet's Kitchen Excellent chicken soup and straightforward family fare— roast chicken with green beans and carrots, fudge layer cake—are available from this unpretentious take-out shop that opens its doors in late afternoon, just when hard-working parents and professionals decide they're not in the mood to cook. ♦ M-Sa 4:30-11PM; Su 4:30-10PM. 502 Amsterdam Ave (between W 84th and W 85th Sts). 721.0045

97 Good Enough to Eat ★★$$ Breakfast or a weekend brunch are the best bets at this tiny Vermont-style outpost. But be prepared to wait in line for pecan-flecked waffles, cinnamon-swirl French toast, or the lumberjack breakfast—it's as big as it sounds. Lunch and dinner are prepared with a homey, if less inventive, touch. Popular picks include

a turkey dinner with gravy, stuffing, and cranberry sauce, meat loaf, and turkey club sandwich. ♦ American ♦ M-F breakfast, lunch, and dinner; Sa-Su brunch and dinner. Reservations recommended for dinner. 483 Amsterdam Ave (between W 83rd and W 84th Sts). 496.0163

98 The Raccoon Lodge West Siders come to this bar for the pool table, friendly atmosphere, great jukebox, and cheap drinks. ♦ M-F 11AM-4AM; Sa-Su 3PM-4AM. 480 Amsterdam Ave (at W 83rd St). 874.9984. Also at: 59 Warren St (at W Broadway). 766.9656; 1439 York Ave (between E 76th and E 77th Sts). 650.1775

98 Cafe Lalo ★$ This dessert-only cafe with brick walls and a wooden floor has long French-style windows that open onto the street. During the day, it's quite pleasant to linger over a cappuccino and such desserts as cappuccino tart, Snicker's Bar cheesecake, lemon mousse cake, chocolate Vienna torte, and assorted fruit pies. At night, it tends to get crowded and loud. ♦ Cafe ♦ Daily until 2AM weeknights, 4AM weekends. 201 W 83rd St (at Amsterdam Ave). 496.6031

99 Children's Museum of Manhattan This educational playground of interactive exhibitions and activity centers is all built around the museum's theme of self-discovery. On the second floor is the **Time Warner Center for Media,** where children can produce their own videotapes, news-casts, and public affairs programs. Exhibition interpreters are always on hand to provide assistance, and entertainers are stationed at key points to provide further understanding through song, dance, or puppetry. There is an art studio where classes in book-and paper-making and other studio arts are held, and a theater where performances are given by theater groups, dancers, musicians, puppeteers, and storytellers, as well as children participating in the museum's education and video programs and workshops. ♦ Admission. M, W-Th 1:30-5:30PM; F-Su 10AM-5PM. 212 W 83rd St (between Amsterdam Ave and Broadway). 721.1223 &

100 Sony Theaters 84th Street Once a grand movie palace, the **Loew's 84th Street** is now a suburban-style, multiscreened venture tucked rather discreetly onto a row of retail shops on the ground floor of the **Bromley.** If you remember the old place, you'll be disappointed; if you want to see a movie, you'll go anyway—they're showing them all. ♦ 2310 Broadway (at W 84th St). 877.3600

101 Ollie's Noodle Shop ★$ Cold sesame noodles; scallion pancakes; vegetable, pork, or shrimp dumplings are all favorites at this bargain-priced Chinese restaurant. ♦ Chinese ♦ Daily lunch, dinner, and late-night meals. 2315 Broadway (at W 84th St). 362.3712 &. Also at: 2957 Broadway (at 116th St). 932.3300; 200 W 44th St (between Broadway and Eighth Ave). 921.5988

102 Patzo $ The pizza at this two-level Italian restaurant has a thin, well-baked crust, and the list of toppings offered will make you dizzy. Good pasta is also available. ♦ Italian ♦ Daily lunch and dinner. 2330 Broadway (at W 85th St). 496.9240 &

103 520 West End Avenue Neighborhood residents vehemently defended their many-gabled "castle" when, in 1987, a misled developer proposed building an apartment house on this site. This survivor was built in 1892 to the designs of **Clarence F. True.** ♦ At W 85th St

104 The Red House Designed by **Harde & Short** and built in 1904, this six-story apartment building is a cross between an Elizabethan manor and a redbrick row house. Note the dragon and crown near the top. ♦ 350 W 85th St (between West End Ave and Riverside Dr)

105 The Clarendon In 1908, William Randolph Hearst moved his family into a 30-room apartment on the top three floors of this 1903 building designed by **Charles Birge.** In 1913, when the landlord refused to ask the residents on the other nine floors to leave so that Hearst, his family, and his art collection could spread out, Hearst simply purchased the building and forced them out himself. Faced with financial woes, he sold the property in 1938. ♦ 137 Riverside Dr (at W 86th St)

106 La Mirabelle ★$$$ A fresh, inviting decor, efficient service, and food that is a notch above the ordinary keep this French bistro busy. Good choices are escargots, soft-shell crabs cooked with lots of garlic and tomatoes, a pink, spicy rack of lamb, and the best steak *frites* (with french fries) on the West Side. Go elsewhere to satisfy your sweet tooth. ♦ French ♦ Daily dinner. Reservations recommended. 333 W 86th St (between West End Ave and Riverside Dr). 496.0458

Child's Play

1 Feel like a shrimp under the 10-ton blue whale or get lost in the stars at the **Planetarium.** Or perhaps you'd rather travel the earth with T-Rex in the **Dinosaur Hall.** All are at the **American Museum of Natural History.**

2 Little sweet teeth will love the fabulously tasty "Bocce Ball" (Italian ice cream covered with chocolate), but even the simple two-scoop cone is grand when eaten at **Rumpelmayer's.**

3 The **New York City Ballet**'s *Nutcracker Suite* brings dancing toy soldiers, evil mice, and sugarplum fairies to **Lincoln Center.**

4 The **New York Philharmonic**'s *Young People's Concerts* at **Avery Fisher Hall** include talks to introduce kids to classical music.

5 Getting into the **Brooklyn Children's Museum** through a 180-foot tunnel and waterway is half the fun.

6 You can climb up on a mushroom and join Alice, the Cheshire Cat, and the Mock Turtle at José de Creeft's statue overlooking **Central Park**'s **Conservatory Water.**

7 One of the best ways to enjoy **Lower Manhattan** is with a view from the river of a replica of an 18th-century steamboat at the **South Street Seaport.**

8 Hear readings from your favorite book by the author at **Books of Wonder.**

9 Produce your own newscasts and public affairs programs at the **Time Warner Center for Media** at the **Children's Museum of Manhattan.**

Upper West Side

A neighborhood in transition, the Upper West Side (the area bordered by **Central Park**, the **Hudson River**, **West 86th Street**, and **Cathedral Parkway/West 110th Street**) is undergoing the same kind of gentrifying process that has taken place farther south. The commercial zone is extending north along **Broadway** and **Amsterdam** and **Columbus Avenues**, and the residential zone that surrounds **Columbia University** is moving south along those same streets. While the **Central Park** blocks (the numbered streets between Columbus Avenue and **Central Park West**) contain brownstones and apartments that are in excellent condition as far north as **West 95th Street**, even the blocks of tenements and middle-income apartments between Amsterdam Avenue and Broadway, in disrepair for years, have become desirable residences—if only for their proximity to the burgeoning shopping and dining strips. The residential **West End Avenue** and **Riverside Drive** remain staunchly unchanged, except perhaps for the parade of new windows in the grand old high-rises, most of which have been converted to co-ops as far north as **Duke Ellington Boulevard (West 106th Street)**.

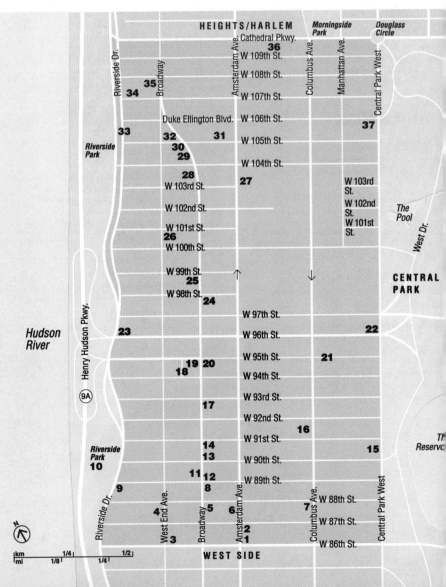

Whereas only a few years ago it seemed to be a fading reminder of the Old World, the West Side north of West 86th Street is now a thriving cosmopolitan mix that feels like the best of both worlds. New high-rise buildings fronted by sidewalk cafes and attractive retail stores are graceful and stabilizing elements to a rapidly changing upper Broadway. Columbus Avenue buzzes with life spilling in and out of its restaurants, bars, antiques shops, and clothing stores. Even the area from **West 96th** to West 110th Streets is sprucing up, particularly east of Broadway, where what was once considered the periphery of Harlem has been given a name of its own— **Manhattan Valley**—and is now more readily associated with the Upper West Side. And while there's easy access to **Central Park** on the eastern side of this area, to the west is **Riverside Park**, a 50-block oasis along the Hudson River, designed by Frederick Law Olmsted, creator of **Central Park.**

1 West Park Presbyterian Church

Originally the **Park Presbyterian Church,** this church was built in 1890 to the designs of **Henry F. Kilburn.** The rough-hewn red sandstone of the Richardsonian Romanesque mass is enlivened by the lightness of the almost Byzantine details of the capitals and doorways and the fineness of the colonettes in the tower. The church's boldness is emphasized by the asymmetrical massing, with the single tower holding the corner between two strong facades. ♦ 165 W 86th (at Amsterdam Ave). 362.4890 ⑰

2 Barney Greengrass (The Sturgeon King) ★★$

Supplying the West Side with appetizing food since 1908, this place, run by Barney's son Moe and grandson Gary, is folksier than **Zabar's,** though not as complete. On one side is a smoked fish counter with perfect smoked salmon, sturgeon, pickled herring, and chopped liver. On the other is an earthy dining room with brown vinyl seats, fluorescent lighting that makes everyone look like they need to be hospitalized. And inscrutably, there's a mural of New Orleans. ♦ Deli ♦ Tu-Su breakfast and lunch. No credit cards accepted. 541 Amsterdam Ave (between W 86th and W 87th Sts). 724.4707

2 Popover Café ★$$

A cozy spot with white brick walls and paisley banquettes, this place has teddy bears scattered around the room for company. Breakfast is a popular meal here—the neighborhood piles in for freshly made popovers. There are also good salads and sandwiches at lunchtime, and at dinner, more serious food is offered. ♦ American ♦ M-F breakfast, lunch, and dinner; Sa-Su brunch and dinner. 551 Amsterdam Ave (at W 87th St). 595.8555 ⑰

3 Church of St. Paul and St. Andrew

Built in 1897 and designed by **R.H. Robertson,** this church has overtones of the manners of Boulee, particularly in the octagonal tower. Note the angels in the spandrels. ♦ 263 W 86th St (at West End Ave). 362.3179 ⑰

4 565 West End Avenue

Designed by **H.I. Feldman** in 1937, this is a Neo-Renaissance building in Art Deco fabric—brick instead of stone, corner windows instead of quoins. At the bottom, banded brick represents the shadow of a traditional plinth, and the cornice is stainless steel. ♦ Between W 87th and W 88th Sts

5 Boulevard $

The wide-ranging menu at this big, comfortable place with a nice outdoor cafe includes so-so barbecue brisket, ribs, roast chicken, burgers, burritos, and angel-hair *pasta primavera*. The Monday dinner special, all-you-can-eat chicken and ribs, is a deal. ♦ American ♦ M-Th lunch and dinner; F lunch, dinner, and late-night meals; Sa-Su brunch, dinner, and late-night meals. 2398 Broadway (at W 88th St). 874.7400 &

6 Ozu ★$ This simple earthy room with exposed-brick walls and wood furniture serves good salmon teriyaki, and such macrobiotic fare as soba (buckwheat) noodle dishes; salads; a variety of grains, steamed vegetables, and seaweeds; and soups that include miso, pea, and carrot ginger. ♦ Japanese ♦ M-F lunch and dinner; Sa-Su brunch and dinner. 566 Amsterdam Ave (between W 87th and W 88th Sts). 787.8316 &

6 Pandit ★$ Save yourself the trek down to the East Village's Little India and have a memorable meal here in this cozy brick-walled room. Try any of the curries, chicken *saag* (cooked with spinach in a spicy sauce), or chicken *biryani* (curried and served on a mound of fragrant rice). ♦ Indian ♦ Daily dinner. 566 Amsterdam Ave (between W 87th and W 88th Sts). 724.1217

6 Les Routiers ★$$ This quaint French bistro with wood beams and baskets of dried flowers has a fairly classic menu that features such items as onion soup; *boeuf bourguignon;* braised lamb shank with tomato, lentils, and Provençal herbs; roast duck with raspberry and green-peppercorn sauce; lemon tart; and chocolate mousse. The wine list is well chosen and reasonably priced. ♦ French ♦ Daily dinner. 568 Amsterdam Ave (between W 87th and W 88th Sts). 874.2742

7 Grossinger's Uptown Bake Shop An old-fashioned kosher bakery, this place sells such traditional Jewish baked goods as coffee cake, cheesecake, chocolate layer cookies, danish, rugalach, hamantaschen, and the kind of buttercream-frosted birthday cakes you had as a kid. ♦ M-Th, Su; F until sundown. 570 Columbus Ave (at W 88th St). 874.6996

7 East West Books A New Age bookstore is home to the **Himalayan Institute of New York,** which offers instruction in many areas, including yoga, meditation, relaxation and breathing, homeopathy, and stress management. ♦ Daily. 568 Columbus

Ave (between W 87th and W 88th Sts). 787.7552 &

8 Westside Judaica Religious articles and a large stock of fiction and nonfiction covering all aspects of the Jewish experience are sold, along with cassette tapes, videos, and holiday decorations for children's parties. ♦ M-Th, F 10:30AM-2PM; Su. 2412 Broadway (between W 88th and W 89th Sts). 362.7846 &

9 Yeshiva Chofetz Chaim Isaac L. Rice had this house built in 1901 and named it **Villa Julia** for his wife, the founder of the now defunct Society for the Suppression of Unnecessary Noise. This and the former **Schinasi Residence** (351 Riverside Drive) are the only two mansions left from the days when Riverside Drive was lined with them. Note the slightly askew porte cochere (a porch large enough for wheeled vehicles to pass through). The architects, **Herts & Tallant,** also designed the **Lyceum Theater.** ♦ 346 W 89th St (at Riverside Dr). 362.1435

10 Riverside Park Originally designed by Frederick Law Olmsted (of **Central Park**) from 1873 to 1910, this welcome strip of greenery stretches for three miles (blessedly covering a rail line below), with space for jogging, tennis, and baseball. When there's snow, people actually sleigh ride and cross-country ski here. Additions were made to the park in 1888 by **Calvert Vaux** and Samuel Parsons Jr., and in 1937 by Clinton F. Lloyd. Not a monument in itself, as is **Central Park,** this piece of land is spattered with a few little memorials—most notably the *Soldiers' and Sailors' Monument* designed in 1902 by **Stoughton & Stoughton** and **Paul E.M. Duboy** at West 89th Street, modeled after the Choragic Monument of Lysicrates in Athens; the *Firemen's Memorial* at West 100th Street, designed in 1913 by sculptor

Attilio Piccirilli and architect **H. Van Buren Magonigle,** and graced by statues of *Courage and Duty;* and the easy-to-overlook but not-to-be-forgotten *Carrère Memorial* (1916), a small terrace and plaque at West 99th Street honoring the great architect **John Merven Carrère,** designed by his partner **Thomas Hastings. Carrère** died in an automobile accident in 1911. ♦ Bounded by Riverside Dr and the Hudson River, and W 72nd and W 145th Sts

11 Docks Oyster Bar and Seafood Grill ★★$$ Fresh seafood is featured in this lively black-and-white–tiled neighborhood haunt. Worth trying are the crab cakes, grilled snapper, and fried calamari. Dessert specials include mud cake and Key lime pie. Stop in on Sunday or Monday night for a full New England clambake. ♦ Seafood ♦ M-F lunch and dinner; Sa-Su brunch and dinner. Reservations recommended. 2427 Broadway (between W 89th and W 90th Sts). 724.5588. Also at: 633 Third Ave (at E 40th St). 986.8080

11 Murray's Sturgeon For more than a half-century, the ultimate Jewish appetizing store has continued to live up to its reputation for high-quality sturgeon, herring, lox, whitefish, and other smoked fish items. The store also carries caviar, coffee beans, and dried fruit. ♦ Daily. 2429 Broadway (between W 89th and W 90th Sts). 724.2650

12 The Armadillo $ If you're in the mood for a lively scene, this is the place. Have the chili, or for something slightly more ambitious, try the pork loin with apple salsa or grilled Gulf shrimp with orange and green-onion salsa. ♦ Tex-Mex ♦ M-F dinner and late-night meals; Sa-Su brunch, dinner, and late-night meals. 2420 Broadway (at W 89th St). 496.1066

13 The Hero's Journey Although this shop carries all the latest crystals, New Age books, trinkets, and paraphernalia, some might feel that spiritualism and commercialism just aren't meant to mix the way they do here. ♦ Daily. 2440 Broadway (at W 90th St). 874.4630

14 Carmine's $$ Come hungry and bring at least one friend to share the huge portions

of Southern Italian fare; all meals are meant for two or more. There's also a take-out shop next door. ♦ Italian ♦ Dinner. 2450 Broadway (between W 90th and W 91st Sts). 362.2200. Also at: 200 W 44th St (between Broadway and Eighth Ave). 221.3800

15 The Eldorado The northernmost of the twin-towered silhouettes on Central Park West, this apartment building, designed by **Margon & Holder** and built in 1931, is characterized by its Art Deco detailing. ♦ 300 Central Park W (between W 90th and W 91st Sts)

16 Trinity School and Trinity House The main building was built in 1894 to the designs of **Charles C. Haight;** the east building was designed by **William A. Potter** in 1892; and the apartment tower and school addition were designed by **Brown, Guenther, Battaglia, Seckler** in 1969. Straight, wonderful Romanesque Revival, now locked to an intricate 1960s tower, it is much better than average. ♦ House: 100 W 92nd St; School: 101 W 91st St (between Columbus and Amsterdam Aves). House: 724.1313. School: 873.1650

17 Murder Ink. The grandmother of all mystery bookstores, this is just the way you picture it: cozy and English, with fat fuzzy cats and a clutter of new and out-of-print mysteries, references, and periodicals. Most major mystery authors do signings here. ♦ Daily. 2486 Broadway (between W 92nd and W 93rd Sts). 362.8905. Also at: 1465 Second Ave (between E 76th and E 77th Sts). 517.3222; 1 Whitehall St (at Broadway). 742.7025 ♿

18 Pomander Walk A surprising little enclave, this double row of mock-Tudor town houses was named after a play that was produced in London and played on Broadway in 1911. The houses, designed in 1922 by **King & Campbell,** were meant to look like the stage set for the New York production. Tenants have included Rosalind Russell, Humphrey Bogart, and Lillian and Dorothy Gish. The building is not open to the public. ♦ W 94th to W 95th Sts (between Broadway and West End Ave)

Restaurants/Clubs: Red   **Hotels:** Blue
Shops/ ♦ Outdoors: Green   **Sights/Culture:** Black

SYMPHONY**SPACE**

19 Symphony Space Constructed during the first decade of this century, this building began as the **Crystal Carnival Skating Rink** and was converted into a movie house in the 1920s. Under the guidance of artistic directors Isaiah Sheffer and the late Allan Miller, it has become a performing arts center that has contributed to a cultural renaissance on the Upper West Side. Every year, usually in March, they present a free-of-charge 12-hour musical marathon featuring composers with such tributes as "Wall to Wall Bach," a free birthday salute to John Cage, and a glorious Aaron Copland celebration. Notable supporters include violinists Itzak Perlman and Pinchas Zuckerman, jazz pianist Billy Taylor, composer John Cage, actor Fritz Weaver, and actresses Estelle Parsons and Claire Bloom. Every June 16 they present *Bloomsday on Broadway,* during which James Joyce's novel *Ulysses* is read.♦ 2537 Broadway (between W 94th and W 95th Sts). 864.5400

20 Key West Diner & Café $ The salmon-and-turquoise decor is straight out of the sunshine state, just as the name suggests. Nevertheless, this place is nothing other than a basic New York coffee shop with decent burgers, sandwiches, salads, omelettes, bagels, and challah French toast. ♦ Diner ♦ Daily breakfast, lunch, dinner, and late-night meals. 2532 Broadway (between W 94th and W 95th Sts). 932.0068

21 West 95th Street These blocks of diverse row houses represent one aspect of the Upper West Side Urban Renewal effort. Between the housing projects on the avenues, side streets such as this one, which provide unique and charming character, are being restored. ♦ Between Central Park W and Amsterdam Ave

22 First Church of Christ, Scientist This is, surprisingly, not particularly Beaux Arts, but more in the style of the English Renaissance, with a touch of Hawksmoor in the energetic facade and steeple. The marble interiors are quite impressive. **Carrère & Hastings,** who designed this structure in 1903, were also responsible for the **New York Public Library**

and the **Frick Residence.** ♦ 1 W 96th St (at Central Park W). 749.3088

23 The Cliff Dwellers' Apartments The facade is decorated with a frieze of mountain lions, snakes, and buffalo skulls—symbols of the Arizona cliff dwellers. Designed in 1914 by **Herman Lee Leader,** this is an unusual example of Art Deco interest in prehistoric art and culture. ♦ 243 Riverside Dr (at W 96th St)

24 The Hunan Balcony ★$ It's hard to ask for more from a neighborhood spot: dependably fresh ingredients, low prices, and clean, bright surroundings—and when they say *spicy,* they mean it. ♦ Chinese ♦ Daily lunch, dinner, and late-night meals. Reservations recommended. 2596 Broadway (at W 98th St). 865.0400

25 Health Nuts Hypoallergenic vitamins, natural breads, and organic goods—grains, nuts, herbs, and honey—are sold here. ♦ Daily. 2611 Broadway (at W 99th St) 678.0054. Also at: Numerous locations throughout the city

26 838 West End Avenue Covered with terra cotta decoration, both in geometric patterns and stylized natural forms, this structure was designed by **George Blum** and **Edward Blum** in 1914. ♦ At W 101st St

27 New York International American Youth Hostel (AYH) $ Clean, safe, and inexpensive accommodations come in the form of 90 dorm-style rooms that sleep from four to twelve; there is no curfew, and the hostel stays open all day long. Like other hostels, all guests must be members of American Youth Hostels (nonmembers can join on the spot) and must bring a sleeping bag or rent sheets. The building itself—designed by **Richard Morris Hunt,** and once a home operated by the Association for the Relief of Respectable Aged Indigent Females—is a Designated Landmark of the City of New York. The maximum stay is seven days, but you can apply for an extension. Bathrooms are shared. ♦ 891 Amsterdam Ave (between W 103rd and W 104th Sts). 932.2300 &

28 Broadway Barber Shop The gilt lettering on the windows is fading, but all the other fixtures seem to be intact in this quaint barbershop, which opened in 1907. "It's the oldest barbershop in New York," a heavily accented barber calls out as he circles a supine head in his chair. In addition to a good shave, it's a great photo opportunity. ♦ M-Sa. 2713 Broadway (between W 103rd and W 104th Sts). 666.3042 &

29 Positively 104th Street Cafe ★$
Simple and cozy, this cafe offers a range of fare. Try one of the well-prepared salads—spinach with goat cheese and sun-dried tomatoes, and Cobb—or such sandwiches as roast beef with homemade coleslaw. ♦ American ♦ Daily breakfast, lunch, and dinner. 2725 Broadway (between W 104th and W 105th Sts). 316.0372

30 Au Petit Beurre $ The eclectic Middle Eastern, French, and Mediterranean menu includes a variety of kabob dishes, good tabbouleh, and such French dishes as chicken cooked slowly in Port. Sandwiches and burgers are also available. ♦ Eclectic ♦ Daily breakfast, lunch, and dinner. 2737 Broadway (at W 105th St). 663.7010

31 Metisse ★★★$ Since the day it opened in the space of the former **Santerello,** this cozy bistro has been wowing the neighborhood with its simple, perfectly prepared French food. Try sautéed sweetbreads with whole-grain mustard, potato and goat-cheese terrine with arugula juice, or salmon with creamy mushroom polenta. ♦ French ♦ M-Sa lunch and dinner. Reservations recommended. 239 W 105th St (between Amsterdam Ave and Broadway). 666.8825

32 Birdland ★$$ This jazz-supper club features the likes of pianist Henry Butler, Mark Morganelli and the Jazz Forum All-Stars, and Arthur Taylor's Wailers. ♦ American/Cajun ♦ No cover; drink minimum. Daily dinner and late-night meals. Call for changing schedule of shows. Reservations recommended. 2745 Broadway (at W 105th St). 749.2228

33 Riverside Drive/West 105th Street Historic District Riverside Drive between West 105th and 106th Streets (plus some of West 105th Street) has an excellent collection of turn-of-the-century French Beaux Arts town houses. Of special interest is **No. 331,** designed in 1902 by **Janes & Leo,** formerly Marion Davies's residence and now part of the **New York Buddhist Church** and **American Buddhist Academy.** ♦ Between W 105th and W 106 Sts

34 Nicholas Roerich Museum Roerich was well known in his native Russia and throughout the world as an artist, philosopher, archaeologist, and founder of an educational institution to promote world peace through the arts. This beautiful old town house, one unit of his **Master Institute,** overflows with his landscapes, books, and pamphlets on art, culture, and philosophy. Lectures and concerts take place here. ♦ Donation suggested. Tu-Su 2-5PM. 319 W 107th St (between Broadway and Riverside Dr). 864.7752

35 107 West ★$$ A mostly young, upscale crowd keeps this three-room establishment bustling. The overall tone is Cajun, but the menu throws a few Mexican and pasta specialties into the mix. The wine list offers decent selections at affordable prices. ♦ Eclectic ♦ Daily dinner. 2787 Broadway (between W 107th and W 108th Sts). 864.1555

36 Cathedral Parkway Houses These two massive apartment towers were carefully articulated in an attempt to accommodate them to the much smaller scale of the neighborhood. They were built in 1975 and designed by **Davis, Brody & Associates** and **Roger Glasgow.** ♦ 125 W 109th St (between Columbus and Amsterdam Aves). 749.1100

37 Towers Nursing Home Typically Victorian with its squat towers and conical roofs, this was originally the **New York Cancer Hospital,** the first in the nation devoted to the care of cancer patients. It was designed in 1887 by **Charles C. Haight,** who was also the architect of the main buildings of the **General Theological Seminary** and **Trinity School.** Today it sits abandoned and neglected, waiting for word from Ian Shrager, formerly of **Studio 54** fame, and currently hotelier about town. He has expressed an interest in incorporating this property into his growing number of hotels—this one as a luxury spa. ♦ 2 W 106th St (between Central Park W and Columbus Ave)

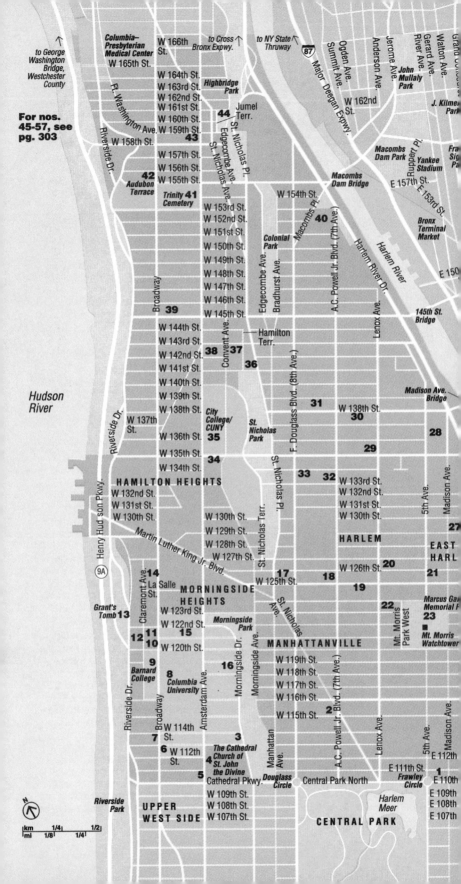

to George
Washington
Bridge,
Westchester
County

**For nos.
45-57, see
pg. 303**

Columbia–
Presbyterian
Medical Center
W 165th St.

W 166th
St.

to Cross
Bronx Expwy.

to NY State
Thruway

87

Major Deegan Expwy.

Ogden Ave.
Summit Ave.
Anderson Ave.

Jerome Ave.

Walton Ave.
Gerard Ave.
River Ave.

grand concourse

John
Mullaly
Park

J. Kilmer
Park

W 164th St.
W 163rd St.
W 162nd St.
W 161st St.
W 160th St.
W 159th St.

Highbridge
Park

Jumel
Terr.

44

43

W 158th St.

W 162nd
St.

Ft. Washington Ave.

Riverside Dr.

St. Nicholas Ave.

Edgecombe Ave.

St. Nicholas Pl.

Macombs
Dam Bridge

Macombs
Dam Park

Ruppert Pl.

Yankee
Stadium

E 157th St.

E 153rd St.

Fra
Sig
Pa

42
Audubon
Terrace

W 157th St.
W 156th St.
W 155th St.

Trinity 41
Cemetery

W 154th St.

Macombs Pl.

40

Bronx
Terminal
Market

Harlem River

E 150

W 153rd St.
W 152nd St.
W 151st St.
W 150th St.
W 149th St.
W 148th St.
W 147th St.
W 146th St.
W 145th St.

Colonial
Park

Edgecombe Ave.

Bradhurst Ave.

A.C. Powell Jr. Blvd. (7th Ave.)

Harlem River Dr.

Lenox Ave.

145th St.
Bridge

Broadway

39

Hudson
River

W 144th St.
W 143rd St.
W 142nd St.
W 141st St.
W 140th St.
W 139th St.
W 138th St.

Hamilton
Terr.

Convent Ave.

38 37

36

City College/
CUNY

F. Douglass Blvd. (8th Ave.)

31

St.
Nicholas
Park

W 138th St.

Madison Ave.
Bridge

30

28

Riverside Dr.

W 137th
St.

W 136th St.

W 135th St.

W 134th St.

35

34

St. Nicholas Terr.

29

33 32

W 133rd St.
W 132nd St.
W 131st St.
W 130th St.

5th Ave.

Madison Ave.

HAMILTON HEIGHTS

W 132nd St.
W 131st St.
W 130th St.

W 130th St.
W 129th St.
W 128th St.
W 127th St.

St. Nicholas Terr.

HARLEM

EAST
HARL

27

Henry Hudson Pkwy.

9A

Martin Luther King Jr. Blvd.

14
La Salle
St.

Claremont Ave.

MORNINGSIDE
HEIGHTS

St. Nicholas Ave.

17

18

W 126th St.

19

20

21

Grant's
Tomb 13

12 11
10

15

W 123rd St.

W 122nd St.

Morningside
Park

Morningside Dr.

Morningside Ave.

22

Mt. Morris
Park West

Marcus Ga
Memorial F

23

Mt. Morris
Watchtower

9
Barnard
College

8
Columbia
University

16

MANHATTANVILLE

W 119th St.
W 118th St.
W 117th St.
W 116th St.
W 115th St.

A.C. Powell Jr. Blvd. (7th Ave.)

Lenox Ave.

5th Ave.

Madison Ave.

E 112th

7
6

Riverside Dr.

Broadway

W 114th
St.

W 112th
St.

3

The Cathedral
Church of
St. John
the Divine

4

5

Amsterdam Ave.

Cathedral Pkwy.

W 109th St.
W 108th St.
W 107th St.

Manhattan
Ave.

Douglass
Circle

2

Central Park North

Frawley
Circle

1

E 111th St.

E 110th

E 109th
E 108th
E 107th

N

Riverside
Park

UPPER
WEST SIDE

CENTRAL PARK

Harlem
Meer

km   1/4   1/2
mi   1/8   1/4

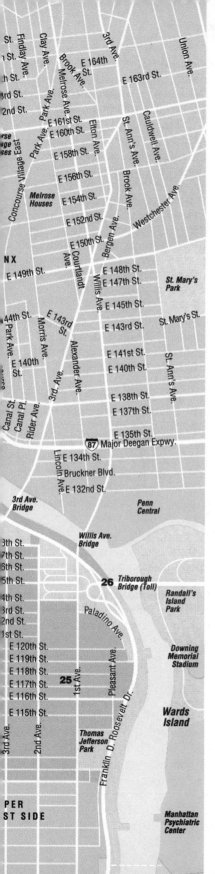

Heights/ Harlem

Located north of **Cathedral Parkway** (West 110th Street), the geographical peaks and valleys of the Heights and Harlem more or less define neighborhood boundaries all the way up to **Spuyten-Duyvil**, where the **Hudson** and **East Rivers** join at **225th Street.**

Morningside Heights, the hilly terrain between Cathedral Parkway and **West 125th Street**, was largely undeveloped until the opening of **Morningside Park** in 1887 and of **Riverside Drive** in 1891. World-renowned scholars began to settle in shortly thereafter, and today the area is dominated by educational giants. **Union Theological Seminary, Jewish Theological Seminary, Columbia University**, and **Barnard College** form the cornerstone of this outstanding academic community. Two other structures stand out in the landscape: the massive work-in-progress of the **Cathedral Church of St. John the Divine**, and the **Riverside Church**, an important religious and cultural center in its own right. While you're in the neighborhood, don't forget **Grant's Tomb**, set high on a hill above the river. **Broadway** is the main drag, just as it is on the **Upper West Side**, but here it's less prettied up, although **Columbia University**, a major property owner in the area, has been bringing in more chic—and consequently more expensive—stores and restaurants.

Hamilton Heights, from West 125th Street north to **Trinity Cemetery** (West 155th St at Riverside Dr), is a former factory and ferry-landing town named for Alexander Hamilton, who built a country estate here in 1802. Other 19th-century buildings survive, but most of the development occurred after 1904, when the **Broadway IRT** subway opened. The area has remained primarily residential, and today, some of the most desirable residences are the turn-of-the-century row houses in the **Hamilton Heights Historic District. City College of New York (CCNY)**, the northernmost Manhattan outpost of the **City University of New York (CUNY)** system, moved into the former campus of **Manhattanville College** (now located in Riverdale) in 1950.

Harlem, which becomes **East Harlem** east of **Fifth Avenue**, is Manhattan's black ghetto, where immigrants from the Caribbean and Africa and economic refugees from the American states live, often in inadequate conditions. Many people of Hispanic origin, mostly from Puerto Rico, have settled in East Harlem, renaming it *El Barrio* ("the neighborhood" in Spanish), while the later wave of Dominicans and Cubans has settled along upper Broadway (Broadway in the 140s is known as "Little Dominica"), and on the east side of Broadway as far north as **Inwood (207th St).** The two Harlems are older than most black urban communities in this country, as well as larger, taking up 6 square miles from West 110th Street north to the **Harlem River** and bounded on the east by the East River. Unlike in many other ghettos in the United States, housing stock was once excellent, and although much of it has deteriorated, it's still worth renovating—which is what increasing numbers of middle-class families are doing.

This section of the island was covered with wooded hills and valleys inhabited by Indians when the Dutch started the settlement of **Nieuw Haarlem** in 1658. Black slaves owned by the West India Company helped build a road, later called Broadway, and the **Haarlem** outpost grew. In the early 19th century, affluent Manhattanites, including James Roosevelt, built estates and plantations here. It was also a haven for the poor, with Irish immigrants among those who built shantytowns on the East River, where they raised free-roaming hogs, geese, sheep, and goats.

Harlem began to develop as a suburb for the well-to-do when the **New York and Harlem Railroad** started service from Lower Manhattan in 1837. More railway lines followed, and as handsome brownstones, schools, and stores went up, immigrant families who had achieved some degree of success, many of them German Jews, moved up from the Lower East Side.

The announcement that work was starting on the **IRT Lenox** subway line touched off another round of development, but this time the boom went bust. When the subway was completed in 1905, most of the buildings were still empty. Blacks began renting, often at inflated rates, after having been squeezed out of other parts of the city by commercial development. Eventually the only whites who remained were poor and lived on the fringes, and Harlem became *the* black community in the United States. The subsequent waves of blacks that poured in were often in need of jobs while lacking in skills and education.

Although many blacks in Harlem were existing at poverty level in the 1920s and 1930s, black culture blossomed here—in dance, drama, literature, and music. Speakeasies flourished in the area during Prohibition, and the smart set came uptown to the **Sugar Cane Club** and the **Cotton Club** to hear Count Basie, Duke Ellington, and other jazz legends. Lena Horne got her start here, and literary giants Langston Hughes and James Baldwin were native sons.

In the 1950s, urban renewal made a dent in the declining housing stock by clearing blocks of slums and replacing them with grim housing developments. Gentrification began in Harlem in earnest in the 1970s and continues today, as middle-class families move into **Striver's Row** in the **St. Nicholas District** and to the **Mount Morris Park Historic District,** where the brownstones are among the city's finest. Still, Harlem is not a safe place to visit at night and, in some neighborhoods, during the day. (Try not to go alone, and always take taxis to and from your destination.) In 1995, Harlem became one of nine zones in the US chosen as the recipient of $100 million in federal aid for job training and social services programs.

Washington Heights, starting at **Trinity Cemetery** and going north to **Dyckman Street,** was once an Irish neighborhood. In addition to the descendants of the Irish, the area now has an ethnic mix of blacks, Puerto Ricans and other Latins, Greeks, and Armenians.

Audubon Terrace, a turn-of-the-century Beaux Arts museum complex, seems out of place at **West 155th** and Broadway, where it's surrounded by housing projects and tenements. But the complex is easy to reach by subway and worth a visit. North and east of Audubon Terrace is the **Jumel Terrace Historic District.**

Another important Heights landmark is **Fort Tryon Park** (pronounced *Try-on*), the site of **Fort Tryon,** the northernmost defense of **Fort Washington.** Its crowning jewel is **The Cloisters,** which houses the medieval collection of the **Metropolitan Museum of Art.** Just south of **The Cloisters** is a little-known shrine, the **St. Frances Cabrini Chapel.** Here, under the altar in a crystal casket, lies the body of Mother Cabrini, the patron saint of all immigrants. It is recorded that shortly after her death in 1917, a lock of her hair restored an infant boy's eyesight; he later became a priest.

Inwood Hill Park, where Indian cave dwellers once lived, caps the northern end of the island with a rural flourish. Playing fields and open parkland with views over the Hudson and the **George Washington Bridge** and as far as the **Tappan Zee Bridge** are highlights, along with a wilderness of hackberry bushes, maples, Chinese white ash, and Oriental pine trees that stretch to the end of the island, where you can wander the trails and imagine what it was like when the Algonquin Indians had this forest paradise all to themselves.

1 Arthur A. Schomburg Plaza These 35-story octagonal apartment towers, completed in 1975 by **Gruzen & Partners** and **Castro-Blanco, Piscioneri & Feder,** are distinguished markers at the corner of **Central Park.** The pairing of the balconies creates an original rhythm in moderating the scale. ♦ 1295 Fifth Ave (between E 110th and E 111th Sts). 289.4465

2 New York Public Library, 115th Street Branch This 1908 Renaissance composition in limestone, a style favored by architects **McKim, Mead & White,** is one of the finest of the branch libraries. ♦ Call for the season's changing hours. 203 W 115th St (between Adam Clayton Powell Jr. and Frederick Douglass Blvds). 666.9393

3 St. Luke's–Roosevelt Hospital At least the central entrance pavilion and east wing remain of **Ernest Flagg**'s Classical/Baroque composition. The 1896 building is charming, dignified, slightly busy, and certainly original. ♦ Morningside Dr (between W 113th and W 114th Sts). 523.4000

4 The Cathedral Church of St. John the Divine Begun in 1892 under the sponsorship of Bishop Henry Codman Potter to designs by **Heins & LaFarge,** this giant, slightly rough Byzantine church (illustrated above) with Romanesque influences is still a work in progress. By 1911, the apse, choir, and crossing were done, the architects and the bishop were dead, and fashions had changed. Gothic enthusiast **Ralph Adams Cram** of **Cram & Ferguson** drew up new plans to complete the church. The nave and western facade are, therefore, fine French Gothic. Work was discontinued in 1941, but resumed in the 1980s in an effort to complete the cathedral, particularly the towers. In the stone yard in operation next to the church, two dozen artisans, many of them neighborhood youths, worked under a master mason from England to carve blocks in a centuries-old tradition until declaring bancruptcy in 1994; the cathedral is launching a major fund-raising campaign to resume building.

When it is finished (a project that will carry over well into the next century), this will be the largest cathedral in the world. The nave is 601 feet long and 146 feet wide; when completed, the transepts will be just as wide and span 320 feet. The floor area is greater than Chartres and Notre Dame together, and the towers will be 300 feet high. Although not entirely complete, four of the five portals have been fitted with Burmese teak doors; the bronze door of the central portal was cast in Paris by M. Barbedienne, who cast the *Statue of Liberty*.The interior is spectacular, with seven apsidal chapels in a variety of styles by a collection of prominent architects. The finest is that of St. Ambrose, a Renaissance-inspired composition by **Carrère & Hastings.** The eight granite columns that ring the sanctuary are 55 feet high and weigh 130 tons each. The dome over the crossing, intended to be temporary, was erected in 1909. Master woodworker George Nakashima's massive heart-shaped *Altar for Peace,* cut from a 125-foot English walnut tree from Long Island and finished with his trademark rosewood inlays, is the site of monthly meditations for peace. The Episcopal church, under the direction of its dean, the Very Rev. James Parks Morton, hosts the visiting Dalai Lama as well as an impressive schedule of concerts, art exhibitions, lectures, and theater and dance events. ♦ Amsterdam Ave (at W 112th St). 316.7540; box office 662.2133

5 V&T Pizzeria ★$ Its fans maintain that this place has the best pizza on the Upper West Side—hefty, thick-crusted, with fresh tomato sauce, whole-milk mozzarella, and flavorful toppings, such as sausage. ♦ Pizza ♦ Daily lunch and dinner. No credit cards accepted. 1024 Amsterdam Ave (between W 110th and W 111th Sts). 663.1708

6 Symposium $ Greek specialties such as moussaka, spinach pie, and peas wrapped in phyllo dough are featured at this popular spot. ♦ Greek ♦ Daily lunch and dinner. 544 W 113th St (between Amsterdam Ave and Broadway). 865.1011

7 Papyrus Booksellers The paperbacks here are geared to Columbia students, and the fine periodical section leans toward politics and the arts. ♦ M-Sa 9:30AM-11PM; Su 10AM-10PM. 2915 Broadway (at W 114th St). 222.3350

8 Columbia University Founded in 1754, this historic Ivy League school has an enrollment of nearly 20,000. Now less politically outspoken than they were in the 1960s, the students have settled down to their studies in the university's three undergraduate schools: **Columbia College, School of General Studies,** and **School of Engineering and Applied Science.** On the site of the **Bloomingdale Insane Asylum** (of which **Buell Hall** is a remnant), the original design and early buildings of the campus (the third one the university has occupied) were planned by **Charles Follen McKim** of **McKim, Mead & White** in a grand Beaux Arts tradition. Although only a segment of his plan was completed in 1897, most of its elements can be discerned. The Italian Renaissance–inspired institutional buildings—in red brick with limestone trim and copper roofs—are arranged around a central quad on a terrace two stories above the street. There were to be six smaller side courts like the one between **Avery** and **Fayerweather Halls** (somewhat changed now due to the extension of **Avery Library**).

McKim's dominant central element is the magnificent **Low Memorial Library** (1897), a monumental pantheon named after the father of university president Seth Low (who was also mayor of New York City from 1902 to 1903). No longer used as a library, **Low** remains the administrative and ceremonial center of the university. The statue of the *Alma Mater* on the front steps—made famous during the riots of 1968—was unveiled by Daniel Chester French in 1903.

Other noteworthy buildings on the campus include **Butler Library,** a colonnaded box facing **Low,** completed in 1934 by **James Gamble Rogers.** The **Sherman Fairchild Center for the Life Sciences,** a 1977 **Mitchell/Giurgola** creation, is an interesting contextual essay in which a glass-and-metal building has been hidden behind a screen of quarry tile that resembles the ground pavers. The **Law School** and the **School of International Affairs** extension, built in 1963 and 1971 by **Harrison & Abramovitz,** forms a great white mass beyond a block-long bridge that spans Amsterdam Avenue. Charming and modest, the Byzantine/Renaissance **St. Paul's Chapel,** a 1907 work by **Howell & Stokes,** has an interior that is lovely, vaulted, and light. Tours of the campus, which originate at **Low Library** (854.4900), are conducted according to public interest and the availability of guides. The main entrance is at West 116th Street. ♦ Bounded by Morningside and Riverside Drs and W 112th and W 123rd Sts. 854.1754 ♿

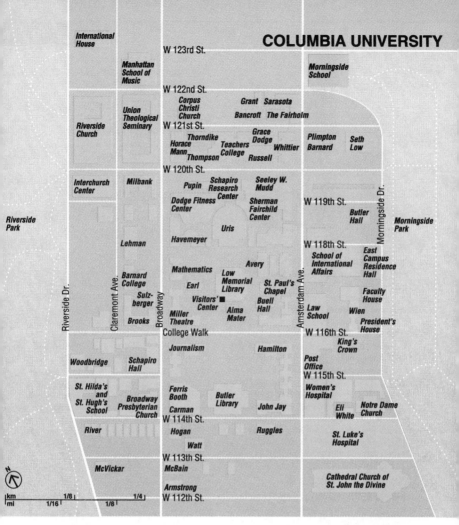

International House

COLUMBIA UNIVERSITY

W 123rd St.

Manhattan School of Music

Morningside School

W 122nd St.

Corpus Christi Church
Grant Sarasota
Bancroft The Fairholm

Union Theological Seminary

Riverside Church

W 121st St.

Thorndike
Grace Dodge
Horace Mann
Teachers College
Whittier
Thompson
Russell

Plimpton Barnard
Seth Low

Interchurch Center

W 120th St.

Milbank

Schapiro Research Center
Pupin
Seeley W. Mudd

Dodge Fitness Center
Sherman Fairchild Center

W 119th St.

Morningside Dr.

Butler Hall

Morningside Park

Riverside Park

Uris

Lehman

Havemeyer

W 118th St.

East Campus Residence Hall

School of International Affairs

Avery

Mathematics

Low Memorial Library

Faculty House

Riverside Dr.

Claremont Ave.

Barnard College

Earl

St. Paul's Chapel

Sulzberger

Visitors' Center

Buell Hall

Law School

Wien

Brooks

Broadway

Miller Theatre

Alma Mater

President's House

College Walk

W 116th St.

Amsterdam Ave.

King's Crown

Journalism

Hamilton

Post Office

Woodbridge

Schapiro Hall

W 115th St.

Women's Hospital

St. Hilda's and St. Hugh's School

Ferris Booth

Butler Library

Eli White

Notre Dame Church

Broadway Presbyterian Church

Carman

John Jay

River

Hogan

W 114th St.

Ruggles

St. Luke's Hospital

Watt

W 113th St.

McVickar

McBain

Cathedral Church of St. John the Divine

N

Armstrong

W 112th St.

km | mi   1/16   1/8   1/4

---

9 Barnard College The 2,200-student women's school, an undergraduate college of **Columbia University,** offers bachelor's degrees in 27 majors, with an emphasis on liberal arts. Across Broadway from the elegant expanse of Columbia, the sister school's campus appears crowded but somehow more lively. The older buildings at the north end—**Milbank, Brinkerhoff,** and **Fiske Halls**—were designed by **Lamb & Rich** in the 1890s in a sort of New England academic style. More interesting is the heart of the campus today: the limestone counterpoints of **MacIntosh Center** and **Altschul Hall,** both built by Philadelphia architect **Vincent G. Kling** in 1969. In 1989, 400 students moved into **Centennial Hall,** a 17-story tower at the southern end of campus, designed by **James Stewart Polshek & Partners.** ♦ Bounded by Broadway and Claremont Ave, and W 116th and W 120th Sts. 854.5262

10 Union Theological Seminary Bookstore This bookstore, affiliated with the seminary next door, stocks any and all in-print books

and periodicals that concern theology. ♦ M-F. 3041 Broadway (at W 120th St). 280.1554

11 Union Theological Seminary In a landscape studded with institutions, this is one of the few that truly manage to keep the city at bay. Designed by **Allen & Collens** in 1910 with alterations by **Collens, Willis & Beckonert** in 1952, the building is an example of collegiate Gothic borrowed from Oxbridge and, in that tradition, it has a secluded interior courtyard. ♦ Bounded by Broadway and Claremont Ave, and W 120th and W 122nd Sts. 662.7100

Billie Holiday called her home at 108 West 193rd Street "a combination YMCA, boardinghouse for broke musicians, soup kitchen for anyone with a hard luck story, community center, and after-hours joint where a couple of bucks would get you a shot of whiskey and the most fabulous fried chicken."

Restaurants/Clubs: Red   Hotels: Blue

Shops/ ♦ Outdoors: Green   **Sights/Culture: Black**

12 Riverside Church This church (shown above) was built in 1930 by **Allen & Collens, Henry C. Pelton,** and **Burnham Hoyt,** with a south wing added in 1960 by **Collens, Willis & Beckonert.** Funded by John D. Rockefeller Jr., it is a steel frame in a thin, institutional Gothic skin. The fine nave is almost overpowered by the tower, which rises 21 stories, and the 74-bell carillon is the largest in the world. Visit the **Observation Deck** in the tower, not only to look at the bells on the way up but for a splendid view of the Hudson, **Riverside Park,** and the surrounding institutions. Forty-five-minute guided tours are offered Sunday, after services. ♦ Daily 9AM-5PM. Carillon bell concerts: Su 10:30AM, noon, 3PM. Tours: Su 12:30PM. Observation deck: Su 12:30-4PM. Riverside Dr (between W 120th and W 122nd Sts). 222.5900

Within Riverside Church:

Theater at Riverside Church For more than a decade, dancers and choreographers tested their mettle on this tiny stage as part of the Riverside Dance Festival. These days, the church no longer sponsors performances, but still opens its doors to theater, music, video, and dance productions. ♦ 864.2929

13 Grant's Tomb/General Grant National Memorial Now's the time to pose the infamous college exam question: Who is buried in **Grant's Tomb?** The massive granite mausoleum, designed in 1897 by **John H. Duncan,** is set on a hill overlooking the river, thereby dominating its surroundings. The walk to the tomb is impressive: You pass along the terrace, up the stairs, through the colonnade and bronze doors, and find yourself under a high dome looking down on the identical black marble sarcophagi of the general and his wife in the center of a rotunda—an open crypt similar to Napoleon's tomb at the Hôtel des Invalides in Paris. It's surrounded by bronze busts of the general's comrades-in-arms and by allegorical figures between the arches representing scenes from his life. Photographs in two flanking rooms fill in with more realistic details. More fun, however, are the benches on the outside, created in 1973 by Pedro Silva of

the Cityarts Workshop. The bright mosaic decorations were done by community residents. Make this trip in daytime only, as the tomb attracts some unsavory characters at night. Oh, yes, the answer: Ulysses S. Grant and his wife, Julia. ♦ Free. Daily. Riverside Dr and W 122nd St. 666.1640

14 The Cotton Club ★$$ The legendary Harlem nightclub (at this location since 1978) is becoming almost as well known for its food as for its entertainment. Try the ribs or fried chicken, and don't forget the greens and ham hocks. The original home of the weekend gospel brunch (seatings at noon and 2:30PM), it offers a prix-fixe buffet. ♦ Southern ♦ W-F dinner; Sa-Su brunch and dinner. Reservations recommended. 656 W 125 St (between Broadway and Riverside Dr). 633.7980

15 Teachers College, Bancroft Hall A stew of abstracted details—basically Beaux Arts Renaissance but with a touch of Spanish and a pinch of Art Nouveau—enliven the facade of this apartment house, designed in 1911 by **Emery Roth.** ♦ 509 W 121st St (between Amsterdam Ave and Broadway)

16 The Terrace ★★$$$$ The sparkling wraparound views of the glittering George Washington Bridge to the northwest and skyscrapers to the south are made even more romantic by the reflection of tabletop candles in the windows and harp music wafting in from the bar area. If only all of the food were as completely wonderful as the ambience. Stick to classic French dishes—*feuilletée* (puff pastry) of seafood with lobster sauce and herb-crusted rack of lamb—that are superb. The wine list is very well chosen but you won't be able to touch a bottle for under $45. ♦ Continental ♦ Tu-F lunch and dinner; Sa dinner. Reservations recommended. 400 W 119th St (at Morningside Dr). 666.9490

Grant's Tomb

Michael Storrings

17 Frank Silvera Writers' Workshop
Founded in 1973 by Garland Lee Thompson, this workshop/theater is a memorial to the late Frank Silvera, who was active in nurturing black writers. Productions include *No Left Turn* by Buriel Clay II and *Inacent Black and Five Brothers* by Marcus Hemphill. Monday evenings feature readings and critiques of new plays. Check the schedule for seminars on play- and screenwriting. ♦ 317 W 125th St (at St. Nicholas Ave), Third floor. 662.8463

18 The Apollo This former vaudeville house, designed by **George Keister** and built in 1914, became the entertainment center of the black community in the 1930s, and by the 1950s it was *the* venue for black popular music. A decade later, however, the theater fell on hard times as big-name acts began playing larger downtown houses. It wasn't until the early 1980s, when it was rescued by **Inner City Broadcasting**, that the faded theater was given a much-needed face-lift and turned into a showplace for black television productions as well as live entertainment. Wednesday amateur nights are always fun and packed with budding talents. No credit cards accepted. ♦ 253 W 125th St (between Adam Clayton Powell Jr. and Frederick Douglass Blvds). 749.5838

19 Studio Museum in Harlem Changing exhibitions of black art and culture from Africa, the Caribbean, and America are featured in this small museum of black fine arts. Year-round education programs, including the well-known "Vital Expression in American Art," offer lectures, concerts, and poetry readings. ♦ Admission. Wed-Su. 144 W 125th St (between Lenox Ave and Adam Clayton Powell Jr. Blvd). 864.4500 ♿

20 Sylvia's ★★$$ The most renowned soul-food restaurant in Harlem, and perhaps in New York City, has added a second dining room, and during the warmer months there's an adjoining open patio next door. Southern-fried and smothered chicken are standouts, as are the dumplings, candied sweets (yams), greens, and desserts—especially the cinnamony sweet-potato pie. ♦ Southern ♦ M-Sa breakfast, lunch, and dinner; Su gospel brunch and dinner. 328 Lenox Ave (between W 126th and W 127th Sts). 996.0660

21 National Black Theater Courses, readings, performance workshops, and productions all take place at this 99-seat theater. ♦ 2033 Fifth Ave (at E 125th St), Second floor. 722.3800

22 Mount Morris Park Historical District
The charming Victorian character of this district, designated historic in 1971, was established during the speculative boom at the end of the 19th century, when it was urbanized by descendants of Dutch, Irish, and English immigrants. After 1900, it became a primarily German-Jewish neighborhood. The houses on Lenox Avenue between 120th and 121st Streets, designed by **Demeuron & Smith** in 1888, are particularly captivating. The **Morris Apartments** at 81-85 East 125th Street, built just a year later by **Lamb & Rich,** now house the Mount Morris Bank and Safety Deposit Vaults. The building is distinguished by Richardsonian Romanesque arches and stained glass.

The district also has a fine collection of religious buildings. Dating from 1907, the Neo-Classical **Mount Olivet Baptist Church,** at 201 Lenox Avenue, was originally designed by **Arnold Brunner** as **Temple Israel,** one of the most prestigious synagogues in the city. **St. Martin's Episcopal Church,** on Lenox Avenue at 122nd Street, is a bulky, asymmetrical Romanesque 1888 composition by **William A. Potter** with a carillon of 40 bells, second in size only to that of **Riverside Church.** Built in 1889 by **Lamb & Rich,** the **Bethel Gospel Pentecostal Assembly,** at 36 West 123rd Street, used to be the **Harlem Club.** The **Greater Bethel AME Church,** built in 1892 by **Lamb & Rich,** was originally the **Harlem Free Library.** Originally the **Dwight Residence, Frank H. Smith**'s 1890 building at 1 West 123rd Street is now the home of the **Ethiopian Hebrew Congregation.** It is a Renaissance mansion with an unusual round- and flat-bayed front that is a strong addition to the block of fine brownstones on West 123rd Street. ♦ Bounded by Mt. Morris Park W and Lenox Ave, and W 119th and W 124th Sts

23 Marcus Garvey Memorial Park When the city purchased this craggy square of land in 1839, it was named **Mount Morris Park.** It was renamed in 1973 for Garvey, who was a brilliant orator and the founder of the Universal Negro Improvement Association and of the now-defunct newspaper *Negro World*. The highland in the center supports an 1856 fire watchtower, the only one surviving in the city. Its steel frame and sweeping spiral stairs, once practical innovations, are now nostalgic. ♦ Bounded by Madison Ave and Mt. Morris Park W, and W 120th and W 124th Sts

24 Harlem Courthouse Constructed with a mix of brick and stone, the Romanesque edifice was built in 1891 to the designs of **Thom & Wilson.** With its gables, archways, and corner tower, the dignified and delicate mass represents the American tradition of great "country" courthouses. ♦ 170 E 121st St (between Third and Lexington Aves)

25 Patsy's Pizzeria ★$ It's worth making the trip uptown for what connoisseurs say is the most delicious thin crust pizza in the city. ♦ Pizza ♦ Daily lunch, dinner, and late-night meals. No credit cards accepted. 2287 First Ave (between E 117th and E 118th Sts). 534.9783

26 Triborough Bridge A lift span connects Manhattan and Randalls Island, a fixed roadway springs from Randalls Island to the Bronx, and a suspension span crosses the Hell Gate. The impressive connector-collection was designed by **Othmar Ammann** (already recognized for his design of the George Washington Bridge) and **Aymar Embury II** in 1936. ♦ From Harlem River Dr at E 125th St, Manhattan to Grand Central Pkwy, Queens to Bruckner Expwy, the Bronx

27 All Saints Church This fine group of buildings shows the Gothic influence of architect **James Renwick Jr.** The firm he founded, **Renwick, Aspinwall & Russell,** built the church in 1894 and the rectory in 1889, and the school was built by **W.W. Renwick** in 1904. Some say this work is more pleasing than **St. Patrick's Cathedral,** also a **Renwick** creation. Especially worthwhile is the harmony of the terra-cotta tracery and buff, honey, and brown brick. ♦ 47 E 129th St (at Madison Ave). 534.3535

28 Riverbend Houses The complex of 625 apartments for moderate-income families is respectful of context and use of material, while assembled with great style and imagination. Built in 1967 by **Davis, Brody & Associates,** the complex is a landmark in the recent tradition of publicly subsidized housing. ♦ Fifth Ave (between E 135th and E 138th Sts)

29 Schomburg Center for Research in Black Culture The largest library of black and African culture in the United States, collected by Puerto Rican black Arthur Schomburg (1874-1938), is housed in this research center. As a young man, Schomberg was disturbed by the absence of information available on black heritage and history. The center hosts revolving exhibits and shows by African and black American artists. The gift shop offers items from the worldwide African diaspora, from hand-carved statues to postcards by Harlem's own African-American artists. ♦ Free. Daily. 515 Lenox Ave (at W 135th St). 491.2200

30 Abyssinian Baptist Church Built in 1923 by **Charles W. Bolton,** this bluestone Gothic Tudor building is renowned for its late pastor, US Congressman Adam Clayton Powell Jr. Founded in 1808, it is New York's oldest black church. ♦ Services: Su 9AM, 11AM. 132 W 138th St (between Lenox Ave and Adam Clayton Powell Jr. Blvd). 862.7474

31 St. Nicholas Historic District/King Model Houses In an unusual and highly successful 1891 venture, speculative builder

David King chose three architects to design the row housing on these three blocks. **Nos. 202** to **250 West 138th Street** and **2350** to **2354 Adam Clayton Powell Jr. Boulevard** are by **James Brown Lord,** all in simple Georgian red brick on a brownstone base. **Nos. 203** to **271 West 138th Street, 2360** to **2390 Adam Clayton Powell Jr. Boulevard,** and **Nos. 202** to **272 West 139th Street** are by **Bruce Price** and **Clarence S. Luce. Nos. 203** to **267 West 139th Street** and **1380** to **1390 Adam Clayton Powell Jr. Boulevard** are the finest—elegantly detailed, Renaissance-inspired designs by **McKim, Mead & White.** The harmony of the ensemble, achieved through similarity of scale and sensitive design, despite the variety of styles and materials, is extraordinary. The area came to be known as "Striver's Row," the home of the area's young and professionally ambitious. It was designated a historic district in 1967. ♦ Bounded by Adam Clayton Powell Jr. and Frederick Douglass Blvds, and W 138th and W 139th Sts

32 Jamaican Hot Pot ★★$ This place turns out fabulous Jamaican specialties—fried chicken, oxtail stew, garlic shrimp, jerk chicken, and curried goat. Locals love this place. ♦ Jamaican ♦ Daily lunch, dinner, and late-night meals. 2260 Adam Clayton Powell Jr. Blvd (at W 133rd St). 491.5270

33 P.S. 92 This 1965 work of **Percival Goodman** is elegantly articulated and warmly detailed. ♦ 222 W 134th St (between Adam Clayton Powell Jr. and Frederick Douglass Blvds). 690.5915

34 135th Street Gatehouse, Croton Aqueduct Built in 1890, this brownstone and granite watchtower, with a Roman echo, was the end of the aqueduct over High Bridge. From here, water was taken in pipes to West 119th Street, by an aqueduct under Amsterdam Avenue, to West 113th Street and then by pipe again to the city. Finely crafted gatehouses still stand at West 119th and West 113th Streets. ♦ At Convent Ave

35 City College/City University of New York Nearly 12,000 students—75 percent of them minorities—attend classes at this 34-acre campus. Bachelor's and master's degrees are offered in liberal arts, education, engineering, architecture, and nursing. The science programs are also noteworthy. The campus is an ornately costumed, energetic collection of white-trimmed, neo-Gothic buildings constructed of Manhattan schist excavated during the construction of the **IRT** subway. The old campus, completed in 1905 by **George B. Post,** is especially wonderful in contrast to the more recent buildings that have grown up around it. The Romanesque south campus used to be **Manhattanville College of the Sacred Heart,** originally an academy and convent. ♦ Bounded by St. Nicholas Terr and

Amsterdam Ave, and W 130th and W 140th Sts. 650.7000

Within City College:

Aaron Davis Hall at City College This multiarts theater is home to, among others, the **Dance Theater of Harlem** and the **City Opera National Company.** ◆ W 135th St and Convent Ave. 650.6900 ♿

The **Harlem** School of the Arts, Inc.

36 Harlem School of the Arts (HSA)
In 1965, soprano Dorothy Maynor began teaching piano in the basement of the **St. James Presbyterian Church Community Center.** From that modest beginning, it has grown to 1,300 students, and has gained national prominence as a performing arts school. Several former students and teachers now have active Broadway careers. With world-famous mezzo-soprano Betty Allen as president, the school now teaches musical instrument study (piano, orchestral string, percussion), ballet and modern dance, and visual and dramatic arts. (The orchestral string department is especially noteworthy; the 23-member **Suzuki Ensemble,** made up of 8- to 17-year-olds, is known throughout the city.) Through the "Opportunities for Learning in the Arts" program, students from other schools are brought in to take classes during the day. The "Community and Culture in Harlem" program hosts concerts, art exhibitions, and readings. The school's award-winning building, a 1977 work of **Ulrich Franzen & Associates,** is a complex marriage of classrooms, practice studios, three large dance studios, auditoriums, offices, and an enclosed garden. An adjacent building holds the 200-seat **Harlem School of the Arts Theater.** ◆ 645 St. Nicholas Ave (at W 141st St). 926.4100 ♿

37 Hamilton Heights Historic District
The Hamilton Heights area, designated historic in 1974, was once the country estate of Alexander Hamilton. His house, the **Grange,** stands at Convent Avenue and West 141st Street next to **St. Luke's Hospital.** The district has a generally high-quality collection of row houses dating from the turn of the century and exhibiting a mixture of styles and a wealth of ornament. **West 144th Street** is exemplary. The row at **Nos. 413 to 423,** designed in 1898 by **T.H. Dunn,** has Venetian Gothic, Italian, and French Renaissance elements. Because there is very little through traffic, the neighborhood has always been slightly secluded and desirable. It is occupied primarily by faculty from nearby **City College.** ◆ Bounded by Hamilton Terr and Convent Ave, and W 141st and W 145th Sts

38 Our Lady of Lourdes Church Truly a scavenger's monument, this 1904 church by the **O'Reilly Brothers** is composed of pieces from three other buildings: the Ruskinian Gothic gray and white marble and bluestone facade on West 142nd Street is from the old **National Academy of Design,** built in 1865 by **P.B. Wight,** that stood at East 23rd Street and Park Avenue South; and the apse and part of the east wall were once the Madison Avenue end of **St. Patrick's Cathedral**—removed for the construction of the Lady Chapel. The pedestals flanking the steps are from A.T. Stewart's palatial department store, which stood on 34th Street at Fifth Avenue when it was built by **John Kellum** in 1867. ◆ 467 W 142nd St (between Convent and Amsterdam Aves). 862.4380

39 Copeland's ★$$ The food here couldn't be any more down-home; try the oxtails, corn fritters, Louisiana gumbo, and barbecued jumbo shrimp. Come on a Friday or Saturday night and be treated to live jazz; the first set starts at 7:30PM (no cover charge). ◆ Southern/Continental ◆ Tu-Sa dinner; Su brunch and dinner. Reservations recommended. 547 W 145th St (between Amsterdam Ave and Broadway). 234.2356

40 Harlem River Houses This exemplary complex consisting of nine acres of public housing developed by the **Federal Administration of Public Works** was built in 1937 by **Archibald Manning Brown** with **Charles F. Fuller, Horace Ginsberg, Frank J. Forster, Will Rice Amon, Richard W. Buckley,** and **John L. Wilson.** Michael Rapuano was the landscape architect. An energetic variety of building shapes are arranged in three groups around a central plaza and landscaped courts, becoming less formal nearer the river. The sculpture inside the West 151st Street entrance is by Paul Manship, who also did the *Prometheus* at **Rockefeller Center.** ◆ Bounded by Harlem River Dr and Macombs Pl, and W 151st and W 153rd Sts

41 Trinity Cemetery This hilly cemetery used to be a part of the estate of naturalist J.J. Audubon, who is among those buried here. Others include many members of families that made New York, such as the Schermerhorns, Astors, Bleeckers, and Van Burens. The grave of Clement Clarke Moore draws special attention—he wrote *A Visit from St. Nicholas.* The boundary walls and gates date from 1876; the gatehouse and keeper's lodge were designed in 1883 by **Vaux & Redford;** and the grounds were laid out in 1881 by Vaux & Co. ◆ Daily 8AM-dusk. Bounded by Amsterdam Ave and Riverside Dr, and W 153rd and W 155th Sts. 602.0787

At Trinity Cemetery:

Chapel of the Intercession Built in 1914 by **Cram, Goodhue & Ferguson,** this chapel is essentially a large country church set in the middle of rural **Trinity Cemetery.** The cloister at the West 155th Street entrance is particularly nice, and the richly detailed interior is marvelous, highlighted by an altar inlaid with stones from the Holy Land and sites of early Christian worship. The ashes of architect **Bertram Goodhue** are entombed in a memorial in the north transept. ♦ Broadway and W 155th St. 283.6200

42 Audubon Terrace This collection of classical buildings was first planned in 1908, and bankrolled by poet and scholar Archer M. Huntington. The master plan was created by **Charles Pratt Huntington,** his nephew, who also designed five of the buildings: the **Museum of the American Indian, Heye Foundation,** built in 1916; the **American Geographic Society,** built in 1916; the **Hispanic Society of America** (north building, constructed in 1916; south building, constructed between 1910 and 1926); the **American Numismatic Society,** built in 1908; and the **Church of Our Lady of Esperanza,** built in 1912. The green-and-gold interior of the church is rather nice; the stained glass, skylight, and lamps were gifts of the king of Spain, who also knighted the architect. The two buildings of the **American Academy and Institute of Arts and Letters** are by **William M. Kendall** (administration building, constructed in 1923) and **Cass Gilbert** (auditorium and gallery, built in 1930). ♦ Broadway (between W 155th and W 156th Sts)

At Audubon Terrace:

Hispanic Society of America The museum of the **Hispanic Society** is in a lavishly appointed building lined with the paintings of old masters—El Greco, Goya,

Velázquez—archaeological finds, ceramics, and other decorative arts of the Iberian Peninsula. The library in the building across the terrace is an important research center. ♦ Free. Tu-Sa; Su 1-4PM. 613 W 155th St (at Broadway). 926.2234

American Numismatic Society Downstairs are rotating examples of the world's coinage—past and present—and a display of medals and decorations. On the second floor is the most comprehensive numismatic library in America. For collectors, a Public Inquiry Counter is staffed by a curator to answer questions. Write or call in advance for help with investigating a specific type of coinage in the collection. ♦ Free. Tu-Sa; Su 1-4PM. 617 W 155th St (at Broadway). 234.3130

American Academy and Institute of Arts and Letters View regular exhibitions of the work of members and nonmembers of this honor society for American writers, artists, and composers. ♦ Free. M-F. Audubon Terr (between W 155th and W 156th Sts). 368.5900

43 Wilson's Bakery & Restaurant ★★$$ You'll be assured of a satisfying meal any day of the week at this Harlem institution. Specialties include chicken and dumplings, barbecued ribs, fried chicken, smothered steak, ham hocks, and meat loaf. Save room for dessert. ♦ Bakery/Southern ♦ Daily breakfast, lunch, and dinner. 1980 Amsterdam Ave (at W 158th St). 923.9821 ♿

44 Morris-Jumel Mansion Built in 1765 by **Roger Morris** as a summer residence on an estate that stretched from river to river, the mansion's two-story portico (illustrated below) became the model for many houses built in Canada and the United States at the turn of the century. During the Revolution, George Washington *did* sleep here, and even briefly used it as a headquarters, until New York City was taken over by the British. After housing a tavern, the mansion was bought and remodeled by French merchant Stephen Jumel. The exterior of the house is Georgian Palladian, with some details added in the Federal period; note the conceit of the quoins—a stone form mimicked in wood.

Michael Storrings

Morris-Jumel Mansion

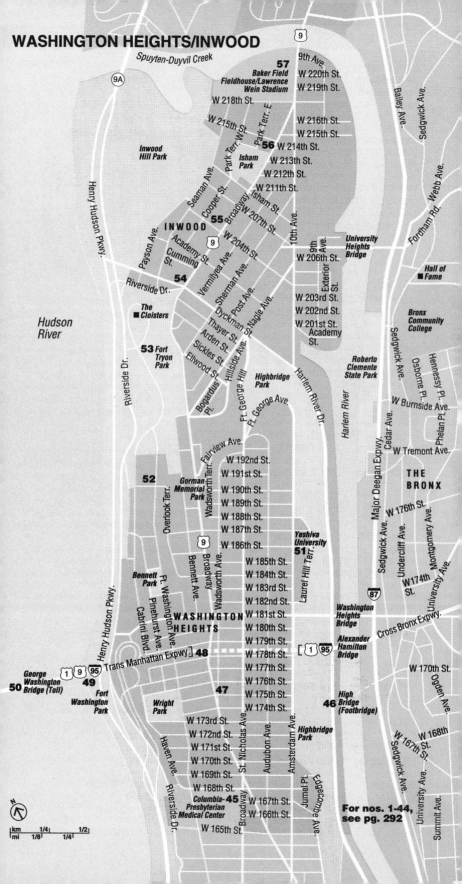

WASHINGTON HEIGHTS/INWOOD

9

Spuyten-Duyvil Creek

9A

57 Baker Field
Fieldhouse/Lawrence
Wein Stadium

9th Ave.
W 220th St.
W 219th St.
W 218th St.
W 216th St.
W 215th St.

Park Terr. E
Park Terr. W.

56 W 214th St.
W 213th St.
W 212th St.
W 211th St.

Inwood Hill Park

Isham Park

Seaman Ave.
Cooper St.
Broadway
Isham St.
55 W 207th St.

INWOOD

Academy St.
Cumming St.

9

W 204th St.

Payson Ave.

Vermilyea Ave.
Sherman Ave.
Post Ave.
Nagle Ave.
Dyckman St.

10th Ave.

9th Ave.
Exterior St.

W 206th St.
W 203rd St.
W 202nd St.
W 201st St.
Academy St.

University Heights Bridge

Hall of Fame

Bronx Community College

54

Riverside Dr.

The Cloisters

Thayer St.
Arden St.
Sickles St.
Ellwood St.
Bogardus Pl.

Hudson River

Riverside Dr.

53 Fort Tryon Park

Ft. George Hill
Hillside Ave.

Ft. George Ave.

Highbridge Park

Harlem River Dr.

Harlem River

Roberto Clemente State Park

Sedgwick Ave.
Cedar Ave.

W Burnside Ave.

W Tremont Ave.

52

Gorman Memorial Park

Overlook Terr.

Fairview Ave.
Wadsworth Terr.

W 192nd St.
W 191st St.
W 190th St.
W 189th St.
W 188th St.
W 187th St.
W 186th St.

Broadway
Wadsworth Ave.

Major Deegan Expwy.
Sedgwick Ave.
Undercliff Ave.
Montgomery Ave.
University Ave.

THE BRONX

W 176th St.

87

W174th St.

9

W 185th St.
W 184th St.
W 183rd St.
W 182nd St.
W 181st St.
W 180th St.
W 179th St.
W 178th St.
W 177th St.
W 176th St.
W 175th St.
W 174th St.

Yeshiva University
51

Laurel Hill Terr.

Bennett Park

Bennett Ave.

Ft. Washington Ave.
Pinehurst Ave.
Cabrini Blvd.

WASHINGTON HEIGHTS

Washington Heights Bridge

Alexander Hamilton Bridge

Cross Bronx Expwy.

W 170th St.

Trans Manhattan Expwy. **48**

1 95

Henry Hudson Pkwy.

George Washington Bridge (Toll)
50

1 9 95

49 Fort Washington Park

Wright Park

47

St. Nicholas Ave.
Audubon Ave.
Amsterdam Ave.

High Bridge (Footbridge) **46**

W 173rd St.
W 172nd St.
W 171st St.
W 170th St.
W 169th St.
W 168th St.
W 167th St.
W 166th St.
W 165th St.

Haven Ave.

Riverside Dr.

Columbia-Presbyterian Medical Center **45**

Broadway

Highbridge Park

Jumel Pl.
Edgecombe Ave.

W 170th St.
Ogden Ave.

W 168th St.
W 167th St.
Sedgwick Ave.
University Ave.
Summit Ave.

Bailey Ave.
Sedgwick Ave.
Fordham Rd.
Webb Ave.

Hennessy Pl.
Osborne Pl.
Phelan Pl.

N

km   1/4   1/2
mi   1/8   1/4

For nos. 1-44, see pg. 292

Inside, the elegant home is decorated with excellent Georgian, Federal, and French Empire–style furnishings, silver, and china. Some draperies were woven by master fabric-maker Franco Scalamandre using period patterns, and some of Napoleon's furniture is here. In 1833, Aaron Burr and the newly widowed Madame Jumel were married in the front parlor room (some accounts claim that her spirit still lingers about the place). Museum educators and volunteers now conduct guided tours of the house, and lectures and concerts are held here as well. Picnickers are welcome to use the colonial herb and rose gardens. Around the mansion is the **Jumel Terrace Historic District,** designated in 1970, a charming neighbor-hood of well-kept 19th-century row houses. ♦ Admission. Tu-Su. 65 Jumel Terr (between W 160th and W 161 Sts). 923.8008

45 Columbia-Presbyterian Medical Center Affiliated with **Columbia University,** this enormous hospital complex continues to grow. The hospital enjoys a reputation as a top-notch teaching facility and working hospital, and it has stabilized the neighbor-hood it serves. ♦ 622 W 168th St (between Broadway and Riverside Dr). 305.2500

46 High Bridge Originally an aqueduct as well, this footbridge is the oldest bridge extant connecting Manhattan to the mainland. Construction lasted from 1839 to 1849. The architect, **John B. Jervis,** also designed the **Highbridge Tower** in 1872, which was used to equalize pressure in the Croton Aqueduct. ♦ From Highbridge Park at W 174th St, Manhattan to W 170th St at University Ave, the Bronx

47 The United Church When it was erected in 1930 by **Thomas W. Lamb,** this building was **Loew's 175th Street Theater.** The Miami-Egyptian concoction is movie palace architecture at the height of its glory. It's one of the few remaining movie palaces in Manhattan *not* to suffer from the sixplex syndrome, but the stage has been given over to Reverend Ike, the "positive-thinking" preacher. ♦ 4140 Broadway (at W 175th St). 568.6700

48 George Washington Bridge Bus Station This concrete butterfly is a noteworthy attempt at celebrating the bus station in the shadow of a grand bridge. It was constructed in 1963 by the Port Authority of New York in collaboration with architect/engineer **Pier Luigi Nervi.** ♦ W 178th St (between Broadway and Fort Washington Ave). Bus information 564.1114

49 Little Red Lighthouse Now over-shadowed by the eastern tower of the George Washington Bridge, this lighthouse was built in 1921 to steer barges away from Jeffrey's Hook. Because navigation lights were put on the bridge, the lighthouse went up for auction in 1951, but the community's support saved

it. The pair is the subject of a well-known children's book by Hildegarde Hoyt Swift entitled *The Little Red Lighthouse and the Great Gray Bridge.* ♦ Fort Washington Park (at Washington Bridge)

50 George Washington Bridge In 1947, French architect and master of Modernism **Le Corbusier** said this spectacularly sited and magnificently elegant suspension bridge (illustrated on page 26) with its 3,500-foot span was "the most beautiful bridge in the world. . . it gleams like a reversed arch. It is blessed." If the original plans had been completed, architectural consultant **Cass Gilbert** would have encased the towers in stone. The work of **Othmar Ammann,** the bridge took four years to build and was completed in 1931. In 1962, it was expanded to become the world's first 14-lane suspension bridge. The roadway peaks at 212 feet above the water and the towers rise 604 feet. Today, the CMI Engineering landmark is the world's busiest bridge, with a hundred million vehicles crossing it yearly. For pedestrians, there is a good view of the bridge from West 181st Street, west of Fort Washington. But the real heart-thumper is a walk across the bridge. ♦ From W 178th St at Hudson River, Manhattan to Fort Lee, New Jersey

51 Yeshiva University The oldest Jewish studies center in the country, this independent university celebrated its centennial in 1986. Offered here are both undergraduate and graduate degrees in programs ranging from Hebraic studies to biomedicine, law, and rabbinics. Also part of the university are the **Albert Einstein College of Medicine** in the Bronx; **Brookdale Center-Cardozo School of Law** in Greenwich Village; and **Stern College for Women** in Midtown. The main building of its Washington Heights campus was built in 1928 by **Charles B. Meyers Associates.** It's characterized by a fanciful, romantic composition of institutional underpinnings overlaid with a Middle Eastern collection of turrets, towers and tracery, minarets, arches, and balconies—all in an unusual orange, with marble and granite striping. The light in the auditorium is especially extraordinary, with mirrored chandeliers and orange and yellow windows. ♦ W 186th St (at Amsterdam Ave). 960.5400

52 Shrine of Saint Frances Xavier Cabrini The remains of St. Frances Cabrini are enshrined in the glass altar here (above her neck is a wax mask; her head is in Rome). There is also a display of personal items belonging to the saint, the first American citizen ever to be canonized (1946) and patron saint of all immigrants. Mother Cabrini was born in Italy in 1850, became an American citizen in 1909, and died in the US in 1917. ♦ 701 Fort Washington Ave (at W 190th St). 923.3536 ♿

53 Fort Tryon Park This 62-acre park, with its sweeping views of the Hudson River, is beyond exquisite. Originally the C.K.G. Billings estate (whose entrance was the triple-arched driveway from Riverside Drive), the land was bought by John D. Rockefeller Jr., in 1909 and given to the city in 1930. (As part of the gift, the city had to agree to close off the ends of several streets above East 60th Street to create the site for **Rockefeller University.**) There are still signs of **Fort Tryon,** a Revolutionary War bulwark. Don't miss the magnificent flower gardens. The landscaping is by Frederick Law Olmsted Jr., who gave us **Central Park.** ♦ Bounded by Broadway and Riverside Dr, and W 192nd and Dyckman Sts

Within Fort Tryon Park:

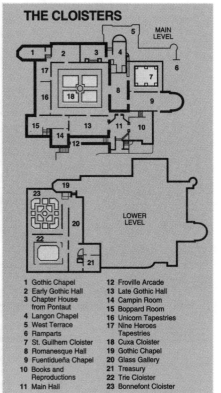

THE CLOISTERS

MAIN LEVEL

5

1 2 3 4
17
16 18 8 7 6
15 13 11 10
14 12

LOWER LEVEL

19
23
20
22
21

1 Gothic Chapel
2 Early Gothic Hall
3 Chapter House from Pontaut
4 Langon Chapel
5 West Terrace
6 Ramparts
7 St. Guilhem Cloister
8 Romanesque Hall
9 Fuentidueña Chapel
10 Books and Reproductions
11 Main Hall
12 Froville Arcade
13 Late Gothic Hall
14 Campin Room
15 Boppard Room
16 Unicorn Tapestries
17 Nine Heroes Tapestries
18 Cuxa Cloister
19 Gothic Chapel
20 Glass Gallery
21 Treasury
22 Trie Cloister
23 Bonnefont Cloister

The Cloisters Both the building and the contents of this branch of the **Metropolitan Museum of Art** were a gift of the munificent John D. Rockefeller Jr. Arranged among cloisters and other architectural elements from monasteries in southern France and Spain, this is very much a medieval ensemble, incorporating both Gothic and Romanesque elements dating from the 12th to 15th centuries. The complex was designed in the mid-1930s by **Charles Collens** to house the **Met's** medieval collection, and the **Fuentidueña** chapel was added in 1962 by **Brown, Lawford &**

Forbes. The best way to see the pastiche of architectural and art fragments is in chronological sequence—discover romantic gardens, ancient stained-glass windows, altar pieces, sculpture, and tapestries along the way. Highlights include the *Treasury,* where precious enamels, 13th- to 15th-century manuscripts, and ivories are on display, and the pièce de résistance, the celebrated *Unicorn Tapestries* from the late 15th and early 16th centuries. Recorded medieval music sets the mood. Special programs, including gallery talks, musical performances, and demonstrations, are scheduled on Saturday at noon and 2PM. A special place to relax is the herb garden (in the Bonnefont Cloister), with a view of the Palisades as Henry Hudson might have seen it. (Rockefeller protected the view by also buying the land on the Palisades opposite and restricting development.) Visiting **The Cloisters** is an absolute must. ♦ Voluntary contribution. Tu-Su. Free tours Tu-F 3PM; Su noon. W 193rd St and Fort Washington Ave. 923.3700

54 International Gourmet and Gift Center China, cutlery, crystal, appliances, food, and cosmetics imported mainly from Germany can be found in this well-stocked store. ♦ M-Th, Su; F until 2PM. 4797 Broadway (between Dyckman and Academy Sts). 569.2611

55 Dyckman House The only 18th-century Dutch farmhouse in Manhattan survives despite the inroads of 20th-century apartment houses and supermarkets. Built in 1783 and given to the city as a museum in 1915, the house has been restored and filled with original Dutch and English family furnishings, and gets high marks for authenticity and charm. An herb garden, smokehouse, and reproduction of a Revolutionary hut are further reminders of life on a farm in the colonies. It's worth a visit. ♦ Free. Tu-Sa 11AM-4PM. 4881 Broadway (at W 204th St). 304.9422

56 Carrot Top Pastries Owner Renee Allen Mancino bakes the single best carrot cake in New York, as well as delicious pecan, sweet-potato, and pumpkin pies. Devoted customers can also enjoy the light cafe menu. Its downtown branch is much bigger and also serves pasta dishes, and chicken, eggplant, and meatball parmigiana. ♦ M-Sa; Su until 4PM. 5025 Broadway (at W 214th St). 569.1532. Also at: 3931 Broadway (at W 164th St). 927.4800

57 Baker Field Fieldhouse/Lawrence Wein Stadium Columbia University's uptown athletic facility features Manhattan's only college football stadium. The views from the stadium (**Inwood Hill Park** is just to the west, **Spuyten-Duyvil** just beyond the northern end zone) are a treat. There's also a soccer field closer to Broadway. ♦ Call for a schedule. W 218th St (between Broadway and Seaman Ave). 567.0404

Boroughs

While Manhattanites refer to Brooklyn, Queens, the Bronx, and Staten Island as the "outer" boroughs, residents of these boroughs refer to Manhattan as "the city." A great deal of attitude is implied therein. The truth is that although they are outside the skyline's media limelight, the boroughs do more than play supporting roles to Manhattan. They lend the city a fair portion of its vitality and character—much of Manhattan's work force commutes from one borough or another—and they hold their own on many fronts, with their own high-caliber restaurants, theaters, parks, and architecture.

Brooklyn

With over 300 years of history and more than 75 square miles of land, Brooklyn has always been a city in its own right. It has also been a step up the ladder for immigrant groups, an oceanfront resort, a shipping capital, a cultural mecca, a teeming slum, and the front-runner of an urban renaissance.

Its national reputation is built on vaudeville jokes, an imitable accent, urban conflict, and a host of famous and often comedic natives—George Gershwin, Woody Allen, Mel Brooks, Barbra Streisand, and Beverly Sills among them. Impressive as it may be, this esteem doesn't begin to do justice to the diverse immensity of what would be, were it still autonomous, America's fourth largest city. Independent until its annexation into New York City in 1898 (Brooklyn-born author Pete Hamill calls this the "great mistake"), it has all the earmarks of a major metropolis.

The borough is divided into many ethnic diversities, among them the Middle Eastern development along **Atlantic Avenue,** the Russian section of **Brighton Beach,** and the Italian enclave in **Bensonhurst.** On any day, you'll see locals and visitors cramming the markets and stores in these vibrant communities—much of the charm of the Old Country can still be found in the heart of Brooklyn.

The River Café

1 River Café ★★★$$$$ The backdrop of this lovely dining spot—the towering, glittering Manhattan skyline visible from its location at the foot of the Brooklyn Bridge—is unequaled. So is the menu, which includes such exciting dishes as salmon and tuna *tartare* with wasabi, ragout of grilled octopus and Manila clams, and sautéed yellowfin tuna

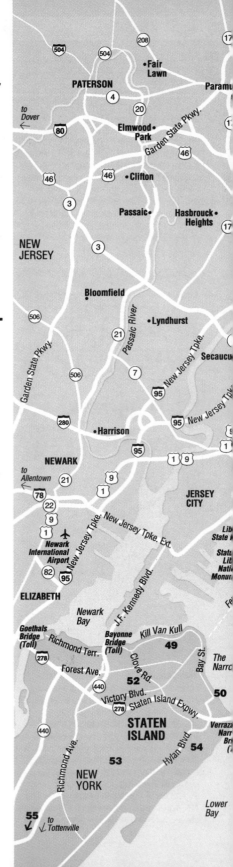

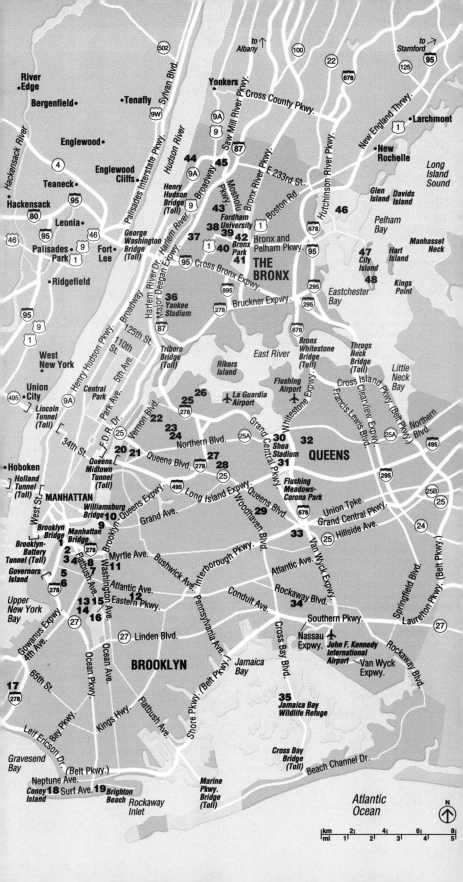

with fennel and hundred-year-old balsamic vinegar. Save the diet for tomorrow; the desserts are worth it. ♦ American ♦ M-F lunch and dinner; Sa-Su brunch and dinner. Reservations required; jacket required. 1 Water St (on the East River under the Brooklyn Bridge), Brooklyn Heights. 718/522.5200

1 Patsy's Pizza ★★$ Patsy Grimaldi learned the art of pizza making from his late uncle (also named Patsy), owner of the famed **Patsy's** pizzeria in East Harlem. The fresh dough is charred in a brick oven and the mozzarella is made fresh, as is the tomato sauce. ♦ Pizza ♦ M, W-Su lunch and dinner. No credit cards accepted. 19 Old Fulton St (between Water and Front Sts), Brooklyn Heights. 718/858.4300 ♿

2 Henry's End ★$$ This cozy—and often loud—neighborhood bistro is known for its wild-game festival, which runs annually from September through January, when the adventurous can dig into such dishes as elk chops, venison, and alligator stew. The American wine list is exceptional. ♦ Continental ♦ Daily dinner. Reservations required for three or more. 44 Henry St (at Cranberry St), Brooklyn Heights. 718/834.1776

3 Montague Street Saloon ★$ A friendly, casual atmosphere fills this local hangout. The basic pub fare is good, and the quaint outdoor cafe is open during the warmer months. Try fried calamari, steamed mussels, Cajun catfish, and steak Delmonico. Finish the meal with mud cake, Key lime pie, or peanut butter pie. ♦ American ♦ Daily lunch, dinner, and late-night meals. 122 Montague St (between Henry and Hicks Sts), Brooklyn Heights. 718/522.6770

4 Brooklyn Borough Hall A palatial sweep of stairs rises to the entrance of this Greek Revival hall of government, designed by **Gamaliel King** and built in 1851. The building, originally fashioned after **Dr. William Thornton**'s competition-winning design, was supposed to mimic Manhattan's **City Hall,** but subsequent design changes dulled the effect. ♦ 209 Joralemon St (at Court St), Downtown. 718/802.3700 ♿

NEW YORK TRANSIT MUSEUM

4 New York Transit Museum Popular with young and old transportation buffs, this small museum takes you back in time with one of the world's finest collections of mass transit artifacts, including vintage cars, signal equipment, turnstiles, mosaics, photographs, and an extensive collection of engineering drawings dating to the beginning of the century. ♦ Admission. Tu-F 10AM-4PM; Sa-Su noon-5PM. Boerum Pl and Schermerhorn St, Brooklyn Heights. 718/330.3060

5 Tripoli ★$$ Atlantic Avenue is the city's center for Middle Eastern fare, and among the numerous small restaurants, this bilevel place is probably the best and most authentic. Order any of the Lebanese dishes, including falafel, hummus, lamb kabobs, stuffed grape leaves, lamb stew, and one of the heavily honeyed desserts. There's live music and entertainment Saturday nights. ♦ Middle Eastern ♦ Daily lunch and dinner. Reservations required Friday and Saturday nights. 156 Atlantic Ave (at Clinton St), Brooklyn Heights. 718/596.5800

6 Casa Rosa ★$$ Good—and inexpensive—home-style cooking is this unpretentious trattoria's trademark. Have pork chops with broccoli rabe; *zuppa di pesce a la Rosa* (fish soup); or clams, shrimp, and calamari in a light tomato sauce. The service can be slow. ♦ Italian ♦ Tu-F lunch and dinner; Sa-Su dinner. Reservations recommended. 384 Court St (at Carroll St), Carroll Gardens. 718/625.8874 ♿

7 Brooklyn Academy of Music This organization, affectionately known as "BAM," was founded in 1859 on Montague Street and is housed in a 1908 **Herts & Tallant**–designed building. Among the superlative performers who have appeared here are Edwin Booth as *Hamlet* and Sarah Bernhardt as *Camille.* Pavlova danced and Caruso sang in the **Opera House. BAM** is the home of the **Brooklyn Philharmonic.** Over the last decade, impresario Harvey Lichtenstein has introduced many innovative programs in music and dance. His annual Next Wave Festival has been the launching pad for artists like Philip Glass, Laurie Anderson, and choreographer Mark Morris. In 1987, the organization reopened the **Majestic,** an 83-year-old theater-turned-movie house that had been lying dormant for nearly 20 years. Interestingly, the shell of the theater was left intact—the wear and tear of the years showing—while two semicircular tiers of seats around a large stage were built, creating an intimate amphitheater-like space with an exciting medieval feel. The interior was designed by **Hardy Holzman Pfeiffer Associates.** Successful engagements at the **Majestic** (located on Fulton Street, a block away from the main structure) have included choreographer-director Martha Clarke's *Endangered Species* and the musical *Township Fever,* from Mbongeni Ngema, the director of *Sarafina!* Theaters: **Opera House** (seats 2,100); **Helen Carey Playhouse** (seats 1,078); **Lepercq Space** (seats 550); **Majestic** (seats 900). A shuttle bus coordinated with scheduled performances at **Opera House** or **Majestic** departs from Lexington Avenue at East 51st Street in Manhattan; call BAM for a schedule. ♦ 30 Lafayette Ave (between St. Felix St and Ashland Pl), Downtown. 718/636.4100 ♿

8 Junior's ★$ Some say the cheesecake here is the best in New York. The rest of the food is standard deli/diner fare, such as pastrami sandwiches and roast chicken, distinguished only by the large size of the portions. Weekend evenings, however, the place jumps, and the cars are double- and triple-parked out front. ♦ Deli ♦ Daily breakfast, lunch, dinner, and late-night meals. 386 Flatbush Ave (at DeKalb Ave), Downtown. 718/852.5257

9 Peter Luger ★★★$$$ One of the oldest and still one of the better, more colorful steak houses in the city, this place is great for one thing only: well-charred porterhouse steak made from prime, aged Iowa corn-fed beef. These hefty heifer parts, for two or more, are always cooked perfectly to order and come presliced unless you request otherwise. Potato side dishes are all serviceable, but skip the other vegetables. For dessert, try cheesecake or ice cream. ♦ Steak house ♦ Daily lunch and dinner. Reservations required. No credit cards accepted. 178 Broadway (at Driggs Ave), Williamsburg. 718/387.7400

9 Planet Thailand ★$ Owners David and Anna Popermhem add pizzazz to the menu using fresh ingredients for their flavorful salads, lemony and tender squid, or charred beef with onions, chiles, and basil. The food contains just the right amount of spices, making it popular with Western palates. Best entrées include chicken in a fragrant coconut curry and the grilled moist marinated chicken. ♦ Thai ♦ M-Sa lunch and dinner; Su brunch and dinner. 184 Bedford Ave(at North St), Williamsburg. 718/559.5758

10 Architectural Salvage Warehouse If you want to recycle some of the charm and detail of old New York into your new home, this warehouse is stocked with authentic architectural artifacts and elements rescued from the city's condemned buildings. Established in 1980 by the New York City Landmarks Preservation Commission, its purpose is to supply New Yorkers who are restoring their homes with bits and pieces of the past. Architects and interior designers come here looking for old woodwork, shutters, doors, mantels, pedestal sinks, and exterior ironwork; you'll need to arrange the transportation of your acquisitions. ♦ By appointment. 337 Berry St (near Broadway at 5th St), Williamsburg. 212/487.6800, 718/388.4527

11 Pratt Institute Architecture, business, science, and fine arts are the strong suits of this 3,200-student school established in 1887. The 25-acre campus has a satellite in Manhattan. ♦ Bounded by DeKalb and Willoughby Aves (between Classon Ave and Hall St), Downtown. 718/636.3600

12 Brooklyn Children's Museum In this museum, which was built in 1976 to the designs of **Hardy Holzman Pfeiffer Associates,** children visit a greenhouse, work with butterflies and fossils, and learn about how animals get energy from food. They can also participate in a dream sequence inside a 25-foot model of a sleeping head and use their five senses to unlock the mystery of objects, using as tools 20,000 cultural artifacts and natural history specimens from the museum's collection. Special events include films, workshops, field trips, concerts, and storytelling sessions. ♦ Donation suggested. W-F 2PM-5PM; Sa-Su, holidays noon-5PM. 145 Brooklyn Ave (at St. Mark's Ave), Crown Heights. 718/735.4432

13 Leaf & Bean Approximately 50 types of coffee beans and 20 types of loose tea are offered here, along with other gourmet items, including truffle candies, fancy jams, and white cocoa. There's also a large supply of kitchen accessories—wine glasses, cookie jars, place mats, Italian ceramic plates, candles, cloth napkins, and, of course, a variety of coffeemakers and teapots. ♦ Daily. 83 Seventh Ave (between Union and Berkeley Sts), Park Slope. 718/638.5791

13 Cucina ★★★$$ This warm inviting place has a stylish decor—maple tables and Art Deco chairs, dried flowers, a vibrant mural, and a colorful antipasto table. Pasta dishes and entrées are also earthy and alluring: Save room for the chocolate tasting plate or richly fruity sorbets. Reasonably priced wines from Italy, France, and California are available. ♦ Italian ♦ Daily dinner. No credit cards accepted. 256 Fifth Ave (between Carroll St and Garfield Pl), Park Slope. 718/230.0711 ♿

13 Santa Fe Grill ★$ The serene Southwestern setting, rich in New Mexican artifacts, is lovely; the noise level, however, makes for a less-than-peaceful mood. The food is quite respectable for this far north—try the vegetable quesadilla, any of the burritos and enchiladas (including a spinach and cheese variety), or one of the decent burgers. ◆ Tex-Mex ◆ Daily dinner. 62 Seventh Ave (at Lincoln Pl), Park Slope. 718/636.0279

14 Aunt Sonia's ★★$$ The perfect conclusion to a late-afternoon stroll through **Prospect Park** or a visit to the **Brooklyn Museum,** this small, crowded restaurant has an eclectic menu that changes with the season—and the chef's mood. The food is dependably decent and sometimes extraordinary. Try the organic chicken couscous with vegetables, or herb-crisped salmon with mussels and scallops in a bouillabaisse sauce. The service is uneven, but good humored. ◆ Eclectic ◆ M-F dinner; Sa-Su brunch and dinner. 1123 Eighth Ave (at 12th St), Park Slope. 718/965.9526 ♿

14 Bed & Breakfast on the Park $$ Former antiques-store owner Liana Paolella has meticulously restored this landmark 19th-century home-turned-inn. Her guests enjoy six spacious, beautifully furnished rooms (two with shared baths) replete with wood-burning fireplaces, canopied beds, stained-glass windows, Oriental rugs, and an extensive collection of museum-quality paintings. A scrumptious breakfast further complements the inn's grand style. ◆ 113 Prospect Park W (between Sixth and Seventh Sts), Park Slope. 718/499.6115; fax 718/499.1385

15 Grand Army Plaza Monuments have been added since the plaza was first laid out in 1870 by Frederick Law Olmsted and Calvert Vaux. The Roman-style *Soldiers' and Sailors' Arch* was raised as a tribute to the Union Army in 1892 and was later encrusted with Frederick MacMonnies's massive sculptures and some less exuberant bas-relief forms. The **Bailey Fountain** was added in 1932 by architect **Edgerton Swarthwout** and sculptor Eugene Savage. **Morris Ketchum, Jr. & Associates** designed the 1965 **John F. Kennedy Memorial.** ◆ Plaza St at Flatbush Ave (between Eastern Pkwy and Prospect Park W), Park Slope–Prospect Heights.

Each John Doe burial in Potter's Field (on the Long Island Sound) costs New York City $300.

Before 1929, the site now occupied by La Guardia Airport was an amusement park.

All that remains of Revolutionary War–era Fort Washington is the outline of the foundation, marked by paving stones, in Bennett Park. Here at Fort Washington Avenue, between West 183rd and West 185th Streets, is the highest point in Manhattan, 267.75 feet above sea level.

15 Prospect Park The Grand Army Plaza is the official entrance to this 526-acre park, as loved by Brooklynites as the larger **Central Park** is by Manhattanites. In fact, these two parks share designers (landscape architects Olmsted and Vaux), and—not surprisingly—landscaping characteristics (meadowlands, footpaths, skating rink, boating lake, carousel, and the recently opened wildlife center, the country's largest children's zoo). The recipient of a recent multimillion-dollar renovation, the park is close to being returned to its original bucolic state. Among other sites, an 18th-century Dutch farmhouse was relocated here to be used as a museum, and an old Quaker cemetery contains Montgomery Clift's tomb. ◆ Bounded by Parkside Ave and Eastern Pkwy, and Flatbush Ave and Prospect Park W, Brooklyn. 718/965.8900

16 Brooklyn Museum This museum always seems to be undergoing construction, which began in 1893 and continued until 1924 by **McKim, Mead & White. Prentice & Chan, Ohlhausen** designed the next addition in 1978, and **Joseph Tonetti** designed the next in 1987. The most recent addition of this massive five-story museum, part of a major $31-million renovation completed in 1993, was designed by **Arata Isosaki** and **James Stewart Polshek & Partners.** It includes three floors of new galleries in the **West Wing,** the 460-seat **Iris and B. Gerald Cantor Auditorium** (which will serve as the museum's first formal gathering place since the original auditorium was converted into the **Grand Lobby** in the early 1930s), and two floors of additional art storage space. Excellent collections include the arts of Egypt, the classical Middle East, and Asia. Exhibitions of primitive arts come from Africa, the South Pacific, and the Americas; other displays feature Greek and Roman antiquities. Costumes, textiles, decorative arts, and period furniture dating from the late 17th century are all beautifully laid out for viewing. The permanent collection includes works by Rodin, Modigliani, Cassatt, Degas, Monet, Chagall, Gauguin, Toulouse-Lautrec, Homer, Sargent, and Bierstadt. The continuing series of exhibitions by contemporary artists has included Joseph Kosuth, Alfredo Jarr, and Reeva Potoff. ◆ Donation suggested. W-Su. 200 Eastern Pkwy (at Washington Ave), Prospect Heights. 718/638.5000 ♿

Within the Brooklyn Museum:

Cafe at Brooklyn Musuem ★$ Rest your tired feet after viewing the museum's exhibits in this bright, cheery room. The small gourmet sandwich menu includes roasted eggplant with mozzarella, tomato, and basil on focaccia. For dessert try raspberry cheesecake or carrot cake. ◆ Cafe ◆ W-Su breakfast, lunch, and afternoon snacks. No credit cards accepted. 718/638.5000 &

16 Brooklyn Botanic Garden Although not as large or as famous as the **New York Botanical Garden** in the Bronx, this one has such celebrated plantings as a Japanese hill-and-pond garden, an herb garden with over 300 specimens, and one of the largest public rose collections in America. A conservatory houses the largest bonsai collection in the country. The 50 acres of flora include a fragrance garden for the blind. The master plan for the garden was designed by the Olmsted brothers and laid down in 1910; the landscaping was completed in 1912 by Harold Caparn; and the **Steinhardt Conservatory,** which was designed by **Davis, Brody & Associates,** was completed in 1988. ♦ Parking fee. Botanic Gardens: free. Steinhardt Conservatory: admission Apr-Nov. Botanic Gardens: Tu-Su. Steinhardt Conservatory: Tu-Su. 1000 Washington Ave (between Empire Blvd and Eastern Pkwy), Prospect Heights. 718/622.4433

17 Areo ★$$ Solid Italian fare is served here. The impressively titled Ram's Feast—veal and filet mignon with mushrooms and fried zucchini—will satisfy nearly every gourmand; other dishes to try include chicken with portobello mushrooms in a Champagne cream sauce, and lobster in a tomato or lemon white sauce. There's also good cheesecake and tiramisù. ♦ Italian ♦ Tu-Sa lunch and dinner; Su dinner. Reservations recommended. 8424 Third Ave (at 85th St), Bay Ridge. 718/238.0079

18 Coney Island Rattling over the tracks since 1927, the wooden *Cyclone* roller coaster still provides thrills, and a **Nathan's** hot dog with everything on it is still a genuine treat, but the golden days of Coney Island are over. The beach has survived somewhat intact, and it sure beats the tar beaches many Brooklynites settle for on the roofs of their apartment buildings on hot summer weekends. In the 1920s, however, this was the Riviera, the "World's Largest Playground" for generations of hard-working immigrants and native New Yorkers. It has since faded into neglect, though it provides a certain nostalgia with a glimpse of other times, ocean views, and a visit to nearby Brighton Beach for a peek into Little Russia. ♦ Surf Ave (between Ocean Pkwy and W 37th St)

On Coney Island:

Nathan's Famous ★$ Indeed, this is probably the most famous and elaborate hot dog stand in the world, having served spicy franks and fabulously greasy, crinkle-cut fried potatoes for nearly a century. There are locations all over Manhattan as well, but this was the first. ♦ American ♦ Surf Ave (at Stillwell Ave), Coney Island. 946.2202. Also at: Numerous locations throughout the city

Aquarium for Wildlife Conservation Native creatures of the *Hudson River Display* and dramatic denizens of the shark tank are on exhibit in the **Native Sea Life** building. Penguins and sea lions provide comic relief, and **Aquatheater** shows provide great entertainment: dolphins in the summer and whales, walruses, and sea lions in the winter. There's also a **Discovery Cove,** where kids can touch sea stars and horseshoe crabs. ♦ Admission; parking fee. Daily. Surf Ave (at W Eighth St), Coney Island. 718/265.3400 &

19 M&I International Considered the **Zabar's** of Brighton Beach, both for its extensive merchandise and constant crowds, this shop sells prepared foods, sausages, and other meats, along with cheeses. There are also good bakery products—try the apple strudel. ♦ Daily. 249 Brighton Beach Ave (between Second and Third Sts), Brighton Beach. 718/615.1011

NATIONAL
Restaurant and Catering

19 National Restaurant ★★$$$ Known for its boisterous good times and late-night bonhomie, this restaurant is the place to come with friends for the rivers of vodka that will have you singing tunes from the motherland with the live band before you know it. The set dinners are huge, featuring a parade of cold appetizers, such as herring with potatoes and beet salad, and five main courses, including shish kebab and roast chicken. ♦ Russian ♦ Daily dinner and late-night meals. 273 Brighton Beach Ave (between Second and Third Sts), Brighton Beach. 718/646.1225

19 Odessa ★★$$$ Make a night of it with the decked-out Eastern European regulars indulging in vodka on ice and an endless parade of "appetizers" (here indistinguishable from the entrées). Try the herring, eggplant caviar, baked salmon, or any of the many other dishes that will come your way. There's dancing and live music nightly. All in all, this is an extraordinary experience. ♦ Russian ♦ Daily lunch and dinner. Reservations required. 1113 Brighton Beach Ave (between 13th and 14th Sts), Brighton Beach. 718/332.3223

Restaurants/Clubs: Red   **Hotels:** Blue

Shops/ ♥ Outdoors: Green   **Sights/Culture:** Black

Past Perfect: The New York City Landmarks Preservation Commission

When the noble, Roman-style **Pennsylvania Train Station** fell victim to the wrecker's ball in 1965, public outrage was not enough to stay its death sentence. In its place rose a modern construction of glass and steel that sorely lacked the elegance and historic significance of its predecessor. The old **Penn Station** was but one of the city's magnificent historic buildings razed in the name of modernism.

To halt further destruction and demolition of New York's past, the New York City Landmarks Preservation Commission was formed by Mayor Robert F. Wagner on 19 April 1965. In October of that year, the Commission designated its first landmark, the former **Astor Library** on **Lafayette Street** in the **East Village.** Built as the first free public library in the 1850s, today it houses Joseph Papp's **Public Theater,** birthplace of *Hair* and *A Chorus Line* and home to the New York Shakespeare Festival.

Celebrating its 30th anniversary, the Commission now protects over 20,000 of New York City's one million buildings. More than 1,000 of these are interspersed one by one throughout the five boroughs; the balance are found clustered within 60 historic districts. The landmarks range from little-known structures in out-of-the-way corners of the city to modest 17th-century houses and graveyards. The roster includes **Grand Central Station, Carnegie Hall,** the **Empire State Building,** the interior of the elegant **Four Seasons** restaurant, and the nostalgic **Cyclone** roller coaster and **Wonder Wheel** rides that once made **Coney Island** America's favorite urban playground.

Although one of New York City's smallest agencies, the Commission is nevertheless the largest municipal preservation agency in the United States. Consisting of 11 commissioners appointed by the mayor for three-year terms (of these, only the chairman receives a salary) and a full-time staff, the agency is responsible for designating city landmarks and historic districts and regulating changes to already designated buildings. The owner of a protected landmark—be it another city agency, a federal government agency, an individual, or a business—must obtain the permission of the Commission before it can alter, reconstruct, or demolish a landmark's exterior or, in some cases, interior features. The Commission itself has very few funds for grants or "brick and mortar" expenses, so the owner is usually the party who absorbs the cost of approved restorations and alterations; the Commission's role is to judge whether they are appropriate.

New York was settled and developed over the centuries by builders from many countries. The mosaic of architectural styles is a source of pride for the city's eight million residents. These landmarks serve as a reminder of the city's history and give it the cachet that tourists have come to expect.

In November 1993, the Commission moved to a landmark building near **South Street Seaport.** Its headquarters, in an Italian Renaissance Revival structure designed in 1909 by **Hunt & Hunt,** stands on the site of the first official marketplace in 17th-century New Amsterdam. The current building served as Manhattan's first police precinct until 1973, then stood vacant for 20 years.

The Commission's research library is open by appointment only to visiting or local historians, architects, and architecture buffs. The Commission also operates Brooklyn's **Architectural Salvage Warehouse** (see page 309), which sells architectural and decorative elements rescued from historic buildings before they were demolished: fireplace mantels, lighting fixtures, doors, and wrought-iron gratings are purchased and recycled back into the homes of New Yorkers.

100 Old Slip (between the East River and Water St). 487.6800

Recommended reading:

Guide to New York City Landmarks, The New York City Landmarks Preservation Commission, by Andrew S. Dolkart (1992, Preservation Press).

The Landmarks of New York and *The Landmarks of New York II,* by Barbaralee Diamonstein (1988 and 1993, Harry Abrams).

Michael Storrings

Queens

This sprawling borough has always been a conglomeration of towns, villages, model communities, and real-estate developments. Suburban in spirit and design, it has grown far too dense to be anything but urban in essence, the type of immigrant staging ground that Manhattan, Brooklyn, and the Bronx used to be (next to Athens, Queens has the world's largest Greek community in **Astoria**). But unlike these older boroughs, it is oriented toward the highways that lace it together, toward the airports (**Kennedy** and **La Guardia**) that sit on either shore, and the suburban reaches of Nassau County. Things have changed considerably since the area of Queens was created in 1683 as one of the 12 counties in the province of New York. It was named for Queen Catherine of Braganza, the Portuguese-born wife of King Charles II of England.

20 Water's Edge ★★$$$ Surrounded by glass walls on three sides, the tables in this swank riverside restaurant all have spectacular west-looking views of Midtown and Lower Manhattan. Don't miss the Oriental crab and lobster dumplings with enoki mushrooms and pea shoots in carrot lobster broth; spinach fettuccine with artichokes, escargots, and parsley in a Pernod lemon sauce; or black bass with arugula vinaigrette. Manhattanites need not fret about transportation to and from Queens—the restaurant runs a complimentary dinner ferry from East 34th Street every hour between 6 and 11PM, Tuesday through Saturday (except during January and February, when it runs only Thursday through Saturday). ♦ Seafood ♦ M-F lunch and dinner; Sa dinner. Reservations required; jacket and tie required. 44th Dr (at the East River), Long Island City. 718/482.0033

21 Manducatis ★★$$ Family atmosphere and a cozy fireplace give this place an authentic trattoria feeling. Chef Ida's fine, straightforward touch with fresh ingredients brings people from all over town to this out-of-the-way spot. One of the best dishes on the menu is *pappardelle* with garlic and white beans. ♦ Italian ♦ M-F lunch and dinner; Sa-Su dinner. Reservations recommended. 13-27 Jackson Ave (at 47th Ave), Long Island City. 718/729.4602

21 P.S. 1 An alternative space of the **Institute for Contemporary Art,** this 19th-century school, under the directorship of Alanna Heiss, is used for exhibitions of new and established artists. Activity is limited during renovations; call for a schedule. ♦ Donation suggested. 46-01 21st St (between Jackson Ave and 45th Rd), Long Island City. 718/784.2084

21 Silvercup Studios In 1983, the **Silvercup Bakery** was converted into a movie studio. Eighteen soundstages are contained within a mammoth three-block-long building. In addition to providing space for work on movies (*Garbo Talks, Street Smart, The Purple Rose of Cairo*), commercials (which account for most of the activity), and music videos, the studio rents screening rooms and production offices, some of whose windows overlook the New York skyline. ♦ 42-22 22nd St (between 43rd Ave and Bridge Plaza S), Long Island City. 718/784.3390

22 Isamu Noguchi Garden Museum Completed in 1985, this is one of the few museums dedicated to the work of a single artist, created by that artist. Isamu Noguchi (1904-88) had a controversial career filled with projects that ranged from immense sculpture gardens to *akari* lamps to set designs for choreographers Martha Graham and George Balanchine. Some of the greatest examples of Noguchi's work are on display in the museum's 12 galleries and outdoor sculpture garden. ♦ Donation suggested. W, Sa-Su 11AM-6PM Apr-Nov. 32-37 Vernon Blvd (at 33rd Rd), Long Island City. 718/204.7088

23 Roumeli Taverna ★$$ A favorite among the abundant supply of Greek eateries in Queens, this place, named after a Greek mountain range, serves high-quality, authentic food. Start with such traditional appetizers as stuffed grape leaves, hummus, and grilled octopus, and then move on to roast suckling pig, charcoal-grilled baby lamb, moussaka, or broiled snapper. ♦ Greek ♦ Daily lunch and dinner. 33-04 Broadway (between 33rd and 34th Sts), Astoria. 718/278.7533

24 American Museum of the Moving Image Designed by **Gwathmey Siegel & Associates** and built in 1988, this museum is all that its name advertises and more, with extensive archives, special showings, and exhibitions. There are no snobbish distinctions between film and TV or technology and art, but it's not about junk culture, either. The artifacts displayed leave an indelible impression of Pop history. ♦ Admission. Tu-F noon-4PM; Sa-Su noon-6PM. 36-01 35th Ave (at 36th St), Astoria. 718/784.0077; tours 718/784.4520 ᕼ

24 Kaufman Astoria Studio/U.S. Army Pictorial Center Rudolph Valentino and Gloria Swanson starred in silent films made here in the heyday of New York City's motion picture boom. Edward G. Robinson made the early talkie *Hole in the Wall* here, and the Marx Brothers used the studio for the filming of *The Cocoanuts.* After the studio's 1932 bankruptcy, the property passed through several hands. During World War II, it was used by the army for training and propaganda films done by Frank Capra. Now a historic landmark—not open to the public—the studio is back in business. It was a favorite location of director Sidney Lumet. ◆ 34-12 36th St (between 34th and 35th Aves), Astoria. 718/392.5600.

25 Elias Corner ★★$ Pick dinner from among the day's catches on the ice-laden counter and have it grilled over charcoal. While you wait, try one of the traditional and richly flavored appetizers, such as *taramasalata* (a creamy mixture of carp roe, lemon juice, milk-soaked breadcrumbs, olive oil, and seasonings) served with crackers or stuffed grape leaves. ◆ Greek/Seafood ◆ Daily dinner. No credit cards accepted. 24-02 31st St (at 24th Ave), Astoria. 718/932.1510

26 Steinway Mansion William Steinway was a great friend of President Grover Cleveland and presented him with a grand piano as a wedding gift. The Steinway home, built in 1856, was once a lively setting for fairy tale social events. Not open to the public. ◆ 18-33 41st St (at Berrian Blvd), Astoria

27 Little India Known as Jackson Heights, this area is a solid, family-oriented neighborhood of Argentinians, Thais, Spaniards, Koreans, Italians, and Pakistanis. But the bold colors and pungent smells of India make it the most foreign and exotic to the curious visitor. Some 60,000 Indian immigrants in the New York City area either live on this one block of 74th Street north of Roosevelt Avenue, or flock here regularly to shop, eat, and visit. Sari shops, aromatic grocery stores, jewelry stores whose windows are laden with 22K-gold wedding jewelry, and about a dozen authentic restaurants are part of the lively scene. ◆ 74th St and Roosevelt Ave

27 Delhi Palace ★★$$ Recently remodeled, this is Queens's most elegant "Little India" dining choice, with crisp white tablecloths, fresh flowers, attentive service, and quiet background music. In addition to selections from the menu, choose from the extensive buffet which appears at both lunch and dinner. Don't miss the chicken with creamy cashew sauce or tandoori shrimp with *masala* (a mild creamy) sauce. ◆ Indian ◆ Daily lunch and dinner. 37-33 74th St (between Roosevelt and 37th Aves), Jackson Heights. 718/507.0666

27 Jackson Diner ★$ Much like a North Indian *dhaba* (truck stop—the connotations are better there), this no-frills Indian restaurant is good for dishes drawn

from owner Gian Saini's family recipes. Local Indian families pack the place for tandoori chicken, *murg lajwab* (chicken simmered with tomatoes, ginger, chili, herbs, and spices), and *paneer palak* (puree of spinach with spices and homemade cheese). ◆ Indian ◆ No credit cards accepted. 37-03 74th St (between Roosevelt and 37th Aves), Jackson Heights. 718/672.1232

28 Jaiya Thai Oriental Restaurant ★★$$ The extensive, original menu at this Thai eatery includes more than 300 choices. Try the excellent spicy chicken and coconut soup; spicy shredded jellyfish; pork with very hot chili peppers and onions; pad thai; naked shrimp (rare shrimp with lime, lemongrass, and chili); and pork with string beans, red chili, and basil. ◆ Thai ◆ Daily lunch and dinner. Reservations recommended for dinner Friday through Sunday. 81-11 Broadway (between 81st and 82nd Sts), Elmhurst. 651.1330. Also at: 396 Third Ave (at E 28th St), Murray Hill. 212/889.1330

29 London Lennie's $$ As befits the name of this place, prints of palace guards grace the dining room wall; otherwise it's a basic, wood-paneled, nautically decorated fish house. Try the chowder, panfried oysters, big pots of steamers, Maryland crab cakes, and fried soft-shell crabs. There's also an extensive wine list. ◆ Seafood ◆ M-F lunch and dinner; Sa-Su dinner. 63-88 Woodhaven Blvd (between 63rd Dr and Fleet Ct), Forest Hills. 718/894.8084

30 Shea Stadium Home of the **New York Mets,** this 55,300-seat stadium, built in 1963 and designed by **Praeger-Waterbury,** also hosted Pope John Paul II in 1979 and the history-making 1965 Beatles concert. The stadium opened for the **Mets'** 1964 season, which coincided with the **World's Fair** next door at **Flushing Meadows–Corona Park.** For its 25th anniversary in 1988, the stadium underwent a modest renovation and now features large neon figures on the outside, new plastic seating to replace old wooden benches, and a "DiamondVision" video screen. Traffic around the stadium is quite congested before and after games; call for directions by public transportation. ♦ 126th St and Roosevelt Ave, Flushing. 718/507.8499 &

31 Flushing Meadows–Corona Park Once a garbage dump, this triumph of reclamation, smack dab in the geographic center of New York City, was later chosen for the **1939-40** and **1964-65 New York World's Fairs.** ♦ Bounded by Union Turnpike and 44th Ave (between Van Wyck Expwy and Grand Central Pkwy), Flushing

Within Flushing Meadows-Corona Park:

Hall of Science Designed by **Wallace K. Harrison** and built as a science pavilion for the **1964-65 World's Fair,** this is New York's only hands-on science and technology museum. The sophisticated collection includes 150 interactive exhibits focusing on color, light, microbiology, structures, feedback, and quantum physics. ♦ Admission; free W-Th 3PM-5PM. W-Su. 47-01 111th St (at 48th Ave). 718/699.0675

Queens Museum of Art Highlights include excellent art and photography shows and the world's largest scale model—a 9,335-square-foot *Panorama of New York City* that has recently been brought up-to-date and now includes just about every street, building, bridge, and park at a scale of one inch to 100 feet. ♦ Donation requested. Tu-F; Sa-Su noon-5PM. Off Grand Central Pkwy. 718/592.5555

32 Jade Palace ★★$ This modern dining room gets absolutely mobbed at night, but regulars patiently wait for what many feel is the best Chinese seafood in the area. Try shark fin soup; steamed, live shrimp; and any of the evening's specials—often striped or sea bass, eel, shrimp, or crab. The dim sum selection is also a standout. If your mood dictates meat instead of fish, you'll have plenty to choose from, as well—lamb baked in a pot is a winner. ♦ Cantonese/Seafood ♦ Daily lunch and dinner. 136-14 38th Ave (between Main and Union Sts), Flushing. 718/353.3366 &

33 Pastrami King ★$ New Yorkers old enough to remember like to reminisce about a time when every neighborhood had delis as good as this one. This place smokes its own pastrami

and corned beef; luckily, these delicacies can be shipped worldwide. Needless to say, pastrami and corned beef sandwiches are the items to order. ♦ Deli ♦ Daily breakfast, lunch, and dinner. 124-24 Queens Blvd (at 82nd Ave), Kew Gardens. 718/263.1717

34 Aqueduct Thoroughbred racing takes place here. ♦ Oct-May. Rockaway Blvd and 110th St, Ozone Park. 718/641.4700 &

35 Jamaica Bay Wildlife Refuge Within the **Center Gateway National Recreation Area,** these vast man-made tidal wetlands and uplands have become a haven for hundreds of species of birds and plants. The fall migratory season, starting in mid-August, is a particularly good time to come. Dress appropriately. ♦ Free. Daily. Cross Bay Blvd and Broad Channel. 718/318.4340

The Bronx

The Bronx not only stands as a study in contrasts, but also typifies the rapid succession of growth and decline experienced throughout New York City—a microcosm of American urban change squeezed into just over half a century. Today it is a mélange of devastated tenements, suburban riverfront mansions, seaside cottages, massive housing superblocks, and fading boulevards of grand Art Deco apartment towers. Although in recent years the Bronx has become a synonym for urban decay, some of the borough remains stable, and heavy philanthropic and governmental investment as well as the energetic efforts of community-based groups are helping to restore some of the more run-down areas.

36 Yankee Stadium In 1973, the **Yankees** celebrated their 50th anniversary in this 57,545-seat horseshoe arena designed in 1923 by **Osborn Engineering Co.** Remodeling has kept the home of the frequent World Series champs one of the most modern baseball facilities in the country. It was almost completely rebuilt in 1976 by **Praeger-Kavanagh-Waterbury.** The park is 11.6 acres, 3.5 of which are taken up by the field itself. Within the park are monuments to such Yankee greats as Lou Gehrig, Joe DiMaggio, Casey Stengel, and, of course, Babe Ruth. It is advised that you exercise caution when visiting the area surrounding the stadium—especially at night. ♦ E 161st St and River Ave, High Bridge. 718/293.6000 &

37 Hall of Fame for Great Americans Bronze busts of nearly a hundred of America's greatest scientists, statesmen, and artists are on display in this handsome building designed in 1901 and 1914 by **McKim, Mead & White.** Sculptures are by Daniel Chester French, Frederick MacMonnies, and James Earle Fraser. Note the classic arcade by **Stanford White.** ♦ Free. Daily. W 181st St and University Ave, Bronx Community College, University Heights. 718/220.6003

38 Edgar Allan Poe Cottage From 1846 to 1848 the writer and his dying wife lived in this house, which dates back to 1812. *Annabel Lee* was among the works written here. The museum displays many of Poe's manuscripts and other memorabilia. ♦ Nominal admission. Sa 10AM-4PM; Su 1-5PM. Grand Concourse and E Kingsbridge Rd, Fordham. 718/881.8900

39 Fordham University One of the nation's foremost Jesuit schools, **Rose Hill Campus** comprises 85 acres and has over 13,000 students enrolled in a traditional arts and sciences curriculum. **Rose Hill Manor** (1838), which now forms part of the **Administration Building,** was the home of the original school, **St. John's College,** begun in 1841 by John Hughes. Hughes later became New York State's first Catholic archbishop. This beautiful campus has a classic collection of Collegiate Gothic structures, most notably **Keating Hall,** designed in 1936 by **Robert S. Reiley.** The university has two satellite campuses in Manhattan, the **Law School** and **Graduate School of Business** at West 62nd Street (212/636.6000). ♦ 441 E Fordham Rd (at Third Ave), Fordham. 718/817.1000

40 Arthur Avenue Retail Market This covered market is packed with stalls selling everything from high-quality Tuscan virgin olive oil to wheels of parmigiano reggiano, fresh eggs, thinly sliced veal, baby eggplant, and zucchini. For the best cheese, stop by **Mike & Sons'** stall. ♦ M-Sa. 2344 Arthur Ave (between E 187th and E 189th Sts), Fordham. 718/367.5686

40 Calabria Pork Store Choose, if you can, among the 500 kinds of sausage dangling from the ceiling; all are delicious, either hot or sweet, and many are studded with peppercorns or garlic. ♦ M-Sa. 2338 Arthur Ave (at E 187th St). Fordham. 718/367.5145

40 Belmont Italian-American Playhouse In a cramped loft above a supermarket in a neighborhood where the newspapers are still read in Italian and social clubs are crowded with old men discussing soccer scores, this 70-seat theater draws crowds from Manhattan for classic and contemporary Italian works, Shakespearean productions, and works by local playwrights of all ethnic backgrounds. The three young Italian-American owners knew their theater would make it when Robert DeNiro used their space to audition for his 1993 film *A Bronx Tale.* ♦ Shows Th-Sa 8:30PM; Su matinee 2:30PM. Call for a schedule. 2385 Arthur Ave (between E 186th and E 187th Sts), Fordham. 718/364.4700 ♿

40 Dominick's ★★$ Don't let the lines outside dissuade you from eating at this noisy and chaotic restaurant. Once you're seated, you'll be greeted with terrific home-style Southern Italian fare and a solicitous staff. ♦ Italian ♦ M, W-Sa lunch and dinner; Su dinner. No credit cards accepted. 2335 Arthur Ave (between E 187th St and Crescent Ave), Fordham. 718/733.2807

40 Calandra Salted braids and unsalted balls of very fresh mozzarella made on the premises are sold here. A wide selection of cheeses from Europe as well as South America is also available. ♦ M-Sa. 2314 Arthur Ave (at E 183rd St). 718/365.7572

41 Bronx Zoo/Wildlife Conservation Park Managed by **NYZS/The Wildlife Conservation Society,** the zoo is home to almost 4,000 animals—650 species—on 265 acres, making it the largest metropolitan zoo in the United States. At its northernmost end is **Astor Court** (built from 1901 to 1922 to the design of **Heins & LaFarge),** a collection of formal zoo buildings that contains the **Zoo Center** (old elephant house), the renovated **Monkey House,** and the **Sea Lion Pool.** These structures, influenced by the **1893 Chicago World's Fair,** were built as part of the original plan, which envisioned a formal central court area surrounded by natural park settings. The balance of the zoo's acreage is designed to re-create naturalistic habitats where African and Asian wildlife roam. ♦ Admission; free Wednesday. Daily. Bounded by Bronx River Pkwy and Southern Blvd, and Bronx Park S and Webster Ave. 718/367.1010

Within the Bronx Zoo:

Paul Rainey Memorial Gate Images of bears and deer decorate this imaginative Art Deco gates, which open onto a 200-year-old Italian fountain donated by William Rockefeller. The gate was designed by **Charles A. Platt** in 1934, and the sculpture is by Paul Manship. ♦ Fordham Rd and Pelham Pkwy

 World of Birds Visitors can observe more than 500 birds in the 25 environments of this well-designed aviary, with no bars or fences to obscure the view. It was designed in 1972 by **Morris Ketchum, Jr. & Associates.**

 Children's Zoo Children can explore prairie dog tunnels or hop like a wallaby in this hands-on zoo. Kids must be accompanied by an adult. ♦ Nominal admission. Last visitors admitted one hour before zoo closes.

Jungle World This award-winning indoor rain forest has four habitats, five waterfalls, giant trees, and Asian animals separated from humans by bridges and small rivers. Look out for proboscis monkeys, silver-leaf langurs (monkey family), white-cheeked gibbons (ape family), and Indian gharials (a crocodilian relative that is believed to have lived 180 million years ago).

World of Darkness Day and night are reversed for the nocturnal animals who live here, so they are awake and active for daytime visitors. This fascinating exhibit was designed by **Morris Ketchum, Jr. & Associates** in 1972.

New York Botanical Gardens

Michael Storrings

42 New York Botanical Garden One of the world's outstanding botanical gardens, its 250 acres include a 40-acre virgin hemlock forest, formal gardens, and the **Enid A. Haupt Conservatory** (built in 1902 and restored in 1978 by **Edward Larrabee Barnes**), which was modeled after the Great Palm House at Kew Gardens in England. A museum houses an herbarium, accessible only to members, of 5.5 million dried plants, and a shop that sells plants and gardening books and supplies. The **Lorillard Snuff Mill** (built in 1840) was converted into a cafe in the 1950s. A massive renovation project with an estimated $165-million price tag is underway in an attempt to draw more visitors, and is expected to be completed in the year 2000. The following projects are in the planning stages: a new library and herbarium, a renovated lecture hall, a restoration of the museum exterior, a new restaurant and catering area, extensive renovation to the **Enid A. Haupt Conservatory,** and a new visitor center. If all goes as planned, the botanical garden will be much more visitor-friendly and less like "a museum of plants." ♦ Gardens: donation suggested. Conservatory: admission. Tu-Su. 200th St and Southern Blvd, Bronx Park. 718/817.8705

43 City University of New York, Herbert H. Lehman College More than 10,000 students attend this school, founded in 1931 as **Hunter College.** The campus's Gothic buildings were designed by **Thompson Holmes & Converse** and **Frank Meyers** in 1928. The **Lehman Center for the Performing Arts,** designed in 1980 by **David Todd & Associates** and **Jan Hird Pokorny,** includes a 2,300-seat concert hall, experimental theater, recital hall, library, dance studio, and art galleries. The complex has become for the Bronx a kind of scaled-down **Lincoln Center,** attracting many of the same events that normally would play Manhattan only. ♦ Bedford Park Blvd W (between Jerome and Goulden Aves), Bedford Park. 718/960.8000

44 Wave Hill The 28-acre Hudson River estate of financier George W. Perkins was given to the city in 1965. Arturo Toscanini, Theodore Roosevelt, and Mark Twain each lived here for a short time. The 19th-century mansion hosts a chamber music series and family-arts projects and presents vintage recordings of Toscanini concerts. The dazzling gardens and greenhouses put on a display each season. ♦ Admission Sa-Su. Tu-Su. 675 W 252nd St (Independence Ave at W 249th St), Riverdale. 718/549.2055 &

45 Van Cortlandt House Museum This Georgian-Colonial mansion is one of those where George Washington actually slept— it was his military headquarters on several occasions. Built in 1748, the mansion has been restored with Dutch, English, and Colonial furnishings. ♦ Nominal admission. Tu-F 10AM-3PM; Sa-Su 11AM-4PM. Broadway and W 246th St, Riverdale. 718/543.3344

46 Bartow-Pell Mansion Museum This Federal home on beautifully manicured grounds, with views of Long Island Sound and outstanding formal gardens, was built from 1836 to 1842. Run by the **International Garden Club,** it's a rare treat. ♦ Nominal admission. W, Sa-Su noon-4PM or by appointment. Shore Rd (Pelham and Split Rock Golf Course), Pelham Bay Park. 718/885.1461

47 City Island A New England atmosphere persists on this small island that served as a US Coast Guard station in World War II. Located in the northeast reaches of the Bronx in Pelham Bay and attached to mainland New York by only one bridge, this picturesque 230-acre island is four blocks across at its widest point. It has the flavor of an island off the coast of Maine, not the Bronx, with marinas (four America's Cup yachts were built here), sea gulls, seafood restaurants, antiques shops, and atmosphere. The **New York Sailing School** (231 Kirby St, near King St, 800/834.SAIL), offers boat rentals and sailing instruction from April through October. Like the island, the only museum is both charming and quirky. The **North Wind Museum and Sea Institute** (610 City Island Ave, near City Island Bridge, 718/885.0701), a nautical museum located in an old sea captain's house, traces the history of the island while offering a cache of old nautical curiosities. The island boasts two 18-hole golf courses and horseback riding on old Indian trails, but a quiet walk along its streets with a brisk off-water breeze may be the most enjoyable. ♦ Over City Island Bridge, the Bronx

47 Le Refuge Bed & Breakfast $ Pierre Saint-Denis, proprietor/chef of Manhattan's East Side's extremely popular **Le Refuge** restaurant, has opened this ultra-charming eight-room inn (shown above) in a restored 19th-century sea captain's house. Replete with widow's walk, chamber music concerts, and the best croissants in town, this is the only spot of its kind in the Bronx or New York City. While it's only a half-hour by subway to Midtown Manhattan (and Pierre's must-visit East Side eatery), it will seem light-years away. With a host who's one of Manhattan's premier chefs, you can count on a wonderful breakfast. ♦ 620 City Island Ave (near City Island Bridge). 718/885.2478; fax 212/737.0384

48 Lobster Box ★★$$$ The Masucchia family turned this small white 1812 house into a restaurant more than 50 years ago. Over the years this popular spot has grown and now serves up to 2,000 pounds of fresh lobster a week. Pick from almost two dozen variations on the lobster theme—beginning with the simple steamed-and-split (lobsters here are never boiled)—or any of the fresh seafood, and watch the fleet of local boats glide by. ♦ Lobster/Seafood ♦ Daily lunch and dinner Apr-Oct. 34 City Island Ave (near Rochelle St), City Island. 718/885.1952

The Bronx is the only borough that is part of mainland New York. Manhattan and Staten Island are islands, and Brooklyn and Queens are on the western end of Long Island. New York City is, in fact, an archipelago.

Staten Island

Geographically distant from the rest of New York, Staten Island seems to be more a spiritual cousin to New Jersey, only a narrow stretch of water away. In fact, Staten Island's political ties to New York City are a historical accident: The island was ceded to Manhattan as a prize in a sailing contest sponsored by the Duke of York in 1687. Before 1964, access was possible only by ferry from Manhattan or by car through New Jersey. In 1964, the **Verrazano-Narrows Bridge** opened, tying Staten Island to Brooklyn. With a new frontier so close at hand, modern-day settlers poured over the bridge and changed the rugged face of the island forever. In 1990, tired of being ignored, residents of the "forgotten borough" voted to create a charter commission to provide for the separation of Staten Island from the rest of New York City. In 1993, residents voted two to one in favor of secession. Final approval rests with the state legislature in Albany and Governor Pataki. If they grant independence to Staten Island, it will become the second-largest city in New York.

49 Snug Harbor Cultural Center This 83-acre center for the performing and visual arts—a retirement village for sailors from 1833 until the mid-1970s—is composed of 28 historic buildings, many of which are fine examples of Greek Revival, Beaux Arts, Italianate, and Victorian architecture. Stop by the **Visitors' Center** for historical exhibitions and information on current and upcoming events, including indoor and outdoor classical, pop, and jazz concerts. A historical tour is held every Saturday and Sunday at 2PM. ♦ Daily dawn to dusk. 1000 Richmond Terr (at Tyson St). 718/448.2500

Within Snug Harbor Cultural Center:

The Newhouse Center for Contemporary Art New and emerging artists not often seen in Manhattan galleries are shown here. The center also hosts an indoor/outdoor sculpture exhibition in the summer. ♦ Donation suggested. W-Su noon-5PM. 718/448.2500 &

Staten Island Children's Museum Hands-on exhibits and related workshops and performances for five- to 12-year-olds are featured. A recent program gave children the opportunity to study bugs from both the scientist's and the artist's perspective. ♦ Admission. Tu-Su noon-5PM; call for extended summer hours. 718/273.2060 &

Staten Island Botanical Garden Located here are an English perennial garden; an herb and butterfly garden; a "White Garden" (all blooms in shades of gray and white) patterned after the famous English garden in Sissinghurst; and a greenhouse with a permanent display of tropicals, including the *Neil Vanderbilt Orchid Collection*. It's best to visit from May

Restaurants/Clubs: Red   Hotels: Blue
Shops/ 🍸 Outdoors: Green   **Sights/Culture: Black**

to October, when the flowers are in bloom. ◆ Free. Daily dawn to dusk. 718/273.8200

49 R.H. Tugs ★$$ Sit on the small outdoor patio and watch the tugboats chug by, or gaze at the twinkling lights of "Joisey" at night. Once an abandoned waterfront shack, this casual and popular restaurant specializes, not surprisingly, in seafood, including its well-known chowder, chunky with shrimp, crab, and fish, and entrées such as simple grilled fish or lobster with fettuccine. Try the occasional Caribbean specialties, especially on Thursday night, when a live Caribbean band will put you in the mood. ◆ Seafood ◆ Daily lunch, dinner, and late-night meals. 1115 Richmond Terr (at Snug Harbor Rd). 718/447.6369

50 The Alice Austen House This is one of the finest records of turn-of-the-century American life from Alice Austen, a photographer whose work was first discovered in *Life* in 1949. ◆ Suggested donation. Th-Su noon-5PM. 2 Hylan Blvd (at Bay St). 718/816.4506

51 Verrazano-Narrows Bridge Built in 1964 and designed by **Othmar Ammann,** this exquisite 4,260-foot minimalist steel ribbon (illustrated on page 26) is the world's longest suspension bridge (San Francisco's Golden Gate comes in a close second). It flies across the entrance to New York Harbor and is especially beautiful when seen from the Atlantic, against the city's skyline. It is named for Giovanni da Verrazano, the first European explorer to see New York (1524). The bridge has become familiar as the starting point for the **New York City Marathon** every November. ◆ From Staten Island Expwy, Staten Island to Gowanus Expwy, Brooklyn

52 The Greenbelt Even New Yorkers are amazed when told that the sprawling 843-acre **Central Park** is not the largest in the city. Measuring in at a remarkable 2,500 acres, the park located on Staten Island offers locals little-known proximity to a variety of landscapes, from shaded woodlands and freshwater swamps to hardwood forests with hiking trails and cross-country skiing in winter. Regular programs, talks, and walking tours are organized by the park service. Call for information and schedules. ◆ Daily. 200 Nevada Ave, High Rock Park. 718/667.2165

Before the 1850s, immigrants afflicted with diseases were kept on a remote spot on Staten Island. Many local residents became sick and died as a result, and others retaliated by setting fire to the quarantined buildings. This action prompted the state to build Hoffman and Swinburne Islands to house the afflicted. The islands are between Staten Island and Brooklyn and date from 1872. They were abandoned in the 1920s following the new immigration laws and serve no purpose today.

52 Staten Island Zoo Popular attractions at this zoo, beloved by many for its small (8.5 acres) scale, include a re-created tropical rain forest, animal hospital, aquarium, and outstanding reptile collection, which features the country's largest collection of rattle-snakes. A Saturday morning program allows children to feed the animals. ◆ Admission. Daily. 614 Broadway (between Forest Ave and Clove Rd), Barret Park. 718/442.3100

53 Historic Richmond Town New York City's answer to Williamsburg is a continuing restoration of 29 buildings that show a picture of 17th- through 19th-century village life. Fourteen are open to visitors, including the **Voorlezer House** (1695), the oldest surviving elementary school; the **General Store** (1840); and the **Bennet House** (1839), which is home to the **Museum of Childhood.** There are demonstrations of Early American trades and crafts, and working kitchens with cooking in progress. The **Museum Store** (in the **Historical Museum**) sells reproductions made by village craftspeople. ◆ Admission. W-F 1PM-5PM Jan-Mar; W-Su 1PM-5PM Apr-June, Sept-Dec; W-F 10AM-5PM, Sa-Su 1PM-5PM July-Aug. 441 Clarke Ave (between Richmond and Arthur Kill Rds), Richmond. 718/351.1611

54 Aesop's Tables ★$$ This rustic restaurant has country-garden wicker furniture, lots of dried flowers, and a patio for alfresco dining. The electic food can be a little uneven, but most dishes are interesting and deeply flavored; try the smoked mozzarella with portobello mushrooms and jerk chicken and beef. ◆ Eclectic ◆ Tu-Sa dinner. No credit cards accepted. 1233 Bay St (at Hylan Blvd), Rosebank. 718/720.2005

55 The Conference House/Billopp House Built in the 1670s, this was the scene of the only peace conference held to try to prevent the Revolutionary War. Admiral Lord Howe, in command of the British forces, hosted the parley on 11 September 1776 for three Continental Congress representatives—Benjamin Franklin, John Adams, and Edward Rutledge. The house is now a National Historic Landmark. ◆ Nominal admission. W-Su 1-4PM 15 Mar to 15 Dec. 7455 Hylan Blvd (at Sutterlee St), Tottenville. 718/984.2086

Robert T. Buck
Director, The Brooklyn Museum

Brooklyn Bests:

River Café—Classic cuisine—one of New York's outstanding menus combined with an unrivaled view from your table of the Manhattan skyline.

Aunt Sonia's—A large choice of inventive pasta dishes—original combination of New York savvy and California ingredients. Desserts not to be believed.

Index

A

Aaron Davis Hall at City College 301
Abbott, Merckt & Co. 134
ABC (American Broadcasting Company Facilities) 272
ABC Carpet 119
Abercrombie & Fitch 24
Abigail Adams Smith Museum 225
Abingdon Square 89
Abramovitz, Max 268
Abrons Arts Center 46
Abyssinian Baptist Church 300
Academy of American Poets 73
Accessibility for the disabled 5
Accommodations 10
AccScentigues 235
Acker-Merrall-Condit 274
Acme Bar & Grill ★$$ 101
Acquavella 238
Acropolis $ 157
Actor's Equity Building 155
Actor's Playhouse 83
Actors Studio, The 147
Adams & Woodbridge 32
Adams, Cindy 15 (bests)
Addison on Madison 220
Ad Hoc Softwares 69
Adler, Dankmar 165
Adrienne ★★$$$ 201
Aesop's Tables ★$$ 319
After the Rain 74
Aggie's ★$ 96
agnès b. 71
Ahlschlager, Walter 276
Aiken, William Martin 122
Airlines 5, 7, 8
Airports 4
Airport Services, John F. Kennedy International Airport 5
Airport Services, La Guardia Airport 7
Airport Services, Newark International Airport 7
Aja ★★★$$$ 121
A.L. Bazzini Company 57
Alexander Cooper & Partners 38
Algonquin Hotel, The 185
Alice Austen House, The 319
Alice Tully Recital Hall 270
Alice Underground 279
Alison on Dominick Street ★★★$$$ 64
Allegria ★$$ 200
Allen & Collens 227, 297, 298
Allerton Hotel for Women $ 208
Alleva Dairy 50
All Saints Church 300
All the Town's a Stage: The New York Theater Scene 152
Alswang, Ralph 159
Alternative Museum 73
Alva ★★$$$ 121
Alwyn Court 166

Ambassador 158
Ambassador Grill Restaurant ★$$$ 178
America ★$$$ 117
American Academy and Institute of Arts and Letters 302
American Bible Society/Bible House 268
American Broadcasting Company Facilities (ABC) 272
American Craft Museum 197
American Federation of the Arts (AFA) 229
American Festival Cafe ★$$$ 188
American Folk Art, Museum of 272
American Institute of Architects 195
American Museum of Natural History 279
American Museum of the Moving Image 313
American Numismatic Society 302
American Place 155
American Renaissance ★★$$$ 59
American-Standard Building 173
American Stock Exchange 32
American Telephone & Telegraph Long Lines Building 56
Americas Society 231
Amici Miei ★$$$ 75
Ammann, Othmar 300, 304, 319
Amon, Will Rice 301
Amsterdam's ★$$ 60
An American Place ★★$$$ 127
Anbar Shoe Steal 56
Angelica Kitchen ★$ 110
Angelika Film Center 97
Angelo's of Mulberry Street ★$$ 51
Anglers & Writers ★$ 81
Anna Z 47
Annabelle ★$$$ 182
Ansonia Hotel 276
Anthology Film Archives 100
Antique Boutique 94
Anvers 69
Apex Fitness Club 244
Aphrodisia 84
Apollo, The 299
Appellate Division of the Supreme Court of the State of New York 123
Applause Theater Books 274
Apple Bank 276
Appleberg, Marilyn J. 111 (bests)
Apthorp Apartments 279
Aquarium for Wildlife Conservation 311
Aquavit ★★★$$$$ 199

Aqueduct 315
Arcadia ★★★$$$$ 220
Architectural Salvage Warehouse 309
Areo ★$$ 311
Argosy Book Store 208
Arizona 206 ★★★$$$ 224
ARKA 101
Armadillo, The $ 289
Armani Boutique 231
Armas, Raoul de 191
Arnold Constable Dry Goods Store Building 119
Arqua ★★$$$ 58
Arsenal, The 260
Art & Tapisserie 249
Arthur A. Schomburg Plaza 295
Arthur Avenue Retail Market 316
Artichoke 192
Artists Space 61
Art Students League 164
Arturo's Pizzeria ★$ 76
Asia Society, The 234, 248
Asser Levy Recreational Center 122
Associated Architects 186
Asti $$$ 92
Astor Place Hairstylists 104
Astor Place Theatre 104
Astor Wines and Spirits 104
Astro Gallery 127
Atterbury, Grosvenor 122
Attia & Perkins 226
Au Cafe ★$ 162
Au Chat Botté 249
Audubon Terrace 302
Au Mandarin ★$$ 35
Aunt Sonia's ★★$$ 310
Au Petit Beurre $ 290
Aureole ★★★$$$$ 221
Austin J. Tobin Plaza 36
Aux Delices des Bois 57
Avery Fisher Hall 268
Avventura 283
A. W. Kaufman 46
AYH (American Youth Hostel, New York International) 290
A. Zito & Sons Bakery 84
Azzurro ★★$$ 245

B

Babb, Cook & Willard 241, 250
Baccarat 215
Baci ★$$ 282
Back From Guatemala 106
Back Pages Antiques 74
Bagel, The ★$ 84
Bag One Arts 279
Baker Field Fieldhouse/Lawrence Wein Stadium 305
Baker, James B. 33
Balducci's 85
Bali Burma ★$ 147
Ballet Shop, The 268
Balto 261
Bancroft Hall, Teachers College 298
B & H Dairy and Vegetarian

Cuisine Restaurant ★$ 107
B&J Fabrics, Inc. 145
Bangkok Cuisine ★★$$ 161
Bankers Trust Building 29
Bank of New York 28
Bank of New York, The/Irving Trust Company Building 29
Bank of Tokyo Trust 32
Baraonda ★★$$$ 239
Barbara Gladstone Gallery 67
Barbetta ★★$$$ 156
Barbizon Hotel, The $$$ 223
Barnard College 297
Barnes & Noble 283
Barnes & Noble Bookstore 116
Barnes & Noble Cafe $ 283
Barnes, Edward Larrabee 210, 234, 317
Barney & Chapman 110, 249
Barney Greengrass (The Sturgeon King) ★★$ 287
Barneys 221
Barneys New York 135
Barocco ★★$$$ 58
Barolo ★★$$$ 65
Barrymore 157
Bartow-Pell Mansion Museum 317
Baskett, Butler Rogers 139
Bath Island 283
Batterson, James C. 123
Battery Maritime Building 21
Battery Park 20
Battery Park City 33, 34 (map)
Battery Park Control House 20
Baum, Dwight James 271
Bayamo ★$$ 103
Bayard Condict Building 100
Bayley, John Barrington 232
B. Dalton Bookseller 196
Beacon Theatre 276
Beau Brummel 69
Beaumont Theater 269
Bébé Thompson 69
Becco ★$$ 157
Beckenstein 47
Bed & Breakfast on the Park $$ 310
Bed Bath & Beyond 135
75½ Bedford Street 81
Beekman Tower Hotel $$$ 191
Belasco 149
Bell Caffè $ 64
Bellevue Hospital Center 124
Belluschi, Pietro 182, 270
Belmont Italian-American Playhouse 316
Belvedere Castle 264
Ben Benson's Steakhouse ★★$$$$ 160
Benito I and Benito II ★$ 50
Benny's Burritos ★$ 90
Beresford, The 281
Bergdorf Goodman 210
Bergdorf Goodman Men 210
Berrys ★$$ 69
Berwind Mansion 228
Bessie Shonberg Theater 136
Bethesda Terrace 262

Betina Riedel **67**
Betsey Johnson **76**
Betsy Senior Contemporary
 Prints **65**
Beverly, The $$$ **193**
Bialystoker Synagogue **46**
Bible House/American Bible
 Society **268**
Bice ★★$$$ **203**
Bicycles **8**
Bien & Prince **237**
Big City Kite Co., Inc. **241**
Billopp House **319**
Bill's Gay Nineties ★$$ **203**
Billy Martin's Western Wear **230**
Biography Bookshop **87**
Birdland ★$$ **290**
Birge, Charles **285**
Birnbaum, Philip **208, 243**
Bistro du Nord ★★$$ **253**
Bitter End **97**
Black Sheep, The ★★$$$ **87**
Blades West **274**
Bleecker Bob's Golden Oldies **95**
Blesch, Otto **115**
Bloomingdale's **223**
Blu ★★$$ **138**
Blue Note Jazz Club **95**
Blue Ribbon ★★$$$ **70**
Blum, Edward **290**
Blum, George **290**
Blum Helman Gallery **213**
Boathouse Cafe ★$$$ **263**
Boats **7**
Boca Chica ★$ **101**
Bogner **231**
Bo Ky Restaurant ★$ **43**
Bolo ★★$$$ **121**
Bolton, Charles W. **300**
Bombay Palace ★$$ **196**
Bonté **238**
Book-Friends Cafe $ **116**
Book Nooks **102**
Books & Co. **236**
Books of Wonder **136**
Boom ★$$$ **68**
Booth **151**
Border Cafe $ **240**
Boring & Tilton **18**
Boroughs **306**
Bosworth, William Welles **37, 195**
Bottomley, Wagner & Whitee **205**
Bottom Line Cabaret **94**
Boulevard $ **287**
Bouley ★★★$$$$ **56**
Boutique Descamps **228**
Bouwerie Lane Theatre **100**
Bow Bridge **263**
Bowery Bar ★$$ **103**
Bowling Green (Central Park) **262**
Bowling Green (Lower
 Manhattan) **22**
Bowlmor Lanes **92**
Boyd's Madison Avenue **222**
Brasserie ★$$$ **194**
Brennan, Beer Gorman **201**
Breslin, Jimmy **255**
Breuer, Marcel **236**
Brewster Gallery **213**
Bridge Cafe ★★$$ **27**
Bridge Kitchenware Corp. **192**
Brill Building, The **158**
Brio ★$$ **223**

Briscola ★★$$$ **109**
Broadhurst **151**
Broadway **161**
26 Broadway **23**
195 Broadway **37**
443 Broadway **60**
478 Broadway **60**
486 Broadway **60**
495 Broadway **60**
521-523 Broadway **60**
560 Broadway **72**
568-578 Broadway **72**
901 Broadway **119**
Broadway Barber Shop **290**
Broadway Diner ★$ **162**
Bronx, The **306, 315**
Bronx Zoo/Wildlife Conservation
 Park **316**
Brooke Alexander **65**
Brooke Alexander Editions **66**
Brooklyn **306**
Brooklyn Academy of Music **308**
Brooklyn-Battery Tunnel **23**
Brooklyn Borough Hall **308**
Brooklyn Botanic Garden **311**
Brooklyn Bridge **27**
Brooklyn Children's Museum
 309
Brooklyn Museum **248, 310**
Brooks Atkinson **157**
Brooks Brothers **184**
Brookstone **24**
Brotherhood Synagogue, The
 118
Brother's Bar-B-Q ★$ **77**
Brown, Archibald Manning **301**
Brown, Guenther, Battaglia,
 Seckler **289**
Brown, Helen Gurley **169**
Brown, Jack **33**
Brown, Lawford & Forbes **305**
Brunner, Arnold W. **46, 299, 122**
Bruno ★$$$ **207**
Bruno The King of Ravioli **148**
Bryant Park **173**
B. Smith's ★$$$ **157**
Buccellati Silver **209**
Buchman & Kahn **148**
Buck, Joan Juliet **215**
Buck, Leffert L. **46**
Buckley, Richard W. **301**
Buck, Robert T. **319**
Buffalo Chips Bootery **67**
Bulgari **211**
Bunshaft, Gordon **204**
Bunting, Charles T. **114**
Burberrys **210**
Burden House **251**
Burgee, John **202, 203, 225, 243**
Burgundy Wine Company **87**
Burlington Book Shop **242**
Burnham, Daniel **176**
Burnham, David H. **121**
Busby's ★$$ **252**
Buses **6, 7, 8, 145**
Butler, Charles **229**
Butterfield House **91**

C

Cabana Carioca ★★$$ **154**
Cable Building **97**
Cady, Berg & See **279**
Cafe at Brooklyn Musuem ★$ **310**

Cafe Centro ★★$$$ **183**
Cafe Crocodile ★★$$ **235**
Cafe de Bruxelles ★$$ **89**
Café des Artistes ★★★$$$
 272
Café Des Sports ★$ **159**
Cafe Español $$ **81**
Cafe Europa ★$ **165**
Cafe Fledermaus $ **24**
Cafe Greco ★$$ **234**
Café La Fortuna ★$ **274**
Cafe Lalo ★$ **284**
Cafe Loup ★★$$ **90**
Cafe Luxembourg ★★$$$ **273**
Cafe Metairie ★$$ **241**
Cafe Mogador ★$$ **107**
Café Nicholson ★$$$ **206**
Cafe Nicole ★$$$ **161**
Cafe Pierre ★★$$$ **220**
Cafe Tabac ★★$$ **108**
Cafe Un Deux Trois ★$$ **149**
Caffe Bianco ★$ **240**
Caffe Bondi ★★$$$ **120**
Caffè Borgia ★$ **96**
Caffè Dante ★$ **96**
Caffè della Pace ★$ **106**
Caffè Napoli ★$ **51**
Caffè Reggio ★$ **95**
Caffè Roma ★★$ **50**
Caffè Vivaldi ★$ **84**
Cajun ★$$ **134**
Calabria Pork Store **316**
Calandra **316**
Cal's ★★$$ **120**
Calvary Church **121**
Calvin Klein **222**
Cambridge Chemists **229**
Campagna ★★$$$ **119**
Can ★$$ **75**
Canal Jean Co. **60**
Candela, Rosario **206, 242**
Canton ★★$$ **44**
Capsouto Frères ★★$$$ **59**
Captain's Table ★$$$ **180**
Caribe ★$ **87**
Carl Schurz Park **245**
Carlyle Hotel $$$$ **237**
Carman, Richard J. **23**
Carmine's $$ **289**
Carnegie Delicatessen ★★$$ **162**
Carnegie Hall **165**
Caroline's Comedy Club **158**
Carol Rollo/Riding High **226**
Carousel, The **261**
Carpenter, J.E.R. **220, 228**
Carrère & Hastings **23, 45, 81,
 91, 156, 174, 208, 214, 233,
 241, 244, 251, 271, 290, 296**
Carrère, John Merven **288**
Carr, Lynch, Hack & Sandell **33**
Carr, Thornton **234**
Car service **9**
Cars, rental **6, 7, 8, 9**
Cartier **195**
Casa di Pré ★$$ **89**
Casa La Femme ★$$ **75**
Casa Rosa ★$$ **308**
Cascabel ★★★$$$ **66**
Casey, Edward P. **234**
Castellano ★$$ **163**
Castelli Graphics **73**
Castillo Cultural Center **64**
Cast Iron Building, The **92**

Castle Clinton National
 Monument **20**
Castro-Blanco, Piscioneri &
 Feder **295**
Caswell-Massey **190**
Catalano, Eduardo **270**
Cathedral Church of St. John the
 Divine, The **295**
Cathedral Parkway Houses **291**
Caughey & Evans **167**
Cavaglieri, Giorgio **85, 104, 175,
 225**
Caviarteria ★★$$$$ **222**
CBGB and OMFUG **100**
CBS Broadcast Center **168**
CBS Building **197**
Cedar Tavern $ **92**
Cellar in the Sky **36**
Cent' Anni ★$$$ **81**
Center for Book Arts **100**
Central Park **256**
Central Park West/76th Street
 Historic District **277**
Central Park Wildlife
 Conservation Center **261**
Central Presbyterian Church **228**
Central Synagogue **204**
Century Apartments **271**
Century Association **184**
Century Cafe ★★$$ **149**
Century 21 **33**
Ceramica **64**
Cerutti **230**
Cesarina ★$$$ **197**
Cesar Pelli & Associates **34,
 198, 206**
Chad, Thornton **234**
Chamber of Commerce of the
 State of New York **33**
Chanel **210**
Chanin Building **177**
Chanin, Irwin S. **271, 277**
Chanterelle ★★★★$$$$ **57**
Chapel of the Intercession **302**
Charging Bull, The **22**
Charivari 72 **274**
Charivari Workshop **281**
Charles A. Dana Discovery
 Center **265**
Charles B. Meyers Associates **304**
Charles Cowles Gallery **69**
Charles Luckman Associates **141**
Chase Manhattan Bank (East
 Side) **228**
Chase Manhattan Bank (Lower
 Manhattan) **33**
Chatham Square **44**
Cheese of All Nations **56**
Chelsea **132**
Chelsea Antiques Building **140**
Chelsea Cafe ★$ **140**
Chelsea Foods **138**
Chelsea Piers **139**
Chelsea Trattoria ★$$ **135**
ChemCort at Chemical Bank
 World Headquarters **190**
Chemical Bank **184**
Chemical Bank World Corporate
 Headquarters **190**
Chen, Paul K.Y. **262**
Cherokee Apartments **239**
Cherry Hill **263**
Cherry Lane Theater **82**

Chess & Checkers House, The 261
Chez Brigitte ★$ 90
Chez Jacqueline ★★$$ 96
Chez Josephine ★★$$$ 145
Chez Michallet ★$$$ 82
Chez Napoléon ★★$$$ 159
Chicago City Limits 225
Chikubu ★★★$$$ 184
Children's Museum of Manhattan 284
Children's Zoo 316
Child's Play 285
China Club 276
China Grill ★★$$$ 197
China House Gallery/China Institute in America 228
Chinatown 40
Chin Chin ★★$$$ 191
Chocolate Soup, The 237
Choshi ★★$$ 117
Christ and St. Stephen's Church 273
Christ Church 222
Christer's ★★★$$$ 163
Christian Dior Boutique 201
Christie's 222
Christopher Park 83
Chrysler Building 177
Chumleys $$ 82
Churchill, Henry S. 221
Church of Our Lady of Pompeii 81
Church of Our Lady of the Rosary 20
Church of Our Savior 128
Church of St. Ignatius Loyola 244
Church of St. Paul and St. Andrew 284
Church of St. Vincent Ferrer 227
Church of the Holy Apostles 139
Church of the Holy Cross 145
Church of the Holy Trinity 249
Church of The Incarnation Episcopal 127
Church of the Transfiguration/ The Little Church Around the Corner 125
Circle in the Square 159
Circle Line 146
Circle Repertory Company 83
Citarella 276
Cité ★★★$$$ 160
Citicorp Center 204
City Bakery, The ★★$ 115
City Center Theater 163
City College/City University of New York 300
City Hall 38
City Island 317
City Lore 101
City University of New York, Herbert H. Lehman College 317
Ci Vediamo ★$ 106
Claiborne Gallery 76
Claire ★$$ 136
Claremont Stables 264
Clarendon, The 285
Clark House 44
Classic Toys 64
Cleopatra's Needle 264
Cliff Dwellers' Apartments, The 290

Climate 10
Clinton & Russell 23, 279
Clinton, Charles W. 230
Cloisters Cafe $ 108
Cloisters, The 305
Cobb Freed & Partners 254
Cockpit, The 73
Coconut Grill ★$ 240
Coco Pazzo ★★$$$$ 236
Codman, Ogden Jr. 219, 234, 250
Coeland, Novak, Israel & Simmon 140
Coffee Shop ★$ 115
Coffin, William Sloane 96
Cohen, Barbara 111
Cola's ★★$ 136
Coliseum Books 164
Collens, Charles 305
Collens, Willis & Beckonert 297, 298
Colonnade Row 104
Colony Club, The 222
Colony Records 158
Colors ★$$$ 182
Columbia-Presbyterian Medical Center 304
Columbia University 296, 297
45 Columbus Avenue 268
Columbus Circle 267
Columbus Park 42
Comic Strip, The 240
Coming or Going ★★$$$ 210
Comme des Garçons 71
Commodities 58
Complete Traveller Bookstore 127
Con Edison Energy Museum 114
Coney Island 311
Conference House, The 319
Confucius Plaza 45
Congregation Adath Jeshurun of Jassy Synagogue 47
Connecticut Muffin Co. 49
Conservatory Garden 265
Conservatory Water 263
Consolidated Edison Building 114
Contrapunto ★★$$$ 224
Convent of the Sacred Heart, The 251
Coolidge, Shepley, Bullfinch & Abbott 235
Cooper, Eckstut Associates 33
Cooper-Hewitt, The 250
Cooper Square 105
Cooper Union 104
Copacabana 168
Copeland's ★$$ 301
Corbett, Harrison and MacMurray 186
Corbett, Harvey Wiley 42, 122
Cornelia Street Café, The ★$ 84
Corner Bistro $ 89
Corner Bookstore 253
Corrado ★$$$ 163
Cort 158
Cory, Russell G. 139
Cory, Walter M. 139
Cosmopolitan Club 227
Cotton Club, The ★$$ 298
Cottonwood Cafe $$ 86
Council on Foreign Relations 231
Country Cafe ★★$ 64

Craft Caravan, Inc. 66
Cram & Ferguson 296
Cram, Goodhue & Ferguson 199, 302
Cram, Ralph Adams 222, 233, 296
Crane, Howard 161
Criminal Courts Building 42
Cronkite, Walter 130
Cross & Cross 190, 193, 206, 211, 242
Cross, H. Page 234
Crouch & Fitzgerald 189
Crown Building, The 211
Crystal Gardens 85
C.T. ★★★★$$$ 121
Cub Room ★$$$ 76
Cucina ★★★$$ 309
Cucina di Pesce ★$ 103
Cucina Stagionale $ 84
Cunningham, Merce 77
Cupcake Cafe 144
Cupping Room Cafe, The ★$$ 65
Curt Marcus Gallery 73

D

DaConha, George 118
Daffy's 116
Daily, Clifford Reed 826
Daily News Building 177
Dairy, The (Central Park Visitors' Center) 261
Dakota Apartments 275
Dallas BBQ $ 275
D & G Bakery 49
Dangerfield's 226
Darbar Indian Restaurant ★★★$$$ 212
Darrow's Fun Antiques 225
Da Silvano ★$$ 96
Dattner, Richard 55
Da Umberto ★★$$$ 135
David Beitzel Gallery 71
David McKee Gallery 210
David Todd & Associates 146, 317
Davis, Alexander Jackson 118, 225
Davis, Brody & Associates 34, 114, 124, 175, 270, 291, 300, 311
Dawat ★★★$$$ 207
Day, William H. 273
Dean & DeLuca 72
Dean & DeLuca Cafe (Midtown) ★$ 188
Dean & DeLuca Cafe (SoHo) ★$ 74
Dean, Clarence 190
De Hirsch Residence $ 252
Delacorte Theatre 264
Delano & Aldrich 206, 220, 222, 231, 254
Delegates' Dining Room ★★$$$ 180
DeLemos & Cordes 116, 144
Del Gaudio, Matthew 81
Delhi Palace ★★$$ 314
Delorenzo 237
Demeuron & Smith 299
Depression Modern 76
DeRobertis Pastry Shop ★$ 108
DeRosa, Eugene 162

Deskey, Donald 187
Detour 68
De Young & Moscowitz 140
Dia Center for the Arts (Chelsea) 137
Dia Center for the Arts (SoHo) 75
Different Light Books 136
Dilthy, William J. 67
Disabled travelers, accessibility 5
Distant Origin 74
Ditmars & Schickel 244
Divino Ristorante ★$$ 240
Docks Oyster Bar and Seafood Grill ★★$$ 288
D'Oench & Yost 115
Dojo ★$ 107
Do Kham 49
Dolce ★$$$ 189
Dolci On Park Caffè ★$$ 127
Dollhouse Antics 254
Dominick's ★★$ 316
Donald Sacks ★$$ 35
Doral Court Hotel $$$ 128
Doral Park Avenue Hotel $$$ 129
Doral Tuscany Hotel $$$ 128
Doran, John 84
Dorilton, The 273
Doubleday 212
Doubletree Guest Suites 155
Down & Quilt Shop 284
Downtown Athletic Club 23
Downtown Sound 35
Doyers Street 43
D. Porthault 232
Drake Swissôtel, The $$$ 209
Drama Bookshop 158
Drawing Center, The 61
Drinking 10
Driving 6, 7, 8
Duane Park Cafe ★★$$$ 56
Dublin House Tap Room 282
Duboy, Paul E.M. 288
Duckworth, Isaac 66
Duckworth, J.F. 61
Duffy Square 155
Duggal Downtown 72
Dumont Plaza Hotel $$$ 128
Duncan, John H. 230, 277, 298
Dunn, T.H. 301
Dyckman House 305

E

Eamonn Doran $$ 192
Ear Inn, The $ 64
216 East 16th Street 114
242 East 52nd Street 192
45 East 66th Street 229
131-135 East 66th Street 227
4 East 67th Street 230
13 and 15 East 67th Street 230
115 East 67th Street 230
6, 8, and 10 East 68th Street 230
9 East 68th Street 230
46 East 70th Street 233
123 East 70th Street 234
124 East 70th Street 234
131 East 71st Street 234
120 and 122 East 92nd Street 252
60 East 93rd Street 253
Eastern Seafood Company ★$ 279
Eastern States Buddhist Temple

of America, Inc. **43**
East Side **216**
East Village **98**
East West Books (Greenwich Village) **91**
East West Books (Upper West Side) **288**
E.A.T. ★★$$$ **242**
Ecce Panis **226**
Ecco $$$ **38**
Eclair $$ **275**
Economy Candy Company **47**
Edgar Allan Poe Cottage **316**
Edison Hotel, The $ **156**
Ed Sullivan **162**
Educational Alliance **46**
Edward Durell Stone House **227**
Edward Mooney House **44**
Edward Thorp Gallery **74**
Eero Saarinen & Associates **269, 270**
Eggars Partnership, The **269**
Eggers & Higgins **38**
E.H. Faile & Co. **188**
Ehrenkranz Group & Eckstut **50**
Eidlitz & MacKenzie **148**
Eidlitz, Cyrus **88**
Eidlitz, Leopold **115**
Eighteenth and Eighth ★$ **136**
Eighth Street **93**
Eileen Lane Antiques **76**
Elaine's ★$$$ **249**
El Charro Español ★$$ **86**
El Cid ★$ **134**
Eldorado, The **289**
Eldridge Street Synagogue **45**
El Faro ★$$ **89**
Elias Corner ★★$ **314**
Eli Attia & Associates **175**
Elio's ★★$$$ **244**
Elizabeth Arden Salon **202**
Elk Candy Company **244**
Ellen's Cafe and Bake Shop ★$ **38**
Ellen's Stardust Diner $ **163**
Ellett, Thomas Harlan **227**
Ellis Island Museum of Immigration **18**
Ellis Island National Monument **18**
Elmer Holmes Bobst Library **94**
El Museo del Barrio **255**
El Parador ★★$$$ **128**
El Pollo ★★$ **251**
El Teddy's ★$$ **58**
Emanuel Ungaro **229**
Embury, Aymar II **144, 234, 263, 300**
Emergencies **11**
Emery, Henry George **115**
Emery, Matthew Lansing **115**
Emery Roth & Associates **182**
Emery Roth & Sons **38, 190, 194, 214**
Emilio Pucci **228**
Emmerich, André **131**
Empire Diner ★$ **139**
Empire State Building, The **126**
Empire State Observatories **126**
Emporio Armani **116**
Enchanted Forest, The **66**
Enchantments **108**
Engelbert, Henry **49, 100, 145**

Ennio & Michael ★★$$$ **971**
Equinox Fitness Club **278**
Equitable Building **32**
Equitable Center **159**
Erbe **70**
Erminia ★★$$$ **245**
Ernie's $$ **277**
E. Rossi & Co. **51**
Essex House $$$ **167**
Estia ★★$$$ **244**
Etats-Unis ★★$$$ **240**
Eugene O'Neill **158**
Eva and Morris Feld Gallery at Lincoln Square **272**
Evergreen Antiques **234**
Excelsior $ **281**

F

Fabricant, Florence **131**
Façonnable **202**
Fairway **276**
Famous Ray's Pizza $ **90**
Fanelli Cafe $ **71**
Fantasticks, The **96**
Fantino ★★$$$ **167**
FAO Schwarz **215**
Farrar & Watmaugh **139**
Fashion Institute of Technology (FIT) **140**
Federal Hall National Memorial **28**
Federal Reserve Bank of New York **33**
Feldman, H.I. **287**
Felidia ★★$$$$ **207**
Felissimo ★★$ **211**
Felix ★$$$ **64**
Fernbach, Henry **58, 204, 120**
Ferrara $ **51**
Ferretti, Fred **215**
Ferrez & Taylor **90**
Ferrier ★$$ **229**
Ferries **9, 20**
200 Fifth Avenue **122**
800 Fifth Avenue **220**
810 Fifth Avenue **220**
820 Fifth Avenue **229**
998 Fifth Avenue **243**
1001 Fifth Avenue **243**
1107 Fifth Avenue **252**
Fifth Avenue Presbyterian Church **201**
54th Street Recreation Center **206**
Filene's Basement **282**
Film Center Building **148**
Film Forum **96**
Fine & Klein **47**
Fine & Schapiro ★$$ **274**
Fiorello's ★$$$ **270**
First Battery Armory, New York National Guard **272**
First Church of Christ, Scientist **290**
First Presbyterian Church **91**
First Reformed Hungarian Church **235**
First Shearith Israel Cemetery **44**
First Taste ★★$$ **45**
Fisher & Levy **205**
Fishin Eddie ★★$$$ **274**
Fishkin **46**
Fishs Eddy **87**
Fitzpatrick Manhattan Hotel, The **207**

Flagg & Chambers **233**
Flagg, Ernest **72, 189, 230, 295**
Flatiron Building **121**
Fletcher Morgan Provisions ★$ **227**
Flower District **140**
Flowers ★★$$$ **116**
Flushing Meadows–Corona Park **315**
Follonico ★★$$$ **123**
Footlight Records **110**
Forbes Building **91**
Forbidden Planet **92**
Ford Foundation Building **178**
Fordham University **316**
Forgotten Woman, The **227**
Forster, Frank J. **301**
Forts, The **265**
Fort Tryon Park **305**
Fortunoff **202**
47th Street Photo **155**
Forum **210**
Forzano Italian Imports Inc. **51**
Foster, Richard **94, 95, 269**
Fouquet, J.D. **273**
Four Seasons Hotel $$$$ **208**
Four Seasons, The ★★★★$$$$ **194**
Fox & Fowle **190**
Fox & Fowle Architects **197**
Fragrance Shoppe, The **106**
Frank E. Campbell Funeral Chapel **242**
Frank, Gerry **52**
Frankie and Johnnie's ★$$$ **151**
Franklin Furnace **58**
Franklin Hotel, The $$ **249**
Frank's ★★$$$ **134**
Frank Silvera Writers' Workshop **299**
Fraunces Tavern **22**
Fraunces Tavern Museum **22**
Fraunces Tavern Restaurant ★$$$ **22**
Freddie and Pepper's Gourmet Pizza ★$ **276**
Frederic York Avenue Patisserie **239**
Fred F. French Building **184**
Fred F. French Company **178, 184**
Freedlander, Joseph **255**
Freed of London **167**
French Embassy **238**
Fresco ★★$$ **194**
Frette **230**
Friars Club **203**
Frick Collection, The **232**
Friedberg, M. Paul **39**
Friend of a Farmer ★$$ **117**
Friends' Meeting House **114**
Friends of Figurative Sculpture **66**
Frontiere ★★$$$ **76**
Frumkin/Adams Gallery **212**
Fujiyama Mama ★$$ **283**
Fuller Building **209**
Fuller, Charles F. **301**
Fulton Fish Market **27**
Fulton Market **25**
Fur District **139**
Fu's ★★$$$ **192**

G

Gabriel's ★★$$$ **267**
Gainsborough Studios **168**
Galerie St. Etienne **213**
Gallagher's Steak House ★★$$$$ **161**
Galleria Hugo **224**
Galleria, The **208**
Gallery of Wearable Art **230**
Gansevoort Market **88**
Garment Center **142**
Gascogne ★★$$ **136**
Gaynor, John **60**
Gay Street **85**
Gazebo, The **208**
Gemini GEL at Joni Weyl **65**
Gem Spa Smoke Shop **107**
General Electric Building **193**
General Post Office **141**
General Society Library of Mechanics and Tradesmen **184**
General Theological Seminary **137**
George P. Post and Sons **200**
George Washington Bridge **304**
George Washington Bridge Bus Station **304**
Georg Jensen/Royal Copenhagen **221**
Gershorn, Irving **33**
Gershwin **159**
Getting around **8**
Getting to New York City **5**
Gibb, James **37**
Gibson, Robert W. **195, 279**
Gilbert, Cass **22, 37, 39, 123, 302, 304, 123**
Gilbert, Cass, Jr. **39**
Gilbert, C.P.H. **251, 253**
Giles, James H. **119**
Gill, Brendan **15**
Ginsberg, Horace **301**
Giorgio Armani Boutique **231**
Girasole ★$$$ **241**
Giselle Sportswear **47**
Givenchy **237**
Glasgow, Roger **291**
Glazer, Samuel **253**
Global 33 ★$ **105**
Goelet Building (Union Square) **119**
Goelet Building, The (Midtown) **188**
Goldberg's Marine Distributors **130**
Golden **151**
Golden Unicorn ★★★$$ **44**
Good & Plenty to Go **146**
Good Enough to Eat ★★$$ **284**
Goodhue, Bertram G. **193, 222, 227, 302**
Goodman, Percival **300**
Goodwin, Philip L. **198**
Gordon, Max **65**
Gorham Hotel $$$ **163**
Gotham Bar and Grill ★★★$$$ **91**
Gotham Book Mart & Gallery **185**
Gourmet Garage **66**
Governors Island **22**
Grace Borgenicht **212**
Grace Church **109**
Grace's Marketplace **234**

Index

Gracie Mansion **249**
Gracious Home **234**
Graham, Ernest R. **32**
Gramercy **112**
Gramercy Park/Gramercy Park Historic District **118**
Gramercy Park Hotel $$ **122**
Gramercy Tavern ★★$$$ **118**
Gran Caffè Degli Artisti ★$ **86**
Grand Army Plaza (Brooklyn) **310**
Grand Army Plaza (Midtown) **214**
Grand Central Terminal **175**
Grand, Frank **167**
Grand Hyatt Hotel $$$ **176**
Grand Ticino ★★$$ **97**
Grange Hall, The ★$ **82**
Grant's Tomb/General Grant National Memorial **298**
Grass Roots Garden, The **68**
Graves & Duboy **276**
Graves, Michael **72**
Gray's Papaya $ **274**
Great Hill **265**
Great Jones Cafe $ **101**
Great Lawn, The **264**
Great Shanghai ★★$ **44**
Greeley Square **125**
Greenacre Park **192**
Greenbelt, The **319**
Greene Street **61**
110 Greene Street **67**
GreenFlea/IS 44 Market **278**
Greenhouse Cafe ★$$ **37**
Green Point Bank **50**
Greenstones & Cie **282**
Greenwich Village **78**
Greer, Seth **104**
Grey Art Gallery **94**
Grolier **125**
Grolier Club, The **222**
Groneburg & Leuchtag **163**
Gropius, Walter **182**
Grossinger's Uptown Bake Shop **288**
Grotta Azzurra ★$$ **50**
Grove Court **82**
Grove Street Cafe ★$$ **83**
Gruzen & Partners **34, 161, 176, 295**
Gruzen, Samton, Steinglass **34, 184**
Gryphon Book Shop **282**
Guardian Angel Church **137**
Guardian Life Insurance Company **115**
Gucci **202**
Guest Quarter Suites by Doubletree $$$ **155**
Guggenheim Bandshell **269**
Guggenheim Museum SoHo **73**
Guggenheim Museum, **248, 249**
Guido's ★$$ **144**
Guinness World Records Exhibit Hall **127**
Gus' Place ★$$ **85**
Guss Pickle Products **46**
Guy Laroche **209**
Gwathmey, Charles **77**
Gwathmey Siegel & Associates **250, 313**

H

Hacker Art Books **213**
Hagmann, John S. **238**

Hagop Kevorkian Center for Near Eastern Studies **95**
Haight, Charles C. **137, 289, 291**
Haines Lundberg Wachler **190**
Hale & Rogers **237**
Hall of Fame for Great Americans **315**
Hall of Science **315**
Halsey, McCormack & Helmer **28**
Hamburger Harry's ★$ **154**
Hamilton Heights **292**
Hamilton Heights Historic District **301**
Hammacher Schlemmer **207**
Hammond House **251**
Hampden-Booth Theatre Library, The **118**
Hampshire House **167**
Hanae Mori **238**
Handblock **284**
H&H Bagels West **282**
Hanover Square **24**
Hans Koch Ltd. **70**
Harde & Short **229, 277, 285**
Harde and Short **166**
Hardenbergh, Henry J. **23, 101, 114, 121, 164, 215, 275**
Hard Rock Cafe $$ **164**
Hardy Holzman Pfeiffer Associates **136, 173, 188, 213, 250, 308, 309**
Harkness House **237**
Harle & Liebman **193**
Harlem **292**
Harlem Courthouse **299**
Harlem Meer **265**
Harlem River Houses **301**
Harlem School of the Arts (HSA) **301**
Harley Davidson Cafe ★$$ **212**
Harmon, Arthur Loomis **190**
Harmonie Club, The **219**
Harriet Love **71**
Harriet's Kitchen **284**
Harrison & Abramovitz **177, 186, 235, 296**
Harrison & Fouilhoux **199**
Harrison Street Row **57**
Harrison, Wallace K. **178, 268, 269, 315**
Harry Cipriani ★★$$$$ **218**
Harry's Burrito Junction ★$ **274**
Harry Winston, Inc. **211**
Harry Zarin Co. Fabric Warehouse **45**
Harvard Club, The **185**
Harvey, David **243**
Hash, Thomas **32**
Hassinger, Herman **109**
Hastings, Thomas **232, 288**
Hatsuhana ★★★$$$ **189**
Hat, The/El Sombrero $ **48**
Haughwout Building **60**
Hausman & Rosenberg **273**
Havemeyer, Horace III **130**
Hayden Planetarium **281**
Health Insurance Building **145**
Health Nuts **290**
Hearst Magazine Building **164**
Heckscher Playground **261**
Hee Seung Fung (HSF) ★$$ **45**
Heights **293, 303**

Heins & LaFarge **20, 109, 230, 274, 295, 316**
Hejduk, John **105**
Helene Arpels **208**
Helen Hayes **150**
Helicopters **6**
Heller Gallery **66**
Helmsley Building, The **182**
Helmsley Middletowne $$$ **190**
Helmsley Park Lane Hotel $$$ **214**
Henderson Place **249**
Henri Bendel **211**
Henry's End ★$$ **308**
Herald Center **140**
Herald Square **144**
Hermes **210**
Hero Boy ★$ **144**
Hero's Journey, The **289**
Herter Bros. **45**
Herts & Tallant **154, 288, 308**
Herts, Henry B. **150, 151, 158**
Hibbs, Jay **96**
High Rock **304**
Hines Building **196**
Hirschl & Adler **233**
Hispanic Society of America **302**
Hiss & Weeks **201**
Historic Richmond Town **319**
H. Kauffman & Sons **124**
Holiday Inn Crowne Plaza $$$ **158**
Holiday Inn Downtown $$ **52**
Holland Tunnel **59**
Hollein, Hans **238**
Holm, Alvin **243**
Home ★★$$ **84**
Home Savings of America **177**
Hood and Fouilhoux **186**
Hood, Godley & Fouilhoux **145**
Hood, Raymond **93, 173**
Hoppin & Koen **50**
Horgan & Slattery **38, 272**
Horowitz & Chun **45**
Hors d'Oeuvrerie at Windows on the World, The **36**
Hotalings News Agency **145**
Hotel Chelsea $$ **138**
Hotel des Artistes **272**
Hotel Dorset $$$ **200**
Hotel Elysée $$$ **203**
Hotel Inter-Continental New York $$$ **190**
Hotel Plaza Athénée $$$$ **228**
Hotel ratings **5**
Hotel Royalton $$$$ **184**
Hotel Wellington $ **163**
Hotel Wolcott $ **125**
Hour Glass Tavern $ **157**
Hours **10**
House of Oldies **81**
Howe, George **191**
Howell & Stokes **296**
Howells & Hood **177**
Howells, John Mead **191**
Hoyt, Burnham **298**
HRC (New York Health & Racquet Club) Tennis **24**
Hubert, Pirrson & Co. **138**
Hudson River Club ★★★$$$$ **34**
375 Hudson Street **77**

Hugh Stubbins & Associates **204**
Hunan Balcony, The ★$ **290**
Hunan Garden ★★$ **43**
Hunt & Hunt **123**
Hunter College **231**
Huntington, Charles Pratt **302**
Hunt, Richard Howland **229, 243**
Hunt, Richard Morris **19, 32, 60, 218, 243, 290**
Hunt Room, The ★★$$$ **195**
Hunt, William Morris **165**

I

IBM Building **210**
If Boutique **76**
Il Bisonte **64**
Il Cantinori ★★$$$ **92**
Il Cortile ★$$$ **52**
Il Monello ★★$$$ **239**
Il Mulino ★★★$$$ **96**
Il Nido ★★$$$$ **205**
Il Ponte Vecchio ★$$ **97**
Il Toscanaccio ★★★$$ **219**
Il Vagabondo ★$$ **226**
Il Valletto ★$$$ **223**
I. Miller Building **155**
Immaculate Conception Church **110**
I.M. Pei & Associates **27**
I.M. Pei & Partners **97, 124, 144**
Imperial **151**
Inagiku Japanese Restaurant ★★$$$$ **189**
Independence Plaza **57**
India House (East Side) **229**
India House (Lower Manhattan) **23**
India Pavilion ★$ **164**
Indochine ★★$$ **104**
Indonesian Pavilion **202**
Ingalls & Hoffman **150**
Inn at Irving Place $$$ **117**
Institute for Contemporary Art **313**
Integral Yoga Institute **89**
International Center of Photography (ICP) **254**
International Education Information Center **180**
International Gourmet and Gift Center **305**
In the Market for a van Gogh? Try New York's Museum Shops **248**
Intrepid Sea Air Space Museum **146**
Inwood **303**
Iridium $$ **268**
Iris Brown's Victorian Doll and Miniature Shop **207**
Irish Secret, The **68**
Irreplaceable Artifacts of North America **48**
Irving Trust Company Building/ The Bank of New York **29**
Isabella ★$$ **278**
Isamu Noguchi Garden Museum **313**
Islamic Center of New York **254**
Island ★$$$ **253**
Island Helicopter Sightseeing **128**
Iso ★$$ **109**

Isola ★$$ **284**
Isozaki, Arata **73**, **110**, **310**
Istanbul Kebap ★★$ **240**
Italian Food Center **50**
I Tre Merli ★$$$ **75**
I Trulli ★★★$$$ **123**
Ives, H. Douglas **178**, **184**

J

Jaap Rietman **68**
Jackson Diner ★$ **314**
Jackson Hole ★$ **226**
Jacob K. Javits Convention Center **144**
Jacob K. Javits Federal Building **39**
Jacob Riis Houses Plaza **107**
Jacobs, Harry Allan **230**
Jacobs, Stephen B. **92**
Jacobs, Steven **155**
Jade Palace ★★$ **315**
Jaiya Thai Oriental Restaurant ★★$$ **314**
Jamaica Bay Wildlife Refuge **315**
Jamaican Hot Pot ★★$ **300**
James B. Duke House **238**
James Beard House ★★★★$$$$ **90**
James II Galleries **210**
James Stewart Polshek & Partners **34**, **165**, **297**, **310**
Janes & Leo **273**, **291**
Jane Street Seafood Cafe ★$$ **89**
Jan Hus Church **235**
Janovic Plaza **227**
Jan Weiss Gallery **59**
Japonica ★★★$$ **92**
Jardine, Hill & Murdock **268**
Jay Gorney Art **67**
J.C. Cady & Co. **279**
Jean Lafitte ★★$$$ **213**
Jean, Patricia **77**
Jefferson Market **86**
Jensen-Lewis **135**
Jerry Ohlinger's Movie Material Store **89**
Jerry's ★★$$ **74**
Jervis, John B. **304**
Jessor, Herman **138**
Jewish Museum **253**
Jezebel ★★$$$ **148**
Jim McMullen ★$$ **239**
Jing Fong ★$ **45**
J.N. Bartfield Galleries & Books **213**
Joan & David **116**
Joe Allen ★$$ **156**
Joe's Dairy **76**
Johansen & Bhavnani **225**
John Burgee Architects **196**
John Carl Warnecke & Associates **56**
John F. Kennedy International Airport (JFK) **4**
John's of Twelfth Street ★$$ **110**
Johnson, Philip **94**, **95**, **172**, **192**, **193**, **198**, **203**, **225**, **243**, **269**
John's Pizzeria ★★$ **83**
Johnston, John Taylor **93**
127 John Street **27**
John Weber **74**
JoJo ★★★$$$ **227**
Joovay **69**

Joseph Patelson Music House **164**
Joseph Tricot **230**
Josie's ★★$ **276**
Jour et Nuit ★★$$$ **61**
Joyce Theater, The **136**
J.P. French Bakery **200**
J. Press **184**
Judge's Chamber **129**
Judson Memorial Baptist Church **94**
Juilliard School **270**
Julie: Artisans' Gallery **221**
Jungle World **316**
Junior League of The City of New York **241**
Junior's ★$ **309**
Just Kidding **58**
Just Shades **49**

K

Kahn & Jacobs **39**, **209**
Kahn, Ely Jacques **127**
Kahn, Louis I. **72**
Kajima International **32**
Kam Man Food Products, Inc. **43**
Kaplan's $$ **222**
Kaplan, Sam Hall **53**
Kate's Paperie **91**
Katz, Bill **57**
Katz's Delicatessen ★$ **48**
Kaufman Astoria Studio/U.S. Army Pictorial Center **313**
Kaufman, A.W. **46**
Kawecki, Charles S. **134**
Keister, George **149**, **299**
Kelley and Ping ★★$ **74**
Kellum, John **38**, **92**, **301**
Kelter/Malce **88**
Kendall, William M. **302**
Kennedy Galleries **212**
Kenneth Cole **278**
Kenn's Broome Street Bar $ **65**
Kessler, S.J. **124**
Kevin Roche, John Dinkeloo & Associates **178**, **196**, **243**, **261**
Key West Diner & Cafe $ **289**
Khyber Pass ★$ **107**
Kiehl's Since 1851 **110**
Kiev ★$ **106**
Kiiroi Hana ★★$$ **212**
Kilburn, Henry F. **287**
Kimball & Thompson **233**
Kimball, Francis H. **32**
Kimball, Richard **233**
King & Campbell **289**
Kin Khao ★★$$ **68**
King & Kellum **118**
King Crab ★$$ **161**
King, Gamaliel **308**
King of Greene Street, The **66**
Kips Bay Plaza **124**
Kirshenblatt-Gimblett, Barbara **52**
Kitchen Arts & Letters **254**
Kitchen, The **137**
Kleine Konditorei ★$$ **244**
Kling, Vincent G. **297**
Knickerbocker Bar & Grill ★$$ **92**
Knickerbocker Club, The **220**
Knitting Factory **57**
Knoedler Gallery **233**
Knowles, H.P. **163**
Kohn Pederson Fox **272**

Kohn, Robert D. **144**, **229**, **271**
Konti, Isadore **168**
Koolhaas, Rem **72**
Kosner, Edward **15**
Koyote Kate's $$ **157**
Krapp, Herbert J. **151**, **156**, **157**, **158**, **161**, **162**
Kyoto Book Center **125**

L

La Bohème ★$$ **95**
La Boîte en Bois ★★$$$ **273**
La Bonne Soupe ★$ **200**
La Caravelle ★★★$$$$ **200**
La Caridad $ **279**
La Colombe d'Or ★★$$$ **123**
La Côte Basque ★★★★$$$$ **200**
376-380 Lafayette Street **101**
Lafever, Minard **44**, **139**
La Fondue $ **200**
La Grenouille ★★$$$$ **196**
La Guardia Airport (LGA) **6**
La Jumelle ★$ **61**
La Lunchonette ★$$ **137**
La Maison du Chocolat **236**
La Mama E.T.C. **103**
La Mangeoire ★★$$$ **205**
Lamb & Rich **60**, **249**, **278**, **297**, **299**
Lamb, Thomas W. **156**, **304**
La Metairie ★★$$ **86**
La Mirabelle ★$$$ **285**
Landmark Tavern ★★$$ **147**
Lang, George **255**
Lansburgh, G. Albert **151**
La Piazzetta di Quisisana ★$$$ **239**
Lapidus, Morris **193**
La Réserve ★★★$$$$ **188**
La Ripaille ★★$$ **89**
Larrabee, Edward **159**
Lasker Rink and Pool **265**
La Tour D'Or ★$$$ **29**
Lattanzi ★$$$ **157**
Laura Ashley **279**
Laura Ashley Home Furnishings **220**
Laurence Miller Gallery **68**
Leader, Herman Lee **290**
Leaf & Bean **309**
Le Bernardin ★★★★$$$$ **160**
Le Bistrot de Maxim's ★$$$ **221**
LeBrun, Napoleon **140**
Le Chantilly ★★★$$$$ **209**
L'Ecole ★★$$ **60**
Le Colonial ★★$$ **207**
Le Corbusier **178**
Lee Manners & Associates **71**
Lee's Art Shop, Inc. **164**
Lee's Studio **164**
Le Figaro Café ★ **96**
Le Madeleine ★$$$ **147**
Le Madri ★★★$$$ **135**
Lenox Hill Hospital **238**
Lenox School, The **234**
Leo Castelli Gallery **69**
Leon & Lionel Levy **267**
Le Pactole ★★$$$ **35**
Le Parker Meridien $$$$ **166**
Le Perigord ★★★$$$ **205**
Le Refuge ★★$$$ **241**
Le Refuge Bed & Breakfast $ **318**

Le Regence ★★★★$$$$ **228**
Le Relais ★★$$$ **220**
L'Ermitage ★★$$ **212**
LeRoy, Warner **262**
Lescaze, Paul **191**
Lescaze Residence **191**
Lescaze, William **234**
Les Célébrités ★★★$$$$ **167**
Les Halles ★$$ **124**
Leslie's Originals **46**
Lespinasse ★★★$$$$ **201**
Les Pyrénées ★$$$ **159**
Les Routiers ★$$ **288**
Les Sans Culottes ★$$$ **207**
Let There Be Neon **58**
Le Train Bleu ★$$ **224**
Le Veau d'Or ★$$$ **223**
Lever House **204**
Levine, Ed **111**
Librairie de France and Librería Hispanica (French and European Publications) **187**
Lighthouse, The **223**
Limelight Discotheque **120**
Limousines **6**, **7**, **8**
Lincoln Center for the Performing Arts **268**
Lincoln Center Guided Tours **270**
Lincoln Center Poster Gallery **270**
Lincoln Square Synagogue **273**
Lincoln Tunnel **144**
Lindenthal, Gustav **45**
Lin, Maya **73**
Lin's Sister Associates Corp. **45**
Lion's Head ★$$ **85**
Lipstick Cafe ★$ **206**
Littel, Emlen T. **127**
Little India **314**
Little Italy **40**
Little Pie Company **146**
Little Red Lighthouse **304**
Little Singer Building **72**
Live Bait $$ **122**
Living Memorial for the Holocaust, The/Museum of Jewish Heritage **34**
Lobster Box ★★$$$ **318**
Loch, The **265**
Loeb Boathouse **263**
Loews New York Hotel $$$ **193**
Lola ★$$$ **120**
Lombardy $$$ **209**
London Lennie's $$ **314**
London Terrace Apartments **139**
Longacre **157**
Long Shine Restaurant ★★$ **44**
Looking Toward the Avenue **160**
Lord & Taylor **130**
Lord, James Brown **123**, **241**, **300**
Lotos Club, The **229**
Louie's Westside Cafe ★$$ **283**
Louise Nevelson Plaza **33**
Louisiana Community Bar and Grill ★$$ **100**
Louis K. Meisel **75**
Louis Vuitton **208**
Lowell, Guy **39**
Lowell, The $$$$ **220**
Lower East Side **40**
Lower East Side Tenement Museum **47**
Lower Manhattan **16**

Lox Around the Clock $ 120
LS Collection 229
Luce, Clarence S. 300
Lucille Lortel Theatre 82
Lucky Cheng's ★$ 101
Lucky Strike $$ 61
Lucy Anna Folk Art & Antique
 Quilts 87
Ludlow & Peabody 148
Ludlow Street Cafe, The ★$ 48
Luma ★★$$$ 138
Luna ★$$ 52
Luna d'Oro 66
Lung Fong Bakery 43
Lunt-Fontanne 156
Lusardi's ★★$$$ 240
Lutèce ★★★$$$$ 191
Lycee Français 233
Lyceum 154

M

Maccioni, Sirio 169
MacDougal Alley 93
MacDougal-Sullivan Gardens
 Historic District 96
Machado & Silvetti 34
MacIntyre Building 117
MacKenzie-Childs 232
Macy's 144
Mme. Romaine de Lyon ★★$$
 223
231 Madison Avenue 129
Madison Avenue Bookshop 232
Madison Square 122
Madison Square Garden Center
 141
Madison Towers Hotel $$ 129
Mad. 61 ★★$$$ 221
Magickal Child 120
Maginnis & Walsh 39
Magonigle, H. Van Buren 288
Main Events 14
Majestic 151
Mall, The 262
Malo 230
ManAlive 244
Mandarin Court ★★$ 43
Mandel, Henry 164
Mandell, Henry 209
M&I International 311
M&J Trimming 130
Manducatis ★★$$ 313
Mangin and McComb 38
Mangin, Joseph 49
Manhattan Address Locator 12
Manhattan Art & Antiques
 Center, The 206
Manhattan Bistro ★$ 68
Manhattan Bridge 45
Manhattan Cafe ★$$$ 226
Manhattan Chili Company, The
 ★$ 150
Manhattan Comics & Cards 138
Manhattan Doll House 137
Manhattan Fruitier 124
Manhattan Mall 140
Manhattan Neighborhoods see
 inside front cover
Manhattan Ocean Club, The
 ★★★$$$ 213
Manhattan Plaza 146
Man Ray ★$$ 136
Mansfield $$ 184

Map key 5
Maraolo 232
Marble Collegiate Church 125
March ★★★$$$ 206
Marchi's ★$$$ 124
Marcus Garvey Memorial Park
 299
Margo Feiden Galleries 221
Margon & Holder 289
Marian Goodman Gallery 213
Marine Midland Bank 32
Mariners' Temple 44
Marino, Peter 221
Marion's Continental Restaurant
 and Lounge ★$$ 103
Markelius, Sven 178
Market at Citicorp Center, The
 205
Mark's ★★$$$$ 237
Mark, The $$$$ 237
Marlborough Gallery 213
Marquis 154
Marriott Marquis $$$ 154
Martha Washington $ 125
Martin Beck 151
Martini's ★★$$ 161
Maruzzella ★$$ 239
Mary Boone 69
Marylou's ★★$$$ 93
Marys ★$ 81
Match ★$$ 73
Matsui, Yasuo 28, 139
Matthew's ★★★$$$ 224
Matthews, Charles T. 195
Maxilla & Mandible 281
MaxMara 230
Max Protetch Gallery 72
Maxwell Davidson Gallery 209
Mayers & Schiff 155
Mayer, Whittlesey & Glass 91
Mayfair Hotel $$$$ 228
Mayflower $$ 268
Mazer Store Equipment Co. 49
McBean, Thomas 37
McBurney YMCA $ 138
McComb, John Jr. 20
McDonald's $ 33
McKim, Charles Follen 129, 199,
 202, 296
McKim, Mead & White 28, 39,
 50, 80, 91, 94, 95, 97, 119,
 124, 129, 140, 141 144, 149,
 176, 184, 185, 194, 195, 199,
 202, 219, 231, 238, 241, 243,
 295, 296, 300 310, 315
McNulty's Tea and Coffee
 Company 82
McSorley's Old Ale House 106
Meader, Herman Lee 90
Melampo Imported Foods 70
Melton, N.C. 229
Menchanko-tei ★$ 200
Mercedes-Benz Showroom 209
Merkin Concert Hall 273
Mesa Grill ★★$$$ 116
Metisse ★★★$ 290
Metro Pictures 74
Metropolitan Club 219
Metropolitan Life Building 182
Metropolitan Life Insurance
 Company 122
Metropolitan Museum of Art
 243, 248

Metropolitan Museum of Art Gift
 Shop 187
Metropolitan Opera House 269
Metropolitan Opera Shop 269
Meyers, Frank 317
Mezzaluna ★$$ 235
Mezzanine, The ★★$$$ 156
Mezzogiorno ★★$$$ 70
Michael Carey American Arts &
 Crafts 66
Michael's ★★$$ 200
Michael's Pub ★$$$ 206
Michelangelo $$$ 160
Mickey Mantle's ★$$ 214
Midtown 170
Mies van der Rohe, Ludwig 172,
 193
Mike's American Bar and Grill
 ★$ 147
Milady ★$ 71
Milburn Hotel $ 278
Milford Plaza $$ 151
Millenium Hilton, The $$$$ 37
Millennium Broadway $$$ 150
Milton Glaser, Inc. 146
Mineral Springs 262
Minetta Lane Theatre 95
1 Minetta Street 95
Minetta Tavern ★★$$ 95
Minna Rosenblatt 232
Minoru Yamasaki & Associates
 35
Minskoff 154
Miracle Grill ★★$$ 106
Mrs. James A. Burden House 251
Mrs. John Henry Hammond
 House 251
Missoni 232
Mitali ★★$$ 106
Mitchell-Giurgola 34, 296
Mitsukoshi ★★★$$$ 208
Mitzi E. Newhouse Theater 270
Miyacaki, Stomu 75
Mobil Building 177
Mocca Hungarian ★$ 245
MoMA Bookstore, The 199
MoMA Design Store, The 197
Money 10
Monkey Bar ★★★$$$ 204
Montague Street Saloon ★$ 308
Montebello, Philippe de 243
Montenapoleone 230
Montrachet ★★★$$$ 58
MONY Tower 163
Moondance Diner ★$ 59
Moore, Albert Preston 202
Moore, Charles 34
Morgan Cafe ★$ 130
Morgan Guaranty Trust
 Company 29
Morgane Le Fay 68
Morgans $$$ 129
Morningside Heights 292
Morrell & Company, The Wine
 Emporium 203
Morris, Benjamin Wistar 28
Morris-Jumel Mansion 302
Morris Ketchum, Jr. &
 Associates 254, 310, 316
Morris Lapidus & Associates 161
Morris, Roger 302
Mortimer's ★$$$ 238
Morton's of Chicago ★★★

$$$ 184
Mother Cabrini Shrine 304
Mould, Jacob Wrey 123, 243,
 261, 262, 279
Mount Morris Park Historical
 District 299
Mount Sinai Hospital 254
Mount, The 265
Movie Star News 135
Mud, Sweat & Tears 147
Mughlai $$ 277
Municipal Building 39
Murder Ink. 289
Murgatroyd & Ogden 223
Murray Hill 112
Murray's Cheese Store 84
Murray's Sturgeon 288
Museum Cafe $$ 278
Museum Company, The 202
Museum for African Art 73
Museum of American Folk Art
 248, 272
Museum of Chinese in the
 Americas 42
Museum of Modern Art (MoMA)
 198
Museum of Television and Radio
 196
Museum of the City of New York
 255
Museum Tower 198
Music & Dance Tickets Booth 173
Music Box 154
Mysterious Bookshop, The 164

N

Nam Wah Tea Parlor ★$ 43
Nancy Hoffman Gallery 69
Nathan's Famous ★$ 311
National Academy of Design 250
National Arts Club 118
National Black Theater 299
National Debt Clock 149
National Museum of the
 American Indian 22
National Restaurant ★★$$$
 311
Nat Sherman's 174
Nature Max Theater 281
Naumburg Bandshell, The 262
NBC Studio Tours 187
Negril Island Spice ★★$ 139
Neil Simon 161
Nello ★★$$$ 220
Nell's 89
Nervi, Pier Luigi 304
Nesle, Inc. 207
Newark International Airport
 (EWR) 7
New Chao Chow ★$ 52
New Dramatists, The 147
Newhouse Center for
 Contemporary Art, The 318
New Lin Heong ★$ 43
New Museum of Contemporary
 Art, The 73
News Bar ★$ 120
New York Academy of Medicine
 255
New York Astrology Center 175
New York Athletic Club, The 167
New York Botanical Garden 317
New York Bound Bookshop 188

New York City area 2
New York City Courthouse 38
New York City Fire Museum 64
New York City in Fact. . . 62
New York City Marble Cemetery 100
New York City on Screen 30
New York County Courthouse 39
New York Doll Hospital 223
New York Gas Lighting Company 49
New York Helmsley Hotel $$$$ 177
New York Hilton and Towers $$$ 162
New-York Historical Society 277
New York, Home Style 12
New York Hospital/Cornell University Medical College 235
New York Hotel Pennsylvania $$ 140
New York International American Youth Hostel (AYH) $ 290
New York Life Insurance Company 123
New York Marble Cemetery 100
New York Marriott East Side $$$ 190
New York Mercantile Exchange (East Village) 100
New York Mercantile Exchange (TriBeCa) 57
New York Open Center 66
New York Palace Hotel, The $$$$ 194
New York Public Library 174
New York Public Library, Donnell Library Center 197
New York Public Library, Hudson Park Branch 81
New York Public Library, Jefferson Market Branch 85
New York Public Library/ Library and Museum of the Performing Arts 270
New York Public Library, Mid-Manhattan Branch 175
New York Public Library, 115th Street Branch 295
New York Public Library, Ottendorfer Branch 108
New York Public Library, Science, Industry, and Business Branch 127
New York Public Library, Yorkville Branch 241
New York Sailing School 317
New York Shakespeare Festival 104
New York Society for Ethical Culture 271
New York Society Library 238
New York Speak 13
New York State Armory 134
New York State Theater 269
New York Stock Exchange 29
New York Studio School of Drawing, Painting & Sculpture 93
New York Times, The 148
New York Transit Museum 308
New York Unearthed 20
New York University (NYU) 94

New York Women's Exchange 226
New York Yacht Club, The 185
Niall Smith Antiques 60
Nice Restaurant ★★★$ 44
Nicholas Roerich Museum 291
Nick & Eddie ★★$$ 70
Nicola Paone ★$$$ 128
Niemeyer, Oscar 178
Night Presence IV 252
92nd Street Y 252
Nippon ★★$$$$ 192
Nobu ★★★$$$$ 58
North Beach Leather 229
North Wind Museum and Sea Institute 317
Norton Books 207
Nostalgia and All That Jazz 97
Novotel $$$ 161
Nuyorican Poet's Cafe ★ 101
Nyborg-Nelson ★★$ 205
N.Y. Noodletown ★$ 44

O
Oak and Rose Rooms ★$$$ 185
Observation Deck, The 35
Oceana ★★★$$$$ 203
O'Connor & Kilhan 137
Odeon, The ★$$ 56
Odessa ★★$$$ 311
Off SoHo Suites $ 49
O.K. Harris Works of Art 65
Old Homestead ★★$$$$ 134
Old Merchants' House 103
Old St. Patrick's Cathedral 49
Old St. Patrick's Convent and Girls' School 49
Old Town Bar ★$ 117
Ollie's Noodle Shop ★$ 285
Olympic Tower 195
Omen ★★$$ 70
Omni Berkshire Place $$$ 194
OMO Norma Kamali 212
On a Clear Day You Can See… 21
O'Neals' ★★$$$ 271
One If By Land, Two If By Sea ★★$$$$ 83
107 West ★$$ 291
1 Penn Plaza 141
One Shubert Alley 150
135th Street Gatehouse, Croton Aqueduct 300
1 Times Square 148
Only Hearts 279
Opal White 76
Oppenheimer, Brady & Vogelstein 57
Orchard Street 47
O'Reilly Brothers 301
Oriental Garden Seafood ★★$$ 45
Oriental Pearl ★$ 52
Original Improvisation, The 141
Original Levi's Store, The 223
Orpheum Theatre 107
Orso ★$$$ 156
Orvis 183
Osadea, Apollinaire 106
Osborn Engineering Co. 315
Osborne, The 165
Oscar Wilde Memorial Bookshop 85
Ottendorfer Library 108

Ottomanelli's Meat Market 83
Our Lady of Lourdes Church 301
Oyster Bar and Restaurant ★★$$$ 176
Ozu ★$ 287

P
Pace Gallery, The (Midtown) 209
Pace Gallery, The (SoHo) 74
Pace University 38
Page, George 131
Palace Theater 155
Paley Plaza 202
Palio ★★$$$ 160
Palladium 110
Palm ★★$$$$ 180
Palmer & Hornbostel 225
Pamir ★$$ 239
Pandit ★ 287
Panevino ★$$ 269
Paola's ★★$$$ 244
Pappardella $$ 277
Papyrus Booksellers 296
Paracelso 69
Paraclete 235
Paragon 117
Paramount Building 150
Paramount Hotel $$$ 156
Parc Vendome Apartments 164
Parioli Romanissimo ★★★$$$$ 242
Parish & Schroeder 138
1 Park Avenue 127
2 Park Avenue 127
3 Park Avenue 127
101 Park Avenue 175
660 Park Avenue 230
680-690 Park Avenue 231
870 Park Avenue 238
1187 Park Avenue 254
Park Avenue Cafe ★★★$$$ 222
Park Bistro ★★$$$ 125
Park Cafe ★★$$$ 200
Park Central $$ 163
Park East Synagogue 227
Parking 9
Parma ★$$$ 241
Parrish-Hadley 167
Parsons School of Design 91
Passage to India ★$ 106
Passenger Ship Terminal 168
Past Perfect: The New York City Landmarks Preservation Commission 312
Pastrami King ★$ 315
Patchin, Aaron D. 85
Patchin Place 85
Patisserie J. Lanciani ★$ 86
Patria ★★★$$$ 118
Patricia Field 93
Patsy's Pizza ★★$ 308
Patsy's Pizzeria ★$ 300
Patzo $ 285
Paula Cooper Gallery 75
Paul Mellon House 234
Paul Rainey Memorial Gate 316
Paul Smith 116
Paul Stuart 183
Peanut Butter & Jane 89
Pearl River Chinese Products 51
Pearl River Mart 59
Peculier Pub 97
Pedro Paramo ★★$ 110

Pei, I.M. 208
Peking Duck House ★★$ 43
Pelham, George F. 228
Pelli, Cesar 198
Pelton, Henry C. 227, 298
Pen & Pencil ★$$$$ 182
Penang ★$ 67
Peninsula New York, The $$$$ 201
Penn Station South 138
Pennsylvania Station 141
Penny Whistle Toys 281
Pen-Top Bar and Terrace $ 201
Performing Arts Gift Shop 270
Performing Garage 61
Periyali ★★★$$$ 120
Personal safety 10
Peruvian Restaurant ★$ 147
Petaluma ★$$$ 235
Peter Fox Shoes 70
Peter Hermann 69
Peterkin, John B. 175
Peter Luger ★★★$$$ 309
Peter Minuit Plaza 21
Peter-Roberts Antiques 68
Petersen, Frederick A. 104
Pete's Tavern ★$ 117
Petrossian ★★★$$$$ 166
Pfeiffer, Carl 201
Phebe's Place 103
Philip Birnbaum & Associates 224
Philip Morris Headquarters 175
Pho Bâng Restaurant ★$ 51
Photographer's Place, A 72
Phyllis Kind Gallery 74
Picholine ★★★$$$ 271
Pickwick Arms Hotel $ 191
Piemonte Ravioli Company 50
Pierpont Morgan Library, The 129
Pierre au Tunnel ★★$$$ 157
Pierre Deux (East Side) 233
Pierre Deux (Greenwich Village) 86
Pierre's ★$$$ 85
Pierre, The $$$$ 219
Pier 17 27
Pig Heaven ★$$ 240
Pillowry, The 223
Pink Teacup ★$ 82
Pipeline ★$$ 35
Pizzeria Uno $ 282
P.J. Clarke's ★$$ 206
Planet Hollywood ★$$ 166
Platt, Charles A. 227, 229, 316
Platypus 67
Players Theatre 95
Playhouse 91 251
Plaza Hotel, The $$$ 214
Plymouth 151
Po ★★★$ 84
Pokorny, Jan Hird 317
Police Academy and Museum 118
Police Building, The 50
Police Plaza 39
Poli Fabrics 166
Pollan, Corky 169
Pollard, George Mort 272
Polo–Ralph Lauren 233
Polo Sport–Ralph Lauren 233
Polo, The ★★$$$ 232
Polshek, James Stewart 34, 61, 118

Pomander Walk **289**
Pond, The **260**
Pong Sri ★$$ **157**
Poor, Alfred Easton **39**
Pope, John Russell **232, 253, 280**
Popover Café ★$$ **287**
Port Authority Bus Terminal **145**
Port Authority Design Staff **145**
Portico **65**
Portland Square Hotel $ **155**
Portman, John **154**
Port of New York Authority Commerce Building/Union Inland Terminal No. 1 **134**
Porto Rico **96**
Poseidon Greek Bakery **147**
Positively 104th Street Cafe ★$ **290**
Poster America Gallery **135**
Post, George B. **29, 243, 300**
Post, George M. **183**
Post House, The ★★★$$$$ **221**
Pot Belly Stove Restaurant $ **82**
Potter, William A. **277, 289, 299**
P.P.O.W. **67**
Prada Milano **208**
Praeger-Kavanagh-Waterbury **315**
Praeger-Waterbury **314**
Pratesi **232**
Pratt, Harold I. **231**
Pratt Institute **309**
Prentice & Chan, Ohlhausen **46, 310**
Price, Bruce **32, 300**
Primavera ★★$$$$ **245**
130 Prince Street **71**
Prince Street Bar & Restaurant ★$ **75**
Printed Matter Bookstore at Dia **65**
Promenade Theatre **278**
Prospect Park **310**
Provence ★★★$$ **77**
Pruyn, John **57**
P.S. 1 **313**
P.S. 92 **300**
P.S. 234 **55**
Publications **10**
Public Theater **104**
Puck Building **48**
Puffy's Tavern **57**
Puglia Restaurant ★$ **51**
Pure Mädderlake **60**
Pushbottom for Kids **224**
Putumayo **278**

Q
Quality Inn by Journey's End Hotel $$$ **175**
Quark International **128**
Queens **306, 313**
Queensboro Bridge **225**
Queens Museum of Art **315**
Quest Book Shop of the New York Theosophical Society **205**

R
Raccoon Lodge, The **284**
Racquet and Tennis Club **194**
Radio City Music Hall **187**
Radisson Empire Hotel, The $$ **268**

Raffetto's **96**
Rainbow Room, The ★★★★$$$$ **188**
Ramble, The **263**
Rand McNally Map and Travel Center **192**
Raoul's ★★$$$ **70**
Rapp & Rapp **150**
Ratner's ★$$ **46**
Red House, The **285**
Red Tulip, The **239**
Reebok Sports Club/NY **272**
Reed & Stem **176**
Regency, The $$$$ **222**
Reiley, Robert J. **39**
Reiley, Robert S. **316**
Reilly, Paul C. **128**
Reinhard & Hoffmeister **186**
Reinstein/Ross **71**
Remi ★★★$$$ **162**
Renaissance New York $$$ **155**
Rene Pujol ★★$$ **159**
Rental cars **6, 7, 8, 9**
Renwick, Aspinwall & Russell **300**
Renwick, James Jr. **109, 121, 195, 193, 225, 300**
Renwick, W.W. **300**
Reservoir, The **264**
Restaurant at Windows on the World, The **35**
Restaurant Daniel ★★★★$$$$ **237**
Restaurant Florent ★★$$ **88**
Restaurant 44 ★★$$$ **184**
Restaurant ratings **5**
Restaurants **10**
Revolution Books **115**
Rhiga Royal Hotel $$$$ **162**
R.H. Tugs ★$$ **319**
Richard Meier Associates **88**
Richard Rodgers **156**
Richardson, Henry Hobson **127**
Richard Stoddard Performing Arts Books **115**
Riddle, Theodate Pope **119**
Ridiculous Theatrical Company, The **83**
Rigo Hungarian Pastry **239**
Rikyu ★$$ **273**
Riles, James **118**
Rink at Rockefeller Center, The **187**
Ristorante Taormina ★$$ **51**
Ritualarium **46**
Ritz-Carlton $$$$ **167**
Ritz Tower **208**
Rive Gauche–Yves Saint Laurent **233**
Riverbend Houses **300**
River Café ★★★$$$$ **306**
River House **205**
Riverrun Cafe ★$$ **58**
Riverside Church **298**
Riverside Drive/West 105th Street Historic District **291**
Riverside Park **288**
Riviera Cafe $$ **86**
Rizzoli Bookstore **213**
Rizzoli Bookstore of SoHo **76**
Road to Mandalay ★★$$ **50**
Robertson, R.H. **117, 233, 287**

Roche, Kevin **253**
Rockefeller Apartments **199**
Rockefeller Center **186**
Rockefeller University **235**
Roebling, John A. **27**
Roebling, Washington **27**
Roerich Museum **291**
Rogers, Butler, Burgun & Bradbury **238**
Rogers, Isaiah **37**
Rogers, James Gamble **183, 296**
Roger Smith Hotel $$$$ **190**
Rolf's Restaurant ★$$ **122**
Ronald Feldman Fine Arts Inc. **59**
Ronin Gallery **209**
Roosevelt Hotel, The $$ **183**
Roosevelt Island **225**
Roosevelt Island Tramway Station **224**
Rosa Mexicano ★★$$$ **206**
Rose Cafe ★★$$ **92**
Roseland **161**
Rosemarie's ★★$$$ **56**
Rosenthal Wine Merchant **241**
Rosenzweig, Anne **53**
Rossant, Conklin **34**
Rossi, Aldo **72**
Rossini's $$$ **128**
Rossiter, Ehrick **184**
Roth, Emery **200, 208, 209, 235, 277, 281, 198**
Roumeli Taverna ★$$ **313**
Roundabout Theatre **154**
Rouse & Goldstone **252**
Royal Athena Galleries **207**
Royale **151**
RTKL Associates **140**
Rudin, Samuel **93**
Rudy's Bar **147**
Rumpelmayer's $$ **214**
Rumsey Field **262**
Rumsey Playground **262**
Russ & Daughters **48**
Russell Sage Foundation Building **122**
Russian & Turkish Baths **107**
Russian Orthodox Cathedral of St. Nicholas **254**
Russian Samovar ★$$ **161**
Russian Tea Room, The ★★$$$ **166**

S
Saarinen, Eero **197**
Saeltzer, Alexander **104**
Safety, personal **10**
Saigon House Restaurant ★★$ **42**
St. Andrew's Church **39**
St. Bartholomew's Church **193**
St. Francis Xavier Church **116**
St. George's Chapel **115**
St. George's Episcopal Church **115**
St. George's Ukrainian Catholic Church **106**
St. James **150**
St. James Episcopal Church **233**
St. James Roman Catholic Church **44**
St. Jean Baptiste Church **238**
St. John the Baptist Church **140**
St. Joseph's Church **84**

Saint Laurie Limited **119**
St. Luke-in-the-Fields **82**
St. Luke's–Roosevelt Hospital **295**
St. Maggie's Cafe ★$$ **28**
St. Mark's Bookshop **109**
St. Mark's-in-the-Bowery Church **109**
St. Mark's Place **106**
St. Mark's Sounds **107**
St. Moritz on the Park $$$ **214**
St. Nicholas Historic District/ King Model Houses **300**
St. Patrick's Cathedral **195**
St. Paul's Chapel **37**
St. Peter's Episcopal Church **137**
St. Peter's Lutheran Church **205**
St. Regis Sheraton, The $$$$ **201**
Saint-Remy Produits de Provence **222**
St. Thomas Church **199**
St. Vartan Cathedral **128**
St. Vincent's Hospital **90**
Saks Fifth Avenue **188**
Salander-O'Reilly Galleries **238**
Sal Anthony's $$ **117**
Sal Anthony's S.P.Q.R $$ **51**
Salisbury Hotel $$ **166**
Saloon, The $$ **271**
Salvation Army Centennial Memorial Temple **90**
Salvatore Ala **72**
Samalita's Tortilla Factory ★$ **241**
Sam Ash Music Store **158**
Sammy's Famous Roumanian Jewish Steakhouse ★★$$$ **49**
Sammy's Noodle Shop & Grill ★$ **86**
Sam's ★$ **151**
Samuel B. & David Rose Building **270**
Samuel Paley Plaza **202**
Samuel Weiser's Bookstore **122**
San Carlos Hotel $$ **192**
San Domenico ★★★★$$$$ **168**
San Pietro ★★$$$ **203**
San Remo **277**
Santa Fe ★$$ **273**
Santa Fe Grill ★$ **309**
Sant Ambroeus ★★$$$ **238**
Sarabeth's at the Whitney ★★$$ **236**
Sarabeth's Kitchen (Upper East Side) ★★$$ **252**
Sarabeth's Kitchen (West Side) ★★$$ **282**
Sarah Delano Roosevelt Memorial House **229**
Saranac ★$ **254**
Sardi's ★$$$ **150**
Sasaki, Dawson, DeMay Associates **192**
Saturnia Restaurant ★$$$ **129**
Savoy ★★$$$ **72**
Sawyer, Philip **230**
Sazerac House ★★$$ **87**
Scaletta ★★$$$ **277**
Schaller & Weber **244**
Schapiro's House of Kosher and Sacramental Wines **47**
Schermerhorn, Peter **25**
Schermerhorn Row **25**

Schickel, William **108**
Schmidt, Mott B. **206, 228, 241, 249**
Schneider & Herter **227**
Schoepfer Studios **140**
Schomburg Center for Research in Black Culture **300**
School of Visual Arts **122**
Schultze & Weaver **189, 218, 219**
Schwartz & Gross **151, 254**
Schwartzmann, Herman J. **100**
Science Fiction Shop **96**
Sculpture Garden, The **199**
Scutt, Der **211**
Seagram Building **193**
SeaGrill, The ★★★$$$$ **188**
Seaport Inn $$ **27**
Seaport Liberty Cruises **27**
Seaport Suites Hotel $$$ **28**
2nd Avenue Deli ★$$ **109**
Secondhand Rose **72**
Ségires à Solanée **227**
Serbian Orthodox Cathedral of St. Sava **123**
Serendipity ★$$ **224**
Serge Sabarsky Foundation, The **244**
Serracino, Nicholas **238**
Sert, Jackson & Associates **225**
Seryna ★★$$$ **203**
Sette Mezzo ★★$$$ **234**
Sette MoMA ★$$$ **199**
Seventh Regiment Armory **230**
Severance, H. Craig **28**
Seward Park **46**
Sfuzzi ★★$$ **271**
Shakespeare & Co. (East Village) **103**
Shakespeare Garden **264**
Shark Bar ★$ **276**
Shea Stadium **314**
Sheep Meadow **262**
Shelburne Murray Hill $$$ **128**
Sheraton Manhattan $$$ **159**
Sheraton New York Hotel & Towers $$$ **161**
Sheraton Park Avenue $$$ **128**
Sheridan Square **83**
Sherle Wagner International **209**
Sherman Square **274**
Sherry Lehman **221**
Sherry-Netherland Hotel $$$$ **218**
Ships, The **25**
Shoofly **283**
Shopping **10**
Shoreham Hotel $$ **201**
Shreve, Lamb & Harmon **38, 126, 127, 163**
Shrine of Saint Frances Xavier Cabrini **304**
Shubert **150**
Shubert Alley **150**
Shun Lee Dynasty ★$$$ **272**
Shun Lee Palace ★★★$$$$ **204**
Siam Inn ★$ **162**
Sichuan Palace ★★$$$ **178**
Siegel-Cooper & Company **116**
Sign of The Dove, The ★★★$$$$ **226**
Silk Road Palace, The ★$$ **283**
Silk Surplus **207**
Sills, Beverly **169**

Silvercup Studios **313**
Silver Palace ★★$$ **45**
Simpson, Lusby **173**
Sirabella ★★$$ **245**
Sistina ★★$$$ **240**
69th Regiment Armory **123**
67 Wine & Spirits **272**
Skidmore, Owings & Merrill **33, 37, 115, 158, 160, 172, 174, 184, 190, 191, 195, 204, 210, 254, 270**
Sky Books International **195**
Skyride **126**
Slade, Jarvis Morgan **75**
Sloan & Robertson **177**
Sloppy Louie's ★$$$ **24**
Smith & Wollensky ★★$$$ **191**
Smithers Alcoholism Center **253**
Smith, Frank H. **299**
Smith, Hamilton **236**
Smith, Henry Atterbury **239**
Smith, Morrel **228**
Smoking **11**
Snaps ★★$$ **182**
Sniffen Court **128**
Snug Harbor Cultural Center **318**
S.O.B.'s Sounds of Brazil ★★$$ **77**
Society of Illustrators **222**
SoHo **54**
SoHo Antiques Fair and Flea Market **60**
SoHo Emporium **65**
SoHo Kitchen and Bar ★$ **67**
SoHo Photo Gallery **58**
SoHo 20 Gallery **66**
SoHo Wine & Spirits **75**
Soleil ★★$$ **227**
Solera ★★$$ **205**
Solomon R. Guggenheim Museum **248, 249**
Solow Houses **226**
Somethin' Else! **137**
Sonnabend Gallery **69**
Sony Building and Sony Plaza, The **203**
Sony Theaters 84th Street **284**
Sony Theaters Lincoln Square **272**
Sotheby's **235**
South Street Seaport **24**
South Street Seaport Museum **24**
South Street Seaport Museums Shops **25**
Soutine **273**
Sparks ★★$$$$ **182**
Specter, David Kenneth **208**
Sperone Westwater **74**
Sporting Club, The $$ **57**
101 Spring Street **67**
Spring Street Books **69**
Spring Street Garden **70**
Spring Street Natural ★$ **66**
Squadron A and Eighth Regiment Armory/Hunter High School **254**
Stacy's ★★★$ **309**
Stage Delicatessen $$ **162**
Stand-Up NY **279**
Stanford $ **125**
Stanhope Hotel, The $$$$ **242**
Stanton Eckstrut **33**

Stark Gallery **73**
Star Magic **275**
Starrett & Van Vleck **23, 32, 229**
Starrett, Goldwyn **185**
Starrett-Lehigh Building **139**
Staten Island **306, 318**
Staten Island Botanical Garden **318**
Staten Island Children's Museum **318**
Staten Island Ferry **20**
Staten Island Zoo **319**
Statue of Liberty Museum, The **19**
Statue of Liberty National Monument **19**
Steak Frites ★$$ **115**
Stein, Clarence **229**
Steinman & Cain **128**
Steinway Hall **166**
Steinway Mansion **314**
Stella Dallas **97**
Stenhouse, J. Armstrong **251**
Stent, Thomas **73, 104**
Sterner, Frederick **234**
Sterner, Frederick J. **118**
Stern, Robert A.M. **131, 238**
Stern's **140**
Stern's Dry Goods Store **120**
Steuben **211**
Stone, Edward Durell **198, 227, 229, 267**
Stonehill, Judith **111**
Stoughton & Stoughton **288**
Strand Bookstore (East Village) **110**
Strand Bookstore (Lower Manhattan) **25**
Strawberry Fields **263**
Street plan **11**
Streit's Matzoth Company **46**
Stuart Moore **71**
Studio Museum in Harlem **299**
Studio Shoo-Ins: How to Get TV Tickets **180**
Stuyvesant Fish House **238**
Stuyvesant High School **38**
Stuyvesant Square **114**
Stuyvesant Town **114**
Style Swami **101**
Suarez **200**
Subways **6, 7, 9, 335**
Sullivan, Louis **100**
Sullivan Street Playhouse **96**
Surma **106**
Surrey, The $$$ **237**
Surrogate's Court **38**
Susan Bennis/Warren Edwards **213**
Susan P. Meisel Decorative Arts **75**
Sushisay ★★$$$ **194**
Sutton Place and Sutton Place South **206**
Swanke, Hayden, Connell & Partners **211**
Swarthwout, Edgerton **310**
Swasey, W.A. **159**
Swedish Cottage **264**
Sweet Basil **83**
Sweetwater's **273**
S. Wyler **231**
Sylvia's ★★$$ **299**

Symphony Space **289**
Symposium $ **296**
Syms **32**
Synod of Bishops of the Russian Orthodox Church Outside Russia **254**

T

T ★$$ **73**
Tachau, William G. **262**
Tafel, Edgar **91**
Tahari **35**
Tai Hong Lau ★$ **43**
Takashimaya **202**
Takesushi ★★$$$$ **183**
Taliesin ★$$ **37**
Taliesin Associates **250**
Tall Ships Bar & Grill ★$$ **37**
Tammany Hall ★★$$ **124**
T&K French Antiques **71**
Tansuya Corporation **74**
Tatou $$$ **192**
Tavern on the Green ★★$$$$ **261**
Taxes **11**
Taxis **6, 7, 8, 9**
Taylor's **87**
Tea and Sympathy ★$ **89**
Tea Box Cafe ★$ **202**
Teachers College, Bancroft Hall **298**
Telephone **11**
Temple Emanu-El **229**
Tender Buttons **223**
Tennessee Mountain ★$$ **68**
Tenth Street Lounge **109**
Terrace, The ★★$$$$ **298**
Teuscher Chocolates of Switzerland **187**
Thai House Cafe ★$ **59**
Thailand Restaurant ★$$ **42**
Theater at Riverside Church **298**
Theater District **142**
Theater for the New City **108**
Theater Row **145**
Theodore Roosevelt Birthplace **119**
Think Big **65**
767 Third Avenue **190**
780 Third Avenue **191**
900 Third Avenue **206**
Third Cemetery of the Spanish & Portuguese Synagogue **138**
Thom & Wilson **299**
Thomas, Andrew J. **230**
Thomas, Griffin **104**
Thomas, Griffith **60, 119**
Thomas, John Rochester **38, 254**
Thomas K. Woodard **230**
Thompson & Churchill **122**
Thompson, Ben **24**
Thompson, Holmes & Converse **154, 317**
Thompson, Jane **24**
Thompson, Martin E. **28, 93, 260**
Thompson, Samuel **90**
Thornton, William **308**
3 Degrees North $$ **70**
Three Lives & Company **85**
Tickets **11**
Tiffany & Co. **211**

Tilberis, Elizabeth 53
Tilly, Stephen 96
Time and Again ★$$$ 128
Time Cafe ★$$ 101
Times Square 148
Time Will Tell 237
Time zone 11
Tinterow, Gary 243
Tiny Doll House 241
Tipping 11
Tirami Sù ★★$ 241
Titanic Memorial Lighthouse 24
TKTS 36, 155
Tobaldi 47
To Boot New York 274
Tompkins Square Park 107
Tonetti, Joseph 310
Tootsi Plohound 68
Top of the Sixes $$$$ 196
Tortilla Flats $ 88
Tours 9
Tower Records 103, 276
Towers Nursing Home 291
Town & Davis 28
Towne, Ithiel 109
Town Hall, The 149
Townsend, Steinle & Haskell 277
Trains 8, 10
Transit Museum Gift Shop 176
Transportation, 8
Trastevere ★★$$$ 245
Trattoria Dell'Arte ★★$$$ 165
Trattoria Pesce Pasta ★★$$ 84
Traveller's Bookstore 196
TriBeCa 54
Tribeca Grill ★★$$$ 57
Tribeca Potters 59
Triborough Bridge 300
Trinity Building 32
Trinity Cemetery 301
Trinity Church 32
Trinity School and Trinity House 289
Triple 8 Palace Restaurant ★★★$$ 44
Triplet's Roumanian Restaurant ★$$$ 59
Tripoli ★$$ 308
Triton Gallery 151
Trois Jean ★★★$$$ 241
Tropica ★★$$$ 182
Trowbridge & Livingston 29, 127, 201, 229, 238, 280
Trowbridge, Samuel 234
True, Clarence F. 285
Trumbauer, Horace 228, 238
Trump Plaza 224
Trump Tower 211
TSE Cashmere 231
Tse Yang ★★$$$ 194
Tuckerman, Arthur 243
Tucker, Marcia 111
Tudor City 178
Tudor, The $$$ 178
Turett, Wayne 120
Turtle Bay Gardens 190
Tuthill, William B. 165
Tutta Pasta Ristorante ★$ 81
20 Mott Street ★★$ 43
21 Club ★★$$$$ 196
26th Street Flea Market 123
Twin Peaks 82
Two Boots ★$ 101

280 Modern 72
Two Two Two ★★★$$$$ 279
Two Worlds Gallery 135

U

Ukrainian ★$ 108
Ulrich Franzen & Associates 34, 175, 220 301
Umberto's Clam House $$ 51
Umeda 122
Umpire Rock 261
Uncle Sam's Umbrella Shop 166
UNICEF House 178
Union Club, The 231
Union Square 112
Union Square Cafe ★★★★$$$ 115
Union Square Greenmarket 114
Union Theological Seminary 297
Union Theological Seminary Bookstore 297
United Church, The 304
United Nations Plaza 178
United Nations Plaza Park Hyatt $$$$ 178
United Nations, The (UN) 178
United States Assay Office 24
United States Courthouse 39
United States Custom House 22
Unity Book Center 138
Universal Pictures Building 209
University Club 199
University Village 97
Untitled 76
Upjohn, Richard 32, 120, 123, 139
Upper East Side 246
Upper West Side 286
Urban Archaeology 49
Urban Center 195
Urban Center Books 195
Urban, Joseph 164, 262
US Realty Building 32
Utrecht Art & Drafting Supplies 110

V

Valentino 231
Van Alen, William 177
Van Cleef & Arpels 210
Van Cortlandt House Museum 317
V&T Pizzeria ★$ 296
Van Dyke, Harry 232
Van Pelt, John 137
Vaux & Redford 301
Vaux, Calvert 85, 118, 243, 279, 288
Vegetarian Paradise 2 ★$ 95
Veniero's Pasticceria & Cafe ★$ 109
Verbena ★★★$$$ 117
Verrazano Monument 20
Verrazano-Narrows Bridge 319
Very Special Flowers 86
Veselka ★$ 108
Vesuvio's Bakery 71
Via Brasil ★★$$ 185
Viceroy, The ★$$ 136
VideoTown Launderette 282
Vietnam ★★★$ 44
View, The ★$$$$ 154
Village Atelier ★$$$ 81

Village Chess Shop 97
Village Community Church 90
Village Vanguard 86
Villard Houses, The 195
Vince & Eddie's ★★★$$ 272
Vince & Linda at One Fifth ★★$$ 93
Vincent's Clam Bar ★$ 51
Vinegar Factory 252
Vinnie's Pizza ★$ 276
Vinoly, Rafael 206
Virginia 161
Virginia Zabriskie 212
Visiting Nurse Service of New York 234
Visitors' Information Centers 11, 267
Vista International Hotel $$$$ 37
Vivian Beaumont Theater 269
Vivolo ★$$ 235
Vong ★★★$$$ 206
Voorhees, Gmelin & Walker 90
Vos, Charles 279
Voulez Vous ★★$$$ 239

W

Wagner, Albert 48
Waid, E. Everett 122
Waldenbooks 29
Waldorf-Astoria Hotel $$$$ 189
Waldorf Towers 189
Wales Hotel $$ 252
Walgrove, George M. 277
Walker & Gillette 21, 209, 231, 234, 253, 277
Walker, Ralph 29
Walking 10
30 Wall Street 28
40 Wall Street 28
55 Wall Street 28
74 Wall Street 28
Wall Street Plaza 27
Walter Kerr 158
Walter Steiger 228
Ware, James E. 165
Warner Brothers Studio Store 210
Warner, Samuel A. 125
Warren & Wetmore 114, 139, 150, 166, 176, 182, 185, 211, 215, 229, 251
Warwick Hotel $$$ 200
Washington Heights 292, 303
Washington Irving High School 115
Washington Market Park 55
Washington Mews 93
Washington Square 94
Washington Square Hotel $ 93
Washington Square North 93
Water Club, The ★★★$$$ 124
Water's Edge ★★$$$ 313
Waterside 124
Wave Hill 317
Wells, James N. 82, 137
Wells, Joseph C. 91
Wentworth $ 185
Werner & Windolph 206
West Bank Cafe ★$$ 145
Westbeth 88
415 West Broadway 68
420 West Broadway 69
Westbury Hotel, The $$$$ 232
343-357 West End Avenue 278

520 West End Avenue 285
565 West End Avenue 287
838 West End Avenue 290
West End Collegiate Church and School 279
Westerman & Miller 270
Western Union Building 121
9 West 57th Street 210
West 14th Street 90
319 West 14th Street 134
West 95th Street 290
Weston, Theodore 228, 243
West Park Presbyterian Church 287
21-131 West 78th Street 279
West Side 266
Westside Judaica 288
Westside Theater 147
West Side YMCA $ 271
West 63rd Street Steakhouse ★★★$$$ 268
406-24 West 20th Street 137
West 21st Street 137
221 West 26th Street 140
Wetmore, James A. 24
Whaler Bar, The 129
Wheelchair accessibility 5
Whitehall Building 23
White Horse Tavern 87
White, Stanford 94, 118, 122, 193, 219, 315
White Street 58
Whitney Museum of American Art 236, 248
Whole Foods 74
Whyte, N. 67
Wight, P.B. 301
Wildenstein & Co. 228
Wilkinson's 1573 Seafood Cafe ★★$$$ 245
William Clark House 44
William Greenberg Jr. Desserts 244
William H. Schab Gallery 213
Williamsburg Bridge 46
William Secord Gallery 237
Williams, Frank 158
Wilson, John L. 301
Wilson's Bakery & Restaurant ★★$$ 302
Windows on Broadway ★★$$$ 156
Winter Drive 263
Winter Garden 159
Withers, Frederick Clarke 85, 123, 225
Witkin Gallery 69
Wolf, Henry 215
Wolfman-Gold & Good Company 67
Wollman Memorial Skating Rink 260
Wong Kee ★$ 51
Woolworth Building 37
59 Wooster Street 65
147 Wooster Street 75
Work Space, The 71
World Cafe ★$$ 273
World Financial Center 34
World Gym 271
World of Birds 316
World of Darkness 316
World Trade Center (WTC) 35
Worldwide Plaza 158

World Yacht Cruises ★★$$$$ 146
Worth & Worth 183
Worth Monument 123
WPA Theater 139
W.R. Grace Building 174
Wright, Frank Lloyd 72, 197, 198, 209, 215, 249
Wylie's ★$$ 191
Wyndham Hotel $$ 213

X
Xanadu 154

Y
Yale Club, The 183
Yankee Stadium 315
Yarn Co., The 283
Yellowfingers ★★$$ 224
Yeshiva Chofetz Chaim 288
Yeshiva University 304
Ye Waverly Inn $$ 90
YIVO Institute for Jewish Research, The (Yidisher Visnschaftlekher Institut) 168
Yohji Yamamoto 60
Yonah Schimmel ★$ 48
York & Sawyer 28, 33, 127, 144, 167, 177, 230, 255, 276, 277
York Theatre Company at St. Peter's Church 205
Yoshi 75
Yura and Company ★★$ 252
Yves Saint Laurent–Rive Gauche 233

Z
Zabar's 282
Zabar's Cafe ★$ 282
Zarela ★★$$ 191
Zeckendorf Plaza 114
Zen Oriental Bookstore 184
Zen Palate ★★★$$ 148
Zero 72
0 to 60s 64
Zinno ★$$ 90
Zion & Breen 198
Zoë ★★$$$ 72
Zona 67
Zucker, Alfred 60, 65

Restaurants

Only restaurants with star ratings are listed below. All restaurants are listed alphabetically in the main (preceding) index.
★★★★ An Extraordinary Experience
★★★ Excellent
★★ Very Good
★ Good
$$$$ Big Bucks ($30 and up)
$$$ Expensive ($20–$30)
$$ Reasonable ($15–$20)
$ The Price Is Right (less than $15)

★★★★
Bouley $$$$ 56
Chanterelle $$$$ 57
C.T. $$$ 121
James Beard House $$$$ 90

La Côte Basque $$$$ 200
Le Bernardin $$$$ 160
Le Regence $$$$ 228
Rainbow Room, The $$$$ 188
Restaurant Daniel $$$$ 237
San Domenico $$$$ 168
Union Square Cafe $$$ 115

★★★
Aja $$$ 121
Alison on Dominick Street $$$ 64
Aquavit $$$$ 199
Arcadia $$$$ 220
Arizona 206 $$$ 224
Aureole $$$$ 221
Café des Artistes $$$ 272
Cafe Pierre $$$ 220
Cascabel $$$ 66
Chikubu $$$ 184
Christer's $$$ 163
Cité $$$ 160
Cucina $$ 309
Darbar Indian Restaurant $$$ 212
Dawat $$$ 207
First Taste $$ 45
Golden Unicorn $$ 44
Gotham Bar and Grill $$$$ 91
Hatsuhana $$$ 189
Hudson River Club $$$$ 34
Il Mulino $$$ 96
Il Toscanaccio $$ 219
I Trulli $$$ 123
Japonica $$ 92
JoJo $$$ 227
La Caravelle $$$$ 200
La Colombe d'Or $$$ 123
La Réserve $$$$ 188
Le Chantilly $$$ 209
Le Cirque $$$$ 228
Le Madri $$$ 135
Le Perigord $$$ 205
Les Célébrités $$$$ 167
Lespinasse $$$$ 201
Lutèce $$$$ 191
Manhattan Ocean Club, The $$$ 213
March $$$ 206
Matthew's $$$ 224
Metisse $ 290
Mitsukoshi $$$$ 208
Monkey Bar $$$ 204
Montrachet $$$ 58
Morton's of Chicago $$$ 184
Nice Restaurant $ 44
Nobu $$$$ 58
Oceana $$$$ 203
Parioli Romanissimo $$$$ 242
Park Avenue Cafe $$$ 222
Patria $$ 118
Periyali $$$ 120
Peter Luger $$$ 309
Petrossian $$$$ 166
Picholine $$$ 271
Po $ 84
Post House, The $$$$ 221
Provence $$ 77
Remi $$$ 162
River Café $$$$ 306
SeaGrill, The $$$$ 188
Shun Lee Palace $$$$ 204
Sign of the Dove, The $$$$ 226
Stacy's $ 309
Triple 8 Palace Restaurant $$ 44

Trois Jean $$$ 241
Two Two Two $$$$ 279
Verbena $$$ 117
Vietnam $ 44
Vince & Eddie's $$ 272
Vong $$$ 206
Water Club, The $$$ 124
West 63rd Street Steakhouse $$$ 268
Zen Palate $$ 148

★★
Adrienne $$$ 201
Alva $$$ 121
American Renaissance $$$ 59
An American Place $$$ 127
Arqua $$ 58
Aunt Sonia's $$ 310
Azzurro $$ 245
Bangkok Cuisine $$ 161
Baraonda $$$ 239
Barbetta $$$ 156
Barney Greengrass (The Sturgeon King) $ 287
Barocco $$ 58
Barolo $$$ 65
Ben Benson's Steakhouse $$$$ 160
Bice $$$ 203
Bistro du Nord $$ 253
Black Sheep, The $$$ 87
Blu $$ 138
Blue Ribbon $$$ 70
Bolo $$ 121
Bridge Cafe $$ 27
Briscola $$$ 109
Cabana Carioca $$ 154
Cafe Centro $$$ 183
Cafe Crocodile $$ 235
Cafe Loup $$ 90
Cafe Luxembourg $$$ 273
Cafe Tabac $$ 108
Caffe Bondí $$$ 120
Caffè Roma $ 50
Cal's $$ 120
Campagna $$$ 119
Canton $$ 44
Capsouto Frères $$$ 59
Carnegie Delicatessen $$ 162
Caviarteria $$$ 222
Century Cafe $$ 149
Chelsea Cafe $ 140
Chez Jacqueline $$ 96
Chez Josephine $$$ 145
Chez Napoléon $$$ 159
China Grill $$$ 197
Chin Chin $$$ 191
Choshi $$ 117
City Bakery, The $ 115
Coco Pazzo $$$$ 236
Cola's $ 136
Coming or Going $$$ 210
Contrapunto $$$ 224
Country Cafe $ 64
Da Umberto $$$ 135
Delegates' Dining Room $$$ 180
Delhi Palace $$ 314
Docks Oyster Bar and Seafood Grill $$ 288
Dominick's $ 316
Duane Park Cafe $$$ 56
E.A.T. $$$ 242
El Cid $ 134

Elias Corner $ 314
Elio's $$$ 244
El Parador $$$ 128
El Pollo $ 251
Ennio & Michael $$$ 971
Erminia $$$ 245
Estia $$$ 244
Etats-Unis $$$ 240
Fantino $$ 167
Felidia $$$$ 207
Felissimo $ 211
Fishin Eddie $$$ 274
Flowers $$$ 116
Follonico $$$ 123
Frank's $$$ 134
Fresco $$ 194
Frontiere $$ 76
Fu's $$$ 192
Gabriel's $$$ 267
Gallagher's Steak House $$$$ 161
Gascogne $$ 136
Good Enough to Eat $$ 284
Gramercy Tavern $$$ 118
Grand Ticino $$ 97
Great Shanghai $ 44
Harry Cipriani $$$$ 218
Home $$ 84
Hunan Garden $ 43
Hunt Room, The $$$ 195
Il Cantinori $$$ 92
Il Monello $$$ 239
Il Nido $$$$ 205
Inagiku Japanese Restaurant $$$$ 189
Indochine $$ 104
Istanbul Kebap $ 240
Jade Palace $ 315
Jaiya Thai Oriental Restaurant $$ 314
Jamaican Hot Pot $ 300
Jean Lafitte $$$ 213
Jezebel $$$ 148
Jing Fong $$ 45
John's Pizzeria $ 83
Josie's $ 276
Jour et Nuit $$$ 61
Kelley and Ping $ 74
Kiiroi Hana $$ 212
La Bo[aci]te en Bois $$$ 273
La Grenouille $$$$ 196
La Mangeoire $$$ 205
La Metairie $$$ 86
Landmark Tavern $$ 147
La Ripaille $$ 89
L'Ecole $$ 60
Le Colonial $$ 207
Le Refuge $$$ 241
Le Relais $$ 220
L'Ermitage $$ 212
Lipstick Cafe $ 206
Lobster Box $$$ 318
Long Shine Restaurant $ 44
Luma $$ 138
Lusardi's $$$ 240
Mme. Romaine de Lyon $$ 223
Mad. 61 $$$ 221
Mandarin Court $ 43
Manducatis $$ 313
Mark's $$$$ 237
Martini's $$ 161
Marylou's $$$ 93
Mesa Grill $$$ 116

Index

Mezzanine, The $$$ 156
Mezzogiorno $$$ 70
Michael's $$ 200
Miracle Grill $$ 106
Mitali $$ 106
National Restaurant $$$ 311
Negril Island Spice $ 139
Nello $$$ 220
Nick & Eddie $$ 70
Nippon $$$$ 192
Nyborg-Nelson $ 205
Odessa $$$ 311
Old Homestead $$$$ 134
Omen $$ 70
O'Neals' $$$ 271
One If By Land, Two If By Sea
    $$$$ 83
Oriental Garden Seafood $$ 45
Oyster Bar and Restaurant $$$
    176
Palio $$$$ 160
Palm $$$$ 180
Paola's $$$ 244
Park Bistro $$$ 125
Park Cafe $$$ 200
Patsy's Pizza $ 308
Pedro Paramo $ 110
Peking Duck House $ 43
Pierre au Tunnel $$$ 157
Polo, The $$$ 232
Primavera $$$$ 245
Raoul's $$$ 70
Rene Pujol $$ 159
Restaurant Florent $$ 88
Restaurant 44 $$$ 184
Road to Mandalay $$ 50
Rosa Mexicano $$$ 206
Rose Cafe $$ 92
Rosemarie's $$$ 56
Russian Tea Room, The $$$ 166
Saigon House Restaurant $ 42
Sammy's Famous Roumanian
    Jewish Steakhouse $$$ 49
San Pietro $$$ 203
Sant Ambroeus $$$ 238
Sarabeth's at the Whitney $$ 236
Sarabeth's Kitchen (Upper East
    Side) $$ 252
Sarabeth's Kitchen (West Side)
    $$ 282
Savoy $$$ 72
Sazerac House $$ 87
Scaletta $$$ 277
Seryna $$$ 203
Sette Mezzo $$$ 234
Sfuzzi $$ 271
Sichuan Palace $$$ 178
Silver Palace $$ 45
Sirabella $$ 245
Sistina $$$ 240
Smith & Wollensky $$$ 191
Snaps $$ 182
S.O.B.'s Sounds of Brazil $$ 77
Soleil $$ 227
Solera $$ 205
Sparks $$$$ 182
Sushisay $$$ 194
Sylvia's $$ 299
Takesushi $$$$ 183
Tammany Hall $$ 124
Tavern on the Green $$$$ 261
Terrace, The $$$$ 298
Tirami Sù $ 241

Trastevere $$$ 245
Trattoria Dell'Arte $$$ 165
Trattoria Pesce Pasta $$ 84
Tribeca Grill $$$ 57
Tropica $$$ 182
Tse Yang $$$ 194
20 Mott Street $ 43
21 Club $$$$ 196
Via Brasil $$ 185
Vince & Linda at One Fifth $$ 93
Voulez Vous $$$ 239
Water's Edge $$$ 313
Wilkinson's 1573 Seafood Cafe
    $$$ 245
Wilson's Bakery & Restaurant
    $$ 302
Windows on Broadway $$$ 156
World Yacht Cruises $$$$ 146
Yellowfingers $$ 224
Yura and Company $ 252
Zarela $$ 191
Zoë $$$ 72

★
Acme Bar & Grill $$ 101
Aesop's Tables $$ 319
Aggie's $ 96
Allegria $$ 200
Ambassador Grill Restaurant
    $$$ 178
America $$$ 117
American Festival Cafe $$$ 188
Amici Miei $$ 75
Amsterdam's $$ 60
Angelica Kitchen $ 110
Angelo's of Mulberry Street $$ 51
Anglers & Writers $ 81
Annabelle $$ 182
Areo $$ 311
Arturo's Pizzeria $ 76
Au Cafe $ 162
Au Mandarin $$ 35
Baci $$ 282
Bagel, The $ 84
Bali Burma $ 147
B & H Dairy and Vegetarian
    Cuisine Restaurant $ 107
Bayamo $$ 103
Becco $$ 157
Benito I and Benito II $ 50
Benny's Burritos $ 90
Berrys $$ 69
Bill's Gay Nineties $$ 203
Birdland $$ 290
Boathouse Cafe $$$ 263
Boca Chica $ 101
Bo Ky Restaurant $ 43
Bombay Palace $$ 196
Boom $$ 68
Bowery Bar $$ 103
Brasserie $$$ 194
Brio $$ 223
Broadway Diner $ 162
Brother's Bar-B-Q $ 77
Bruno $$$ 207
B. Smith's $$$ 157
Busby's $$ 252
Cafe at Brooklyn Musuem $ 310
Cafe de Bruxelles $$ 89
Café Des Sports $ 159
Cafe Europa $ 165
Cafe Greco $$ 234
Café La Fortuna $ 274

Cafe Lalo $ 284
Cafe Metairie $$ 241
Cafe Mogador $$ 107
Café Nicholson $$$ 206
Cafe Nicole $$$ 161
Cafe Un Deux Trois $$ 149
Caffe Bianco $ 240
Caffè Borgia $ 96
Caffè Dante $ 96
Caffè della Pace $ 106
Caffè Napoli $ 51
Caffè Reggio $ 95
Caffè Vivaldi $ 84
Cajun $$ 134
Can $$ 75
Captain's Table $$$ 180
Caribe $ 87
Casa di Pré $$ 89
Casa La Femme $$ 75
Casa Rosa $$ 308
Castellano $$$ 163
Cent' Anni $$$ 81
Cesarina $$$ 197
Chelsea Trattoria $$ 135
Chez Brigitte $ 90
Chez Michallet $$$ 82
Ci Vediamo $ 106
Claire $$ 136
Coconut Grill $ 240
Coffee Shop $ 115
Colors $$$ 182
Copeland's $$ 301
Cornelia Street Café, The $ 84
Corrado $$$ 163
Cotton Club, The $$ 298
Cub Room $$$ 76
Cucina di Pesce $ 103
Cupping Room Cafe, The $$ 65
Da Silvano $$ 96
Dean & DeLuca Cafe (Midtown)
    $ 188
Dean & DeLuca Cafe (SoHo) $ 74
DeRobertis Pastry Shop $ 108
Divino Ristorante $$ 240
Dojo $ 107
Dolce $$ 189
Dolci On Park Caffè $ 127
Donald Sacks $$ 35
Eastern Seafood Company $ 279
Eighteenth and Eighth $ 136
Elaine's $$$ 249
El Charro Español $$ 86
El Faro $$ 89
Ellen's Cafe and Bake Shop $ 38
El Teddy's $$ 58
Empire Diner $ 139
Felix $$$ 64
Ferrier $$ 229
Fine & Schapiro $$ 274
Fiorello's $$$ 270
Fletcher Morgan Provisions $ 227
Frankie and Johnnie's $$$ 151
Fraunces Tavern Restaurant $$$
    22
Freddie and Pepper's Gourmet
    Pizza $ 276
Friend of a Farmer $$ 117
Fujiyama Mama $$ 283
Girasole $$$ 241
Global 33 $ 105
Gran Caffè Degli Artisti $ 86
Grange Hall, The $ 82
Greenhouse Cafe $$ 37

Grotta Azzurra $$ 50
Grove Street Cafe $$ 83
Guido's $$ 144
Gus' Place $$ 85
Hamburger Harry's $ 154
Harley Davidson Cafe $$ 212
Harry's Burrito Junction $ 274
Hee Seung Fung (HSF) $$ 45
Henry's End $$ 308
Hero Boy $ 144
Hunan Balcony, The $ 290
Il Cortile $$$ 52
Il Ponte Vecchio $$ 97
Il Vagabondo $$ 226
Il Valletto $$$ 223
India Pavilion $ 164
Isabella $$ 278
Island $$$ 253
Iso $$ 109
Isola $$ 284
I Tre Merli $$$ 75
Jackson Diner $ 314
Jackson Hole $ 226
Jane Street Seafood Cafe $$ 89
Jerry's $$ 74
Jim McMullen $$ 239
Joe Allen $$ 156
John's of Twelfth Street $$ 110
Junior's $ 309
Katz's Delicatessen $ 48
Khyber Pass $ 107
Kiev $ 106
Kin Khao $$ 68
King Crab $$ 161
Kleine Konditorei $$ 244
Knickerbocker Bar & Grill $$ 92
La Bohème $$ 95
La Bonne Soupe $ 200
La Jumelle $ 61
La Lunchonette $$ 137
La Mirabelle $$$ 285
La Piazzetta di Quisisana $$$ 239
La Tour D'Or $$$ 29
Lattanzi $$$ 157
Le Bistrot de Maxim's $$$ 221
Le Madeleine $$$ 147
Le Pactole $$ 35
Les Halles $$ 124
Les Pyrénées $$$ 159
Les Routiers $$ 288
Les Sans Culottes $$$ 207
Le Train Bleu $$ 224
Le Veau d'Or $$$ 223
Lion's Head $$ 85
Lola $$$ 120
Louie's Westside Cafe ★$$ 283
Louisiana Community Bar and
    Grill $$ 100
Lucky Cheng's $ 101
Ludlow Street Cafe, The $ 48
Luna $$ 52
Manhattan Bistro $ 68
Manhattan Cafe $$$ 226
Manhattan Chili Company, The $
    150
Man Ray $$ 136
Marchi's $$ 124
Marion's Continental Restaurant
    and Lounge $$ 103
Maruzzella $$ 239
Marys $ 81
Match $$ 73
Menchanko-tei $$ 200